SKOKIE PUBLIC LIBRARY

31232002576371

S0-ABY-601

FERGUSON

CAREER RESOURCE GUIDE FOR

PEOPLE

WITH

DISABILITIES

Third Edition

VOLUME 1

Ferguson
An imprint of Infobase Publishing

SKOKIE PUBLIC LIBRARY

Ferguson Career Resource Guide for People with Disabilities, Third Edition

Copyright © 2006 by Infobase Publishing

All rights reserved. No part of this book may be reproduced or utilized in any form or by any means, electronic or mechanical, including photocopying, recording, or by any information storage or retrieval systems, without permission in writing from the publisher. For information contact

Ferguson
An imprint of Infobase Publishing
132 West 31st Street
New York NY 10001

Library of Congress Cataloging-in-Publication
Ferguson career resource guide for people with disabilities. — 3rd ed.
    p. cm.
    Rev. ed. of: Ferguson's guide for people with disabilities. 2nd ed. c2001.
    Includes bibliographical references and index.
    ISBN 0-8160-6127-0 (set) (hc : alk. paper)
    ISBN 0-8160-6128-9 (vol. 1)— ISBN 0-8160-6129-7 (vol. 2)
    1. People with disabilities—Services for—United States—Directories.   2. People with disabilities—Services for—United States—Finance—Directories.   3. Self-help devices for people with disabilities—United States—Directories.   4. People with disabilities—Vocational guidance—United States.   I. J.G. Ferguson Publishing Company.   II. Resources for people with disabilities.
    HV1553.F47 2006
    362.4'04802973—dc22

Ferguson books are available at special discounts when purchased in bulk quantities for businesses, associations, institutions, or sales promotions. Please call our Special Sales Department in New York at (212) 967-8800 or (800) 322-8755.

You can find Ferguson on the World Wide Web at http://www.fergpubco.com

Text design by David Strelecky
Cover design by Salvatore Luongo

Printed in the United States of America

VB FOF 10 9 8 7 6 5 4 3 2 1

This book is printed on acid-free paper.

Ref.
362.4048
F
ed. 3
v. 1

CONTENTS

PART IV: INDEXES

PART I
INTRODUCTION AND OVERVIEW

FOREWORD

by T. Alan Hurwitz, Ph.D.

My success as a deaf professional is in no way a chance event. Growing up profoundly deaf with deaf parents, in the 1940s and 1950s, when opportunities were scarce, I was fortunate to have had both a strong family support system and a fierce desire to succeed.

My mother was always working at different jobs while other mothers stayed home. She was headstrong—a leader in her own way—and really my best friend during my development years.

I attended Central Institute for the Deaf in St. Louis, some 500 miles from home. Each summer when I returned home, my mother made sure she was always there for me and asked for a leave of absence so she could be with me. But she was always refused this privilege, so she'd quit. For 10 years, when I returned to school each fall, she'd find a new job.

Every summer, she would make me read a book (including reading aloud) one hour every day, before I could go outside to play with my friends. As I matured, my mother made sure that I'd meet with everyday deaf people, always encouraging me to talk with them about their jobs. I met a farmer, linotype operator, barber, baker, seamstress, assembly worker, and mechanic, among others.

She also took me to events sponsored by deaf organizations, such as picnics and bowling tournaments, and encouraged me to talk with the leaders of these groups. She showed me the occasional article about successful deaf people, including those who went to college, and told me if they could do it, I could do it.

When I finished my studies at Central Institute for the Deaf, I lived at home and attended a mainstream junior and senior high school. My mother applied for a job as a radio assembler at Zenith, a prestigious job in the eyes of many deaf people. They wouldn't hire her because she was deaf. She applied again and again but still received rejection letters. Finally, she went to the personnel office and told them that she wanted to meet with a manager about a job. They kept trying to send her home, but she was persistent and said she'd wait. The manager finally came out at 5 P.M. and apologized for making her wait so long. He told her they didn't have anything for her. She suggested that he allow her to work for two weeks without pay. He agreed. She ended up working there for 25 years until her retirement.

Thanks to her, I grew up with the conviction that nothing is impossible and knowing that I could dream of big things and believe in myself.

For three summers, I worked alongside my father—a quiet, unassertive man who worked as a furniture upholsterer. I delivered newspapers at 4:30 each morning for four-and-a-half years while working in a variety of other jobs, including busboy, cabinetmaker, and dishwasher. I chased turkeys at a farm and washed hundreds of cars at a car wash.

No job was too trivial for me. By trying so many things, I learned what I wanted to do and what I didn't want to do. I learned that education would be the ticket to my success.

At one point in my college career, when I considered quitting, my father bluntly asked me if, for the rest of my life, I wanted to have the kind of job he had.

Without any interpreters, note takers, or tutors, classrooms were extremely challenging. It was impossible to read my teachers' lips because they either spoke too fast or moved around too much in the classroom. Although exhausted from trying to read lips all day, I would read and re-read my textbooks and my notes every evening.

My mother's "I can" mentality stuck with me, and my perseverance paid off. It was a proud day for my family and me when I earned my bachelor's degree in electrical engineering and started working at McDonnell Douglas. I later earned my master's in the same field and started teaching math, electronics, and computer science to deaf college students at the newly established National Technical Institute for the Deaf (NTID) at Rochester Institute of Technology (RIT). I eventually earned my doctoral degree in teaching and curriculum.

For the last 35 years, I worked in key roles with the NTID, became its first dean who is deaf, and now the first to hold the dual position of RIT vice president and CEO/dean of the NTID. Having consulted at the local, state, and national levels and served in leadership roles within most of the major national deaf organizations, like the National Association of the Deaf, I have had an incredible experience participating in the exciting evolution for people with disabilities.

Fifteen years ago, President George H. W. Bush signed the Americans with Disabilities Act into law, guaranteeing equal opportunity for people with disabilities in public accommodations, commercial facilities, employment, transportation, government services, and telecommunications.

But change comes slowly. While it has taken longer than hoped, this law has been successful in enlightening many of those who have misunderstood disabilities or whose actions have been clouded by prejudice and ignorance.

Despite any remaining barriers, it is important to remember that it is the responsibility of each person—with or without disability—to succeed.

The government has passed laws to enable equal access to all its diverse citizens, which helps level the playing field in the job market. But the support and the equal opportunities are just that—opportunities. People with disabilities must use these opportunities to take action. The person who uses a wheelchair, or who is blind, deaf, or learning disabled, and all others with a disability, have an obligation to work to attain the self-sufficiency necessary to lead a productive and happy life.

Our society can build ramps, but you need to wheel the chair up the ramp, through the portal, to apply for that job. And you must be qualified to do the job. In the end, you are responsible. No one can learn for you. No one can do the job for you. You must write the new software or design the new product. The opportunity is given and you must take it. It is an opportunity to shine.

A combination of adaptive technology and better-educated people with disabilities has encouraged more integration in the workforce. Many of the large companies are hiring people with disabilities. Some—including Eastman Kodak Company, Xerox, and Bausch and Lomb—now have specific disability hiring initiatives under their corporate diversity programs. IBM also has a well-defined disability-hiring program, as does Citigroup. These companies have all hired engineers, computer specialists, and software technicians with disabilities.

The benefits are universal. Businesses can tap into a skilled labor pool to fill the gap caused by retiring baby boomers, and the person with a disability becomes a contributing member of society, no longer needing taxpayer support. Hiring people with disabilities is not charity. It's simply good business.

For this successful trend to continue, it is essential for everyone to contribute. The family contributes to the early education and support of their disabled children. The educators contribute by teaching the necessary skills so people can communicate with each other and the world. Technological advances will continue to close the gap for disabled people both in and out of the workplace. As a society, we must bring ourselves to embrace difference and see everyone individually, for his or her contribution.

I urge the 50 million-plus Americans with disabilities to get educated. Education will open the door to interesting jobs, and will give you choices in life. Use all the wonderful tools available to you today, such as this directory, to get information and help yourself. Persevere, take risks, and don't forget to give back.

Dr. T. Alan Hurwitz leads the internationally known National Technical Institute for the Deaf, providing curriculum and marketable skills to its 1,200 students. A past president of the National Association of the Deaf, he has served on countless boards and earned many honors for his work.

INTRODUCTION: INFORMATION—THE FIRST STEP TO ACCESS

Over the last 25 years, a portion of our society has come forward after being invisible and forgotten—invisible because they could not access public spaces, forgotten because the adage "out of sight, out of mind" holds true far too often. Rather than being themselves handicapped, people with disabilities have found that their environment and the attitudes of the people around them have handicapped them. With new technologies, changing attitudes, and better legislation, however, things have begun to improve. Now, for example, people with disabilities are finding it easier to shop for their own groceries, attend universities, use the Internet and other technologies, and remain active members of the workforce.

As this population speaks up, it reminds us repeatedly of its need to escape the old stereotype of being "taken care of" and move on toward the idea of independence and self-determination. Fulfilling this need requires access to information about assistive technologies, about funding to purchase those technologies, and about organizations that can help people with disabilities to take their places as active and productive members of society.

Ferguson Career Resource Guide for People with Disabilities provides easy access to this information. With more than 8,000 listings (nearly 3,000 of which are new to this edition), it is the most comprehensive directory of its kind. Among other options, readers can explore and compare choices for purchasing assistive computer devices, participating in vocational rehabilitation, joining an online support group, or seeking legal aid. Librarians and teachers will find that this one-point reference work is an excellent resource for launching people on their quests to make personal decisions about their lives.

WHO ARE PEOPLE WITH DISABILITIES?

The U.S. Census Bureau reports that nearly 50 million people with disabilities live outside institutions. This number is approximately 20 percent of the population. One out of every five people has trouble performing one or more daily-living tasks; these are the people with permanent disabilities. Other people, perhaps as many as one out of three, experience a temporary disability, such as a broken arm or leg. As the American population continues to grow, disability numbers will no doubt continue to increase as well. Whether these disabilities are permanent or temporary, people need assistance to make up for the losses they experience.

The following statistics for people with disabilities come from the U.S. Census Bureau. Visit the bureau's Web site, http://www.census.gov, for more information.

People with Disabilities, Ages 5 and Older, 2000

Total	49,746,248
Male	24,439,531
Female	25,306,717
Ages 5-15	2,614,919 people (5.8 percent of this age group)
Ages 16-64	33,153,211 people (18.6 percent of this age group)
Ages 65 and older	13,978,118 people (41.9 percent of this age group)

Disability Status by Ethnicity, Ages 5 and Older, 2000

Ethnic Group	Percent with a Disability
African American	24.3
American Indian and Alaska Native	24.3

Ethnic Group	Percent with a Disability
Hispanic or Latino	20.9
Native Hawaiian and Other Pacific Islander	19.0
White	18.5
Asian	16.6

Employment Status, 2000

Total Employed Persons Aged 21-64	99,206,689
Total Employed Persons with Disabilities	17,288,292
Men	9,606,846
Women	7,681,446
Total Employed Persons with Severe Disabilities	2,900,000
Men	1,300,000
Women	1,600,000

Specific Disabilities, 2003

Following are some of the most prevalent disabilities of Americans.

Number of adults with hearing trouble	32.5 million
Number of adults with vision trouble	18.6 million
Number of adults who are unable or find it very difficult to walk a quarter mile	14.9 million
Number of adults with any physical functioning difficulty	14.7 million

ATTITUDES AND STEREOTYPES

People with disabilities still depend heavily on the government for health care and general living expenses. This perpetuates negative stereotypes and attitudes toward disabilities.

One of the most common stereotypes about the disabled is that all people with disabilities are impoverished and, therefore, are not viable consumers. Although 26 percent of the disabled have an annual household income below $15,000 (as compared to 9 percent for the general population), a large percentage of disabled people have earnings that match or exceed the average per capita income (approximately $44,389 in 2004) for all Americans. This belief, that people with disabilities are all poor, makes businesses less willing to spend the money necessary to make their buildings and products accessible. The more people with disabilities are seen in the workplace, however, the more this misconception is dispelled. But in order for most people with disabilities to be employed, some sort of resource modification to overcome a particular limitation is usually needed. This demonstrates the importance of access to information about helpful resources. When people with disabilities have access to modern resources, they are able to become more independent. This helps to dispel the negative stereotypes and leads to greater accessibility.

Another common misconception is that a physical limitation prevents a person from making and communicating his or her own decisions. Many times, for example, store clerks or waiters will talk to a companion rather than speak directly to a person using a wheelchair. This mistake often involves the method of payment, which is tied to the poverty stereotype. As individuals use modern technologies to become more independent, people will see that consumers with disabilities are able to handle their own business. Demonstrating changing attitudes means responding to people as people first, without concentrating on their particular disability. It means understanding that the expressions, such as "overcome a disability" or "in spite of a disability," inaccurately reflect the problems faced by people with disabilities, who succeed not in spite of their disabilities but in spite of an inaccessible and discriminatory society.

HISTORY OF THE INDEPENDENT LIVING AND DISABILITY RIGHTS MOVEMENTS

As it did with the civil rights movement and affirmative action programs, government has stepped in with laws and mandates to level the playing field and help eliminate stereotypes for people with disabilities. It began in 1962, when Ed Roberts rolled onto the campus at the University of California-Berkeley to begin classes. Nobody knew how to handle the "helpless cripple" who wouldn't take no for an answer. Buildings were inaccessible, alternate formats of learning materials were inconceivable, and there were no appropriate living quarters.

As he chipped away at the barriers, Roberts saw the need for laws to help with enforcing accessibility. Ed Roberts completed his education and, in 1975, was made director of California's Department of Rehabilitation. Because of the efforts of Ed Roberts, the government provided funds to set up regional independent living centers and he is known as "the father of the independent living movement." The philosophy is simple: "Provide a curb cut and a person gets off their block; teach them how to get their own curb cut, and they gain access to the whole world." These centers teach people to advocate for themselves and change deficiencies in laws as well as in structures. The following list shows the major pieces of legislation that have resulted from such advocacy. (Visit http://www.usdoj.gov/crt/ada/cguide.htm for more information.)

- 1964: Civil Rights Act prohibits discrimination against various minority groups in America, most notably women and minorities categorized by race, religion, and national origin.
- 1968: Architectural Barriers Act prohibits architectural barriers in all federally owned or leased buildings.
- 1970: Urban Mass Transit Act requires that all newly purchased mass-transit vehicles be equipped with lifts. The American Public Transit Association sought and won a court injunction barring implementation of the proposed regulations, virtually holding this law hostage until the Americans with Disabilities Act passed.
- 1973: Rehabilitation Act Title V (particularly Sections 503 and 504) forbids discrimination on the basis of disability in programs receiving federal funds. The language used is parallel to that of the Civil Rights Act of 1964.
- 1975: Individuals with Disabilities Education Act (formerly called the Education of All Handicapped Children Act) requires a free, appropriate public education in an integrated setting for children with disabilities. This law has been the least effective of all those passed to support the integration of people with disabilities into our society because it has created, essentially, a separate, segregated system of "special education." It was reauthorized in 2004.

- 1988: Air Carrier Access Act provides for equal access on private airlines and air carriers and forbids discrimination on the basis of disability in air travel.
- 1988: Civil Rights Restoration Act clarifies that any organization or corporation receiving federal funds may not discriminate in any of its programs on the basis of race, ethnicity, religion, national origin, gender, age, or disability. For the first time, people with disabilities were included as a protected class with other classes protected by the Civil Rights Act of 1964.
- 1988: Fair Housing Amendments Act prohibits discrimination against people with disabilities (along with families that have children) in housing and provides for universal design (architectural accessibility) in new construction of housing units of various types and sizes beginning in March 1991.
- 1988: Technology-Related Assistance for Individuals with Disabilities Act (Tech Act) established money to form state agencies that help people with disabilities to obtain assistive devices by evaluating their needs and finding sources for equipment and funding.
- 1990: Americans with Disabilities Act creates broad civil rights protections for people with disabilities; modeled after the Civil Rights Act of 1964 and Section 504 of the Rehabilitation Act of 1973.
- 1992: Civil Rights Act permits women and individuals with disabilities to sue for punitive damages (up to a maximum of $250,000) when employment discrimination has been proven in court.
- 1996: The Telecommunications Act of 1996 requires manufacturers of telecommunications equipment or customer-premises equipment to ensure that the equipment is designed, developed, and fabricated to be accessible to and usable by people with disabilities.
- 1996: The Small Business Job Protection Act of 1996 creates the Work Opportunity Tax Credit to encourage employers to hire certain groups of individuals, including people with disabilities.
- 2004: The Individuals with Disabilities Education Act of 2004 revised the Individuals with

Disabilities Education Act of 1975 to reflect the educational goals and strategies of President Bush's No Child Left Behind Act of 2002. It now serves approximately 6.8 children and youth with disabilities.

Examining four of these more carefully increases an understanding of the rights of people with disabilities and the opportunities that they can pursue when the proper connections and resources are available.

Individuals with Disabilities Education Act (IDEA)

This law guarantees people with disabilities, especially children and young adults, educational opportunities. These are some of its basic principles:

- All children with disabilities are entitled to a free public education appropriate to their needs.
- As much as possible, children with disabilities should be educated with students without disabilities, as close to home as possible, and in the least restrictive environment.
- Children with disabilities must be provided with supplemental services, such as physical therapy and assistive technologies.
- A fair assessment, with parental agreement, must be completed to determine the student's educational needs.

The Individual Education Program (IEP) for each child must be reviewed annually to incorporate products and services that maximize educational goals. Assistive technologies cannot be denied a student, if they are part of the IEP. Assistive technology devices are not restricted to those used in school; the law applies to devices used in an individual's home as well. See the "Assistive Technology" section in Part III of this book for a list of vendors of assistive technology.

Americans with Disabilities Act (ADA)

This law expands upon earlier accessibility mandates and other civil rights legislation that made discrimination illegal, since disabilities were not included in those previous laws. The act covers more than 900 separate disabilities. In specific sections, it covers accessibility and accommodation requirements for all public places, state and local government services, transportation, employment, and communications. This law strives to ensure equal opportunities for people with disabilities in all these areas.

Employers must make reasonable accommodations for qualified workers with disabilities, so that job requirements and structure do not become barriers to employment. These accommodations must be made unless the employer shows that it would cause undue hardship. Accommodations usually include assistive technologies or technology access. If you have had trouble with an employer, potential employer, or public facility, see the section "Legal Assistance Organizations" in "Other Organizations and Associations" in Part III of this book.

Technology-Related Assistance for Individuals with Disabilities Act (Tech Act)

The act mandates that federal funds be provided to assist states in developing programs that allow easy access to assistive technologies, technology services, and information. A landmark phrase in this legislation is "consumer responsive," which means that states must evaluate and respond to the concerns of people with disabilities.

The act set standard definitions for assistive technologies that have been used in subsequent legislation. Assistive technology is defined as "any tool that increases, maintains, or improves functional capabilities of individuals with disabilities" in such areas as seating, mobility, daily living, and environmental control. These devices are not necessarily computerized. They can be as simple as a hand-held magnifier.

For a list of agencies funded by the Tech Act, see "State Tech Act Programs and Organizations" in "Organizations and Associations" in Part III of this book. Funds are generally used to provide information and referral in order to eliminate barriers that prevent access to assistive technologies by consumers. A list of funding sources for purchasing assistive technology can be found in the section "Assistive Technology" in Part III.

Rehabilitation Act Amendments of 1992

People with significant disabilities have benefited the most from these amendments by gaining access to rehabilitative services. Earlier laws evaluated people on their "employability," "feasibility of employment," and "rehabilitation potential." The amendments are based on the presumption that a person with a severe disability can achieve employment and other rehabilitation goals. The older laws did not provide for rehabilitative support except in cases of "full employment" potential.

Vocational rehabilitation agencies are now required to look for employment solutions rather than evaluate needs. Support to gain employment must now be given unless there is absolutely no possibility that an individual is employable, even with the aid of assistive devices. This way of regarding disabilities is a significant change from previous attitudes. Unfortunately, the burden of finding the proper technology is placed upon government agencies that are, in most cases, unaware of the most recent technologies. By using this book, people can match their needs to the proper equipment and receive support from state vocational agencies in order to purchase the equipment. See the sections "Vocational Assistance and Employment Organizations" and "Rehabilitation Centers" in Part III for more information.

HOW TO USE THIS BOOK

Ferguson Career Resource Guide for People with Disabilities is divided into four main parts. Part I contains this introduction and a foreword by T. Alan Hurwitz, Ph.D., vice president, Rochester Institute of Technology and CEO/dean, National Technical Institute for the Deaf. Part II contains essays on various topics, such as assistive technology, caregiving, locating resources for education, and making libraries accessible for people with disabilities, among others. Part III, "Directory," makes up the majority of the book and has eight main sections. The entries in each section in Part III are typically presented in alphabetical format for ease of use, although some sections are alphabetized by state if the services provided are specific to a particular state. Contact information (including mailing address, telephone numbers, e-mail address, and URLs) is provided for each organization that is included in this directory. Where appropriate, a brief description is provided of the organization's services, products, or other resources.

A disability identifier (i.e., the "Disability Served" line) is also included in each listing to help the user determine whether the organization offers products, services, or other resources that are applicable to his or her needs. For example, the identifier for the American Cancer Society is "Disability Served: cancer patients and survivors." The identifier for the National Hemophilia Foundation is "Disability Served: inherited bleeding disorders." The identifier "Disability Served: various" is used when an organization offers resources that are applicable to people who have a variety of disabilities. Organizations that would fall under this classification

include state departments of disability services, general product vendors, and professional associations such as the National Organization on Disability. The following identifiers are used in *Ferguson Career Resource Guide for People with Disabilities:*

Disability Served: AIDS
Disability Served: amputees
Disability Served: Asperger Syndrome
Disability Served: asthma
Disability Served: attention deficit disorder
Disability Served: autism
Disability Served: back injury
Disability Served: behavioral disorders
Disability Served: burns
Disability Served: cancer patients and survivors
Disability Served: cerebral palsy
Disability Served: Charcot-Marie-Tooth Disease
Disability Served: chemical dependency
Disability Served: chronic pain
Disability Served: communication
Disability Served: cystic fibrosis
Disability Served: developmentally disabled
Disability Served: diabetes
Disability Served: Down Syndrome
Disability Served: dyslexic
Disability Served: ectodermal dysplasias
Disability Served: elderly
Disability Served: emotionally disabled adolescents
Disability Served: epilepsy
Disability Served: Glycogen Storage Disease
Disability Served: hearing
Disability Served: hydrocephalus
Disability Served: immune deficiency disorders
Disability Served: inherited bleeding disorders
Disability Served: kidney disease
Disability Served: knee injury
Disability Served: learning disabled
Disability Served: Lowe Syndrome
Disability Served: mental health (includes anxiety disorders, bipolar disorder, depression, and other related disabilities)
Disability Served: mental retardation
Disability Served: mentally disabled
Disability Served: multiple sclerosis
Disability Served: neck injury
Disability Served: orthopedic
Disability Served: oxygen-dependent individuals
Disability Served: Parkinson's Disease

Disability Served: physically disabled (covers a wide array of disabilities that are otherwise not specifically categorized, including Amytrophic Lateral Sclerosis, arthritis, ataxia, cleft lip and other craniofacial anomalies, Creutzfeldt-Jakob Disease and other brain disorders, heart disease, and muscular dystrophy)

Disability Served: severe communication disorders

Disability Served: sickle cell anemia

Disability Served: spina bifida

Disability Served: spinal-cord injury

Disability Served: stroke

Disability Served: Tourette Syndrome

Disability Served: traumatic brain injury

Disability Served: various

Disability Served: vision

Part IV, "Indexes," features three indexes: a Disabilities Index, a Geographic Location Index, and an Organization Name Index.

PART II
ESSAYS

ASSISTIVE TECHNOLOGY: UNDERSTANDING THE BASICS

When he's on a baseball diamond coaching his team of Little Leaguers, Bill Chatterton doesn't think much about technology. He's more concerned about whether the 11-year-old outfielder will be able to catch a pop fly.

Ask Chatterton about the assistive technology that allows him to use a computer, though, and he'll say without hesitation that it has "opened up a new life" for him. In 1991, Chatterton was in a motorcycle accident that resulted in a severe spinal injury causing paralysis from the neck down. After five years on a ventilator, Chatterton discovered that he could function without the machine and began attending a state university. At first, he didn't have a computer and was reliant on other people for a number of tasks, including carrying books and papers back and forth from school and turning pages as he read from textbooks. "It was very time consuming," he recalls. After one semester, he purchased a computer, which he operates via an infrared dot placed with adhesive on his nose. Now, his textbooks are scanned and put on disk by the college's disability services, and notes and assignments are sent directly to his computer so that he can view them without assistance. "I have an incredible amount of freedom," he says. In fact, despite his studies and his part-time research work at the university, Chatterton has time left over to coach not just the Little League team but also a YMCA basketball team.

For an increasing number of people with disabilities, computers and assistive technology are making it possible to tackle everyday tasks and activities more independently than ever before. This equipment has also drawn people with disabilities into the workplace, public libraries, and classrooms, where they can be recognized as peers and given equal opportunities.

In its simplest definition, assistive technology is anything that provides alternatives to the standard way of using a computer's keyboard, monitor, or printer. What paved the way for the explosion of new assistive equipment was the Technology-Related Assistance for Individuals with Disabilities Act. Better known as the Tech Act, it focused on developing state-by-state programs that have a lasting impact on the way people with disabilities access and obtain technology devices. In every state, Tech Act projects offer such services as referral centers, assistance in obtaining devices, equipment exchange and recycling, financial loans, and training.

In spite of the advancements of the past two decades, the science of making computer hardware and programs accessible to everyone with a disability is still evolving. "Universal access is, and will continue to be, a tough nut to crack, until there are widely accepted protocols [for input and output] that can be put into a modality each computer user can access," points out Denis Anson, author of *Alternative Computer Access: Making Appropriate Selections*. "A software package that is perfectly accessible to a blind user might still be completely inaccessible to a person with a spinal injury or a person with spastic cerebral palsy."

As Anson indicates, it's not a one-size-fits-all selection process, and it's important to find assistive equipment that accommodates your individual needs. The following sections will get you started exploring the assistive technologies available to specific disability populations and the possible methods of obtaining funding to acquire this technology. For more personalized guidance, contact the Tech Act project in your state, a vocational rehabilitation counselor, or one of the other resources listed in the section on assistive technology.

MOBILITY IMPAIRMENTS

For people with mobility impairments, the key word is adjustability. Components such as the desk, chair, armrests, monitor, and keyboard all need to be positioned according to an individual's needs. An adjustable-height desk, for example, allows someone in a wheelchair to get close enough to the monitor, even for a computer that is shared by several users. This is more than an issue of comfort. "The height of a computer in relation to the wheelchair is critical for someone with a severe spinal cord injury. You don't want to do something that causes secondary strain," emphasizes Jude Monson, education coordinator for an independent living center.

A person who cannot use a standard keyboard because of limited use of his or her hands can use a headpointer, mouthstick, or other mechanical pointing device to press keys on the keyboard. There also are lightweight head-tracking devices that require only a small, dot-sized item placed on a person's face. These devices utilize an infrared beam to access an on-screen keyboard on the computer. In addition, there are a number of keyboard adaptations. Expanded keyboards have keys that are spaced farther apart to help people with limited fine motor control. Conversely, smaller-than-standard keyboards are useful for those who use one hand to type or who lack the range of motion to use a larger keyboard.

Other assistive solutions are the result of new software utilities. Someone who types using one of the devices mentioned above, for instance, cannot easily use programs that require a person to simultaneously press two or more keys (such as "Shift" and "D"). Sticky keys have solved that problem; they stay pressed down so that sequential, rather than simultaneous, keystrokes will work. Repeat keys eliminate the problem of unwanted key repetitions, caused when a person with limited motor control can't release a key before it starts to repeat. Slow keys are helpful for people who often strike unwanted keys before hitting the one they want. These keys have to be pressed longer in order to be decisively selected, thus eliminating excessive corrections. Another item that can help with making a precise selection on the keyboard is a keyboard guard, a simple template with holes over each key.

Word-prediction software is useful for people with limited mobility and for people who tire easily from typing. It reduces input strokes by "guessing" the rest of a word or phrase after several keystrokes are made. Word abbreviation software (in which you could type "imdy" or "imy" for the word "immediately") is also effective.

As an alternative to typing, voice-recognition systems (also called speech-input systems) respond to voice commands. These systems require "discrete" speech; that is, the person has to pause between words to indicate that sounds should be interpreted as words. Speech input can enable a person to compose an essay on word processing software, use the Internet, or search for files on the hard drive, among other functions. Bill Chatterton says that it took some time to "train" his system to recognize his speech patterns. "But now, I've got the computer set up to respond to voice commands to open doors in my house and turn the stereo on and off," he says.

VISUAL IMPAIRMENTS

More than 40 million people in the world are blind or vision impaired. A variety of assistive technology has been developed to help this disability group take advantage of computers, the Internet, and related technologies.

Low Vision

Two of the most common assistive technologies for people with low vision are screen-enlargement software and a large (ideally, at least 17-inch) monitor. The screen-enlargement software allows everything on the computer screen to appear in a larger-than-standard font. Some people also find that adjusting the foreground and background colors on the monitor can be helpful. For instance, people with light sensitivity can usually read white text on a black background best.

A scanner allows a person to input text from any source (such as a magazine article or class syllabus), and then use screen enlargement software to enlarge it.

Inputting on a standard keyboard is usually not problematic for people with low vision, but those just learning to type might find large-print key labels helpful.

Blindness

While most people who are blind are comfortable using standard keyboards, Braille keyboards are another option. Other available Braille devices include Braille printers and refreshable displays that provide detailed, line-by-line Braille translation of the text on the computer screen.

HEARING IMPAIRMENTS

Generally, hearing impairments do not affect a person's ability to use a computer. Most computer operating systems now have built-in visual cues—such as a flashing screen or musical note in one corner of the screen—as alternatives to computer sound cues.

SPEECH IMPAIRMENTS

A person with a serious speech impairment who wants to communicate verbally in class, at work, or in other settings can use a portable communication device (also called a speech synthesizer) as his or her voice. The user can input frequently used sentences or can type out an original sentence, then press a button to make the device "speak."

LEARNING DISABILITIES

Many computer users with learning disabilities are utilizing adaptive tools designed originally for visually impaired users. Scanners and voice-output systems, for instance, can help people who have trouble comprehending what they read directly from books. Screen-enlargement software can assist people who have certain reading difficulties.

Other helpful software features are real-time spell checking, vocalized text (which talks as you type), word highlighting, and word prediction.

Paul Peterson works full time, running both a community disability advocacy program and a peer-support program. His disabilities stem from diabetes; he has no vision, is hearing impaired in one ear, and uses a wheelchair because of nerve damage. To do his job, he makes extensive use of screen-reading software and a speech synthesizer that speaks the text out loud. Since he types on a standard keyboard, he finds it particularly useful to have the computer read aloud as he types. He also uses a scanner to scan printed material into his computer in order to store or read it easily. "I wouldn't be able to do my work without [my computer]," he acknowledges. "It would be monumentally expensive for my office to hire a full-time person to read everything to me." For taking notes and keeping track of his schedule, Paul also uses a small portable device that has a seven-key Braille keyboard and a "voice." Paul truly understands the importance of access to technology.

FINDING FUNDING FOR ASSISTIVE TECHNOLOGY

Aid in acquiring assistive technology, which can be extremely expensive, is available through a variety of sources. It is usually is advantageous to individuals with disabilities to know their rights under the law and apply for funding from a combination of available avenues. Both public and private sources offer funding. The following information serves as a starting point for individuals initiating their search.

Public Sources of Funding

Public sources of funding, or those that are mandated by local, state, or national governments, are usually a good place to start. If you or a family member requires assistive technology, and can be substantiate this claim through a medical professional, you should consider what programs such as Medicaid or Medicare can offer.

Medicaid and Medicare

Medicaid and Medicare both have specific requirements regarding who is able to receive benefits under the respective plans. If you know that you have a right to benefits under one of these plans, contact your provider for information about what they will cover regarding assistive technology. Keep in mind that you will need to document your need for assistive technology as a medical necessity. A good place to start is by contacting the Centers for Medicare and Medicaid Services at http://www.cms.hhs.gov.

State Vocational Rehabilitation Agencies

State vocational rehabilitation agencies provide another source of public funding. This source is particularly applicable to those who can demonstrate a need for assistive technology in their professional and/or work life. Documenting such need in as much detail as possible, by illustrating the impact assistive technology would have on your ability to perform specific work-related tasks, is essential in applying for these types of grants. For a listing of these agencies by state, visit http://www.parac.org/svrp.html.

State Grants to Small Businesses

If you work for a small employer, you may also consider discussing with the owner the option of applying for a state grant. You might discuss the benefits of assistive technology and how it could impact your productivity and overall job performance. Many states have funds available, in the form of grants to small businesses that enable them to make special accommodations for workers with disabilities. Contact your state government for information on this type of funding.

Schools

If assistive technology will help your child perform better in school, you should talk with school administrators about including this information in the student's Individualized Education Program (IEP) that is required for every disabled child. Public schools are required to provide assistive technology for students, but as more and more advances are made, often it is in a parent's best interest to make sure the school knows about new devices that may impact a child's learning. Because this technology is often specific to a particular disability, staying on top of technological advances that are specific to your child's needs is important. Because recommendations for assistive technology devices must be included in a child's IEP for the school to provide it at no cost, it is useful for parents to stay involved with the process.

Private Sources of Funding

Private, nongovernmental institutions and organizations also provide funding sources for assistive technology. Some organizations will provide grants, while others will offer loan programs for obtaining assistive technology.

Private Insurance

Private insurance can be overlooked sometimes because insurance plans seldom come right out and state that they will cover assistive technology. However, it is always useful to seek out opportunities through private health insurance. It goes without saying that you should do your homework, be extremely knowledgeable, and have a doctor or doctors who will prescribe the device(s) as medically necessary. Being able to show that assistive technology will improve you or your family members' condition also can help in attaining funding from private insurance. Because insurance plans often are vague as to what they will and will not cover, be persistent in pursuing this avenue of funding.

Nonprofit Organizations and Foundations

Nonprofit disability organizations and/or foundations often provide funding for both individuals and organizations for assistive technology. Because there are so many of these organizations it is best if you contact the organizations that you may be involved with or those that support individuals with your specific disability. Your local library is a good place to find listings of such organizations. A few of these organizations include the following: National Easter Seals Society (http://www.easterseals. com), March of Dimes (http://www.marchofdimes.com), Muscular Dystrophy Association (http://www.mdausa. org), and United Way (http://national.unitedway.org).

Several nonprofit organizations also exist to help individuals in their quest for funding. These organizations don't provide funding themselves, but they will provide resources and referrals on how to find additional sources of funding: The Alliance for Technology Access (http://www.ataccess.org), United Cerebral Palsy Association, Inc. (http://www.ucp.org), Independent Living centers (http://ilusa.com/links/ilcenters.htm), state Tech Act Projects (http://www.resna.org/taproject/at/statecontacts.html),

regional Disability and Business Technical Assistance Centers (http://www.adata.org/centers.htm), and Parent Training and Information Centers (http://www.taalliance. org/centers).

Local Service and Civic Organizations

Your local chamber of commerce is an excellent source of information on civic and service organizations that may provide funding for assistive technology. Clubs and organizations such as the Lions Club (http://www. lionsclubs.org), Elks Club (http://www.elks.org), Rotary Club (http://www.rotory.org), or Kiwanis (http://www. kiwanis.org), often select a disability that they support. Others will simply raise funds at the local level for a particular person in need of a device.

Private Corporations

Corporations that are privately owned also provide funding for assistive technology. If you are aware of a corporation that has been known to support a particular disability, it is best to start by contacting that corporation. Also, if you work for a corporation and can demonstrate that you will become a more productive employee with the aid of assistive technology, your employer may be willing to fund the purchase of the device. Make an appointment to meet with the appropriate company administrators and pitch the idea to them. Many companies may want to capitalize on the opportunity to create positive public relations for themselves through funding such technology. If you are open to that possibility, don't be afraid to sell your request as a win-win situation for everybody involved.

Fund-raising

Sometimes local community religious organizations, friends, and neighbors can help with fund-raising efforts. Approach leaders of any groups that you have an affiliation with and discuss your circumstances and the impact that assistive technology would have on your life or the life of your child. Create your own fund-raising strategy and speak to organizations on behalf of yourself or someone you know who would benefit from assistive technology.

Loans

When you've exhausted all sources for grants and free funding, commercial loans are another option. Many states, though not all, provide loans for individuals who wish to purchase assistive technology. Further information about obtaining loans in your state can be found at http://www.resna.org/AFTAP/state.

THINGS TO CONSIDER WHEN SEEKING FUNDING OR PURCHASING ASSISTIVE TECHNOLOGY

Before purchasing assistive technology, and even before seeking funding, you should carefully research the types of technology available and access your needs. Knowing exactly how much funding you need, as well as being able to articulate effectively the purpose of a particular device and the impact it will have on your work/life situation, is imperative to successfully reaching your goals.

Be Able to Prove Need

Your evidence of need is essential in seeking funding. You must be able to provide documentation of this need. Find technology resource centers that will loan you equipment or find suppliers that will allow you to try a product before buying. Take photos, notes, and videos of the experience. Illustrate how the device affects your daily functioning.

Do your research and be thorough. By the time you are ready to approach funding sources, be sure you know exactly what you need and want so that you can articulate effectively the purpose of the device and how it will affect your work/life situation.

Develop an Action Plan

Your financial situation, combined with the cost of assistive technology, will determine your plan of action. How much financing are you able to provide on your own? Decide exactly what device you need, and how much outside funding you must find. Know your rights in regard to disability law. This is imperative, especially when seeking public funding. Gather necessary documents and reports that outline agency requirements for funding. Keep detailed records of your fund-seeking progress, especially if you are working with more than one funder. If you need to appeal a case, careful documentation will mean that revising applications won't be such an ordeal. Keep records of all correspondence, including phone calls, with organizations. Diversify your requests. Seek funding from multiple sources. Finally, find yourself an advocate. Assistive technology manufacturers have funding coordinators available, or you can try advocacy groups, support groups, family members, or others. The process of raising funds can be exhausting. Don't try to do it alone.

THE FUTURE OF ASSISTIVE TECHNOLOGY

Typically, when a new computer technology becomes popular, there's a lag before computer users with disabilities are provided with adaptive solutions. However, more technology manufacturers are recognizing the potential in this large group of consumers and incorporating accessible technology into their hardware and software. These changes will make it possible for people with disabilities to work and study on a level playing field with their non-disabled peers. Look for accessible technology to become incorporated into the original design of many electronic and computer products in the future.

Another obstacle for people with disabilities is the technology that exists outside the home and workplace. Going out into the "real world" and trying to use an ATM, for example, was a barrier until very recently. To use the touchscreen, a person had to be able to both reach and visually read the screen. Today, "talking ATMs" and other assistive technology can be found in banks and other financial institutions throughout the United States. The Trace Center (http://trace.wisc.edu) at the University of Wisconsin-Madison works with designers to integrate disability access features into many technologies. Its EZ Access technology can be found in automated postal kiosks, the first fully accessible paging and information system at an airport (Phoenix Sky Harbor International Airport), and other public settings.

A primary technological focus of the next decade will be making the Internet more accessible to people who are disabled—especially the blind, the visually impaired, and those with impaired mobility. While computers and related technology have become much more user-friendly in the past decade, most Web sites are still not easily accessible for persons with certain disabilities.

In 1998, Congress amended the Rehabilitation Act to require that federal agencies make their information technology and electronics (including computers, telephones, and the Internet) accessible to the disabled. Under Section 508, federal agencies must provide access to their employees and the general public that is comparable to that received by those who are not disabled. While this act applies only to federal agencies and departments, many states, private organizations, and companies are also integrating the guidelines stipulated in Section 508 into their programs, products, and services.

FOR MORE INFORMATION

Action Without Borders
360 West 31st Street, Suite 1510
New York, NY 10001
212-843-3973
http://www.idealist.org

This organization is a network of individuals and organizations that share ideas, information, and resources in order to help people live free, dignified, and productive lives.

Alliance for Technology Access

1304 Southpoint Boulevard, Suite 240
Petaluma, CA 94954
707-778-3011, 707-778-3015 (TTY)
atainfo@ataccess.org
http://www.ataccess.org
The alliance is a nationwide network of resource centers that are dedicated to providing information on assistive technology and funding and support services to children and adults with disabilities, as well as increasing their use of standard, assistive, and informative technologies.

Center for Information Technology Accommodation (CITA)

Office of Governmentwide Policy
U.S. General Services Administration
1800 F Street, NW, Room 1234
Washington, DC 20405
202-501-4906
section.508@gsa.gov
http://www.section508.gov
Visit the center's Web site for more information on Section 508 of the Rehabilitation Act.

Centers for Medicare and Medicaid Services

7500 Security Boulevard
Baltimore MD 21244-1850
877-267-2323, 866-226-1819 (TTY)
http://www.cms.hhs.gov
Contact the Centers for Medicare and Medicaid Services for information on possible funding for assistive technology under the Medicare or Medicaid programs.

DO-IT

University of Washington
PO Box 355670
Seattle, WA 98195-5670
206-685-3648 (Voice/TTY), 888-972-3648 (Voice/TTY)
doit@u.washington.edu
http://www.washington.edu/doit
DO-IT (Disabilities, Opportunities, Internetworking, and Technology) works to increase the participation of individuals with disabilities in academic programs and careers.

Information Technology Technical Assistance and Training Center

Center for Assistive Technology and Environmental Access
Georgia Institute of Technology
490 10th Street, NW
Atlanta, GA 30318
866-948-8282 (Voice/TTY)
ittatc@ittatc.org
http://www.ittatc.org
This organization works to increase the availability of accessible technology in the United States. It is funded by the National Institute on Disability and Rehabilitation Research.

Rehabilitation Engineering and Assistive Technology Society of North America (RESNA)

1700 North Moore Street, Suite 1540
Arlington, VA 22209-1903
703-524-6686, 703-524-6639 (TTY)
info@resna.org
http://www.resna.org
Contact RESNA or visit its Web site to find information about Tech Act projects in your home state and funding options.

Trace Research and Development Center

University of Wisconsin-Madison
College of Engineering
2107 Engineering Centers Building
1550 Engineering Drive
Madison, WI 53706
608-262-6966, 608-263-5408 (TTY)
info@trace.wisc.edu
http://www.trace.wisc.edu
This is an interdisciplinary research, development, and resource center on technology and disability located at the University of Wisconsin-Madison.

United Cerebral Palsy Association Inc.

1660 L Street, NW, Suite 700
Washington, DC 20036
800-872-5827, 202-973-7197 (TTY)
http://www.ucp.org
This organization provides information on assistive technology and referrals to funding sources.

COMMUNICATING WITH PEOPLE WHO HAVE DISABILITIES

Martha Knowles, of Orlando, Florida, will never forget the time she went to renew her driver's license at the Department of Motor Vehicles. When her number came up, she handed the clerk her paperwork and told him that she was deaf. He became flustered and asked, "And you currently have a driver's license?" Martha laughs about it now, but, at the time, she was indignant. "He was clearly surprised that a person who was deaf could drive a car," she says. "Communication goes beyond just what people say; [it's] their attitudes and body language as well."

If you ask 10 people who have disabilities to describe moments when communicating with other people has been strained or unpleasant, you'll hear recurring themes in their stories. For instance, there's the theme of being treated like a child. A middle-aged woman who has a speech impairment as the result of a stroke says she wishes that people wouldn't talk to her in a high-pitched, singsong voice. Another woman who uses a wheelchair says she has been patted on the head countless times. One man with multiple sclerosis who uses a wheelchair is not even taken aback anymore when waiters and waitresses hand a menu to his wife instead of directly to him.

If you haven't spent much time around people with disabilities, you might read these anecdotes and feel nervous about doing or saying the wrong thing yourself. But, if you learn some very simple guidelines, communicating with people who have disabilities doesn't have to be awkward. Jude Monson, who works at the Summit Independent Living Center in Missoula, Montana, says, "The most common mistake people make is forgetting that it's a person they're dealing with, someone with feelings, thoughts, and their own personality." She offers an easy rule of thumb, which is to just relax and think how you would want to be treated. Don't tiptoe and dwell on the way that the person is different from you; focus on the many things you have in common.

COMMUNICATION BASICS

The best guide to communication is always the person with whom you are communicating. But there are some basic guidelines—specific to the type of disability—that you can follow as you're getting to know someone.

Visual Impairments

Be sure to identify yourself and anyone with you when you are meeting a person who is visually impaired. In talking to or working with people who have visual impairments, be as descriptive and specific as possible. For instance, say, "The chair is on your left, about two feet away." If you are guiding a person, don't grab or push. Instead, offer your arm and walk at their pace. In addition, remember that you should ask permission to interact with a person's guide dog.

Mobility Impairments

For people who are in wheelchairs, try to position yourself at eye level when you're speaking. Don't patronize someone by patting him or her on the head or shoulder. Treat the wheelchair as you would someone's personal body space, and don't lean on it. Feel free to offer assistance. After all, think about how grateful you are when someone holds open a door when you're carrying packages. Simply ask the person if he or she needs help and then act accordingly. If the answer is no, don't insist on it. Never move anyone's crutches, walker, cane, or other mobility aid without asking the person.

Speech Impairments

When you are talking to someone with a speech disability, the goal is communication. Don't pretend to understand what they've said if you haven't. Repeat what you've understood, using a regular tone of voice, and let the person respond. Listen carefully. Be patient and wait for the person to finish. Don't step in to speak for him or her. If it's easier, the person may write it down. If you need to get information quickly, try to ask brief questions that can be answered by a nod of the head or a simple response. However, don't insult the person's intelligence by oversimplifying.

Hearing Impairments

To get the attention of a person who is deaf, tap him or her lightly on the shoulder. If the person can read lips, face the person so that he or she can see your mouth. Speak clearly and with natural expressiveness, but keep in mind that not all people who are deaf can read lips. If you are speaking through an interpreter, remember to pause occasionally to allow him or her to translate completely and accurately—particularly if there are technical terms or names that need to be fingerspelled. Even though the person you are speaking to will be looking at the interpreter, speak directly to the person who is deaf.

Cognitive Impairments

An adult with a cognitive disability should be treated as an adult. As with speech impairments, don't pretend to understand someone with a cognitive impairment if you don't. Give the person time to respond and be supportive. Use language that is concrete rather than abstract. People with brain injuries may have short-term memory deficits and will need information to be repeated. People with auditory perceptual problems might need to take notes to remember directions. Some persons with cognitive impairments may benefit from having a task demonstrated. Others have a problem with sensory overload and will find it disorienting to have to absorb too much information at once. Finally, don't interpret the person's distractedness as rudeness.

LANGUAGE MATTERS

Are you worried about using the politically correct terminology and perhaps opting instead to say nothing at all? The more you work or talk with people who are disabled, the more of a handle you'll get on this. Generally speaking, however, remember this perspective: put people first. Say "person with a disability" rather than "disabled person." Having a disability is just one aspect of a person's life. Use words that emphasize the wholeness of the person. A woman with prosthetic arms might also be a mother, a skier, a singer, and a stockbroker. Think about how you would feel if people constantly referred to you as "the knock-kneed person," "the tea-drinking person," or "the shaky-hands person."

June Isaacson Kailes, a disability policy consultant in Playa del Rey, California, was one of the earliest advocates for the thoughtful use of language about disabilities. She argues that while some people feel it's a trivial matter, "language plays a role in perpetuating negative stereotypes and in shaping ideas and attitudes." It really isn't any more complicated than learning the language of a new sport, hobby, or job. Once you get used to phrasing things "people first," it will become second nature.

Considering the subtle power that words carry, it's worthwhile to take a look at a few other phrases that are inappropriate. The phrases "confined to a wheelchair" and "wheelchair bound" carry negative connotations. A person uses a wheelchair to increase his or her mobility and is anything but confined to it. Likewise, you've probably read articles in the newspaper that talked about how someone "overcame his or her disability." In fact, people live with their disabilities. What they overcome are social, economic, psychological, architectural, transportation, educational, and employment barriers. Other terms that are considered outdated and even offensive are "handicapped," "sightless," "lame," "deformed," "crippled," and "deaf mute."

Remember that the language that is considered appropriate now will change and evolve. But, if you treat people who have disabilities as equal human beings, you will learn more along the way and forge reciprocal the kind of relationships. "I try to teach in my style of language," comments Jude Monson. "People who have the willingness to learn tend to pick up on it and begin mirroring how I've phrased things."

Some people with disabilities say that when you are in doubt about how to relate to a person, imagine how a child would handle the situation. A man who is deaf comments, "If I'm at the park, kids aren't afraid to walk over to me. They're curious, and they'll come right out and ask, 'Can you read my lips?'" Jude Monson reiterates that sentiment. As part of her job as educational coordinator for an independent living center, she goes into the local schools to do presentations. "Kids are great because they'll ask questions. Their parents are often the ones who are embarrassed or trying to be tactful," she says. "It's good to think that we can educate future generations to feel at ease with people who have disabilities."

FOR MORE INFORMATION

National Center on Disability and Journalism
10 Milk Street, Suite 423
Boston, MA 02108
617-728-7772
http://www.ncdj.org/styleguide.php

Register at the National Center on Disability and Journalism Web site to review a style guide on disability and journalism.

Office of Disability Employment Policy
U.S. Department of Labor
Frances Perkins Building
200 Constitution Avenue, NW
Washington, DC 20210
866-633-7365, 877-889-5627 (TTY)
http://www.dol.gov/odep/pubs/fact/comucate.htm
Contact the Office of Disability Employment Policy to review the publication *Communicating with and about People with Disabilities.*

Ten Commandments of Etiquette for Communicating with People with Disabilities
http://www.ucp.org/ucp_generaldoc.cfm/161/9/6573/6573-6573/190
This Web site is a good resource for communicating with people with disabilities.

University of Kansas, Publications
Research and Training Center on Independent Living
1000 Sunnyside Avenue, Room 4089, Dole
Lawrence, KS 66045-7555
785-864-4095, 785-864-0706 (TTY)
rtcil@ku.edu
http://www.lsi.ku.edu/lsi/internal/guidelines.html
Contact the University of Kansas for a copy of the *Guidelines for Reporting and Writing about People with Disabilities.*

LOCATING THE RESOURCES TO GO TO COLLEGE

"I've always known I would go to college," says Joe Coombs Jr., a freshman with cerebral palsy at Delaware Technical College. "To make decent money these days you really have to." Eric Patterson, a freshman at Mt. Hood Community College, echoes that sentiment. He began toying with the idea of going to college while he was a high school student at the Oregon School for the Blind. He explains, "I started researching careers and talking to a lot of people who worked in technology. Almost everyone had a college degree."

Joe and Eric are among an increasing number of people with disabilities who are heading off to college—and thriving there. The percentage of first-year college students who report having a disability has more than tripled since the late 1970s. A rise in the awareness and diagnosis of learning disabilities accounts for some of this tremendous enrollment jump. More significantly, however, students with disabilities who would have been steered away from college in the past now recognize that it's a great way to prepare for an interesting career and to take fuller control of their lives.

Heading off to college ranks right up there as one of life's major transitions. For the disabled student, it's particularly important to start laying the foundation for a good college experience early. Here are some tips to help you get into the school of your choice, locate a variety of financial aid options, and make a smooth transition once you're on campus.

STARTING NOW

You can't start preparations too soon. Even if you're only in the ninth or 10th grade, it's time to begin considering your options. Talk with school counselors or independent-living-center counselors about careers that pique your interest. Sign up for college-prep courses or consider taking a few college-level classes at a community college. Tackling tough courses now will make it easier once you're in college. And purchase the best computer you can afford, since they've become a necessity on most cam-

puses. You should also obtain extensive documentation from medical professionals regarding your disability (in addition to the information that is found in your Individualized Education Program). This documentation will be necessary for you to obtain many accommodations when you are in college.

Doing well on precollege exams such as the SAT (http://www.collegeboard.com/ssd/student/index.html) and ACT (http://www.act.org/aap/disab/index.html) is also going to give you a head start on getting into the college of your choice. If you need any sort of test-taking accommodations, don't be shy about asking for them. If you're disappointed with your score and feel you could improve on it, consider retaking the exam.

CHOOSING A SCHOOL

You've decided what kind of career or degree program interests you. Now it's time to make a list of schools that offer those programs. Your high school counselor will have some suggestions, but you should also do your own research on colleges and universities by using reference books and the Internet, and talking to people who have been to college about their experiences. Don't forget to consider two-year colleges. It is estimated that 60 percent of all students with disabilities choose two-year colleges.

After you've made a preliminary list of schools that offer your chosen course of study, start narrowing the list based on other criteria. One of the things you'll need to decide is how important a school's disability services are to you. This question often evokes strong reactions. "I feel that someone with a disability should not choose a school because of its disability services," says Jim Marks, Director of Disability Services for Students at the University of Montana. "They should choose one because it's in a cool city, or because the academic program is what they want, or because their friends are all going there." Carolyn Tyjewski, who is blind, wholeheartedly agrees. She has earned degrees in Black studies and English and is working toward a Ph.D. in Rhetoric at Ohio State University. She advises, "The law is quite clear that all schools have to make themselves accessible. Make your decision based on what you want to get out of the [college] experience."

Yet a number of students believe that the strength of a college's disability services can have a huge impact on their academic success or failure. Chuck Hurlburt was born with spina bifida and has learning disabilities. He earned an associate degree from Mitchell College in New London, Connecticut, and a bachelor's degree from New Hampshire College. "I was not a terrific student and knew I needed to attend a college with small classes and lots of support," he says. "I worked with my guidance counselor to select a college that had excellent disability services."

Whatever the criteria on which you ultimately base your decision, you'll definitely want to inquire about disability services at all of the colleges on your list. One of the most important things you can do is to prepare of list of questions for potential colleges and universities regarding your needs and how they will address them. After you come up with your questions, share your list with your parents, teachers, counselors, and case managers in case they have any additional suggestions. Having as many people as possible who are familiar with you and your needs review your list of questions will help ensure that your questions are comprehensive and address all of your needs. Some general topics to cover in your questions:

- How much money does the school spend on its disability services?
- Is financial support available for continuing services?
- What's the enrollment of disabled students on campus?
- What is the graduation rate for students with disabilities?
- Is the staff knowledgeable about my disability?
- What services does the school offer?
- How can I obtain any services that I need that the school does not currently provide?
- What equipment and assistive technology is available, where is it, how often will I have access to it, and how will I be trained on it, if necessary.
- How are services or equipment funded? Will I be expected to pay for any portion of it?
- What types of accommodations will be made for me as I attend class, prepare assignments, and take exams?

If you anticipate living on campus while you attend school, ask about residential options: How accessible are they for you?

Inquire about the layout of campus, taking into consideration the buildings you are most likely to live in and attend classes in—especially if you have a physical disability:

- How easily will I be able to maneuver between buildings?
- Are all buildings accessible to me?
- Are all of the classrooms accessible to me? If not, how likely is it that all of my classes can be held in accessible areas?
- What type of public transportation is available on campus and in the surrounding community? Is it accessible to me?
- Does the university offer transportation for disabled students?
- Are there any support groups or mentoring options on campus for students with disabilities?

When you find an institution that you are interested in, take the time to meet with staff from the school's office that coordinates disability services. Try to get a feel for the personnel of the office: how helpful they are, how comfortable you are with them. While your overall impression of them should not be the only reason you decide whether or not to attend that institution, you should have a clear idea of what you can or cannot expect from them, and factor that into your planning process. Be sure to attend any orientations or programs for prospective students with disabilities that the school may have. Besides being informative, they will also serve to introduce you to other students with disabilities who might have already encountered some of the same obstacles that you have, and might be able to offer useful suggestions. They will also provide you with an opportunity to forge friendships with others who are facing many of the same things you are, as you anticipate your postsecondary education options.

FINDING THE FUNDS

If you're worried about how to pay for college, you're not alone. Every three years, the HEATH Resource Center, a national clearinghouse on postsecondary education for individuals with disabilities, publishes a statistical profile on first year college students with disabilities. Among its findings, the 2001 study showed that students with disabilities are more likely than their peers without disabilities to be significantly concerned about paying for their education. The good news is that with some perseverance, you can find financial aid that will cover—or at least offset—the expense of college.

One of the sources that many college students with disabilities depend on is Vocational Rehabilitation (VR), a government-funded program. The purpose of VR is to help individuals with disabilities maximize their employment, economic self-sufficiency, and integration into society. It's very important to contact your local VR office as early as possible. If you're a junior in high school, you should apply now to find out if you're eligible for assistance. Once VR determines your eligibility, you'll begin meeting with a counselor who will help you map out a long-term career plan. In most states, VR will pay for tuition, books, reader and interpreter services, and technological aids or devices. Kathy Cook, a former disabled services counselor at the University of Washington, cautions that getting assistance from VR requires patience and persistence: "To go this route, you need to go through a lot of red tape, but it can definitely pay off. Last year, two of my students with learning disabilities had VR pay for their laptop computers."

It's unlikely, however, that all of your expenses will be covered by VR. You'll need to look into funding from other sources, too, such as grants, scholarships, loans, and work-study. The benefit of grants and scholarships is that they do not have to be repaid. Some scholarships are given to specific disability populations (contact the Heath Resource Center for a partial list). However, these scholarships are usually limited and in small amounts ranging from $500 to $1,000. Some colleges and universities also offer scholarships for students with disabilities, so it's important to contact disability services at the colleges you're considering. For a broader choice of scholarships, consider those that have nothing to do with your disability, but depend instead on your career goals, military experience, ethnic background, religious affiliation, extracurricular activities, and so forth. To search for current scholarships, see the *Funding Sources* section. You can also research scholarships on the Internet (see *For More Information* for specific Web sites) and at your local or school library.

Loans are a form of financial aid that must be repaid over an extended period of time after you finish college. Work-study allows you to work to earn money to cover your college expenses. One of the best sources of information about loans and work-study programs is the financial aid officer at each college to which you apply.

Other sources of financial assistance for students with disabilities include Supplemental Security Income (http://www.ssa.gov/notices/supplemental-security-income), a federal program that provides assistance to people who are aged, blind, or disabled and have little or no income, and Social Security Disability Insurance (http://www.ssa.gov/dibplan/index.htm), which assists certain students who have been employed, who have a parent who has filed for Social Security, or who have a deceased parent. Discuss these options with your VR counselor or contact the Social Security administration office.

Here are some final thoughts about applying for financial aid: You'll be dealing with reams of paperwork. It's vital that you meet the deadlines and provide accurate information. Ask someone to proofread your forms and applications. During the application process, contact the colleges' financial aid offices to confirm that your data is being processed. It doesn't hurt to ask your VR counselor to stay in touch with the colleges, too.

NOW YOU'RE IN COLLEGE!

One of the most important differences between high school and college for a person who is disabled is the manner in which his or her needs are addressed and served. In college, you are your own advocate, you are responsible for making your needs known. In high school, the educational system creates your IEP for you, identifies which services you need, and you can expect to receive the necessary support and services. In college, there is no IEP—you must request the same services that were previously identified and provided for you. In high school, classes are modified for you according to your disability; in college they are not. Prepare yourself for this and create strategies to deal with the difference. You can request certain modifications, but the actual coursework requirements will not be modified. Consider things like assistive technology or using a facilitator in class to assist with note taking. These are things you may be required to fund yourself—its good idea to research how you'll do this while you're still in high school.

The 1973 Rehabilitation Act and 1990 Americans with Disabilities Act states: "No otherwise qualified individual with a disability shall, solely by reason of his/her disability, be excluded from participation in, be denied the benefits of, or be subjected to discrimination under any program or activity of a public entity." But, as Jim Marks, Director of Disability Services for Students at the University of Montana, says, "As a college student, you have a civil right to access, but the responsibility to advocate is up to you. If you see discrimination, you have to fight it."

No matter how excellent a college or university is at providing accommodations for disabled students, you know better than anyone what your needs are. So it's up to you to make requests. Some accommodations are simple, such as a student with low vision asking to be seated in the front row. Other accommodations require creativity, like the student with a learning disability who asks a professor to incorporate tactile demonstrations into her instruction. Getting to know other students with disabilities on campus will give you a chance to share ideas and accommodation strategies.

Shifting into self-advocacy can be a dramatic change for students who have previously relied on counselors, parents, or teachers to handle matters for them. Students with disabilities find that one of their biggest adjustments is learning to speak up for themselves. Because they were assisted via an IEP in high school, they may have never talked about their disability and how it affects them academically. It's a good idea to start practicing these types of conversations before you get to college.

Learning how to be a self-advocate is, in itself, a powerful skill, something you should aspire to gain from your time in college. You'll need to remind yourself of that occasionally when you face obstacles along the way to getting your degree. As Jim Marks says, however, "I can't think of a better way to prepare for the world of work."

FOR MORE INFORMATION

ACT Inc.
Services for Students With Disabilities
http://www.act.org/aap/disab/index.html
ACT Inc. provides reasonable accommodations to students with disabilities who are taking the ACT Assessment.

Association on Higher Education and Disabilities (AHEAD)
PO Box 540666
Waltham, MA 02454
781-788-0003 (TTY)
ahead@ahead.org
http://www.ahead.org
AHEAD is an organization that addresses the need for upgrading the quality of services and support available to persons with disabilities in postsecondary education. It provides a variety of useful brochures to disabled students at a low cost.

College and Career Programs for Deaf Students
http://gri.gallaudet.edu/ccg/index.html
At this Web site, you'll find excellent information that is intended for deaf students but is applicable to other disabilities as well.

The College Board
Services for Students With Disabilities
609-771-7137
ssd@info.collegeboard.org
http://www.collegeboard.com/ssd/student/index.html
The College Board offers testing accommodations (SAT Reasoning and Subject Tests, Advanced Placement Tests, PSAT/NMSQT) for students with disabilities. It also offers a scholarship search engine (http://apps.collegeboard.com/cbsearch_ss/welcome.jsp) that lists awards that total more than $3 billion. You can search by specific major and a variety of other criteria.

CollegeNET
http://mach25.collegenet.com/cgi-bin/M25/index
The CollegeNET Web site features a scholarship database of more than 600,000 scholarships worth more than $1.6 billion. You can search by keyword or by creating a personality profile of your interests.

DO-IT
University of Washington
PO Box 355670
Seattle, WA 98195-5670
206-685-3648 (Voice/TTY), 888-972-3648 (Voice/TTY)
doit@u.washington.edu
http://www.washington.edu/doit
DO-IT (Disabilities, Opportunities, Internetworking, and Technology) works to increase the participation of individuals with disabilities in academic programs and careers. It offers a variety of useful publications and resources, including *College: You Can Do It!, College Funding Strategies for Students with Disabilities* and *Preparing for College: An Online Tutorial.*

FastWeb
http://www.fastweb.com
The FastWeb Web site is an excellent source of information for planning for college and beyond. It includes information on admissions, scholarships, and financial aid, and tips on college life. It offers a free search of the nation's largest database of local, national, and college-specific scholarships.

Federal Trade Commission
600 Pennsylvania Avenue, NW
Washington, DC 20580
202-326-2222
http://www.ftc.gov/bcp/conline/edcams/scholarship
Contact the Federal Trade Commission to report fraud
and for tips on avoiding scholarships scams.

FinAid
http://www.finaid.org
FinAid is excellent Web site that focuses on financial aid.
It offers calculators to help determine total school
costs and financial need and links to free financial aid
searches. It also reviews many books on financial aid
for undergraduates and for graduates.

Funding Your Education
Federal Student Aid Information Center
PO Box 84
Washington, DC 20044-0084
800-433-3243
http://studentaid.ed.gov/students/publications/FYE/
index.html
This is a free booklet for students from the U.S. Depart-
ment of Education. It is available in both English and
Spanish.

Heath Resource Center
2121 K Street, NW, Suite 220
Washington, DC 20037
202-973-0904 (Voice/TTY)
askheath@gwu.edu
http://www.heath.gwu.edu
The Heath Resource Center is the American Council on
Education's national clearinghouse on postsecondary education for people with disabilities. Its Web
site features useful publications (such as *Financial
Aid for Students with Learning Disabilities* and *Creating
Options: A Resource on Financial Aid for Students With
Disabilities*) and articles written by disabled students.

Institute on Disability
University of New Hampshire
250 Commercial Street, Suite 4107
Manchester, NH 03101
603-628-7681
http://www.iod.unh.edu
The institute seeks to "provide a coherent university-
based focus for the improvement of knowledge,

policies, and practices related to the lives of persons
with disabilities and their families." It publishes
Postsecondary Education: A Choice for Everyone, which
provides tips on preparing for college while in high
school, an overview of the differences between high
school and college for students with disabilities, and
advice on choosing the right college.

Landmark College
River Road South
Putney, VT 05346
802-387-6718
http://www.landmarkcollege.org
Landmark College is one of the few colleges in the
United States that is designed exclusively for students
with dyslexia, attention deficit hyperactivity disorder,
or other specific learning disabilities.

**National Center on Secondary Education
and Transition**
Institute on Community Integration
University of Minnesota
150 Pillsbury Drive, SE, 6 Pattee Hall
Minneapolis MN 55455
612-624-2097
ncset@umn.edu
http://www.ncset.org
The center provides support and information to students
with disabilities who are pursuing higher education
and other postsecondaryoptions.

National Technical Institute for the Deaf
Rochester Institute of Technology
52 Lomb Memorial Drive
Rochester, NY 14623
585-475-6400 (Voice/TTY)
ntidmc@rit.edu
http://www.ntid.rit.edu
The National Technical Institute for the Deaf is the
world's largest technological college for students
who are deaf or hard of hearing. It is affiliated with
the Rochester Institute of Technology.

**Parent Advocacy Coalition for Educational
Rights Center**
8161 Normandale Boulevard
Minneapolis, MN 55437
952-838-9000, 952-838-0190 (TTY)
pacer@pacer.org

http://www.pacer.org
This is a network of parents that advocates for educational opportunities for young people and adults with disabilities.

Scholarship America
One Scholarship Way
St. Peter, MN 56082
800-537-4180
http://www.scholarshipamerica.org
Scholarship America works through its local Dollars for Scholars chapters in 41 states and the District of Columbia. In 2003, it awarded more than $29 million in scholarships to students.

Scholarships.com
http://www.scholarships.com
Scholarships.com offers a free college scholarship search engine (although you must register to use it) and financial aid information.

Social Security Administration
Benefits for People With Disabilities
6401 Security Boulevard
Baltimore, MD 21235
800-772-1213, 800-325-0778 (TTY)
http://www.ssa.gov/disability
Contact the Social Security Administration for more information on financial aid options available through its Supplemental Security Income and Social Security Disability Insurance programs.

Talent Search and Educational Opportunity Centers
U.S. Department of Education
1990 K Street, NW, 7th Floor
Washington, DC 20006-8510
http://www.ed.gov/programs/trioeoc
These programs provide counseling and other services to disadvantaged students and students with disabilities. The programs can help to negotiate financial assistance with postsecondary institutions.

Vocational Rehabilitation Offices
To find one in your community:

- Look under the "State Government" pages of the phone book.
- Check with the local health and human services office.
- Call your local independent living center.
- Request a list from the National Rehabilitation Information Center, 4200 Forbes Boulevard, Suite 202, Lanham, MD 20706, 800-346-2742 or 301-459-5984 (TTY), naricinfo@heitechservices.com, http://www.naric.com.
- See the Government Bodies section of this book to locate your state's vocational rehabilitation office.

TEACHING STUDENTS WITH LEARNING DISABILITIES: SUGGESTIONS FOR IMPROVING THE CLASS ENVIRONMENT

One in seven Americans experiences some degree of learning disability, so it's almost certain that as you look out over your class, you are looking into the faces of some students who find some type of learning virtually impossible without specialized instruction. These children have average or above-average intelligence but have difficulty learning because of how their minds process information. There's Allison, a freckled fifth-grader in Omaha, Nebraska, who doesn't know how to spell her first or last name and whose attention can be whisked away by the sound of a tapping pencil. And there's four-year-old Stuart in Pekin, Illinois. Although he hasn't been officially diagnosed as learning disabled, his early childhood teacher notices that he can't tell the difference between a question and a statement.

As a teacher, you've already witnessed for yourself how learning disabilities like these can take their toll on children's futures. But there are many reasons to believe that students with learning disabilities can succeed— especially with the dedicated work of education professionals just like you. Dr. Kathleen Spencer, former director of the Starpoint School at Texas Christian University, says, "Early and strong intervention can make the difference. Learning differences don't go away, but students can be taught strategies to understand text and be able to study."

Whether you're a special-education teacher, a general education teacher who has students with learning disabilities integrated into the class, or a librarian, you have the chance to make a difference for these kids. A successful educational experience starts with an adult who sets high expectations for students with learning disabilities, believing that they can fulfill them. Obviously, it helps enormously when the whole school or district believes that students with learning disabilities can learn. Here are some ideas and options for improving the learning environment for your students who have learning disabilities. Making these changes will always require a process of trial and error to find what works for each individual child.

TAKE A SEAT

Simply finding the right spot in the classroom can make a world of difference. Think about the row of seats near the window, for instance. Since everything in the surrounding environment competes for this child's attention, a view out the window will always win out over schoolwork. For you, the trick is getting the student seated where there won't be many distractions. This might mean the front row, where he or she almost has to pay attention to you. But the solution isn't always so simple. If there's a boisterous neighbor or a bustling hallway visible to the student, you'll have to move the neighbor and shut the classroom door.

When it comes to test taking, putting students who have learning disabilities in a private place can be crucial. The Disabilities Education Improvement Act of 2004 requires that solitude and quiet be provided for learning disabled students of all ages if classroom distractions keep them from performing well on tests. Creating a private place can be as simple as putting up a study carrel or three-walled cubicle. Special-education teacher Karen Kazemi works with fourth- and fifth-graders at a public school near Denver, Colorado. "If you talk to the student and explain that it's a positive thing, most students really appreciate having a carrel placed in the classroom for them. I just describe it as their second desk, a place where they can sit and concentrate."

Then again, maybe your student would benefit from not sitting down at all. Some children with learning disabilities find it hard to concentrate when they're seated at a desk. Suzanne Stevens has written a book about classroom success for students with learning disabilities or attention-deficit disorder. She writes that "whole-body involvement" can draw students into their work more effectively than standard seated positions. Some teachers have set up a tall counter at the side of the class where the student can stand, lean, and move around. Stevens emphasizes the need to put firm limits on the student's behavior, however, so that the rest of the class is not disturbed. Talk to your student one-on-one and agree on what amount of movement is acceptable during the class.

IT'S ONLY ROCK AND ROLL

A silent classroom was anything but peaceful for seventh-grader David in Fort Worth, Texas. Diagnosed late with a reading disability, David was also hyperacoustic. That is, he could pick up the sound of a fan in the next room but could not hear what his teacher was saying. He found reading with his classmates in a quiet classroom nearly impossible. The solution came when his teacher suggested that he wear headphones and listen to music, which allowed him to focus on reading instead of on incidental noises.

Many other students with learning disabilities have discovered that they can concentrate best with a steady background noise. Consider letting your students use an iPod or other musical device with headphones, and don't be shy about experimenting with different types of music if the first time doesn't work. Try classical music, rock and roll, a recording of the ocean, or just white noise. For students who find even music distracting, Dr. Barbara Guyer, director emeritus of the learning disabilities graduate program at Marshall University in West Virginia, recommends headphones that significantly decrease the noise level, such as those worn by airport workers.

Like sounds, certain types of lighting can be distracting. The overhead lighting in most classrooms, especially in older schools, is usually too bright. Dim lighting often helps students feel calm, but some will just get sleepy. Brighter light helps some students stay alert, while others get fidgety. Sometimes it's a matter of changing the lighting on a student's page. Some students have benefited by wearing visors. Other students' reading skills have improved when they have placed a red or blue plastic laminating sheet on the text.

PEER POWER

Another critical ingredient to a successful learning environment is involving other students. By including everyone in the class, you can avoid stigma to the student with a learning disability. Start out by dividing the class into five-person cooperative learning groups, then breaking it down so that students are working one-on-one. You can rotate the two-person teams, which gives you a chance to see which students are especially good study buddies.

TEACH THE WAY THEY LEARN

Textbooks can tell you all about different learning styles of students. In a nutshell, people learn by seeing, by listening, by touching, by doing, or—most commonly—by using a combination of these styles.

By accident or design, teachers can discover ways to work with a student's unique learning style. For example, Nancy McKinney, an early education teacher in Pekin, Illinois, sometimes teaches young children to write their letters in shaving cream or finger paint. Other ways to increase students' tactile involvement include having them shape the letters in clay, or running their fingertips along words written on sandpaper.

Computers often grab the attention of a student with a learning disability because they offer both visual and tactile involvement. The method of processing makes sense to them in a way that written language does not. There are CD-ROMs available for all subjects and levels that help keep the student motivated and involved by highlighting key ideas, reading the material out loud, or asking frequent comprehension questions.

Believe it or not, munchies are another way to get some students focused on the subject. Oral stimulation is the fancy name for it, and some experts explain that it "integrates" the nervous system. At any rate, it's worth a try for those students who have trouble getting focused. Suzanne Stevens suggests trying chewing gum if it's allowed in your school, or something less sticky, such as popcorn, pretzels, or sugarless candy.

To work successfully with a child who has a learning disability, you have to teach the way the student learns. This means paying attention so that you can discover what makes every student unique and teachable. "So often in a classroom, we place a value on certain academic styles. Students with learning differences have remarkable talents that get hidden behind a rock," says Dr. Kathleen Spencer. "We need to teach to the student's strength and not dwell on their weakness."

Here are a few simple modifications you can make in the classroom:

Instruction

- Reduce the number of concepts that you present at one time.
- Reduce the amount of copying from the chalkboard.
- Alternate quiet and active class activities.
- Give advance warning when a transition is going to take place.

Grading

- Set realistic and mutually agreed upon expectations for neatness and spelling.

- Let students type, tape record, or give answers orally instead of in writing.
- Accept key word responses instead of complete sentences.
- Provide practice questions for study.

Organization

- Help keep students' work areas free of unnecessary materials.
- Frequently check the organization of the students' notebooks.
- Provide a daily chart to help students keep track of homework.

RESOURCES FOR TEACHERS AND PARENTS

***Classroom Success for the LD and ADHD Child* (ISBN 0-89587-159-9, 1997)**

***The Complete Learning Disabilities Directory, 2005–06 Edition* (ISBN 1-59237-092-6, 2005)**
This annual directory, which offers a wealth of resources pertaining to learning disabilities, can be ordered by contacting Grey House Publishing, Pocket Knife Square, Lakeville, CT 06039, 860-435-0868, 800-562-2139, http://www.greyhouse.com/learningdisabilities.htm.

Council for Exceptional Children
1110 North Glebe Road, Suite 300
Arlington, VA 22201
703-620-3660, 866-915-5000 (TTY)
service@cec.sped.org
http://www.cec.sped.org
This is the largest international professional organization dedicated to improving educational outcomes for individuals with exceptionalities, students with disabilities, and/or the gifted. Among its many services, it provides teachers with newsletters discussing classroom practices that really work.

Learning Disabilities Online: Teaching Techniques
http://www.ldonline.org/ld_indepth/teaching_
techniques/teaching-tech.html
This site offers excellent resources for teachers, including expert articles and recent research

***The LD and the ADHD Child: Ways Parents and Professionals Can Help* (0-89587-142-4, 1996)**
Both titles are by Suzanne H. Steven, and can be ordered by contacting John F. Blair, Publisher, Customer Order Department, 1406 Plaza Drive, Winston-Salem, NC 27103, 800-222-9796, http://www.blairpub.com.

***Postsecondary Education and Transition for Students with Learning Disabilities* (ISBN 0-89079-872-9, 2002)**
This book—written by Loring C. Brinckerhoff, Joan M. McGuire, and Stan F. Shaw—is designed to assist persons who work with college students with learning disabilities. It can be ordered by contacting PRO-ED Inc., 8700 Shoal Creek Boulevard, Austin, TX 78757-6897, 800-897-3202, http://www.proedinc.com..

A BUDGET-FRIENDLY GUIDE TO MAKING YOUR LIBRARY MORE ACCESSIBLE

Libraries have long played a vital role in connecting people with disabilities to information that can help them lead independent lives. Federal legislation has affirmed that role by mandating equal access for patrons with disabilities. Thanks to that legislation, most new library facilities are designed from the start to be user-friendly for all people. The San Francisco Public Library (http://sfpl.lib.ca.us/librarylocations/accessservices/access.htm), for instance, was built in 1996 according to universal design principles, which ensure that an environment is usable by people with a broad range of abilities and disabilities. Throughout the library, patrons with vision impairments can browse the online card catalog on audio headsets; deaf patrons can rent more than 250 descriptive videos, which feature descriptive narration when the characters are not speaking; and people with mobility impairments can access every nook and cranny of the building's seven floors. "We wanted the library to be accessible right from the time that a patron approaches the building," says Marti Goddard, Access Services Manager at the San Francisco Public Library. Community meetings and advisory groups representing various disabilities ensured that the goal of accessibility was met.

But what if your library is situated in an architecturally outdated, 50-year-old building? What if recent budget cuts don't allow it to stay open evenings, let alone buy new computers? Believe it or not, making your library more accessible to people with disabilities doesn't have to drain the coffers.

Here's how you can improve accessibility at your library through a combination of staff training, structural changes, technology, and outreach. Start by contacting a few similarly sized libraries near your own to ask if and how they have gone about improving accessibility. More often than not, they will be proud of the work they have done and enthusiastic about sharing their findings and plans. It is also crucial to include people with disabilities in the planning process.

STAFF TRAINING AND AWARENESS

A library's staff is often the most overlooked resource when it comes to creating a great, usable environment for people with disabilities. Solicit ideas and opinions from the staff. They might have low-cost solutions, such as putting a nonskid surface on an entryway or creating large-print directional signs using the photocopier or computer printer.

It's also important to help staff members become comfortable communicating with people with disabilities. As part of regular meetings, set aside time when staffers can discuss their concerns. At this time, you can also explore ways for staff members to expand their training. Ask if anyone is interested in learning specialized skills such as using telecommunication devices for the deaf (TTD/TTY) or setting up and managing assistive technology on the computers. Is anyone interested in learning American Sign Language or taking a course in guiding people who are blind? These are also skills and interests to consider when interviewing and hiring new employees.

As new equipment or services for people with disabilities are incorporated, be sure to keep staff members up-to-date. For instance, has your staff stayed current on state and federal organizations such as talking book and Braille libraries that provide services to people with disabilities? Is every staff member trained on at least the very basics of using the assistive technology that's installed on library computers? At one library in central Illinois, several part-time librarians didn't even realize that computer equipment for visually impaired users was available on site.

ACCESSING THE BUILDING AND ITS SERVICES

To get a book from the business section, just go to the information desk and ask if someone can escort you. A librarian will then take you up a steep ramp, through some closed stacks, then onto a freight elevator. You'll get off the freight elevator and go through some more closed stacks, then, presto, you're in the business section. That's the odyssey that mobility-impaired patrons in wheelchairs used to face at one city's public library, prior to redesign. Imagine how many people thought twice before undergoing that trial.

With universal design, there is at least one route, preferably the main entrance, where people with disabilities can enter a library as freely and with as much dignity as everyone else. Equally important, once a person with a disability is inside the library, he or she needs to be able to access its services as easily as possible. To accomplish that, you'll need to determine what obstacles are currently standing in the way at your facility. The following checklist will get you started. To get a more extensive checklist, along with suggested solutions, contact your regional Disability and Business Technical Assistance Center (see "For More Information" at the end of this essay).

- Can a person in a wheelchair navigate the parking areas, sidewalks, and doors to the building?
- Is there a way of entering that does not involve using stairs? Is the route of travel stable, firm, and slip-resistant?
- Are all doorways at least 32 inches wide, with a bottom lip no higher than half an inch?
- Are ramps or elevators provided as an alternative to stairs? Can someone in a wheelchair reach the elevator controls? Are the controls also written in Braille and large print?
- Are hallways kept clear for wheelchair users? Is carpeting low-pile, tightly woven, and securely attached along its edges? Can a person with a visual disability, who uses a cane, detect all protruding objects in the hallway?
- Does the emergency system have both visible and audible signals?
- At book return/checkout counters and information desks, is there a section of the counter accessible for wheelchair users that is no more than 36 inches high?
- Are there Braille and large-print shelf identifiers? Are call numbers on the spines of books in large print for low-vision users?
- Are telecommunications devices (TTD/TTY) for the deaf available?
- Are wheelchair-accessible restrooms available and marked with large-print signs?

COMPUTERS AND ASSISTIVE TECHNOLOGY

Computers have made it possible for libraries to serve a previously untapped segment of the population. For example, a person with a lifelong mobility impairment who has never handled a book can now have it scanned into a computer and read back aloud using a speech-output system. To create a facility that's more accessible to people with disabilities, your library should plan on purchasing and installing assistive hardware and software.

But how do you choose this technology? In an article outlining an eight-part library access strategy, Alan Cantor, a workplace accommodation consultant, tries to reassure librarians who feel they lack the expertise to select appropriate technology for disabled patrons. He writes, "The accessibility of your library will not be judged by the sophistication of the technologies you have, but the comprehensiveness of services you offer." That said, how much or how little equipment you have is ultimately dependent upon the needs of your patrons, and your budget. Again, many of the best suggestions will come from people with disabilities. A designated staff member or committee can evaluate and respond to patrons' requests and keep abreast of technology developments.

It pays to evaluate various dealers for the best prices. Price differences of $100 to $400 per device are not unusual, and your library can save by shopping wisely. The list below offers a good—and affordable—selection of what's common at many libraries, as well as the basic features of an accessible Web site. (For greater detail about specific pieces of equipment, see the essay *Assistive Technology: Understanding the Basics*.)

Basic Computer Access/Internet

- Adjustable-height worktables that a wheelchair can easily fit beneath
- Adjustable chairs
- Large-print and Braille key labels for people with blindness or low vision
- Keyboard trays and alternate keyboards such as mini-keyboards or extended keyboards to help people with various mobility impairments
- Mouse alternatives such as trackballs or keyboard control of the mouse
- Wrist rests for people who require extra wrist support while typing

Software and Hardware

- Screen-enlargement software that enlarges images to assist patrons with low vision and learning disabilities
- A speech-output system that converts text on the computer screen to speech for patrons with low vision, blindness, and learning disabilities
- A scanner that allows books to be scanned into the computer and can be converted to speech for patrons with low vision or blindness
- Braille conversion software and a Braille printer for patrons who are blind
- Large-screen monitors for patrons with low vision
- Software that "speaks" text back as it is typed for those with blindness, low vision, or learning disabilities
- Software that modifies keyboard response (such as sticky keys or slow keys) for people with impaired mobility or dexterity
- Dictation software that allows people who are blind or mobility impaired to input text using their voice rather than a keyboard

Library Web Site

- Choice of font for people with low vision
- Choice of text size for people with low vision and learning disabilities
- A simple, clean layout throughout the entire site
- Good contrast to assist people with low vision
- Links that feature descriptive text so that they can be understood out of context
- Video and audio that features captioning for people with low vision and learning disabilities
- Text-based alternatives for forms, databases, and software programs (such as JavaScript and Adobe Acrobat)

REACHING OUT

Sometimes, reaching out to patrons who have disabilities can literally mean finding ways of transporting them to the library (minibus or taxi) or delivering books to them (bookmobile). Reaching out also means offering text in alternative formats to patrons. Does your library have print materials available on cassette or CD-ROM or via other electronic delivery methods? Captioned videocassettes and DVDs? A CD-ROM dictionary in American Sign Language? A talking dictionary and calculator? Do your meeting rooms have assistive-listening devices for people with hearing impairments?

A number of accessibility solutions can sometimes be found in an office supply store. Whether you have a formal disability advisory council or not, be sure to talk to your patrons with disabilities to gather ideas. Probably they've come up with low-cost solutions in their own homes that you can transfer to the library. For instance, a simple bookholder and a magnifying glass mounted on an adjustable arm can help people with low vision, as can a good desk lamp. A tape recorder will work nicely as a note-taking machine for people who can't use their hands, are blind, or have a learning disability. And having a basic walker with a hanging bin for books will greatly assist patrons who tire on their feet.

Lastly, once your library has achieved its goal of improved accessibility, don't forget to tell people about all you now have to offer. That means going beyond the mailing list of those who have already identified themselves as library patrons with disabilities. Put together a brochure in formats that everyone can access—such as Braille, large-print, and audio versions—and put the information on a Web site. Send a press release to the local newspaper as well as radio and television stations. Get the word out! There are probably many people with disabilities in your community who would be happy to become patrons.

FOR MORE INFORMATION
"The A-D-A-P-T-A-B-L-E Approach: Planning Accessible Libraries."
http://www.rit.edu/~easi/itd/itdv02n4/article2.htm
This article was written by Alan Cantor for *Information Technology and Disabilities* (December 1995).

***Adaptive Technology for the Internet: Making Electronic Resources Accessible to All* (American Library Association, ISBN 0-8389-0752-0, 2000)**
http://www.ala.org/ala/productsandpublications/books/editions/adaptivetechnology.htm
This useful resource, written by Barbara T. Mates, Head, Library for the Blind and Physically Handicapped at the Cleveland Public Library, provides a wealth of suggestions to librarians interested in making their electronic resources available to people with disabilities.

Checklist for Readily Achievable Barrier Removal
http://www.usdoj.gov/crt/ada/checkweb.htm
This publication was created by Adaptive Environments,
Inc. and Barrier Free Environments, Inc., which were
authorized by the National Institute on Disability and
Rehabilitation Research to develop information and
materials on the Americans with Disabilities Act.

**Americans with Disabilities Act Technical Assistance
Program**
http://www.adata.org
Visit the Web site of the Americans with Disabilities Act
Technical Assistance Program for information on
regional disability and business technical assistance
centers.

**Association of Specialized and Cooperative Library
Agencies**
Libraries Serving Special Populations Section
http://www.ala.org/ala/ascla/asclaourassoc/
asclasections/lssps/lssps.htm
Visit this organization's Web site for information and Web
forums on library services for people with special
needs.

Center for Universal Design
North Carolina State University
College of Design
Campus Box 8613
Raleigh, NC 27695-8613
800-647-6777
cud@ncsu.edu
http://www.design.ncsu.edu:8120/cud
This organization evaluates, develops, and promotes
universal design.

Disability Resources
http://www.disabilityresources.org
This Web site's librarians section has a wealth of information on assistive technology for patrons with disabilities, connections to listservs and e-zines about library
services for people with disabilities, and connections
to libraries that have special collections for or about
people with disabilities. Its section (http://www.
disabilityresources.org/WEB.html) on accessible Web
site design will also be useful.

DO-IT
University of Washington
PO Box 355670
Seattle, WA 98195-5670
206-685-3648 (Voice/TTY), 888-972-3648 (Voice/TTY)
doit@u.washington.edu
http://www.washington.edu/doit
http://www.washington.edu/doit/UA (resources on
universal design)
DO-IT (Disabilities, Opportunities, Internetworking, and
Technology) works to increase the participation of
individuals with disabilities in academic programs
and careers. It provides comprehensive information
on universal design at its Web site.

**International Federation of Library Associations
and Institutions**
Libraries Serving Disadvantaged Persons Section
http://www.ifla.org/VII/s9/index.htm
Visit the federation's Web site for information on issues
of interest to librarians who serve people with
disabilities.

Usability.gov
U.S. Department of Health and Human Services
200 Independence Avenue, SW, Room 638 E
Washington, DC 20201
202-619-0257, 877-696-6775
http://www.usability.gov
This Web site provides comprehensive resources on
designing accessible Web sites and user interfaces.

PART III
DIRECTORY

ASSISTIVE TECHNOLOGY

COMPUTERS AND TECHNOLOGY

These companies develop, sell, or distribute items related to technology and computers. These items may include computer hardware and software, communication aids, and adaptive controls.

ABBYY USA
47221 Fremont Boulevard
Fremont, CA 94538
510-226-6717
sales@abbyyusa.com
http://www.abbyyusa.com
Disability Served: vision
This company manufactures optical character recognition software.

Ability Research Inc.
PO Box 1721
Minnetonka, MN 55345-1721
952-939-0121
ability@skypoint.com
http://www.abilityresearch.com
Disability Served: communication, learning disabled, vision
This company manufactures and markets the Hand Held Voice, a dynamic touch screen digital voice communicator.

AbleLink Technologies
528 North Tejon, Suite 100
Colorado Springs, CO 80903
719-592-0347
support@ablelinktech.com
http://www.ablelinktech.com
Disability Served: developmentally disabled, learning disabled, traumatic brain injury
This company designs software and other technology that allows people with cognitive and related disabilities access to computers.

AbleNet Inc.
2808 Fairview Avenue
Roseville, MN 55113-1308
800-322-0956
customerservice@ablenetinc.com
http://www.ablenetinc.com
Disability Served: various
This company manufactures a wide variety of adaptive switches, including pull switches, touch switches, button switches, and switch adapters. AbleNet also makes direct selection communicators, mounting hardware, and adaptive devices designed to convert appliances and toys to switch-activated units.

Able-Phone
1246 Losser Avenue
Gridley, CA 95948
530-846-PHONE
ablephone@juno.com
http://www.ablephone.com
Disability Served: various
This company manufactures a variety of telephones to accommodate persons with disabilities, including voice-activated telephones and hands-free telephones. It also manufactures wireless remote controls.

Academic Software Inc.
3504 Tates Creek Road
Lexington, KY 40517-2601
859-552-1040
asistaff@acsw.com
http://www.acsw.com
Disability Served: physically disabled
This company develops academic software programs and games, as well as adaptive switch interfaces.

Access Solutions
4536 Edison Avenue
Sacramento, CA 95821
916-481-3559
info@axsol.com
http://www.axsol.com
Disability Served: communication
This company manufactures speech synthesizers.

Access to Recreation
8 Sandra Court
Newbury Park, CA 91320
800-634-4351
dkrebs@accesstr.com
http://www.accesstr.com
Disability Served: physically disabled
This company offers a mouth controller for the Playstation II game console.

AccuCorp Inc.
PO Box 66
Christiansburg, VA 24073
703-961-2001

Disability Served: physically disabled
This company manufactures chording keyboards.

Active Words Systems Inc.
support@activewords.com
http://www.activewords.com
Disability Served: physically disabled
This company manufactures software that allows users to operate their computers more efficiently using typed keywords and shortcut keys.

Adamlab
55 East Long Lake Road, Suite 337
Troy, MI 48085
248-362-9603
customerservice@adamlab.com
http://www.adamlab.com
Disability Served: communication
Adamlab sells augmentative communication devices and accessories to speech-challenged individuals.

Adaptivation Inc.
2225 West 50th Street, Suite 100
Sioux Falls, SD 57105
605-335-4445, 800-723-2783
info@adaptivation.com
http://www.adaptivation.com
Disability Served: various
This company manufactures environmental control switches, auditory paging systems, a mouse emulator program, remote controls, and communication devices.

Adaptive Computer Systems
16 Gingham Street
Trabuco Canyon, CA 92679
949-459-5241
sales@compuaccess.com
http://www.compuaccess.com
Disability Served: various
This company distributes screen-reading software, screen magnification software, real-time translation devices, and other assistive technology devices for people with disabilities.

Adaptive Switch Labs
125 Spur 191, Suite C
Spicewood, TX 78669
800-626-8698
http://www.asl-inc.com

Disability Served: various
This company designs and sells a variety of adaptive switches, as well as driver control hardware for wheelchairs.

ADCO Hearing Products
4242 South Broadway
Englewood, CO 80113
303-794-3928
http://www.adcohearing.com
Disability Served: hearing
This company offers TTYs, closed caption decoders, group listening systems, personal listening systems, TV listening systems, amplified and special needs telephones, and adaptive alarm clocks and watches.

Adesso Inc.
565 Brea Canyon Road, #C
Walnut, CA 91789
800-467-1195
info@adesso.com
http://www.adesso.com
Disability Served: physically disabled
This company offers keyboards, touchpads, and ergonomic mice.

Advanced Access Devices
2066-C Walsh Avenue
Santa Clara, CA 95050
408-970-9760
inquiry@aadbrl.com
http://www.aadbrl.com
Disability Served: vision
This company offers the SuperBraille-2000, a portable computer for people with low vision or blindness.

Advanced Peripheral Technologies
14416 Erin Court
Lockport, IL 60441
708-301-4508
apt@advancedperipheral.com
http://www.advancedperipheral.com
Disability Served: physically disabled
This company manufactures mouse emulators, sip and puff interface modules, and remote adaptive switches.

Ai Squared
PO Box 669
Manchester Center, VT 05255
800-859-0270

sales@aisquared.com
http://www.aisquared.com
Disability Served: vision
This company develops screen magnification software and screen-reading software for the visually impaired.

ALDS Inc. (Assistive Listening Device Systems)
20540 Duncan Way, Unit #103
Langley, BC V3A 7A3
Canada
604-514-0037
kstead@alds.com
http://www.alds.com
Disability Served: hearing
This company manufactures products for the hearing impaired. The products include a telephone amplifier, workplace training devices, and communication devices for one-on-one meetings or large gatherings.

All Devices Network
c/o Arizona Hearing Online Corporation
5975 West Western Way, Suite 119
Tucson, AZ 85713
866-674-3549
http://assistivedevices.net
Disability Served: various
This company offers listening systems, telephones, TTYs, talking watches, CCTVs, magnification systems, big button telephones, speech aids, and mobility devices.

AllVoice Computing
20 Courtenay Park
Newton Abbot TQ12 2HB
United Kingdom
information@allvoice.co.uk
http://www.allvoice.co.uk
Disability Served: physically disabled
This company offers voice-recognition software.

AlphaSmart Inc.
973 University Avenue
Los Gatos, CA 95032
408-355-1000, 888-274-0680
info@alphasmart.com
http://www.alphasmart.com
Disability Served: various
This company manufactures and sells the AlphaSmart 3000, a portable keyboard and screen device that lets students enter and edit text and transfer it easily to a Macintosh or PC for formatting and printing.

ALVA Access Group Inc.
436 14th Street, Suite 700
Oakland, CA 94612
888-318-2582
info@aagi.com
http://www.aagi.com
Disability Served: vision
This company develops and manufactures Braille displays, computer screen readers, speech synthesizers, screen magnification software, and Braille software and printers.

Always Thinking Inc.
27 James Byrnes Street
Beaufort, SC 29907
800-556-9559
info@alwaysthinking.com
http://www.alwaysthinking.com
Disability Served: physically disabled
This company offers voice-activated home automation software that can be used to control lights and appliances.

AMDi
200 Frank Road
Hicksville, NY 11801
516-822-0808, 888-353-AMDI
Info@amdi.net
http://www.amdi.net
Disability Served: communication, physically disabled
This company manufactures augmentative and alternative communication devices, adaptive switches, and mounting systems for wheelchairs.

American Thermoform Corporation
1758 Brackett Street
La Verne, CA 91750
909-593-6711, 800-331-3676
service@americanthermoform.com
http://www.americanthermoform.com
Disability Served: vision
This company markets equipment and supplies for the blind. Products include Braille embossers, Braille printers, Braille paper, Braille translation software, labeling material, and Braille displays.

America Online
22000 AOL Way
Dulles, VA 20166
703-265-1000

http://www.corp.aol.com
Disability Served: various
This company offers a variety of services to its sub-
     scribers, including closed captions for select news
     and entertainment video streams, voice access for
     reading and writing e-mail, and keyboard overlays
     customized for the AOL service.

Amherst-Merritt International
5565 Red Bird Center Drive, Suite 150
Dallas, TX 75237
800-627-7752
information@amherst-merritt.com
http://www.amherst-merritt.com/product1.htm
Disability Served: various
This company makes a keyboard protector.

Amtel Systems Corporation
1955 Ticonderoga Boulevard, Suite 800
Chester Springs, PA 19425
800-999-8903
amtel@amtel.com
http://www.amtelsystemscorp.com
Disability Served: hearing
This company manufactures text communication systems
     for interoffice communication and for personal use.

Apple Computer Inc.
One Infinite Loop
Cupertino, CA 95014
800-767-2775
http://www.apple.com/accessibility
Disability Served: various
This manufacturer offers technologies geared toward
     people with disabilities who use its Mac OS X
     operating system, including talking alerts, speech
     recognition, zoom, Quick Time closed-captioning,
     keyboard mouse keys, spoken interfaces, keyboard
     navigation shortcuts, and TextEdit, which allows users
     to have an entire document spoken aloud.

Applied Future Technologies Inc.
11615 West 75th Avenue
Arvada, CO 80005
303-403-0457
aft@appliedfuture.com
http://www.appliedfuture.com
Disability Served: physically disabled
This company manufactures voice-controlled home
     automation systems.

Applied Human Factors Inc.
PO Box 228
Helotes, TX 78023
210-408-0098
sales@ahf-net.com
http://www.ahf-net.com
Disability Served: physically disabled
This company offers on-screen keyboard software, word
     prediction software, and other computer interface
     products.

Aroga Group
5055 Joyce Street, #150
Vancouver, BC V5R 6B2
Canada
800-561-6222
sales@aroga.com
http://www.aroga.com
Disability Served: various
This company offers low-vision TVs, computer-
     compatible CCTVs, portable CCTVs, screen
     magnification software, large print keyboards,
     scanning and reading systems, voice-recognition
     software, and other products.

Artic Technologies International Inc.
1000 John R. Road, Suite 108
Troy, MI 48083
248-588-7370
info@artictech.com
http://www.artictech.com
Disability Served: vision
This company manufactures speech synthesizers,
     talking note takers, Braille note takers, voice-output
     document scanning programs, large-print programs,
     video telescopes, and low-vision reading systems.

Artificial Language Laboratory
Michigan State University
405 Computer Center
East Lansing, MI 48824-1042
517-353-5399
http://www.msu.edu/~artlang/Switches.html
Disability Served: physically disabled
The laboratory develops adaptive switches, including
     optical and touch switches.

ArtisSoftware
Austria
contact@artissoftware.com

http://www.artissoftware.com
Disability Served: vision
This company offers the Artis Screen Lupe, a desktop
   utility for Mac computers that shows a magnified
   view of whatever is underneath a user's mouse
   cursor. The product is available for purchase and
   download at the company's Web site.

Ash Technologies
Ireland
info@ashtech.ie
http://www.ashtech.ie
Disability Served: vision
This company offers electronic full-color portable
   magnifiers.

AssisTech Inc.
PO Box 137
Stow, NY 14785
716-789-4197
info@assisttech.com
http://www.assisttech.com
Disability Served: physically disabled
This company offers adaptive computer keyguards.

Assis-TECH Inc.
2 Ponderosa Drive
Townsend, MA 01469
978-597-0921 (Voice/TDD)
sales@assis-tech.com
http://www.assis-tech.com
Disability Served: various
This company offers TDD/TTY devices; reading, writing,
   and special needs software; environmental controls;
   fire safety devices; automotive backup alert devices;
   mobility products; and adjustable furniture.

Assistive Technology Inc.
333 Elm Street
Dedham, MA 02026
781-461-8200, 800-793-9227
customercare@assistivetech.com
http://www.assistivetech.com
Disability Served: learning disabled
This company offers hardware and software tools
   for communication and learning disabilities.

Attainment Company Inc.
PO Box 930160
Verona, WI 53593-0160

800-327-4269
info@attainmentcompany.com
http://www.attainmentcompany.com
Disability Served: various
This company develops and distributes a wide variety
   of educational materials, including augmentative
   communication devices, printed materials, software,
   videos, and DVDs.

The Attention Builders
707 East Main Street, Suite 1700
Richmond, VA 23219
804-342-5888
customerservice@attention.com
http://www.attention.com
*Disability Served: attention deficit disorder, elderly,
   learning disabled, traumatic brain injury*
This company offers the Attention Trainer, a video game
   for people with attention deficit disorder.

Attention Control Systems Inc.
650 Castro Street, Suite 120, PMB 197
Mountain View, CA 94041
650-494-2002
cortex@brainaid.com
http://www.brainaid.com
Disability Served: attention deficit disorder
This company manufactures PEAT, a talking handheld
   scheduler for people with ADD and other cognitive
   disorders.

Audex/Audiometrics Inc.
710 Standard Street
Longview, TX 75604
800-237-0716
paula@audex.com
http://www.audex.com
Disability Served: hearing
This company manufactures infrared amplification
   systems for a variety of uses, including televisions,
   wide-area applications, and personal amplification.
   Audex also manufactures hearing-aid compatible
   cellular and cordless telephones.

Audio Enhancement
14241 South Redwood Road, PO Box 2000
Bluffdale, UT 84065
801-254-9263, 800-383-9362
http://www.audioenhancement.com

Disability Served: hearing
This company provides personal and classroom amplification systems for the hearing impaired.

Audiological Engineering Corporation
9 Preston Road
Somerville, MA 02143
617-623-5562, 800-283-4601
feedback@tactaid.com
http://www.tactaid.com
Disability Served: hearing
This company manufactures tactile sound amplification systems that turn sounds into vibrations.

Augmentative Communication Consultants Inc.
PO Box 731
Moon Township, PA 15108
412-264-6121, 800-982-2248
acci1@earthlink.net
http://www.ACCIinc.com
Disability Served: various
This company distributes communication devices, educational software, games, adaptive switches, resource books, environmental controls, and wheelchair mounting systems.

Aurora Systems Inc.
Box 43005
Burnaby, BC V5G-3H0
Canada
604-291-6310, 888-290-1133
service@aurora-systems.com
http://www.aurora-systems.com
Disability Served: various
This company provides software solutions for individuals with speech impairments, motor control disabilities, learning disabilities, and physical disabilities. Aurora 3.0 for Windows provides assistance with writing and spelling through spoken feedback.

Automated Voice Systems Inc.
17059 El Cajon Avenue
Yorba Linda, CA 92686
714-524-4488
http://www.mastervoice.com
Disability Served: physically disabled
This company supplies an environmental control system that gives complete voice control over appliances, lighting, and heating.

Bavisoft
PO Box #8
Dewitt, NY 13214
help@bavisoft.com
http://www.bavisoft.com
Disability Served: vision
This company offers computer games for people with low or no vision. These games replace graphics with sound imagery.

Bellaire Electronics
4 Broadgate
Bellaire Barnstaple, Devon EX31 1QZ
United Kingdom
chris@bellaire.co.uk
http://www.bellaire.co.uk
Disability Served: physically disabled
This company manufactures chording keyboards.

Beyond Sight Inc.
5650 South Windermere Street
Littleton, CO 80120
303-795-6455
support@beyondsight.com
http://www.beyondsight.com
Disability Served: vision
This company offers more than 800 products for the blind and visually impaired.

BioControl Systems Inc.
PO Box 19596
Stanford, CA 94309
707-824-9703
http://www.biocontrol.com
Disability Served: physically disabled
This company manufactures technology that allows users to control computers, PDAs, laptops, or game consoles by using nerve or muscle signals.

Biolink Computer Research and Development Ltd.
4770 Glenwood Avenue
North Vancouver, BC V7R 4G8
Canada
604-984-4099
sales@biolink.bc.ca
http://www.biolink.bc.ca
Disability Served: vision
This company designs products for the vision-impaired, including a screen magnification program and voice output/Braille screen-reading software.

Bitstream Inc.
245 First Street, 17th Floor
Cambridge, MA 02142
617-497-6222, 800-522-3668
oemsales@bitstream.com
http://www.bitstream.com/font_rendering/products/
    dev_fonts/tiresias.html
Disability Served: vision
This company offers electronic typefaces that have
    been developed for ease of reading by the vision-
    impaired.

BlindSoftware.com LLC
PO Box 145
East Palestine, OH 44413
support@blindsoftware.com
http://www.blindsoftware.com
Disability Served: vision
This Web site offers accessible shareware, freeware, and
    demo software downloads for people with vision
    problems.

Blissymbolics Communication International
1011 Grey Street, PO Box 222
Bala, ON P0C 1A0
Canada
705-762-0028
info@blissymbolics.org
http://www.blissymbolics.org
Disability Served: communication
This company develops Blissymbol tutorial programs
    and Blissymbol reference aids, including flash cards,
    stamps, dictionaries, and software.

Boost Technology
1702 Rosemary Lane
Redwood City, CA 94061
415-794-2937
service@boosttechnology.com
http://www.boosttechnology.com
Disability Served: physically disabled
This company offers a computer mouse that can
    be controlled by movements of the head.

Boys Town Press
14100 Crawford Street
Boys Town, NE 68010
800-282-6657
btpress@girlsandboystown.org
http://www.boystownpress.org

Disability Served: hearing
This company produces sign language tutorial videos.

Brain Actuated Technologies Inc.
1350 President Street
Yellow Springs, OH 45387-1815
937-767-2674
sales@brainfingers.com
http://www.brainfingers.com
Disability Served: physically disabled
This company offers hands-free computer pointing
    devices.

Brainchild Corporation
2706 South Horseshoe Drive
Naples, FL 34104
800-811-2724
http://www.brainchild.com
*Disability Served: learning disabled, traumatic brain
    injury*
This company manufactures a handheld electronic
    educational device.

BrainTrain Inc.
727 Twin Ridge Lane
Richmond, VA 23235
804-320-0105
info@braintrain.com
http://www.braintrain.com
Disability Served: learning disabled
This company offers cognitive training software.

Bridges LearningSystems Inc.
49 Old Solomons Island Road, Suite 206
Annapolis, MD 21401
800-639-4423
info@bridgeslearning.com
http://www.bridgeslearning.com
Disability Served: learning disabled
This company offers software programs that assess and
    develop students' cognitive abilities and perceptual
    skills.

BrightEye Technology
2 Westwood Place
Asheville, NC 28806
877-233-7323
info@brighteye.com
http://www.brighteye.com
Disability Served: various

This company provides software for learning disabled, ESL, sight and hearing impaired, and adult students. One of its products is Scan-A-Page, which allows users to hear out loud what they are attempting to read.

BRL Inc.
110 Commerce Drive, Suite 210
Fayetteville, GA 30214-1369
877-993-4994
comments@wyfiwyg.com
http://www.wyfiwyg.com
Disability Served: dyslexic, vision
This company offers talking Internet browsers, text-to-audio software, and talking checkbooks, dictionaries, and word processors.

Broderbund
c/o Riverdeep, Inc.
100 Pine Street, Suite 1900
San Francisco, CA 94111
800-395-0277
http://www.broderbund.com
Disability Served: learning disabled
This company develops educational software programs for children with learning disabilities. Products include the Edmark Reading Program series, the Reader Rabbit series, and the Achieve! series.

BRYTECH Inc.
600 Peter Morand Crescent, Suite 240
Ottawa, ON K1G 5Z3
Canada
613-731-5800
inquiries@brytech.com
http://www.brytech.com
Disability Served: vision
This company manufactures reading systems for the blind and visually impaired that provide voice-output identification of U.S. and Canadian paper currency. It also offers a product that helps people who are blind or who have color vision impairment identify the color of materials and objects.

BSC Games
559-224-2436
sales@BscGames.com
http://www.bscgames.com
Disability Served: vision
This company offers accessible computer games for the visually impaired or blind.

C-CAD Center for Computer Assistance to the Disabled
1950 Stemmons Freeway, Suite 2019
Dallas, TX 75207
214-800-2223
info@c-cad.org
http://www.c-cad.org
Disability Served: various
This organization provides evaluation and training for individuals with disabilities. Services cover a full range of disabilities, assistive technologies, and computer skills.

Celadon
50 Mitchell Boulevard
San Rafael, CA 94903
707-648-1098
http://www.celadon.com
Disability Served: physically disabled
This company manufactures programmable remote control devices.

CellularOne
3650 131st Avenue Southeast, Suite 600
Bellevue, WA 98006
media@wwireless.com
http://www.cellularone.com
Disability Served: hearing, physically disabled
This company offers voice-amplifying accessories and One Touch Headsets for its cell phones.

Centrum Sound Systems
572 La Conner Drive
Sunnyvale, CA 94087
408-736-6500
info@centrumsound.com
http://www.centrumsound.com
Disability Served: hearing
This company offers assistive listening devices and portable sound field systems for the hearing impaired.

Cingular
5565 Glenridge Connector
Atlanta, GA 30342
866-CINGULAR
http://www.cingular.com/about/disability_resources
Disability Served: hearing, vision
This company manufactures accessible telephones for persons who are hearing or visually impaired.

Cirque Corporation

2463 South 3850 West, Suite A
Salt Lake City, UT 84120
801-467-1100, 800-454-3375
http://www.cirque.com
Disability Served: various
This company manufactures touch pads and modified keyboards.

Clarity (A Division of Plantronics Inc.)

4289 Bonny Oaks Drive, Suite 106
Chattanooga, TN 37406
423-629-3500, 800-426-3738
http://www.clarityproducts.com
Disability Served: hearing
This company manufactures aids for the hearing impaired, including amplification systems, telephone accessories, text telephones, signaling devices, and wireless signal transmitters.

Clarity Solutions

2222 Park Place, Suite 1C
Minden, NV 89423
800-575-1456
clarity@clarityusa.com
http://www.clarityusa.com
Disability Served: vision
This company manufactures video magnifiers.

Code-It Software Inc.

PO Box 171
Midwest, WY 82643
mb@code-it.com
http://www.code-it.com
Disability Served: vision
This company offers a talking Web browser.

CommandSets.com

c/o Chuck Rogers Consulting
PO Box 15276
New Orleans, LA 70115
support@commandsets.com
http://www.commandsets.com
Disability Served: physically disabled
This company offers speech recognition software for Mac computers.

Commodio

info@commodio.com
http://www.commodio.com

Disability Served: physically disabled
This company offers technology that allows users to control computers by keyboard only, voice only, or a combination of keyboard and voice.

Common Cents Systems

PO Box 110514
Nashville, TN 37222
800-805-9278
box-talk@Commoncentssystems.com
http://www.box-talk.com
Disability Served: communication
This company develops communication devices to assist the speech impaired.

Compucare Inc.

12 Depot Street, Unit A, PO Box 578
Peterborough, NH 03458
603-924-7664
compucare@abilities.com
http://www.abilities.com
Disability Served: physically disabled
This company offers voice recognition technology interface systems and trains people in their use.

Compusult Limited

40 Bannister Street
Mount Pearl, NL A1N 1W1
Canada
888-388-8180
hear-it@compusult.nf.ca
http://www.hear-it.com
Disability Served: various
This company manufactures speech synthesizers; talking bar code readers; speech-enabling telephone indicators and message displays; electronic magnifiers; mouth-activated joysticks, and closed-caption display units for the workplace and home.

CompuTALK

245 Alden Drive
Madison, WI 53705
888-773-2599
jim@speak-it.com
http://www.speak-it.com
Disability Served: physically disabled
This company offers speech-recognition software.

Computerade Products

2346 Wales Drive
Cardiff, CA 92007

760-942-3343
mbirch@computerade.com
http://www.computerade.com
Disability Served: communication
This company is a consulting and software development firm. Its products include Calcu-Scan, Picture Sentence Key, and Board Builder.

Computers to Help People Inc.
6033 Monona Drive, Suite 205
Madison, WI 53716
608-257-5917
http://www.chpi.org
Disability Served: various
This nonprofit company provides Braille transcription, computer consulting, assistive technology, and special software to help people with disabilities.

Computer Vision and Voice
504 North Avenue East
Westfield, NJ 07090
908-317-8255
Sales@cvv.com
http://www.cvv.com
Disability Served: vision, physically disabled
This company offers speech-recognition software for people with visual or physical disabilities.

Compu TTY Inc.
3408 Indale Road
Ft Worth, TX 76116
817-738-2485 (Voice/TTY)
info@computty.com
http://www.computty.com
Disability Served: hearing
This company manufactures telephone accessories for the hearing impaired. It also offers signaling devices, alarm clocks, and closed captioning equipment.

Conover Company
2926 Hidden Hollow Road
Oshkosh, WI 54904
920-231-4667
conover@execpc.com
http://www.conovercompany.com
Disability Served: developmentally disabled, learning disabled
This company offers the TOOLS FOR LIFE software program, which helps users become functionally literate.

Consultants for Communication Technology
508 Bellevue Terrace
Pittsburgh, PA 15202
412-761-6062
CCT@ConCommTech.com
http://www.concommtech.com
Disability Served: severe communication disorders
This company offers software and hardware for children and adults with severe speech problems. This includes technology for use with telephones, computers, VCRs, lights, and appliances.

Contact Assistive Technology
3101 Hobbs Road, Suite 116
Amarillo, TX 79109
888-567-2175 (Voice/TTY)
http://www.contactassist.com
Disability Served: various
This company offers TDDs and TTYs, closed-caption decoders, signaling devices, mobility aids, and other products.

Conversational Computing Corporation
15375 NE 90th Street
Redmond, WA 98052
888-487-4373
customerservice@conversay.com
http://www.conversa.com
Disability Served: physically disabled
This company offers voice-activated software and hardware.

Crestwood Communication Aids Inc.
6625 North Sidney Place
Milwaukee, WI 53209-3259
414-352-5678
crestcomm@aol.com
http://www.communicationaids.com
Disability Served: communication
This company is a manufacturer and distributor of communication aids for children and adults. The company offers more than 325 products through its mail order catalog.

Crick Software
14687 Northeast 95th Street
Redmond, WA 98052
425-467-8260, 866-33-CRICK
info@cricksoft.com
http://www.cricksoft.com

Disability Served: various
This company offers literacy, word processing, and communication software. It also offers adaptive switches and on-screen keyboards.

CrissCross Technologies
110-64 Queens Boulevard, #406
Forest Hills, NY 11375
212-569-7432
info@crisscrosstech.com
http://www.crisscrosstech.com
Disability Served: vision
This company offers audio tutorials for Windows 98, Internet Explorer, Word, WordPerfect, and other Windows applications.

C TECH
2 North Williams Street
Pearl River, NY 10965
845-735-7907
info@lowvisionproducts.com
http://www.lowvisionproducts.com
Disability Served: learning disabled, vision
This company distributes video magnifiers; reading systems; screen and portable magnifiers; enlarging software; and Braille printers, displays, note takers, and embossers.

Dancing Dots
1754 Quarry Lane, PO Box 927
Valley Forge, PA 19482-0927
610-783-6692
http://www.dancingdots.com
Disability Served: vision
This company offers Braille music notation translators and music software for blind and visually impaired musicians.

DataCal Enterprises LLC
1345 North Mondel Drive
Gilbert, AZ 85233
480-813-3100, 800-223-0123
http://www.datacal.com
Disability Served: physically disabled, vision
This company manufactures special use computer keyboards, including keyboards with trackballs, large print keyboards, and keyboards with touchpads.

Data Collection and Dispersal Inc.
42 Skinner Road
East Windsor, CT 06016

860-623-7364
info@dcdinc.com
http://www.dcdinc.com
Disability Served: communication, hearing
This company manufactures portable communication aids and designs custom systems.

Datadesk Technologies
10598 Northeast Valley Road, #100
Bainbridge Island, WA 98110
206-842-5480, 888-446-3222
support@datadesktech.com
http://www.datadesktech.com
Disability Served: physically disabled
This company offers ergonomic keyboards.

DataHand Systems
3032 North 33rd Avenue
Phoenix, AZ 85017-5247
800-875-7171
datahand@datahand.com
http://www.datahand.com
Disability Served: physically disabled
This company offers ergonomic keyboards and furniture and a hands-free mouse.

Dazor Manufacturing Corporation
4483 Duncan Avenue
St Louis, MO 63110-1111
800-345-9103
info@dazor.com
http://www.dazor.com
Disability Served: vision
This company manufactures fluorescent, incandescent, and halogen task lights, as well as illuminated magnifiers.

Deaf Resources
341 East Weisheimer Road
Columbus, OH 43214
jsochor@columbus.rr.com
http://www.deafresources.com
Disability Served: hearing
This company offers assistive listening devices, notification systems, bed vibrators, timers, watches, and other devices for the hearing impaired.

Deafworks
PO Box 1265
Provo, UT 84603-1265

801-465-1957 (TTY), 800-855-2881
info@deafworks.com
http://www.deafworks.com
Disability Served: hearing
This company manufactures, sells, and repairs assistive
    devices and products for the deaf and hard of
    hearing. These include videophones, alarm clocks,
    signalers, TTY screeners, and signalers.

Digital Acoustics Corporation
1 Compobeach Road, Suite 100
Westport, CT 06880
203-226-0041
salesinfo@digitalacoustics.com
http://www.textspeak.com
Disability Served: communication
This company offers a portable text-to-speech keyboard
    that works without a personal computer.

Dimango Products
c/o Lord Henry Enterprises, Inc.
3524 Central Pike, Suite 304
Hermitage, TN 37076
800-366-7235
sales@dimango.com
http://www.dimango.com
Disability Served: physically disabled
This company manufactures several remote switches
    that can control lights, televisions, stereos, and other
    small appliances.

DiRAD Technologies Inc.
14 Computer Drive East
Albany, NY 12205
518-438-6000
sales@dirard.com
http://www.dirad.com
Disability Served: hearing
This company offers a telecommunication program that
    enables companies with phone menu systems to
    accommodate callers with hearing impairments.

Dolphin Computer Access
60 East Third Avenue, Suite 301
San Mateo, CA 94401
650-348-7401, 866-797-5921
info@dolphinusa.com
http://www.dolphinuk.co.uk
Disability Served: vision

This company manufactures screen magnifiers; screen
    readers; speech synthesizers; and Braille translators
    and printers.

Don Johnston Inc.
26799 West Commerce Drive
Volo, IL 60073
847-740-0749, 800-999-4660
info@donjohnston.com
http://www.donjohnston.com
Disability Served: various
This company manufactures talking word processors,
    software programs, and a variety of other products.

Dunamis Inc.
3545 Cruse Road, Suite 312
Lawrenceville, GA 30044
770-279-1144, 800-828-2443
info@dunamisinc.com
http://www.dunamisinc.com
Disability Served: various
This company sells assistive software programs,
    including an expanded keyboard modification
    program, vocational skills program, and pre-reading
    tutorial programs.

Duxbury Systems Inc.
270 Littleton Road, Unit 6
Westford, MA 01886-3523
978-692-3000
info@duxsys.com
http://www.duxburysystems.com
Disability Served: vision
This company produces Braille word processing
    and translation software.

DynaVox Systems, LLC
2100 Wharton Street, Suite 400
Pittsburgh, PA 15203
412-381-4883, 800-344-1778
http://www.dynavoxsys.com
Disability Served: communication
This company manufactures voice-output
    communication boards.

EconoNet International Inc.
11404 Lakeview Drive
Coral Springs, FL 33071
http://www.econointl.com

Disability Served: vision
This company offers computer screen readers and
a talking web browser.

Educational Furniture Inc.
15 Alden Street, Suite 7
Cranford, NJ 07016
908-276-8393, 800-545-4474
info@efurnitureinc.com
http://www.kinderlink.com
Disability Served: physically disabled
This company manufactures a children's wheelchair-
accessible computer workstation.

EduSpeak
c/o SRI International
333 Ravenswood Avenue
Menlo Park, CA 94025
650-859-5865
info@eduspeak.com
http://www.eduspeak.com
Disability Served: physically disabled
This company offers speech-recognition software.

EKEG Electronics Company Ltd.
26227 62nd Avenue
Aldergrove, BC V4W 1L8
Canada
604-857-0828, 866-721-3534
ekeg@ekegelectronics.com
http://www.ekegelectronics.com
Disability Served: various
This company manufactures a variety of keyboards
for people with disabilities, including expanded
computer keyboards and expanded keyboards for
automatic telephones. The company also produces
a communication training aid.

Electronic Keyboards Inc.
110 Corporate Drive
Elizabeth City, NC 27909
877-368-6824
http://www.electronickeyboards.com
Disability Served: various
This company offers industrial and custom computer
keyboards.

Electronic Vision Access Solutions (EVAS)
39 Canal Street, PO Box 371
Westerly, RI 02891

401-596-3500 (TTY), 800-872-3827
contact@evas.com
http://www.evas.com
Disability Served: various
EVAS designs and manufactures plug and play accessible
computer systems for the visually, physically, hearing,
or learning disabled.

ENABLE
1603 Court Street
Syracuse, NY 13208
315-455-7591, 315-455-1794 (TDD)
info@enablecny.org
http://www.enablecny.org
Disability Served: various
This organization provides assessment, training, services,
and support for children and adults with disabilities.
Among the services provided are augmentative
communication, adapted computer access,
ergonomics, seating and positioning, splinting
and bracing, sensory integration, environmental
modifications, and adaptive equipment.

EnableMart
4210 East 4th Plain Boulevard
Vancouver, WA 98661
888-640-1999
sales@enablemart.com
http://www.enablemart.com
Disability Served: various
This company offers a wide variety of software and
hardware for the disabled.

Enabling Devices and Toys for Special Children
385 Warburton Avenue
Hastings-on-Hudson, NY 10706
914-478-0960, 800-832-8697
info@enablingdevices.com
http://www.enablingdevices.com
Disability Served: various
This company offers augmentative communication
devices, capability switches, alternative keyboards,
keyboard additions, mounting systems, ADHD/autism
aids and training devices, and adapted toys for the
physically challenged.

Enhanced Vision
17911 Sampson Lane
Huntington Beach, CA 92647

888-811-3161
info@enhancedvision.com
http://www.enhancedvision.com
Disability Served: vision
This company manufactures video magnifiers.

Enkidu Research Inc.
2100 Wharton Street, Suite 400
Pittsburgh, PA 15203
800-344-1778
sales@dynavoxsys.com
http://www.enkidu.net
Disability Served: communication
This company manufactures augmentative
  communication devices.

Envirotrol Association
6575 Burger Drive, SE
Grand Rapids, MI 49546-7209
616-940-0122
http://home.earthlink.net/~trwood/envirotrol/home.html
Disability Served: physically disabled
This nonprofit organization offers remote controls for
  telephones, televisions, VCRs, radios, lights, electric
  bed, and air conditioners.

En-Vision America
2012 West College Avenue, Suite 200
Normal, IL 61761
309-452-3088, 800-890-1180
envision@envisionamerica.com
http://www.envisionamerica.com
Disability Served: dyslexic, vision
This company offers a product that allows visually
  impaired and blind people, as well as those with
  cognitive impairments, to use bar codes to identify
  items at work or in the home.

Epson
3840 Kilroy Airport Way
Long Beach, CA 90806
800-463-7766
support@epson.com
http://www.epson.com
Disability Served: vision
This company manufactures scanners.

Essex Electronics Inc.
1130 Mark Avenue
Carpinteria, CA 93013

805-684-7601, 800-539-5377
essex@keyless.com
http://www.keyless.com
Disability Served: hearing, vision
This company manufactures keypad-based access
  control systems, including Braille keypads for the
  blind, keypads with LED readback for the deaf, and
  illuminated keypads with large buttons for the sight
  impaired.

Exceptional Computing Inc.
9519 Southwest 38th Lane
Gainesville, FL 32608
352-331-8847
RHM@exceptionalcomputing.com
http://www.exceptionalcomputing.com
Disability Served: physically disabled
This company offers adaptive switch software and
  adaptive switches, alternate keyboards, and other
  assistive technology products.

Exceptional Teaching Aids Inc.
5673 West Las Positas Boulevard
Pleasanton, CA 94588
800-549-6999
ExTeaching@aol.com
http://www.exceptionalteaching.com
Disability Served: various
This company sells teaching aids for the blind and
  visually impaired, as well as other students with
  special needs.

Eye Control Technologies Inc. (dba NaturalPoint)
PO Box 2317
Corvallis, OR 97339
541-753-6645
sales@naturalpoint.com
http://www.eyecontrol.com
Disability Served: physically disabled
This company manufactures electronic head-pointing
  devices that can be used as computer mouse
  alternatives.

Eye Response Technologies
100 2nd Street, NW
Charlottesville, VA 22902
434-296-3846
info@eyeresponse.com
http://www.eyeresponse.com

Disability Served: physically disabled

This company offers a gaze-controlled computer mouse.

EyeTech Digital Systems
1750 East McLellan Road
Mesa, AZ 85203
480-704-3158
info@etmail.net
http://www.eyetechds.com
Disability Served: physically disabled

This company manufactures electronic gaze-controlled devices that can be used to operate computers.

Ezscreen
4955 Gulf Freeway
Houston, TX 77023
888-868-2439
sales@ezscreen.com
http://www.ezscreen.com
Disability Served: physically disabled

This company offers touch screen technology for people who are unable to use a computer mouse.

Failure Free Reading
140 Cabarrus Avenue West
Concord, NC 28025
800-542-2170
http://www.failurefree.com/au_overview.htm
Disability Served: learning disabled

This company offers software products to help children with reading difficulties.

FastPoint Technologies
8381 Katella Avenue
Stanton, CA 90680
714-484-6300, 800-962-3900
info@fastpoint.com
http://www.fast-point.com
Disability Served: various

This company produces alternative input devices for computers, including light pens, on-screen virtual keyboards, and LCD computer touch screens.

Fellowes Inc.
1789 Norwood Avenue
Itasca, IL 60143
800-955-0959
http://www.fellowes.com
Disability Served: various

This company manufactures glare filters for computer monitors; headsets; trackballs; and wrist and foot rests.

Fentek Industries Inc.
470 South Main Street, Suite G, PO Box 2278
Cottonwood, AZ 86326
928-639-0161, 800-639-0710
sales@fentek-ind.com
http://www.fentek-ind.com
Disability Served: physically disabled, vision

This company manufactures adapted and ergonomic keyboards, mice, and screen magnifiers.

1st Voice
2470 El Camino Real, #110
Palo Alto, CA 94306
650-747-0275
http://www.1stvoice.com
Disability Served: physically disabled

This company offers voice-recognition software.

Fonix Corporation
629 Massachusetts Avenue
Boxborough, MA 01719
978-266-0100
support@fonix.com
http://www.fonix.com
Disability Served: communication, physically disabled

This company offers voice-activated phones and PDAs, and text-to-speech software.

Franklin Electronic Publishers
One Franklin Plaza
Burlington, NJ 08016-4907
800-266-5626
service@franklin.com
http://www.franklin.com
Disability Served: learning disabled, vision

This company produces voice output dictionaries, thesauri, and tutorial software programs. It also offers the Reading Pen II, a handheld scanning device that allows users with learning disabilities to improve reading comprehension.

Freedom of Speech
5100 Eden Avenue, Suite 204
Edina, MN 55436
952-929-3456
info@freedomofspeech.com

http://www.freedomofspeech.com
Disability Served: various
This company offers speech-recognition software. It also offers products for people with learning disabilities, blindness, and mobility impairments.

Freedom Scientific
11800 31st Court North
St. Petersburg, FL 33716-1805
800-444-4443
Info@FreedomScientific.com
http://www.freedomscientific.com
Disability Served: vision
This company develops hardware and software for the visually impaired, including note takers; Braille displays, embossers, and scanners; speech-assisted learning systems; teletypewriter/telecommunication devices; hand-held electronic dictionaries; bar code readers; and screen-reading, screen magnification, and speech- and Braille-based Internet access software programs.

FrogPad Inc.
3310 West Main
Houston, TX 77098
713-960-9611
info@frogpad.com
http://www.frogpad.com
Disability Served: physically disabled
This company offers a one-handed keyboard that can be used with compatible PDAs and pocket, tablet, and wearable PCs.

Frontier Computing
2221 Yonge Street, Suite 406
Toronto, ON M4S 2B4
Canada
416-489-6690, 888-480-0000
sales@frontiercomputing.on.ca
http://www.frontiercomputing.on.ca
Disability Served: learning disabled, vision
This company offers a variety of products, including large print keyboards; magnification software; note takers; voice-recognition software; Braille displays, readers, printers, and translation software; digital audio book players; color detectors; and talking clocks.

GenesisOne Technologies Inc.
343 West Milltown Road, PMB-143
Wooster, OH 44691
330-259-1304, 888-221-5032
http://www.genesisone.net
Disability Served: physically disabled
This company provides assistive devices to people with physical disabilities, including a joystick mouse, environmental controls, and adaptive switches.

GenoVation Inc.
17741 Mitchell North
Irvine, CA 92614-6028
949-833-3355
sales@genovation.com
http://www.genovation.com
Disability Served: various
This company manufactures numeric keypads for notebook computers, custom keyboards, and terminals.

gh Braille
1305 Cumberland Avenue
West Lafayette, IN 47906
866-693-3687
ghinfo@ghbraille.com
http://www.ghbraille.com
Disability Served: vision
This company offers a software player that allows users to access digital talking books, as well as document reading software.

GN Netcom Inc.
77 Northeastern Boulevard
Nashua, NH 03062
800-826-4656
salesna@gnnetcom.com
http://gnnetcom.com
Disability Served: various
This company makes wireless telephone headsets, corded headsets, and digital amplifiers.

Grant Enterprises
2510 Wigwam Parkway, Suite 101
Henderson, NV 89074
800-338-5370
emailus@grant-ent.com
http://www.grant-ent.com/safco/2gsc01.htm
Disability Served: physically disabled
This company offers ergonomic equipment for computer users, including back rests, wrist support systems, adjustable footrests, foot cushions, articulating mouse trays, and forearm platforms.

The Great Talking Box Company
2245 Fortune Drive, Suite A
San Jose, CA 95131
408-456-0133, 877-275-4482
http://www.greattalkingbox.com
Disability Served: communication
This company manufactures augmentative and
alternative communication devices.

Greystone Digital Inc.
PO Box 1888
Huntersville, NC 28078-1888
800-249-5397
gdi@bigkeys.com
http://www.bigkeys.com
Disability Served: various
This company makes BigKeys, a computer keyboard
with large keys for PCs and Macintosh computers.
Greystone also sells educational and assistive-
technology computer products.

Gus Communications Inc.
1006 Lonetree Court
Bellingham, WA 98229
360-715-8580, 866-487-1006
admin@gusinc.com
http://www.gusinc.com
Disability Served: various
This company develops augmentative communication
software programs, touch screens, keyboards,
scanning cursors, talking keyboards, speech
synthesizers, and other products.

GW Micro Inc.
725 Airport North Office Park
Ft Wayne, IN 46825
260-489-3671
sales@gwmicro.com
http://www.gwmicro.com
Disability Served: vision
This company produces voice output software programs, large-print programs, Braille text translation
programs, voice output database management
programs, voice output word processing programs,
speech synthesizers, and screen-reading programs.

Handykey Corporation
1565 Adams
Denver, CO 80206
303-558-2019

info@handykey.com
http://www.handykey.com
Disability Served: physically disabled
This company manufactures a combination mouse and
keyboard that can be operated with one hand.

Handy Tech Consulting
1149 Main Street East
Hamilton, ON L8M 1P3
Canada
905-544-7551, 866-207-9526
info@htconsulting.ca
http://www.htconsulting.ca
*Disability Served: developmentally disabled, learning
disabled, vision*
This company offers Braille displays and embossers,
screen magnification systems, and CCTVs.

Harcourt Assessment
19500 Bulverde Road
San Antonio, TX 78259
800-232-1223
https://harcourtassessment.com
Disability Served: learning disabled
This company manufactures assessment tools.

Harris Communications
15155 Technology Drive
Eden Prairie, MN 55344
800-825-6758, 800-825-9187 (TTY)
info@harriscomm.com
http://www.harriscomm.com
Disability Served: communication, hearing
This company offers TTYs; amplified telephones and
other assistive listening devices; speech assistance
keyboards; signalers; hearing aid products; and
vibrating clocks.

Hartling Communications Inc.
85 Wilmington Road, Unit 16
Burlington, MA 01803
781-272-7634, 781-270-6710 (TTY)
hartcom@ultranet.com
http://www.hartling.com
Disability Served: hearing, vision
This company offers a wide variety of products for
the hearing and vision impaired, including TTYs;
speakerphones and cordless phones; remote control
speakerphones; large numbered phones; assistive
listening devices; and door, phone, and other
signaling devices.

HATCH

PO Box 11927
Winston-Salem, NC 27106
800-624-7968
http://www.computersforkids.com
Disability Served: various
This company provides assistive technology to individuals with special needs. Products include educational software and hardware, as well as adaptive switches, keyboards, and switch interfaces.

Hello Direct Inc.

5893 Rue Ferrari
San Jose, CA 95138
408-972-1990, 800-435-5634
xpressit@hellodirect.com
http://www.hellodirect.com
Disability Served: hearing
This company offers telephone amplifiers, telephone signaling devices, and TTY systems.

Herzog Research

1433 East Broadway
Tucson, AZ 85719
520-792-2550
Office@HerzogKeyboarding.com
http://herzogkeyboarding.com
Disability Served: various
This company has developed a quick and easy way to learn computer keyboarding that provides accurate hand positioning, facilitates range of motion, and prevents errors caused by hand drift, hand pull-off, and hand contortions.

HomeTOVA Attention Deficit Screening Test

c/o Universal Attention Disorders, Inc.
4281 Katella Avenue, Suite 215
Los Alamitos, CA 90720
714-229-8770, 877-PAY-ATTN
info@hometova.com
http://www.hometova.com
Disability Served: attention deficit disorder
This company offers a performance-based computerized screening test for attention and impulsivity problems.

Hooleon Corporation

304 West Denby Avenue, PO Box 589
Melrose, NM 88124
505-253-4503, 800-937-1337
sales@hooleon.com
http://www.hooleon.com
Disability Served: vision
This company manufactures large print and Braille keyboard overlays.

IBM Corporation

Special Needs Systems
1133 Westchester Avenue
White Plains, NY 10604
800-IBM-4YOU, 800-IBM-3383 (TTY)
http://www-306.ibm.com/able
Disability Served: various
This company manufactures hardware and software to assist disabled users. For example, the blind or visually impaired can use Home Page Reader to hear the contents of Web pages.

Image Management LLC

1501 Chester Road
Raleigh, NC 27608-2023
888-462-4346
info@image-management.com
http://www.image-management.com
Disability Served: various
This company offers voice-recognition software, screen readers, and recorders, as well as mobility, access, and transport products.

Inclusive TLC

2206 Legacy Oak Drive
Waxhaw, NC 28173
704-243-3622, 800-462-0930
info@inclusiveTLC.com
http://www.inclusivetlc.com
Disability Served: various
This company offers special educational needs software; switches, keyboards, and alternative computer access devices; augmentative communication aids; and assistive technology devices.

Infogrip Inc.

1794 East Main Street
Ventura, CA 93001
805-652-0770, 800-397-0921
info@infogrip.com
http://www.infogrip.com
Disability Served: communication, physically disabled, vision
This company manufactures software and hardware to assist people with disabilities, including adaptive switches, mice, trackballs, keyboards, and handheld communication devices.

Information Services Inc.
Water Street, PO Box 7056
St. John's, NL A1E 3Y3
Canada
888-492-4925
sales@is-inc.com
http://www.is-inc.com
Disability Served: various
This company, in collaboration with the Institute on
Applied Technology of the Boston Children's Hospital,
developed and markets Write Away, a word processor
that incorporates assistive technologies, including
text-to-speech output, word prediction, and multiple
access modes.

Innovation Management Group Inc.
21350 Nordhoff Street, Suite 112
Chatsworth, CA 91311
818-701-1579, 800-889-0987
cs@imgpresents.com
http://www.IMGPresents.com
Disability Served: various
This company provides software for on-screen keyboards
with macro buttons and optional word prediction;
operating Windows with joystick or any pointing
device; and screen magnification.

Innovative Rehabilitation Technology Inc.
13465 Colfax Highway
Grass Valley, CA 95945
800-322-4784
Info@IRTI.net
http://www.irti.net
*Disability Served: autistic, dyslexic, learning disabled,
vision*
This company offers screen and portable magnifiers;
Braille note takers and compasses; digital recording
devices; bar code readers; speech synthesizers;
and talking thermometers, color identifiers, clocks,
watches, and dictionaries.

Institute for Disabilities Research and Training Inc.
11323 Amherst Avenue
Wheaton, MD 20902
301-942-4326 (Voice/TTY)
http://www.idrt.com
Disability Served: hearing
This company offers TTY software and modems; foreign
language/ sign language translators; and sign
language dictionaries and software.

Intelligent Products
91 Dartmouth Street
Marlborough, MA 01752
508-251-1308 (TTY)
sales@softtty.com
http://www.softtty.com
Disability Served: hearing
This company offers TTY software and modems for Mac
computers.

IntelliTools Inc.
1720 Corporate Circle
Petaluma, CA 94954
707-773-2000, 800-899-6687
info@intellitools.com
http://www.intellitools.com
Disability Served: various
This company develops alternative keyboards for users
with physical, visual, or cognitive disabilities and
software to help students meet state and national
standards in math and language arts.

In Touch Systems
11 Westview Road
Spring Valley, NY 10977
800-332-6244
sc@magicwandkeyboard.com
http://www.magicwandkeyboard.com
Disability Served: physically disabled
This company manufactures an adaptive miniature
computer keyboard with a built-in mouse.

ION Systems Inc.
107 Mississippi Avenue
Crystal City, MO 63019
636-937-9094
help@WebEyes.us
http://www.ionwebeyes.com
Disability Served: various
This company offers Web Eyes, an Internet Explorer plug-
in that allows users to adjust type size and eliminate
the need for scrolling.

James Sentman
james@sentman.com
http://www.sentman.com/x2web
Disability Served: physically disabled
This company offers software for Mac computers that
allows remote control of lights and appliances. The
software is available for purchase and download at
the company's Web site.

JBliss Imaging Systems
PO 7382
Menlo Park, CA 94026
888-452-5477
info@jbliss.com
http://www.jbliss.com
Disability Served: vision
This company manufactures text-to-voice and
magnifying systems for the PC.

J. E. Stewart-Teaching Tools
PO Box 15308
Seattle, WA 98115
206-262-9538
Disability Served: developmentally disabled
This company provides software and instructional
materials to teach community sign reading and
vocational skills.

Judy Lynn Software Inc.
PO Box 373
East Brunswick, NJ 08816
908-390-8845
techsupt@judylynn.com
http://www.judylynn.com
Disability Served: mentally disabled, physically disabled
This company produces adaptive switch software
for PCs.

Kare Products
1644 Conestoga Street, Suite 2
Boulder, CO 80301
303-443-4243, 800-927-5273
http://www.kareproducts.com
Disability Served: physically disabled
This company offers ergonomic computer products, such
as wrist rests, adjustable keyboards, keyboards with
trackballs, document holders, upright mice, foot pedal
mice, trackballs, monitor risers, anti-glare devices,
footrests, back supports, and headsets. It also offers
ergonomic chairs, support pillows, and air filters.

Kensington Technology Group
333 Twin Dolphin Drive
Redwood Shores, CA 94065
800-235-6708
http://www.kensington.com
Disability Served: physically disabled
This company manufactures a trackball that emulates
mouse functions.

Keybowl Inc.
206 South Park Avenue
Winter Park, FL 32789
877-363-7774
http://www.keybowl.com
Disability Served: physically disabled
This company offers a keyless keyboard that allows users
to access computers without using fingers or wrist
motion.

Keytec Inc.
1293 North Plano Road
Richardson, TX 75081
800-624-4289
sales@magictouch.com
http://www.magictouch.com
Disability Served: physically disabled
This company manufactures touch screen systems
for computer monitors.

Keytools Ltd.
PO Box 700
Southampton SO17 1LQ
United Kingdom
info@keytools.com
http://www.keytools.com
Disability Served: various
This company offers assistive technology, including
keyboards for people with visual and physical
impairments; ergonomic mice; alternative mice;
touch screens; digital magnifiers; adaptive switches;
and access and communication software.

Key TronicEMS Corporation
North 4424 Sullivan Road
Spokane, WA 99214
509-928-8000
http://www.keytronic.com
Disability Served: physically disabled
This company designs modified keyboards.

Kinesis Corporation
22121-17th Avenue, SE, Suite 112
Bothell, WA 98021-7404
800-454-6374
sales@kinesis.com
http://www.kinesis-ergo.com
Disability Served: physically disabled
This company offers ergonomic keyboards, pointing
devices, and office chairs.

Kurzweil Educational Systems Inc.
100 Crosby Drive
Bedford, MA 01730-1402
800-894-5374
info@kurzweiledu.com
http://www.kurzweiledu.com
Disability Served: learning disabled, vision
This company provides text-to-speech technology for persons with learning difficulties and those who are blind or visually impaired.

KY Enterprises
246 East Tobiano Trail
Belgrade, MT 59714
406-388-3970
info@quadcontrol.com
http://www.quadcontrol.com
Disability Served: physically disabled
This company provides adaptive products for operation of household devices, including mouth-operated video game joysticks, big button electric bed controls, and sip-puff adaptive switches.

LAB Resources
161 West Wisconsin Avenue, Suite 2G
Pewaukee, WI 53072
262-691-3476
info@elabresources.com
http://www.elabresources.com
Disability Served: various
This company offers alternative keyboards, adaptive switches, pointing devices, on-screen keyboards, speech recognition software, and augmentative software and devices.

Laetare Solutions
2409 Belair Drive
Bowie, MD 20715
888-HOORAY-4
laetaresolutions@comcast.net
http://www.mdtap.org/tt/Laetare/Laetare.html
Disability Served: various
This company distributes augmentative communication products, as well as adaptive switches and alternate computer access products from a variety of manufacturers.

Lake Software
30 Phyllis Lane
Fairfield, NJ 07004

CNT@LakeFolks.com
http://www.lakefolks.org/cnt
Disability Served: physically disabled
This company offers free on-screen virtual keyboard software.

Laureate Learning Systems Inc.
110 East Spring Street
Winooski, VT 05404-1898
802-655-4755, 800-562-6801
customer-service@llsys.com
http://www.llsys.com
Disability Served: communication, developmentally disabled, physically disabled
This company creates educational software.

LC Technologies Inc.
3955 Pender Drive, Suite 120
Fairfax, VA 22030
703-385-7133, 800-393-4293
info0309@eyegaze.com
http://www.eyegaze.com
Disability Served: physically disabled
This company manufactures a computer interface controlled by eye movement.

LeapFrog
6401 Hollis Street, Suite 100
Emeryville, CA 94608-1071
800-701-5327
http://www.leapfrog.com
Disability Served: various
This company offers software that helps children develop their reading, language, logic, and motor skills.

Leithauser Research
3624 Royal Fern Circle
DeLand, FL 32724-1223
386-738-0418
Leithauser@aol.com
http://leithauserresearch.com
Disability Served: physically disabled
This company offers a shareware program called No-Keys that allows the user to input text via a mouse or trackball rather than by a standard keyboard.

Less Gauss Inc.
1164 Route 9G
Hyde Park, NY 12538

877-828-4817
info@lessgauss.com
http://www.lessgauss.com
Disability Served: vision
This company manufactures computer enhancement
products, including magnifiers and clarifiers.

Lexia Learning Systems Inc.
2 Lewis Street, PO Box 466
Lincoln, MA 01773
800-435-3942
info@lexialearning.com
http://www.lexialearning.com
Disability Served: learning disabled
This company manufactures an award-winning reading
skills assessment programs for use with Windows and
Macintosh computers.

Lighthouse International
111 East 59th Street
New York, NY 10022-1202
800-829-0500, 212-821-9713 (TTY)
info@lighthouse.org
http://www.lighthouse.org
Disability Served: vision
This nonprofit organization provides rehabilitation
services, education, and research for vision
impairment. The Lighthouse Professional Products
Catalog sells assistive devices.

Lind Electronic Design
6414 Cambridge Street
Minneapolis, MN 55426
800-697-3702
lrlind@lindelectronics.com
http://www.lindelectronics.com
Disability Served: various
This company manufactures portable battery packs
for computers.

Linemaster Switch Corporation
29 Plaine Hill Road, POB 238
Woodstock, CT 06281-0238
800-974-3668
information_0267@linemaster.com
http://www.linemaster.com/main.shtml
Disability Served: physically disabled
This company manufactures several foot switches.

Lingraphicare Inc.
580 Second Street, Suite 210
Oakland, CA 94607
888-274-2742
info@lingraphicare.com
http://www.aphasia.biz
Disability Served: communication
This company manufactures the Lingraphica, a selection-
to-speech device for persons unable to speak.

Listen Technologies Corporation
14912 Heritagecrest Way
Sandy, UT 84065-4818
801-233-8992, 800-330-0891
info@ListenTech.com
http://www.listentech.com
Disability Served: hearing
This company rents and sells assistive listening
transmitters and receivers.

Logitech Inc.
6505 Kaiser Drive
Fremont, CA 94555
510-795-8500, 800-231-7717
http://www.logitech.com/index.cfm/US/EN
Disability Served: various
This company manufactures a cordless mouse, an
ergonomically designed mouse, headsets, and
numerous trackballs.

MacChampion
info@macchampion.com
http://www.macchampion.com/pinpoint_ddownload.
shtml
Disability Served: vision
This company offers PinPoint, Mac-based software
that projects an image around or behind the
regular mouse pointer on a computer. The product
is available for purchase and download at the
company's Web site.

MacLaboratory Inc.
314 Exeter Road
Devon, PA 19333-1710
610-688-3114
info@bc.drexel.edu
http://bc.drexel.edu/publish.html
Disability Served: communication, developmentally
disabled, traumatic brain injury

This company designs assessment and assistive software for persons with motor or cognitive impairments.

MacSpeech
50A Northwestern Drive
Salem, NH 03079
603-251-1477
http://www.macspeech.com
Disability Served: physically disabled
This company offers voice-recognition software for Macintosh computers.

Madentec Ltd.
4664 99 Street
Edmonton, AB T6E 5H5
Canada
780-450-8926, 877-623-3682
sales@madentec.com
http://www.madentec.com
Disability Served: physically disabled
This company offers head pointing devices, on-screen keyboards, and other assistive computer interface products.

The Magnifying Center
3950 Northwest 120th Avenue
Coral Springs, FL 33065
800-364-1608
http://www.magnifyingcenter.com
Disability Served: vision
This company offers Braille keyboards, note takers, embossers, and displays; bar code readers; screen magnification software; voice-recognition software; screen readers; magnifying devices; and a variety of daily living aids for the visually impaired, such as bold line paper, signature guides, big print check registers, large print playing cards, and large print and talking watches.

Marblesoft
12301 Central Avenue, NE, Suite 205
Blaine, MN 55434
763-755-1402
mail@marblesoft.com
http://www.marblesoft.com
Disability Served: various
This company manufactures early learning and special needs educational software.

Maryland Relay
301 West Preston Street, Suite 1008A
Baltimore, MD 21201
800-552-7724 (Voice/TTY)
http://www.mdrelay.org
Disability Served: various
This organization links persons using standard voice telephones with persons who are using text telephones.

Mas Systems
1116 North Harbor Boulevard, Unit B
Santa Ana, CA 92703
714-554-3898
massystems@earthlink.net
http://www.massystems.com
Disability Served: physically disabled
This company offers adapted controllers for computer games.

Matias Corporation
129 Rowntree Dairy Road, Unit #20
Vaughan, ON L4L 6E1
Canada
905-265-8844, 888-663-4263
info@half-qwerty.com
http://www.half-qwerty.com
Disability Served: physically disabled, vision
This company offers Half-QWERTY, a one-handed keyboard.

Maui Innovative Peripherals
300 Ohukai Road, Suite C-325
Kihei, HI 96753
808-875-0555, 866-875-5556
support@maui-innovative.com
http://www.miracle-mouse.com
Disability Served: physically disabled
This company offers Miracle Mouse, a head-pointing computer interface device.

Maxess Products
The Chinestone
Dancers Hill, Charlbury
Oxfordshire OX7 3RZ
United Kingdom
sales@maxessproducts.co.uk
http://www.maxesssite.co.uk
Disability Served: physically disabled

This company offers keyguards, adaptive keyboards, switches, switch trays, switch mounts, joysticks, keyboard gloves, and wrist rests.

Mayer-Johnson Company
PO Box 1579
Solana Beach, CA 92075-1579
858-550-0084, 800-588-4548
mayerj@mayer-johnson.com
http://www.mayer-johnson.com
Disability Served: communication
This company produces books, hardware, and software for use in augmentative communication and special education.

McDowell-Craig
13146 Firestone Boulevard
Norwalk, CA 90650
562-921-4441, 877-921-2100
info@mcdowellcraig.com
http://www.mcdowellcraig.com
Disability Served: physically disabled
This company manufactures adaptive office equipment, including adjustable-height computer tables and workstations, keyboard platforms, monitor stands, and ergonomic chairs.

Med Labs Inc.
28 Vereda Cordillera
Goleta, CA 93117
805-968-2486, 800-968-2486
Medlabsinc@aol.com
http://hometown.aol.com/medlabsinc
Disability Served: physically disabled
This company manufactures signal devices for calling a hospital nurse, electronic muscle stimulators, and portable alarms.

Mextel Inc.
159 Beeline Drive
Bensenville, IL 60106
630-595-4146
Disability Served: physically disabled
This company manufactures an expanded keyboard modification program for computers.

Micro Ed
PO Box 24750
Edina, MN 55424
612-929-2242

tory@ttinet.com
http://www.ttinet.com/microed
Disability Served: learning disabled
This company designs a reading tutorial software program.

Microsoft Corporation
One Microsoft Way
Redmond, WA 98052-6399
425-882-8080, 800-642-7676
http://www.microsoft.com
Disability Served: various
Microsoft makes keyboard modification programs, trackballs to emulate standard mouse controls, and voice output programs. Its Windows operating system offers many built-in features specifically geared for people with disabilities.

Micro Video Corporation
1935 Pauline Boulevard, Suite H
Ann Arbor, MI 48103
734-996-0626, 800-537-2182
http://www.videovoice.com
Disability Served: communication
This company produces a speech training software program.

Millennium Software
PO Box 1306
Torrance, CA 90505
310-378-7525
peuapeu@aol.com
http://members.aol.com/peuapeu
Disability Served: developmentally disabled
This company offers cognitive training software.

Mindplay
440 South Williams Boulevard, Suite 206
Tucson, AZ 85711
520-888-1800
mail@mindplay.com
http://www.mindplay.com
Disability Served: learning disabled
This company produces curriculum-based software for special needs learners.

MONS International Inc.
6595 Roswell Road, NE, Suite 224
Atlanta, GA 30328
800-541-7903

salesinfo@magnifiers.com
http://www.magnifiers.com
Disability Served: vision
This company offers screen and portable magnifiers, talking devices, and related accessories.

Multimedia Designs Inc.
10 Woodcutter Court
Palm Harbor, FL 34683
888-353-3996
Dan@MultimediaDesigns.com
http://www.multimediadesigns.com
Disability Served: physically disabled
This company manufactures Multimedia Max, a voice-activated computer system that controls lights, electrical appliances, telephones, fax machines, door openers, window openers, thermostats, and more. It also offers a voice-activated telephone, a hands-free mouse and an on-screen keyboard.

NanoPac Inc.
4823 South Sheridan Road, Suite 302
Tulsa, OK 74145-5717
918-665-0329, 800-580-6086
info@nanopac.com
http://www.nanopac.com
Disability Served: various
This company provides a wide range of assistive technology products.

National Discount Battery Service
PO Box 15
Northampton, MA 01061-0015
413-586-5295 (Voice/TTY)
mailto:h2u1@aol.com
http://members.aol.com/h2u1/hears.htm
Disability Served: hearing
This company offers hearing aid supplies and batteries, TDD/TTYs, amplified telephones, and wake-up alarms.

newAbilities Systems Inc.
2938 Scott Boulevard
Santa Clara, CA 95054
408-988-9969, 800-829-8889
http://www.newabilities.com
Disability Served: physically disabled
This company manufactures a tongue-controlled device that allows users to operate power wheelchairs, computers, cordless telephones, home electronics, and other electromechanical devices.

Nextel
2001 Edmund Halley Drive
Reston, VA 20191
http://nextelonline.nextel.com
Disability Served: vision
This company offers cell phones with adaptations for the vision-disabled.

nFinity Inc.
c/o Kagi
1442A Walnut Street, PMB 392
Berkeley, CA 94709-1405
http://www.quick-voice.com
Disability Served: physically disabled
This company offers software that allows people to use the microphone on their Mac computers to create voice notes and send audio e-mails.

NotePage Inc.
PO Box 296
Hanover, MA 02339
781-829-0500
products@notepager.net
http://www.notepager.net
Disability Served: hearing
This company offers alphanumeric paging and wireless messaging software solutions to the hearing impaired.

NXi Communications Inc.
4505 South Wasatch Boulevard, Suite 120
Salt Lake City, UT 84124
801-274-6001, 801-274-6004 (TTY)
nxi@nextalk.com
http://www.nextalk.com
Disability Served: hearing
This company manufactures software designed for TTY communication via computer.

OMS Development
1013 West 32nd Street, Suite 3F
Chicago, IL 60608
773-247-1632
ebohlman@omsdev.com
http://www.omsdev.com
Disability Served: various
This company offers text-to-speech applications; adaptive software and hardware for users with disabilities; and text processing including XML.

Optimum Resource Inc.
18 Hunter Road
Hilton Head Island, SC 29926
843-689-8000
stickyb@stickybear.com
http://www.stickybear.com
Disability Served: various
This company develops educational software programs including the Stickybear series.

ORCCA Technology Inc.
444 East Main Street, Suite 101
Lexington, KY 40507
859-226-9625
orcca@orcca.com
http://www.orcca.com
Disability Served: physically disabled
This company manufactures switches, switch-adapted products, and adapted photography products.

Origin Instruments Corporation
854 Greenview Drive
Grand Prairie, TX 75050-2438
972-606-8740
support@orin.com
http://www.orin.com
Disability Served: physically disabled
This company manufactures computer access devices, including HeadMouse Extreme (which allows users to access a computer using head-controlled technology), SofType (an on-screen keyboard), Dragger (which replaces the functions of the left and right buttons on a computer mouse), sip/puff switches, and other products.

OVAC Magnification Systems
67-555 East Palm Canyon, Building C-103
Cathedral City, CA 92234
800-325-4488
info@ovac.com
http://www.ovac.com
Disability Served: vision
This company manufactures video magnification devices.

PageMinder
10580 Barkley, Suite 450
Overland Park, KS 66212
888-882-7787
remindme@pageminderinc.com
http://www.pageminderinc.com
Disability Served: various

This company manufactures PageMinder, an alert system that sends task reminders, such as taking pills and keeping appointments, via a person's pager or cell phone.

Parrot Software
PO Box 250755
West Bloomfield, MI 48325
800-727-7681
catalog@parrotsoftware.com
http://www.parrotsoftware.com
Disability Served: various
This company develops reading and language tutorial software programs for people who suffer from aphasia, Alzheimer's disease, closed head injuries, and other disorders affecting, speech, memory, and cognitive functioning.

PCD Maltron Limited
15 Orchard Lane
East Molesey, Surrey KT8 0BN
United Kingdom
sales@maltron.com
http://www.maltron.com
Disability Served: physically disabled
This company offers single-handed, single-fingered, or head/mouth stick keyboards.

PC Squared
2914 Russell Avenue North
Minneapolis, MN 55411-1068
888-588-7019
sales@pc-squared.com
http://www.pc-squared.com
Disability Served: various
This company offers magnifiers, screen readers, and adaptive mice.

Perceptive Automation LLC
sales@perceptiveautomation.com
http://www.perceptiveautomation.com
Disability Served: physically disabled
This company offers Indigo, Mac-based software that allows users to control household appliances and lights remotely. This product is available for purchase and download at the company's Web site.

Personal Data Systems Inc.
PO Box 1008
Campbell, CA 95009-1008
408-866-1126

info@PersonalDataSystems.com
http://www.personaldatasystems.com
Disability Served: *various*
This company designs and installs data systems that
help people with visual or reading impairments. It
also sells speech synthesizers, magnification software,
Braille translation software, and other products.

PESCO International
21 Paulding Street
Pleasantville, NY 10570
800-431-2016
http://www.pesco.org
Disability Served: *various*
This company manufactures and sells career assessment
tools that evaluate an individual's aptitudes, reasoning,
math and language skills, interests, temperament, work
attitude, ethics, and learning styles. The system then
matches these assessments to appropriate training and
jobs. These products are available in Braille, large print,
and Spanish, Vietnamese, and Russian.

Phillip Roy Inc.
13064 Indian Rocks Road
Largo, FL 33774
800-255-9085
info@philliproy.com
http://www.philliproy.com
Disability Served: *various*
This company offers more than 90 educational software
programs and books addressing life, academic, and
vocational skills.

Phone TTY Inc.
1246 Route 46 West
Parsippany, NJ 07054-2121
973-299-6627, 973-299-6626 (TTY)
phonetty@aol.com
http://www.phone-tty.com
Disability Served: *hearing*
This company manufactures aids for the hearing
impaired. Products include doorbell signalers,
telephone ring signalers, specialized alarm clocks,
TDD emulation software programs, text telephones,
and emergency devices.

Phonic Ear Inc.
3880 Cypress Drive
Petaluma, CA 94954-7600
707-769-1110, 800-227-0735
customerservice@phonicear.com

http://www.phonicear.com
Disability Served: *hearing*
This company makes items for the hearing impaired,
including amplification systems and electronic
communication aids.

Plantronics
345 Encinal Street
Santa Cruz, CA 95060
831-426-5858, 800-544-4660
http://www.plantronics.com
Disability Served: *physically disabled*
This company makes a cordless, headset telephone.

Possum Controls Limited
8 Farmbrough Close
Aylesbury, Buckinghamshire HP20 1DQ
United Kingdom
unit8@possum.co.uk
http://www.possum.co.uk
Disability Served: *various*
This company offers communication aids and software;
page turners; and adaptive switches.

Potomac Technology
One Church Street, Suite 101
Rockville, MD 20850-4158
800-433-2838 (Voice/TTY)
info@potomactech.com
http://www.potomactech.com
Disability Served: *hearing*
This company offers text telephones; amplified and
cordless phones; assistive listening devices; flashing
or vibrating clocks, timers, and watches; flashing and
vibrating signalers and smoke detectors; and wireless
communication devices.

Premier
1309 North William Street
Joliet, IL 60435
517-668-8188, 815-722-5961
info@readingmadeeasy.com
http://www.readingmadeeasy.com
Disability Served: *vision*
This company offers a variety of reading machines,
including talking checkbooks, dictionaries, word
processors, and scanners.

Prentke Romich Company
1022 Heyl Road
Wooster, OH 44691

330-262-1984, 800-262-1984
info@prentrom.com
http://www.prentrom.com
Disability Served: various
This company provides a variety of augmentative
communication devices, computer access products,
and other assistive technology devices.

Pres Air Trol Corporation
1009 West Boston Post Road
Mamaroneck, NY 10543
914-698-2026, 800-431-2625
info@presair.com
http://www.presair.com
Disability Served: physically disabled
This company makes a variety of adaptive switches,
including foot switches.

Psychological Software Services Inc.
6555 Carrollton Avenue
Indianapolis, IN 46220
317-257-9672
nsc@netdirect.net
http://www.neuroscience.cnter.com/pss/index.htm
Disability Served: various
This company develops and markets rehabilitation
software for use in clinical or educational settings.
The software is used to improve the cognitive skills
compromised by head injury, stroke, and tumor, as
well as problems associated with learning disabilities.

Pulse Data HumanWare
175 Mason Circle
Concord, CA 94520
800-722-3393
usa@pulsedata.com
http://www.pulsedata.com
Disability Served: learning disabled, vision
This company provides adaptive technology to people
who need equal access due to blindness, low vision,
and/or learning disabilities.

Quartet Technology Inc.
87 Progress Avenue
Tyngsboro, MA 01879
978-649-4328
info@qtiusa.com
http://www.qtiusa.com
Disability Served: physically disabled

This company manufactures voice-operated
environmental control units for appliances,
telephones, lights, and other household devices.

Radio Shack
300 Radio Shack Circle
Ft Worth, TX 76102
800-843-7422
http://www.radioshack.com
Disability Served: various
This company manufactures electronic goods, including
disabled-friendly telephones, telephone amplifiers,
dictionaries, calculators, phone flashers, universal
remotes, door knock signalers, and switches.

Rapidtext
1801 Dove Street, Suite 101
Newport Beach, CA 92660
949-399-9200
info@rapidtext.com
http://www.rapidtext.com
Disability Served: hearing
This company offers a full line of captioning services,
including real-time captioning for classrooms,
seminars, meetings, and television. Rapidtext also
offers closed or open captioning for videos and sells
captioning software and hardware.

RC Systems Inc.
1609 England Avenue
Everett, WA 98203
425-355-3800
sales@rcsys.com
http://www.rcsys.com
Disability Served: various
This company develops voice output software programs
and speech synthesizers.

Reading Machines.com
c/o Benetech
480 California Avenue, Suite 201
Palo Alto, CA 94306-1609
703-620-1125
info@readingmachines.com
http://www.shrinknet.com/RM-site
Disability Served: vision
This company offers the Bookcourier, a small, portable
device that provides access to text, Braille, and mp3
sound files for the visually disabled.

Realize Software Corporation
5255 Stevens Creek Boulevard, Suite 276
Santa Clara, CA 95051
http://www.realizesoftware.com
Disability Served: physically disabled
This company offers speech-recognition software.

Rehabilitation Consultants Inc.
2221 Peachtree Road, NE, Suite D, #481
Atlanta, GA 30309
404-575-4331
marilyn@oakes.org, barry@oakes.org
http://www.oakes.org
Disability Served: various
This company provides rehabilitation, safety, and
    technical consultation for life-care planning, pain
    management, wheelchair accessibility, industrial
    safety, and catastrophic injury.

RehabTool.com
PO Box 572190
Houston, TX 77257
281-531-6106
info@rehabtool.com
http://www.rehabtool.com
Disability Served: various
This company offers assistive technology products,
    augmentative and alternative communication devices,
    computer access equipment, and multilingual speech
    synthesis and voice-recognition software. It offers help
    in the selection and use of assistive products .

Research Press
Department 24W, PO Box 9177
Champaign, IL 61826
217-352-3273, 800-519-2707
rp@researchpress.com
http://www.researchpress.com
Disability Served: developmentally disabled
This company produces educational software,
    books, and videos including materials for the
    developmentally disabled.

Riverdeep Inc.
100 Pine Street, Suite 1900
San Francisco, CA 94111
800-542-4222
info@riverdeep.net
http://www.riverdeep.net/edmark

Disability Served: learning disabled
This company publishes children's educational software.
    The software is intended to develop self-esteem,
    higher-level thinking, and problem-solving skills.

R. J. Cooper and Associates
27601 Forbes Road, Suite 39
Laguna Niguel, CA 92677
949-582-2572, 800-752-6673
info@rjcooper.com
http://www.rjcooper.com
Disability Served: various
This company provides adaptive switch training programs,
    speech-training programs, and game programs, and
    also sells assistive hardware and software.

Robo Systems Corporation
PO Box 290
Newtown, PA 18940-0290
215-604-4006
http://www.robosys.com
Disability Served: various
This company develops computer-aided design software
    programs.

Runge Enterprises
10522 Covington Circle
Villa Park, CA 92861
714-685-1066
voicecnx@aol.com
http://www.voicecnx.com
Disability Served: physically disabled
This company develops voice-recognition, synthesis,
    and digitized speech products.

Safe Reading and Computer Box Company
4407 Swinson Road
Rhodes, MI 48652
989-689-6369
http://www.mcsrelief.com/safe.html
Disability Served: various
This company manufactures protective boxes for
    persons who are chemically sensitive, including
    a computer box and a reading box. It also sells a
    sauna for persons who need to detoxify.

Saia-Burgess
801 Scholz Drive
Vandalia, OH 45377

937-454-2345, 800-998-2298
http://www.saia-burgess-usa.com
Disability Served: physically disabled
This company manufactures microswitches.

Saltillo Corporation
2143 TR112
Millersburg, OH 44654
330-674-6722, 800-382-8622
aac@saltillo.com
http://www.saltillo.com
Disability Served: various
This company offers communication devices, computer
access software, memory assistance products,
mounting systems, adaptive switches, and voice
amplifiers.

Scan Soft
9 Centennial Drive
Peabody, MA 01960
978-997-2000, 800-654-1187
http://www.scansoft.com
Disability Served: physically disabled
This company offers speech recognition and optical
character recognition software.

Scholastic
557 Broadway
New York, NY 10012
800-724-6527
http://www.scholastic.com
Disability Served: various
This company develops reading tutorial software
programs, spelling tutorial programs, and voice
output word processing programs.

SEMCO
2012 North 15th Street
Sheboygan, WI 53081
877-736-2663
info@quadjoy.com
http://www.quadjoy.com
Disability Served: physically disabled
This company manufactures the Quadjoy Mouse, a
computer mouse for quadriplegics. The mouse can
be mounted on the computer workstation and is sip
and puff activated .

Serac Software
support@seracsoftware.com
http://seracsoftware.com

Disability Served: physically disabled
This company offers Mac-based software that allows
users to control household appliances, lights, and
computers and printers remotely. The product
is available for purchase and download at the
company's Web site.

Serotek Corporation
1128 Harmon Place, Suite 310
Minneapolis, MN 55403
866-202-0520
support@freedombox.info
http://www.freedombox.info
Disability Served: physically disabled
This company offers the FreedomBox, a product that
allows disabled users access to the Internet via voice
commands.

Seventh Generation Technologies
PO Box 18381
Boulder, CO 80308
800-500-2921
info@7gt.com
http://www.7gt.com
Disability Served: developmentally disabled
This company offers SpeechTeach, software that teaches
children and adults with language delays, autism, and
developmental disabilities to speak.

Sighted Electronics Inc.
69 Woodland Avenue
Westwood, NJ 07675
800-666-4883
sales@sighted.com
http://www.sighted.com/index.htm
Disability Served: vision
This company offers Braille note takers, displays,
keyboards, embossers, and software.

Silent Call Communications Corporation
5095 Williams Lake Road
Waterford, MI 48329
248-673-7353 (Voice/TTY), 800-572-5227
http://www.silent-call.com
Disability Served: hearing, vision
This company manufactures and distributes alerting
devices for persons who are hearing impaired or
deaf-blind.

Simtech Publications
22 Spring Hill Road
Harwinton, CT 06791

866-485-1052
support@hsj.com
http://www.hsj.com
Disability Served: physically disabled
This company offers adaptive switch training software.

Slater Software Inc.
351 Badger Lane
Guffey, CO 80820
877-306-6968
http://www.slatersoftware.com
Disability Served: learning disabled
This company offers writing composition software
    programs.

Slosson Educational Publications Inc.
538 Buffalo Road, PO Box 280
East Aurora, NY 14052
716-652-0930, 888-756-7766
slosson@slosson.com
http://www.slosson.com
Disability Served: various
This company offers an extensive product line that
    includes testing and assessment materials, learning
    enhancement materials, books, games, videos,
    cassettes, and computer software. These products
    are intended for psychologists, teachers, counselors,
    students, and parents.

SofDesign International Inc.
701 East Plano Parkway, Suite 500
Plano, TX 75074
972-644-0098
http://www.sofdesign.com/dyslexia
Disability Served: learning disabled
This company offers software and computer keyboards
    for training people with dyslexia.

SoftTouch
4300 Stine Road, Suite 401
Bakersfield, CA 93313
877-763-8868
sales@softtouch.com
http://www.softtouch.com
Disability Served: various
This company offers software programs for young
    people with various disabilities.

Solutions for Humans
365A Tesconi Circle
Santa Rosa, CA 95401

707-544-8000, 800-953-9262
staff@sforh.com
http://www.sforh.com
Disability Served: physically disabled
This company offers adapted keyboards; pointing
    devices; speech recognition software; telephone
    headsets; document holders; magnification software
    and hardware; Braille note takers, embossers, and
    printers; and augmentative communication devices.

Sound Associates Inc.
424 West 45th Street
New York, NY 10036
888-772-7686
http://www.soundassociates.com
Disability Served: hearing
This company offers I-Caption, an individual captioning
    system for use by the hearing-disabled at Broadway
    shows. It also offers infrared assistive listening
    systems.

SoundBytes
PO Box 9023
Hicksville, NY 11802
888-816-8191 (Voice/TTY)
info@soundbytes.com
http://www.soundbytes.com
Disability Served: hearing
This company offers amplified telephones and
    answering machines; TTYs; alerting systems; cell
    phones and pagers for the deaf; hearing aid batteries
    and accessories; vibrating and loud alarm clocks and
    watches; flashing smoke detectors; flashing and loud
    doorbells; and telephone ring amplifiers.

Sound Choice Assistive Listening Inc.
PO Box 843
Doylestown, PA 18901
215-230-8600, 877-896-5048
sndchoice@aol.com
http://www.eclipse.net/~synergy/soundchoice.html
Disability Served: hearing
This company offers infrared audio transmitters and
    accessories.

Startly Technologies LLC
PO Box 65580
West Des Moines, IA 50265
515-221-1801, 800-523-7638
http://www.cesoft.com
Disability Served: various

This company produces a keyboard expansion software program that allows the user to customize keys and create macros.

Steck-Vaughn Company
c/o Harcourt Achieve, Attn: Customer Service, 5th Floor
6277 Sea Harbor Drive
Orlando, FL 32887
800-531-5015
http://www.steck-vaughn.com
Disability Served: various
This company develops language and personal skills training programs.

Stoelting
620 Wheat Lane
Wood Dale, IL 60191
630-860-9700
psychtests@stoeltingco.com
http://www.stoeltingco.com
Disability Served: various
This company offers a skills training evaluation program.

SubRosaSoft.com Ltd
sales@SubRosaSoft.com
http://www.subrosasoft.com
Disability Served: vision
This company offers the SubRosaSoft Macnifier, Mac-based software that allows users to magnify portions of their computer monitor for improved viewing. The product is available for purchase and download at the company's Web site.

Sunburst Technology
1550 Executive Drive
Elgin, IL 60123
800-321-7511
Service@sunburst.com
http://www.sunburst.com
Disability Served: various
This company develops software programs, including writing skills programs, math tutorial programs, and typing tutorial programs.

Switch in Time
172 Harvard Road
Littleton, MA 01460
978-486-9433
adams@switchintime.com
http://www.switchintime.com
Disability Served: various

This company manufactures a music composition program for computers.

Symbol Graphics
1047 West Sixth Street
Corona, CA 92882
951-736-4040, 800-736-4045
symbolsgi@aol.com
http://www.symbolgraphics.com
Disability Served: vision
This company offers a Braille graphics software program.

Tapeswitch Corporation
100 Schmitt Boulevard
Farmingdale, NY 11735
800-234-8273
http://www.tapeswitch.com
Disability Served: physically disabled
This company manufactures a variety of adaptive switches, sensing bumpers, safety/sensing mats, light curtain safety systems, touch pads, foot/hand/grip switches, and interface controllers.

TASH International Inc.
3512 Mayland Court
Richmond, VA 23233
800-463-5685
tashinc@aol.com
http://www.tashinc.com
Disability Served: physically disabled
This company manufactures and markets assistive technology devices for people with physical disabilities, including mouse movers; computer single access switches; and the Five Finger Typist, a typing program for individuals who want to keyboard with one hand.

Teachers' Institute for Special Education
9933 Northwest 45th Street
Sunrise, FL 33351
954-572-6220
TISE@special-education-soft.com
http://www.special-education-soft.com
Disability Served: various
This company develops typing instruction software programs for the disabled.

Tech-Able Inc.
1114 Brett Drive, Suite 100
Conyers, GA 30094
770-922-6768
techweb@techable.org

http://www.techable.org
Disability Served: physically disabled
This company offers switch-adapted mice, plug-
in adapters that make small appliances switch
accessible, and keyguards.

Technology Assistance Group
944 Madison Avenue
Valdosta, GA 31602
888-293-0060
info@tagrp.com
http://tagrp.com
Disability Served: various
This company offers a variety of software and hardware
for the disabled, including one-handed keyboards,
Braille translators and keyboards, amplified phones,
and dictation software.

Technos America Ltd., LLC
386 Quartz Circle
Bailey, CO 80421
303-562-9797
info@mctos.com
Disability Served: physically disabled
This company offers adaptive switches and software.

Tek-Talk
8224 East Brandscreek Way
Nampa, ID 83687
208-724-6321
mwilson@tek-talk.net
http://www.tek-talk.net
Disability Served: vision
This company manufactures reading machines, note
takers, cell phones with talking software, talking GPS
systems, and related software.

Teltex Inc.
404 East 13th Avenue
North Kansas City, MO 64116
816-221-6316 (Voice/TTY), 888-515-8120
info@teltexinc.com
http://www.teltexinc.com
Disability Served: hearing
This company offers amplified telephones, TTYs, TDDs,
and assistive devices.

Texthelp Systems Inc.
Northern Ireland Technology Center
545 Boylston Street
Boston, MA 021116

888-333-9907 (U.S. toll-free voicemail)
info@Texthelp.com
http://www.texthelp.com
Disability Served: various
This company offers software products for people with
disabilities, including accessibility software, dyslexia
software, and text-to-speech software.

Textware Solutions
58 Lexington Street
Burlington, MA 01803-4005
781-272-3200, 800-355-5251
support@textware.com
http://www.fitaly.com
Disability Served: physically disabled
This company offers on-screen keyboards.

3M Touch Systems
3M Corporate Headquarters
3M Center
St. Paul, MN 55144-1000
866-407-6666
US-TS-CustomerService@mmm.com
http://www.3m.com/3mtouchsystems
Disability Served: various
This company manufactures touch screens for computers

TriTek Corp.
5263 Stewart Road
Sumerduck, VA 22742
Sales@TriTekCorp.com
http://www.tritekcorp.com
Disability Served: physically disabled
This company develops and sells scientific tools that can
be used by people with severe mobility deficits. The
PC-Scope is a computer-controlled microscope that
can be operated using voice-activated commands or
a trackball.

Troll Touch
25530 Avenue Stanford, Suite 201
Valencia, CA 91355-1131
661-257-1160, 800-201-1160
sales@trolltouch.com
http://www.trolltouch.com
Disability Served: physically disabled
This company manufactures touch screens.

Turning Point Therapy and Technology Inc.
PO Box 310751
New Braunfels, TX 78131-0751

830-608-9812, 877-608-9812
sales@turningpointtechnology.com
http://www.turningpointtechnology.com
Disability Served: *various*
This company offers key guards; large-key keyboards and other adapted keyboards; mounting systems; talking books and game boards; and wheelchair and gait trainer trays.

21st Century Eloquence
800-245-2133
info@voicerecognition.com
http://www.voicerecognition.com
Disability Served: *physically challenged*
This company offers voice-recognition software.

UCLA Microcomputer Project
1000 Veteran Avenue, Room 23-10
Los Angeles, CA 90095
310-825-4821
Disability Served: *various*
A variety of educational software programs are offered by the project, including programs designed to teach cognitive skills and prereading skills.

Ultratec Inc.
450 Science Drive
Madison, WI 53711
608-238-5400
http://www.ultratec.com
Disability Served: *hearing*
This company manufactures text telephones; amplified phones and ringers; and simplicity signalers.

United TTY Sales and Service
21004 Brooke Knolls Road
Laytonsville, MD 20882
866-889-4872 (Voice/TTY)
help@unitedtty.com
http://www.unitedtty.com
Disability Served: *hearing, vision*
This company offers TTYs, computer TTY software, Braille TTYs, amplified telephones, assistive listening systems, closed caption decoders, and wireless two-way pagers.

Valpar International Corporation
2450 West Ruthrauff Road, Suite 180
Tucson, AZ 85705
800-528-7070

valpar@valparint.com
http://www.valparint.com
Disability Served: *various*
This company designs a software program that assesses vocational interests and aptitude.

Verizon
Customer Service Department
777 Big Timber Road
Elgin, IL 60123-1488
800-922-0204, 800 256-4646
http://www.verizonwireless.com/b2c/aboutUs/accessibility/index.jsp
Disability Served: *hearing, vision*
This company offers wireless communication devices with voice command and text-to-speech features; hearing aid-compatible products; and digital wireless phones that are compatible with TTY devices. It also offers text messaging products, as well as its bills and brochures in Braille, large print, and audio formats.

VideoEye! Corporation
9465 West Emerald Street
Boise, ID 83704
208-323-9577, 800-416-0758
info@videoeye.com
http://www.videoeye.com
Disability Served: *vision*
This company offers VideoEye!, a screen magnifier that helps people with low vision to read, write, enjoy hobbies, and tackle a variety of daily living tasks.

Vision Aid Systems Inc.
PO Box 1369
Greenwood, IN 46142
317-888-0323, 800-765-7483
info@visionaidsystems.com
http://www.visionaidsystems.com
Disability Served: *vision*
This company's products include video magnifiers, TV remotes, large number phones, talking caller ID technology, and voice-recognition remotes.

Vision Technology Inc.
8501 Delport Drive
St. Louis, MO 63114
314-890-8300, 800-560-7226
vti@vti1.com
http://www.visiontechinc.com
Disability Served: *vision*

This company offers video magnification systems and other products for people with macular degeneration and low vision.

Visuaide Inc.
841 Jean-Paul-Vincent Boulevard
Longueuil, QC J4G 1R3
Canada
450-463-1717, 888-723-7273
info@visuaide.com
http://www.visuaide.com
Disability Served: vision
This company develops talking book readers and screen reading hardware.

The Visual-Tech Connection
8174 Rookery Way, PO Box 1996
Westerville, OH 43096
800-589-8835
cs@visual-techconnection.com
http://www.visual-techconnection.com
Disability Served: vision
This company offers Telesensory video magnifiers.

Vocational Research Institute
1528 Walnut Street, Suite 1502
Philadelphia, PA 19102
215-875-7387, 800-874-5387
info@vri.org
http://www.vri.org
Disability Served: various
This company develops career-assessment systems that focus on interest and aptitude testing.

VoiceIt Technologies
Minneapolis, MN 55408
612-807-0909
http://www. voiceit-tech.com/index.php
Disability Served: physically disabled
This company offers voice-recognition software that can be used with many Windows-based applications.

Vort Corporation
PO Box 60132-W
Palo Alto, CA 94306
650-322-8282
custserv@vort.com
http://www.vort.com
Disability Served: developmentally disabled
This company designs developmental assessment software programs and books.

WCI
926 Colorado Avenue
Santa Monica, CA 90401-2717
800-233-9130 (Voice/TTY)
sales@weitbrecht.com
http://www.weitbrechtcom.com
Disability Served: communication, hearing
This company offers assistive listening devices, including alerting systems (alarm clocks, wake-up devices, telephone ring signalers, and door signalers); text, amplified, and other specialty telephones; speech-assistance technology; and large-area listening systems.

Western Psychological Services
12031 Wilshire Boulevard
Los Angeles, CA 90025-1251
310-478-2061, 800-648-8857
http://www.wpspublish.com
Disability Served: various
This company designs tests and software programs that assess and evaluate persons with developmental, speech, language, hearing, and other disabilities.

WesTest Engineering Corporation
810 West Shepard Lane
Farmington, UT 84025
801-451-9191
webmail@westest.com
http://www.westest.com
Disability Served: physically disabled
This company designs alternate input devices that emulate mouse and keyboard controls.

Williams Sound Corporation
10321 West 70th Street
Eden Prairie, MN 55344-3459
952-943-2252, 800-328-6190
info@williamssound.com
http://www.williamssound.com
Disability Served: hearing
This company manufactures personal amplifiers and listening systems, amplified phones and ringers, listening systems, and related accessories.

WizCom Technologies Inc.
257 Great Road
Acton, MA 01720
978-635-5357, 888-777-0552
usa.info@wizcomtech.com

http://www.wizcomtech.com
Disability Served: various
This company offers a variety of scanning pens that
can be used to translate text to other languages
and to transfer text to PCs and other devices. It also
offers the Readingpen, a portable reading device for
dyslexic users.

Woodlake Technologies
650 West Lake Street, Suite 320
Chicago, IL 60661
800-253-4391
info@woodlaketechnologies.com
http://www.woodlaketechnologies.com
Disability Served: various
This company offers screen magnifiers, voice amplifiers,
TDD/TTYs, signaling and alerting devices, speech
synthesizers, Braille embossers and translation
software, and a variety of other products.

WyndTell
c/o GoAmerica
433 Hackensack Avenue, Third Floor
Hackensack, NJ 07601
800-549-9991, 800-501-0555 (TTY)
help@goamerica.com
http://www.wyndtell.com
Disability Served: hearing
This company manufactures a compact pager that
allows wireless communication via e-mail, TTY, fax,
alphanumeric paging, and voice telephone.

Xerox Inc.
800 Long Ridge Road
Stamford, CT 06904
800-275-9376
http://www.xerox.com
Disability Served: vision
This company offers optical character recognition
software and reading machines.

YoMax Communications
5711 East Waltann Lane
Scottsdale, AZ 85254
800-808-0966, ext. 600
comments@yomax.com
http://www.yomax.com
Disability Served: hearing
This company offers pagers and other text-based
communication devices.

DAILY LIVING AIDS

These companies manufacture, sell, and distribute daily living aids, which may include home management aids; personal care items, such as adapted utensils or clothing; safety devices, such as bathroom grab bars and shower seats; cushions and positioning devices; therapeutic aids; orthotics and prosthetics; and other products.

A and E Industries Inc.
525 South 17th Street
Belleville, IL 62226-7417
618-233-6176
Disability Served: various
This company manufactures a back support for toilets.

Abilitations
3155 Northwoods Parkway
Norcross, GA 30071
800-850-8603
customer.service@sportime.com
http://www.abilitations.com
Disability Served: various
This company provides pediatric equipment for the improvement of physical functioning, including, exercise, sensory stimulation, aquatic, and positioning equipment.

ABLEDATA
8630 Fenton Street, Suite 930
Silver Spring, MD 20910
301-608-8912 (TTY), 800-227-0216
abledata@orcmacro.com
http://www.abledata.com
Disability Served: various
ABLEDATA is an electronic database of assistive technology and rehabilitation equipment listing more than 20,000 products from more than 2,500 companies.

Able Table Company
227 Fern Street
Santa Cruz, CA 95060
831-425-5767
Disability Served: various
This company manufactures bookholders that raise books to eye level.

Access-Able Designs Inc.
2851 Elderwood Road
Salem, OR 24153
877-853-7816
xsable@adelphia.net
http://www.accessabledesigns.com

Disability Served: physically disabled
This company manufactures shower and toilet transfer benches, as well as pool lifts and related accessories.

Accessible Designs Inc.
7626 Grissom Road
San Antonio, TX 78251
210-684-6794, 888-684-2234
email@accessibledesigns.com
http://accessibledesigns.com
Disability Served: various
This company offers accessible exercise equipment, ramps, and wheelchair accessories.

Accessible Environments Inc.
PO Box 2208
Gloucester, VA 23601
804-694-5321, 800-643-5906
pweis@acessinc.com
http://www.acessinc.com
Disability Served: various
This company offers a variety of assisted living and rehabilitation products.

Access Mobility Inc.
4855 South Emerson Avenue
Indianapolis, IN 46203
317-784-2255
alan@accesstoday.com
http://www.accesstoday.com
Disability Served: various
This company offers bathroom safety devices, adjustable beds, daily living aids, wheelchairs, lifts, and vehicle modifications.

Accessible Threads Design Studio
4545 River Parkway, #13-L
Atlanta, GA 30339
770-355-3281
http://www.accessiblethreads.com
Disability Served: various
This company offers clothing and alterations for people with special needs.

Access to Recreation
8 Sandra Court
Newbury Park, CA 91320-4302
800-634-4351
dkrebs@accesstr.com
http://www.accesstr.com
Disability Served: physically disabled
This is a mail order company specializing in exercise and recreation equipment for the physically challenged.

Access with Ease
1755 Johnson, PO Box 1150
Chino Valley, AZ 86323-1150
928-636-9469, 800-531-9479
http://store.yahoo.com/capability
Disability Served: various
This company makes independent living aids, such as reachers, lamp switches, touch pads, book holders, arthritis pens, large-print address books, wall clocks, key turners, bed canes, dressing aids, bathroom safety rails, kitchen utensils, and gardening tools.

Ace Medical
94-910 Moloalo Street
Waipahu, HI 96797
866-678-3601
acemed@hula.net
http://www.acemedicalinc.com
Disability Served: various
This company sells and rents beds, daily living aids, respiratory care products, wheelchairs, and scooters.

Achievement Products Inc.
PO Box 9033
Canton, OH 44711-9033
800-373-4699
info@specialkidszone.com
http://www.specialkidszone.com
Disability Served: various
This company manufactures innovative therapy, exercise, stimulation, and education products for children with special needs.

Ackley Appliance Service
4301 Park Avenue, #540
Des Moines, IA 50321
515-288-3931
aackley@braillerman.com
http://www.braillerman.com
Disability Served: vision

This company offers Perkins Brailler repair, updating, and reconditioning.

Acor Inc.
18530 South Miles Parkway
Cleveland, OH 44128
216-662-4500, 800-237-2267
email@acor.com
http://www.acor.com
Disability Served: various
Acor makes orthopedic footwear and orthotic shoe inserts.

Action Products Inc.
22 North Mulberry Street
Hagerstown, MD 21740
301-797-1414, 800-228-7763
service@actionproducts.com
http://www.actionproducts.com
Disability Served: various
This company manufactures wheelchair cushions and seating systems, heel and elbow pads, and mattress overlays.

Activa Brand Products Inc.
6845 Davand Drive
Mississauga, Ontario L5T 1L4
Canada
800-991-4464
Info@Advantajet.com
http://www.advantajet.com
Disability Served: diabetes
This company makes a needle-free jet injector for insulin delivery to persons with diabetes.

Activeaid Inc.
101 Active Road, PO Box 359
Redwood Falls, MN 56283-0359
800-533-5330
activeaid@activeaid.com
http://www.activeaid.com
Disability Served: physically disabled
This company manufactures assistive devices for the bathroom, including bariatric chairs; commode and shower chairs; bath and shower benches; raised toilet seats; and adult and pediatric shower wheelchairs.

ActiveForever
c/o Independent Living Products
10799 North 90th Street

Scottsdale, AZ 85260
800-377-8033
CustomerService@ActiveForever.com
http://www.activeforever.com
Disability Served: various
This company offers a wide variety of daily living aids,
including dressing aids, ergonomic products, and
mobility aids.

Adapt-A-Lap Inc.
44 East Main, Suite 503
Champaign, IL 61820
800-419-2354
adaptalap@adaptalap.com
http://www.adaptalap.com
Disability Served: physically disabled
This company manufactures an adjustable, portable
easel that can support a book, magazine, or
notebook computer.

Adaptations by Adrian
PO Box 7
San Marcos, CA 92079-0007
877-6-ADRIAN
adrians1@infostations.com
http://www.adaptationsbyadrian.com
Disability Served: physically disabled
This company provides adaptive clothing and
accessories for children and adults with limited
mobility.

Adaptations Inc.
5 F Street, SW
Ardmore, OK 73401
866-353-3506
customerservice@adaptations4u.com
http://adaptations4u.com
Disability Served: cancer patients and survivors
This company offers hats, headwear, and wigs for people
experiencing hair loss as a result of chemotherapy.

Adaptive Apparel Designs
43 Oak Street
Middleboro, MA 02346
508-946-4036
info@adaptive-apparel.com
http://www.adaptive-apparel.com
Disability Served: physically disabled
This company offers adaptive clothing for people
in wheelchairs.

Adaptive Design Shop
12847 Point Pleasant Drive
Fairfax, VA 22033
800-351-2327
rickerso@email.com
http://www.adaptivedesignshop.com
Disability Served: cerebral palsy, physically disabled
This company designs and builds bath chairs and toilet
supports for those with significant balance problems.

Adaptive Engineering Ltd.
419 34th Avenue, SE
Calgary, AB T2G 1V1
Canada
403-243-9400, 800-448-4652
info@adaptivelifts.com
http://www.adaptivelifts.com
Disability Served: physically disabled
This company manufactures portable wheelchair lifts
for buildings, boats, and trains.

Adaptive Mall
c/o Bergeron Health Care
15 Second Street
Dolgeville, NY 13329
800-371-2778
info@adaptivemall.com
http://www.adaptivemall.com
Disability Served: various
This company offers special needs seating, toileting
equipment and commodes, adult adaptive equipment, exercise balls, tables and trays, strollers, walkers, and pediatric wheelchairs.

Adaptive Tools
1700 Sullivan Street, PO Box 20411
Greensboro, NC 27420
336-273-9101
info@elec-tra-mate.com
Disability Served: physically disabled
This company offers adaptive equipment for disabled
people who enjoy fishing.

AD-AS
2728 South Cole Road
Boise, ID 83709
800-208-2020
customerservice@ad-as.com
http://www.ad-as.com
Disability Served: various

This company manufactures accessible furniture and cabinets for the office, library, kitchen, bath, and rehabilitation center.

Adjustable Bed Company Inc.
13610 North Scottsdale Road, Suite 10-500
Scottsdale, AZ 85254
800-738-4000
info@craftmaticbeds.com
http://www.craftmaticbeds.com
Disability Served: physically disabled
This company manufactures the Craftmatic adjustable bed.

Aiphone Corporation
PO Box 90075
Bellevue, WA 98009
800-692-0200
cust-serv@aiphone.com
http://www.aiphone.com
Disability Served: hearing, physically disabled
This company manufactures the Aiphone Freedom Environment Control System, which allows immobile users to control everyday devices such as lights, heating and cooling systems, sound systems, motorized beds, room-to-room or door-answering intercoms, and any other device that is activated by a relay, switch, or infrared control.

Aircast Inc.
92 River Road
Summit, NJ 07901
800-526-8785
USInq@Aircast.com
http://www.aircast.com
Disability Served: physically disabled
This company manufactures orthotics and support braces.

Air Lift Oxygen Carriers
1212 Kerr Gulch
Evergreen, CO 80439
303-526-4700, 800-776-6771
info@airlift.com
http://www.airlift.com
Disability Served: oxygen-dependent individuals
Air Lift manufactures carriers for portable and cylinder oxygen systems, including backpacks, fanny packs, and shoulder carriers.

AliMed Inc.
297 High Street
Dedham, MA 02026
781-329-2900, 800-225-2610
info@alimed.com
http://www.alimed.com
Disability Served: various
This company offers more than 20,000 items, including cushions, supports, orthotics, wheelchairs and accessories, lapboards, copy stands, computer accessories, bathroom safety devices, and decubitus ulcer pads.

All Hands Interpreting Service
PO Box 201025
Bloomington, MN 55420
612-242-5122, 952-888-3461 (TTY)
info@deafstuffnmore.com
http://www.deafstuffnmore.com
Disability Served: hearing
This company offers amplified telephones, alarm locks, and a variety of daily living aids. It also offers sign language interpreter services.

Allied Medical
690 South Mendenhall
Memphis, TN 38117
901-683-3543, 800-422-2126
http://www.alliedmedical.com
Disability Served: various
This company offers a wide variety of medical and rehabilitation products, including ostomy, urological, and wound care products; power wheelchairs; lifts; bathroom safety products; incontinence supplies; and support cushions and seating systems, including foam in-place seating systems, vacuum-molded seating systems, and lower back support cushions.

Allyn Air Cycle
30 Millstream Road
Woodstock, NY 12498
845-679-2051
Airman@netstep.net
http://woodstock-ny.com/allynair
Disability Served: physically disabled
This company manufactures air cushions for wheelchairs.

Alsto Company
PO Box 1267
Galesburg, IL 61402-1267
800-447-0048
customerservice@alsto.com
http://www.alsto.com
Disability Served: various
This company offers moist heat pads, portable massage
tables, scales, and AeroBeds.

Amana Refrigeration Inc.
403 West 4th Street North
Newton, IA 50208
800-843-0304
http://www.amana.com
Disability Served: various
This company manufactures Easy Reach refrigerators.

Amcest Corporation
1017 Walnut Street
Roselle, NJ 07203
800-631-7370
info@amcest.com
http://www.amcest.com
Disability Served: various
This company manufactures a personal emergency
alert system.

American Bidet Company
PO Box 1500
Hollywood, FL 33022-1500
877-981-1111
info@bidet.com
http://www.bidet.com
Disability Served: various
This company manufactures bidets.

American Craftsmen Inc.
PO Box 484
Coffeyville, KS 67337
800-835-0687
amcrafts@amcrafts.com
http://www.amcrafts.com
Disability Served: physically disabled
This company manufactures the Rok-A-Chair,
a rocking chair for people with back problems.

American Discount Home Medical Equipment
PO Box 1855
Boulder Creek, CA 95006

800-956-6616
service@home-med-equip.com
http://www.home-med-equip.com
Disability Served: various
This company offers adjustable beds, commodes, bath
safety products, nebulizers, walkers, wheelchairs,
scooters, and more.

American Ergonomics Corporation
PO Box 4285
San Rafael, CA 94913
415-492-0325, 800-332-5635
info@AmericanErgonomics.com
http://www.americanergonomics.com
Disability Served: various
This company manufactures ergonomic office chairs
and vehicular seating.

American Health Care Apparel Ltd.
302 Town Center Boulevard
Easton, PA 18040
800-252-0584
info@clothesforseniors.com
http://www.clothesforseniors.com
Disability Served: physically disabled
This company provides clothing and footwear for those
with restricted mobility.

American Medical Alert Corporation
3265 Lawson Boulevard
Oceanside, NY 11572
800-286-2622
info@amac.com
http://amacalert.com
Disability Served: various
This company makes an emergency alert system
activated by pushing a button on a pendant worn by
the user. Activation allows two-way communication
with the alert center. The company also offers
medicine organization kits and in-home health
monitoring appliances.

American Medical Industries
330 East 3rd Street, Suite 2
Dell Rapids, SD 57022-1918
605-428-5501
s.skinner@ezhealthcare.com
http://www.ezhealthcare.com
Disability Served: physically disabled

This company manufactures products that assist individuals with limited strength and mobility to crush, split, and store their medication.

American Olean
1000 Cannon Avenue
Lansdale, PA 19446-0271
215-855-1111
http://www.americanolean.com
Disability Served: vision
This company manufactures nonslip floor tiles and tactile floor surfaces designed for persons with low vision.

American Standard Inc.
1 Centennial Plaza, PO Box 6820
Piscataway, NJ 08855-6820
800-442-1902
http://www.americanstandard-us.com
Disability Served: various
American Standard manufactures ADA-compliant faucets, sinks, and toilets.

AmerTac
25 Robert Pitt Drive
Monsey, NY 10952
800-777-0802
questions@amertac.com
http://www.amertac.com
Disability Served: various
Westek manufactures motion activated light sensor controls, lamp dimmers, and touch lamps.

AMI Inc.
PO Box 808
Groton, CT 06340-0808
860-536-3735, 800-248-4031
http://www.amiaqua.com
Disability Served: various
This company manufactures the Aqua PT, a dry hydrotherapy, massage therapy, and dry heat therapy machine.

Amoena Corporation
1955 West Oak Circle
Marietta, GA 30062
800-726-6362
info@amoena.com
http://www.us.amoena.com
Disability Served: cancer patients and survivors
This company manufactures prosthetic breast forms and post-mastectomy bras and swimwear.

Ampco Products Inc.
11400 Northwest 36th Avenue
Miami, FL 33167
305-821-5700
info@ampco.com
http://www.ampco.com
Disability Served: physically disabled
This company manufactures wheelchair-accessible bathroom cabinets.

Andermac Inc.
2626 Live Oak Highway
Yuba City, CA 95991
800-824-0214
info@hygenique.com
http://www.hygenique.com
Disability Served: various
This company manufactures Hygenique, a combination bidet and whirlpool sitz bath. It also offers patient transport systems.

Anitavee's Adaptive Apparel
3000B East Main Street, #277
Columbus, OH 43209
888-246-8203
info@anitavee.com
http://www.anitavee.com
Disability Served: physically disabled
This company offers adaptive clothing and a tote bag for use with walkers, wheelchairs, and scooters.

Anna-Dote Inc.
PO Box 40, Pullam Drive
West Middlesex, PA 16159-2108
724-346-6132sales@anna-dote.com
http://www.anna-dote.com
Disability Served: physically disabled
This company manufactures and distributes support cushions for wheelchairs and geriatric chairs.

Ann Morris Enterprises Inc.
PO Box 9022
Hicksville, NY 11802-9022
516-937-1848, 800-537-2118
http://www.annmorris.com
Disability Served: hearing, vision
This company manufactures tactile kitchen scales, button battery testers, tactile thermometers, and other products for the hearing- and vision-impaired.

Ansa Bottle Company Inc.
1200 South Main Street
Muskogee, OK 74401
918-687-1664
ansaco@muskogee.com
http://www.theansacompany.com
Disability Served: various
This company manufactures easy-to-hold baby bottles, teethers, rattles, and cups.

Anthros Medical Group
807 East Spring Street
Highland, KS 66035
800-258-0782
anthros@carsoncomm.com
http://www.anthrosmedical.com
Disability Served: various
This company manufactures bath and shower chairs, commode chairs, shower gurneys, and adjustable walkers.

Apex Dynamics Inc.
800-742-0453
info@apexdynamics.com
Disability Served: various
This company offers patient lift and transfer products.

Apex Medical Corporation
800 South Van Eps Avenue
Sioux Falls, SD 57104
800-328-2935
http://www.apexmedical.com
Disability Served: various
This company makes health care aids, including pill organizers, medicine spoons, nitroglycerine tablet holders, and forehead thermometers.

Apollo Light Systems Inc.
376 South Commerce Loop
Orem, UT 84058
800-545-9667
info@apollohealth.com
http://www.apollolight.com
Disability Served: mental health
This company manufactures lighting systems for the treatment of seasonal affective disorder.

Aqua Glass Corporation
320 Industrial Park Drive
Adamsville, TN 38310

731-632-2501
http://www.aquaglass.com
Disability Served: physically disabled
This company manufactures and distributes bathing fixtures, including a complete line of products for the physically challenged.

Aquatic Access Inc.
417 Dorsey Way
Louisville, KY 40223-2833
502-425-5817, 800-325-5438
info@aquaticaccess.com
http://www.aquaticaccess.com
Disability Served: physically disabled
This company manufactures water-powered lifts for in-ground and above-ground pools, spas, and therapy tanks.

Aquatic Development Group
13 Green Mountain Drive, PO Box 648
Cohoes, NY 12047-4807
518-783-0038
http://www.aquaticgroup.com
Disability Served: physically disabled
This company manufactures movable swimming pool floors that allow disabled people to use swimming pools.

ArcMate Manufacturing
637 South Vinewood Street
Escondido, CA 92029
888-637-1926
customerservice@arcmate.com
http://www.arcmate.com
Disability Served: physically disabled
This company manufactures reaching and gripping devices for the home. Products include the EZ Reacher, a reaching aid; Dress EZ, a dressing aid; and EZ ShoeOn, a tool to help people pick up and put on shoes.

Aristoplay
901 Lincoln Parkway
Plainwell, MI 49080
800-433-GAME
http://www.aristoplay.com
Disability Served: various
This company manufactures educational games for toddlers and up.

ArmchairFitness.com
7755 16th Street, NW
Washington, DC 20012
800-453-6280
info@armchairfitness.com
http://www.armchairfitness.com
Disability Served: physically disabled
This company produces Armchair Fitness videos and
DVDs, a series of exercise and fitness workouts.

Ascension
3526 East Fort Lowell Road
Tucson, AZ 85716
520-881-3993, 800-459-0400
sales@wheelchairlift.com
http://www.wheelchairlift.com
Disability Served: physically disabled
This company manufactures a portable wheelchair lift
for access to stages and platforms in public facilities.

ASF Lightware Solutions
Box 625
Merrick, NY 11566
516-868-6897, 800-625-6897
ASF@readinglight.com
http://www.readinglight.com
Disability Served: vision
This company offers hands-free reading lights, book
lights, and magnifiers. It also offers notebook and
palmtop computer lights, visibility-improving
computer keyboard stickers, and high-visibility
playing cards.

ASI American Specialties Inc.
441 Saw Mill River Road
Yonkers, NY 10701-4913
914-476-9000
Info@AmericanSpecialties.com
http://www.americanspecialties.com
Disability Served: physically disabled
This company manufactures grab bars for bathrooms,
shower and tub seats, mirrors, and towel
dispensers.

ASKOInc.
PO Box 851805
Richardson, TX 75085-1805
800-898-1879
http://askousa.com
Disability Served: physically disabled

This company manufactures dishwashers, washers,
and dryers designed to accommodate persons with
physical disabilities.

Assembled Products Corporation
115 East Linden Street
Rogers, AR 72756
800-548-3373
techservice@assembledproducts.com
http://www.martcart.com
Disability Served: physically disabled
This company manufactures electric shopping carts
and a home-use cart.

Assisted Access Inc./NFSS Communications
822 Preston Court
Lake Villa, IL 60046
800-950-9655 (Voice/TTY)
http://www.nfss.com
Disability Served: various
This company distributes and services assistive
devices for the deaf and hard of hearing, including
alerting and signaling systems, amplification
systems, assistive listening devices, Braille products,
calculators, closed-caption decoders, clocks, watches,
timers, radios, fire alarms and smoke detectors,
talking products, walkers, magnifiers, jar and can
openers, pens and pen grippers, and bold-line
writing paper.

Assistive Devices Inc.
800-856-0889
http://www.geocel.com/ADI/HOME.htm
Disability Served: various
This company offers writing grips, nonslip placemats,
hand exercisers, reusable hot/cold packs, reachers,
sock aids, jar openers, weighted utensils, transfer
boards, and playing card holders.

Assistive Devices Network
c/o Arizona Hearing Online Corporation
5975 West Western Way, Suite 119
Tucson, AZ 85713
866-674-3549
http://assistivedevices.net
Disability Served: various
This company offers talking watches, amplified
telephones, TTYs, magnification systems, speech
aids, walkers, canes, shower seats, commodes,
transfer boards and benches, and raised toilet seats.

Atlantic Rubber Products Inc.
3065 Cranberry Highway
East Wareham, MA 02538
800-585-0446 (MA only), 800-695-0446 (outside MA)
mats@atlrubber.com
http://www.atlrubber.com
Disability Served: various
This company makes nonslip floor coverings.

A2i Transcription Services
Bell Business Centre
196-198 Cheltenham Road
Bristol BS6 5QZ
United Kingdom
info@a2i.co.uk
http://www.a2i.co.uk
Disability Served: vision
This company offers text-to-Braille, large print, audio, and disk transcription services.

Audio Book Contractors Inc.
PO Box 40115
Washington, DC
20016-0115
202-363-3429
flogibsonabc@aol.com
http://www.audiobookcontractors.com
Disability Served: various
This company produces unabridged classic books on cassettes.

AudioBooks Online
3325 Hinesburg Road
Richmond, VT 05477-9210
802-434-5550, 800-639-1862
help@audiobooksonline.com
http://www.audiobooksonline.com
Disability Served: vision
This company offers audio books.

Audio-Reader
1120 West 11th Street, PO Box 847
Lawrence, KS 66044
800-772-8898
reader@ku.edu
http://reader.ku.edu
Disability Served: vision
This organization offers a free reading service for residents of Kansas and western Missouri via electronic media and other technologies.

Babee Tenda Corporation
123 South Belmont Boulevard
Kansas City, MO 64123
816-231-2300
babeetenda@babeetenda.com
http://www.babeetenda.com
Disability Served: various
This company manufactures tables for children and an adjustable crib.

Back Be Nimble
2405 Rice Boulevard
Houston, TX 77005
713-521-0003, 800-639-3746
sales@backbenimble.com
http://www.backbenimble.com
Disability Served: various
This company offers mattresses, adjustable beds, pillows, wedges, sleep aids, supports, and ergonomic furniture for the relief and prevention of back and body pain.

Back Ease Inc.
4229 Bardstown Road, Suite 118
Louisville, KY 40218
502-458-2000
Disability Served: various
This company manufactures back support cushions and other medical devices.

BackSaver Products Company
53 Jeffrey Avenue
Holliston, MA 01746
800-251-2225
customerservice@BackSaver.com
http://www.backsavercorp.com
Disability Served: back injury
This company manufactures back aids, including support cushions, foot rests, pillows, recliner chairs, and positioning chairs.

Bailey Manufacturing Company
PO Box 130
Lodi, OH 44254-0130
800-321-8372
baileymfg@baileymfg.com
http://baileymfg.com
Disability Served: various
This company offers therapeutic aids and equipment, including positioning pillows, parallel bars, and wheelchair aids, such as worktables, desks, training stools, and ramps.

Ball Dynamics International LLC
14215 Mead Street
Longmont, CO 80504
800-752-2255
orders@balldynamics.com
http://www.balldynamics.com
Disability Served: various
This company manufactures inflatable exercise balls, therapy and exercise mats, and exercise equipment designed for therapeutic and rehabilitative activities.

Barrier Free Lifts Inc.
c/o Horcher Lifting Systems
324 Cypress Road
Ocala, FL 34472
800-582-8732
info@horcherUSA.com
http://www.barrierfreelifts.com
Disability Served: physically disabled
This company manufactures battery-operated overhead lifts.

Bassmatic
PO Box 7117
Canton, OH 44705-0117
330-455-3983
Disability Served: physically disabled
This company manufactures a fishing-reel adapter for hand amputees.

Bath Ease Inc.
3815 Darston Street
Palm Harbor, FL 34685-3119
727-786-2604
bathease@aol.com
http://www.bathease.com
Disability Served: various
This company manufactures acrylic bathtubs with doors.

Bath Unlimited
1578 Sussex Turnpike
Randolph, NJ 07869
973-598-4300, 800-635-2731
http://www.franklinbrass.com
Disability Served: various
This company manufactures grab bars, folding shower seats, and toilet arm supports.

Battle Creek Equipment Company
307 West Jackson Street
Battle Creek, MI 49017-2306
616-692-6181, 800-253-0854
bcec@prodigy.net
Disability Served: various
This company manufactures a variety of products including the moist heat packs, cervical pillows, and fitness and massage products.

Bauerfeind USA Inc.
55 Chastain Road, NW
Kennesaw, GA 30144
800-423-3405
http://www.bauerfeindusa.com
Disability Served: various
This company manufactures support cushions, splints, and orthotics.

Bay Home Medical and Rehab
707 Parsons
Traverse City, MI 49686
231-933-1200
info@bayhomemedical.com
http://www.bayhomemedical.com
Disability Served: various
This company offers beds, chairs, magnifiers, patient lifts, scooters, wheelchairs, and stair lifts.

Becton, Dickinson and Company
1 Becton Drive
Franklin Lakes, NJ 07417
888-232-2737
http://www.tru-fit.com
Disability Served: various
This company makes home healthcare and sports injury treatment products, including braces, support hosiery, thermometers, blood glucose monitors, and syringes.

Bed Check Corporation
PO Box 170
Tulsa, OK 74101
800-523-7956
webinquiry@bedcheck.com
http://www.bedcheck.com
Disability Served: various
This company manufactures nonrestrictive patient monitoring systems.

Bed Handles Inc.
4825 South Tierney Drive
Independence, MO 64055
800-725-6903
mail@Bed Handles.com
http://www.bedhandles.com
Disability Served: various
This company manufactures bed handles and a hand-
or mouth-operated Singer sewing machine.

Bell-Horn
7952 Zionsville Road
Indianapolis, IN 46268
317-228-1144
customerservice@bell-horn.com
http://www.bell-horn.com
Disability Served: various
Bell-Horn makes compression hosiery, orthotics, diabetic
socks, bandages, and braces.

Bemis Manufacturing Company
300 Mill Street
Sheboygan Falls, WI 53085-0901
920-467-4621, 800-558-7651
toiletseats@bemismfg.com
http://www.bemismfg.org
Disability Served: various
This company manufactures toilet seats for home
healthcare and commercial applications. These seats
contain an antimicrobial agent and fit round and
elongated bowls.

Bernafon LLC
200 Cottontail Lane, Building B
Somerset, NJ 08873
888-941-4203
http://www.bernafon-maico.com
Disability Served: hearing
This company develops hearing aids.

Bernina of America Inc.
3702 Prairie Lake Court
Aurora, IL 60504
630-978-2500
question@berninausa.com
http://www.berninausa.com
Disability Served: physically disabled
Bernina manufactures hand-operated sewing
machines.

Best Bath Systems
4545 Enterprise
Boise, ID 83705
208-342-6823, 800-727-9907
cince@best-bath.com
http://www.fsidaho.com
Disability Served: various
This company offers custom bathing units for people
with disabilities.

BEST Orthopedic Products
2356-B Springs Road, NE
Hickory, NC 28601
828-256-1933, 800-344-5279
customerservice@best-ortho.com
Disability Served: various
This company manufactures support pillows and wrist
and hand splints.

Better Sleep Inc.
80 Industrial Road, PO Box 288
Berkeley Heights, NJ 07922
908-464-2200
info@better-sleep.com
http://better-sleep.com
Disability Served: various
This company manufactures pillows, support cushions,
leg rests, reachers, nonslip bath and shower mats,
and portable beds.

The Bidet Company
205 Berg Street
Algonquin, IL 60102
847-854-7292
support@biobidet.com
http://www.biobidet.com
Disability Served: physically disabled
This company offers bidets.

Bio Compression Systems Inc.
120 West Commercial Avenue
Moonachie, NJ 07074
800-ABC-PUMP
http://www.biocompression.com
Disability Served: various
This company manufactures compression sleeves
and appliances to treat edema and other
conditions.

Bio Concepts Inc.
2424 East University Drive
Phoenix, AZ 85034-6911
800-421-5647
http://www.bio-con.com
Disability Served: various
This company manufactures custom-made elastic
pressure garments, ready-made pressure gloves,
and gel for use with elastic pressure garments.

BIOflex Medical Magnets Inc.
3370 Northeast Fifth Avenue
Oakland Park, FL 33334
954-565-8500, 800-619-2717
info@bioflexmagnets.com
http://www.bioflexmagnets.com
Disability Served: physically disabled
This company offers magnetic therapy products,
including braces and supports, foot care products,
and mattress overlays.

Bioject Medical Technologies Inc.
20245 Southwest 95th Avenue
Tualatin, OR 97062
800-683-7221, ext. 4122
customerservice@bioject.com
http://www.bioject.com
Disability Served: various
This company manufactures needle-free injection
systems.

Biosig Instruments Inc.
PO Box 860
Champlain, NY 12919
514-637-0016, 800-463-5470
biosig@biosig.net
http://www.biosiginstruments.com
Disability Served: various
This company manufactures biofeedback units, heart
rate monitors, and no-impact running shoes.

Blind Children's Fund
311 West Broadway, Suite 1
Mt. Pleasant, MI 48858
989-779-9966
bcf@blindchildrensfund.org
http://www.blindchildrensfund.org
Disability Served: vision
This organization offers Braille toys.

B. M. Brantman Inc.
207 East Westminster
Lake Forest, IL 60045
800-232-7987
nursebeasy@aol.com
http://www.beasytrans.com
Disability Served: physically disabled
This company makes transfer boards with sliding seats.

Body Glove
201 Herondo Street
Redondo Beach, CA 90277
310-374-3441
pr@bodyglove.com
http://www.bodyglove.com
Disability Served: various
Body Glove manufactures ankle, wrist, and knee
supports made of neoprene, as well as ice and
heat wraps.

Bodyline Comfort Systems
3730 Kori Road
Jacksonville, FL 32257
904-262-4068, 800-874-7715
info@bodyline.com
http://bodyline.com
Disability Served: various
Among the items this company manufactures are mattress pads, braces, support pillows, and sleeping
aids.

BodyTrends.com
304 Tequesta Drive
Tequesta, FL 33469
800-549-1667
customerservice@bodytrends.com
http://bodytrends.com
Disability Served: various
This company offers a wide variety of health and fitness
products, including fitness balls, exercise cycles,
exercise mats, heart rate monitors, massagers, spas,
balance therapy products, treadmills, and yoga
equipment.

Bogen Imaging Inc.
565 East Crescent Avenue
Ramsey, NJ 07446
201-818-9500
info@bogenimaging.com

http://www.bogenimaging.us
Disability Served: various
Bogen distributes a camera mount for wheelchairs and
    tables.

Bossert Specialties Inc.
5130 North 19th Avenue, Suite 7
Phoenix, AZ 85015
602-956-6637, 800-776-5885
http://www.wemagnify.com
Disability Served: hearing, vision
This company offers a full line of products for the visually
    impaired, including electronic read/write systems. It
    also offers products for the hearing-impaired.

BPS Architectural Products Inc.
10816 Fallstone Road, Suite 505
Houston, TX 77099
281-568-9945, 800-255-9513
cabinetman1839@yahoo.com
http://www.bpsproducts.com
Disability Served: physically disabled
This company manufactures accessible vanity systems
    and wardrobes.

Braille It
4910 Dawnview Terrace
Golden Valley, MN 55422
763-522-2501
maureensmusic@comcast.net
http://www.brailleit.com
Disability Served: vision
This company offers text-to-Braille translation services.

Braille Jymico Inc.
4545 Iere Avenue
Charlesbourg, QB G1H 2S8
Canada
418-624-2105
info@braillejymico.com
http://www.braillejymico.com
Disability Served: vision
This company translates books, music scores, greeting
    cards, and business cards into Braille and produces
    tactile graphics.

Braille Works
2207 Jaudon Road
Dover, FL 33527

800-258-7544
brailleworks@brailleworks.com
http://www.brailleworks.com
Disability Served: vision
This company offers text-to-Braille, large print, audiocas-
    sette, and disk transcription services.

Breast Enhancers by Olga's
2753 Nostrand Avenue
Brooklyn, NY 11210
877-654-2272
info@breastenhancers.com
http://breastenhancers.com
Disability Served: cancer
This company offers breast enhancers, breast forms,
    and surgical bras.

Brio
PO Box 1013
Germantown, WI 53022
888-274-6869
CusServ@briotoy.com
http://www.brioplay.com
Disability Served: various
Brio makes tactile tic-tac-toe games and other toys.

Brookstone Company
One Innovation Way
Merrimack, NH 03054
800-846-3000
customerservice@brookstone.com
http://www.brookstone.com
Disability Served: various
This company manufactures aids for daily living.
    Products include voice-activated remote controls,
    talking thermometers, massage chairs, temperature-
    sensitive bedding, air purifiers, and gardening tools.

Brown Engineering Corporation
289 Chesterfield Road
Westhampton, MA 01027
413-527-1800, 800-726-4233
info@bedbar.com
http://www.bedbar.com
Disability Served: various
This company manufactures support rails for beds.

Brown Medical Industries
1300 Lundberg Drive West
Spirit Lake, IA 51360-7246

712-336-4395, 800-843-4395
customer.service@brownmed.com
http://www.brownmed.com
Disability Served: various
This company manufactures cast and bandage covers; compression supports; wrist supports, splints, wound care products, fracture walkers; and ice therapy wraps and packs.

Bruce Medical Supply
411 Waverly Oaks Road, Suite 154
Waltham, MA 02452
800-225-8446
http://www.brucemedical.com
Disability Served: various
This company manufactures arthritis, incontinence, hearing loss, laryngectomy, mastectomy, ostomy, and wound care products. It also offers mobility aids, bathroom safety products, and bedroom comfort equipment.

BTE Technologies Inc.
7455-L New Ridge Road, Suite L
Hanover, MD 21076-3143
410-850-0333, 800-331-8845
info@btetech.com
http://www.btetech.com
Disability Served: various
This company provides musculoskeletal evaluation and therapy products and services.

Buck and Buck Inc.
3111 27th Avenue South
Seattle, WA 98144-6502
800-458-0600
info@buckandbuck.com
http://www.buckandbuck.com
Disability Served: various
This company manufactures a full line of adaptive clothing and footwear.

Camp Healthcare
2010 East High Street, PO Box 89
Jackson, MI 49204
800-492-1088
info@camphealthcare.com
http://www.camphealthcare.com
Disability Served: various
This company manufactures post-mastectomy products; casts; support systems and stabilizers; and therapeutic compression stockings.

Canine Assistants
3160 Francis Road
Alpharetta, GA 30004
800-771-7221
info@canineassistants.org
http://www.canineassistants.org
Disability Served: various
This nonprofit organization provides and trains service dogs for adults and children who have physical disabilities or other special needs.

Canine Companions for Independence
PO Box 446
Santa Rosa, CA 95402-0446
866-224-3647
http://www.caninecompanions.org
Disability Served: various
This nonprofit organization provides service dogs to the disabled.

Canine Helpers for the Handicapped Inc.
5699-5705 Ridge Road
Lockport, NY 14094
716-433-4035
chhdogs@aol.com
http://caninehelpers.netfirms.com
Disability Served: various
This organization trains assistance dogs for people with any type of disability.

Canine Partners for Life
PO Box 170
Cochranville, PA 19330-0170
610-869-4902
info@k94life.org
http://www.k94life.org
Disability Served: various
This organization trains and places assistance dogs with people who have a variety of disabilities.

Canoe Creek Rehabilitation Products Inc.
2508 Collins Road
Pittsburgh, PA 15235
800-753-1788
canoecreek@aol.com
http://www.canoe-creek.com
Disability Served: physically disabled
This company manufactures ergonomic devices and rehabilitation equipment, including the Stable Slide, a self-feeding support, and Mary's Aide, a support device that helps caregivers to transfer patients.

Canton Enterprises
701 West Railroad
Canton, KS 67428
888-323-3123
http://www.stormshelters.biz
Disability Served: various
This company manufactures handicapped-accessible
storm shelters.

Care Electronics Inc.
4700 Sterling Drive, Suite D
Boulder, CO 80301
303-444-2273, 888-444-8284
donna@medicalshoponline.com
http://www.medicalshoponline.com
Disability Served: various
This company distributes patient monitoring systems;
emergency phones; therapy pillows and mattresses;
wheelchairs; uplifts seats; and incontinence monitors,
undergarments, and pads.

Care4u
PO Box 377
Wayne, NJ 07474
877-538-6568
custservice@care4u.com
http://www.care4u.com
Disability Served: various
This company offers a variety of daily living aids for the
elderly and the disabled.

Carex Health Care
921 East Amidon Street
Sioux Falls, SD 57104
800-526-8051
http://www.apex-carex.com
Disability Served: various
This company manufactures bathroom safety products
(bath and shower seats, raised toilet seats, and
transfer benches), mobility aids (walkers, canes, and
crutches), and patient room equipment (bed rails, IV
poles, mattress protectors, and overbed tables).

Carolyn's Low Vision Products
1415 57th Avenue West
Bradenton, FL 34207
800-648-2266
sales@carolynscatalog.com
http://www.carolynscatalog.com
Disability Served: vision
This mail order catalog features more than 700 visual aids.

CASIO Inc.
570 Mount Pleasant Avenue
Dover, NJ 07801
800-836-8580
http://www.casio.com
Disability Served: various
Casio manufactures a wide variety of electronic
products, including vibrating alarm clocks with
pill storage features and mobile handheld
computers.

C. D. Denison Orthopaedic Appliance Corporation
220 West 28th Street
Baltimore, MD 21211
410-235-9645
denison@erols.com
http://www.cddenison.com
Disability Served: physically disabled
This company manufactures custom orthotics and
prostheses for children and adults.

C. D. Sparling Company
498 Farmer Street
Plymouth, MI 48170
734-455-3121
info@cdsparling.com
http://www.cdsparling.com
Disability Served: various
This company manufactures shower seats, grab bars,
and folding tub benches.

Center for Sutton Movement Writing
PO Box 517
La Jolla, CA 92038-0517
858-456-0098
Sutton@SignWriting.org
http://www.signwriting.org
Disability Served: hearing
This company offers materials that instruct students and
teachers about SignWriting. SignWriting can be used
to read, write, and learn sign language.

Cepco Products Inc.
9540 Owensmouth Avenue
Chatsworth, CA 91311
818-998-8569
pbelcher@cepcoproducts.com
http://www.cepcoproducts.com
Disability Served: various
This company manufactures a sick room call system
and a home security unit.

CFI Medical Solutions
14241 Fenton Road
Fenton, MI 48430
810-750-5300
sales@cfimedical.com
http://www.contourfab.com
Disability Served: various
This company manufactures home health care aids, including seat cushions and supports, wheelchair accessories, and pediatric positioning devices.

Chattanooga Corporation
4717 Adams Road,
Hixson, TN 37343-9903
423-870-2281, 800-592-7329
http://www.chattgroup.com
Disability Served: various
This company manufactures a wide variety of rehabilitation products, including hot and cold packs and pads; paraffin baths; continuous passive motion systems; bath seats; pressure pads; orthotics; exercisers; and massage and therapy tables.

Chesapeake Rehab Equipment Inc.
2700 Lord Baltimore Drive
Baltimore, MD 21244
410-298-4555, 800-777-6981
Custserv@chesrehab.com
http://www.chesrehab.com
Disability Served: various
This company sells and repairs home care beds, bath safety products, wheelchair cushions, power tilt/ recline systems, pediatric equipment, manual and power wheelchairs, scooters, scooter lifts, stair lifts, and other products.

Chicago Faucet Company
2100 South Clearwater Drive
Des Plaines, IL 60018-5999
847-803-5000
customerservice.us@chicagofaucets.com
http://www.chicagofaucets.com
Disability Served: physically disabled
This company manufactures a lever faucet handle for persons with limited hand dexterity or strength.

Children's Factory
245 West Essex Avenue
St Louis, MO 63122
314-821-1441, 877-726-1696
kvogel@childrensfactory.com
http://www.childrensfactory.com
Disability Served: various
This company manufactures aids for developing and practicing fine motor skills for children, such as shoes for practicing lacing and bow tying, buckle boards, and button boards, as well as foam play blocks and other play equipment.

Clark Medical Products Inc.
5510 Ambler Drive, Unit 10
Mississauga, ON L4W 2V1
Canada
905-238-6163, 800-889-5295
info@clarkmedical.com
http://www.clarkmedical.com
Disability Served: various
This company manufactures products for the bathroom, including a wall grab bar, an elevating toilet seat lift, a bathtub seat, and a hydraulic bath lift.

Clark's Orthopedic and Medical
816 Ninth Street South
Great Falls, MT 59405
800-325-6347
http://www.clarksorthopedic.com
Disability Served: various
This company offers post-mastectomy products, orthotics and prosthetics, incontinence supplies, lifts, wheelchairs, walkers, and scooters.

Clothing Solutions
1525 West Alton Avenue
Santa Ana, CA 92704
800-336-2660
info@ClothingSolutions.com
http://www.clothingsolutions.com
Disability Served: various
This company designs and manufactures adaptive apparel for men and women.

Cochlear Corporation
61 Inverness Parkway, Suite 200
Englewood, CO 80112
800-523-5798
http://www.cochlearamericas.com
Disability Served: hearing
This company manufactures cochlear implants for severe to profound hearing loss in adults and profound hearing loss in children as young as 12 months.

Collis Curve Toothbrush
6110 California Road
Brownsville, TX 78521
800-298-4818
brushteeth@aol.com
http://www.colliscurve.com
Disability Served: physically disabled
This company provides a therapeutic toothbrush designed
for limited range brushers and assisted brushing. The
toothbrush fits over the teeth for easy placement and
allows for a thorough cleaning in 30 seconds.

Coloplast Inc.
1955 West Oak Circle
Marietta, GA 30062-2249
800-533-0464
us.ga@coloplast.com
http://www.us.coloplast.com
Disability Served: various
This company manufactures incontinence aids and
wound, skin care, and ostomy products.

Columbia Medical Manufacturing Corporation
13368 Beach Avenue
Marina Del Rey, CA 90292
310-454-6612, 800-454-6612, ext. 100
http://www.columbiamedical.com
Disability Served: various
This company manufactures bath chairs, positioning
chairs, bath lifters, strollers, gait systems, and
specialty wheelchairs.

Comfort Clothing
PO Box 1396
Standish, ME 04084
888-640-0814
info@comfortclothing.com
http://www.comfortclothing.com
Disability Served: various
This company offers adaptive clothing.

The Comfort Company
851 Bridger Drive
Bozeman, MT 59715
800-564-9248
http://www.comfortcompany.com
Disability Served: various
This company offers wheelchair cushions, back rests,
drop seats, arm supports, lateral supports, and foot
supports.

Comfortex Inc.
1680 Wilkie Drive
Winona, MN 55987
800-445-4007
sales@comfortexinc.com
http://www.comfortexinc.com
Disability Served: various
Comfortex manufactures foam mattresses, foam
mattress overlays, and bedside injury prevention
floormats.

Community Advocates Inc.
PO Box 83304
Lincoln, NE 68501
402-486-3091 (TTY)
clickrule@cs.com
Disability Served: vision
This company sells measuring devices, Braille labelers,
and other products for the blind and visually
impaired.

Compex Technologies
1811 Old Highway 8
New Brighton, MN 55112-1828
651-631-0590, 800-676-6489
info@rehabilicare.com
http://www.compextechnologies.com
Disability Served: physically disabled
This company makes an electrical stimulator for home
or clinical use. It also offers pain management and
rehabilitation products.

Composite Medical Equipment
17310 Jackie Street
Ramona, CA 92065
760-788-0828, 800-253-1523
duane@ultraslick.com
http://www.ultraslick.com
Disability Served: physically disabled
This company manufactures transfer and support boards.

Comtek Communications Technology
357 West 2700 South
Salt Lake City, UT 84115
800-496-3463
sales@comtek.com
http://www.comtek.com
Disability Served: hearing
This company manufactures amplification systems for
the hard of hearing.

Consumer Care Products Inc.
1446 Pilgrim Road
Plymouth, WI 53073
920-893-4614, 800-977-2256
ccpi@consumercareinc.com
http://www.consumercareinc.com
Disability Served: various
This company manufactures and distributes
    rehabilitation equipment for children and adults.
    Products include positioning equipment, fasteners,
    slant boards, floor desks, communication aids, easels,
    walkers, walking aids, and hand-driven tricycles.

Contour Form Products
38 Stewart Avenue, PO Box 328
Greenville, PA 16125
724-588-4452, 800-223-8808
info@contourform.com
http://www.contourform.com
Disability Served: various
This company manufactures medical supports for the
    back, knee, and wrist.

Convatec
PO Box 5254
Princeton, NJ 08543-5254
800-422-8811
http://www.convatec.com/US_en
Disability Served: various
Convatec offers ostomy, skin, and wound care products.

Cord-Mate Inc.
705 Wallingford Road
Cheshire, CT 06410-2914
800-922-7990
Sales@Cord-Mate.com
http://www.cord-mate.com
Disability Served: various
This company manufactures an emergency alert system.

Corometrics Medical Systems Inc.
61 Barnes Park Road North
Wallingford, CT 06492
203-265-5631, 800-243-3952
Disability Served: various
This company manufactures a respiration and cardiac
    monitor for use with infants.

Crazy Creek Products Inc.
1401 South Broadway, PO Box 1050
Red Lodge, MT 59068

406-446-3446, 800-331-0304
chairs@crazycreek.com
http://www.crazycreek.com
Disability Served: various
This company manufactures portable chairs and
    loungers equipped with padded seat and back
    supports.

Creations in Space
PO Box 508
Garfield, WA 99130
800-635-1547
bags@creationsinspace.com
http://www.creationsinspace.com
Disability Served: physically disabled
This company manufactures carrying accessories
    for use with wheelchairs, walkers, and crutches.
    Products include crutch bags, backpacks for
    wheelchairs, and beverage holders for wheelchairs.
    The company also manufactures assistant dog side
    pouches.

Creative Adaptations for Learning
38 Beverly Road
Great Neck, NY 11021-1330
516-466-9143
calinfo@cal-s.org
http://www.cal-s.org
*Disability Served: autism, dyslexic, learning disabled,
    vision*
This nonprofit organization produces embossed, tactile
    illustrations.

Creative Designs
3704 Carlisle Court
Modesto, CA 95356
800-335-4852
robes4you@aol.com
http://www.robes4you.com
Disability Served: physically disabled
This company manufactures a robe that users can put on
    without standing up.

C. R. Newton Company Ltd.
1575 South Beretania Street
Honolulu, HI 96826
800-545-2078
http://www.crnewton.com
Disability Served: various
This company sells and rents bathroom equipment, beds
    and bed supplies, and mobility equipment.

CS Mounting Systems Inc.
3079 West 43rd Avenue
Vancouver, BC V6N 3J4
Canada
604-726-6214
david@csmountingsystems.com
http://www.csmountingsystems.com
Disability Served: physically disabled
This company manufactures a mounting kit for attaching
augmentative communication devices, computers,
and trays to wheelchairs, beds, and tables.

Cybex International Inc.
10 Trotter Drive
Medway, MA 02053
508-533-4300, 888-GO-CYBEX
http://www.cybexinternational.com
Disability Served: physically disabled
This company manufactures exercise and rehabilitation
equipment.

Daedalus Technologies Inc.
2491 Vauxhall Place
Richmond, BC V6V 1Z5
Canada
604-270-4605
daessy@daessy.com
http://www.daessy.com
Disability Served: various
This company manufactures wheelchair mounting
systems for augmentative communication devices,
laptops, and switches, as well as wheelchair-
accessible workstations and desks.

Dale Medical Products
7 Cross Street, PO Box 1556
Plainville, MA 02762-0556
800-343-3980
info@dalemed.com
http://www.dalemed.com
Disability Served: physically disabled
This company manufactures orthotics and therapeutic
aids, including abdominal binders, catheter tube
holders, and tracheostomy tube holders.

Danmar Products, Inc.
221 Jackson Industrial Drive
Ann Arbor, MI 48103-9104
800-783-1998
http://www.danmarproducts.com
Disability Served: various

This company manufactures adaptive equipment,
including seating and positioning equipment,
helmets, flotation devices, and toileting aids.

Dean Rosecrans
PO Box 310
Nampa, ID 83653
800-237-3699
deana@deanrosecrans.com
http://www.deanrosecrans.com
Disability Served: communication
This company manufactures foam stoma filters, stoma
shower shields, a cloth stoma cover, and a speech aid
for persons who have lost the use of their larynxes.

Delta Faucet Company
55 East 111th Street, PO Box 40980
Indianapolis, IN 46280
800-345-3358
customerservice@deltafaucet.com
http://deltacom.deltafaucet.com
Disability Served: physically disabled
This company manufactures water temperature control
monitors, lever handles for faucets, and controls for
adjusting water flow volume.

Designs for Comfort Inc.
PO Box 761044
Marietta, GA 30066
800-443-9226
headliner@mindspring.com
http://www.headlinerhats.com
Disability Served: various
This company manufactures hairpieces and hats with
hairpieces for women experiencing hair loss.

Designs for Vision Inc.
760 Koehler Avenue
Ronkonkoma, NY 11779
631-585-3300, 800-727-6407
info@designsforvision.com
http://www.designsforvision.com
Disability Served: vision
This company develops lens systems for persons with
low vision or specific visual problems.

Detecto
203 East Daugherty Street
Webb City, MO 64870
800-641-2008
detecto@cardet.com

http://www.detectoscale.com
Disability Served: physically disabled
This company manufactures scales, including wheelchair scales, chair scales, and electronic in-bed scales.

Diabetes Home Care
PO Box 265
Crescent City, FL 32112
800-544-5433
info@diabeteshomecare.com
http://www.diabeteshomecare.com
Disability Served: diabetes
This company offers a variety of products for people with diabetes, including syringes and other insulin delivery systems, blood glucose monitors, and glucose bars and tablets.

Diabetes Sentry Products Inc.
1200 Dupont Street, Suite 1-D
Bellingham, WA 98225
866-270-5675
info@sleepsentry.com
http://www.sleepsentry.com
Disability Served: diabetes
This company manufactures an insulin monitor that can be worn on the wrist while sleeping.

Dial A Hearing Screening Test
PO Box 1880
Media, PA 19063-8880
800-222-EARS
Disability Served: hearing
This company provides automated hearing screening tests via telephone. Call the 800 number for instructions and a local test number.

Diestco Manufacturing Corporation
PO Box 6504
Chico, CA 95927
800-795-2392
info@diestco.com
http://www.diestco.com
Disability Served: physically disabled
This company manufactures accessories for wheelchairs, scooters, and walkers. Products include canopies, backpacks, threshold ramps, cup holders, and lap trays.

Different Roads to Learning Inc.
12 West 18th Street, Suite 3E
New York, NY 10011

212-604-9637, 800-853-1057
info@difflearn.com
http://www.difflearn.com
Disability Served: autism
This company offers a variety of products for children with autism, including handwriting tools; puzzles and games; software and videos; flashcards; and books.

Disability Products
5447 East Elmwood Street
Mesa, AZ 85205
800-688-4576
info@disabilityproducts.com
http://www.disabilityproducts.com
Disability Served: various
This company offers a wide variety of daily living aids, including bath, shower, and toilet aids; dressing and grooming aids; eating and drinking aids; kitchen aids; low vision aids; walkers; canes; wheelchair accessories; and writing aids.

Dixon Industries Inc.
877-288-6673
http://www.dixon-ztr.com
Disability Served: physically disabled
This company manufactures a hand-controlled riding lawnmower.

Donegan Optical Company
PO Box 14308
Lexena, KS 66285-4308
913-492-2500
info@doneganoptical.com
http://www.doneganoptical.com
Disability Served: vision
This company manufactures a variety of magnifying lenses.

Dor-O-Matic
121 West Railroad Avenue, PO Box 100
Princeton, IL 61356-0100
800-815-1517
domdoorsclosersinfo@irco.com
http://www.doromatic.com
Disability Served: physically disabled
This company manufactures mechanical door closers.

Dragonfly Toy Company
291 Yale Avenue
Winnipeg, MB R3M 0L4

Canada
800-308-2208
http://www.dftoys.com
Disability Served: various
This company offers a variety of daily living aids and toys
for children with disabilities, including adjustable
computer desks, switch-adapted products, talking
products, and games and puzzles.

Drew Karol Industries Inc.
PO Box 1066
Greenville, MS 38702-1066
662-378-2188
Disability Served: physically disabled
This company manufactures and distributes a
toothbrush for persons with limited or no hand use.

Driving Systems Inc.
16141 Runnymede Street
Van Nuys, CA 91406
818-782-6793
Disability Served: various
This company manufactures wall grab bars for bathrooms,
power and manual wheelchairs, and driving systems
for people with a variety of disabilities.

Drymids Protective Underwear
1918 Ruffin Mill Road
Colonial Heights, VA 23835
866-379-6437
http://www.drymids.com
Disability Served: various
This company offers reusable protective undergarments
for children with special needs.

Duralife Inc.
195 Phillips Park Drive
South Williamsport, PA 17702
570-323-9743, 800-443-5433
sales@duralife-usa.com
http://www.duralife-usa.com
Disability Served: various
This company manufactures commode chairs, shower
chairs, walkers, geriatric chairs, shower beds, and
bath transfer benches.

Duro-Med Industries Inc.
800-526-4753
cs@duromed.com
http://www.duro-med.com

Disability Served: various
This company manufactures a number of health care
products, including orthopedic supports, daily living
aids, and footcare products.

Dwyer Kitchens
320 West Ohio Street
Chicago, IL 60610
800-822-0092
http://www.dwyerkitchens.com
Disability Served: physically disabled
This company manufactures custom compact kitchens
for the physically challenged.

Dynamic Living Inc.
428 Hayden Station Road
Windsor, CT 06095-1302
888-940-0605
http://www.dynamic-living.com
Disability Served: various
This company offers hundreds daily living aids. It also
offers mobility aids.

Dynamic Systems Inc.
235 Sunlight Drive
Leicester, NC 28748
828-683-3523
dsi@sunmatecushions.com
http://www.sunmatecushions.com
Disability Served: various
This company manufactures orthopedic foam seating for
anyone requiring special seating.

Dynasplint Systems Inc.
River Reach, W21
770 Ritchie Highway
Severna Park, MD 21146
800-638-6771
info@Dynasplint.com
http://www.dynasplint.com
Disability Served: orthopedic
This company manufactures dynamic splints designed to
increase joint movement.

DynaWave Corporation
2520 Kaneville Court
Geneva, IL 60134
630-232-4945
dynawave@inil.com
http://my.inil.com/~dynawave

Disability Served: various
This company manufactures ultrasound units to promote healing and reduce pain.

Earglasses
c/o The Listening Institute
1807 Alabama Street
Huntington Beach, CA 92648
sales@earglasses.com
http://www.earglasses.com
Disability Served: hearing
This company offers Earglasses, sound magnifying headsets that allow users to hear voices and sounds more clearly.

Earmark Inc.
1125 Dixwell Avenue
Hamden, CT 06514
203-777-2130, 888-EAR-MARK
staff@earmark.com
http://www.earmark.com
Disability Served: hearing
This company manufactures products for the hard of hearing, including headsets and amplification systems.

The Easel Shop
717-232-6301
joefoster@pa.net
http://www.theeaselshop.com
Disability Served: physically disabled
This company offers adjustable easels for artists who are in wheelchairs.

Easier Ways Inc.
3022 South Wheeling Way, Suite 310
Aurora, CO 80014
303-751-9876
info@EasierWays.com
Disability Served: vision
This company offers Braille equipment and supplies, digital recorders, talking watches and clocks, talking bathroom and food scales, and a variety of other talking products.

Easy Access Clothing
PO Box 6521
San Rafael, CA 94903
800-775-5536
http://www.easyaccessclothing.com

Disability Served: various
This company offers adaptive clothing.

Easy Motion Wood Splitter
PO Box 1285
Vestal, NY 13850
woodwiz@woodwiz.com
http://www.woodwiz.com
Disability Served: physically disabled
This company manufactures a safe, easy-to-use log splitter for use by physically challenged individuals.

Ebco Manufacturing Company
265 North Hamilton Road
Columbus, OH 43213
800-646-2747
psimpson@oasiswatercoolers.com
http://www.oasiswatercoolers.com
Disability Served: physically disabled
This company manufactures wheelchair-accessible water coolers and fountains.

EFCO Corporation
1000 County Road
Monett, MO 65708
800-221-4169
contactus@efcocorp.com
http://www.efcocorp.com
Disability Served: various
This company makes a mechanical, belt-driven, automatic door operator.

EHOB Inc.
250 North Belmont Avenue
Indianapolis, IN 46222
317-972-4600, 800-899-5553
corporate@ehob.com
http://www.ehob.com/consumers
Disability Served: various
This company manufactures mattresses, cushions, foam limb positioners, back support belts, heel elevators, and ostomy systems.

ElderCorner
89 Rio Drive
Ponte Vedra, FL 32082
877-883-5337
info@eldercorner.com
http://www.eldercorner.com
Disability Served: various

This company offers a variety of daily living aids, including adjustable tables; bathroom aids; dressing aids; pill dispensers; large-number and talking calculators; talking clocks and watches; extra large print bingo cards; and magnifiers.

Electone Inc.
PO Box 521727
Longwood, FL 32752-1727
407-831-2555
info@electoneonline.com
http://www.electoneonline.com
Disability Served: hearing
Electone manufactures products for the hearing-impaired, including behind-the-ear hearing aids and miniature hearing aids.

Electric Fishing Reel Systems Inc.
PO Box 20411
Greensboro, NC 27420
336-273-9101
info@elec-tra-mate.com
http://www.elec-tra-mate.com
Disability Served: physically disabled
This company manufactures electric fishing reel drives.

ElectroEase
907 Hollywood Way
Burbank, CA 91505-2816
800-551-2010
Electropedic@hotmail.com
http://www.electroease.com
Disability Served: various
This company offers adjustable beds.

Electromedical Products Inc.
2201 Garrett Morris Parkway
Mineral Wells, TX 76067-9484
800-367-7246
alpha-stim@epii.com
http://alpha-stim.com
Disability Served: various
This company manufactures Alpha Stim, a neuromuscular stimulator that treats pain and stress-related disorders.

E. L. Foust Company Inc.
754 Industrial Drive, PO Box 105
Elmhurst, IL 60126
800-353-6878
sales@foustco.com
http://www.foustco.com
Disability Served: various
This company manufactures and sells air purifiers for the chemically sensitive. Products include water filters, face masks, specialty ventilation system filters, and books.

Eljer Plumbingware Inc.
14801 Quorum Drive
Dallas, TX 75254
972-560-2000, 800-423-5537
http://www.eljer.com
Disability Served: physically disabled
This company manufactures plumbing fixtures and supplies, including bathtubs, faucets, bidets, handles, and showers.

Elkay Manufacturing Company
2222 Camden Court
Oak Brook, IL 60523
630-574-8484
http://www.elkay.com
Disability Served: physically disabled
This company manufactures hot and cold water dispensers, kitchen sink accessories, and wheelchair-accessible water fountains.

Elsafe Inc.
c/o ASSA ABLOY Hospitality Inc.
631 International Parkway, Suite 100
Richardson, TX 75081
800-367-8094
usa@elsafe.com
http://www.elsafe.com
Disability Served: physically disabled
This company manufactures a safe with keypad access.

Empi Inc.
599 Cardigan Road
St Paul, MN 55126-4099
800-328-2536
http://www.empi.com
Disability Served: physically disabled
This company offers orthopedic rehabilitation products.

Enabling Technologies
1601 Northeast Braille Place
Jensen Beach, FL 34957
772-225-3687, 800-777-3687

info@brailler.com
http://www.brailler.com
Disability Served: vision
This company manufactures Braille embossers.

Endorphin
6901 90th Avenue North
Pinellas Park, FL 33782
727-545-9848
sales@endorphin.net
http://www.endorphin.net
Disability Served: physically disabled
This company makes exercise equipment for wheelchair users, including treadmills, bicycle exercisers, and weight machines.

Eneslow-The Foot Comfort Center
924 Broadway
New York, NY 10010
800-ENESLOW
info@eneslow.com
http://www.eneslow.com
Disability Served: physically disabled
This company designs, manufactures, fits, and modifies shoes and foot appliances.

Enhancement Corporation of America
4839 SW 148 Avenue, Box/Suite 529
Davie, FL 33330
customersupport@enhancementcorp.com
http://www.enhancementcorp.com
Disability Served: cancer
This company offers external silicone breast prostheses and adapted clothing.

Equalizer Exercise Machines
62 Everett Crescent
Red Deer, AB T4R 1M1
Canada
403-341-5192
james@equalizerexercise.com
http://www.equalizerexercise.com
Disability Served: physically disabled
This company makes exercise machines for wheelchair users.

Equipment Shop
PO Box 33
Bedford, MA 01730
800-525-7681

info@equipmentshop.com
http://www.equipmentshop.com
Disability Served: physically disabled
This company offers pediatric physical therapy equipment, including adjustable chairs, mats, exercise balls, feeding tools, books, videos, and tricycles with accessories.

Eschenbach
904 Ethan Allen Highway
Ridgefield, CT 06877
203-438-7471
info@eschenbach.com
http://www.eschenbach.com
Disability Served: vision
This company offers low vision aid products including hand and stand magnifiers, telescopes, filters, and electronic reading devices.

Everest and Jennings (A Division of Graham Field)
2935 Northeast Parkway
Atlanta, GA 30360
800-347-5678
http://www.everestjennings.com
Disability Served: physically disabled
This company manufactures more than 200 items for persons with physical disabilities, including wheelchairs, seat cushions, shower chairs, and grab bars.

Extensions for Independence
555 Saturn Boulevard, #B-368
San Diego, CA 92154
866-632-7149
http://www.mouthstick.net
Disability Served: physically disabled
This company develops home and office equipment, including adaptive workstations, desk lapboards, motorized easels, telephone receiver holders, mouthsticks, computer disk loading systems, and keyboard keylocks.

Extreme Adaptive Sports
504 Brett Place
South Plainfield, NJ 07080
908-313-5590
eas@sitski.com
http://www.sitski.com
Disability Served: physically disabled
This company offers mono-skis and adaptive ski equipment.

EZ-ACCESS (A Division of Homecare Products Inc.)
1704 B Street, NW, Building E, Suite 110
Auburn, WA 98001
800-451-1903
custservice@ezaccess.com
http://www.homecareproducts.com
Disability Served: various
This company makes ramps; portable showers and
baths to accommodate the bedridden; and packs,
pouches, and covers for wheelchairs, scooters, and
crutches.

EZ On Products Inc. of Florida
605 Commerce Way West
Jupiter, FL 33458
800-323-6598
info@ezonpro.com
http://www.ezonpro.com
Disability Served: various
This company manufactures a vehicle vest restraint for
children.

Fabrication Enterprises Inc.
PO Box 1500
White Plains, NY 10602
914-345-9300, 800-431-2830
info@FabricationEnterprises.com
http://www.fabricationenterprises.com
Disability Served: various
This company manufactures heat and cold packs, heat
pads, resistance exercisers, and therapeutic weights.

Fabrico Manufacturing Corporation
4222 South Pulaski Road
Chicago, IL 60632
773-890-5350
marketing@fabricoinfo.com
http://www.fabricoinfo.com/bathomatic
Disability Served: various
This company manufactures the BATH-O-MATIC bathing
system to assist with independent bathing.

Farberware Inc.
800-809-7166
http://www.farberware.com
Disability Served: physically disabled
This company manufactures a variety of kitchen
tools and appliances, including an electric peeler,
a battery-operated can opener, electric skillets,
convection ovens, indoor grills, and mixing bowls.

Fashion Ease
1541 60th Street
Brooklyn, NY 11219-5023
800-221-8929
http://www.fashionease.com
Disability Served: various
This company sells adaptive clothing.

Fashion Magic Apparel
859 Battle Street
Kamloops, BC V2C 2M7
Canada
250-314-1849
rjclark@fashionmagic.bc.ca
http://www.fashionmagic.bc.ca
Disability Served: various
This company offers custom clothing for people in
wheelchairs and those with other disabilities.

Fellowes Inc.
1789 Norwood Avenue
Itasca, IL 60143
800-945-4545
http://www.fellowes.com
Disability Served: various
This company manufactures desktop accessories and
office aids, including copyholders and stands,
ergonomic computer mice, wrist rests, and foot rests.

Ferno Performance Pools
70 Weil Way
Wilmington, OH 45177
888-206-7802
info@ fernoperformancepools.com
http://www.fernoperformancepools.com
Disability Served: various
This company manufactures a complete line of aquatic
rehabilitation products.

The First Years
One Kiddie Drive
Avon, MA 02322-1171
800-225-0382
http://www.thefirstyears.com
Disability Served: various
This company manufactures feeding, play, and care
products for children from birth to age three,
including spill-proof cups and bowls, thermometers,
soft tip medicine dispensers, medicine droppers,
baby monitors, and sleep positioners.

Fishburne Enterprises Inc.
140 East Stetson Avenue, Suite 319
Hemet, CA 92543
951-765-9276
Disability Served: vision
This company makes large-print embossed labels for persons with vision impairments who are unable to read Braille.

Fisher-Price Inc.
c/o Mattel, Inc.
636 Girard Avenue
East Aurora, NY 14052
800-432-5437, 800-382-7470 (TTY)
http://www.fisher-price.com
Disability Served: various
Fisher-Price manufactures toys and activities for children and infants that are designed to stimulate and enhance fine motor and eye-hand coordination skills. Products include blocks, puzzles, touch-activated toys, and electronic learning toys.

Fisher Scientific International
Liberty Lane
Hampton, NH 03842
800-776-7000
https://www1.fishersci.com
Disability Served: physically disabled
This company builds a portable science workstation to accommodate wheelchair users who wish to conduct laboratory work.

Fishing Has No Boundaries Inc.
PO Box 175
Hayward, WI 54843
800-243-3462
info@fhnbinc.org
http://www.fhnbinc.org
Disability Served: physically disabled
This nonprofit organization helps people with disabilities enjoy the sport of fishing. It offers information on companies that sell power-driven electric reels, rod holders, reel grippers, ergonomic fishing rods, and adapted boats and ice houses.

Fitter International Inc.
3050, 2600 Portland Street, SE
Calgary, AB T2G 4M6
Canada
800-348-8371

general@fitter1.com
http://www.fitter1.com
Disability Served: various
Fitter supplies balance and fitness products, including balance boards, hand exercisers, and hot and cold packs.

FJR Industries Inc.
PO Box 968
Painesville, OH 44077
440-352-9333
fjrinc@ameritech.net
http://www.fishingrodstuff.com
Disability Served: various
This company manufactures a fishing rod holder.

Flaghouse
601 FlagHouse Drive
Hasbrouck Heights, NJ 07604-3116
201-288-7600, 800-793-7900
sales@flaghouse.com
http://www.flaghouse.com
Disability Served: various
Flaghouse manufactures a wide variety of sports equipment, therapeutic toys, and daily living aids for children, including developmental balls, scooter boards, tricycles, helmets, standing frames, walkers, wheelchairs, communication devices, indoor wheelchair soccer sets and goals, balance boards, wheelchair swings, and games.

Flex-A-Bed Inc.
PO Box 568
LaFayette, GA 30728
800-648-1256
info@flexabed.com
http://www.flexabed.com
Disability Served: various
This company manufactures a motorized, adjustable bed.

Floating Swimwear Inc.
3001 South Madison
Wichita, KS 67216-2143
316-524-0444, 800-374-8111
http://www.floatingswimwear.com
Disability Served: various
This company makes a one-piece bathing suit that provides buoyancy and flotation assistance. It also manufactures a reusable swimsuit diaper.

Follow Me Outdoors
chada@ev1.net
http://users.ev1.net/~chada
Disability Served: physically disabled
This site offers information on adaptive devices for the physically disabled who like to fish, hunt, and do other outdoor activities.

Forde's Functional Fashions Inc.
8020 East Drive, Suite 317
North Bay Village, FL 33141-4157
305-754-4457, 800-531-7705
fashions@fordes.com
http://www.fordes.com
Disability Served: various
This company offers adaptive clothing for people with disabilities.

Fox Bay Industries Inc.
4150 B Place, NW, #101
Auburn, WA 98001
253-941-9155, 800-874-8527
info@foxbay.com
http://www.foxbay.com
Disability Served: various
This company manufactures office and computer equipment, including adjustable laptop platforms, ergonomic office chairs, keyboard wrist supports, keyboard trays, and foot supports.

Frame Technologies
W677 Pearl Street
Oneida, WI 54155
920-869-2979
cframe@netnet.net
http://www.frame-tech.com
Disability Served: communication
This company develops communication aids for children with speech disabilities.

Freedom Machine Inc.
PO Box 321
Greer, AZ 85927
928-735-7746
kjstewart@cybertrails.com
http://freedommachineco.com
Disability Served: physically disabled
This company manufactures a weight exercise machine for wheelchair users.

Freeman Manufacturing Company Inc.
PO Box J
Sturgis, MI 49091
269-651-2371, 800-253-2091
freeman@freemanmfg.com
http://www.freemanmfg.com
Disability Served: physically disabled
Freeman is a manufacturer and supplier of orthopedic soft goods. Its products include a full line of back-support garments, spinal braces, and lower-limb prosthetic supplies.

Frigidaire
c/o Electrolux Home Products
PO Box 212378
Martinez, GA 30917
800-374-4432
http://www.frigidaire.com
Disability Served: various
Frigidaire makes home appliances, including cooktops, air conditioners, and oven ranges that are adapted for people with disabilities.

Front Row Experience
540 Discovery Bay Boulevard
Byron, CA 94514-9454
923-634-5710, 800-524-9091
service@frontrowexperience.com
http://www.frontrowexperience.com
Disability Served: physically disabled
This company manufactures children's motor coordination games and equipment. Products include wood and foam balance beams, foam balls, coordination ladders, scooter boards, beanbag kits, rhythm stick kits, ribbon stick kits, and rubber-band ball kits.

Fun-Attic Inc.
3719 Jasmine, NE
Grand Rapids, MI 49525
877-293-5315
sales@funattic.com
http://www.funattic.com
Disability Served: various
This company sells toys and games for children with disabilities.

Future Forms
http://www.futureforms.com
Disability Served: vision
This company offers continuous Braille paper.

Gaggenau

c/o BSH Home Appliances Corporation
5551 McFadden Avenue
Huntington Beach, CA 92649
800-828-9165
questions@bshg.com
http://www.gaggenau.com
Disability Served: physically disabled
This company manufactures wall ovens that feature side-hinged doors.

Garaventa Accessibility

PO Box 1769
Blaine, WA 98231-1769
604-594-0422, 800-663-6556
productinfo@garaventa.ca
http://www.garaventa.ca
Disability Served: physically disabled
This company manufactures emergency evacuation carriers for persons with limited mobility, as well as wheelchair and stair lifts.

Gardener's Supply Company

128 Intervale Road
Burlington, VT 05401
800-876-5520
info@gardeners.com
http://www.gardeners.com
Disability Served: various
This company provides gardening tools and equipment, such as the Garden Kneeler and Tractor Scoot, for physically challenged people.

G. E. Miller Inc.

45 Saw Mill River Road
Yonkers, NY 10701
800-431-2924
Disability Served: various
This company sells items for daily living and home health care. Products include height-adjustable commodes, walkers, crutches, shower chairs, grab bars, accessible tables, patient lifts, dressing aids, eating aids, protective helmets, child tricycles, and wheelchair swings.

Gendron Inc.

400 East Lugbill Road
Archbold, OH 43502
800-537-2521
http://www.gendroninc.com
Disability Served: physically disabled
This company manufactures wheelchairs; wheelchair accessories; bariatric lifts, beds, chairs, and wheelchairs; wheeled commode chairs; and transport stretchers.

General Electric Appliances

800-626-2005
http://www.geappliances.com
Disability Served: various
This company manufactures appliances and housewares that can be adapted for persons with disabilities. Products include wall ovens, ranges, washers and dryers, microwave ovens, and Braille controls for household appliances.

General Partitions Manufacturing Corporation

1702 Peninsula Drive
Erie, PA 16505-0370
814-833-1154
mikez@erie.net
http://www.genpartitions.com
Disability Served: various
This company manufactures accessible bathroom stall partitions for public facilities.

Gentleman Door Company

c/o Enabling Solutions
814, 743 Railway Avenue
Canmore, Alberta AB T1W 1P2
Canada
877-656-6566
info@gentlemandoor.com
http://www.gentlemandoor.com
Disability Served: physically disabled
This company manufactures automatic door and window openers for residential and light commercial use.

Gentle Touch Medical Products Inc.

800-989-5726
http://www.gentlet.com
Disability Served: cancer
This company offers a mastectomy and lumpectomy camisole.

Gerber Plumbing Fixtures Corporation

4600 West Touhy Avenue
Lincolnwood, IL 60712
847-675-6570
literature@gerberonline.com

http://www.gerberonline.com
Disability Served: various
This company produces bathroom and plumbing
fixtures, including lever faucets, electronic faucets,
bidets, and valves to control water temperature.

Geri-Care Products
250 Moonachie Avenue
Moonachie, NJ 07074-1897
201-440-0409, 800-654-8322
sales@geri-careproducts.com
http://www.geri-careproducts.com
Disability Served: various
This company manufactures incontinence aids,
including underpads, undergarments, diapers, bibs,
and sheets.

Gestetner Corporation
c/o Ricoh Corporation
Five Dedrick Place
West Caldwell, NJ 07006
973-882-2000
http://www.gestetnerusa.com
Disability Served: physically disabled
This company manufactures a copy machine for
employees who are physically disabled.

GKR Industries Inc.
13653 South Kenton Avenue
Crestwood, IL 60445
708-389-2003, 800-526-7879
http://www.gkrindustries.com
Disability Served: physically disabled
This company produces a disposable urine and vomit
bag.

Glacier Cross Inc.
1694 Whalebone Drive
Kalispell, MT 59901-7341
800-388-4828
http://www.glaciercross.com
Disability Served: physically disabled
This company manufactures cervical and lumbar traction
equipment.

Global Assistive Devices, Inc.
4950 North Dixie Highway, Suite 121
Ft Lauderdale, FL 33334-3947
954-776-1373 (Voice/TTY)
info@globalassistive.com

http://www.globalassistive.com
Disability Served: hearing
This company manufactures assistive devices for the
deaf and hard of hearing. Products include wake-up
alarms , door knock signalers, phone signalers, and
vibrating watches.

Glynn-Johnson
2720 Tobey Drive
Indianapolis, IN 46219
877-613-8766
gjinfo@irco.com
http://www.glynn-johnson.com
Disability Served: various
This company manufactures a door handle that can be
manipulated by pushing or pulling.

GN ReSound Corporation
8001 Bloomington Freeway
Bloomington, MN 55420
800-248-4327
http://www.gnresound.com
Disability Served: hearing
This company manufactures digital hearing aids.

Golden Wear Clothing Inc.
1833 Portage Avenue
Winnipeg, MN R3J 0G4
Canada
888-551-9484
info@goldenwearclothing.com
http://www.goldenwearclothing.com
Disability Served: various
This company offers adaptive clothing for nursing home
and home health care residents.

Goodman Specialty Pillows Inc.
PO Box 29027
Dallas, TX 75229-0027
800-423-1233
Disability Served: various
This company manufactures foam support pillows.

GPK Inc.
535 Floyd Smith Drive
El Cajon, CA 92020
619-593-7381, 800-468-8679
info@gpk.com
http://www.gpk.com
Disability Served: spinal-cord injury

This company manufactures products for people with quadriplegia, including UPPERTONE, a device that allows users to perform upper body exercises without any assistance; QuadTrac, assistive technology that helps users to use a computer; and QuadDesk, a worktable for wheelchair users who are unable to lean and reach or lack grip strength.

Grabber Performance Group
4600 Danvers Drive, SE
Grand Rapids, MI 49512
616-940-1914, 800-518-0938
info@warmers.com
http://www.warmers.com
Disability Served: various
This company manufactures disposable heating pads.

GRACO Children's Products Inc.
Attn: Consumer Services
150 Oaklands Boulevard
Exton, PA 19341
800-345-4109
http://www.gracobaby.com
Disability Served: various
This company manufactures a variety of car seats, strollers, high chairs, swings, bouncers, cribs, bassinets, monitors, and activity centers for children.

GRAHL
One Grahl Drive
Coldwater, MI 49036
888-289-4724
http://www.grahl.com/Product.htm
Disability Served: various
This company offers ergonomic chairs.

Greatest of Ease Company
3022 Buchanan Street
San Francisco, CA 94123
415-606-4416
GreatestOfEase@AOL.com
http://personalpagers.tripod.com/go
Disability Served: various
This company designs paging systems and emergency alert systems that are activated by pushing a button.

Great Wave Software
c/o School Specialty Publishing
PO Box 141487
Grand Rapids, MI 49514-1487
800-417-3261
http://www.greatwave.com
Disability Served: various
Great Wave Software publishes K-12 educational software.

Greenwald Surgical Company
2688 De Kalb Street
Lake Station, IN 46405-1519
219-962-1604, 888-962-1829
custserv@greenwaldsurgical.com
Disability Served: physically disabled
This company manufactures male incontinence clamps.

Griffin Laboratories
27636 Ynez Road, Suite L7199
Temecula, CA 92591
800-330-5969
http://www.griffinlab.com
Disability Served: communication
This company manufactures augmentative communication aids for persons with laryngectomies.

Grimm Scientific Industries
Box 2143
Marietta, OH 45750
800-223-5395
grimm@ee.net
http://www.grimmscientific.com
Disability Served: various
This company manufactures paraffin baths.

Grip Mate Products Inc.
4850 Oak Arbor Drive
Valdosta, GA 31602
800-941-4505
info@gripmate.com
http://www.gripmate.com
Disability Served: physically disabled
This company is the manufacturer of a handle adapter for people who cannot use their fingers.

Grohe America Inc.
241 Covington Drive
Bloomingdale, IL 60108
630-582-7711
http://www.groheamerica.com
Disability Served: various
This company manufactures kitchen faucets, handshowers, and thermostats to control water temperature.

Guerdon Homes Inc.
5556 Federal Way
Boise, ID 83716
800-473-3586
info@guerdon.com
http://www.guerdon.com
Disability Served: various
This company manufactures customized mobile homes.

Guidecraft USA
66 Grand Avenue, Suite 207
Englewood, NJ 07631
800-524-3555
orders@guidecraft.com
http://www.guidecraft.com
Disability Served: various
This company manufactures educational games and
activities for children.

Guiding Eyes for The Blind Inc.
611 Granite Springs Road
Yorktown Heights, NY 10598
800-942-0149
http://www.guiding-eyes.org
Disability Served: vision
This company offers guide dogs and training for people
who are visually disabled.

Gunnell Inc.
8440 State Street
Millington, MI 48746
989-871-4529, 800-551-0055
info@gunnell-inc.com
http://www.gunnell-inc.com
Disability Served: physically disabled
This company manufactures recliners, chairs on wheeled
bases, walkers, wheelchairs, and specialized seating
systems for wheelchairs.

Gyro Tech Inc.
PO Box 906
Muskego, WI 53150
414-679-0045
jpedersen@nabcoentrances.com
http://www.nabcoentrances.com
Disability Served: various
This company manufactures an electric door operator.

Hal-Hen Company
35-53 24th Street
Long Island City, NY 11106
718-392-6020, 800-242-5436
http://www.halhen.com
Disability Served: hearing
This company offers alarm clock awakening devices,
amplified telephones, fire and doorbell signaling
devices, hearing aid accessories, ear plugs, hearing
protectors, and magnifiers. These devices are only
available through healthcare professionals.

Halsey Taylor
2222 Camden Court
Oak Brook, IL 60523
630-574-3500
sales@halseytaylor.com
http://www.halseytaylor.com
Disability Served: physically disabled
This company manufactures accessible drinking
fountains and water coolers.

Handi Ramp Inc.
510 North Avenue
Libertyville, IL 60048
847-680-7700, 800-876-RAMP
rampmarketing@aol.com
http://www.handiramp.com
Disability Served: physically disabled
This company manufactures metal ramps, portable
metal tracks, concrete deck ramps, and folding van
ramps.

Han-D-Products Inc.
3999 Parkway Lane, Suite 1
Hilliard, OH 43026-1252
614-876-6625
Disability Served: various
This company manufactures a bathtub grab bar.

Hands On Toys Inc.
14 Jewel Drive
Wilmington, MA 01887
978-988-1141, 888-442-6376
Disability Served: various
This company manufactures foam toys.

Hanger Orthopedic Group Inc.
Two Bethesda Metro Center, Suite 1200
Bethesda, MD 20814
301-986-0701, 877-442-6437
info@hanger.com
http://www.hanger.com

Disability Served: orthopedic
This company designs and fabricates orthotic and prosthetic devices.

Happy Baby Products
791 Palermo Drive
Santa Barbara, CA 93105
800-549-8973
info@happybabyproducts.com
http://www.happybabyproducts.com
Disability Served: various
This company offers seats and back supports for children riding in grocery cart seats, as well as other products.

HARC Mercantile Ltd.
1111 West Centre Street
Portage, MI 49024
269-324-1615 (Voice/TTY), 800-445-9968
info@harc.com
http://www.harcmercantile.com
Disability Served: hearing
This company manufactures an electronic stethoscope with an amplifier. HARC also offers a wide range of assistive listening devices, including alerting and signaling systems, personal and wide-area listening systems, wake-up systems, hearing aid accessories, amplified telephones, and voice amplifiers.

HARD Manufacturing Company Inc.
230 Grider Street
Buffalo, NY 14215-3797
800-873-4273
http://www.hardmfg.com
Disability Served: various
This company manufactures hospital beds and cribs, including manual adjustable beds, motorized beds, and safety cribs.

Harriet Carter Inc.
425 Stump Road
North Wales, PA 19454
800-377-7878
customerservice@harrietcarter.com
http://www.harrietcarter.com
Disability Served: various
This company offers adjustable tilt-top tables, lap trays, bed wedges, tub support bars, tube squeezers, swivel seats for use in automobiles, and other products.

Hartwell Medical
6352 Corte Del Abeto, Suite J
Carlsbad, CA 92009-1408
800-633-5900
info@hartwellmedical.com
http://www.hartwellmedical.com
Disability Served: physically disabled
This company manufactures emergency medical equipment.

Hasten Help System
c/o AC Corporation
301 Creek Ridge Road, PO Box 16367
Greensboro, NC 27416
336-271-6395
molsen@accorporation.com
Disability Served: various
This company offers a telephone emergency response unit.

Hats with Heart Inc.
801-567-0066
hwh@hatswithheart.com
http://www.hatswithheart.com
Disability Served: various
This company manufactures turbans, scarves, and hats for women who have experienced hair loss.

Health-E-Quip
803 East 30th
Hutchinson, KS 67502
800-247-0292
info@health-e-quip.com
http://www.health-e-quip.com
Disability Served: various
This company offers home health care, wellness, and relaxation products.

HealthGuard
c/o Bay Street Manufacturing
155 Rowntree Dairy Road, Unit #3
Woodbridge, ON L4L 6E1
Canada
800-624-2436
breathe@healthguard.com
http://www.healthguard.com
Disability Served: asthma
This company offers products for people with asthma and other respiratory illnesses. These include mattress and pillow covers, nonallergenic pillows,

mattresses, sleeping pillows, air cleaners, and anti-bacterial spray.

HealthGuard HealthCare Limited

707 High Road, First Floor
London N12 0BT
United Kingdom
enquiries@HealthGuardTM.com
http://www.healthguardtm.com
Disability Served: various
This company makes cleaning solutions that are effective against bacteria, spores, viruses, fungi, algae, and dust mites.

Hear-More Inc.

42 Executive Boulevard
Farmingdale, NY 11735
800-881-4327, 800-281-3555 (TTY)
http://www.hearmore.com
Disability Served: various
This company offers a wide variety of products, including phone signalers, amplified telephones, portable voice amplifiers, voice-activated universal remotes, vibrating alarm clocks with pill storage options, low-vision calculators, television screen enlargers, emergency call systems, closed-caption decoders, TTY screeners, canes, scooters, walkers, and wheelchairs.

Heart Rate Inc.

3190-East Airway Loop
Costa Mesa, CA 92626
800-237-2271
http://www.heartrate.com
Disability Served: various
This company manufactures a climbing and stepping exercise machine that allows the user to exercise just the arms, just the legs, or both the arms and legs.

Heide's Mastectomy Shop

Southdale Place
3400 West 66th South, Suite 160
Edina, MN 55435
800-777-4596
http://www.class.net/heide/heidi.htm
Disability Served: cancer
This company offers bras, breast forms, swimwear, and other products for women who have had breast cancer surgery.

Helluva Hunt

1562 Esterbrook Road
Douglas, WY 82633-9592
307-358-6580
Disability Served: various
This company coordinates an annual antelope hunt for sportsmen and sportswomen with disabilities.

Hermell Products Inc.

9 Britton Drive, PO Box 7345
Bloomfield, CT 06002
860-242-6550, 800-233-2342
hermell@hermell.com
http://www.hermell.com
Disability Served: physically disabled
This company manufactures orthopedic softgoods, including wheelchair cushions, cervical and lumbar pillows, wedges, elastic supports, cervical collars, and foot care products.

Hitchcock Shoes Inc.

225 Beal Street
Hingham, MA 02043
800-992-WIDE
hitchcock@wideshoes.com
http://www.hitchcockshoes.com
Disability Served: various
This company makes men's shoes in extra wide sizes.

HITEC Group International

8160 Madison Avenue
Burr Ridge, IL 60527
800-288-8303, 800-536-8890 (TTY)
info@hitec.com
http://www.hitec.com
Disability Served: various
This company distributes hundreds of assistive products for people who are deaf, hard of hearing, speech impaired, visually impaired, and mobility impaired.

HK EyeCan Ltd.

36 Burland Street
Ottawa, ON K2B 6J8
Canada
613-860-0333, 800-356-3362
info@eyecan.ca
http://www.eyecan.ca
Disability Served: physically disabled
This company produces a computer that is controlled by eye movements.

Hold-It Inc.
PO Box 611391
Port Huron, MI 48061-1391
810-984-4213
neolube@comcast.net
Disability Served: physically disabled
This company manufactures and distributes thermoplastic materials that can be applied to a handle of any shape and custom molded to the user's hand.

Hollister Inc.
2000 Hollister Drive
Libertyville, IL 60048
800-343-4060
http://www.hollister.com
Disability Served: various
This company manufactures incontinence aids and catheters.

Home Delivery Incontinent Supplies Inc.
9385 Dielman Industrial Drive
Olivette, MO 63132
800-269-4663
custcare@hdis.com
http://www.hdis.com
Disability Served: various
This company provides incontinence supplies.

Homedics Inc.
3000 Pontiac Trail, Department 168
Commerce Township, MI 48390
800-466-3342
http://www.homedics.com
Disability Served: various
This company manufactures heating pads, massage chairs, foot massagers, hand held massagers, massage cushions and mats, and related products.

Honeywell International Inc.
101 Columbia Road
Morristown, NJ 07962
800-328-5111
http://www.honeywell.com
Disability Served: vision
This company provides a touch-screen thermostat designed with large numbers.

Hosmer Dorrance Corporation
561 Division Street
Campbell, CA 95008
800-827-0070

http://www.hosmer.com
Disability Served: physically disabled
This company manufactures a large variety of prosthetic devices, including a baseball glove attachment, a bowling attachment, a skiing attachment, a fishing attachment, buttonhooks to facilitate dressing, a steering wheel spinner ring, and a prosthetic elbow.

Housing Devices Inc.
407 R Mystic Avenue
Medford, MA 02155
781-395-5200, 800-392-5200
sales@housingdevices.com
http://www.housingdevices.com
Disability Served: vision
This company produces visitor and emergency signal systems.

Howbrite Solutions Inc.
PO Box 880
Cokato, MN 55321
800-505-6284
mathline@howbrite.com
http://www.howbrite.com
Disability Served: physically disabled, vision
This company manufactures a manipulative, math tool to help people learn basic arithmetic. It is made in large print, Braille, and for the physically disabled.

Howda Designz Inc.
PO Box 451
Newburyport, MA 01950
978-462-6260
http://www.howda.com
Disability Served: back injury
This company manufactures a posture chair to provide support for persons with lower back problems.

Howell Design Inc.
287 Mountain Road, #7
Stowe, VT 05672
800-867-7869
rick@readerswindow.com
http://www.readerswindow.com
Disability Served: physically disabled
This company manufactures an overhead, hands-free book holder. Normal finger dexterity is required.

Howell's Tackle
PO Box 5323
Emerald Isle, NC 28594

252-393-2311
sardeh@howellstackle.com
http://www.howellstackle.com
Disability Served: physically disabled
This company offers a fishing rod that can be used with one arm.

Howe Press of Perkins School for the Blind
175 North Beacon Street
Watertown, MA 02472
617-924-3434
howepress@perkins.com
http://www.perkins.org
Disability Served: vision
This company manufactures items for persons with visual impairments. Products include Braille paper, Braille styluses, Braille embossers, erasers, rulers, and copyholders.

Hoyle Products Inc.
10675 Highway 155, PO Box 490
Glennville, CA 93226
800-345-1950
HoyleGrips@aol.com
http://www.hoylegrips.com
Disability Served: various
This company manufactures grips for pens and utensils and book holders.

Hughes Toy Company
24675 Glenwood Drive
Los Gatos, CA 95033-8592
408-353-2137
Disability Served: various
This company manufactures a swimming aid to help persons stay afloat.

Humanicare International Inc.
9 Elkins Road
East Brunswick, NJ 08816
800-631-5270
info@humanicare.com
http://www.humanicare.com
Disability Served: various
This company manufactures incontinence garments, t pads, guards, liners, and bedding for men and women.

Hydro-Care Inc.
PO Box 19074
West Palm Beach, FL 33416
561-688-9771, 877-859-4397

hygina100@aol.com
http://www.hygina.com
Disability Served: various
This company offers a portable personal showering system.

HYDRO-FIT Inc.
2790 Montgomery Highway
Pelham, AL 35124-9977
800-346-7295
http://www.wetvest.com
Disability Served: various
This company manufactures wet suit vests, belts, and collars to use when exercising or running in water.

Hygenic Corporation
1245 Home Avenue
Akron, OH 44310
330-633-8460, 800-321-2135
http://www.thera-band.com
Disability Served: various
This company manufactures a resistive exercise band designed to strengthen and stretch upper and lower extremities. It also offers exercise mats, hand exercisers, exercise balls, paraffin therapy, water therapy, and other fitness products.

Hygienics Direct
c/o National Fulfillment Services
100 Pine Avenue
Holmes, PA 19043
888-463-7337
hygienics@aol.com
http://www.hygienics.com
Disability Served: various
This company makes incontinence briefs and pads.

Hy-Ko Products Company
60 Meadow Lane
Northfield, OH 44067-1415
800-292-0550
cservice@hy-ko.com
http://www.hy-ko.com
Disability Served: vision
This company manufactures driveway markers, safety markers, and reflectors.

Ida-Joy Shoppes
The Gunderson Building
24800 Chagrin Boulevard, #105
Beachwood, OH USA

888-551-1017
info@ida-joy.com
http://www.ida-joy.com
Disability Served: cancer
This company offers post-surgical products including bras, swimwear, and external silicone enhancement forms.

Independent Living Aids Inc.
200 Robbins Lane
Jericho, NY 11753
800-537-2118
can-do@independentliving.com
http://www.independentliving.com
Disability Served: hearing, vision
This company sells aids to the blind and visually and hearing-impaired, including Braille displays, embossers, slates, and watches; talking and large number calculators; canes and walkers; talking alarm clocks, vibrating clocks, and timers; screen magnifiers and talking software; cooking accessories; pill organizers; sign language dictionaries; bathing aids; and telephones for the hearing-impaired, and vision-impaired.

Innovative Products Unlimited Inc.
4351 West College Avenue, Suite 505
Appleton, WI 54914
920-738-9090, 800-424-3369
ipu@ipu.com
http://www.ipu.com
Disability Served: various
This company manufactures healthcare equipment, including shower chairs, commodes, walkers, transfer chairs, and low beds.

Innoventions Inc.
9593 Corsair Drive
Conifer, CO 80433-9317
303-797-6554, 800-854-6554
magnicam@magnicam.com
http://216.247.168.247
Disability Served: vision
This company manufactures a portable electronic magnification system that utilizes a television set to magnify printed materials.

Interbath Inc.
665 North Baldwin Park Boulevard
City of Industry, CA 91746-1502
626-369-1841, 800-423-9485

cs@interbath.com
http://www.interbath.com
Disability Served: various
This company manufactures hand showers and accessories.

Intermatic Inc.
Intermatic Plaza
Spring Grove, IL 60081
815-675-7000
http://www.intermatic.com
Disability Served: various
Intermatic manufactures a timed switch that automatically activates appliances and lights.

International Sani-fem Inc.
PO Box 4117
Downey, CA 90241
800-542-5580
http://www.freshette.com
Disability Served: various
This company manufactures a portable urinal for women.

Invacare Corporation
One Invacare Way
Elyria, OH 44036
800-333-6900
http://www.invacare.com
Disability Served: various
This company manufactures durable medical equipment such as power wheelchairs; custom, standard, and rehabilitation manual chairs; seating and positioning products; patient aids; respiratory products; and homecare beds.

Iron-A-Way Inc.
220 West Jackson
Morton, IL 61550
800-536-9495
info@ironaway.com
http://ironaway.com
Disability Served: physically disabled
This company manufactures a wheelchair accessible ironing board.

JACO Enterprises Inc.
PO Box 22084
Phoenix, AZ 85028
800-678-0078
info@earbandit.com

http://www.earbandit.com
Disability Served: hearing
This company makes a neoprene ear protector for swimmers with ear tubes or those who are prone to swimmer's ear. It also produces extra-soft silicone earplugs in a variety of colors.

James Stanfield Company Inc.
PO Box 41058
Santa Barbara, CA 93140-1058
800-421-6534
maindesk@stanfield.com
http://www.stanfield.com
Disability Served: developmentally disabled, learning disabled
This company produces and distributes video programs and curricula for persons with mild to moderate learning or developmental disabilities.

Jaypro Sports LLC
976 Hartford Turnpike
Waterford, CT 06385
800-243-0533
info@jaypro.com
http://www.jaypro.com
Disability Served: various
This company manufactures exercise bars and other sports and exercise equipment.

JEEZ Specialty Clothing
8780 19th Street, #110, PO Box 9000
Alta Loma, CA 91701
909-987-9512
http://www.jeez-ca.com
Disability Served: various
This company offers undershirts and camisoles for people who have problems with excessive sweating.

Jetta Products Inc.
425 Centennial Boulevard
Edmond, OK 73013-3714
405-340-6661, 800-288-7771
sales@jettacorp.com
http://www.jettaproducts.com
Disability Served: various
This company manufactures hydrotherapy whirlpools.

Jobst
800-537-1063
http://www.jobst-usa.com
Disability Served: various

This company manufactures therapeutic stockings and a water flotation pad.

Jokari/US Inc.
1815 Mometary Lane, #100
Carrollton, TX 75006-7029
972-416-5202
http://www.jokari.com
Disability Served: various
This company offers tools to open bottles, cans, and other containers.

JoMarie's Creative Braille Inc.
jomarie@creativebraille.com
http://www.creativebraille.com
Disability Served: vision
This company offers Braille greeting cards and text-to-Braille transcription services.

JTL Enterprises Inc.
15395 Roosevelt Avenue, Suite 200
Clearwater, FL 33760
800-699-1008
info@aquamed.com
Disability Served: various
This company manufactures a water therapy system in which the patient stays dry.

Just Manufacturing Company
9233 King Street
Franklin Park, IL 60131
847-678-5150
http://www.justmfg.com
Disability Served: various
This company manufactures ADA-compliant stainless steel plumbing fixtures, faucets, and related accessories.

Kardex Systems Inc.
119 Westview Avenue
Marietta, OH 45750
614-374-9300, 800-234-36
Sales@kardex.com
http://www.kardex.com
Disability Served: physically disabled
This company makes a power filing cabinet, ADA-compliant shelving, and file folders.

Kaye Products Inc.
535 Dimmocks Mill Road
Hillsborough, NC 27278-2352

800-685-5293
http://www.kayeproducts.com
Disability Served: various
This company manufactures and distributes a number of daily living aids for children, including toilet seats, walkers, therapy mats, positioning chairs, incontinence garments, and adjustable benches.

Kees Goebel Medical Specialties Inc.
9663 Glades Drive
Hamilton, OH 45011
513-874-2201, 800-354-0445
info@keesgoebel.com
http://www.keesgoebel.com
Disability Served: various
This company manufactures a variety of products, including paraffin baths, exercise bikes, treadmills, whirlpools, treatment tables, foam wheelchair cushions, and foam mattresses.

Keitzer Check Writing Guide
5324 Ingleside
Leesburg, FL 34748
info@checkwritingguide.com
http://www.checkwritingguide.com
Disability Served: various
This company manufactures a plastic check-writing guide to assist persons with various disabilities.

Keller Enterprises
930 East Lake Street
Aurora, IL 60506
630-859-2864
Disability Served: physically disabled
This company makes a long-handled stocking and trouser aid.

Kimberly-Clark Corporation
Department INT, PO Box 2020
Neenah, WI 54957-2020
888-525-8388
http://www.depend.com
Disability Served: various
This company manufactures Depend incontinence undergarments and pads.

Kinetic Concepts Inc.
PO Box 659508
San Antonio, TX 78265-9508
800-275-4524
http://www.kci1.com

Disability Served: physically disabled
This company manufactures a support bed designed to prevent pressure sores; seat cushions; commodes; wheelchairs; walkers; battery powered patient lift/transfer systems; anti-embolism stockings; and other products.

Kinetic Diversified Industries Inc.
PO Box 26730
San Diego, CA 92196-0730
858-566-4850, 800-451-6206
kindiv@aol.com
http://www.tushcush.com
Disability Served: various
This company manufactures foam, orthopedic seat cushions and lumbar support products .

KLOZ-EZ
800-848-5540
http://www.kloz-ez.com
Disability Served: various
This company makes incontinence briefs, disposable incontinence pads, and hospital gowns.

K'NEX Industries
2990 Bergey Road
Hatfield, PA 19440-0700
800-543-5639
http://www.knex.com
Disability Served: various
This company manufactures toy construction sets with pieces that snap together into cars, roller coasters, and other structures. Its toys are designed to stimulate and enhance cognitive skills and eye-hand coordination.

Knork Flatware
1840 East Northern, PO Box 782734
Wichita, KS 67216
877-KNORKIT
http://www.knork.net
Disability Served: physically disabled
This company offers the Knork, a combination fork/knife that helps people with arthritis, limited motor skills, and other physical disabilities to cut food. It is available in both disposable and reusable models.

Kohler Company
444 Highland Drive
Kohler, WI 53044

800-456-4537
http://www.kohlerco.com
Disability Served: various
This company makes bathroom and plumbing fixtures, including hand showers, bidets, baths, whirlpools, faucets, toilets, and drinking fountains.

Kopptronix Company

Box 367
Stanhope, NJ 07874
973-543-6819
kopptronix@kopptronix.com
http://www.kopptronix.com
Disability Served: hearing
This company manufactures sign-language games.

Koregon Enterprises Inc.

9735 Southwest Sunshine Court, Suite 100
Beaverton, OR 97005
800-544-4240
info@nitetrain-r.com
http://www.nitetrain-r.com
Disability Served: various
This company manufactures an incontinence alarm to prevent bed-wetting.

Krissie Products Inc.

232 Taylor Road
Portsmouth, RI 02871
401-846-1701, 401-846-1702, 800-846-1701
jrrd@1connect.com
Disability Served: physically disabled
This company offers machine-washable bibs for persons with arthritis or physical disabilities.

Labac Systems Inc.

4965 Kingston Street
Denver, CO 80239
800-445-4402
http://www.labaconline.com
Disability Served: physically disabled
This company manufactures reclining seat systems for power and manual wheelchairs.

Ladies First Inc.

PO Box 4400
Salem, OR 97302
800-497-8285
info@ladiesfirst.com
http://www.ladiesfirst.com
Disability Served: cancer

This company offers a variety of post-mastectomy products.

Lakeshore Learning Materials

2695 East Dominguez Street
Carson, CA 90810
800-428-4414
http://www.lakeshorelearning.com
Disability Served: learning disabled
This company supplies developmentally appropriate educational supplies, including blocks, science materials, and arts and crafts.

Landscape Structures Inc.

601 7th Street South
Delano, MN 55328-0198
763-972-3391, 888-438-6574
info@playlsi.com
http://www.4funlsi.com
Disability Served: physically disabled
This company manufactures playground equipment, including an adjustable basketball backstop, an infant maze, playground systems with wheelchair accessibility, and rubber mats for playground surfaces.

Lane Bryant

PO Box 850
Milford, OH 45150-0850
800-228-3120
http://www.lanebryantcatalog.com
Disability Served: various
This company manufactures women's clothing for sizes 14 to 44.

LASCO Bathware

Attn: Customer Service
8101 East Kaiser Boulevard, Suite 130
Anaheim, CA 92808
800-94LASCO
http://www.lascobathware.com
Disability Served: various
This company manufactures shower units equipped with support bars, a seat, and plumbing hardware. Other units may be ordered with factory-installed handicapped grab bars. The company also manufactures whirlpools, bubblers, soaking tubs, and steam rooms.

Lavin Inc.

PO Box 91
Belleville, MI 48112-0091
888-545-5438

manuel@lavinlift.com
http://www.lavinlift.com
Disability Served: physically disabled
This company offers a device that can be used to lift
   bedridden patients.

LCN Closers
121 West Railroad Avenue, PO Box 100
Princeton, IL 61356
800-526-2400
http://www.lcnclosers.com/app_ada.asp
Disability Served: physically disabled
This company manufactures power door operators.

Leading Lady
24050 Commerce Park
Beachwood, OH 44122
216-464-5490, 800-321-4804
http://www.leadinglady.com/arthritis_bras
Disability Served: physically disabled
This company offers bras for women with limited hand
   or upper body mobility.

Learning Curve
1111 West 22nd Street, Suite 320
Oak Brook, IL 60523
630-573-7200
cs@learningcurve.com
http://www.learningcurve.com
Disability Served: various
This company offers toys for children who have
   disabilities.

Learning disAbilities Resources
c/o Center for Alternative Learning
6 East Eagle Road
Havertown, PA 19083
610-446-6126
rcooper-ldr@comcast.net
http://www.learningdifferences.com
Disability Served: various
This company offers carbonless duplicating notebooks,
   tablets, loose leaf sheets, and assignments books;
   a variety of books and workbooks for students with
   learning disabilities; page magnifiers; speaking
   dictionaries; talking calculators; and a variety of other
   useful resources.

Learning Products Inc.
5111 Southwest Avenue
St Louis, MO 63110

800-859-3815
info@learningproducts.com
http://www.learningproducts.com
Disability Served: various
This company develops early childhood products
   including infection control mats, sand and water
   tables, large plastic blocks, scooters, tricycles, and
   plastic toys.

Levenger
420 South Congress Avenue
Delray Beach, FL 33445
800-667-8034
Cservice@levenger.com
http://www.levenger.com
Disability Served: various
This company provides reading and writing aids,
   including magnifiers, bookstands, and lap desks.

Life@Home
3630-F Trousdale Drive
Nashville, TN 37204
800-653-1923
info@lifehome.com
http://www.lifehome.com
Disability Served: various
This company offers arthritis, sleep, medication, mobility,
   and dressing aids, as well as bath safety
   and emergency responses devices.

Lifeguard Lift Inc.
3070-B Bay Vista Court
Benicia, CA 94510
800-688-3958
Lifeguard20A@aol.com
http://www.lifeguardlift.com
Disability Served: physically disabled
This company manufactures hydraulic pool lifts.

Life Like Laboratory
2718 Hollandale Lane
Dallas, TX 75234
972-620-0203
http://www.lifelikelab.com
Disability Served: physically disabled
This company manufactures custom hand and foot
   prostheses.

Lifeline International Inc.
3201 Syene Road
Madison, WI 53713

608-288-9252, 800-553-6633
info@lifelineusa.com
http://www.lifelineusa.com
Disability Served: various
This company manufactures a pulley exerciser for use
in physical rehabilitation.

Lifeline Systems Inc.
111 Lawrence Street
Framingham, MA 01702-8156
617-923-4141, 800-380-3111
http://www.lifelinesys.com
Disability Served: various
This company provides an emergency call system that
sends a signal to Lifeline's emergency response
center when the system is activated.

LifeScan Inc.
1000 Gibraltar Drive
Milpitas, CA 95035
800-227-8862
CustomerService@LifeScan.com
http://www.lifescan.com
Disability Served: diabetes
This company manufactures blood glucose monitoring
systems.

Life Solutions Plus
877-785-8326
sales@lifesolutionsplus.com
http://www.lifesolutionsplus.com
Disability Served: various
This company offers bath, dressing, household, kitchen,
medical, and gardening aids, as well as magnifiers
and medicine organizers.

Life with Ease
PO Box 302
Newbury, NH 03255
800-966-5119
questions@lifewithease.com
http://www.lifewithease.com
Disability Served: various
This company offers a wide variety of daily living
aids, including dressing aids, bedding and pillows,
ergonomic keyboards, gardening tools, support
devices, magnifiers, and talking products.

LiftAid Transport LLC
100 Bloomfield Hills Parkway, Suite 195
Bloomfield Hills, MI 48304

800-951-4243
info@liftaid.com
http://www.liftaid.com
Disability Served: physically disabled
This company manufactures patient lifts with a capacity
of up to 500 pounds.

Liko Inc.
842 Upper Union Street, Suite 4
Franklin, MA 02038
508-553-3993, 888-545-6671
info@likoinc.com
http://www.liko.com/na
Disability Served: physically disabled
This company offers mobile and stationary lifts.

Lindustries Inc.
21 Shady Hill Road
Weston, MA 02193
781-237-8177
Disability Served: physically disabled
This company manufactures a door handle lever
that accommodates persons with limited hand
strength.

LiteTouch Inc.
3400 South West Temple
Salt Lake City, UT 84115
888-548-3824
info@litetouch.com
http://www.litetouch.com
Disability Served: various
This company manufactures lighting control systems.

Living Wall Garden Company
33 Lyon Street
Naples, NY 14512
585-374-2907
bobkharris@livingwallgardens.com
http://www.livingwallgardens.com
Disability Served: various
This company manufactures accessible garden
structures.

Loving Paws Assistance Dogs
PO Box 12005
Santa Rosa, CA 95406
707-586-0798
info@lovingpaws.org
http://www.lovingpaws.com
Disability Served: physically disabled

This nonprofit organization trains dogs to assist children who are physically disabled.

The Low Vision Store
2200 University Avenue, Suite 180
St. Paul, MN 55114
800-871-8780
eriknelson@thelowvisionstore.com
http://www.thelowvisionstore.com
Disability Served: vision
This company offers magnifiers; CCTV reading machines; and talking watches, thermometers, calendars, and clocks.

LS&S LLC
PO Box 673
Northbrook, IL 60065
800-468-4789, 866-317-8533 (TTY/TDD)
info@LSSproducts.com
http://www.lssgroup.com
Disability Served: hearing, vision
This company distributes aids and appliances for the visually and hearing-impaired. Products include voice activated phone dialers; talking, low-vision, and Braille watches; talking and low-vision clocks; universal remotes; television enlargers; assistive technology software and hardware; and magnifying glasses, binoculars, and lamps.

Lubidet USA Inc.
c/o DesignCrew Inc.
820 South Monaco Parkway, #353
Denver, CO 80224
800-582-4338
http://www.lubidet.com
Disability Served: various
This company manufactures a bidet.

Luminaud Inc.
8688 Tyler Boulevard
Mentor, OH 44060
440-255-9082, 800-255-3408
info@luminaud.com
http://www.luminaud.com
Disability Served: various
This company manufactures, sells, and services artificial larynges, voice amplifiers, small communications boards, switches for limited motion capability, and other specialized products for people with communication impairments.

Lutron Electronics Company Inc.
7200 Suter Road
Coopersburg, PA 18036
888-LUTRON1
custsvc@lutron.com
http://www.lutron.com
Disability Served: various
This company manufactures lighting control systems for persons with disabilities.

Maddak Inc.
661 Route 23 South
Wayne, NJ 07470
973-628-7600, 800-443-4926
custservice@maddak.com
http://www.maddak.com
Disability Served: various
This company is the manufacturer of Ableware self-help products for daily-living needs. Ableware products are designed to increase mobility and facilitate everyday activities such as dressing, bathing, grooming, and eating.

MagEyes Inc.
PO Box 293010
Kerrville, TX 78029-3010
800-210-6662
sales@mageyes.com
http://www.mageyes.com
Disability Served: vision
This company offers head-mounted magnification devices.

MagniSight Inc.
3631 North Stone Avenue
Colorado Springs, CO 80907
719-578-8893
info@magnisight.com
http://www.magnisight.com
Disability Served: vision
This company manufactures video magnifiers.

Magnistitch Inc.
3756 Rockhill Road
Birmingham, AL 35223
205-967-8326
magnistitch@bellsouth.net
http://magnistitch.com
Disability Served: vision

This company manufactures magnifying lenses, including a magnifier for use with sewing machines.

Mailhawk Manufacturing Company
5292 Whitehouse Parkway, PO Box 445
Warm Springs, GA 31830-0445
800-331-5070
http://www.mailhawkmfg.com
Disability Served: various
This company manufactures a reaching device.

Manning Holoff Company
8565 Canoga Avenue
Canoga Park, CA 91304
818-988-3185
info@magna-lite.com
http://www.magna-lite.com
Disability Served: vision
This company offers handheld illuminated magnifiers and other visual aids.

Maramed Orthopedic Systems
2480 West 82nd Street
Hialeah, FL 33016
305-823-8300, 800-327-5830
maramed@oandp.com
http://www.maramed.com
Disability Served: various
This company manufactures orthopedic devices, including leg splints, hand immobilizers, and leg braces.

Marlen Manufacturing and Development Company
5150 Richmond Road
Bedford, OH 44146
216-292-7060
info@marlenmfg.com
http://www.marlenmfg.com
Disability Served: various
This company develops personal care medical products, including colostomy pouches, colostomy irrigating systems, cleaning brushes, and ostomy supplies.

Mason Medical Products (A Division of MRC Industries, Inc.)
85 Denton Avenue
New Hyde Park, NY 11040
516-328-6900, 800-233-4454
info@masonmedical.com
http://www.masonmedical.com

Disability Served: physically disabled
This company manufactures mattress systems, support cushions, wheelchair and chair cushions, positioners, wedges, floor mats, and equipment covers.

Mat Factory Inc.
760 West 16th Street, Building E
Costa Mesa, CA 92627
949-645-3122, 800-628-7626
info@matfactoryinc.com
http://www.matfactoryinc.com
Disability Served: physically disabled
This company manufactures Safety Deck II, an interlocking tile system that installs directly on the ground, providing wheelchair access over grass.

MAX-Ability Inc.
1275 Fourth Street, Suite 304
Santa Rosa, CA 95404
800-577-1555
mail@max-ability.com
http://www.max-ability.com
Disability Served: various
This company offers technologies for barrier free living, including overhead lifts, stair lifts, and transfer systems.

Maxi-Aids
42 Executive Boulevard
Farmingdale, NY 11735
800-522-6294, 800-281-3555 (TTY)
http://www.maxiaids.com
Disability Served: various
This company sells products to enable independent living, including Braille clocks, calendars, watches, books, printers, and signs; telephones for the hearing-impaired; alarm clocks with extra large displays; wheelchairs; scooters; folding canes; kitchen aids; and large-print wireless keyboards and wireless mice.

Maxi-Signal Products (A Division of Mill Specialties Inc.)
5 East 49th Street
La Grange, IL 60525
800-227-9636
http://www.maxi-signal.com
Disability Served: hearing
This company manufactures signals and alarms that use flashing lights.

Mayline Group
619 North Commerce Street, PO Box 728
Sheboygon, WI 53082-0728
800-822-8037
mayline@mayline.com
http://www.mayline.com
Disability Served: physically disabled
This company produces a height-adjustable, electrically
powered drafting table, as well as modular workstations, mobile computer carts, filing caddies, and
other furniture items for home offices.

McCarty's SACRO-EASE
3329 Industrial Avenue South
Coeur d'Alene, ID 83815
208-765-8408, 800-635-3557
sacroease@aol.com
http://www.mccartys.com
Disability Served: various
This company manufactures pillows, cushions, and back
supports.

McDavid Sports/Medical Products
10305 Argonne Drive
Woodridge, IL 60517
800-237-8254
info@mcdavidinc.com
http://www.mcdavidinc.com
Disability Served: various
This company manufactures ankle guards, knee guards,
stability braces, hot and cold therapy products, and
compression clothing.

Medco Supply Company Inc.
500 Fillmore Avenue
Tonawanda, NY 14150
800-556-3326
Sales@MedcoSupply.com
http://www.medcosupply.com
Disability Served: physically disabled
This company offers wound dressings, blood pressure
kits, hot and cold therapy products, braces, and
supports.

MedDev Corporation
730 North Pastoria Avenue
Sunnyvale, CA 94085
800-543-2789
info@meddev-corp.com

http://www.meddev-corp.com
Disability Served: physically disabled
This company manufactures equipment used for the
rehabilitation of patients suffering from hand injuries.
Products include a resistance exerciser; an isometric
exerciser; and specialized exercisers for the thumb
and individual fingers.

Medical Care Products Inc.
PO Box 10239
Jacksonville, FL 32247-0239
800 741-0110
mcp@ostomymcp.com
http://www.ostomymcp.com
Disability Served: various
This company offers ostomy, incontinence, urological,
and wound care products.

Medic Bath
United Kingdom
sales@medic-bath.co.uk
http://www.medic-bath.co.uk
Disability Served: various
This company offers walk-in baths and bathing
equipment.

Medic ID International
PO Box 571687
Tarzana, CA 91357
818-705-0595, 800-926-3342
medicid@medicid.org
http://medicid.com
Disability Served: various
This company makes medical identification bracelets,
pendants, and watch charms.

Medicool Inc.
20460 Gramercy Place
Torrance, CA 90501
800-433-2469
service@medicool.com
http://www.medicool.com
Disability Served: various
This company makes health care products, such as
portable coolers to carry insulin; glucose testing
supplies; blood pressure monitors; food scales;
emergency phones and pagers; pill organizer with
reminder alarms; medical identification jewelry; and
exercise products for people with limited mobility.

Medi Crush and Supplies Company LLC
PO Box 321381
Flowood, MS 39232
800-262-6334
info@medicrush.com
http://www.medicrush.com
Disability Served: various
This company offers medical products, including pill
    splitters, pill crushers, pill cases, diabetes testing
    products, disposable and reusable undergarments,
    thermometers, and wound care products.

Medinorm Ergonomic Kitchens
48525 Yale Road East, R.R. #2
Chilliwack, BC V2P 6H4
Canada
604-792-1450
medinorm@uniserve.com
http://www.medinorm-kitchens.com
Disability Served: physically disabled
This company designs and manufactures height-
    adjustable and adaptable kitchens and vanities.
    Electric height-adjustable systems are available,
    as are shallow sinks with single or double bowls,
    shallow sinks with two sloped sides, and long-
    handled faucets.

MediUSA
6481 Franz Warner Parkway
Whitsett, NC 27377-3000
847-640-8400, 800-633-6334
info@mediusa.com
http://www.mediusa.com
Disability Served: various
This company makes therapeutic stockings, pressure
    wraps, and orthopedic products for the knee, ankle,
    elbow, wrist, and back.

Med-Lift and Mobility Inc.
PO Box 1249
Calhoun City, MS 38916
800-748-9438
sales@medlift.com
http://www.medlift.com
Disability Served: physically disabled
This company manufactures lift chairs and a motorized
    bed for residential use. It also distributes lift chairs,
    scooters, and power wheelchairs.

Medmart Inc.
888-832-7545
info@mymedmart.com
http://www.mymedmart.com
Disability Served: various
This company offers a variety of daily living aids,
    including commodes, bath benches, catheters, door
    alarms, doorknob grippers, spoon and fork holders,
    hot and cold compresses and pads, orthopedic
    devices, scales, patient lifts, wheelchairs and related
    accessories, scooters, and stair lifts.

Medtek Resources Inc.
204 North Clay Avenue
St Louis, MO 63122-4004
314-966-0221, 800-397-0222
medtekres@aol.com
Disability Served: various
This company manufactures bathroom safety devices,
    including grab bars, flip-up safety bars, toilet roll
    accessories, and back rests.

Merillat Industries Inc.
PO Box 1946
Adrian, MI 49221
517-263-0771
http://www.merillat.com
Disability Served: physically disabled
This company manufactures accessible kitchen cabinet
    accessories.

Miller's Adaptive Technologies
2023 Romig Road
Akron, OH 44320
330-753-9799, 800-837-4544
http://www.millersadaptive.com
Disability Served: physically disabled
This company manufactures wheelchair support systems
    and accessories.

Misty Mate
1171 North Fiesta Boulevard, Suite 4
Gilbert, AZ 85233
480-967-6446, 800-233-6478
customerservice@mistymate.com
http://www.mistymate.com
Disability Served: various
This company makes a device that sprays a water mist in
    order to cool the user.

MJ Designs
800-722-2021
contact@mjdesignsinc.com
http://www.mjdesignsinc.com
Disability Served: various
This company offers adaptive clothing.

Mobility Limited
PO Box 838
Morro Bay, CA 93443-0838
805-772-3560, 800-366-6038
shsh@mobilityltd.com
http://www.mobilityltd.com
Disability Served: physically disabled
This company produces and distributes exercise videos
    for people with physical disabilities.

Mobility Transfer Systems Inc.
PO Box 253
Medford, MA 02155
888-854-4687
info@mtsmedequip.com
http://www.mtsmedequip.com
Disability Served: various
This company makes a variety of daily living aids and
    mobility products, including doorknob grippers;
    easy risers for chairs; reachers; magnified readers;
    commodes and accessories; dressing aids; handheld
    showers; medication reminders; raised toilet seats;
    urinals; tub benches and seats; transfer aids; ramps;
    walkers; and wheelchairs.

Moen Incorporated
25300 Al Moen Drive
North Olmsted, OH 44070
800-BUY-MOEN
http://www.moen.com
Disability Served: physically disabled
This company manufactures ADA-compliant kitchen
    sinks, faucets, and hand showers.

Morfam Inc.
3002 North Home Street
Mishawaka, IN 46545
574-259-4581, 800-338-7014
suemorey@morfam.com
http://www.morfam.com
Disability Served: various
This company manufactures portable electric massagers
    and massage tables.

Mount Sinai Medical Center
Patient Service Center
1 Gustave Levy Place, Box 1161
New York, NY 10029
212-659-8990
Disability Served: communication
The center manufactures a portable communication
    board.

Murphy Bed Company Inc.
42 Central Avenue
Farmingdale, NY 11735
631-420-4330, 800-845-2337
info@murphybedcompany.com
http://murphybedcompany.com
Disability Served: various
This company manufactures space-saving beds and
    cabinetry.

Nada-Chair
2448 Larpenteur Avenue West
St. Paul, MN 55113
651-644-4466, 800-722-2587
info@nadachair.com
http://www.nadachair.com
Disability Served: back injury
This company makes a back support belt that affixes
    to a chair, car seat, or other seating area to provide
    extra support for the lower back.

Nady Systems Inc.
6701 Shellmound Street
Emeryville, CA 94608
510-652-2411
ussales@nady.com
http://www.nadywireless.com
Disability Served: hearing
This company makes amplification systems and assistive
    listening systems.

National Association for Visually Handicapped
22 West 21st Street, 6th Floor
New York, NY 10010
212-255-2804
staff@navh.org
http://www.navh.org
Disability Served: vision
The association offers products to accommodate
    persons with limited vision including magnifiers,
    telephone accessories, writing aids, watches, playing
    cards, and computer hardware.

National Captioning Institute Inc.
1900 Gallows Road, Suite 3000
Vienna, VA 22182
703-917-7600
http://www.ncicap.org
Disability Served: hearing
NCI, a nonprofit corporation founded in 1979, is the nation's largest provider of closed-captioned television services for the broadcast, cable, and home video industries.

Nearly Me
c/o Capital Marketing Technologies Inc.
PO Box 21475
Waco, TX 76702-1475
254-662-1752, 800-887-3370
custserv@nearlymefashion.com
http://www.nearlymefashion.com
Disability Served: cancer
This company designs breast enhancers, gel bras, foam bra cups, and related accessories for women who have had mastectomies.

Nearly You
PO Box 938
Forney, TX 75126
866-722-6168
contactus@nearlyou.com
http://www.nearlyou.com
Disability Served: cancer
This company offers breast forms, breast prostheses, mastectomy bras, breast enhancers, and other products.

Neuropedic
10 New King Street
White Plains, NY 10604
914-684-2665, 800-327-6759
neuropedic@aol.com
http://www.neuropedic.com
Disability Served: various
This company manufactures electric, adjustable beds, orthopedic mattresses, support surfaces, and pillows.

The New Vision Store
919 Walnut Street, First Floor
Philadelphia, PA 19107
215-629-2990
http://www.thenewvisionstore.com
Disability Served: vision
This organization sells products for the visually impaired, including talking clocks, magnifiers, canes, and calculators.

Nex Gen Products
779 Circuit Street
Hanover, MA 02339
781-608-8519
nexgenproducts@nexgenproducts.com
http://www.nexgenproducts.com
Disability Served: hearing
This company offers loud vibrating alarm clocks and wireless visual alerting products.

Next To Me Intimate Apparel
8920 Mentor Avenue
Mentor, OH 44060
866-820-BRAS
info@nexttomeintimateapparel.com
http://www.nexttomeintimateapparel.com
Disability Served: cancer
This company offers post-mastectomy bras, bustiers, and breast forms.

NIKKEN Inc.
800-669-8859, ext. 2
http://www.nikken.com
Disability Served: various
This company manufactures therapeutic aids, including foam mattresses, massagers, support pillows, massaging shoe inserts, and support wraps.

NoIR Medical Technologies
PO Box 159
South Lyon, MI 48178
734-769-5565, 800-521-9746
AGleichert@aol.com
http://www.noir-medical.com
Disability Served: vision
This company offers eyewear for people with achromatopsia, night blindness, diabetic retinopathy, albinism, macular degeneration, retinitis pigmentosa, glaucoma, and cataracts.

No-Rinse Laboratories LLC
868 Pleasant Valley Drive
Springboro, OH 45066
937-746-7357, 800-223-9348
http://www.NoRinse.com
Disability Served: various

This company makes no-rinse hair-care and body-care products, including shampoo, hair conditioner, and lotion.

North Coast Medical Inc.
18305 Sutter Boulevard
Morgan Hill, CA 95037-2845
408-776-5000, 800-235-7054
custserv@ncmedical.com
http://www.beabletodo.com
Disability Served: various
This company offers a wide array of daily living aids and health care products. Items include back supports, jar openers, dressing aids, and automated feeders.

Northern Tool and Equipment
2800 Southcross Drive West
Burnsville, MN 55306
800-221-0516
http://www.northerntool.com
Disability Served: physically disabled
This company manufactures a telescoping wheelchair ramp for vehicles.

Northport Inc.
6311 Trap Line Circle
Chanhassen, MN 55317
952-474-7996
northport77@msn.com
http://www.theadjustable.com
Disability Served: physically disabled
This company manufactures height-adjustable desks and work stations.

Novo Nordisk Inc.
100 College Road West
Princeton, NJ 08540
800-727-6500
http://www.novonordisk-us.com
Disability Served: diabetes
This company makes an insulin injection pen.

Nu-Hope Laboratories Inc.
PO Box 331150
Pacoima, CA 91333-1150
800-899-5017
info@nu-hope.com
http://www.nu-hope.com
Disability Served: various

This company manufactures catheters, colostomy pouches, skin care products for stoma protection, and urinary pouches.

Nurion-Raycal
Station Square, Building 2, Suite B
Paoli, PA 19301
610-640-2345, 877-577-2263
info@nurion.net
http://www.lasercane.com
Disability Served: hearing, vision
This company manufactures electronic guiding devices for blind, deaf-blind, and visually impaired persons. Products include handheld units and devices for mounting on wheelchairs, scooters, or walkers.

Nytone Inc.
2424 South 900 West
Salt Lake City, UT 84119
801-973-4090
nytonemsg@aol.com
http://www.nytone.com
Disability Served: various
This company manufactures an alarm for children with nighttime enuresis. It is also used as a moisture detector for incontinence.

Oakworks Inc.
923 East Wellspring Road
New Freedom, PA 17349
800-558-8850
http://www.oakworks.net
Disability Served: various
This company manufactures treatment tables and chairs.

OBUS Forme
125 Tycos Drive
Toronto, ON M6B 1W6
Canada
416-785-1386, 888-225-7378
info@obusforme.com
http://www.obusforme.com
Disability Served: various
This company manufactures support cushions and pillows, belts, supports, hot and cold compresses, massage rollers, and therapeutic seat panels.

Ocutech Inc.
919-967-6460, 800-326-6460
http://www.ocutech.com

Disability Served: vision
This company offers magnification eyewear.

Olympic Medical
5900 First Avenue South
Seattle, WA 98108
206-767-3500, 800-426-0353
customerservice@olympicmedical.com
http://www.olympicmedical.com
Disability Served: various
This company manufactures a seating and positioning
system that molds to the patient's figure.

Omni Hearing Systems
3418 Midcourt, Suite 105
Carrollton, TX 75006
800-527-0872
contact_us@omnihearing.com
http://www.omnihearing.com
Disability Served: hearing
This company manufactures hearing aids.

OMNI Medical Technologies
981 Park Center Drive
Vista, CA 92081
760-734-1550, 800-448-6664
support@bw-omni.com
http://www.bw-omni.com/usa-home.htm
Disability Served: orthopedic
This company manufactures custom and noncustom
knee braces, ankle supports, and neoprene sports
supports.

Omron Healthcare Inc.
1200 Lakeside Drive
Bannockburn, IL 60015
847-680-6200
http://www.omronhealthcare.com
Disability Served: various
This company manufactures automatic, manual, and
wrist blood pressure monitors; ear and digital stick
thermometers; heart rate monitors; pedometers;
body fat analyzers; nebulizer systems; and peak flow
meters.

One Shoe Crew
PO Box 285
Rio Linda, CA 95673
sally_tavarez@hotmail.com
Disability Served: physically disabled

This company provides a shoe-sharing service for
persons who need only one shoe. The company
matches persons with the same shoe sizes.

Open Sesame
1933 Davis Street, Suite 279
San Leandro, CA 94577
800-673-6911
http://www.opensesamedoor.com
Disability Served: spinal-cord injury
This company manufactures remote control door
systems primarily for individuals in wheelchairs.

Optelec US Inc.
321 Billerica Road
Chelmsford, MA 01824
800-828-1056
http://www.optelec.com
Disability Served: vision
This company manufactures video and handheld
magnifiers. It also offers a variety of communication
and Braille products including software for cell
phones that converts text into speech.

Oralgiene USA Inc.
8460 Higuera Street
Culver City, CA 90032
310-204-7888, 800-933-6725
http://www.timemachinetoothbrush.com
Disability Served: various
This company manufactures a battery-powered
toothbrush for children.

Orthopedic Physical Therapy Products
3800 Annapolis Lane, Suite 165, PO Box 47009
Minneapolis, MN 55447-0009
763-553-0452, 888-819-0121
customerservice@optp.com
http://www.optp.com
Disability Served: various
This company distributes aquatic and physical therapy
products including fin and flipper exercise logs,
lumbar rolls, Swiss balls, medicine balls, and
stretching products.

Orthoshirt
1645 Red Oak Road
Williamstown, NJ 08094-2023
609-472-4031
corporate@orthoshirt.com

http://www.orthoshirt.com
Disability Served: various
This company offers an orthopedic unisex medical shirt that provides ease in dressing and treating patients.

Oval Window Audio

33 Wildflower Court
Nederland, CO 80466-9638
303-447-3607 (Voice/TDD)
http://www.ovalwindowaudio.com
Disability Served: hearing
This company manufactures assistive technologies and multisensory sound systems for hearing-impaired children and adults.

OXO International

75 Ninth Avenue, Fifth Floor
New York, New York 10011
800-545-4411
http://www.goodgrips.com
Disability Served: various
This company manufactures cooking, serving, cleaning, organizing, and gardening utensils with rubber grips.

Paille Industries LLC

6033 Old Antonia Road
Imperial, MO 63052
800-443-4926, ext. 3210
cservice@selfwipe.com
http://www.selfwipe.com
Disability Served: various
This company offers SelfWipe, a bathroom toileting aid.

Palco Laboratories

8030 Soquel Avenue, Suite 104
Santa Cruz, CA 95062-2032
831-476-3151, 800-346-4488
info@palcolabs.com
http://www.palcolabs.com
Disability Served: various
This company manufactures medical aids, including puncture devices for blood tests, syringe injection aids, and pediatric incontinence alarms.

Panasonic Corporation

c/o Consumer Affairs Division
One Panasonic Way, Panazip 2F-3
Secaucus, NJ 07094
http://www.panasonic.com/flash.html
Disability Served: various

Panasonic manufactures computer and telephone headsets, air purifiers, massage chairs, and blood pressure monitors.

PaperPak

PO Box 3240
San Dimas, CA 91773
800-4-ATTENDS
info@paperpak.com
http://www.attends.us/us
Disability Served: various
This company makes disposable diapers for adults.

Parent's Helper Inc.

PO Box 293
Waterville Valley, NH 03215
800-709-SAFE
information@childsafety.com
http://www.childsafety.com
Disability Served: various
This company manufactures and markets the warning signs to help protect playing children.

Park Surgical Company Inc.

5001 New Utrecht Avenue
Brooklyn, NY 11219
718-436-9200
info@parksurgical.com
http://www.parksurgical.com
Disability Served: communication
This company makes speech amplifiers and speech aids.

Passy-Muir Inc.

4521 Campus Drive, PMB 273
Irvine, CA 92612
949-833-8255, 800-634-5397
info@passy-muir.com
http://www.passy-muir.com
Disability Served: communication
This company manufactures a patented tracheostomy and ventilator speaking valve.

Paws With A Cause

4646 South Division
Wayland, MI 49348
800-253-7297
paws@pawswithacause.org
http://www.pawswithacause.org
Disability Served: various
This organization provides service dogs to the disabled.

Pedicraft
PO Box 5969
Jacksonville, FL 32247-5969
800-223-7649
custserv@pedicraft.com
http://www.pedicraft.com
Disability Served: various
This company manufactures pediatric aids, including
cribs, mesh-enclosed beds, infant slings, and
therapeutic foam wedges.

Personal Touch Health Care Apparel Inc.
PO Box 230321
New York, NY 11223
888-626-1703
http://www.adaptiveapparel.com
Disability Served: various
This company offers adaptive apparel for the incontinent
and disabled.

Phoenix Poke Boats, Inc.
800-354-0190
pokeboat@pokeboat.com
http://www.pokeboat.com
Disability Served: various
This company produces lightweight kayaks and poke
boats used for paddling, fishing, hunting, and
photography.

Phonak Inc.
4520 Weaver Parkway
Warrenville, IL 60555-3927
630-821-5000, 800-679-4871
info@phonak.com
http://www.phonak-us.com
Disability Served: hearing
This organization manufactures hearing aids, including
programmable and digital units, as well as wireless
communication systems.

PillowTalk USA
348 Pond Road
Freehold, NJ 07728
732-780-9483
Info@pillowtalkusa.com
http://www.pillowtalk-usa.com
Disability Served: various
This company makes waterproof mattress pads, foam
mattresses, and bed pillows and blankets.

PI Professional Therapy Products
PO Box 669
Athens, TN 37371-0669
888-818-9632
http://www.pi-inc.com
Disability Served: various
This company manufactures physical therapy products.

Pip Squeakers LLC
11 Myrtle Avenue
Lebanon, NJ 08833
866-722-4535
pipsqueakers@earthlink.net
http://www.pipsqueakers.com
Disability Served: vision
This company offers squeaky footwear for children,
which can help parents with low-vision to keep track
of their children.

Playskool
800-752-9755
http://www.hasbro.com/playskool
Disability Served: various
Playskool offers toys and activities that help children
develop their cognitive and motor skills.

Plow and Hearth
Route 29 North
Madison, VA 22727
800-494-7544
http://www.plowhearth.com
Disability Served: physically disabled
This company makes a device that makes it easy to grab
high and low objects.

Plum Enterprises,Inc.
500 Freedom View Lane, PO Box 85
Valley Forge, PA 19481-0085
610-783-7377, 800-321-PLUM
info@plument.com
http://www.plument.com
Disability Served: various
This company makes protective helmets and hip
protectors.

Poppin and Company
PO Box 176
Unity, ME 04988
207-437-2746
poppin@uninets.net

http://www.poppinandcompany.com
Disability Served: communication
This company specializes in communication and language materials that use DynaSyms, the symbols on DynaVox devices.

Port-A-Bar
c/o Grabit, Inc.
1077 Old Highway 35
Hudson, WI 54016
800-542-5076
info@GrabItOnline.com
http://www.grabitonline.com
Disability Served: various
This company offers a portable grab bar for use in showers or tubs.

Posey Company
5635 Peck Road
Arcadia, CA 91006-0020
626-443-3143, 800-447-6739
http://www.aidsfordailyliving.com
Disability Served: various
This company manufactures a variety of health care products, including wander and fall prevention devices; wheelchair cushions; wound prevention boots, guards, stabilizers, and related products; straps and holders for urine collection systems; bed safety devices; self-releasing belts; and therapy aids.

Positive Image Orthotics and Prosthetics Inc.
515 East 63rd Street, Suite 5
Savannah, GA 31405
912-354-7500
dmpuckett@pipoinc.com
http://www.pipoinc.com
Disability Served: physically disabled
This company provides orthotic and prosthetic devices with cosmetic enhancement.

Postcraft Company
625 West Rillito Street
Tucson, AZ 85705
520-624-2531, 800-528-4844
sales@postcraft.com
http://www.postcraft.com
Disability Served: various
This company manufactures mattress and pillow protectors, as well as shower curtains.

Pos-T-Vac Inc.
1701 North 14th Avenue, PO Box 1436
Dodge City, KS 67801
866-52-ERECT
erect@postvac.com
http://www.postvac.com
Disability Served: various
This company makes an erection aid for impotence.

Power Access Corporation
170 Main Street, PO Box 1050
New Hartford, CT 06057-0980
800-344-0088
salesint@power-access.com
http://www.power-access.com
Disability Served: physically disabled
This company makes a power door opener.

PPN Inc.
800-289-4776
customer.service@ppninc.com
http://www.ppninc.com
Disability Served: various
This company offers adaptive clothing for men and women, lift chairs, wheelchair accessories, and scooters.

PPP Enterprises
2027 Pheasant Creek Drive
Martinez, GA 30907
706-855-7059
pppent@webehave.com
http://www.webehave.com
Disability Served: various
This company manufactures 'Lastic Laces that convert shoes to slip-ons, as well as other adaptive clothing. PPP Enterprises also manufactures incentive tools for encouraging positive behavioral change in children.

Prairie Seating Corporation
7515 Linder Avenue
Skokie, IL 60077
847-568-0001
prairieusa@aol.com
http://www.prairieseating.com
Disability Served: physically disabled
This company manufactures custom cushions for wheelchairs.

PrePak Products
4055 Oceanside Boulevard, Suite L
Oceanside, CA 92056-5821
800-544-7257
info@prepakproducts.com
http://www.prepakproducts.com
Disability Served: various
This company manufactures exercise and therapeutic
equipment, including shoulder pulleys and weight
bags. The company also offers arm slings and
massage creams.

Prevent Care Products Inc.
1006 Arnold Avenue
Point Pleasant, NJ 08742
800-443-6743
http://improvetoothbrush.com
Disability Served: various
This company makes a toothbrush designed for effective
plaque reduction at the gumline.

Principle Business Enterprises Inc.
Pine Lake Industrial Park
Dunbridge, OH 43414
800-467-3224
http://www.tranquilityproducts.com
Disability Served: various
This company manufactures disposable incontinence
garments and pads.

Priva Inc.
PO Box 448
Champlain, NY 12919-0448
514-356-8881, 800-761-8881
piv@priva-inc.com
http://www.priva-inc.com
Disability Served: various
This company manufactures and distributes reusable
incontinence care products, daily living aids, and anti-
allergen bedding.

Professional Fit Clothing
831 North Lake Street, Suite 1
Burbank, CA 91502
800-422-2348
sales@professionalfit.com
http://www.professionalfit.com
Disability Served: various
This company offers adaptive clothing.

Pro Orthopedic Devices Inc.
2884 East Ganley Road
Tucson, AZ 85706
520-294-4401, 800-523-5611
info@proorthopedic.com
http://www.proorthopedic.com
Disability Served: various
This company manufactures neoprene braces for ankles,
knees, elbows, lower backs, and wrists.

Prospect Designs
11 Prospect Street
New Hartford, CT 06057
860-379-3755
info@prospectdesigns.com
http://www.prospectdesigns.com
Disability Served: various
This company manufactures pediatric seating and positioning equipment, including classroom positioning
chairs, desk/standers, tilt-in-space positioning chairs,
adjustable tilt-in-space chairs, and prone and supine
standers.

Qualitone
6415 Flying Cloud Drive
Eden Prairie, MN 55344
952-927-7161, 800-328-3897
http://www.qualitonehearing.com
Disability Served: hearing
This company manufactures hearing aids.

Quality Health Products Inc.
PO Box 433
Indiana, PA 15701
724-349-9394, 800-834-7058
info@qhpinc.com
http://www.qhpinc.com
Disability Served: various
This company offers exercise equipment, orthotic insoles,
pillows, supports, and hot and cold therapy equipment.

Quik-Scrybe
1723 Sumac Street
Longmont, CO 80501
888-820-7845
quikscrybe@comcast.net
http://www.quikscrybe.com
Disability Served: vision
This company offers Braille transcription services.

R and H Adaptive Equipment Company
PO Box 175
Thompson, IA 50478
800-255-6956
rhadaptive@wctatel.net
http://www.wctatel.com/web/rhadaptive
Disability Served: physically disabled
This company manufactures support frames and seating systems for persons with physical disabilities.

Rand-Scot Inc.
401 Linden Center Drive
Ft. Collins, CO 80524
970-484-7967, 800-467-7967
info@randscot.com
http://randscot.com
Disability Served: physically disabled
This company manufactures a strain-free lifting system, therapeutic pressure reduction cushions, and mattress overlays for the prevention of decubitus ulcers.

RD Equipment Inc.
230 Percival Drive
West Barnstable, MA 02668
508-362-7498
info@rdequipment.com
http://www.rdequipment.com
Disability Served: various
This company produces an electric leg bag emptier and a tub slide shower chair.

R.E.A.L. Design Inc.
187 South Main Street
Dolgeville, NY 13329-1455
800-696-2041
Disability Served: various
This company manufactures pediatric rehabilitation products, including seating systems and wheelchair tables.

Recording for the Blind and Dyslexic
20 Roszel Road
Princeton, NJ 08540
866-732-3585
http://www.rfbd.org
Disability Served: dyslexia, vision
This company offers recorded books.

Rehab Specialists Inc.
2557 Wyandotte Street
Mountain View, CA 94043

650-965-8282
mikem@rehabspecialists.com
http://www.rehabspecialists.com
Disability Served: various
This company sells and repairs a wide variety of independent living aids and mobility devices.

Relaxo Bak Inc.
PO Box 2613
Anderson, IN 46018-2613
800-527-5496
prgold1@aol.com
http://www.relaxobak.com
Disability Served: orthopedic
This company manufactures orthopedic cushions and seats.

Reliable Medical Supply Inc.
7111 West Broadway Avenue
Brooklyn Park, MN 55428
763-566-4060
csr@reliamed.com
http://www.reliamed.com
Disability Served: various
This company offers bath safety, rehabilitation, and respiratory care products, as well as medical supplies, lift chairs, and patient lifts.

The Respiratory Group
4150 Carr Lane
St. Louis, MO 63119
314-659-4300, 877-877-3774
info@respiratorygroup.com
http://www.penox.com
Disability Served: various
The Respiratory Group offers oxygen concentrators and containers, ultra-lightweight liquid oxygen portable units, lift chairs, and scooters.

Respironics Inc.
1001 Murry Ridge Drive
Murrysville, PA 15668-8517
800-345-6443
http://www.respironics.com
Disability Served: various
This company manufactures asthma products and apnea respiration monitors.

R. G. Abernethy Inc.
PO Box 11733
Winston-Salem, NC 27116

800-334-0128
abernethyshoes@aol.com
http://www.rgabernethy.com
Disability Served: orthopedic
This company makes custom orthopedic shoes.

Rhamdec Inc.
MYDESC Division
Santa Clara, CA 95056
408-496-5590, 800-4-MYDESC
sales@mydesc.com
http://www.mydesc.com
Disability Served: physically disabled
This company manufactures lapboards and mounting
hardware to be used on wheelchairs and scooters.

Rifton Equipment
c/o Community Products LLC
359 Gibson Hill Road
Chester, NY 10918-2321
800-777-4244
sales@riftonequipment.com
http://www.rifton.com
Disability Served: physically disabled
This company offers gait trainers; dynamic and prone
standing equipment; supine boards; seated bathing
and toileting systems; and tricycles.

Roberts Home Medical
9003 Yellow Brick Road, Suite K
Baltimore, MD 21237
http://www.robertshomemedical.com
Disability Served: various
This company offers homecare, respiratory, and
rehabilitation equipment.

ROHO Inc.
100 North Florida Avenue
Belleville, IL 62221
618-277-9173, 800-851-3449
cs@therohogroup.com
http://www.roho.com
Disability Served: various
This company manufactures therapeutic cushions,
chairs, and accessories.

Royce Medical Products
742 Pancho Road
Camarillo, CA 93012
800-521-0601
info@roycemedical.com

http://www.roycemedical.com
Disability Served: various
This company manufactures splints, supports, and
immobilizers.

Rugg Manufacturing Company
105 Newton Street
Greenfield, MA 01301-3122
413-773-5471
sales@rugg.com
http://www.rugg.com
Disability Served: back injury
This company manufactures snow shovels, push brooms,
and lawn rakes designed to minimize back stress.

Safe Guard Surfacing Corporation
9 Brandywine Drive
Deer Park, NY 11729
800-899-8703
sales@safeguardsurfacing.com
http://www.safeguardsurfacing.com
Disability Served: various
This company makes a rubber mat and ground retention
grid designed to prevent injuries and falls on
playgrounds and athletic surfaces.

Salk Inc.
320 Washington Street
Brookline, MA 02445
800-343-4497
info@salkcompany.com
http://www.salkcompany.com
Disability Served: various
This company manufactures incontinence garments and
aids for men and women.

Sammons Preston Rolyan
Four Sammons Court
Bolingbrook, IL 60440-5071
630-226-1300, 800-323-5547, 800-325-1745 (TDD)
spr@abilityone.com
http://www.sammonspreston.com
Disability Served: physically disabled
This company provides daily living products including
household helpers, dressing aids, personal care items,
and exercise products.

S & S Worldwide
PO Box 513
Colchester, CT 06415-0513
800-243-9232

http://www.ssww.com
Disability Served: various
This company manufactures daily living and home
    health care aids, including commodes, restraints,
    tables, orthotics, support systems, recreational items
    and games, clothing and dressing aids, canes, and
    eating utensils. It also offers cross-stitch patterns for
    persons with low vision, magnifying lenses, large
    crayons, and self-opening scissors.

S. A. Richards Inc.
PO Box 1037
Ft Lee, NJ 07024
201-947-3850, 800-722-6403
Disability Served: physically disabled
This company makes a bookholder for hands-free
    reading.

Scale-Tronix
200 East Post Road
White Plains, NY 10601
914-948-8117, 800-873-2001
sales@scale-tronix.com
http://www.scale-tronix.com
Disability Served: various
This company manufactures scales, including chair, floor,
    ramp, and wheelchair scales.

SCAN Medical Company
PO Box 253
Medford, MA 02155
888-593-0377
info@scanmedical.com
http://www.scanmedical.com
Disability Served: various
This company offers transfer boards, belts, and slings.

Schlage Lock Company
1010 Santa Fe
Olathe, KS 66051
800-847-1864
http://www.schlagelock.com
Disability Served: various
This company manufactures security systems and door
    locks, including keyless door locks.

Schukra
Attn: Order Department
310 Carlingview Drive

Toronto, ON M9W 5G1
Canada
800-663-7248
backrest@schukra.com
http://www.schukra.com/prd_portable.html
Disability Served: various
This company designs portable back support cushions
    for use in the home, office, or motor vehicles.

Schwinn
http://www.schwinn.com
Disability Served: various
This company manufactures bicycles and fitness
    equipment.

Science Products for the Blind
PO Box 888
Southeastern, PA 19399
800-888-7400
Disability Served: vision
This company offers a variety of science-related products
    for the blind and visually impaired.

Scott Specialties
512 M Street
Belleville, KS 66935
785-527-5627, 800-255-7136
CustomerService@ScottSpecialties.com
http://www.scottspecialties.com
Disability Served: various
This company manufactures a number of restraints,
    pads, orthopedic shoes, and supports.

Seiko Corporation of America
1111 MacArthur Boulevard
Mahawah, NJ 07430
201-529-5730
custserv@scamahwah.com
http://www.seikousa.com, http://www.pulsarwatches.
    com
Disability Served: vision
Seiko manufactures watches with Braille dials and
    talking clocks for persons with limited vision.

Senior Shopping Service Inc.
319 Anderson Road
Chesterfield, IN 46017
800-334-2897
seniorshoppingservice@yahoo.com

https://www18.safesecureweb.com/
  seniorshoppingservice
Disability Served: various
This company offers adaptive clothing.

**Senior Technologies (A Division of Stanley Security
  Solutions, Inc.)**
1620 North 20th Circle
Lincoln, NE 68503
800-824-2996
http://www.seniortech.com
Disability Served: elderly, physically disabled
This company manufactures a wireless monitoring
  system, fall prevention equipment, and wandering
  detection alarms.

Sennheiser Electronic Corporation
One Enterprise Drive
Old Lyme, CT 06371
860-434-9190, 877-736-6434
http://www.sennheiserusa.com/newsite
Disability Served: hearing
This company manufactures personal amplification
  systems.

Sensaphone
901 Tryens Road
Aston, PA 19014
610-558-2700, 877-373-2700
http://www.sensaphone.com
Disability Served: various
This company makes an emergency alert system for
  the home that is activated by water leaks, furnace
  failures, and power failures.

Shake Awake
200 Winston Drive, Suite 815
Cliffside Park, NJ 07010
800-599-5321
cs@shakeawake.com
http://www.shakeawake.com
Disability Served: hearing
This company offers clocks and timers for people with
  hearing difficulties.

Shamrock Medical Inc.
3620 Southeast Powell Boulevard
Portland, OR 97202
503-233-5055, 800-231-2225

info@shamrockmedical.com
http://www.shamrockmedical.com
Disability Served: physically disabled
This company manufactures traction systems.

Sharn Inc.
4517 George Road
Tampa, FL 33634
813-889-9614, 800-325-3671
mailbox@sharn.com
http://www.sharn.com
Disability Served: various
This company makes specialized medication dispensers
  and thermometers for babies.

Shower Aide
PO Box 339
Pelzer, SC 29669-0339
800-680-4187
sales@showeraide.com
http://www.showeraide.com
Disability Served: physically disabled
This company manufactures a bath chair that swivels
  360 degrees and has folding arms.

Siemens Hearing Instruments Inc.
PO Box 1397
Piscataway, NJ 08855
800-766-4500
http://www.siemens-hearing.com
Disability Served: hearing
This company manufactures aids for the hearing-
  impaired, including hearing aids, personal
  amplification systems, amplification systems for
  televisions, infrared amplification systems, and
  speech amplifiers.

Sigvaris Inc.
1119 Highway 74 South
Peachtree City, GA 30269
800-322-7744
http://www.sigvarisusa.com
Disability Served: various
This company manufactures medical compression socks,
  stockings, armsleeves, and bandages.

Silver Creek Industries
1909 Silver Creek Road, PO Box 1988
Manitowoc, WI 54221

800-533-3277
electronics@silvercreekindustries.com
http://www.silvercreekindustries.com
Disability Served: hearing
This company makes personal amplification systems in headset form and a handheld unit with separate headphones.

Silver Ring Splint Company
PO Box 2856
Charlottesville, VA 22902-2856
434-971-4052, 800-311-7028
cindy@silverringsplint.com
http://www.silverringsplint.com
Disability Served: various
This company manufactures a finger splint.

Silverts Easy-Wear Clothing
3280 Steeles Avenue West, Suite 18
Concord, ON L4K 2Y2
Canada
800-387-7088
customercare@silverts.com
http://www.silverts.com
Disability Served: various
This company offers adaptive clothing.

Sinties Scientific Inc.
5151 South 110th East Avenue
Tulsa, OK 74146
918-359-2000, 800-278-3933
info@scifit.com
http://www.scifit.com
Disability Served: various
This company provides fitness and healthcare products, including wheelchair-accessible exercise equipment.

Snug Seat Inc.
12801 East Independence Boulevard, PO Box 1739
Matthews, NC 28106
800-336-7684
http://www.snugseat.com
Disability Served: various
This company manufactures and distributes pediatric and adult wheelchairs, walkers, shower and commode products, aids for daily living, gait trainers, standing frames, strollers, and car seats for children with special needs.

Solar World
2807 North Prospect
Colorado Springs, CO 80907
719-635-5125
Sales@solarworld.com
http://www.solarworld.com
Disability Served: hearing
This company makes a button battery tester and a solar-powered hearing aid battery charger.

Sonic Alert Inc.
1050 East Maple Road
Troy, MI 48083
248-577-5400 (Voice/TDD)
sonic-info@sonicalert.com
http://www.sonicalert.com
Disability Served: hearing
This company manufactures daily living aids for persons with hearing impairments. Products include doorbell signalers, alert systems, alarm clocks, sound monitors, and various sound signalers.

SOS Rehabilitation Products
3359 Griffith Street
St Laurent, QB H4T 1W5
Canada
800-667-3422
mitchell@sosrehab.com
http://www.sosrehab.com
Disability Served: physically disabled
This company offers commode, bath, and shower chairs; standing frames; cushions; wheelchairs; gait trainers; and walkers.

Southeastern Health Plus Inc.
11816 Highway 17 By-Pass
Murrells Inlet, SC 29576
843-651-5795, 877-386-0600
http://www.sehealthplus.com
Disability Served: various
This company offers bath safety equipment, walking aids, seat lift chairs, and incontinence supplies. It also sells, rents, and repairs wheelchairs and scooters.

South Mountain Health Supply Inc.
1402 East South Mountain Road
Phoenix, AZ 85042
800-324-5804
customerservice@smhs-medsupply.com

http://www.smhs-medsupply.com
Disability Served: various
This company offers incontinence products, nutritional supplements, and protective gloves.

Southpaw Enterprises Inc.
PO Box 1047
Dayton, OH 45401
937-252-7676, 800-228-1698
therapy@southpawenterprises.com
http://www.southpawenterprises.com
Disability Served: developmentally disabled, physically disabled
This company manufactures and distributes equipment for children with special needs in the area of sensory integration and developmental delay. Products include tactile massage therapy balls, fine motor toy boxes, swings, and air walkers.

Southwest Medical
513 West Thomas Road
Phoenix, AZ 85013
800-236-4215
information@southwestmedical.com
http://www.southwestmedical.com
Disability Served: various
This company offers a variety of daily living aids and health care products, including home assistance products, bathroom devices, diabetic care products, incontinence supplies, cushions, gloves, gowns, masks, scooters, and wheelchairs.

Space Tables Inc.
11511 95th Avenue North
Maple Grove, MN 55369
800-328-2580
http://www.spacetables.com
Disability Served: physically disabled
This company manufactures height-adjustable, accessible tables and work stations.

Span-America Inc.
PO Box 5231
Greenville, SC 29606
800-888-6752
http://www.spanamerica.com
Disability Served: various
This company makes support pillows, cushions, and splints. It also offers skin care products for the treat-

ment and prevention of diaper rash, pressure ulcers, and dry skin.

Spanners Inc.
17621 Sampson Lane
Huntington Beach, CA 92647
714-841-6292
info@spannersinc.com
http://www.spannersinc.com
Disability Served: physically disabled
This company manufactures backpacks and totes for wheelchairs.

Speak To Me
330 SW 43rd Street, Suite K, PMB #154
Renton, WA 98055-4976
800-248-9965
info@speaktomecatalog.com
http://www.speaktomecatalog.com
Disability Served: vision
This company offers talking products, including blood pressure kits, keychains, and toys.

Special Clothes
PO Box 333
East Harwich, MA 02645
508-385-9171
Specialclo@aol.com
http://www.special-clothes.com
Disability Served: various
This company manufactures clothing for children and adults with disabilities.

Special Fit Clothing
18323 234th Circle
Hutchinson, MN 55350
320-587-8777
ddesens@hutchtel.net
http://www.specialfitonline.com
Disability Served: Down Syndrome
This company offers adaptive clothing for people with Down Syndrome.

Specially for You Inc.
15621 309th Avenue
Gettysburg, SD 57442
605-765-9396
speciallyforyou@sbtc.net
http://www.speciallyforyou.net

Disability Served: various
This company designs and sews custom adaptive
 clothing.

Spectrum Aquatics
7100 Spectrum Lane
Missoula, MT 59802
406-543-5309, 800-776-5309
info@spectrumaquatics.com
http://www.spectrumaquatics.com
Disability Served: physically disabled
This company manufactures swimming pool access
 products for people with disabilities, including lifts,
 ramps, railings, and ladders, as well as stainless steel
 hydrotherapy tanks.

The Speech Bin Inc.
1965 25th Avenue
Vero Beach, FL 32960
772-770-0007, 800-477-3324
info@speechbin.com
http://www.speechbin.com
Disability Served: various
This company publishes and distributes books and
 materials on rehabilitation, speech-language
 pathology, special education, and related fields.
 Among the major product lines are computer
 software, diagnostic tests, educational games
 and materials, and specialty items.

Spenco Medical Corporation
PO Box 2501
Waco, TX 76702
800-877-3626
cservice@spenco.com
http://www.spenco.com
Disability Served: various
Spenco makes support pillows, pads, positioners, burn
 care products, and hot and cold packs.

Sports Health Products
527 West Windsor Road
Glendale, CA 91204
800-289-7889
Disability Served: physically disabled
This company manufactures Power Putty, hand therapy
 putty in four color-coded resistances. This putty
 is used for hand rehabilitation and carpal tunnel
 prevention and treatment.

Staplex Company
777 Fifth Avenue
Brooklyn, NY 11232-1695
718-768-3333, 800-221-0822
info@staplex.com
http://www.staplex.com
Disability Served: various
This company makes an electric mail opener and electric
 staplers, including a handheld, battery-powered
 stapler.

Starkey Labs Inc.
6700 Washington Avenue South
Minneapolis, MN 55344
800-328-8602
http://www.starkey.com
Disability Served: hearing
This company develops hearing aids and tinnitus
 maskers. Its Web site offers useful information about
 hearing loss and hearing instruments.

Stern Williams Company Inc.
PO Box 8004
Shawnee Mission, KS 66208
913-362-5635
sales@sternwilliams.com
http://www.sternwilliams.com
Disability Served: physically disabled
This company makes bath equipment, including shower
 cabinets and shower floors. The company also makes
 wheelchair-accessible water fountains.

Streamlight Inc.
30 Eagleville Road
Eagleville, PA 19403
610-631-0600, 800-523-7488
cs@streamlight.com
http://www.streamlight.com
Disability Served: vision
Streamlight manufactures flashlights to assist those with
 night blindness.

SunBox Company
19217 Orbit Drive
Gaithersburg, MD 20879
301-869-5980, 800-548-3968
sunbox@aol.com
http://www.sunbox.com
Disability Served: mental health

This company manufactures lights for the treatment of seasonal affective disorder.

Sunnyfield Supplies Inc.
4821 Elk Road, RR #5
Victoria, BC V8X 4M6
Canada
ralph@sunnyfieldsupplies.com
http://www.sunnyfieldsupplies.com
Disability Served: physically disabled
This company makes a manual transfer sling.

Sunrise Medical
2842 Business Park Avenue
Fresno, CA 93727
559-292-2171
http://www.sunrisemedical.com
Disability Served: various
This company manufactures bath and shower products, lifts, beds, wheelchairs, sports wheelchairs, wheelchair cushions, crutches, walkers, canes and daily living accessories.

Support Dogs Inc.
11645 Lilburn Park Road
St. Louis, MO 63146
314-997-2325
supportdogs@MSN.com
http://www.supportdogs.org
Disability Served: various
This organization provides support or therapy dogs to the disabled.

Support Plus
99 West Street, PO Box 500
Medfield, MA 02052
877-808-0024
cs@supportplus.com
http://www.abdominalbelt.com
Disability Served: various
This company sells support hosiery, comfort shoes, and daily living aids, such as easy-grip jar openers, bathtub benches, dressing tools, comfort pillows and cushions, and wheelchair packs.

SureHands
982 Route 1
Pine Island, NY 10969-1205
845-258-6500, 800-724-5305
http://www.surehands.com
Disability Served: physically disabled
This company distributes patient lift and transfer systems, including ceiling-mounted track systems, wall lifts, mobile units, pool lifts, and frictionless slides.

S. Walters Inc.
30423 Canwood Street, Suite 115
Agoura Hills, CA 91301
818-706-2202, 800-992-5837
walterslv@cs.com
http://www.walterslowvision.com
Disability Served: vision
This company provides low-vision optics and manufactures and distributes a device for projecting reading material on the TV screen.

Swede-O Inc.
6459 Ash Street, PO Box 610
North Branch, MN 55056
651-674-8301, 800-525-9339
info@swedeo.com
http://www.swedeo.com
Disability Served: various
This company manufactures ankle supports, braces, and splints.

Symmetric Designs Ltd.
125 Knott Place
Salt Spring Island, BC V8K 2M4
Canada
800-537-1724
sales@symmetric-designs.com
http://www.symmetric-designs.ca
Disability Served: various
This company manufactures neck braces; cervical collars; limb orthoses; and adaptive devices for wheelchairs, such as fishing rod holders, lap desks, and trays.

TACK-TILES Braille Systems LLC
PO Box 475
Plaistow, NH 03865
800-822-5845
http://www.tack-tiles.com
Disability Served: vision
This company offers Tack-Tiles, a teaching tool to encourage Braille literacy that is based on LEGO-type blocks.

Tag Toys Inc.
1810 South Acacia Avenue
Compton, CA 90220
800-488-4824
info@tagtoys.com
http://www.tagtoys.com
Disability Served: various
This company develops wooden puzzles and toys
designed to teach shapes, names, and numbers.

Talking RX
PO Box 649
Southington, CT 06489
888-798-2557
http://www.talkingrx.com
Disability Served: vision
This company offers an audio guidance tool for people
who take medications.

Tamarack Habilitation Technologies Inc.
1670- 94th Lane, NE
Blaine, MN 55449
866-795-0057
tamarack@oandp.com
http://www.oandp.com/tamarack
Disability Served: various
This company provides orthotic and prosthetic products.

Tecogics Scientific Limited
72 Pretoria Avenue, Unit #4
Ottawa, ON K1S 1W9
Canada
613-238-8403, 800-541-0002
exnflex@pacificcoast.net
http://www.selene.com/selene/exnflex
Disability Served: physically disabled
This company offers a passive/active exerciser for people
who have little or no control over their lower bodies.

Telex Communications Inc.
12000 Portland Avenue South
Burnsville, MN 55337
952-884-4051
info@telex.com
http://www.telex.com
Disability Served: hearing
This company manufactures amplification systems,
personal listening systems, auditory trainer systems
for students, talking book players, and signaling
products.

Tescor Technology Inc.
PO Box 606
Cedarburg, WI 53012
262-377-4208, 877-383-7267
info@tescortech.com
http://www.tescortech.com
Disability Served: various
This company manufactures a strobe light that can be
connected to security or fire detection systems.

TFH (USA) Ltd.
4537 Gibsonia Road
Gibsonia, PA 15044-7964
800-467-6222
http://www.tfhusa.com
Disability Served: various
This company manufactures adaptive toys and products
for education, rehabilitation, and recreation.

TFI HealthCare
600 West Wythe Street
Petersburg, VA 23803
804-861-0063
Service@tfihealthcare.com
http://www.tfihealthcare.com
Disability Served: various
This company manufactures bathroom fixtures,
including commodes, bathtub and shower benches,
stools, and toilet rails. The company also makes canes,
walkers, and oxygen carts.

Thames Valley Children's Centre
779 Base Line Road East
London, ON N6C 5Y6
Canada
519-685-8680
tvcc@tvcc.on.ca
http://www.tvcc.on.ca
Disability Served: various
The center offers a wheelchair mounting and positioning
system for augmentative communication devices,
positioning interface frames, and useful books for
children with disabilities.

Thelma's Mastectomy Boutique
251 Park Avenue
Rochester, NY 14607
585-256-2460
sandy@thelmasboutique.com
http://www.thelmasboutique.com

Disability Served: cancer

This company offers post-mastectomy breast forms, mastectomy bras, swimwear, lymphedema sleeves, wigs, and caps.

TherAdapt

11431 North Port Washington Road, Suite 105-5
Mequon, WI 53092
800-261-4919
http://www.theradapt.com
Disability Served: various

This company offers basic, therapeutic, adaptive, modular, and specialty chairs for home, classroom, or clinic use. It also offers mobility aides, such as walkers and quad poles.

Therafin Corporation

19747 Wolf Road
Mokena, IL 60448
708-479-7300, 800-843-7234
info@therafin.com
http://www.therafin.com
Disability Served: various

This company offers aids to daily living, including dressing and grooming aids, kitchen utensils, armrests, and standing frames.

Thera-P-Cushion Inc.

331 Bowes Road, #2
Concord, ON L4K 1J2
Canada
800-567-9926
http://www.therapyproducts.com
Disability Served: various

This company provides support cushions, including anti-snoring pillows, as well as a solar/electric pedal assist bicycle.

Therapeutic Alliances Inc.

333 North Broad Street
Fairborn, OH 45324
937-879-0734
TAIinfo@aol.com
http://www.musclepower.com
Disability Served: various

This company manufactures rehabilitation equipment for home and clinical use. Products are appropriate for those with head trauma, cerebral palsy, spinal cord injury, and others who need to restore muscle control.

Therapeutic Health and Equipment Specialists

14000 Northwest 1st Avenue
North Miami, FL 33168-4851
800-533-0178
THEREQUIP@aol.com
http://www.unlimitedversatility.com
Disability Served: various

This company manufactures therapeutic aids, including therapy mats, large foam shapes, wedges, rolls, and blocks.

Thetford Corporation

PO Box 1285
Ann Arbor, MI 48106
800-521-3032
http://www.thetford.com
Disability Served: various

This company manufactures portable toilets.

Thomas Fetterman Inc.

1680 Hillside Road
Southampton, PA 18966
888-582-5544
allen.burns@verizon.net
http://www.fetterman-crutches.com
Disability Served: physically disabled

This company provides custom-made crutches, crutch tips, telescoping travel crutches, and accessories.

Thought Technology Ltd.

8396 Route 9
West Chazy, NY 12992
514-489-8251, 800-361-3651
mail@thoughttechnology.com
http://www.biofeedbackrus.com
Disability Served: various

This company manufactures biofeedback systems.

Tie Tech Inc.

PO Box 5226
Lynnwood, WA 98046
425-743-5863
info@tietechinc.com
http://tietechinc.com
Disability Served: physically disabled

This company manufactures wheelchair restraint systems for vehicles, evacuation devices for removing physically disabled persons during emergency situations, and webbing cutters.

Timm Medical Technologies Inc.
6585 City West Parkway
Eden Prairie, MN 55344
952-947-9410, 800-438-8592
Customerservice@endocare.com
http://www.timmmedical.com
Disability Served: various
This company manufactures an erection aid for impotence.

Tip Top Mobility Inc.
PO Box 5009
Minot, ND 58702-5009
701-857-1182, 800-735-5958
tiptop@minot.com
http://www.minot.com/~tiptop
Disability Served: physically disabled
This company manufactures a wheelchair lift for use with
automobiles.

Todd Brickhouse Accessibility Associates
8 Joan Lane
Massapequa Park, NY 11762
516-541-1509
info@brickhousedesigns.net
http://www.brickhousedesigns.net
Disability Served: various
This firm offers home redesign consulting services to the
physically challenged and seniors.

The Total Woman Boutique
745 Rio Vista Lane
Cottageville, SC 29435
866-533-8304
http://www.thetotalwomanboutique.com
Disability Served: cancer
This company offers a variety of post-mastectomy
products, including breast forms, bras, prostheses,
and accessories.

Toto USA Inc.
1155 Southern Road
Morrow, GA 30260
888-295-8134
http://totousa.com/toto/totohome.asp
Disability Served: various
This company manufactures toilets, bidets, and
electronic flush systems and faucets.

Toys For Special Children
385 Warburton Avenue
Hastings-on-Hudson, NY 10706

914-478-0960, 800-TEC-TOYS
http://www.enablingdevices.com
Disability Served: various
This company adapts toys for use by handicapped
children. The company also provides augmentative
devices, communication devices, and capability
switches for people of all ages.

Trademark Medical
449 Sovereign Court
St. Louis, MO 63011
800-325-9044
info@trademarkmedical.com
http://www.trademarkmedical.com
Disability Served: various
This company manufactures medical products, including
oral suction toothbrushes, patient communication
aids, waterproof cast covers, fever strips for monitoring temperature, and disposable wound-measuring
guides.

Transpo-Industries Inc.
20 Jones Street
New Rochelle, NY 10801
914-636-1000
info@transpo.com
http://www.transpo-industries.com/step-safe.htm
Disability Served: vision
This company manufactures a tactile safety surface
designed to help alert persons with visual
disabilities.

Trendware Phone Systems
4448 West El Segundo Boulevard, Suite 165
Hawthorne, CA 90250
310-644-3014
trendware@pacbell.net
Disability Served: hearing
This company manufactures a telecommunications
Voice/TTY/VCO device that works as a standard
telephone and can also record TTY calls.

Triad Technologies Inc.
105 Spencer Street
Syracuse, NY 13204-1333
315-422-7607, 800-729-7514
http://www.triadtec.com/TRIADPRO.htm
Disability Served: physically disabled
This company manufactures a fiberglass and stainless
steel transfer system that enables users to enter and
exit a swimming pool.

TRS Inc.
3090 Sterling Circle, Studio A
Boulder, CO 80301-2338
303-444-4720, 800-279-1865
http://www.oandp.com/trs
Disability Served: physically disabled
This company manufactures prosthetic recreational
devices for persons with disabilities who are missing
a hand or hands. Products include devices for skiing,
camera mounts for prosthetic arms, amputee golf
grips, and bicycle brakes.

Truxes Company
16 Stone Hill Road
Oswego, IL 60543
630-554-8448, 888-554-8448
sales@truxes.com
http://truxes.com
Disability Served: vision
Truxes makes Braille signs for commercial use.

Tubular Specialties Manufacturing Inc.
PO Box 60262
Los Angeles, CA 90060
310-515-4801, 800-225-5876
tsm@calltsm.com
http://www.calltsm.com
Disability Served: various
This company manufactures grab bars, shower seats,
commercial washroom accessories, corner guards,
and railing systems in stainless steel, aluminum,
brass, and bronze.

Tucker Designs Ltd.
PO Box 740031
New Orleans, LA 70114
888-236-9275
info@tuckerdesigns.com
http://www.tuckerdesigns.com
Disability Served: various
This company makes a positioning system to elevate
infants while they sleep.

Tuffcare
3999 East La Palma Avenue
Anaheim, CA 92807
Contact@tuffcare.com
http://www.tuffcare.com
Disability Served: physically disabled
This company manufactures home care beds and bath
equipment, including shower benches, grab bars,

and commodes. It also offers wheelchairs, scooters,
walkers, and canes.

Turn-EZ
c/o Med-E-Z, Inc.
3400 Tupper Drive, PO Box 8026
Greenville, NC 27835
252-757-0279, 800-522-4464
lbatech@lbagroup.com
http://lbagroup.com/turnez
Disability Served: physically disabled
This company offers a patient turning system.

Tyco Healthcare/Mallinckrodt
675 McDonnell Boulevard, PO Box 5840
Hazelwood, MO 63042
314-654-2000
http://www.mallinckrodt.com/respiratory/resp
Disability Served: various
This company makes ventilators and apnea respiration
monitors.

uCan Health
PO Box 54965
Irvine, CA 92619-4965
949-387-9165
info@ucanhealth.com
http://www.ucanhealth.com
Disability Served: various
This company offers a variety of daily living products,
including transfer chairs, shower benches, hospital
beds, wheelchairs, and walkers.

Ulster Scientific Inc.
c/o American Scientific Resources
PO Box 819
New Paltz, NY 12561-0819
845-255-2200, 877-206-3225
info@americansci.com
http://www.americansci.com
Disability Served: various
This company distributes a variety of products, including a medication administration device for infants,
peak-flow meters for children and adults to monitor pulmonary function, and temperature warning
devices.

UltraVoice
3612 Chapel Avenue
Newtown Square, PA 19073
800-721-4848

http://www.ultravoice.com
Disability Served: communication
Ultravoice manufactures a speech aid for laryngectomies that consists of a unit that fits inside the mouth and a handheld controller.

United Hearing Systems Inc.
137 Norwich Road
Central Village, CT 06332
800-835-2001
mail@unitedhearing.com
http://www.unitedhearing.com
Disability Served: hearing
This company manufactures hearing aids.

United Steel and Wire Company
4909 Wayne Road
Battle Creek, MI 49016
800-227-7887
uswsales@unitedsteelandwire.com
http://www.unitedsteelandwire.com
Disability Served: physically disabled
This company manufactures a shopping cart that attaches to wheelchairs.

Uplift Technologies
125-11 Morris Drive
Dartmouth, NS B3B 1M2
Canada
902-422-0804
http://www.up-lift.com
Disability Served: various
This company offers lifting cushions, commodes, wheelchair seating devices, and light therapy products.

Urocare Products Inc.
2735 Melbourne Avenue
Pomona, CA 91767-1931
909-621-6013, 800-423-4441
support@urocare.com
http://www.urocare.com
Disability Served: various
This company manufactures health care aids, including skin care products, leg bags, catheters, and enuresis alarms.

USA Wheelchair Jeans
9062 East 28th Street
Tulsa, OK 74129

800-935-5170
Darlene@wheelchairjeans.com
http://www.wheelchairjeans.com
Disability Served: physically disabled
This company designs jeans for people in wheelchairs or who have limited mobility.

Valley Braille Service Inc.
4615 Swenson Street, Suite 210-B
Las Vegas, NV 89119
702-733-6941
richard@valleybraille.com
http://www.valleybraille.com
Disability Served: vision
This company offers text-to-Braille transcription services.

Value Medical Supplies
7328 Chase Avenue
Hesperia, CA 92345
877-246-1766
http://www.valuemedicalsupplies.com
Disability Served: various
This company offers urinals, shower chairs, transfer benches, grab bars, alternating pressure pads, blood pressure monitors, thermometers, wedge and cervical pillows, wheelchairs, walkers, canes, and crutches.

Van Duerr Industries
820 West Seventh Street
Chico, CA 95928
530-893-1596
http://www.vanduerr.com
Disability Served: physically disabled
This company manufactures floor transition matting and ramps.

Variety Ability Systems Inc.
2 Kelvin Avenue, Unit 3
Toronto, ON M4C 5CB
Canada
416-698-1415, 800-891-4514
mmifsud@vasi.on.ca
http://www.vasi.on.ca
Disability Served: various
This company manufactures a variety of products for children, including electric prosthetic limbs, toileting systems, walkers, seating and positioning systems, standing frames, and mounting hardware for wheelchair accessories.

VARILITE
4000 1st Avenue South
Seattle, WA 98134
800-827-4548
customerservice@varilite.com
http://www.varilite.com
Disability Served: physically disabled
This company develops postural support systems for
people who use wheelchairs.

V. B. Schaeffer Inc.
PO Box 15892
Pittsburgh, PA 15244
412-494-4846
deevbs@sightsheet.com
http://www.sightsheet.com
Disability Served: vision
This company offers magnifiers in various sizes.

Vecta
1800 South Great Southwest Parkway
Grand Prairie, TX 75051
http://www.vecta.com
Disability Served: various
This company manufactures an ergonomically designed
office chair that provides lower back support.

Velcro USA Inc.
406 Brown Avenue
Manchester, NH 03103
800-225-0180
http://www.velcro.com
Disability Served: various
This company makes Velcro fasteners and straps.

Vesture Corporation
120 East Pritchard Street
Asheboro, NC 27203
800-462-4201
info@vesture.com
http://www.vesture.com
Disability Served: various
This company manufactures hot and cold packs.

Villeroy and Boch
PO Box 1120
Mettlach, D 66688
Germany
http://www.villeroy-boch.com
Disability Served: various

This company manufactures a variety of products,
including water- and temperature-controlled faucets,
bidets, and slip-resistant tile.

Viscot Industries Inc.
32 West Street, PO Box 351
East Hanover, NJ 07936
973-887-9273
info@viscot.com
http://www.viscot.com
Disability Served: various
This company manufactures both male and female
urinals designed to be used in bed.

Voicewave Technology Inc.
12156 Natural Bridge Road
Bridgeton, MO 63044
877-786-2266
Service@SpeechEnhancer.com
http://www.speechenhancer.com
Disability Served: communication
This company manufactures an assistive device that
processes and clarifies speech.

Von Duprin Inc.
2720 Tobey Drive
Indianapolis, IN 46219
317-613-8944
vonduprin_info@irco.com
http://www.vonduprin.com
Disability Served: various
This company manufactures panic bars for doors.

Walker Equipment
4289 Bonny Oaks Drive, Suite 106
Chattanooga, TN 37406
423-622-7793, 800-HANDSET
information@handset.com
http://www.handset.com
Disability Served: hearing
This company manufactures amplifiers for telephones.

Walt Nicke Company
36 McLeod Lane, PO Box 433
Topsfield, MA 01983
978-887-3388
http://gardentalk.com
Disability Served: various
This company offers ergonomically designed gardening
tools and a water-saving hose nozzle.

Wardrobe Wagon Inc.
555 Valley Road
West Orange, NJ 07052-5115
800-992-2737
info@wardrobewagon.com
http://www.wardrobewagon.com
Disability Served: physically disabled
This company designs, produces, and sells adaptive
    clothing and footwear for people with limited
    mobility. A free catalog is available.

Wayne Engineering
8242 North Christiana Avenue
Skokie, IL 60076
847-674-7166
wayne@wayneengineering.com
http://www.wayneengineering.com
Disability Served: various
This company manufactures an electronic pen that
    produces auditory feedback for the development of
    fine motor skills.

WearABLES
2200 North George Mason Drive, PO Box 7407
Arlington, VA 22207
703-841-7274
wearable@erols.com
Disability Served: various
This company develops sewing patterns for adaptive
    clothing. Patterns can be purchased by mail order.

Wear-With-All.com
PO Box 8276
Longboat Key, FL 34228
888-808-4888
info@wear-with-all.com
http://wear-with-all.com
Disability Served: various
This company offers compression garments for post-
    surgery patients.

Wenzelite Re/hab
220 36th Street
Brooklyn, NY 11232
516-998-4600, 800-706-9255
http://www.wenzelite.com
Disability Served: various
This company manufactures wheeled walkers,
    positioning chairs, standing frames, bathing chairs,
    and oxygen tank holders and baskets.

Western Medical Inc.
760 East McDowell Road
Phoenix, AZ 85006
800-643-9347
info@westernmedical.net
http://www.westernmedicalinc.net
Disability Served: various
This company offers bed products, clothing, daily living
    aids, lift chairs, lifts and slings, ramps, scooters, and a
    variety of other products.

Westinghouse Security Electronics
5452 Betsy Ross Drive
Santa Clara, CA 95054-1102
408-727-5170, 800-624-8999
Disability Served: physically disabled
This company manufactures a door opener that can
    be used in the workplace by persons with physical
    disabilities.

Wheelchairs of Kansas
204 West 2nd Street
Ellis, KS 67637
800-537-6454
wokinfo@go2wok.com
http://www.wheelchairsofkansas.com
Disability Served: physically disabled
This company manufactures, electric beds, bath aids,
    manual and power wheelchairs, and power bariatric
    transfer lifts.

Whirlpool Corporation
2000 North M-63
Benton Harbor, MI 49022-2692
800-253-1301
http://www.whirlpool.com
Disability Served: various
This company manufactures home appliances such as
    cooktops and ovens. It offers Braille, large print, and
    audiocassette product use and care manuals.

White Home Products Inc.
400 North 14th Street
Kenilworth, NJ 07033
800-896-0902
sales@closets.net
http://www.closets.net
Disability Served: various
This company manufactures a motorized clothing rack
    and a rotating kitchen shelving system.

Whitespa USA
12155 Magnolia Avenue
Riverside, CA 92503-4967
800-707-0567
http://www.softbathtubs.com
Disability Served: various
This company manufactures cushioned bathtubs.

Whitestone Products
4265 West Vernal Pike
Bloomington, IN 47404
812-332-3703
customerservice@whitestonecorp.com
http://www.whitestonecorp.com
Disability Served: various
This company manufactures incontinence garments and
pads, as well as bed underpads.

Whitmyer Biomechanix Inc.
1833 Junwin Court
Tallahassee, FL 32308
877-944-8246
http://www.whitbio.com
Disability Served: physically disabled
This company manufactures head supports, wheelchair
bases, and mounting hardware for wheelchairs.

Wimmer Ferguson
c/o Manhattan Toy Company
430 First Avenue North, Suite 500
Minneapolis, MN 55401
612-337-9600, 800-541-1345
cs@manhattantoy.com
http://www.manhattantoy.com
Disability Served: various
This company makes products for infants and children,
including activities and mobiles for developing gross
motor skills and providing visual stimulation.

Winco Inc.
5516 SW First Lane
Ocala, FL 34474-9307
352-854-2929, 800-237-3377
customerservice@wincomfg.com
http://www.winco-medquip.com
Disability Served: various
This company manufactures recliner chairs, travel
chairs, treatment tables, footstools, and privacy
screens.

Window Ease (A Division of A-Solution Inc.)
1332 Lobo Place, NE
Albuquerque, NM 87106
505-256-0115
info@windowease.com
http://www.windowease.com
Disability Served: physically disabled
This company manufactures a handicapped-accessible
retrofit for windows.

Wis Ent Health Care Products
c/o Wise Enterprises
5017 El Don Drive
Rocklin, CA 95677
916-624-3848, 888-947-3368
http://www.wisent.com
Disability Served: physically disabled
This company features a wide variety of adaptive daily
living, communication, and mobility products.
Products include feeding devices, golf playing aids,
pill organizers, button hooks, dressing sticks, shoe
removers, adapted kitchen utensils, writing devices,
card holders, cushions, walkers, bath benches, bidets,
and exercise devices.

The Woman's Personal Health Resource
400 Route 59
Monsey, NY 10952
877-463-1343
wphrinc@hotmail.com
http://www.womanspersonalhealth.com
Disability Served: cancer
This company offers a variety post- surgery products,
including mastectomy bras, camisoles, silicone and
nonsilicone breast forms, mastectomy swimsuits,
mastectomy exercise wear and sportswear, compression stockings, lymphedema sleeves, wigs, turbans,
and headwear.

Woodbury Products Inc.
Department 250
Island Park, NY 11558
800-777-1111
info@woodburyproducts.com
http://www.woodburyproducts.com
Disability Served: various
This company manufactures incontinence products,
including adult disposable diapers, briefs, and pads.
The company offers a free sample program.

Words+ Inc.
1220 West Avenue J
Lancaster, CA 93534-2902
661-723-6523, 800-869-8521
info@words-plus.com
http://www.words-plus.com
Disability Served: various
Words+ provides augmentative and alternative communications systems as well as computer access programs, input switches, and wheelchair mounting devices.

Work Connections
525 Wall Street
Tiffin, OH 44883
419-448-4655, 800-589-2572
Disability Served: various
This company sells ergonomically designed office chairs.

The Wright Stuff
75 Esaias Road
Grenada, MS 38901
662-294-1444, 877-750-0376
info@thewright-stuff.com
http://www.thewright-stuff.com
Disability Served: various
This company offers a variety of daily living and health care products, including raised toilet seats, tube squeezers, walker accessories, adapted gardening tools, mattresses and cushions, folding commodes, and transfer boards.

Wright Therapy Products
305 High Tech Drive
Oakdale, PA 15071
800-631-9535
info@wrighttherapy.com
http://www.wrightlinearpump.com
Disability Served: various
This company makes an electrically operated pressure system designed to reduce lymphedema. It also offers gradient pressure support garments.

WristSaver Rods Inc.
PO Box 223
Prior Lake, MN 55372
877-721-0020
http://www.wristsaverrods.com
Disability Served: physically disabled

This company offers a specially designed fishing rod for people with wrist pain.

X10 Inc.
800-675-3044
support@x10.com
http://www.x10.com
Disability Served: various
This company manufactures a variety of environmental control units and switches designed to control appliances and lights. X10 also makes personal assistance voice dialers, timing switches, security systems and alarms, and thermostat controllers.

YogaBack Company
PO Box 9113
Rochester, MN 55903
800-748-8464
http://www.yogaback.com
Disability Served: various
This company makes a back support system designed to fit office chairs, as a core posture cushion for driving.

Young Medical Equipment
4062 Technology Drive
Maumee, OH 43537
800-426-6654
http://www.hmeiv.com
Disability Served: various
This company offers a variety of home health care products.

Your Medical Stop
888-264-0628
info@yourmedicalstop.com
http://www.yourmedicalstop.com
Disability Served: various
This company offers daily living aids, such as bath benches, transfer seats, bathroom safety rails, pillboxes, raised toilet seats, and commodes. It also offers wheelchairs, walkers, and scooters.

Zero International Inc.
415 Concord Avenue
Bronx, NY 10455
718-585-3230
http://www.zerointernational.com

Disability Served: physically disabled
This company manufactures accessible thresholds and portable ramps to facilitate wheelchair access.

Zygo Industries Inc.
PO Box 1008
Portland, OR 97207-1008
503-684-6006, 800-234-6006
zygo@zygo-usa.com
http://www.zygo-usa.com
Disability Served: communication
This company manufactures and distributes communication systems, such as text-to-speech products, touchscreen tablet computers, alternative computer mice and keyboards, screen communication software, and pictogram symbol reference books.

MOBILITY AND TRANSPORTATION

These companies develop, design, and sell wheelchairs, scooters, carts, vehicles, driving aids, lifts, and other products designed to increase the mobility of persons with disabilities. Companies that assist the disabled with travel throughout the United States and the world are also included.

AAA Medical
2095 West Hampden Avenue
Englewood, CO 80110
800-525-8586
http://www.aaamedical.com
Disability Served: various
This company offers manual and power wheelchairs, scooters, sports chairs, standers, and other products.

Access-Ability Inc.
610 Sample Road
Pompano Beach, FL 33064
954-942-1882
http://www.access-ability.com
Disability Served: various
This company offers residential elevators, lifts, ramps, and power door systems. It also offers power scooters and wheelchairs, bathroom and shower grab bars, environmental control systems, height-adjustable cabinets, and amplified and Braille telephones.

Access-Able Travel Source
PO Box 1796
Wheat Ridge, CO 80034
303-232-2979
access-able@comcast.net
http://access-able.com
Disability Served: various
This organization offers comprehensive information for disabled travelers.

Access Aloha
414 Kuwili Street, #101
Honolulu, HI 96817
800-480-1143
info@accessalohatravel.com
http://www.accessalohatravel.com
Disability Served: various
This full-service travel agency offers services for disabled travelers.

Accessible Italy/H Travel
34 Via C. Manetti
47891 Dogana
Republic of San Marino, Italy
info@accessibleitaly.com
http://www.accessibleitaly.com
Disability Served: various
This company offers tourism services for visitors to Italy who have disabilities.

Accessible Journeys Inc.
35 West Sellers Avenue
Ridley Park, PA 19078
800-846-4537
sales@disabilitytravel.com
http://www.disabilitytravel.com
Disability Served: various
This company offers travel-planning services for disabled travelers.

Accessible Vans of America LLC
888-AVA-VANS
rental101request@accessiblevans.com
http://www.accessiblevans.com
Disability Served: physically disabled
This company is a nationwide network of companies that offer wheelchair-accessible van rentals. Visit its Web site for a list of vendors in your state.

Access Industries Inc.
901-323-5438, 800-264-4304
info@access-ind.com
http://www.access-ind.com
Disability Served: physically disabled
This company manufactures a wide array of lifts and residential elevator systems.

Access Unlimited
570 Hance Road
Binghamton, NY 13903
800-849-2143
http://www.accessunlimited.com
Disability Served: physically disabled
This company offers adaptive and mobility devices for cars, vans, SUVs, trucks, and other types of vehicles. It also offers home lifts.

Accredited Home Elevator Company
800-488-5905
sales@accelevator.com

http://www.accelevator.com
Disability Served: physically disabled
This company installs residential elevators, stair chairs, platform lifts, and dumbwaiters in New Jersey and Philadelphia.

Acme Home Elevator Inc.
4740 East 2nd Street, Suite 20
Benicia, CA 94510
800-888-5267
info@acmehe.com
http://www.acmehe.com
Disability Served: physically disabled
This company offers stair lifts, home elevators, wheelchair lifts, and dumbwaiters to residents of Northern California and Nevada.

Acorn Stairlifts
6450 Kingspointe Parkway, Unit 1
Orlando, FL 32819
866-782-4754
http://www.acornstairlifts.com
Disability Served: physically disabled
This company offers stair lifts.

Action VW Enterprises
621 Forest Lake Drive
Brea, CA 92821-2849
888-521-2053
Actionvw@earthlink.net
http://www.actionvw.com
Disability Served: physically disabled
This company offers wheelchairs, scooters, and walkers.

Adaptive Engineering Lab Inc.
17907 Bothell-Everett Highway
Mill Creek, WA 98012
425-806-5568, 800-327-6080
http://www.aelseating.com
Disability Served: physically disabled
This company manufactures abductor pads, mounting hardware for wheelchairs, restraints, and support systems.

Adaptive Environments
43600 Utica Road
Sterling Heights, MI 48314
586-739-9300, 800-355-LIFT (Michigan only)
mbosley@ameritech.net
http://www.adaptive-environments.com

Disability Served: physically disabled
This company offers stairway lifts, inclined platform lifts, vertical platform lifts, residential elevators, scooters, and spa lifts to Michigan residents.

Adaptive Equipment Systems
7128 Ambassador Road
Baltimore, MD 21244
800-237-2370
http://www.aesys.com
Disability Served: physically disabled
This company offers seating and positioning products for wheelchairs.

Advacare Medical Corporation
14801 West 117th Street
Olathe, KS 66062
913-780-4700
KGribble@AdvaCare.com
http://www.advacare.com
Disability Served: physically disabled
This company designs and sells customized wheelchairs and adaptive seating systems.

Advanced Medical Concepts
9-H Gwynns Mill Court
Owings Mills, MD 21117
800-860-3185
http://www.amcbaltimore.com
Disability Served: physically disabled
This company offers electric scooters, power wheelchairs, and lift chairs.

Advanced Mobility Inc.
7720 North Sepulveda Boulevard
Van Nuys, CA 91401
818-780-1788, 800-687-4446
http://www.advanced-mobility.com
Disability Served: physically disabled
This company manufactures a portable, aluminum wheelchair ramp; rents wheelchair-friendly vans; and customizes vans to meet the needs of disabled customers.

Advanced Mobility of Maryland
8740-6 Cherry Lane
Laurel, MD 20707
800-678-3178
advancedmobility@erols.com
http://www.advancedmobility-md.com

Disability Served: physically disabled
This company repairs and sells stair glides, vehicle lifts, wheelchairs, scooters, and ramps.

Advanced Mobility Systems
621 Justus Drive
Kingston, ON K7M 4H5
Canada
613-384-7460, 800-661-6716
info@amstilt.com
http://www.amstilt.com
Disability Served: physically disabled
This company makes the iTilt, a tilt and recline wheelchair, and related accessories.

Advantage Bag Company
22633 Ellinwood Drive
Torrance, CA 90505-3323
310-540-8197, 800-556-6307
advantagebag@verizon.net
Disability Served: physically disabled
This company manufactures backpacks and other carrying devices for use with wheelchairs, walkers, crutches, and scooters.

Advantage Mobility Outfitters
3990 Second Street
Wayne, MI 48184
800-990-8267
sales@advantagemo.com
http://www.advantagemobility.net
Disability Served: physically disabled
This company offers wheelchair lifts, scooter lifts, full-sized vans, lowered-floor minivans, ramps, and driving aids.

Alaska Welcomes You! Inc.
7321 Branche Drive, PO Box 91333
907-349-6301, 800-349-6301
akwy@customcpu.com
http://www.accessiblealaska.com
Disability Served: various
This organization plans Alaskan travel and cruises for travelers with disabilities.

All In One Mobility Inc.
12833 Northeast Airport Way
Portland, OR 97230
503-255-5005
sales@AllinOneMobility.com

http://www.allinonemobility-shop.com
Disability Served: physically disabled
This company offers scooters, power wheelchairs, patient lifts, lift chairs, and accessible van conversions.

AllWebScooters
c/o Tracy Leigh Enterprises
PO Box 831
Brodheadsville, PA 18322
877-570-6961
http://www.allwebscooters.com
Disability Served: physically disabled
This company offers scooters, power wheelchairs, and power-assisted bicycles and mountain bikes.

AlumiRamp Inc.
855 East Chicago Road
Quincy, MI 49082
800-800-3864
sales@alumiramp.com
http://www.alumiramp.com
Disability Served: physically disabled
This company manufactures modular aluminum access ramps, platforms, and stairs for vehicle and home use.

American Access Inc.
5674 Cleaves Circle, Suite 106
Arlington, TN 38002
888-790-9269
sales@americanaccess.net
http://www.wheelchairramps.com
Disability Served: physically disabled
This company offers portable, modular, and van ramps; wheelchair carriers; standing aids; and bed handles.

American Airless
7216 East Alondra Boulevard
Paramount, CA 90723
800-248-4737
http://www.americanairless.com
Disability Served: physically disabled
This company manufactures foam core tires and air-free tires and tubes for wheelchairs.

American Wheelchairs Inc.
12547 66th Street North
Largo, FL 33773
727-538-0604, 800-449-8991
sales@americanwheelchairs.com
http://www.americanwheelchairs.com

Disability Served: physically disabled
This company offers new and used wheelchairs, scooters, lifts, and ramps.

Amigo Mobility International Inc.
6693 Dixie Highway
Bridgeport, MI 48722-9725
989-777-0910, 800-248-9130
info@myamigo.com
http://www.myamigo.com
Disability Served: physically disabled
This company manufacturers power operated vehicles and scooters.

Angletech
318 North Highway 67, PO Box 1893
Woodland Park, CO 80866-1893
800-793-3038
angletech@att.net
http://www.angletechcycles.com
Disability Served: physically disabled
This company offers recumbent bicycles, tricycles, and tandems.

Anthony Brothers Manufacturing
1945 South Rancho Santa Fe Road
San Marcos, CA 92069-5195
760-744-4763
kids@kidtrikes.com
http://www.kidtrikes.com
Disability Served: physically disabled
This company manufactures hand-propelled tricycles for children and adults with physical disabilities.

A1 Electric Wheelchairs
207 Red Field Street
Cary, NC 27511
800-797-4654
inquiry@a1-electric-wheelchairs.com
http://www.a1-electric-wheelchairs.com
Disability Served: various
This company offers wheelchairs, ramps, rolling walkers, and adjustable beds; and wheelchair, stair, bath, and patient lifts.

APA Medical Equipment
3867 Minnehaha Avenue South
Minneapolis, MN 55406
800-333-3214
http://www.apamedical.com

Disability Served: various
This company offers mobility devices and hospital beds.

Arcola Mobility
51 Kero Road
Carlstadt, NJ 07072-2604
201-507-8500, 800-272-6521
brianp@arcolasales.com
http://www.arcolasales.com
Disability Served: physically disabled
This company provides wheelchair lifts, ramps, stair lifts, platform lifts, and accessible and paratransit vehicles for the disabled.

Area Access Inc.
7131 Gateway Court
Manassas, VA 20109
800-333-AREA
http://www.areaaccess.com
Disability Served: physically disabled
This company sells and rents scooters, and sells, rents, and installs stair lifts, and residential elevators. Installation of wheelchair lifts in commercial buildings and private residences is provided. Area Access also sells hand controls, van lifts, and lowered-floor minivans.

ATS Wheelchair and Medical
1610 North Orchard
Boise, ID 83704
800-287-5550
questions@atswheelchair.com
http://www.atswheelchair.com
Disability Served: physically disabled
This company offers power and manual wheelchairs, scooters, seat lifts, and walking aids.

Autofold Inc.
188 East Street
Fitchburg, MA 01420
866-300-2263
info@autofold.com
http://www.autofold.com
Disability Served: physically disabled
This company manufactures folding canes, specialty canes, and walking sticks.

Baan Khun Daeng
Chiang Mai, Thailand
tulip@loxinfo.co.th

http://members.ams.chello.nl/danblokker/e_home.html
Disability Served: various
This company offers tourism services for visitors to
    Thailand who have disabilities.

Baby Jogger Company
2042 Westmoreland Street
Richmond, VA 23230
800-241-1848
specialneeds@babyjogger.com
http://www.babyjogger.com
Disability Served: physically disabled
This company develops racing and heavy-duty strollers.

Bach Mobilities Inc.
1617 North 28th Street
Escanaba, MI 49829
800-828-2224
bachmobilities@chartermi.net
http://www.bachmobilities.com
Disability Served: physically disabled
This company sells and services lifts, scooters, and
    vehicle controls.

Balder
580 T.C. Jester
Houston, TX 77007
888-4-BALDER
RCarmichael@balderusa.com
http://www.balderusa.com
Disability Served: physically disabled
This company distributes power wheelchairs, stand-up
    wheelchairs, and elevating wheelchairs.

Best Wheelchairs
PO Box 215
Millington, MI 48746
866-827-3529
info@bestwheelchairs.com
http://www.bestwheelchairs.com
Disability Served: physically disabled
This company offers manual and power wheelchairs,
    mobility scooters, walking aids, and related
    accessories.

Bike-On.com
54 Tiffany Road
Coventry, RI 02816
888-424-5366
info@bike-on.com

http://www.bike-on.com
Disability Served: physically disabled
This company offers new and used hand cycles.

BlackBerry Technologies Inc.
3813 Coventryville Road
Pottstown, PA 19465-8905
800-413-4824
BlkBerry@Bellatlantic.net
http://www.blackberrytech.com
Disability Served: physically disabled
This company manufactures wheelchair brakes and
    mounts.

Bluechip Industries
1088 Plymouth Avenue
Fall River, MA 02721-2559
800-336-1300
bluechip.industries@verizon.net
http://www.bluechipindustries.com
Disability Served: physically disabled
This company offers lift chairs, adjustable chairs, and
    scooters.

Bodypoint Inc.
558 First Avenue South, Suite 300
Seattle, WA 98104
206-405-4555
http://www.bodypoint.com
Disability Served: physically disabled
This company offers wheelchair seating accessories.

Braun Corporation
800-THE-LIFT
referrals@braunlift.com
http://www.braunlift.com
Disability Served: physically disabled
Braun offers vans and vehicle accessories, including
    lifts, ramps, power seat bases, and automatic door
    controls.

Brooks Stairlifts
866-412-7665
http://www.brooksstairlifts.com
Disability Served: physically disabled
This company offers stair lifts.

Bruno Independent Living Aids Inc.
1780 Executive Drive, PO Box 84
Oconomowoc, WI 53066

262-567-4990, 800-882-8183
http://www.brunousa.com
Disability Served: physically disabled
This company manufactures wheelchair and scooter lifts for cars, trucks, and vans. It also produces battery-powered scooters, stair lifts, and Turning Automotive Seating for people who have difficulty entering and exiting a vehicle.

Burr Engineering Company
730 East Michigan Avenue, PO Box 460
Battle Creek, MI 49016-0460
800-537-9940
sales@burractuators.com
http://www.burractuators.com
Disability Served: physically disabled
This company manufactures scooter lifts and transporters.

Butler Mobility Products Inc.
390 Eberts Lane
York, PA 17403
717-854-7720, 800-326-2418
Geness@blazenet.net
http://www.butlermobility.com
Disability Served: physically disabled
This company manufactures interior seat lifts, wheelchair stair lifts, and vertical wheelchair lifts.

Campanian Society
PO Box 243
Rhinecliff, NY 12574
845-876-0303
campania@one.net
http://www.campanian.org
Disability Served: vision
This organization offers travel programs for the blind and visually impaired.

Canemate Inc.
26 Kamway Drive
Whiting, ME 04691
207-733-2980
jaydee@maineline.net
http://www.caneaccessories.com
Disability Served: physically disabled
This company offers a portable cane stand.

Canes and Such
10119 Southwest 122nd Street
Gainesville, FL 32608-5843
888-383-CANE
canes@canesandsuch.com
http://www.canesandsuch.com
Disability Served: physically disabled
This company offers a wide variety of canes and walking sticks.

Canes Galore
2712 Beaver Court
Fort Collins, CO 80526
800-346-6400
info@canesgalore.com
http://www.canesgalore.com
Disability Served: physically disabled
This company offers canes and walking sticks.

Carolina Mobility and Seating Inc.
541 New Hill/Olive Chapel Road
Apex, NC 27502
800-488-9170
info@CarolinaMobility.com
http://www.carolinamobility.com
Disability Served: various
This company offers power and manual wheelchairs; positioning strollers; seating and positioning systems; standing and walking aids; helmets; car seats; and bath and toiletry aids.

Castleton Inc.
11300 Coloma, #A6
Rancho Cordova, CA 95670
916-638-8291
info@rearguard.com
http://www.rearguard.com
Disability Served: physically disabled
This company manufactures Rear Guard, a driving aid that mounts on vehicles and detects objects near the rear of the vehicle by using ultrasound. The system can be adapted for wheelchair applications.

CNC Medical
1804 Glenview Road
Glenview, IL 60025
866-668-5775
http://www.cncmedical.com
Disability Served: various
This company offers scooters, lift chairs, electric and manual wheelchairs, stair lifts, walkers, ramps, beds, and bath safety devices.

Colours In Motion
860 East Parkridge Avenue
Corona, CA 92879
951-808-9131, 800-892-8998
http://www.colourswheelchair.com
Disability Served: physically disabled
This company manufactures colorful, stylish wheelchairs, lightweight sport wheelchairs, and children's wheelchairs.

Colson Caster Corporation
3700 Airport Road
Jonesboro, AR 72401
800-643-5515
info@colsoncaster.com
http://www.colsoncaster.com
Disability Served: physically disabled
This company manufactures casters and wheels for industrial and institutional applications.

Companion Walker Ltd.
1324 Norfolk Drive, NW
Calgary, AB T2K 5P6
Canada
403-250-1888
info@companionwalker.com
http://www.companionwalker.com
Disability Served: physically disabled
This company designs and manufactures mobility aid products for senior citizens and the disabled. Products include wheelchairs, walkers, oxygen carts, and canes.

Complete Mobility Systems
1915 West County Road C
Roseville, MN 55113
651-635-0655, 800-788-7479
http://www.completemobility.com
Disability Served: physically disabled
This company manufactures vehicle accessories, including power seats, driving aids, automatic van door controls, power parking brakes, and van lifts. It also sells vans and scooters and offers driver training to people with disabilities.

Concorde Battery Corporation
2009 San Bernardino Road
West Covina, CA 91790
626-813-1234
http://www.concordbattery.com
Disability Served: physically disabled
This company is a manufacturer of wheelchair batteries.

Concord Elevator Inc.
107 Alfred Kuehne Boulevard
Brampton, ON L6T 4K3
Canada
905-791-5555, 800-661-5112
info@concordelevator.com
http://www.concordelevator.com
Disability Served: physically disabled
This company manufactures and designs residential elevators and lifts.

Connecticut Rehab and Medical Products
11 Progress Circle
Newington, CT 06111
800-457-3422
http://www.ctrehab.com
Disability Served: various
This company sells and repairs a variety of mobility devices.

Connie George Travel Associates
PO Box 312
Glenolden, PA 19036
888-532-0989
info@cgta.com
http://www.cgta.com
Disability Served: various
This company offers travel services to wheelchair users, slow walkers, deaf, and non-disabled travelers.

Convaid
PO Box 4209
Palos Verdes, CA 90274
310-618-0111, 888-266-8243
custservice@convaid.com
http://www.convaid.com
Disability Served: physically disabled
This company manufactures wheelchairs and transport chairs for children and adults. The chairs are lightweight, stylish, and fold compactly. Positioning, support, tilt, and tilt/recline chairs are available.

Convaquip Industries Inc.
PO Box 3417
Abilene, TX 79604

800-637-8436
info@convaquip.com
http://www.convaquip.com
Disability Served: physically disabled
This company manufactures aids for obese patients.
Items offered include wheelchairs, scooters, commodes, bath seats, crutches, canes, and more. Product weight specifications range from 250 pounds to
1,500 pounds.

Creative Controls Inc.
1470 Souter Boulevard
Troy, MI 48083-2824
248-577-9800, 800-539-7237
http://www.creativecontrolsinc.com
Disability Served: physically disabled
This company designs and manufactures vehicle and
driving accessories, such as hand controls, pedal
extenders, and electric park brakes. It also sells
vehicles, lifts, and ramps.

Crutch Solutions
c/o Hessa Medical Inc.
PO Box 2744
Sunnyvale, CA 94087
408-431-3720
info@crutchsolutions.com
http://www.crutchsolutions.com
Disability Served: physically disabled
This company offers underarm and forearm crutches.

Curtis Instruments Inc.
200 Kisco Avenue
Mt Kisco, NY 10549
914-666-2971
mtkcustserv@curtisinst.com
http://www.curtisinst.com
Disability Served: physically disabled
This company manufactures speed limiters for
wheelchairs, battery fuel gauges, and battery
chargers.

Custom Home Elevators of St. Louis Inc.
8582 St. Charles Rock Road, PO Box 142725
St. Louis, MO 63114-2725
314-423-1620, 800-783-1620
Disability Served: physically disabled
This company furnishes and installs stairway chairs,
residential elevators, on-slope and vertical wheelchair

lifts, small dumbwaiters, accessibility elevators, and
barrier-free lifts.

Cyclo Manufacturing Company
PO Box 2038
Denver, CO 80201
303-744-8043, 800-525-0701
cyclomfg@worldnet.att.net
http://www.nomorflats.com
Disability Served: physically disabled
This company manufactures a self-sealing inner tube for
wheelchair tires.

Cyncor Roller Racer
185 Hanmer Street West
Barrie, ON L4N 7J9
Canada
705-792-5557
http://www.rollerracer.com
Disability Served: physically disabled
This company manufactures the Roller Racer, a riding toy
propelled by pushing and pulling the handlebars.

Davis Mobility Company
1228 North Beltline Road
Irving, TX 75061
800-239-0102
info@davismobility.com
http://www.accessusaonline.com/davismobility
Disability Served: physically disabled
This company offers scooters, lift chairs, and power
chairs.

Daytona Elevators
440 Spring Forest Drive
New Smyrna Beach, FL 32168
386-423-7226
info@daytonaelevator.com
http://www.daytonaelevator.com
Disability Served: physically disabled
This company installs residential stair lifts, vertical
platform lifts, and elevators.

Deming Designs
1090 Cobblestone Drive
Pensacola, FL 32514
850-478-5765
kmdeming@aol.com
http://www.beachwheelchair.com

Disability Served: physically disabled
This company manufactures beach wheelchairs.

Dialysis at Sea Cruises
13555 Automobile Boulevard, Suite 220
Clearwater, FL 33762
800-544-7604
dasc1@dialysisatsea.com
http://www.dialysisatsea.com
Disability Served: physically disabled
This company provides dialysis services aboard cruise
    ships.

Disability Systems Inc.
6834 South University Boulevard, #222
Centennial, CO 80122-1515
303-995-9008
info@disabilitysystems.com
http://www.disabilitysystems.com
Disability Served: physically disabled
This company offers wheelchair ramps, portable ramps,
    stair lifts, and handicap door openers.

Discount Scooters
149 Reservoir Avenue
Lincoln, RI 02865
401-726-5400
http://www.discountscooters.com
Disability Served: physically disabled
This company offers scooters; electric and manual
    wheelchairs; lift chairs; walkers; trailers; and ramps.

Door-Aid Corporation
7700 Sprinkle Road
Portage, MI 49002
800-493-8377
bedoor@door-aid.com
http://www.door-aid.com
Disability Served: physically disabled
This company manufactures and markets the Door-Aid
    automatic door opener.

Doron Precision System Inc.
174 Court Street, PO Box 400
Binghamton, NY 13902-0400
607-772-1610
service@doronprecision.com
http://www.doronprecision.com
Disability Served: physically disabled
This company manufactures a driving simulator for
    training persons with disabilities.

Drive-Master Company Inc.
37 Daniel Road West
Fairfield, NJ 07004
973-808-9709
drivemaster@drivemaster.net
http://www.drivemaster.net
Disability Served: physically disabled
This company manufactures driving and vehicle
    accessories, including hand and foot controls,
    wheelchair and scooter lifts and ramps, electronic
    driving aids, and steering and braking devices.

Driving Aids Development Corporation
9417 Delancey Drive
Vienna, VA 22182
800-767-6435
dadc500@drivingaids.com
http://www.drivingaids.com
Disability Served: physically disabled
This company offers hand control systems for
    automobiles.

Dynamic Controls Ltd.
31335 Industrial Parkway, Suite 2
North Olmsted, OH 44070
440-979-0657
sales@dynamic-controls.com
http://www.dynamicmobility.co.nz
Disability Served: physically disabled
This company offers power wheelchair and scooter
    control systems.

Eagle Sportschairs
2351 Parkwood Road
Snellville, GA 30039
770-972-0763, 800-932-9380
bewing@bellsouth.net
http://www.eaglesportschairs.com
Disability Served: physically disabled
This company sells sports wheelchairs and products.

Edmond Wheelchair Repair and Supply
3800 East 2nd Street, Suite H
Edmond, OK 73034
888-343-2969
Sales@edmond-wheelchair.com
http://www.edmond-wheelchair.com
Disability Served: various
This company offers wheelchairs, scooters, lifts, ramps,
    hospital beds, bath safety equipment, reachers, and
    patient alarms.

Electric Mobility Corporation
One Mobility Plaza, PO Box 156
Sewell, NJ 08080
800-662-4548
service@electricmobility.com
http://www.electricmobility.com
Disability Served: physically disabled
This company produces Rascal Scooters and power
chairs, lightweight and compact folding scooters,
and related accessories.

Electric Scooters 4 Less
510 Heritage Lane
Winder, GA 30680
800-710-4964
http://www.electricscooters4less.com
Disability Served: physically disabled
This company offers scooters, scooter lifts, stair lifts,
and ramps.

Environmental Coating Systems Inc.
668 North Coast Highway, #511
Laguna Beach, CA 92651
800-ALL-DECK
info@alldeck.com
http://www.alldeck.com
Disability Served: various
This company manufactures nonslip floor-covering
systems for indoor or outdoor use.

Epic Enabled
Fish Hoek, South Africa
info@epic-enabled.com
http://www.epic-enabled.com
Disability Served: various
This company offers adventure tourism services for
visitors to South Africa.

EVAC+CHAIR Corporation
PO Box 2396
New York, NY 10021
212-369-4094
sales@evac-chair.com
http://www.evac-chair.com
Disability Served: physically disabled
This company manufactures an emergency wheelchair
for stairway evacuation.

Extended Home Living Services Inc.
555 Wolf Road
Wheeling, IL 60090-3027

847-215-9490
info@ehls.com
http://www.ehls.com
Disability Served: physically disabled
This company offers residential construction services for
exterior and interior elevators, platform lifts, stair lifts,
and ramps.

EZ-International
3275 Intertech Drive, Suite 500
Brookfield, WI 53045
262-790-5200, 800-824-1068
info@ez-international.com
http://www.ez-international.com
Disability Served: physically disabled
This company manufactures electric shopping scooters,
motorized utility carts, and electric transport chairs.

EZ Lock Inc.
2001 Wooddale Boulevard
Baton Rouge, LA 70806-1516
225-214-4620
http://www.ezlock.net
Disability Served: physically disabled
This company manufactures an electric docking system
that secures wheelchairs to vehicle floors.

Factory Direct Ramps LLC
PO Box 1288
Southgate, MI 48195
800-509-RAMP
sales@factoryramps.com
http://www.factoryramps.com
Disability Served: physically disabled
This company offers lifts, carriers, scooter trailers, and
modular ramps.

Falcon Rehabilitation Products Inc.
800-370-6808
http://www.falconrehab.com
Disability Served: physically disabled
This company manufactures customized power
wheelchairs and accessories.

Florlift of New Jersey Inc.
893 Franklin Avenue
Newark, NJ 07107
973-484-1717
sales@florlift.com
http://florlift.com
Disability Served: physically disabled

This company makes interior and exterior wheelchair lifts and elevators.

Flying Wheels Travel Inc.
143 West Bridge Street
Owatonna, MN 55060
507-451-5005
thq@ll.net
http://www.flyingwheelstravel.com
Disability Served: various
This travel agency specializes in travel for people with disabilities.

Forward Motions Inc.
214 Valley Street
Dayton, OH 45404-1839
937-222-5001, 877-364-8267
fmotions@aol.com
http://www.forwardmotions.com
Disability Served: physically disabled
This company modifies vehicles for people with physical disabilities. It also sells, installs, and services wheelchair and scooter lifts, tie-down systems, and hand controls.

4 Lift Chairs
801 South Power Road, #205
Mesa, AZ 85206
800-711-8209
http://www.4liftchairs.com
Disability Served: physically disabled
This company offers electric lift recliner chairs.

4 Wheelchairs
801 South Power Road, #205
Mesa, AZ 85206
800-339-6329
inquiry@4-wheelchairs.com
http://www.4-wheelchairs.com
Disability Served: physically disabled
This company offers manual and electric wheelchairs, lifts, ramps, walkers, adjustable beds, and oxygen supplies.

Frank Mobility Inc.
1003 International Drive
Oakdale, PA 15071
724-695-7822, 888-426-8581
info@frankmobility.com
http://www.frankmobility.com

Disability Served: physically disabled
This company offers power and manual wheelchairs.

Freedom Concepts Inc.
PO Box 45117, RPO Regent
Winnipeg, MB R2C 5C7
Canada
800-661-9915
Mobility@freedomconcepts.com
http://www.freedomconcepts.com
Disability Served: physically disabled
This company manufactures mobility devices for disabled people of all ages.

Freedom Designs Inc.
2241 Madera Road
Simi Valley, CA 93065
805-582-0077, 800-331-8551
nancy@freedomdesigns.com
http://www.freedomdesigns.com
Disability Served: physically disabled
This company offers wheelchairs, adaptive seating and positioning systems, restraint systems, and mounting hardware for wheelchairs.

Freedom Factory
1943 Karen Circle
Cookeville, TN 38506
931-520-4898
info@freedomfactory.org
http://www.freedomfactory.org
Disability Served: physically disabled
This company manufactures mono-skis and other winter sports equipment for the disabled.

Freedom Rentals
4996 Westminster Avenue
Delta, BC V4K 2H9
Canada
604-952-4499
waverent@aol.com
http://www.wheelchairvanrentals.com
Disability Served: physically disabled
This company rents wheelchair-accessible vans.

Freedom Ryder
800-800-5828
ack@frii.com
http://www.freedomryder.com

Disability Served: physically disabled
This company offers performance hand cycles.

Gary E. Colle Inc.
12300 Stowe Drive, Suite A
Poway, CA 92064-6814
858-748-9414
info@garyecolleinc.com
http://www.garyecolleinc.com
Disability Served: physically disabled
This company modifies vehicles for people with physical
    disabilities. It also sells modified vehicles as well as
    used and rebuilt equipment, such as wheelchairs,
    scooters, stair lifts, and vehicle lifts.

Giant Lift Equipment Manufacturing Company Inc.
185 Lafayette Road, PO Box 626
North Hampton, NH 03862
603-964-5127, 800-52-GIANT
GiantLift@aol.com
http://www.giantlift.com
Disability Served: physically disabled
This company manufactures a hydraulic wheelchair lift.

Global Dialysis
PO Box 200
Stourbridge DY8 4ZL
United Kingdom
info@globaldialysis.com
http://www.globaldialysis.com
Disability Served: physically disabled
This Web site provides information for dialysis patients
    who want to travel. It features lists of dialysis
    centers, accommodations with dialysis services, and
    information on cruises, tours, and travel agents.

Golden Technologies Inc.
401 Bridge Street
Old Forge, PA 18518
800-624-6374
cjcopley@goldentech.com
http://www.goldentech.com
Disability Served: various
This company manufactures power scooters, motorized
    beds, seat lift chairs, armchairs, and replacement
    seats for wheelchairs.

Goshen Coach
1110 D.I. Drive
Elkhart, IN 46514

574-264-7511
service@goshencoach.com
http://www.goshencoach.com
Disability Served: physically disabled
This company manufactures small- to medium-sized
    vans.

Gresham Driving Aids
30800 South Wixom Road
Wixom, MI 48393
248-624-1533, 800-521-8930
Disability Served: physically disabled
This company sells and installs driving aids, including
    steering devices, extension levers for parking brakes
    and gear selectors, hand controls, restraint systems,
    and wheelchair lifts.

The Guided Tour
7900 Old York Road, Suite 114-B
Elkins Park, PA 19027-2339
800-783-5841
gtour400@aol.com
http://www.guidedtour.com
Disability Served: developmentally disabled, physically
    disabled
This company offers varied tours for people with
    developmental and physical challenges.

Gulf Coast Rehab Equipment Inc.
801 Lakeside Drive
Mobile, AL 36693
888-666-5560
http://www.gulfcoastrehab.com
Disability Served: various
This company sells and repairs wheelchairs and scooters.
    It also offers specialty bathing aides and cushions.

Handicaps Inc.
4335 South Santa Fe Drive
Englewood, CO 80110
303-781-2062, 800-782-4335
forest77@earthlink.net
http://www.handicapsinc.com
Disability Served: physically disabled
This company manufactures driving aids and accessories
    for persons with disabilities. Products include hand
    brakes, hand controls, motor home lifts, left-foot
    accelerators, wheelchair restraints, ramps, pedal
    extensions, shoes, scooters, trailers, golf carts, and
    more.

Harness Designs Inc.
516 Middlebrooks Circle
Tallahassee, FL 32312
850-523-7890
myk3h@harnessdesigns.com
http://www.harnessdesigns.com
Disability Served: physically disabled
This company offers wheelchair day and racing gloves.

Harris Company
781-595-5414, 800-943-5646
bob@walkingstickcom, doug@walkingstick.com
http://www.walkingstick.com
Disability Served: physically disabled
This company offers walking sticks.

Haseltine Systems Corporation
2181 Jamieson Avenue, #1606
Alexandria, VA 22314
888-445-8751
http://www.haseltine.com
Disability Served: physically disabled
This company offers containers that protect wheelchairs
during travel.

Haverich Ortho Sport Inc.
160 Emerald Street
Keene, NH 03431
603-358-0438, 800-529-9444
info@haverich.com
http://www.haverich.com
Disability Served: physically disabled
This company manufactures tricycles, bicycles, and
tandems for physically challenged individuals. Cycles
are available to fit ages from one-and-a-half years to
adult.

Heartland Mobility
1810 Megan Circle
El Dorado, KS 67042
316-322-3502
customerservice@heartlandmobility.com
http://www.heartlandmobility.com
Disability Served: physically disabled
This company offers scooters, wheelchairs, lift chairs,
carriers, and ramps.

Henley Medical
1090 McCallie Avenue
Chattanooga, TN 37404

423-698-4200
http://www.henleymedical.com
Disability Served: physically disabled
This company sells a wide range of mobility products.

Hill Hiker Inc.
3565 County Road 6
Orono, MN 55356
952-476-2422
hillhikerinc@msn.com
http://www.hillhiker.com
Disability Served: physically disabled
This company offers motorized hillside lifts.

HomeExchange Inc.
Post Office Box 787
Hermosa Beach, CA 90254
800-877-8723
http://www.homeexchange.com/n_category.
    php?type=hcapa&print_type=Accessible
Disability Served: various
This Web site offers information on accessible
    homes throughout the world for travelers with
    disabilities.

Horizon Mobility Equipment Inc.
PO Box 362
Kerhonkson, NY 12446
info@hmeny.biz
http://www.hmeny.biz
Disability Served: various
This company offers scooters, wheelchairs, lifts, seating
    and positioning devices, beds and related products,
    and other medical equipment.

House of Canes and Walking Sticks
PO Box 574
Wilderville, OR 97543
800-458-5920
http://www.houseofcanes.com
Disability Served: physically disabled
This company offers canes, walking sticks, and
    ambulatory aids.

Hoveround Corporation
2151 Whitfield Industry Way
Sarasota, FL 34243
800-542-7236
http://www.hoveround.com
Disability Served: physically disabled

This company manufactures power wheelchairs and scooters.

Hutchinson Medical Inc.
333 Highland Avenue
Salem, MA 01970
978-741-1770, 800-287-1770
hutmed@aol.com
http://www.hutchinsonmedical.com
Disability Served: various
This company offers power and manual wheelchairs, walking aids, bathroom safety devices, and other products.

Inclinator Company of America
601 Gibson Boulevard, PO Box 1557
Harrisburg, PA 17104-1557
717-234-8065
isales@inclinator.com
http://www.inclinator.com
Disability Served: physically disabled
This company manufactures residential lifts, elevators, and dumbwaiters.

Independence Technology
PO Box 7338
Endicott, NY 13760
877-794-3125
https://www.independencenow.com
Disability Served: physically disabled
This company offers a mobility device that can climb stairs and curbs, raise the user to eye-level, and traverse rugged terrain such as grass, gravel, sand, mud, and puddles.

Innovative Products Inc.
830 South 48th Street
Grand Forks, ND 58201
800-950-5185
http://www.iphope.com
Disability Served: physically disabled
This company manufactures mobility equipment for children with disabilities. It also offers equipment that allows people who are physically challenged to bowl.

Invisible Structures Inc.
1600 Jackson Street, Suite 310
Golden, CO 80401
800-233-1510
sales@invisiblestructures.com

http://www.invisiblestructures.com
Disability Served: physically disabled
This company manufactures paving products, such as plastic beach matting systems, which increase accessibility.

Island Dialysis
Barbados
Puerto Rico
St. Lucia
800-408-6031
info@islanddialysis.com
http://www.islanddialysis.com
Disability Served: physically disabled
This Web site provides information for travelers to the Caribbean who need dialysis services.

Just Two Bikes Inc.
15449 Forest Boulevard North, #C
Hugo, MN 55038
800-499-1548
http://www.justtwobikes.com
Disability Served: physically disabled
This company manufactures dual recumbent cycles for the disabled.

Kempf-Katalavox
PO Box 61103
Sunnyvale, CA 94086
408-773-0219, 800-255-6174
kempf@katalavox.com
http://www.katalavox.com
Disability Served: physically disabled
This company designs and manufactures a voice-activation system that can be used to operate power wheelchairs and control the electrical functions in automobiles.

Kettler International Inc.
PO Box 2747
Virginia Beach, VA 23450-2747
757-427-2400
info@kettlerusa.com
http://www.kettlerusa.com
Disability Served: physically disabled
This company manufactures a pedal-powered car for children.

Kik Tire Inc.
590 Airport Road
Oceanside, CA 92054

800-545-8221
kiktire@aol.com
http://www.kiktire.com
Disability Served: physically disabled
This company manufactures tires for scooters, and manual and power wheelchairs.

Kinedyne Corporation
3701 Greenway Circle
Lawrence, KS 66046-5442
913-841-4000, 800-848-6057
http://www.kinedyne.com
Disability Served: physically disabled
This company designs and manufactures wheelchair securement and occupant restraint systems.

Kroepke Kontrols Inc.
104 Hawkins Street
Bronx, NY 10464
718-885-1100
kkontrols@aol.com
http://www.kroepkekontrols.com
Disability Served: physically disabled
This company manufactures hand controls for automobiles.

Lefever and Associates
220 Centerville Road, Suite 2
Lancaster, PA 17603
866-533-3837
CRLNO1@aol.com
http://www.electricscooter.com
Disability Served: various
This company offers three- and four-wheel electric scooters, power wheelchairs, adjustable beds, and van lifts.

Leisure-Lift Inc.
1800 Merriam Lane
Kansas City, KS 66106
800-255-4147
leisure-Lift@kc.rr.com
http://www.pacesaver.com
Disability Served: physically disabled
This company manufactures nine scooter models; six power wheelchair models; a lift for cars, vans, pick-ups, and SUVs; and a 600-pound-capacity bariatric home care bed. This company does not sell to the general public, but offers its products through local dealers. Contact the company for more information.

LeMans Industries Corporation
79 Express Street
Plainview, NY 11803
516-942-9800, 800-289-5667
sales@lemansind.com
http://www.lemansindustries.com
Disability Served: physically disabled
This company manufactures a wheelchair cover made of clear plastic.

Leslie´s Modern Mobility
126 South Main
Frankenmuth, MI 48734
989-652-6693
scooterman2@aol.com
http://custommobility.pridedealer.com
Disability Served: physically disabled
This company sells electric scooters, power wheelchairs, walkers, canes, and other mobility-related devices. It also sells and installs lifts for autos, trucks, and vans and offers home remodeling services.

Lester Electrical Inc.
625 West A Street
Lincoln, NE 68522
402-477-8988
http://www.lesterelectrical.com
Disability Served: physically disabled
This company manufactures battery chargers for wheelchairs.

Levo USA Inc.
211 Fulton Court
Peachtree City, GA 30269
770-486-0033, 888-538-6872
request@levousa.com
http://www.levousa.com
Disability Served: physically disabled
This company manufactures wheelchairs with power lifting features so the user can stand up.

Life Essentials
8796 South US 231
Brookston, IN 47923
765-742-6707
info@life-essentials.net
http://www.life-essentials.net
Disability Served: physically disabled
This company offers agricultural, recreational, van, truck, and equestrian lifts; motorized wheelchairs, scooters,

and mobility modules; home elevators; and hand controls for many applications.

LifeStand
c/o Frank Mobility Systems, Inc.
1003 International Drive
Oakdale, PA 15071
888-426-8581
http://www.lifestand-usa.com
Disability Served: physically disabled
This company manufactures lightweight, standing wheelchairs.

Liftavator, Inc.
5299 Enterprise Drive
Lockport, NY 14094
716-434-1300, 800-660-2629
sales@liftavator.com
http://www.liftavator.com
Disability Served: physically disabled
This company offers residential elevators, vertical wheelchair lifts, and stair lifts.

LIFTnWALK
Box 742855
Dallas, TX 75374-2855
214-343-6496
sales@liftnwalk.com
http://www.safetyrollers.com
Disability Served: physically disabled
This company manufactures LIFTnWALK, a combined conventional gait walker and transporter hoist device.

Lightning Handcycles
360 Sepulveda Boulevard, Suite 1005
El Segundo, CA 90245
888-426-3292
drfranks@handcycle.com
http://www.handcycle.com
Disability Served: physically disabled
This company offers hand cycles.

Mac's Lift Gate Inc.
2715 Seaboard Lane
Long Beach, CA 90805
800-795-6227
macslift@blvd.com
http://www.macslift.com
Disability Served: physically disabled

This company manufactures van lifts, home wheelchair lifts, stair lifts, and scooter lifts. It also sells new and used vans that are adapted for people with disabilities.

MADA Medical Products Inc.
625 Washington Avenue
Carlstadt, NJ 07072
201-460-0454, 800-526-6370
dianelind@mail.madamedical.com
http://www.madamedical.com
Disability Served: various
This company manufactures wheelchairs, transport chairs, canes, walkers, crutches, bath benches, grab bars, folding commodes, and an extensive line of respiratory equipment.

Maintenance Specialties
2002 Riverside Drive
Bradenton, FL 34208
866-753-2289
apartsman4u@yahoo.com
http://wheelchairparts.com
Disability Served: various
This company offers manual and power wheelchairs, accessories, and parts; wheelchair ramps; shower and commode chairs; scales; and other health care and daily living products.

Matot
2501 Van Buren
Bellwood, IL 60104-2459
800-369-1070
sales@matot.com
http://www.matot.com
Disability Served: physically disabled
This company manufactures residential elevators.

Maxim Mobility
90 Hamilton Street
New Haven, CT 06511
800-411-1388
http://www.maximmobility.com
Disability Served: physically disabled
This company offers power wheelchairs and scooters.

MedAid Medical
78 Bay Creek Road
Loganville, GA 30052
800-743-7203

Stuff@medaidmedical.com
http://www.medaidmedical.com
Disability Served: various
This company offers wheelchairs, ramps, and a wide
variety of daily living aids.

Medical Equipment Distributors
2200-109 Millbrook Road
Raleigh, NC 27604
919-873-9168
sdl6015@aol.com
http://www.medequipnc.com
Disability Served: various
This company distributes power wheel chairs, scooters,
personal mobility vehicles, and lift chairs.

Medical Travel Inc.
16555 White Orchid Lane
Delray Beach, FL 33446
800-778-7953
info@medicaltravel.org
http://www.medicaltravel.org
Disability Served: various
This company arranges travel for people with disabilities.

Merry Walker Corporation
21350 South Sylvan Drive
Mundelein, IL 60060
847-837-9580
office@merrywalker.com
http://www.merrywalker.com
Disability Served: physically disabled
This company manufactures wheeled walkers and therapeutic canes.

MidWest Mobility Inc.
437 West Wise Road
Schaumburg, IL 60193
800-809-3738
sales@midwestmobility.com
http://www.midwestmobility.com
Disability Served: physically disabled
This company adapts vehicles for the disabled, adding
or altering such features as wheelchair lifts, hand
controls, power seats, raised roofs and doors, lowered
floors, door openers, and manual and electric wheelchair tie-downs. It also rents and sells vans.

Minnesota Mobility Systems Inc.
800-828-3944
mmsi@mobilityscootersonthenet.com

http://www.mobilityscootersonthenet.com
Disability Served: physically disabled
This company offers scooters, power chairs, and lifts.

Missouri Stairway Lift Corporation
601 North College Avenue
Columbia, MO 65201-4770
800-392-2591
http://www.missouristairwaylift.com
Disability Served: physically disabled
This company offers stairway lifts, elevators, and lift
chairs for residences and businesses in Missouri.

MK Battery
1645 South Sinclair Street
Anaheim, CA 92806
714-937-1033, 800-372-9253
info@mkbattery.com
http://www.mkbattery.com
Disability Served: physically disabled
This company manufactures batteries for power
wheelchairs.

Mobility-Care.com
1349 El Prado Avenue
Torrance, CA 90501
800-464-3258
orders@MobilityCare.com
http://www.mobilitycare.com
Disability Served: various
This company offers scooters, power lift chairs, walkers,
power wheelchairs, bath safety products, and
support stockings.

Mobility Concepts Inc.
1017 54th Avenue East
Fife, WA 98424
888-227-6375
http://www.mobilityconceptsinc.com
Disability Served: physically disabled
This company sells adapted vehicles, patient lifts, ceiling
lifts, stair lifts, and elevators.

Mobility Direct
3478 Shadow Ridge Drive
Loveland, OH 45140
513-774-9475, 877-914-1830
info@affordableoption.com
http://www.affordableoption.com
Disability Served: various

This company offers wheelchairs and related parts, scooters, batteries, lift chairs, canes, walkers, and ramps. It also offers bath safety products, bedrails, grabbers, reachers, raised toilets, and wheelchair trays, bags, and backpacks.

Mobility Freedom Inc.
800-910-VANS
mobilityfreedom@yahoo.com
http://www.rainbowwheels.com
Disability Served: physically disabled
This company sells and rents wheelchair-accessible vans.

Mobility Medical Equipment
4009 Lindbergh Drive
Addison, TX 75001
888-350-1616
info@mobilitymed.com
http://www.mobilitymed.com
Disability Served: various
This company offers wheelchairs, scooters, ramps, vehicle lifts and carriers, ambulatory aids, cushions and back supports, and bathroom safety devices.

Mobility Solutions Inc.
1001 East Cooley Drive, Suite 104
Colton, CA 92324
888-400-1533
sales@mobility-solutions.com
http://www.mobility-solutions.com
Disability Served: various
This company offers manual and power wheelchairs, scooters, sports chairs, standing positioning systems, walkers, walking aids, lifts, and beds.

Mobility Systems
6015 160th Avenue East, PO Box 928
Sumner, WA 98390
253-863-4744, 800-830-4744 (in Washington only)
http://www.mobilitysystemsinc.com
Disability Served: physically disabled
This company offers conversion vans, wheelchair lifts, scooter lifts, and driving aids.

Mobility Unlimited
505 North Del Prado Boulevard
Cape Coral, FL 33909-2244
941-772-5155
http://www.mobilityunlimited.com
Disability Served: various

This company offers power and manual wheelchairs, walkers, electric scooters, bathroom safety equipment, and rehabilitation devices.

Mobility Works
800-638-8267
info@mobilityworks.com
http://www.mobilityworks.com
Disability Served: physically disabled
This company builds and adapts vehicles for the handicapped. It also offers lifts, power wheelchairs, and scooters.

Modern Mobility
849 Virginia Beach Boulevard
Virginia Beach, VA 23451
757-437-2501
sales@modernmobilityinc.com
http://www.modernmobilityinc.com
Disability Served: physically disabled
This company sells, rents, and repairs scooters, lift chairs, stair glides, scooter lifts, and power and manual wheelchairs.

Monmouth Vans, Access & Mobility Equipment
5105 Route 33/34
Farmingdale, NJ 07727
732-919-1444, 800-221-0034
http://www.monmouthvans.com
Disability Served: physically disabled
This company provides complete modifications to vans and cars, stairway or vertical lifts, automatic door openers, modular ramp systems, and patient transfer systems. Additionally, the company has modified full-size and mini-vans available for sale.

Motion Concepts
716-447-0050, 888-433-6818
ann@medbloc.com
http://www.medbloc.com
Disability Served: physically disabled
This company manufactures powerpositioning systems for wheelchairs.

Motovator
716B San Antonio Road
Palo Alto, CA 94303
650-494-2162
http://motovatorsales.pridedealer.com
Disability Served: physically disabled
This company offers scooters and lift chairs.

Mr. Mobility
15 Minneakoning Road, Suite 309
Flemington, NJ 08822
800-872-5229
questions@mrmobility.com
http://www.mrmobility.com
Disability Served: physically disabled
This company offers power wheelchairs, scooters, strollers, standing positioning systems, and walkers.

Mulholland Positioning Systems Inc.
215 North 12th Street, PO Box 391
Santa Paula, CA 93060
805-525-7165, 800-543-4769
customer_service@mulhollandinc.com
http://mulhollandinc.com
Disability Served: physically disabled
This company designs, manufactures, markets, and sells pediatric seating and standing positioning devices for individuals with motor development disorders.

National Scooters
PO Box 3518
Post Falls, ID 83877
800-596-6607
sales@nationalscooters.com
http://www.nationalscooters.com
Disability Served: physically disabled
This company offers scooters, wheelchairs, lifts, and ramps.

National Wheel-O-Vator Company Inc.
509 West Front Street
Roanoke, IL 61561
800-551-9095
http://www.wheelovator.com
Disability Served: physically disabled
This company manufactures vertical platform lifts, inclined platform lifts, limited use/limited application low-rise elevators, and private residence elevators.

Natural Access
PO Box 5729
Santa Monica, CA 90409-5729
800-411-7789
natural@superlink.net
http://www.natural-access.com/home
Disability Served: physically disabled
This company manufactures all-terrain wheelchairs for use on beaches and trails.

NeverLand Adventures Inc.
3940 7th Avenue, Suite #103
San Diego, CA 92103-3294
800-717-8226
info@neverland-adventures.com
http://www.neverland-adventures.com
Disability Served: various
This company arranges tours to New Zealand and Australia for people with disabilities.

NobleMotion Inc.
PO Box 5366
Pittsburgh, PA 15206
412-720-6425, 800-234-9255
info@noblemotion.com
http://www.noblemotion.com/letter.htm
Disability Served: physically disabled
NobleMotion manufactures Swedish-style, four-wheeled roller walkers and other products for the walking impaired.

1A Discount Electric Scooters
4608 Colby Road
Winchester, KY 40391
800-974-9590
inquiry@1adiscountelectricscooters.com
http://www.1adiscountelectricscooters.com
Disability Served: physically disabled
This company offers scooters, power wheelchairs, ramps, lifts, and trailers.

1800Wheelchair.com
174 Broadway, Suite 515
Brooklyn, NY 11211
718-302-1923, 800-320-7140
info@1800Wheelchair.com
http://www.1800wheelchair.com
Disability Served: various
This company offers manual and electric wheelchairs; scooters; walking aids, such as walkers, canes, and crutches; daily living aids, such as adapted kitchenware, reachers, and dressing aids; shower chairs; transfer benches; incontinence supplies; pillows and support devices; and assistive furniture.

One-Off Titanium Inc.
494 Stage Road
Cummington, MA 01026
413-634-5591
mike@titaniumarts.com

http://www.titaniumarts.com
Disability Served: physically disabled
This company offers custom titanium hand cycles.

Ontario Drive and Gear Ltd.
220 Bergey Court
New Hamburg, ON N0B 2G0
Canada
519-662-4000
http://www.argoatv.com
Disability Served: physically disabled
This company manufactures and distributes amphibious all-terrain vehicles that can be operated with hand controls.

Orthofab Inc.
2160 De Celles Street
Quebec City, QC G2C 1X8
Canada
418-847-5225, 800-463-5293
cplourde@orthofab.com
http://www.orthofab.com/Anglais/index-ang2.shtml
Disability Served: physically disabled
This company manufactures power wheelchairs and scooters.

Palmer Industries Inc.
PO Box 5707
Endicott, NY 13763
607-754-2957, 800-847-1304
palmer@palmerind.com
http://www.palmerind.com
Disability Served: physically disabled
This company manufactures outdoor power scooters, powertricycles, manual tricycles, and all-terrain carts.

Permobil of America Inc.
6961 Eastgate Boulevard
Lebanon, TN 37090
800-736-0925
info@permobilusa.com
http://www.permobil.com
Disability Served: physically disabled
This company manufactures power wheelchairs.

Planet Mobility
14986 Technology Drive
Shelby Township, MI 48315
866-465-4387
http://www.planetmobility.com

Disability Served: various
This company offers new and used power wheelchairs, manual wheelchairs, scooters, lifts, elevators, ramps, and a variety of daily livings aids.

Pride Mobility Products Corporation
182 Susquehanna Avenue
Exeter, PA 18643
800-800-8586
http://www.pridemobility.com
Disability Served: physically disabled
This company manufactures lift chairs, power wheelchairs, recliner chairs, scooters, and travel lifts.

Prime Engineering
4202 Sierra Madre
Fresno, CA 93722
800-82-STAND
info@primeengineering.com
http://www.primeengineering.com
Disability Served: physically disabled
This company manufactures standing aids for children and adults.

Q'Straint
5553 Ravenswood Road, Building 110
Ft Lauderdale, FL 33312
954-986-6665, 800-987-9987
qstraint@qstraint.com
http://qstraint.com
Disability Served: physically disabled
This company designs and manufactures wheelchair restraint systems for vehicles.

Quick Deck Inc.
PO Box 537
Byron, CA 94514
925-516-0603, 800-903-7772
ramps@quick-deck.com
http://www.quick-deck.com
Disability Served: physically disabled
This company rents and leases modular ramps for home and industrial use.

Quickie Wheelchairs
c/o Southwest Medical
513 West Thomas Road
Phoenix, AZ 85013
800-236-4215
Info@quickiewheelchairs.com

http://www.quickie-wheelchairs.com
Disability Served: physically disabled
This company manufactures manual and power
    wheelchairs, positioning wheelchairs, sports
    wheelchairs, hand cycles, and standing frames.

Radventure Inc.
20755 Southwest 238th Place
Sherwood, OR 97140
971-219-4897
radyetti@aol.com
http://www.radventures-yetti.com
Disability Served: various
This company manufactures and distributes Yetti mono-
    skis and outriggers for snow skiing.

Ranger All Season Corporation
PO Box 132
George, IA 51237
800-225-3811
sales@rangerallseason.com
http://www.rangerallseason.com
Disability Served: physically disabled
This company manufactures three- and four-wheeled
    scooters, scooter lifts, and related accessories.

Recreatives Industries Inc.
60 Depot Street
Buffalo, NY 14206
800-255-2511
http://www.maxatvs.com
Disability Served: physically disabled
This company manufactures an all-terrain vehicle with
    hand controls.

REDD Team Manufacturing Inc.
c/o Alcoa Engineered Products
6599 State Route 21
Keystone Heights, FL 32656
352-473-7246, 800-648-3696
http://www.reddteam.com
Disability Served: various
This company builds prefabricated modular aluminum
    access systems that include ramps, stairs, pedestrian
    bridges, docks, and walkways. Custom and standard
    applications are available.

Rehab Designs Inc.
11700 Commonwealth Drive
Louisville, KY 40299

888-889-1114
http://www.rehabdesigns.com
Disability Served: various
This company offers wheelchairs, ramps, scooters, and
    daily living aids, such as bath aids, commodes, grab
    bars, raised toilet seats, shower chairs, and transfer
    benches.

RGK Wheelchairs
Burntwood, United Kingdom
info@rgklife.com
http://www.rgklife.com
Disability Served: physically disabled
This company offers custom-made, lightweight
    wheelchairs.

Ricon Corporation
7900 Nelson Road
Panorama City, CA 91402
818-267-3000, 800-322-2884
customerservice@riconcorp.com
http://www.riconcorp.com
Disability Served: physically disabled
This company makes power transfer seats and van lifts.

Rock N' Roll Marketing
PO Box 1558
Levelland, TX 79336
806-894-5700
funmachines@rocknrollcycles.com
http://www.rocknrollcycles.com
Disability Served: physically disabled
This company provides cycles for disabled riders from age
    two to adult. It also offers wheelchair pusher bikes.

RolControl Products
6750 Worth Way
Camarillo, CA 93012
805-386-4191, 800-281-7791
rolcontrol@msn.com
http://www.rolcontrol.com
Disability Served: physically disabled
This company sells new or used mobility aides, including
    power wheelchairs, manual wheelchairs, walkers,
    power lift and recline chairs, and power scooters.

Roleez
c/o Primex Marketing Inc.
3890 Industrial Way
Benicia, CA 94510

707-746-6855
http://www.primexmarketing.com
Disability Served: physically disabled
This company offers an all-terrain platform wheelchair dolly suitable for trails, beaches, and other difficult terrain.

RollingSA
South Africa
http://www.rollingsa.co.za
Disability Served: various
This company offers adventure tourism services for disabled visitors to South Africa.

Safety Chairs
c/o Concept Development Associates Inc.
1375 Central Avenue
Santa Rosa, CA 95401
877-379-2638
info@cda-designs.com
http://www.safetychairs.net
Disability Served: physically disabled
This company offers chairs that can be used during emergencies to evacuate the mobility-impaired.

Savaria Inc.
4150 Highway #13
Laval, QB H7R 6E9
Canada
800-931-5655
savaria@savaria.com
http://www.savaria.com
Disability Served: physically disabled
This company makes straight stair lifts, curved stair lifts, inclined and vertical wheelchair platform lifts, and residential elevators.

ScootAround
208-584 Pembina Highway
Winnipeg, MB R3M 3X7
Canada
881-441-7575
http://www.scootaround.com
Disability Served: physically disabled
This company offers scooter rentals. It has locations throughout Canada and the United States.

Scooter Discounters
1945 Winterhaven Drive
Virginia Beach, VA 23456

757-430-2664, 800-229-1317
Disability Served: physically disabled
This company offers discount pricing on new electric scooters.

Scooter Discounts of Florida
3320 Wind Chime Drive
Clearwater, FL 33761
866-265-0060
scooterdiscounts@tbi.net
http://www.scooterdiscounts.net
Disability Served: physically disabled
This company offers scooters, lifts, walkers, power chairs, and related accessories.

Scooter411
11030 Arrow Route, #103
Rancho Cucamonga, CA 91730
888-466-1651
info@scooter411.com
http://www.scooter411.com
Disability Served: physically disabled
This company offers a variety of three- and four-wheeled scooters, as well as scooter lifts and ramps.

ScootersOnline.com
1699 Stevenson Station Road
Chandler, IN 47610
812-925-7745, 888-420-2278
info@mapv.com
http://www.scootersonline.com
Disability Served: physically disabled
This company sells scooters.

The Scooter Store
PO Box 310709
New Braunfels, TX 78131-0709
800-391-7237
http://www.thescooterstore.com
Disability Served: physically disabled
This company offers scooters, power chairs, home ramps, car lifts, and related accessories.

Scooterville
1536 Myrtle Avenue
Monrovia, CA 91016
800-994-0454
http://www.scooterville.net
Disability Served: physically disabled
This company offers scooters, manual and power wheel chairs, ramps, walkers, lift chairs, and stair lifts.

SeatCase Inc.
6108 Dedham Lane
Austin, TX 78739
512-301-3703, 800-221-7328
info@seatcase.com
http://www.seatcase.com
Disability Served: physically disabled
This company manufactures SeatCase, a lightweight, durable, and compact wheelchair chair for traveling.

SeeMore Scenic Tours
Australia
seemore@goldlink.aunz.com
http://www.geocities.com/TheTropics/Island/4245
Disability Served: various
This company offers accessible tourism services for visitors to Australia.

Segway LLC
14 Technology Drive
Bedford, NH 03110
866-4SEGWAY
http://www.segway.com
Disability Served: physically disabled
This company manufactures the Segway, a self-balancing, electric transportation device.

SFH Products Inc.
1951 East Myrna Lane
Tempe, AZ 85284
888-224-1425
http://www.lectraaid.com
Disability Served: physically disabled
This company manufactures a personal lift for use with trucks and mobile homes.

Silver Cross
rharvey@silvercross.com
http://www.silvercross.com
Disability Served: physically disabled
This company offers new and recycled residential stair and wheelchair lifts, elevators, scooters, wheelchairs, patient lifts, bath lifts, and door openers. It has more than 100 locations and affiliates in the United States.

Skyway Machine Inc.
4451 Caterpillar Road
Redding, CA 96003
530-243-5151, 800-332-3357
Info@SkywayWheels.com
http://www.skywaytuffwheels.com
Disability Served: physically disabled
This company manufactures wheels and casters.

SpinLife.Com
1108 City Park Avenue
Columbus, OH 43206
800-850-0335
http://www.spinlife.com
Disability Served: various
This company offers manual and power wheelchairs, scooters, lifts, ramps, walking aids, and bathroom safety devices.

Spokes 'n Motion
2226 South Jason Street
Denver, CO 80223
303-922-0605
info@spokesnmotion.com
http://www.spokesnmotion.com
Disability Served: physically disabled
This company offers adaptive sports equipment, including mono-skis, all-terrain beach wheelchairs, custom crutches, hand cycles, and car hand controls.

Sportaid
78 Bay Creek Road
Loganville, GA 30052
800-743-7203
stuff@sportaid.com
http://www.sportaid.com
Disability Served: various
This company offers wheelchairs and related accessories; wheelchair ramps; scooters; transfer benches; daily living aids; and health care supplies, such as urinals, suppositories, and catheters.

Stand Aid of Iowa Inc.
1009 Second Avenue, PO Box 386
Sheldon, IA 51201
712-324-2153, 800-831-8580
sales@stand-aid.com
http://www.stand-aid.com
Disability Served: various
This company makes hydraulic standing aids, wheelchair ramps, an attachment that converts a manual wheelchair into a power chair, and power toilet lifts.

Stannah Stairlifts
101 Constitution Boulevard, Suite C
Franklin, MA 02038
800-877-8247
inquiries@stannah.com
http://www.stannah.com/us
Disability Served: physically disabled
This company offers stair lifts for home and business
use.

Sun Metal Products Inc.
PO Box 1508
Warsaw, IN 46581-1508
574-267-3281
info@sunmetal.com
http://www.sunmetal.com
Disability Served: physically disabled
This company manufactures hubs, rims, and wheels for
wheelchairs.

Sunrise Medical
2382 Faraday Avenue, Suite 200
Carlsbad, CA 92008-7220
800-333-4000
http://www.sunrisemedical.com
Disability Served: various
This company offers manual and power wheelchairs,
sports wheelchairs, wheelchair cushions, crutches,
walkers, and canes.

Superior Mobility
2172 Torrance Boulevard
Torrance, CA 90501
310-533-4840
http://www.superiormobility.com
Disability Served: various
This company offers manual and power wheelchairs,
scooters, pediatric positioning products, lift chairs,
and bathroom safety products.

Tag-a-Long Trailers Inc.
c/o Centreville Manufacturing Inc.
601 Ruthsburg Road
Centreville, MD 21617
410-758-1333
info@centrevilletrailer.com
http://www.centrevilletrailer.com
Disability Served: physically disabled
This company manufactures a hitch-mounted scooter lift
and carrier.

Telecom Pioneers of America
PO Box 13888
Denver, CO 80201-3888
800-872-5995
info@telecompioneers.org
http://www.telecompioneers.org
Disability Served: physically disabled
This organization manufactures the HOT Trike, a tricycle
for children who do not have the use of their legs.

Theradyne Corporation
395 Ervin Industrial Drive
Jordan, MN 55352
800-328-4014, ext. 6197
kurt-theradyne-cs@kurt.com
Disability Served: physically disabled
This company manufactures a wide variety of
wheelchairs.

ThyssenKrupp Access
4001 East 138th Street
Grandview, MO 64030
800-829-9760
info@stairlift.com
http://www.chair-lift.com
Disability Served: physically disabled
This company manufactures interior stair lifts, as well as
inclined and vertical platform lifts.

ThyssenKrupp Elevator
2595 Dallas Parkway, Suite 400
Frisco, TX 75034
877-230-0303
sales@thyssenkruppelevator.com
http://www.thyssenelevator.com
Disability Served: various
This company manufactures residential elevators.

TIRALO LLC
42 Cove Way
Brinnon, WA 98320
877-244-2810
http://www.tiralo-usa.com
Disability Served: physically disabled
This company offers beach wheelchairs.

T.L. Shield and Associates Inc.
PO Box 6845
Thousand Oaks, CA 91359
818-509-8228

info@tlshield.com
http://www.tlshield.com
Disability Served: physically disabled
This company manufactures residential elevators, wheelchair lifts, stair chairs, and dumbwaiters.

Trailex Aluminum Products
One Industrial Park Drive, PO Box 553
Canfield, OH 44406
877-TRAILEX
sales@trailex.com
http://www.trailex.com
Disability Served: physically disabled
This company manufactures hitch-mounted scooter carriers.

Trailmate
800-777-1034
http://www.trailmate.com
Disability Served: physically disabled
This company manufactures tricycles and tandem bicycles for physically challenged children and adults.

Travel Ramp Inc.
13818 NW 126th Terrace, PO Box 2015
Alachua, FL 32616
386-462-5267, 888-661-7267
Disability Served: physically disabled
This company manufactures lightweight fiberglass ramps for wheelchair and scooter users.

Treadle Power Inc.
6 Linden Terrace
Burlington, VT 05401-4928
802-862-2980, 800-648-7335
info@stepngo.com
http://www.stepngo.com
Disability Served: various
This company manufactures a three-wheeled, step-action, self-balancing cycle.

Triaid Rehabilitation Products
PO Box 1364
Cumberland, MD 21501-1364
301-759-3525, 800-306-6777
sales@triaid.com
http://www.triaid.com
Disability Served: physically disabled
This company manufactures three-wheeled cycles, gait trainers, and walkers.

Triketrails
1621 McEwen Drive, Unit #5
Whitby, ON L1N9A5
Canada
905-434-1409, 866-587-4537
contact@triketrails.com
http://www.triketrails.com
Disability Served: physically disabled
This company offers recumbent bicycles and recumbent tricycles.

Trips Inc.
PO Box 10885
Eugene, OR 97440
800-686-1013
trips@tripsinc.com
http://www.tripsinc.com
Disability Served: developmentally disabled
This company offers travel outings for people with developmental disabilities.

Tri Quality Inc.
8590 Younger Creek Drive
Sacramento, CA 95828
800-567-9090
support@triquality.com
http://www.triquality.com
Disability Served: physically disabled
This company offers wheelchair replacement parts and accessories.

Tri State Lift
10048 37th Avenue, SW
Ellendale, MN 56026
507-455-3553, 800-626-6017 (Minnesota, Iowa, and Wisconsin only)
moreinfo@tri-state-lift.com
http://www.tri-state-lift.com
Disability Served: physically disabled
This company offers stairway lifts, commercial and residential wheelchair lifts, residential elevators, limited-use elevators, power door operators, and dumbwaiters to residents of Minnesota, Wisconsin, and Iowa.

Trus-T-Lift
c/o RAM Manufacturing Ltd.
10812 181 Street
Edmonton, AB T5S 1K8
Canada

780-484-4776, 800-563-4382
trustram@trustram.com
http://www.trustram.com
Disability Served: physically disabled
This company offers residential and commercial lifts.

21st Century Scientific Inc.
4915 Industrial Way
Coeur d'Alene, ID 83815-8931
208-667-8800, 800-448-3680
21st@wheelchairs.com
http://www.wheelchairs.com
Disability Served: physically disabled
This company manufactures powered wheelchairs and
     replacement power drives for powered wheelchairs.

Union Battery Corporation
205 Berg Street
Algonquin, IL 60102
847-854-1295
jason@unionbattery.com
http://www.unionbattery.com
Disability Served: physically disabled
This company makes rechargeable batteries for
     wheelchairs.

Uplift Mobility Inc.
1625 Starkey Road
Largo, FL 33771
727-535-4645, 800-237-8268
doris@upliftmobility.com
http://www.upliftmobility.com
Disability Served: physically disabled
This company sells, services, and rents medical
     equipment, including scooters, manual wheelchairs,
     power wheelchairs, lift chairs, walkers, and lifts.

USA Mobility Inc.
409 North Tejon Street
Colorado Springs, CO 80903
800-309-1667
http://www.usamobilityinc.com
Disability Served: physically disabled
This company offers power wheelchairs, lift chairs,
     scooters, and ramps.

U.S. Medical Supply
3901A Commerce Park Drive
Raleigh, NC 27610
800-922-3659

ausmed@ausmed.com
http://www.adlmedicalsupply.com
Disability Served: various
This company offers power wheelchairs, walkers, lift
     chairs, scooters, and crutches. It also offers magnifiers,
     adapted eating utensils, reachers, turners, blood pres-
     sure monitoring equipment, foot care products, incon-
     tinence supplies, convalescent care products, and a
     variety of health care and rehabilitation products.

Vacation Home Exchange
Independent Living Institute
Stockholm, Sweden
http://www.independentliving.org/vacex
Disability Served: various
This Web site offers a bulletin board for people who are
     interested in exchanging accessible vacation homes.

Varna Cycles
1635 Queequeg
Gabriola Island, BC V0R 1X5
Canada
250-247-8379
varna@varnahandcycles.com
http://www.varnahandcycles.com
Disability Served: physically disabled
This company makes hand-propelled bicycles, tricycles,
     and other cycles for the disabled.

Vartanian
2550 Central Point Parkway
Lima, OH 45804
888-324-7895
http://www.vartanian.com
Disability Served: physically disabled
This company provides custom van conversions for
     physically challenged individuals.

Ventura Enterprises Inc.
35 Lawton Avenue
Danville, IN 46122
317-745-2989
info@venturaenterprises.com
http://www.venturaenterprises.com
Disability Served: physically disabled
This company manufactures mobility aids.

Venture Products Inc.
PO Box 148
Orrville, OH 44667

866-836-8722
info@ventrac.com
http://www.venturepro.com
Disability Served: physically disabled
This company manufactures riding lawn mowers, plows,
and other outdoor equipment for the disabled.

Volkswagen United States Inc.
PO Box 3
Hillsboro, OR 97123-0003
800-428-4034
http://www.vw.com
Disability Served: physically disabled
Volkswagen of America provides up to $500 toward the
purchase and installation of lift equipment or carriers,
hand controls, or pedal extensions on any eligible
Volkswagen model.

Walk Easy Inc.
PO Box 812432
Boca Raton, FL 33481-2432
800-441-2904
info@walkeasy.com
http://www.walkeasy.com
Disability Served: various
This company manufactures crutches, canes, crutch and
cane tips, and crutch bags.

WalkerWorks
4580 Hickmore
Montreal, QB H4T 1K2
Canada
604-944-8990, 800-667-4111
sales@walkerworks.com
http://www.walkerworks.com
Disability Served: physically disabled
This company manufactures adjustable walkers.

WalkingEquipment
5539 Park Street North
St. Petersburg, FL 33709
877-890-7677
generalinformation@walkingequipment.com
http://www.walkingequipment.com
Disability Served: physically disabled
This company offers canes, walking sticks, walkers,
forearm crutches, and accessories.

Waupaca Elevator Company Inc.
1726 North Ballard Road
Appleton, WI 54911

920-991-9082, 800-238-8739
info@waupacaelevator.com
http://www.waupacaelevator.com
Disability Served: physically disabled
This company manufactures home elevators and dumb
waiters.

Wells-Engberg Company Inc.
PO Box 6388
Rockford, IL 61125-1388
815-227-9765, 800-642-3628
wellseng@aol.com
http://www.wells-engberg.com
Disability Served: physically disabled
This company manufactures driving accessories,
including hand controls, parking brake extensions,
and pedal extensions.

Wheelcare Inc.
12691 Monarch Street
Garden Grove, CA 92841
800-448-5999
customerservice@wheelcare-inc.com
http://www.wheelcare-inc.com
Disability Served: physically disabled
This company offers scooters and wheelchairs.

Wheelchair Carrier Inc.
203 Matzinger Road
Toledo, OH 43612
419-478-4423, 800-541-3213
CustomerService@LockreyManufacturing.com
http://www.wheelchaircarrier.com
Disability Served: physically disabled
This company manufactures wheelchair carriers,
including hitch-mounted carriers.

Wheelchair Getaways Inc.
PO Box 605
Versailles, KY 40383
800-642-2042
corporate@wheelchairgetaways.com
http://www.wheelchair-getaways.com
Disability Served: physically disabled
This company rents and sells wheelchair-accessible vans.

Wheelchair Lifts 'n Ramps
510 Heritage Lane
Winder, GA 30680
800-710-4964
inquiry@ wheelchair-lifts-ramps.com

http://www.wheelchair-lifts-ramps.com
Disability Served: physically disabled
This company offers patient lifts and wheelchair ramps,
   lifts, and carriers.

The Wheelchair Site
editor@thewheelchairsite.com
http://www.thewheelchairsite.com
Disability Served: physically disabled
This Web site offers advice on renting and buying electric
   wheelchairs, lifts, scooters, and related accessories.

Wheelchairs Plus
3004 River Watch Lane
Augusta, GA 30907-2035
877-737-9877
sales@wheelchairsplus.net
http://www.wheelchairsplus.net
Disability Served: various
This company offers wheelchairs, walkers, canes, hospital
   beds, and transfer boards.

Wheel Chair Tours Australia
Bicton, Australia
david@wheeltours.com.au
http://www.wheeltours.com.au
Disability Served: physically disabled
This company offers tours of Western Australia for people
   in wheelchairs.

Wheelchair Travel
1 Johnston Green
Guildford GU2 9XS
United Kingdom
info@wheelchair-travel.co.uk
http://www.wheelchair-travel.co.uk
Disability Served: various
This company rents adapted vehicles for disabled
   travelers to the United Kingdom and can also provide
   a chauffeur/guide for assistance.

Wheelchair Works Inc.
4211 Southeast International Way, Suite C
Milwaukie, OR 97222
503-654-4333
http://www.wheelchairworks.com
Disability Served: physically disabled
This company sells and repairs a variety of mobility
   devices.

Wheel Coach Services Inc.
4000 Beeston Hill Medical Building, Suite 1
Christiansted, St. Croix
U.S. Virgin Islands 00820-4007
340-719-9335
info@wheelcoach.com
http://www.wheelcoach.com
Disability Served: various
This company offers tours of the U.S. Virgin Islands for
   people with disabilities.

WheelSource
340 Stuyvesant Drive
San Anselmo, CA 94960-1145
415-456-6134, 800-424-1516
JimHood@WheelSource.com
http://www.wheelsource.com
Disability Served: physically disabled
This company offers wheelchair, scooter, walker, and
   crutch bags.

World Class Motor Specialists (WCMS) Inc.
9920 Painter Avenue, PO Box 4023
Santa Fe Springs, CA 90670
562-944-8555, 800-359-1892
http://www.wcmsmotors.com
Disability Served: physically disabled
WCMS rebuilds electric motors for powered
   wheelchairs.

Wright-Way Inc.
175 East I-30
Garland, TX 75043
972-240-8839, 800-241-8839
stefani@wrightwayinc.com
http://www.wrightwayinc.com
Disability Served: physically disabled
Wright-Way manufactures driving aids for the physically disabled, including steering devices, restraint
   systems, vehicle modification kits, and hand controls.

RESOURCES
FOR CAREGIVERS

RESOURCES FOR CAREGIVERS

The following organizations provide useful services and resources to caregivers including information and referral, support programs, publications, peer counseling, respite care, and networking programs.

Alzwell
c/o Prism Innovations Inc.
50 Amuxen Court
Islip, NY 11751
prisminnovations@hotmail.com
http://www.alzwell.com
Disability Served: dementia
Alzwell provides support to caregivers of people with dementia and Alzheimer's.

Caregiving.com
c/o Center for Family Caregivers
PO Box 224
Park Ridge, IL 60068
denise@caregiving.com
http://www.caregiving.com
Disability Served: various
This organization provides support to caregivers via support groups, publications, and other resources.

CaringToday.com
151 Fairchild Avenue, Suite 2
Plainview, NY 11803-9828
800-480-4851
http://www.caringtoday.com
Disability Served: various
CaringToday.com, an online version of *Caring Today Magazine,* offers advice and support to caregivers.

Children of Aging Parents
PO Box 167
Richboro, PA 18954
800-227-7294
info@caps4caregivers.org
http://www.caps4caregivers.org
Disability Served: elderly
This organization provides information and support to caregivers of the elderly.

ElderCare Online
c/o Prism Innovations, Inc.
50 Amuxen Court
Islip, NY 11751
http://www.ec-online.net/index.htm
Disability Served: elderly

This online resource for caregivers of the elderly provides useful articles, publications, and support groups.

Exceptional Parent Magazine
877-372-7368
EPAR@kable.com
http://www.eparent.com
Disability Served: various
This magazine has provided support, ideas, and outreach to parents of disabled children for more than 30 years.

Family Resource Center on Disabilities
20 East Jackson Boulevard, Room 300
Chicago, IL 60604
312-939-3513, 312-939-3519 (TDD)
http://www.frcd.org
Disability Served: various
This is an organization of parents, professionals, and volunteers who seek to improve services for children with disabilities.

The Fathers Network
c/o Washington State Fathers Network
16120 Northeast Eighth Street
Bellevue, WA 98008
425-747-4004, ext. 4286
cmorris@fathersnetwork.org
http://www.fathersnetwork.org
Disability Served: various
The network provides support to fathers of children with special health care needs and developmental disabilities. Its Web site lists local fathers' support organizations throughout the United States.

Federation of Families for Childrens' Mental Health
1101 King Street, Suite 420
Alexandria, VA 22314
703-684-7710
ffcmh@ffcmh.org
http://www.ffcmh.org
Disability Served: mental health
This organization provides support and resources to parents of children with mental health disabilities.

Mothers United for Moral Support National Parent to Parent Network
150 Custer Court
Green Bay, WI 54301-1243
877-336-5333
mums@netnet.net
http://www.netnet.net/mums
Disability Served: various
This organization provides information and support to parents or care providers of children with disabilities.

National Alliance for Caregiving
4720 Montgomery Lane, 5th Floor
Bethesda, MD 20814
info@caregiving.org
http://www.caregiving.org
Disability Served: various
The alliance is a nonprofit coalition of 40 national organizations that focus on issues of caregiving.

National Association for Parents of the Visually Impaired Inc.
PO Box 317
Watertown, MA 02272-0317
617-972-7441, 800-562-6265
napvi@perkins.org
http://www.napvi.org
Disability Served: vision
This organization helps parents find information and resources for their blind and visually impaired children.

National Family Caregivers Association
10400 Connecticut Avenue, Suite 500
Kensington, MD 20895-3944
301-942-6430, 800-896-3650
info@thefamilycaregiver.org
http://thefamilycaregiver.org
Disability Served: various
This is an advocacy organization for family caregivers.

National Respite Locator Service
800 Eastowne Drive, Suite 105
Chapel Hill, NC 27514
919-490-5577
http://www.archrespite.org/index.htm
Disability Served: various
This Web site provides links to respite care services for caregivers.

Parents Helping Parents
3041 Olcott Street
Santa Clara, CA 95054-3222
408-727-5775
info@php.com
http://www.php.com
Disability Served: various
This organization provides information and referral, support programs, peer counseling, siblings programs, and networking programs to families of children with disabilities or illness.

Parents of Children with Down Syndrome
c/o The Arc of Montgomery County
PO Box 10416
Rockville, MD 20849
301-916-4985
information@podsmc.org
http://www.podsmc.org
Disability Served: Down Syndrome
This organization is a support group of parents who have children with Down Syndrome.

Parent to Parent-USA
http://www.p2pusa.org
Disability Served: various
This is an alliance of statewide Parent to Parent programs. These programs provide support to parents of disabled children in the form of an experienced parent who dispenses advice and information on caring for children with disabilities.

Sharethecaregiving Inc.
http://www.sharethecare.org
Disability Served: various
This organization educates the public, health professionals, and clergy about how to organize groups of caregivers for the sick or disabled.

The Sibling Support Project
c/o Arc of the United States
6512 23rd Avenue, NW, #213
Seattle, WA 98117
206-297-6368
donmeyer@siblingsupport.org
http://www.thearc.org/siblingsupport
Disability Served: developmentally disabled, mental retardation

The Sibling Support Project provides support to the six million brothers and sisters of people with special health, mental health, and developmental needs.

Special Needs Advocate for Parents
11835 West Olympic Boulevard, #465
Los Angeles, CA 90064
888-310-9889
info@snapinfo.org
http://www.snapinfo.org/home.html
Disability Served: developmentally disabled, mental retardation
This organization for parents of children with special needs provides educational seminars on special needs estate planning, referrals, and networking opportunities. It also offers information on medical insurance.

EDUCATIONAL AND
VOCATIONAL ASSISTANCE

COLLEGE DISABILITY SERVICES OFFICES

Disability services offices ensure that students with disabilities receive equal access to education in accordance with statutes in Section 504 of the Rehabilitation Act of 1973 and Title II of the Americans with Disabilities Act of 1990. In addition to ensuring that classrooms and other facilities are accessible to the disabled, these offices provide counseling, advocacy, adaptive and assistive technology, auxiliary aids, academic and testing accommodations, and assessment and testing. Although some offices provide financial assistance in the form of scholarships, grants, and loans, these services are more commonly provided by an institution's financial aid or admissions office. See the Educational Funding Resources section for more information on college financial aid .

Disabled students who are seeking more information on preparing for college should read Students with Disabilities Preparing for Postsecondary Education: Know Your Rights and Responsibilities, *a useful resource published by the U.S. Department of Education's Office for Civil Rights. The brochure can be read online at http://www.ed.gov/about/offices/list/ocr/transition.html.*

Agnes Scott College
Disability Services
141 East College Avenue, Buttrick 104B
Decatur, GA 30030
800-868-8602
http://www.agnesscott.edu/academics/p_disability.asp
Disability Served: various
Available Accommodations/Facilities/Services: accessible facilities; counseling and advocacy; assistive technology; tape recording of lectures; scribes; distraction-free environments; and extra time provided for quizzes, tests, or exams.

Alabama, University of
Office of Disability Services
PO Box 870185
Tuscaloosa, AL 35487-0185
205-348-4285
ods@bama.ua.edu
http://ods.ua.edu
Disability Served: various
Available Accommodations/Facilities/Services: counseling and advocacy; adaptive technology laboratories (featuring screen readers, magnifiers, voice synthesizers, and voice-to-text and text-to-voice software); accessible facilities and parking; and more.

Alaska-Fairbanks, University of
Center for Health and Counseling
PO Box 755580
Fairbanks, AK 99775
907-474-7043
fyheaco@uaf.edu
http://www.uaf.edu/chc/disability.html
Disability Served: various
Available Accommodations/Facilities/Services: disability shuttles; note takers, readers, audio-taped texts; test proctoring and other alternative testing arrangements; sign language interpreters; and an assistive technology laboratory (which offers an Optelec color video magnification system, an Arkenstone Ruby Open Book reading program, a Dragon Naturally Speaking program, and a Duxbury Braille Translator program).

Alberta, University of
Specialized Support and Disability Services
2 - 800 Students' Union Building
Edmonton, AB T6G 2J7
Canada
780-492-3381, 780-492-7269 (TTY)
sadvisor@ualberta.ca
http://www.uofaweb.ualberta.ca/SSDS/ssdsmain.cfm
Disability Served: various
Available Accommodations/Facilities/Services: accessible facilities; adaptive technology and assistive devices (e.g., Braille devices and software, ergonomic supports, computer laboratories, assistive listening devices, screen magnification devices and software, voice input software, voice output devices and software, note taking devices, and wheelchairs and scooters); advocacy; alternate formats for print materials (including Braille, large-print, and voice output formats); counseling; exam accommodations; interpreting services; library research assistance; new student orientation; note taking services; parking accommodations; psycho-educational assessments; real-time transcribing (captioning) services; referrals; and tutoring. The university also offers a program for students with learning disabilities.

Alfred University
Services for Students with Disabilities
Special Academic Services, Crandall Hall
Alfred, NY 14802

607-871-2148
sas@alfred.edu
Disability Served: various
Available Accommodations/Facilities/Services: support services, consultation, advocacy, accessible facilities, academic and testing accommodations, and more.

American University
Disability Support Services
4400 Massachusetts Avenue, NW
206 Mary Graydon Center
Washington, DC 20016-8001
202-885-3315
dss@american.edu
http://www.american.edu/ocl/dss
Disability Served: various
Available Accommodations/Facilities/Services: disabled access to classrooms and events; reader services in the form of recorded material; transcription services (such as Braille and large-print materials); counseling; note takers and scribe services during class or test-taking situations; sign language and oral interpreters; assistive listening devices; access to adaptive technology and auxiliary aids; and proctor services and testing accommodations.

Aquinas College
Student Achievement Services
1607 Robinson Road, SE
Grand Rapids, MI 49506
616-632-2163
tylermon@aquinas.edu
http://www.aquinas.edu/sss/index.html
Disability Served: various
Available Accommodations/Facilities/Services: advocacy and counseling, readers, scribes, tutors, note takers, taped lectures, books on tape, accessible facilities, and more.

Arizona, University of
Disability Resource Center
1224 East Lowell Street
Tucson, AZ 85721
520-621-3268 (Voice/TTY)
uadrc@email.arizona.edu
http://drc.arizona.edu
Disability Served: various
Available Accommodations/Facilities/Services: assistive technology (such as alternative mice, alternative keyboards, and Braille translation software), and an assistive technology computer facility.

Arizona State University
Disability Resource Center
PO Box 873202
Tempe, AZ 85287-3202
480-965-1234, 480-965-9000 (TDD)
Disability-Q@asu.edu
http://www.west.asu.edu/drc
Disability Served: various
Available Accommodations/Facilities/Services: adaptive technology (four-track tape recorders/players, adjustable height tables, and closed-circuit televisions); academic and test accommodation (scribes, note takers, alternative print); text conversion services; American Sign Language and oral interpreting, equipment checkout (manual wheelchairs, assistive listening devices, note taking keyboards, spelling aids and talking calculators, and TDDs); and library assistance.

Arkansas-Fayetteville, University of
Center for Students with Disabilities
ARKU 104
Fayetteville, AR 72701
479-575-3104
ada@uark.edu
http://www.uark.edu/ua/csd
Disability Served: various
Available Accommodations/Facilities/Services: scribes, note takers, test accommodations, personal listening systems, disability-accessible facilities, adapted computer technology, document conversion services, and more.

Arkansas State University
Office of Disability Services
PO Box 360
State University, AR 72467
870-972-3964
jrmason@astate.edu
http://disability.astate.edu
Disability Served: various
Available Accommodations/Facilities/Services: priority orientation and registration; note taking services; test administration with accommodations; reader services; physical adaptations, guidance and counseling; adaptive physical education courses; and interpreter services.

Auburn University
Program for Students with Disabilities
1244 Haley Center

Auburn, AL 36849-5250
334-844-2096 (Voice/TDD)
http://www.auburn.edu/academic/disabilities
Disability Served: various
*Available Accommodations/Facilities/Services: priority
    registration; accessible facilities; an assistive technology
    laboratory (with Braille printers and displays, and voice
    recognition, speech output, and screen enhancement
    software); alternate format services; loans of assistive
    devices; note takers; interpreters; and disabled parking
    and accessible transportation.*

Barnard College

Office of Disability Services
3009 Broadway, 105 Hewitt
New York, NY 10027
212-854-4634 (Voice/TTY)
ods@barnard.edu
http://www.barnard.edu/ods
Disability Served: various
Available Accommodations/Facilities/Services:
    *advocacy and counseling; readers; note takers; tutors;
    disability-related classroom and test accommodations;
    wheelchairs; tape recorders; large-print/taped books;
    accessible facilities; and disability-related workshops
    and seminars. The College also hosts the Annual
    Women and Disability Film Festival and offers a
    variety of useful publications, including the* ODS
    Accommodative Aide Directory, A Parent Guide to
    Disability Services, Survival Tools for LD Students,
    and What We've Learned: Thoughts on Disability from
    Graduating Seniors to Entering Students at Barnard.

Baylor University

Office of Access and Learning Accommodation
One Bear Place, #97204
Waco, TX 76798-7204
254-710-3605
Sheila_Graham@baylor.edu
http://www.baylor.edu/oala
Disability Served: various
*Available Accommodations/Facilities/Services: advocacy
    and counseling, accessible facilities, academic and
    testing accommodations, disabled parking, and more.*

Boston College

Disability Services Office
Office of the Dean for Student Development
140 Commonwealth Avenue, Campanella Way, Suite 212
Chestnut Hill, MA 02467

617-552-3470, 617-552-2548 (TTY)
conwaymh@bc.edu
http://www.bc.edu/offices/odsd/services/
    disabilityservices
Disability Served: various
*Available Accommodations/Facilities/Services: advocacy
    and counseling, accessible facilities, academic and
    testing accommodations, and more. The College's
    Connors Family Learning Center provides academic
    support and accommodations to students with learning
    disabilities and attention deficit/ hyperactivity disorder.*

Boston University

Office of Disability Services
19 Deerfield Street
Boston, MA 02215
617-353-3658
access@bu.edu
http://www.bu.edu/disability
Disability Served: various
*Available Accommodations/Facilities/Services: academic
    accommodations, auxiliary aids and services, accessible
    university housing, special dietary accommodations,
    career development and personal counseling, academic
    support, and more.*

Brandeis University

Disabilities Support and Services
PO Box 9110
Waltham, MA 02454-9110
781-736-3470
brodgers@brandeis.edu
http://www.brandeis.edu/uaafys/acacom/prospective-
    new.html
Disability Served: various
*Available Accommodations/Facilities/Services: accessible
    facilities; counseling and advocacy; and academic and
    testing accommodations (e.g., note takers, books on
    tape, and adaptive technology).*

Brigham Young University

University Accessibility Center
1520 WSC
Provo, UT 84602
801-422-2767
uac@byu.edu
http://campuslife.byu.edu/uac
Disability Served: various
*Available Accommodations/Facilities/Services: accessible
    facilities; academic accommodations (including priority*

registration, accommodation letters, and tutoring); textbooks on tape; interpreters; note takers; and assistive hardware and software.

British Columbia, University of
Disability Resource Centre
Brock Hall, 1203-1874 East Mall
Vancouver, BC V6T 1Z1
Canada
604-822-5844, 604-822-9049 (TTY)
disability.resource@ubc.ca
http://students.ubc.ca/access/drc.cfm
Disability Served: various
Available Accommodations/Facilities/Services:
interpreting and captioning services, mobility assistance, tutoring, accommodated examinations, accessible facilities, counseling and advocacy, and more.

Calhoun Community College
Disability Services
PO Box 2216
Decatur, AL 35609-2216
256-306-2635
iwh@calhoun.edu
http://www.calhoun.edu/Student_Affairs/disabilities.html
Disability Served: various
Available Accommodations/Facilities/Services:
vocational education counseling (including personal counseling, financial aid counseling, academic advising, career planning, and tutorial assistance); a book loan library; and accessibility accommodations.

California-Los Angeles, University of
Office for Students with Disabilities
PO Box 951426
Los Angeles, CA 90095-1435
310-825-2651
kmolini@saonet.ucla.edu
http://www.saonet.ucla.edu/osd
Disability Served: various
Available Accommodations/Facilities/Services: priority enrollment; campus orientation; note taking and transcription services; test-taking accommodations; alternative formats (such as Braille, large-print, or speech-synthesized reading programs); interpreting/captioning services; mobility assistance; disability parking; adaptive equipment; accessible facilities; and advocacy and counseling.

California-Santa Cruz, University of
Disability Resource Center
1156 High Street, 146 Hahn Student Services
Santa Cruz, CA 95064
831-459-2089
drc@ucsc.edu
http://www2.ucsc.edu/drc
Disability Served: various
Available Accommodations/Facilities/Services: advocacy and counseling, accessible facilities, academic and testing accommodations, and more.

California State University-Bakersfield
Services for Students with Disabilities
9001 Stockdale Highway, 55SA
Bakersfield, CA 93311-1099
661-664-3360
jclausen@csub.edu
http://www.csubak.edu/UnivServices/SSD
Disability Served: various
Available Accommodations/Facilities/Services:
assistance with registration; priority registration; counseling and advising not duplicated by regular counseling and advising services; learning disability assessment, review and support services; American Sign Language interpreters, readers, scribes, note takers, and test proctors; adaptive equipment (including assistive technology, Braille printers, Kurzweil reading machines, CCTV large-text displays, assistive listening devices, and books on tape); testing accommodations (including extended time, adaptive equipment, readers, scribes, and individually proctored examinations); and assistance with classroom and campus accessibility.

California State University-Fresno
Services for Student with Disabilities
Henry Madden Library
5200 North Barton Avenue, Room 1049
Fresno, CA 93740
559-278-2811
siteadmin_ssd@csufresno.edu
http://studentaffairs.csufresno.edu/SSD
Disability Served: various
Available Accommodations/Facilities/Services:
adaptive technology (such as screen and text readers, assistive listening devices, and voice recognition software); an adaptive computer laboratory; testing accommodations (including readers and scribes, large-print exams, and sign language interpreters);

note taking services, interpreting and related services; transportation services; and priority registration.

California State University-Fullerton
Office of Disabled Student Services
PO Box 6830
Fullerton, CA 92834-6804
714-278-3117
dsservices@fullerton.edu
http://www.fullerton.edu/disabledservices
Disability Served: various
Available Accommodations/Facilities/Services:
counseling and advising; interpreter services (including manual, steno, and oral interpreting for hearing-impaired students); reader services; test-taking facilitation; transcription services (such as providing Braille and large-print materials); note taker services; access to adaptive educational equipment and technology; priority registration; disabled parking; and a computer access laboratory.

Calvin College
Student Academic Services
Hiemenga Hall, 1855 Knollcrest Circle, SE, #446
Grand Rapids, MI 49546
616-526-6113
kbroeskt@calvin.edu
http://www.calvin.edu/academic/sas
Disability Served: various
Available Accommodations/Facilities/Services:
auxiliary aids (such as books on tape, note takers, and interpreters); special advising/early registration; tutoring services; diagnostic screening; alternative testing arrangements; counseling and vocational assistance and referral; assistance in housing assignment modifications; and accessible campus facilities.

Canyons, College of the
Disabled Students Programs and Services
26455 Rockwell Canyon Road, #C-103
Santa Clarita, CA 91355
661-362-3341
info@mail.coc.cc.ca.us
http://www.canyons.edu/offices/dsps
Disability Served: various
Available Accommodations/Facilities/Services: accessible
facilities; adapted furniture; alternate media (such as Braille, books on tape, e-text, large-print, and tactile graphics); assistive technology; counseling; extended

time for tests; preferential seating; priority registration; sign language interpreters; tape-recorded lectures; and more.

Carleton University
Paul Menton Centre for Persons with Disabilities
1125 Colonel By Drive, 500 University Centre
Ottawa, ON K1S 5B6
Canada
613-520-6608, 613-520-3937 (TTY)
pmc@carleton.ca
http://www.carleton.ca/pmc
Disability Served: various
Available Accommodations/Facilities/Services: accessible
facilities; counseling; scribes; note-takers; tutors; sign language interpreters; academic accommodations; specialized equipment loans (e.g., variable speed and four-track tape recorders, telephone devices for the deaf, adaptive listening systems, and laptop computers); and learning disability assessments.

Carnegie Mellon University
Accessibility and Accommodation
Whitfield Hall, 143 North Craig Street
Pittsburgh, PA 15213
412-268-2013
lpowell@andrew.cmu.edu
http://hr.web.cmu.edu/prospective/eos/accessibility
Disability Served: various
Available Accommodations/Facilities/Services:
interpreters; note-takers; extended time for class assignments and exams; alternative testing arrangements; books on tape; large-print books, exams, and materials; voice recognition software; use of tape recorders, dictionaries, and calculators; advocacy and counseling; disabled parking; and accessible facilities.

Central Arkansas, University of
Disability Support Services
PO Box 5145
Conway, AR 72035
501-450-3135
crystalh@mail.uca.edu
http://www.uca.edu/divisions/student/disability
Disability Served: various
Available Accommodations/Facilities/Services: academic
accommodations and counseling; priority registration and scheduling; alternative testing, auxiliary aids and services; note takers; readers and/or scribes; sign

language/oral interpreters; assistive listening devices; assistive technology; alternative formats for printed materials; and accessible residential accommodations.

Central Michigan University
Student Disability Services
Park Library 120
Mt Pleasant, MI 48859
989-774-3018
sds@cmich.edu
http://www.cmich.edu/student-disability
Disability Served: various
Available Accommodations/Facilities/Services: an adaptive technology room, adaptive computers, tape-recorded texts, note takers, extended time for tests, enlarged print tests, on-campus transportation, readers, scribes, and interpreters.

Central Piedmont Community College
Services for Students with disAbilities
PO Box 35009
Charlotte, NC 28204-2240
704-330-6556
http://www.cpcc.cc.nc.us/disabilities
Disability Served: various
Available Accommodations/Facilities/Services: disabled parking, counseling services, interpreting services, assistive listening devices, reader/note taker services, tutorial services, and testing services.

Central Washington University
Disability Support Services
400 East University Way
Ellensburg, WA 98926-7495
509-963-2171
campbelr@cwu.edu
http://www.cwu.edu/~dss
Disability Served: various
Available Accommodations/Facilities/Services: inter-preters and transcribers for deaf and hard of hearing students; academic and testing accommodations; counseling; accessible facilities; and advocacy.

Cerritos College
Disabled Student Programs and Services
11110 Alondra Boulevard
Norwalk, CA 90650
562-860-2451
dsps-info@cerritos.edu
http://www.cerritos.edu/dsps

Disability Served: various
Available Accommodations/Facilities/Services: advocacy; academic and personal counseling; mobility assistance; note taking assistance; disabled parking; reader services; registration assistance; tutoring services; typing assistance; wheelchair loans; assistive software; and captioning services.

Chicago, University of
Disabilities Services
5801 South Ellis, Room 219
Chicago, IL 60637
773-702-7770
http://dos.uchicago.edu/disab_index.shtml
Disability Served: various
Available Accommodations/Facilities/Services: sign language interpreting, note taking services, advocacy and counseling, accessible facilities, academic and testing accommodations, disabled parking, and more.

Cincinnati, University of
Disability Services Office
University Pavilion, Suite 210, PO Box 210213
Cincinnati, OH 45221-0125
513-556-6823
disabisv@ucmail.uc.edu
http://www.uc.edu/sas/disability
Disability Served: various
Available Accommodations/Facilities/Services: note-takers; readers; sign language interpreters; open and closed captioning of classroom videos; communication access real-time translation services; books on tape; scribes; real-time captioning of lectures; time extensions for tests; individual testing rooms; and proofreaders.

Clemson University
Disability Services
R. M. Cooper Library, Academic Success Center, 3rd Level
Clemson, SC 29634-5126
864-656-6848 (Voice/TTY)
asc@clemson.edu
http://www.clemson.edu/asc/sds_student_guide.html
Disability Served: various
Available Accommodations/Facilities/Services: priority registration; assistive technology (e.g., closed-circuit TVs, speech recognition software, assistive listening devices, computer-assisted note-taking, and real-time captioning); auxiliary aids and services (e.g., note-takers, readers, and transcribers); document conversion (e.g., Braille, tape, large-print, and electronic format);

alternative test formats; interpreters; tutors; testing for learning disabilities and ADHD/ADD; accessible facilities; and disabled parking.

Colorado-Boulder, University of
Disability Services
Willard Administrative Center 322
Boulder, CO 80309-0107
303-492-8671
DSInfo@colorado.edu
http://www.colorado.edu/disabilityservices
Disability Served: various
Available Accommodations/Facilities/Services:
examination and classroom accommodations; auxiliary aids; disability parking; interpreting services; note taking services; and an assistive technology laboratory with speech controlled computers, screen readers and screen enlargement technology, alternate and ergonomic keyboards, adaptive and ergonomic pointing devices, scanning and optical character recognition systems with voice output for access to hard-copy items, closed-circuit TV for enlarging hard copy material, ergonomic furniture and workstation accessories, and Braille printers.

Columbia State Community College
Counseling and Disability Services
PO Box 1315
Columbia, TN 38402-1315
931-540-2572, 800-848-0298 (TDD)
petty@columbiastate.edu
http://www.columbiastate.edu/studentsvcs/disability.htm
Disability Served: various
Available Accommodations/Facilities/Services:
vocational and career counseling, academic planning and registration support, technology services, tutors, note takers, and reader services.

Columbia University
Office of Disability Services
Lerner Hall, Suite 802
New York, NY 10027
212-854-2388, 212-854-2378 (TDD)
http://www.health.columbia.edu/ods
Disability Served: various
Available Accommodations/Facilities/Services: academic and testing accommodations (including extended time, reader services, note takers, tutors, interpreters, books on tape, and use of computers and tape recorders

during exams); accessibility tours; adaptive equipment loan services (e.g., tape recorders, manual wheelchair, and TDDs); advocacy and counseling; and accessible facilities. The university also sponsors the Students with Disabilities Coalition for graduate and undergraduate students.

Concordia University
Office for Students with Disabilities
Hall Building, 1455 de Maisonneuve Boulevard West, Room 580
Montreal, QB H3G 1M8
Canada
514-848-2424, ext. 3525 (Voice/TTY)
http://supportservices.concordia.ca/disabilities
Disability Served: various
Available Accommodations/Facilities/Services:
alternative media transcription (e.g., large-print, Braille transcription, audio cassette, and computer disk); readers; note takers; transcribers; tutors; oral and sign language interpreters; exam accommodations; wireless handsets; equipment loans; screening and referral for learning disability assessment; accessible facilities; and counseling and advocacy.

Connecticut-Storrs, University of
Center for Students with Disabilities
233 Glenbrook Road
Storrs, CT 06269-4116
860-486-2020, 860-486-2077 (TDD)
jennifer.lucia@uconn.edu
http://www.csd.uconn.edu
Disability Served: various
Available Accommodations/Facilities/Services: academic accommodations and counseling; priority registration and scheduling; alternative testing services; taped texts; auxiliary aids and services; note takers; laboratory assistants, readers and/or scribes; sign language/oral interpreters and captioning services; assistive listening devices; assistive technology; alternative formats for printed material; residential accommodations and counseling; transportation services; and disability parking.

Curry College
Disability Services
1071 Blue Hill Avenue
Milton, MA 02186
617-333-2120 (Voice/TYY)
info@curry.edu

http://www.curry.edu/Student+Life/Student+Services/
  Disability+Services.htm
Disability Served: various
Available Accommodations/Facilities/Services: vocational
  and career counseling, tutors, note takers, reader services,
  and academic planning and registration support.

Cuyamaca College
Disabled Student Program and Services
900 Rancho San Diego Parkway
El Cajon, CA 92019
619-660-4205, 619-660-4386 (TTD)
yvonettepowell@qcccd.net
http://www.cuyamaca.edu/EOPS/DSPS.asp
Disability Served: various
Available Accommodations/Facilities/Services:
  enrollment and registration assistance, counseling
  services, speech-language services, mobility orientation,
  tutors, note takers, sign language interpreters, test
  proctoring/facilitation, and disabled parking.

Davis and Elkins College
Supported Learning Program
100 Campus Drive
Elkins, WV 26241
304-637-1900, 800-624-3157
sneedd@devisandelkins.edu
http://www.davisandelkins.edu/studentlife/
  supportedlearning.htm
Disability Served: attention deficit disorder, dyslexic,
  learning disabled
Available Accommodations/Facilities/Services: a support
  program for students with learning disabilities.

Daytona Beach Community College
Student Disability Services Office
1200 West International Speedway Boulevard
Daytona Beach, FL 32114
386-255-8131, ext. 3807, 386-254-3043 (TDD)
http://dbcc.cc.fl.us/html/departments/sds
Disability Served: various
Available Accommodations/Facilities/Services: note
  takers, readers, taped materials, sign language
  interpreters, scribes, private testing rooms, an adaptive
  computer laboratory, documents in alternative format,
  priority registration, SNAPS (a student organization for
  students with disabilities), tutoring services, campus
  mobility assistance, computers with voice output,
  closed circuit TVs, portable CCTVs, magnification
  software, talking scientific calculators, talking four-

function calculators, TDDs, phonic ear assistive listening
  devices, Braille embossers, four-track tape players, tape
  recorders, scooters, luggage carts, on-screen keyboards,
  and adaptive mice.

De Anza College
SPED-Disabled Students Programs and Services
21250 Stevens Creek Boulevard, ATC 209
Cupertino, CA 95014
408-864-8407
http://www.deanza.fhda.edu/specialed
Disability Served: various
Available Accommodations/Facilities/Services: a
  computer access laboratory (featuring assistive
  technology, assistive computer technology instruction,
  assistive computer technology support, Web content
  accessibility support, and alternate media production);
  counseling and advisement; interpreting and captioning
  services; note taking services; reader/tutor referral;
  disabled parking; materials in alternative media; Braille
  printing stations; test accommodations; transition
  planning services; and educational diagnostic services.

Delaware-Newark, University of
Services for Students With Disabilities
413 Academy Street, Room 165
Newark, DE 19716
302-831-3679, 302-831-4563 (TDD)
http://www.udel.edu/main/cur-students/currdisab.html
Disability Served: various
Available Accommodations/Facilities/Services: academic
  accommodations, career planning services, accessible
  facilities, an assistive technology center, and more.

Drexel University
Office of Disability Services
3141 Chestnut Street
Philadelphia, PA 19104
215-895-2506
http://www.drexel.edu/edt/disability
Disability Served: various
Available Accommodations/Facilities/Services: advocacy
  and counseling, recorded textbooks, tape recorders,
  spellers, interpreters, readers, note-takers, specialized
  computer equipment and software, accessible facilities,
  and more.

Duke University
Student Disability Access Office
402 Oregon Street, Suite 102

Durham, NC 27708
919-668-1267, 919-668-1329 (TTY)
eswain@duke.edu
http://www.access.duke.edu/studentIssues.asp
Disability Served: *various*
Available Accommodations/Facilities/Services: *assistive technology (e.g., voice-recognition software, scanners, note taking devices, assisted living devices, reading software, closed-circuit TVs, and portable listening systems); advocacy; counseling; accessible facilities; campus accessibility maps; and more.*

DuPage, College of
Special Student Services
425 Fawell Boulevard, Berg Instructional Center, Rooms 2123/2125
Glen Ellyn, IL 60137
630-942-2306, 630-858-9692 (TTY)
Ricketts@cdnet.cod.edu
http://www.cod.edu/service1/Health/special_student_services.htm
Disability Served: *various*
Available Accommodations/Facilities/Services: *sign language interpreters, note takers, academic accommodations, large-print/Braille formats for course materials, testing accommodations, mobility assistance, preferential seating, assistive technology, books on audiotape, barrier-free parking, and TTYs.*

Eastern Kentucky University
Office of Services for Individuals with Disabilities
361 Student Service Building
Richmond, KY 40475
859-622-1500 (Voice/TDD)
Teresa.Belluscio@eku.edu
http://www.disabled.eku.edu
Disability Served: *various*
Available Accommodations/Facilities/Services: *disabled parking permits, sign language interpreters, assistive listening devices, note taking services, specialized tutoring, books on tape, and accessible housing and other facilities.*

East Los Angeles College
Disabled Student Program and Services
1301 Avenida Cesar Chavez
Monterey Park, CA 91754
323-265-8650
http://www.elac.edu/departments/dsps/index.html
Disability Served: *various*

Available Accommodations/Facilities/Services: *specialized advisement and registration assistance, academic accommodations, adapted computer-assisted instruction, and campus transportation (via electric carts).*

Edinboro University of Pennsylvania
Office for Students with Disabilities
Shafer Hall
Edinboro, PA 16444
814-732-2462 (Voice/TDD)
McConnell@edinboro.edu
http://www.edinboro.edu/cwis/tac/dis_serv/ds_start.htm
Disability Served: *various*
Available Accommodations/Facilities/Services: *academic aides, alternative testing, wheelchair repair services, occupational therapy services, an assistive technology center, a computer laboratory, transportation services, and tactile and Braille services.*

Edmonds Community College
Services for Students with Disabilities
Woodway Hall, 20000 68th Avenue West, Room 114
Lynnwood, WA 98036
425-640-1320, 425-774-8669 (TTY)
ssdmail@edcc.edu
http://www.edcc.edu/ssd
Disability Served: *various*
Available Accommodations/Facilities/Services: *academic advising, campus orientation, one-on-one tutoring, interpreters for the deaf, test scribes, readers, priority registration, taped books, large-print materials, and Braille services.*

El Camino College
Special Resource Center
16007 Crenshaw Boulevard
Torrance, CA 90506
310-660-3295, 310-660-3445 (TDD)
http://www.elcamino.edu/src/table.html
Disability Served: *various*
Available Accommodations/Facilities/Services: *Braille transcription services; testing assistance; counseling; disabled parking permits; registration assistance; wheelchair loans; textbook recording services; readers; instructional aides; real-time captioning; wheelchairs; a Braille library; and assistive technology (including cassette tape recorders, reading machines, large-print typewriters, Braille embossers, large-print copiers, talking calculators, illuminated magnifiers, and videotape recorders).*

Faulkner State Community College
Student Support Services
McGowan Hall, 1900 US Highway 31 South
Bay Minette, AL 36507
251-580-2106
http://www.faulknerstate.edu/fa/faother/other/view?sea
    rchterm=student%20support%20services
Disability Served: various
Available Accommodations/Facilities/Services: individual
    tutoring; individual and group counseling; advocacy;
    accessible facilities; and more.

Florida, University of
Disability Resources Program
Peabody Hall, P202
Gainesville, FL 32611-4025
352-392-1261, 352-392-3008 (TDD)
accessuf@dso.ufl.edu
http://www.dso.ufl.edu/drp
Disability Served: various
Available Accommodations/Facilities/Services: accessible
    facilities, taped textbook recordings, note takers,
    interpreter services, educational assistants, scribes,
    readers, assistive technology, and more.

Florida International University
Disability Resource Center
University Park Campus, GC 190
Miami, FL 33199
305-348-3532, 305-348-3852 (TTY)
garciaj@fiu.edu
http://www.fiu.edu/~disser
Disability Served: various
Available Accommodations/Facilities/Services: academic
    and testing accommodations, accessible facilities,
    speech recognition software, screen-reading software,
    note takers, and more.

Florida State University
Student Disability Resource Center
108 Student Services Building, 97 Woodward Avenue
    South
Tallahassee, FL 32306-2430
850-644-9566, 850-644-8504 (TDD)
sdrc@admin.fsu.edu
http://www.fsu.edu/~staffair/dean/StudentDisability
Disability Served: various
Available Accommodations/Facilities/Services: test and
    classroom accommodations, accessible housing, a
    mentorship program, disabled parking permits, and more.

Fordham University
Disability Services
Lincoln Center Campus
New York, NY 10023
212-636-6282
disabilityservices@fordham.edu
http://www.fordham.edu/Student_Affairs/Student_
    Services/Disability_Services/index.html
Disability Served: various
Available Accommodations/Facilities/Services: sign
    language interpreters, assistive technology, specialized
    tutoring, accessible housing and facilities, advocacy,
    counseling, and more.

Friends University
Disability Services
2100 West University Street
Wichita, KS 67213
316-295-5779
ADA@friends.edu
http://www.friends.edu/CurrentStudents/
    StudentServices/ada.asp
Disability Served: various
Available Accommodations/Facilities/Services: advocacy
    and counseling, accessible facilities, academic and
    testing accommodations, disabled parking, and more.

Frostburg State University
Disability Support Services Office
150 Pullen Hall
Frostburg, MD 21532
301-687-4483 (Voice/TTY)
lpullen@frostburg.edu
http://www.frostburg.edu/clife/dss/frontpage.htm
Disability Served: various
Available Accommodations/Facilities/Services: test
    accommodation, books on tape and reader services,
    note taker services, sign language interpreters,
    advocacy and self-advocacy training, tutoring services,
    and academic advising.

Gallaudet University
Office for Students with Disabilities
800 Florida Avenue, NE, Student Academic Center, Room
    1220
Washington, DC 20002
202-651-5256 (Voice/TTY)
oswd@gallaudet.edu
http//depts.gallaudet.edu/oswd/index.htm
Disability Served: various

Available Accommodations/Facilities/Services: audiological and psychological evaluations; diagnostic/prescriptive services; interpreting; note taking; orientation and mobility services; Braille and large-print services; counseling; specialized materials and equipment (such as low-vision equipment/computers, Braille and large-print materials/maps, assistive listening devices, instructional television, and captioned media); a learning resource room; transportation; tutoring; and wheelchair repair.

Galveston College
Services for Students with Special Needs
4015 Avenue Q
Galveston, TX 77550
409-944-1227
Mclark@gc.edu
http://www.gc.edu/counsel/special.htm
Disability Served: various
Available Accommodations/Facilities/Services: test and classroom accommodations, career and vocational counseling, advocacy, accessible facilities, and more.

Gardner-Webb University
Noel Program for the Disabled
PO Box 7274
Boiling Springs, NC 28017
704-406-4270, 704-406-3991 (Voice/TTY)
http://www.noel.gardner-webb.edu/index.html
Disability Served: various
Available Accommodations/Facilities/Services: accessible computer laboratories, alternative testing, assisted science laboratories, textbooks in alternate format, career and counseling services, note taker services, interpreter services, orientation and mobility assistance, reader services, and hearing captionists (transcribers). The university's John R. Dover Memorial Library provides a resource room for the blind and visually impaired.

GateWay Community College
Disability Resources
108 North 40th Street
Phoenix, AZ 85034
602-286-8888, 602-286-8171 (TDD)
bluestein@gwmail.maricopa.edu
http://students.gatewaycc.edu/resources/
    disabilityresources
Disability Served: various
Available Accommodations/Facilities/Services:
    interpreters for the deaf, note takers, advisement, test reading, and adaptive equipment.

Georgetown University
Academic Resource Center
Leavey Center, Third Floor
Washington, DC 20057
202-687-8354
http://ldss.georgetown.edu
Disability Served: various
Available Accommodations/Facilities/Services: academic advising, audiovisual aids, enlarged texts, extended time for testing, note takers, interpreters, readers, books on tape, telecommunication devices, accessible facilities, orientation for new students, lift-equipped transportation, and campus maps with accessibility routes for wheelchair users.

George Washington University
Disability Support Services
800 21st Street, NW, Marvin Center, Suite 242
Washington, DC 20052
202-994-8250 (Voice/TDD)
dss@gwu.edu
http://gwired.gwu.edu/dss
Disability Served: various
Available Accommodations/Facilities/Services: assistive technology; sign language and oral interpreting services; laboratory assistance; learning disability screening; note taking assistance; priority registration; reading services; test accommodations (including extended time, readers, scribes, and/or use of adaptive equipment); and writing services.

Georgia, University of
Disability Resource Center
114 Clark Howell Hall
Athens, GA 30602-3338
706-542-8719, 706-542-8778 (TTY)
voda@uga.edu
http://www.drc.uga.edu
Disability Served: various
Available Accommodations/Facilities/Services:
    accessible facilities; disabled parking; priority registration; academic assistants; alternative text services (e.g., large-print, Braille, digital format, and audiotape); assistive listening systems; note takers; real-time captioning and note taking; sign language interpreters; telecommunication devices for the deaf; test accommodation (e.g., extended testing time, scribe services, low distraction testing environment, Braille test conversion, and the use of assistive technology); video closed captioning; and an assistive technology lab.

Georgia Institute of Technology
ADAPTS Office
Smithgall Student Services Building, 353 Ferst Drive,
    Suite 210
Atlanta, GA 30332-0460
404-894-2564, 404-894-1664 (TDD)
adapts@vpsa-mail.gatech.edu
http://www.adapts.gatech.edu
Disability Served: various
Available Accommodations/Facilities/Services: priority
    registration and assistance; counseling; advocacy; test
    accommodations and proctoring; enlarged print or
    Braille resources; conversions of textbooks into cassette
    tape or electronic format; readers; tutors; note takers;
    sign language and oral interpreting services; a library
    retrieval service for students with physical disabilities;
    disabled parking; and adapted campus shuttle bus
    service.

Georgia Southwestern University
Disability Support Services
800 Wheatley Street
Americus, GA 31709
229-931-2661
http://www.gsw.edu/services/sss/ds.html
Disability Served: various
Available Accommodations/Facilities/Services: test
    accommodations; adaptive equipment; advocacy
    and advising; alternative media (e.g., audio textbooks,
    scanned test, enlarged print, and Braille note takers):
    diagnostic testing referrals; sign language interpreters;
    real-time captioning; readers; scribes; and books on tape.

Glendale Community College
Disability Services and Resources
600 West Olive Avenue, TDS 100
Glendale, AZ 85302
623-845-3080, 623-845-3086 (TTY)
http://gecko.gc.maricopa.edu/dsr
Disability Served: various
Available Accommodations/Facilities/Services: books-
    on-tape, interpreters, note-taking services, advocacy,
    academic accommodations, accessible facilities,
    counseling, and more.

Gonzaga University
Disability Resources, Education, and Access Management
502 East Boone Avenue, AD Box 19
Spokane, WA 99258-0019
509-323-4093

shearer@gonzaga.edu
 http://www.gonzaga.edu/Campus+Resources/
    Offices+and+Services+A-Z/Disability+Resources+Ed
    ucation+and+Access+Management/default.htm
Disability Served: various
Available Accommodations/Facilities/Services: advocacy;
    enrollment assistance (including help with registration
    and campus orientation); alternate media (such as
    Brailled materials, textbooks on tape, and large-print
    materials); alternative testing (e.g., distraction-reduced
    environments, extended time, and use of scribes,
    readers, and computers); classroom accommodations
    (e.g., sign language interpreters, note takers, and
    readers); adaptive technology (e.g., text-to-speech
    software, speech-to-text software, closed caption
    decoders, CCTVs, MP3 players, and screen magnifiers);
    and accessible facilities.

Grand Valley State University
Disability Support Services
1 Campus Drive, 200 STU
Allendale, MI 49401-9403
616-331-2490
http://www.gvsu.edu/dss
Disability Served: various
Available Accommodations/Facilities/Services: academic
    and career advising, tutoring, recorded textbooks
    or electronic texts, referrals for testing, note taking
    assistance, alternative testing accommodations,
    assistive software and hardware, peer mentoring, and
    counseling.

Grays Harbor College
Disability Support Services
1620 Edward P. Smith Drive
Aberdeen, WA 98520
360-538-4068, 360-538-4223 (TDD)
jrajcich@ghc.edu
http://ghc.ctc.edu/support/index.htm
Disability Served: various
Available Accommodations/Facilities/Services:
    counseling; adaptive equipment (such as tape recorders,
    reading computers, voice-assisted and other adapted
    computers, and adapted physical fitness equipment);
    disabled parking; transportation services; and
    accessible facilities.

Harding University
Student Support Services
PO Box 12235

Searcy, AR 72149-0001
501-279-4028
sss@harding.edu
http://www.harding.edu/sss/faq.html
Disability Served: various
Available Accommodations/Facilities/Services: test
accommodations, note-takers, taping of lectures,
textbooks on tape, accessible facilities, and counseling.

Harper College
Access and Disability Services
Building D, Room D119
Palatine, IL 60067-7398
847-925-6266, 847-397-7600 (TTY)
tthompso@harpercollege.edu
http://www.harpercollege.edu/services/ads/index.shtml
Disability Served: various
Available Accommodations/Facilities/Services:
priority registration; reduced course loads; test
accommodations; note taking assistance; readers
or scribes for exams; sign language interpreters;
specialized technology; counseling; accessible facilities;
and conversion of educational/support materials into
Braille, large-print, audio, or other formats.

Hartford, University of
Services for Students with Medical, Physical, and
Psychological Disability
200 Bloomfield Avenue, Gengras, #307
West Hartford, CT 06117-1599
860-768-5129
fitzgeral@hartford.edu
http://hartford.edu/support/desc.asp?id=9
Disability Served: various
Available Accommodations/Facilities/Services: academic
and career advising, tutoring, testing accommodations,
assistive software and hardware, and more.

Hawaii-Hilo, University of
University Disability Services Office
200 West Kawili Street, Hale Kauanoe A Wing Lounge
Hilo, HI 96720-4091
808-933-0816, 808-933-3334 (TTY)
shirachi@hawaii.edu
http://www.uhh.hawaii.edu/studentaffairs/uds
Disability Served: various
Available Accommodations/Facilities/Services: test
and academic accommodations; accessible facilities;
counseling; and assistive technology (e.g., screen
enlargement software, screen reader software,
speech recognition software, note taking devices,
voice-activated tape recorders, TTYs, talking desktop
calculators, and split-key design keyboards).

Hawkeye Community College
Student Disabilities
Hawkeye Center, PO Box 8015
Waterloo, IA 50704
319-296-4027
sudlife@hawkeyecollege.edu
http://www.hawkeye.cc.ia.us/currentstudents/
studentdisabilities.asp?
Disability Served: various
Available Accommodations/Facilities/Services:
orientation, academic support, testing
accommodations, books on tape, text-reading software
and other assistive technology, interpreters, note takers,
peer tutoring services, priority scheduling, accessible
facilities, and disabled parking.

Hofstra University
Program for the Higher Education of the Disabled
101 Memorial Hall
Hempstead, NY 11549
516-463-6972, 516-463-5108 (TTY)
advkjs@hofstra.edu
http://www.hofstra.edu/StudentServ/Advise/adv_phed.
cfm
Disability Served: various
Available Accommodations/Facilities/Services: assistance
with registration, interpreters, counseling, equipment
loans, books on tape, test administration, and referrals
to readers, writers, and attendant care. The university's
Program for Academic Learning Skills offers support
services to students with learning disabilities.

Holy Cross, College of the
Office of Disability Service
1 College Street, Hogan Campus Center, Room 209
Worcester, MA 01610-2395
508-793-3693, 508-793-3591 (TTY)
info@holycross.edu
http://www.holycross.edu/departments/dos/website/
disability_services
Disability Served: various
Available Accommodations/Facilities/Services:
counseling, academic accommodations, tutors, readers,
interpreters, note takers, library/laboratory assistance,
preferential course scheduling, accessible housing,
special diets, and disabled parking.

Houston, University of
Center for Students with Disabilities
CSD Building, 4800 Calhoun Road, Room 100
Houston, TX 77204-2010
713-743-5400, 713-749-1527 (TTY)
camoruso@bayou.uh.edu
http://www.uh.edu/csd
Disability Served: various
Available Accommodations/Facilities/Services: academic and test accommodations, tutoring, job placement, counseling, and academic advising.

Howard University
Office of the Dean for Special Student Services
2225 Georgia Avenue, NW, Suite 725,
Washington, DC 20059
202-238-2420
bwilliams@howard.edu
http://www.howard.edu/specialstudentservices/disabledstudents.htm
Disability Served: various
Available Accommodations/Facilities/Services: advocacy, counseling, assistive technology, sign language and oral interpreting services, learning disability screening, note taking assistance, reading services, test accommodations, accessible facilities.

Humboldt State University
Student Disability Resource Center
1 Harpst Street
Arcata, CA 95521-8299
707-826-4678, 707-826-5392 (TDD)
sdrc@humboldt.edu
http://www.humboldt.edu/~sdrc
Disability Served: various
Available Accommodations/Facilities/Services: disability-related counseling and advising; adaptive technologies (e.g., TDDs, CCTVs, assistive listening devices, and adaptive computer hardware or software); oral and manual interpreters; note takers; reading services; on-campus mobility assistance; registration assistance; real-time captioning; alternate educational formats (e.g., audiotape, Braille, large print); disabled parking; and test accommodations.

Idaho, University of
Disability Support Services
Idaho Commons, Room 333, PO Box 442550
Moscow, ID 83844-4291
208-885-7200
dss@idaho.edu

http://www.access.uidaho.edu/default.aspx?pid=56098
Disability Served: various
Available Accommodations/Facilities/Services: readers; note takers; sign language interpreters; real-time captioning; assistive devices (e.g., assistive listening devices, audiotape four-track and two-track players, Braille labelers, handheld audiotape recorders, headsets, and microphones); accessible campus housing and other facilities; priority registration; disability parking; and advocacy.

Idaho State University
The ADA Disabilities and Resource Center
Gravely Hall, Room 123, Campus Box 8121
Pocatello, ID 83209-8077
208-282-3599 (Voice/TYY)
tonedenn@isu.edu
http://www.isu.edu/ada4isu/ada%20info.htm
Disability Served: various
Available Accommodations/Facilities/Services: in-class note-takers, test-taking accommodations, priority registration, scribes, priority seating arrangements, sign language interpreters, test proctors, textbooks on tape, transcribers, accessible transportation, tutoring, and counseling services.

Illinois State University
Disability Concerns
350 Fell Hall, Campus Box 1290
Normal, IL 61790-2320
309-438-5853, 309-438-8620 (TTY)
ableisu@ilstu.edu
http://www.disabilityconcerns.ilstu.edu
Disability Served: various
Available Accommodations/Facilities/Services: testing accommodations (e.g., separate testing rooms, extended times, readers, and writers); classroom accommodations (e.g., typists, note takers, and other assistants); communication accommodations (e.g., sign language interpreters, real-time captioning services, and FM systems); alternative format accommodations (e.g., electronic text, voice-recognition programs, enlarged print, and Braille); and assistive technology (e.g., scanners, telecommunications devices for the deaf, closed-circuit TVs, screen readers, and accessible campus computer laboratories).

Illinois-Urbana-Champaign, University of
Division Of Rehabilitation-Education Services
1207 South Oak Street
Champaign, IL 61820

217-333-4603 (Voice/TTY)
disability@uiuc.edu
http://www.disability.uiuc.edu
Disability Served: various
Available Accommodations/Facilities/Services: assistive technology (e.g., optical character recognition/speech output systems, Braille translators and embossers, keyboards, switches, specialized adaptive software, and assistive devices for the hearing-impaired); interpreter services; learning disability services; note taker services; registration assistance; testing accommodations; counseling; accessible facilities; and text conversion (including Braille, large print, and other formats).

Indiana-Purdue University at Fort Wayne
Services for Students with Disabilities
2101 East Coliseum Boulevard, Walb Student Union, Room 113
Ft Wayne, IN 46805
260-481-6657
borrors@ipfw.edu
http://www.ipfw.edu/ssd
Disability Served: various
Available Accommodations/Facilities/Services: special test proctoring services; reader and sign interpreter services; specialized academic and career counseling; and a disabled resource facility (which offers talking and large-display computers, a reading machine, electronic spell checkers, cassette transcription machines, specially adapted cassette recorder/players, Braille equipment, carbonless note-taking paper, and more).

Indiana State University
Disabled Student Services
200 North Seventh Street
Terre Haute, IN 47809
812-237-2301
http://www.indstate.edu/sasc/dss/index.htm
Disability Served: various
Available Accommodations/Facilities/Services: counseling, mobility services, special orientation for new students, advocacy, accessible facilities, and more.

Indiana University-Bloomington
Disability Services for Students
Franklin Hall 096
Bloomington, IN 47405
812-855-7578
http://www.dsa.indiana.edu/dss.html
Disability Served: various
Available Accommodations/Facilities/Services: testing

modifications (e.g., quiet setting, extended time, readers, and scribes); note takers; interpreters; audio versions of texts; accessible van transportation, elevators and lift keys; counseling; accessible facilities; and learning disability screenings.

Iowa, University of
Student Disability Services
3100 Burge Hall
Iowa City, IA 52242-1214
319-353-1462, 319-353-1498 (TTY)
http://www.uiowa.edu/~sds
Disability Served: various
Available Accommodations/Facilities/Services: academic accommodations, interpreters, English transliterators, on-site and remote captioning services, note takers, alternative instructional materials, accessible facilities, disabled parking, counseling, and more.

Iowa State University
Disability Resources
1076 Student Services Building
Ames, IA 50011-2028
515-515-294-6624, 515-294-6635 (TTY)
dsoweb@iastate.edu.
http://www.dso.iastate.edu/dr
Disability Served: various
Available Accommodations/Facilities/Services: academic and testing accommodations (e.g., note takers, extended time for exams, sign language interpreters, captioning, Braille formats for tests, and accommodation letters to instructors); orientation for new students; advocacy; counseling; and more.

Iowa Western Community College
Office of Disability Services
2700 College Road
Council Bluffs, IA 51502
712-325-3390
shollowell@iwcc.edu
http://iwcc.cc.ia.us/student_life/stu_services/disability.html
Disability Served: various
Available Accommodations/Facilities/Services: counseling, tutoring, note takers, sign language interpreters, academic and testing accommodations, accessible facilities, and more.

Irvine Valley College
Disabled Students Programs and Services
SC171

Irvine, CA 92720
949-451-5630
czucker@ivc.edu
http://www.ivc.edu/dsps
Disability Served: various
Available Accommodations/Facilities/Services:
counseling and advising; interpreters; note takers;
readers; special classroom aides; special diagnostic
testing; disabled parking; testing accommodations;
tutors; accessible facilities; and special equipment (e.g.,
adaptive computer equipment, books on tape, Brailling
handouts/syllabi, course material enlargement, talking
calculators; tape recorders, and video decoders).

Johns Hopkins University
Office of Equal Opportunity and Affirmative Action
Programs-Disability Services
Garland Hall, 3400 North Charles Street, Suite 130
Baltimore, MD 21218
410-516-8949, 410-516-6225 (TTY)
http://www.jhuaa.org/DSS
Disability Served: various
Available Accommodations/Facilities/Services: Priority
registration and course substitutions; classroom
accommodations (such as readers, scribes, note takers,
sign interpreters, and testing accommodations);
accessible facilities; and academic, career, and short-
term counseling.

Kansas, University of
Disability Resources
Strong Hall, 1450 Jayhawk Boulevard, Room 22
Lawrence, KS 66045-7576
785-864-2620
mrasnak@ku.edu
http://www.disability.ku.edu
Disability Served: various
Available Accommodations/Facilities/Services:
counseling and advising, accessible facilities, test
accommodations, note takers, interpreters, typists,
readers, accessible transportation, and more.

Kent State University
Student Disability Services
Michael Schwartz Center, Room 181
Kent, OH 44242-0001
330-672-3391 (Voice/TTY)
ajannaro@kent.edu
http://www.registrars.kent.edu/disability
Disability Served: various

Available Accommodations/Facilities/Services:
counseling and advising; accessible facilities;
interpreters; adaptive technology (e.g., magnification
and reading software, Braille translation programs,
screen readers, optical character recognition software,
Braille printers, Braille dictionaries, and assistive
listening devices); wheelchair loans; disabled parking;
and more.

Kentucky, University of
Disability Resource Center
2 Alumni Gym
Lexington, KY 40506-0029
859-257-2754
msfogg0@uky.edu
http://www.uky.edu/StudentAffairs/
DisabilityResourceCenter
Disability Served: various
Available Accommodations/Facilities/Services: accessible
facilities; registration and housing priority; academic
and testing accommodations; transportation services;
radio reading services, interpreters; note takers; referral
to diagnostic testing; and adaptive aids (e.g., Braille
printers, assistive listening devices, electronic visual aids,
TTDs, and adapted computers).

Kentucky State University
Disability Resource Center
400 East Main Street
Frankfort, KY 40601
502-597-5093
ewhite@gwmail.kysu.edu
http://www.kysu.edu/student_affairs/campus_life/
disability_resource_center.cfm
Disability Served: various
Available Accommodations/Facilities/Services: tape
recorders, listening devices, screen readers, note takers,
readers, counseling and advising, accessible facilities,
academic and testing accommodations, and tutors.

Lake-Sumter Community College
Office for Students with Disabilities
9501 U.S. Highway 441
Leesburg, FL 34788
352-365-3574
http://www.lscc.edu/osd.asp
Disability Served: various
Available Accommodations/Facilities/Services:
counseling, academic and testing accommodations,
readers, scribes, note-takers, books on tape, large-

print materials, sign language interpreters, accessible facilities, and assistive technologies.

Lamar University
Services for Students with Disabilities
101 Wimberly
Beaumont, TX 77710
409-880-8347 (Voice/TTY)
callie.trahan@lamar.edu
http://dept.lamar.edu/sfswd
Disability Served: various
Available Accommodations/Facilities/Services:
counseling; academic and testing accommodations; priority registration; sign language interpreters; and adaptive equipment (e.g., headphones, tape players/ recorders, four-track tape players, assistive listening devices, Braille keypads, screen readers, and screen enlargers).

Landmark College
River Road South
Putney, VT 05346
802-387-6718
http://www.landmark.edu
Disability Served: attention deficit disorder, dyslexic, learning disabled
Available Accommodations/Facilities/Services: assistive technology, individual and group counseling, educational programs, tutoring services, advocacy, and more.

Las Positas College
Disability Resource Center
Building 1500, 3033 Collier Canyon Road
Livermore, CA 94550
925-373-4921
http://lpc1.clpccd.cc.ca.us/lpc/altmedia/dsps/index.htm
Disability Served: various
Available Accommodations/Facilities/Services: priority registration; accessible facilities; academic and testing accommodations; books on tape; note taking assistance; interpreters; alternate media services; tutorial assistance; registration assistance; closed-captioning services; and academic-, career-, and disability-related counseling.

Lewis-Clark State College
Office of Disability Services for Students
Reid Centennial Hall, 500 Eighth Avenue, Room 111
Lewiston, ID 83501
208-792-2211, 800-933-5272

oslws@lcsc
http://www.lcsc.edu/osl/ada.htm
Disability Served: various
Available Accommodations/Facilities/Services: advocacy and counseling, accessible facilities, academic and testing accommodations, and more.

Lipscomb University
Office of Disability Services
3901 Granny White Pike
Nashville, TN 37204
615-269-1781
ashley.dumas@lipscomb.edu
http://counseling.lipscomb.edu/page.asp?SID+58&Page=159
Disability Served: various
Available Accommodations/Facilities/Services: classroom and campus accommodations, referrals to psychologists and physicians for assessment and testing, and counseling services.

Los Medanos College
Disabled Students Programs and Services
2700 Leland Road, Room CC 3429
Pittsburg, CA 94565
925-439-2181, ext. 3133, 925-439-5709 (TDD)
http://www.losmedanos.net/hightechcenter/default.htm
Disability Served: various
Available Accommodations/Facilities/Services: academic and testing accommodations, accessible facilities, adaptive computer hardware and software, alternate media formats, counseling, hearing amplification technology, interpreters, priority registration, readers, specialized tutoring, and tape recorders.

Louisiana-Lafayette, University of
Services for Students With Disabilities
PO Drawer 41650
Lafayette, LA 70504-1650
337-482-5252
ssd@louisiana.edu
http://disability.louisiana.edu
Disability Served: various
Available Accommodations/Facilities/Services: sign language interpreters; readers; note takers; tape recording services; tutoring; disabled parking; priority scheduling; counseling; accessible facilities; and academic and testing accommodations (e.g., extended test time, exams in large print, Brailled tests, scribe services, computer access, and oral testing).

Louisiana State University
Office of Disability Services
112 Johnston Hall
Baton Rouge, LA 70803
225-578-5919, 225-578-2600 (TDD)
disability@lsu.edu
http://appl003.lsu.edu/slas/ods.nsf/index
Disability Served: various
Available Accommodations/Facilities/Services: accessible facilities; assistive listening devices; books on tape; counseling; accessible facilities; priority registration; cued speech transliterating; enlarged tests; exams in a distraction-reduced environment; extended time for exams; note taking services; readers; real-time captioning; scribes; sign language interpreting (including ASL, PSE, and signed English); and tape recorders.

Loyola University Chicago
Office of Services for Students with Disabilities
Damen Hall, Lake Shore Campus, Suite 105
Chicago, IL 60626
773-508-2741
http://www.luc.edu/depts/lac/disabilities
Disability Served: various
Available Accommodations/Facilities/Services: advocacy and counseling; academic modifications (such as priority registration, reduced course load, and extended time to complete assignments); exam modifications (such as use of a scribe or reader, rest periods, and alternative test areas); auxiliary services (such as assistive technology, sign language interpreters, note takers, readers, researchers, real-time captioning, alternate forms of text, and photocopy enlargement); and accessible facilities.

Madonna University
Office of Disability Resources
36600 Schoolcraft Road, Room 1113C
Livonia, MI 48150
734-432-5641 (Voice/TTY)
mmeldrum@madonna.edu
http://www.munet.edu/pages/odr.cfm
Disability Served: various
Available Accommodations/Facilities/Services: adaptive computer equipment (e.g., Braille printers, screen-reading programs, and screen magnification software); accessible facilities; alternative testing accommodations (e.g., private testing rooms, extended testing times, readers, transcribers, and enlarged print materials); assistive listening devices; counseling and advising;

in-class note taking; sign language and oral interpreting services; and tutoring/academic support services.

Maine-Augusta, University of
Learning Support Services
Jewett Hall, Room 195J
Augusta, ME 04330
207-621-3066, 800-621-3600
donald.osier@maine.edu
http://www.uma.edu/ss/uossdisability.html
Disability Served: various
Available Accommodations/Facilities/Services: counseling, accessible facilities, academic and testing accommodations, adaptive equipment, and more.

Marin, College of
Disabled Students Programs and Services
835 College Avenue
Kentfield, CA 94914
415-485-9406
marie@marin.cc.ca.us
http://www.marin.cc.ca.us/disabled/index.html
Disability Served: various
Available Accommodations/Facilities/Services: counseling; accessible facilities; academic and testing accommodations (e.g., readers, note takers, books on tape, interpreters, and extended time on tests); an accessible computer center; and special equipment and learning aids (e.g., computers with adaptive software, large-print materials, books on tape, wheelchairs, and print magnification machines).

Marquette University
Office of Disability Services
PO Box 1881
Milwaukee, WI 53201-1881
414-288-1645
http://www.marquette.edu/oses/disabilityservices
Disability Served: various
Available Accommodations/Facilities/Services: advance notice of assignments; time extensions for assignments and tests; alternative ways of completing assignments; note takers; laboratory/library assistants; readers; sign language interpreters; captioning; scribes; taped textbooks; document conversion to alternate formats (Braille, large print, tape, etc.); priority registration; counseling; and accessible facilities.

Marshalltown Community College
Special Needs Accommodations
3700 South Center Street

Marshalltown, IA 50158
641-752-7106
http://www.iavalley.cc.ia.us/mcc/Students/SpecialNeeds.
   htm
Disability Served: various
Available Accommodations/Facilities/Services: academic
   and testing accommodations; counseling (including
   vocational evaluation and planning, financial assistance, course selection, career assistance, and personal
   counseling); assistive devices (including reading magnifiers, talking tests, and audio and visual enhancers); and
   accessible facilities.

Maryland-College Park, University of
Disability Support Services
0126 Shoemaker Hall
College Park, MD 20742
301-314-7682
jahutch@umd.edu
http://www.counseling.umd.edu/DSS
Disability Served: various
Available Accommodations/Facilities/Services: priority
   registration; note-taking services, laboratory/library
   assistance; individualized mentoring; advocacy; testing
   accommodations (e.g., extended exam time, private
   examination space, testing readers and/or scribes,
   computer access for exams, and enlarged print); reading
   accommodations (e.g., books on tape, taping of text
   materials, and enlarged print); and deaf and hard
   of hearing services (e.g., assistive learning devices,
   interpreting services, and FM systems).

Massachusetts-Dartmouth, University of
Disabled Student Services Office
285 Old Westport Road, Group I, Room 016
North Dartmouth, MA 02747
508-999-8711
http://www.umassd.edu/studenthandbook/
   univservices/univservices2.cfm
Disability Served: various
Available Accommodations/Facilities/Services: accessible
   facilities, note takers, counseling, advocacy, orientation
   for new students, and more.

McGill University
Office for Students with Disabilities
Brown Student Services Building, 3600 McTavish Street,
   Room 3100
Montreal, QB H3A 1Y2
Canada
514-398-6009, 514-398-8198 (TTY)

disabilities.students@mcgill.ca
http://www.mcgill.ca/osd
Disability Served: various
Available Accommodations/Facilities/Services: sign
   language interpreters; oral interpreters; tutors; note
   takers; an adaptive laboratory; reading services; Braille
   transcription services; photocopying services; testing for
   learning disabilities; equipment loans (including four-
   track tape recorders, laptop computers, portable speech
   synthesizers, talking dictionaries, FM systems, books
   on tape, and portable word processors); accessible
   facilities; adapted transport service; and disabled
   parking. The university also offers the pamphlet Library
   Service for Users with Disabilities.

McLennan Community College
Services for Students with Disabilities
1400 College Drive
Waco, TX 76708
254-299-8067
msweatt@mclennan.edu
http://www.mclennan.edu/students/dis.php
Disability Served: various
Available Accommodations/Facilities/Services: accessible
   facilities, academic and testing accommodations,
   counseling and advocacy, disabled parking, and more.

Memorial University of Newfoundland
Glenn Roy Blundon Centre for Students with Disabilities
Smallwood Centre, Room 4007
St. John's, NF A1C 5S7
Canada
709-737-2156, 709-737-4763 (TTY)
blundon@mun.ca
http://www.mun.ca/student/disabilities
Disability Served: various
Available Accommodations/Facilities/Services: adaptive
   technology (e.g., screen-reading software, scanners,
   closed-circuit televisions, screen magnifiers, text-to-
   speech software, and microfilm readers); academic
   and testing accommodations (e.g., scribes, extended
   time, alternative formats, and note-taking assistance);
   orientation and mobility training; disabled parking;
   accessible transportation; tutors; readers; counselors;
   and accessible accommodations.

Michigan, University of
Office of Services for Students with Disabilities
G-664 Haven Hall, 505 South State Street
Ann Arbor, MI 48109-1316
734-763-3000

http://www.umich.edu/~sswd
Disability Served: various
Available Accommodations/Facilities/Services:
  accommodations for placement testing and student
  orientation; counseling; accessible housing and
  facilities; academic and testing accommodations (e.g.,
  adjustments in physical access, testing procedures,
  teaching techniques, seating arrangements, auxiliary
  aids, and copies of lecture notes, as well as alternative
  format course materials); note takers; sign language
  and oral interpreters; computer assisted real-time
  captioning; assistive listening devices and other assistive
  technology; and tutors.

Michigan State University
Resource Center for Persons with Disabilities
120 Bessey Hall
East Lansing, MI 48823
517-353-9642, 517-355-1293 (TTY)
rcpd@msu.edu
http://www.rcpd.msu.edu/Home
Disability Served: various
Available Accommodations/Facilities/Services:
  academic and testing accommodations; an assistive
  technology center, which offers voice-input and -output
  systems, large-print software, and Braille translation
  and embossing equipment; advocacy and training;
  accessible facilities; counseling; a library of Braille, large-
  print, electronic and recorded texts with a computerized
  inventory and search system; assistive technology
  tutorials and training materials; and equipment loans
  of portable electronic note-takers, portable electronic
  dictionaries, talking calculators, Braille writers, four-
  track cassette recorders, and handheld magnifiers.

Midlands Technical College
Services to Students with Disabilities
PO Box 2408
Columbia, SC 29202
803-738-8324
counseling@midlandstech.com
http://www.midlandstech.edu/counseling/csds.html
Disability Served: various
Available Accommodations/Facilities/Services:
  counseling; accessible facilities; note taking services and
  assistive technology (e.g., Braille translation software
  and embossers, computers with speech output, screen
  magnification software, text scanning and reading
  software, and voice dictation software).

Minnesota-Twin Cities, University of
Disability Services
McNamara Alumni Center
200 Oak Street, SE, Suite 180
Minneapolis, MN 55455
612-626-1333 (Voice/TTY)
ds@umn.edu.
http://ds.umn.edu
Disability Served: various
Available Accommodations/Facilities/Services: accessible
  facilities; classroom and program modifications; testing
  and exam accommodations; document conversion
  services (including audiotape, Braille, electronic, and
  large-print formats); interpreter and captioning services;
  access assistance; counseling; and adaptive technology.

Mississippi, University of
Office of Student Disability Services
PO Box 1848
University, MS 38677
662-915-7128, 662-915-7907 (TTY)
sds@olemiss.edu
http://www.olemiss.edu/depts/sds
Disability Served: various
Available Accommodations/Facilities/Services: priority
  registration; counseling; accessible facilities; alternate
  format reading materials (e.g., books on tape, readers,
  etc.); alternate testing environments; an assistive
  computer laboratory; equipment loans (e.g., tape
  recorders, four-track tape players, etc.); preferential
  classroom seating; assistive listening devices; and
  American Sign Language signers.

Mississippi State University
Disability Resource Center
PO Box 806, Mail Stop 9724
Mississippi State, MS 39762
662-325-3335
http://www.msstate.edu/dept/sss/disabilities
Disability Served: various
Available Accommodations/Facilities/Services:
  counseling; classroom and testing accommodations;
  priority registration; advocacy; accessible facilities; and
  assistive technology (e.g., closed-circuit televisions,
  Braille printers, adapted computers, TTYs, and TDDs).
  The T.K. Martin Center for Technology and Disability
  and the Rehabilitation Research and Training Center
  on Blindness and Low Vision are also located at the
  university.

Missouri-Columbia, University of

Office of Disability Services
A038 Brady Commons
Columbia, MO 65211
573-882-4696, 573-882-8054 (TTY)
disabilityservices@missouri.edu
http://web.missouri.edu/~accesscm
Disability Served: various
Available Accommodations/Facilities/Services:
advocacy; laboratory/classroom assistants; note
takers, campus transportation; assistive technology;
personal care attendants; readers; counseling;
accessible facilities; and an adaptive computing
technology center (which offers voice-activated
software, magnification software and equipment,
speech output devices, and more). The Office also
offers Transition to College, an excellent guide for
disabled students preparing for college. It can be
accessed by visiting http://www.missouri.edu/
~accesscm/transition.htm.

Molloy College

Disability Support Services
1000 Hempstead Avenue, PO Box 5002
Rockville Centre, NY 11570
888-4-MOLOY
http://www.molloy.edu/acad_affairs/steep/dss.htm
*Disability Served: attention deficit disorder, dyslexia,
learning disabled*
*Available Accommodations/Facilities/Services: The
college offers the Success Through Expanded Education
Program for students with learning disabilities.*

Montana, University of

Disability Services for Students
Lommasson Center, #154
Missoula, MT 59812
406-243-2243 (Voice/TTY)
jim.marks@umontana.edu
http://www.umt.edu/dss
Disability Served: various
Available Accommodations/Facilities/Services:
accessible facilities; counseling; advocacy; academic
and testing accommodations; interpreters; captioning;
alternate formats for educational materials (such
as Braille, audio recordings, and electronic text);
and assistive technology (including software and
hardware).

National Technical Institute for the Deaf

Rochester Institute of Technology
52 Lomb Memorial Drive
Rochester, NY 14623
585-475-6400 (Voice/TTY)
ntidmc@rit.edu
http://www.ntid.rit.edu
Disability Served: hearing
*Available Accommodations/Facilities/Services: advocacy
and counseling, accessible facilities, on-campus
audiology and hearing aid services, tutors, note takers,
sign language interpreters, speech-to-text transcription,
and more.*

Nazareth College of Rochester

Services for Students with Disabilities
Smyth Hall, Room 22A
Rochester, NY 14618
585-389-2754
avhouse@naz.edu
http://www.naz.edu/dept/acad_advisement/disabilities.
html
Disability Served: various
*Available Accommodations/Facilities/Services: advocacy
and counseling, accessible facilities, academic and
testing accommodations, and more. The college also
offers the* Handbook for Students with Disabilities.

Nebraska-Lincoln, University of

Services for Students with Disabilities
132 Canfield Administration Building, PO Box 880401
Lincoln, NE 68588-0411
402-472-3787, 402-472-0053 (TDD)
vcheney2@unl.com
http://www.unl.edu/ssd
Disability Served: various
Available Accommodations/Facilities/Services:
advocacy, accessible facilities, note takers, testing
accommodations, technological assistance, interpreters,
taped textbooks, real-time captioning services,
accessible transportation, and disabled parking.

Nevada-Las Vegas, University of

Learning Enhancement Services
4505 Maryland Parkway, Box 452015
Las Vegas, NV 89154-2016
702-895-0866, 702-895-0652 (TDD)
les@ccmail.nevada.edu
http://studentlife.unlv.edu/disability

Disability Served: various
Available Accommodations/Facilities/Services:
   counseling; advocacy; equipment loans (including
   four-track recorders/players, standard cassette
   recorders/players, and pocket talkers); alternative
   textbook formats (including audio, enlarged print, or
   computerized text); testing accommodations; accessible
   facilities; American Sign Language interpreters; real-
   time captioning services; note taking accommodations;
   research/laboratory assistants; and an adaptive
   computer laboratory (which offers hands-free mice,
   screen enlargers, large-size trackballs, on-screen
   keyboards, and other adaptive technology).

New Brunswick, University of
Services for Students with Disabilities
Marshall d'Avray Hall, Room 212
Fredericton, NB E3B 5A3
Canada
506-453-3515
unbds@unb.ca
http://www.unbf.ca/studentservices/departments/
   disabilities.html
Disability Served: various
Available Accommodations/Facilities/Services: academic
   and testing accommodations, advocacy and support
   services, counseling, accessible facilities, accessibility
   software for computers, and more.

New Hampshire, University of
Disability Service for Students
118 Memorial Union Building
Durham, NH 03824
603-862-2607(Voice/TTY)
http://www.unh.edu/access/disabilityservices.html
Disability Served: various
Available Accommodations/Facilities/Services: note takers; scribes; readers; interpreters; proctors; academic and
   testing accommodations; advocacy; accessible facilities;
   texts on tape or e-text; enlarged or Brailled texts and
   other course materials; and assistive technology (e.g.,
   four- and two-track tape machines and tape copiers,
   portable closed-circuit television units, and text-to-
   speech software). The university's Dimond Library also
   features the Parker Adaptive Technology Room.

New Jersey, College of
Office of Disability Services
Eickhoff Hall, Room 159
Ewing, NJ 08628
609-771-2571, 609-771-2451 (TDD)
yamiolko@tcnj.edu
http://www.tcnj.edu/~wellness/disability/generalinfo.
   html
Disability Served: various
Available Accommodations/Facilities/Services: American
   Sign Language interpreters, transcriptionists, note
   takers, academic and testing accommodations,
   advocacy, taped textbooks, accessible facilities,
   counseling, and more.

New Mexico, University of
Learning Support Services
Zimmerman Library, 3rd Floor
Albuquerque, NM 87131
505-277-8291
lpdu@unm.edu
http://www.unm.edu/~ovpsa/learning.htm
Disability Served: attention deficit disorder, dyslexic,
   learning disabled
Available Accommodations/Facilities/Services: Learning
   Support Services, an educational program for students
   suspected of having learning disabilities or who have
   previously diagnosed learning disabilities.

New York University
The Moses Center for Students with Disabilities
240 Greene Street, 2nd Floor
New York, NY 10012-1119
212-998-4980 (Voice/TTY)
http://www.nyu.edu/csd
Disability Served: various
Available Accommodations/Facilities/Services:
   counseling; advocacy; accessible facilities; course
   materials in Braille, audio, and large-print formats; and
   assistive technology (including screen enlargement
   software, synthetic speech output software, speech
   input software for exam accommodation use, CCTV
   enlargement systems, four- and two-track track tape
   players/recorders, and FM assistive listening devices).

Northampton Community College
Disability Services
3835 Green Pond Road
Bethlehem, PA 18017
610-861-5342, 610-861-5351 (TTY)
Ldemshock@Northhampton.edu
http://www.northampton.edu/Office/St_Services/
   Disability/default.htm
Disability Served: various

Available Accommodations/Facilities/Services: academic
support and advisement, accessible facilities, an
adaptive computer laboratory, assistance in securing
taped textbooks, note takers, taped lectures, test
accommodations, readers, scribes, sign language
interpreters, and disabled parking.

North Carolina-Chapel Hill, University of
Disability Services
05 Steele Building, CB 5100
Chapel Hill, NC 27514-1080
919-962-8300
disabilityservices@unc.edu
http://disabilityservices.unc.edu
Disability Served: various
Available Accommodations/Facilities/Services:
advocacy; disability parking; orientation for new
students; counseling; assistive technology (e.g.,
closed-circuit televisions, assistive listening devices,
tape recorders, and laptops/computers); testing
accommodations; tutors; sign language interpreters;
note takers; cued speech transliteration; library
assistance; modified course schedules; adaptive
physical education courses; and accessible course
materials and services.

North Carolina State University
Disability Services for Students
1900 Student Health Center, Campus Box 7509
Raleigh, NC 27695-7509
919-515-7653, 919-515-8830 (TTY)
http://www.ncsu.edu/provost/offices/affirm_action/dss
Disability Served: various
Available Accommodations/Facilities/Services: priority registration; testing accommodations (such as
extended time on tests and reduced-distraction testing
rooms); academic accommodations (such as priority
seating, note takers, and access to tape recorders);
alternate format materials; interpreters; transliteration; assistive listening devices; accessible facilities;
counseling; and more.

North Dakota, University of
Disability Support Services
McCannel Hall, Room 190, PO Box 9040
Grand Forks, ND 58202-8371
701-777-3425 (Voice/TTY)
dss@und.nodak.edu
http://www.und.edu/dept/dss
Disability Served: various

Available Accommodations/Facilities/Services: disabled
parking; accessible transportation; adaptive technology
(e.g., trackballs, alternate keyboards, voice output
technology, and large-print software); accessible
facilities; TTYs; advocacy; and counseling.

North Dakota State College of Science
Disability Support Services
800 Sixth Street North, Library 225
Wahpeton, ND 58076
701-671-2623
joy.eichhorn@ndscs.nodak.edu
http://www.ndscs.nodak.edu/student/asc/dss.html
Disability Served: various
Available Accommodations/Facilities/Services: career and
vocational counseling, advocacy, accessible facilities,
academic and testing accommodations, and more.

Northeastern University
Disability Resource Center
20 Dodge Hall, 360 Huntington Avenue
Boston, MA 02115
617-373-2675, 617-373-2730 (TTY)
d.auerbach@neu.edu
http://www.access-disability-deaf.neu.edu
Disability Served: various
Available Accommodations/Facilities/Services: tape-
recorded lectures, note takers, scribes, American Sign
Language interpreters, Signed English transliterators,
computer access real-time reporters, extra time
on exams, alternate formatted material, campus
orientation, accessible classrooms and facilities, and
counseling.

Northern Arizona State University
Disability Support Services
PO Box 5633
Flagstaff, AZ 86001-4108
928-523-8773, 928-523-6906 (TTY)
disability.support@nau.edu
http://www2.nau.edu/dss
Disability Served: various
Available Accommodations/Facilities/Services: disabled
parking; accessible computer laboratories; registration
assistance and priority registration; advocacy;
alternative format services; alternative testing
accommodations; assistive technology; interpreter
accommodation (including the following language
modes: American Sign Language, Pidgin Signed English,
Signed English, or Oral); and transportation services.

North Harris College

Disability Services Office
2700 W.W. Thorne Drive
Houston, TX 77073-3499
281-618-5690
tgarza@nhmccd.edu
http://wwwnhc.nhmccd.cc.tx.us/Templates/content.
    aspx?pid=21891
Disability Served: various
*Available Accommodations/Facilities/Services: advocacy
    and counseling, accessible facilities, academic and
    testing accommodations, and more.*

North Lake College

Disability Services Office
5001 North MacArthur Boulevard
Irving, TX 75038
972-273-3165, 972-273-3169 (TTY)
http://www.northlakecollege.edu/scresources/
    disabilitysvcs.htm
Disability Served: various
*Available Accommodations/Facilities/Services:
    assistance with registration; vocational and academic
    counseling and guidance; note taking assistance;
    sign language interpreting; special classroom seating
    arrangements; academic and testing accommodations
    (e.g., extra time, scribes, etc.); accessible facilities; and
    assistive technology (e.g., taped or digital textbooks,
    magnification devices, telecommunication devices, and
    assistive hearing equipment).*

Northwestern University

Services for Students with Disabilities
Scott Hall, 601 University Place
Evanston, IL 60208-1270
847-467-5530, 847-467-5533 (TTY)
ssd@northwestern.edu
http://www.northwestern.edu/disability
Disability Served: various
*Available Accommodations/Facilities/Services: note-
    taking services; interpreter and captioning services;
    scribe and reader services; materials in e-text and
    audio format; counseling; accessible facilities; testing
    accommodations (such as alternative test environments
    and extended time); assistance in obtaining elevator
    and lift keys: and access to adaptive equipment and
    software (including personal assistive listening devices,
    voice dictation, screen-reading and text-reading
    software, adaptive personal computers for taking tests,
    audiotape recorders, and four-track recorders).*

Norwalk Community-Technical College

Services for Students with Disabilities
188 Richards Avenue
Norwalk, CT 06854
203-857-7192
http://www.ncc.commnet.edu/disabledservices.asp
Disability Served: various
*Available Accommodations/Facilities/Services:
    counseling, advocacy, accessible facilities, academic
    and testing accommodations, disabled parking, and
    more.*

Oakland Community College

Disability Services
2480 Opdyke Road
Bloomfield Hills, MI 48304
248-341-2000
http://www.oaklandcc.edu/pass
Disability Served: various
*Available Accommodations/Facilities/Services: note
    takers, readers, recorded materials, sign language
    interpreters, tutors, learning station modification,
    counseling, accessible facilities, and special instructional
    equipment.*

Odessa College

Students with Disabilities
201 West University
Odessa, TX 79764
432-335-6357
rhernandez@odessa.edu
http://www.odessa.edu/dept/counseling/students.htm
Disability Served: various
*Available Accommodations/Facilities/Services: academic
    advocacy and counseling; accessible facilities;
    specialized aids and equipment (such as wheelchairs,
    tape recorders, and large-print books); and a resource
    library of books, periodicals, and videos on disability-
    related topics.*

Ohio State University

Office for Disability Services
150 Pomerene Hall, 1760 Neil Avenue
Columbus, OH 43218-3029
614-292-3307, 614-292-0901 (TDD)
carlton.1@osu.edu
http://www.ods.ohio-state.edu
Disability Served: various
*Available Accommodations/Facilities/Services: test
    accommodations (e.g., readers, scribes, adaptive*

technology, scanned exams, extended time, distraction-reduced space, and tape-recorded exams); alternative media (options include: scanned, scanned and edited, taped, enlarged, Brailled and image enhancements); note taking assistance; interpreters; transcribers; assistive technology (e.g., word prediction software, screen reader software, CCTV text magnification systems, large and flat screen monitors, refreshable Braille displays, adaptive mice and keyboards, and scan-to-speech, text-to-speech, web-to-speech, and screen reader software); disabled parking; adaptive transportation; counseling; accessible facilities; and learning disability testing.

Ohio University
Disability Services
101 Crewson House
Athens, OH 45701
740-593-2620, 740-593-0193 (TTD)
fahey@ohio.edu
http://www.ohio.edu/equity/disabilityservices/index.cfm
Disability Served: various
Available Accommodations/Facilities/Services:
alternative format course materials, priority registration, counseling, academic accommodations, amplified listening devices, sign language interpreting services, peer tutoring, Braille services, advocacy, accessible facilities, and adaptive physical education classes.

Oklahoma, University of
Office of Disability Services
620 Elm Avenue, Suite 166
Norman, OK 73019-4078
405-325-3852, 405-325-4173 (TDD)
ods@ou.edu
http://www.sa.ou.edu/ods
Disability Served: various
Available Accommodations/Facilities/Services: counseling and advocacy, accessible facilities, interpreter and real-time reporting services, note taking services, alternative testing, tutoring, adaptive computer laboratories, priority enrollment, assistive technology, and library assistance.

Oklahoma State University
Office of Disability Services
315 Student Union
Stillwater, OK 74078
405-744-7116
http://www.okstate.edu/ucs/stdis

Disability Served: various
Available Accommodations/Facilities/Services: priority enrollment; counseling; assistive technology (e.g., screen-reading software, screen magnification software, etc.); testing accommodations (e.g., separate rooms, readers, scribes, extended testing time, and use of computers); disabled parking; tutoring services; note taking and typing services; and library assistance.

Old Dominion University
Disability Services
1525 Webb Center
Norfolk, VA 23529
757-683-4655
http://www.odu.edu/disabilityservices
Disability Served: various
Available Accommodations/Facilities/Services: advocacy and counseling, accessible facilities, academic and testing accommodations, and more.

Olivet Nazarene University
Student Success Services
One University Avenue
Bourbonnais, Il 60914-2345
815-939-5011
http://www.olivet.edu/academics/ldc/success.asp
Disability Served: various
Available Accommodations/Facilities/Services: tutors, note takers, counseling and advocacy, accessible facilities, and accommodations for exams.

Oregon, University of
Disability Services
164 Oregon Hall, 5278 University of Oregon
Eugene, OR 97403-1278
541-346-1155, 541-346-1083 (TTY)
disabsrv@darkwing.uoregon.edu
http://ds.uoregon.edu
Disability Served: various
Available Accommodations/Facilities/Services: priority registration; academic advising; adaptive technology; books on tape; note taking services; sign language interpreting; specialized equipment (including tape recorders, TTYs, personal FM systems, and lightweight word processors for classroom use); accessible facilities; and testing accommodations.

Pacific, University of the
Office of Services for Students with Disabilities
Educational Resource Center

Stockton, CA 95211
209-946-2879 (Voice/TDD)
ssd@pacific.edu
http://www.pacific.edu/education/departments/
   educational_resource_center/support_for_students.
   html
Disability Served: *various*
Available Accommodations/Facilities/Services:
   *alternative testing procedures, taped texts/reading
   machines, CCTV equipment, taped lectures, note takers,
   cart transportation to and from class, advocacy and
   counseling, accessible facilities, and more.*

Pennsylvania, University of
Office of Learning Resources
3702 Spruce Street, Suite 300
Philadelphia, PA 19104-6270
215-573-9235, 215-746-6320 (TDD)
sdsmail@pobox.upenn.edu
http://www.vpul.upenn.edu/lrc/sds
Disability Served: *various*
Available Accommodations/Facilities/Services:
   *orientation for new students, counseling and
   advocacy, interpreters, computer-aided transcription
   services, assistive listening systems, readers, note
   takers, taped texts, materials in Braille, accessible
   housing and transportation services, and auxiliary
   aids and services.*

Pennsylvania State University
Office for Disability Services
116 Boucke Building
University Park, PA 16802
814-863-1807 (Voice/TTY)
wjw9@psu.edu
http://www.equity.psu.edu/ods
Disability Served: *various*
Available Accommodations/Facilities/Services: *academic
   and testing accommodations; advocacy and counseling;
   auxiliary aids; an assistive technology laboratory; library
   assistance; and accessible transportation, parking, and
   facilities.*

Pennsylvania State University-Harrisburg
Disability Services
777 West Harrisburg Place
Middletown, PA 17057
drh2@psu.edu
http://www.hbg.psu.edu/studaf/disability/dsmain.htm
Disability Served: *various*

Available Accommodations/Facilities/Services: *large-
   print class materials; tape-recorded lectures; taped or
   electronic texts; extended time and alternate locations
   for tests; counseling and advocacy; scribes; note
   takers; sign language interpreters; oral interpreters;
   assistive listening devices; accessible facilities; and a
   campus library assistive technology room (which offers
   screen readers, screen magnifiers, and text-to-speech
   software).*

Pepperdine University
Disability Services Office
24255 Pacific Coast Highway
Malibu, CA 90263
310-506-4000
http://www.pepperdine.edu/disabilityservices
Disability Served: *various*
Available Accommodations/Facilities/Services: *American
   Sign Language interpreters; note takers; extended time
   on exams; distraction-free exam rooms; alternative
   text formats (e.g., taped books, digital text, etc.); real-
   time captioning services; accessible facilities; assistive
   listening devices; counseling; and workshops (to help
   freshman transition to college and seniors land a job).*

Portland State University
Disability Resource Center
435 Smith Memorial Student Union
Portland, OR 97207-0751
503-725-4150, 503-725-6504(TTY)
drc@pdx.edu
http://www.pdx.edu/iasc/drc.html
Disability Served: *various*
Available Accommodations/Facilities/Services: *priority
   registration; note taking; assistive listening devices;
   interpreting and captioning services; alternate testing
   accommodations; taped texts and electronic texts;
   counseling and advocacy; accessible facilities; furniture
   for special needs; and referral services for learning
   disabilities assessment, psychological disabilities
   assessment, and assistive technology assessment.*

Potomac State College of West Virginia University
Office of Disability Services
104 Science Hall
Keyser, WV 26726
304-788-6936, 304-293-7740 (TTY)
access2@mail.wvu.edu
http://www.potomacstatecollege.edu/student-life/
   disabilities.html

Disability Served: various

Available Accommodations/Facilities/Services: priority pre-registration; sign language interpreters and/or auxiliary aids; enlarged reading materials; accessible transportation for class-related activities; disabled parking; advocacy and counseling; and referrals for arrangements for specific dietary needs, speech and hearing evaluations, career services, diagnostic evaluations, and access to assistive technology in academic computing laboratories.

Rhode Island, University of

Disability Services
330 Memorial Union
Kingston RI 02881
401-874-2098, 800-745-5555
rohland@uri.edu
http://autocrat.uri.edu/841.html
Disability Served: various

Available Accommodations/Facilities/Services: priority registration; counseling and advocacy; wheelchair-accessible vans; disabled parking; accessible facilities; tape-recorded lectures; note takers; books on tape; readers; sign language interpreters, exam accommodations (including extended time on exams, private testing areas, and alternate exam formats); and adaptive equipment and software (including FM assistive listening devices, closed-circuit TV text enlargers, screen enlarging software, and voice-recognition programs).

Roane State Community College

Disability Services
Counseling and Career Services Department
276 Patton Lane
Harriman, TN 37748
865-882-4550
Bonner@roanestate.edu
http://www.roanestate.edu/keyword.
    asp?keyword=COUNSELING
Disability Served: various

Available Accommodations/Facilities/Services: interpreting for the deaf, note takers, spell checkers, counseling and advocacy, academic and testing accommodations, and accessible facilities.

Roosevelt University

Disability Services
430 South Michigan Avenue, HCC 310
Chicago, IL 60605

312-341-3810
info@roosevelt.edu
http://www.roosevelt.edu/dss/default.htm
Disability Served: various

Available Accommodations/Facilities/Services: counseling and advocacy; academic and testing accommodations (e.g., extended time for tests, separate testing areas, use of a tape recorder in class, typists, scribe, readers, and note takers); assistive technology; and accessible facilities.

Rutgers, The State University of New Jersey

Office of Disability Services
151 College Avenue, Suite 123
New Brunswick, NJ 08901
732-932-2848
dsoffice@rci.rutgers.edu
http://studentaffairs.rutgers.edu/disability
Disability Served: various

Available Accommodations/Facilities/Services: advocacy and counseling, accessible facilities, academic and testing accommodations, and more.

Saint Anselm College

Disability Services
100 Saint Anselm Drive, PO Box 1747
Manchester, NH 03102
603-641-7465
http://www.anselm.edu/administration/
    academic+advisement/disability
Disability Served: various

Available Accommodations/Facilities/Services: reduced course loads, counseling and advocacy, accessible facilities, extended time for exams, books on tape, assistance with note-taking, special seating arrangements, course materials in enlarged print, distraction-reduced environments for taking exams, and the use of tape recorders in class.

Saint Cloud State University

Student Disability Services
720 Fourth Avenue
St Cloud, MN 56301-4498
320-308-4080
sds@stcloudstate.edu
http://www.stcloudstate.edu/sds
Disability Served: various

Available Accommodations/Facilities/Services: priority registration, sign language/oral interpreting services, note takers, testing accommodations, taped textbooks, orientation to buildings for new students (including elevators, accessible routes, restrooms, automatic doors, etc.), and counseling and advocacy.

Saint Elizabeth, College of

Services For Students With Learning Disabilities
Academic Skills Center
2 Convent Road
Morristown, NJ 07960
cepp@cse.edu
http://www.cse.edu/index.php?id=354
Disability Served: attention deficit disorder, dyslexic, learning disabled
Available Accommodations/Facilities/Services: academic support, advocacy, tutoring services, note-takers, tape recorders, and academic and testing accommodations.

Salisbury State University

Office of Disability Support Services
Guerrieri University Center, 1101 Camden Avenue, Room 212
Salisbury, MD 21801
410-453-6080, 410-543-6083 (TTY)
http://www.salisbury.edu/Students/DSS/welcome.html
Disability Served: various
Available Accommodations/Facilities/Services: priority registration, academic and testing accommodations, carbonixed notebooks for note takers, recorded books, tutoring services, interpreters, dining hall assistance, counseling and advocacy, and accessible facilities.

San Diego City College

Disability Support Services Program
1313 Park Boulevard
San Diego, CA 92101
619-388-3513, 616-338-3313 (TTY)
bmason@sdcc.net
http://www.sdcity.edu/studentresources/dsps/default.asp
Disability Served: various
Available Accommodations/Facilities/Services: priority registration; counseling and advocacy; specialized tutoring; sign language interpreting and real-time captioning services; adapted computer software and hardware; assistive listening devices; closed-circuit televisions; computer access and assistive devices; learning disability assessments; magnifiers; note taking paper; talking calculators; tape recorders; test proctoring; and accessible facilities.

San Francisco, University of

Student Disability Services
2130 Fulton Street
San Francisco, CA 94117
415-422-2613 (Voice/TTY)
sds@usfca.edu
http://www.usfca.edu/acadserv/academic/services/drs/index.html
Disability Served: various
Available Accommodations/Facilities/Services: counseling and advocacy; accessible facilities; exam accommodations, readers; note takers; certified sign language interpreters; real-time captioning services; laboratory assistance; tape-recorded lectures, educational materials in alternate format (including Braille, large print, audiotape, and audio/video captioning); and assistive technology (e.g., electronic reading machines, assistive listening devices, closed-circuit televisions, screen reader software, screen magnification software, voice-activated software, hands-free mice, accessible computer workstations, and assistive listening devices).

San Jose State University

Disability Resource Center
Administration Building, One Washington Square, #110
San Jose, CA 95192-0036
408-924-6000, 408- 924-6542 (TTY)
info@drc.sjsu.edu
http://www.drc.sjsu.edu
Disability Served: various
Available Accommodations/Facilities/Services: priority registration; alternative formats for curriculum-related print materials (e.g., Braille, enlarged print, CD-ROM, or audiotape); assistive listening devices; audio taping of course lectures, scribes, note takers, sign language interpreters, counseling and advocacy, accessible facilities; disabled parking; and more. The university also hosts the Alternative Media Center and the Emma E. Legg Adaptive Technology Center, one the largest adaptive computing centers in the United States.

Saskatchewan, University of

Disability Services for Students
1 Campus Drive, Lower Place Riel, Room 60
Saskatoon, SK S7N 5A3
Canada
306-966-7273, 306-966-7276 (TTY)
dss@usask.ca

http://www.students.usask.ca/disability
Disability Served: various
Available Accommodations/Facilities/Services: advocacy;
exam accommodations (including extra time, scribes,
readers, laptop computers, and alternative test site
locations); a mentoring program; note taking services;
orientation for new students; campus accessibility
maps; an adaptive technology room; and accessible
facilities. The university also offers a library assistance
program for students with physical disabilities who
have difficulty accessing library facilities and services.

Shawnee State University
Disability Services
940 Second Street
Portsmouth, OH 45662
740-351-4SSU, 740-351-3159 (TTY)
To_SSU@shawnee.edu
http://www.shawnee.edu/off/ssc/disability.html
Disability Served: various
Available Accommodations/Facilities/Services:
interpreter/note taking services, tape recorder loans,
individual and group counseling, adapted testing,
disabled parking accommodations, and accessible
facilities.

Shenandoah University
Office of Disability Services
1460 University Drive, Academic Support Center,
Howe 106
Winchester, VA 22601
800-432-2266
http://www.su.edu/studaffs/disability/index.asp
Disability Served: various
Available Accommodations/Facilities/Services:
counseling and advocacy; accessible facilities; in-class
accommodations (e.g., scribes, note takers, interpreters,
preferred seating, extended time on assignments/
projects, adaptive equipment, and tape-recorded
lectures); testing accommodations (e.g., readers,
separate testing rooms, alternate formats, and adaptive
equipment); and out-of-class accommodations (e.g.,
books on tape, tutoring, and special diets).

Sierra College
Disabled Student Programs and Services
5000 Rocklin Road
Rocklin, CA 95677
916-781-0592

http://www.sierracollege.edu/stu_services/dsps
Disability Served: various
Available Accommodations/Facilities/Services: academic
counseling, academic accommodations, accessible
facilities, assistive technology, Braille services, CCTVs,
interpreter services, mobility assistance, note-takers,
priority registration, readers, recorded textbooks, test
proctoring, test-taking facilitation, and vocational
counseling.

South Carolina, University of
Center for Disability Resources
LeConte College, Room 106
Columbia, SC 29208
803-777-6142, 803-777-6744 (TDD)
http://www.sa.sc.edu/dss
Disability Served: various
Available Accommodations/Facilities/Services: priority
registration; orientation; interpreters; readers; note
takers; tutors; textbooks and supplementary readings
on tape; and disabled parking, transportation, and
facilities. The university's Thomas Cooper Library has an
adapted resource room that offers auxiliary aids such as
large-print typewriters, closed-circuit magnifiers, tape
recorders, and Braille printers.

South Dakota, University of
Center for Disabilities
414 East Clark Street, Room 119B
Vermillion, SD 57069
605-677-6389
cd@usd.edu
http://www.usd.edu/ds
Disability Served: various
Available Accommodations/Facilities/Services:
counseling and advocacy, accessible facilities, academic
and testing accommodations, disabled parking, and
more.

South Dakota State University
Office of Disability Services
110 West Hall
Brookings, SD 57000-0001
605-688-4504, 605-688-4394 (TTD)
Nancy.Crooks@sdstate.edu
http://www3.sdstate.edu/StudentLife/DisabilityServices
Disability Served: various
Available Accommodations/Facilities/Services: advocacy
and counseling, accessible facilities, sign language

interpreters, note takers, alternative format text and other educational materials, testing accommodations, and more.

Southern Idaho, College of
Student Disability Services
Taylor Building, Second Floor, PO Box 1238
Twin Falls, ID 83303-1238
208-732-6260, 208-734-9929 (TDD)
AccessAbility@csi.edu
http://www.csi.edu/prospectiveStudents_/
    studentServices/Disabilities/index.asp
Disability Served: various
*Available Accommodations/Facilities/Services: CCTVs,
    note takers, scribes, sign language interpreters,
    counseling and advocacy, accessible facilities, and
    more.*

Southern Illinois University-Carbondale
Disability Support Services
Woody Hall B-150, Mailcode 4705
Carbondale, IL 62901
618-453-5738, 618-453-2293 (TTY)
DSSsiu@siu.edu
http://www.siu.edu/~dss
Disability Served: various
*Available Accommodations/Facilities/Services: American
    Sign Language or Signed English interpreters; real-
    time typists; oral interpreters; note takers; assistive
    listening devices; electronic and Braille textbooks;
    alternate media (such as electronic text, Braille text,
    and large print and raised line drawings); assistive
    technology (such as tape recorders/players, talking
    calculators, Braillers, slates and styluses, and note
    taking systems); personal attendant services; accessible
    facilities; counseling and advocacy; disabled parking;
    information technology computer learning centers;
    accessible transportation; and more. The university also
    offers the Achieve Program for students with learning
    disabilities and/or attention deficit disorders. Program
    services include mentoring, advocacy, tutoring,
    proctored testing, note takers, readers, adapted
    textbooks, and access to a writing class and a computer
    laboratory.*

Southern Illinois University-Edwardsville
Office of Disability Support Services
Rendleman Hall, Room 1218, Campus Box 1611
Edwardsville, IL 62026-1611
618-650-3782 (Voice/TTY)

jfloydh@siue.edu
http://www.siue.edu/DSS
Disability Served: various
*Available Accommodations/Facilities/Services: priority
    registration, academic referral services, counseling and
    advocacy, local resource identification, and disabled
    parking. The university also offers New Horizons, a
    student organization for students with disabilities.*

Southern Indiana, University of
Counseling Center
8600 University Boulevard
Evansville, IN 47712-3596
812-464-1961
http://www.usi.edu/cou/disres.asp
Disability Served: various
*Available Accommodations/Facilities/Services: test
    accommodations, reader/taping services, tutoring, sign
    language services, note taker supplies and copy services,
    advocacy and counseling, temporary disability parking,
    scheduling of accessible tables and chairs, orientation
    presentations, and accessible facilities.*

Southern Vermont College
Support Services and Accommodations for Students
    with Disabilities
982 Mansion Drive
Bennington, VT 05201
802-442-5427
http://www.svc.edu/student/disabilities_services.html
Disability Served: various
*Available Accommodations/Facilities/Services: tutorial
    sessions, note taking, extended time for exams,
    textbooks on tape, accessible facilities, and counseling
    and advocacy. The college also offers the Learning
    Differences Support Program (http://www.svc.edu/
    student/disability_program.html).*

South Mountain Community College
Disability Resources and Services
Student Enrollment Services Building, 7050 South 24th
    Street, Room 130
Phoenix, AZ 85042
602-243-8027
drs@smcmail.maricopa.edu
http://www.southmountaincc.edu/Services/Disability
Disability Served: various
*Available Accommodations/Facilities/Services: adaptive
    computer software/equipment, readers, note takers,
    scribes, sign language interpreters, alternative print*

formats, counseling and advocacy, accessible facilities, and more.

Southwest Missouri State University

Disability Services
901 South National Avenue, Plaster Student Union, Suite 405
Springfield, MO 65804
417-836-4192, 417-736-6792 (TTY)
DisabilityServices@smsu.edu
http://www.smsu.edu/disability
Disability Served: various
Available Accommodations/Facilities/Services:
   academic and testing accommodations, interpreting services, assistive technology, adaptive computer technology devices, accessible facilities, and advocacy and counseling. The university also offers a learning diagnostic clinic and Gates to Adventure (http:// outcome.mcpo.org/GatesToAdventure), a program to help deaf and hard of hearing students transition to the postsecondary level.

Spoon River College

Disability Support Services
Centers Building, 23235 North County 22, Room C134
Canton, OH 61520
309-649-6273, 309-649-7005 (TTY)
http://www.spoonrivercollege.net/services/ specialneeds.html
Disability Served: various
Available Accommodations/Facilities/Services: accessible facilities, academic and testing accommodations, counseling and advocacy, disabled parking, and more.

Stanford University

Student Disability Resource Center
Office of Accessible Education
563 Salvatierra Walk
Stanford, CA 94305
650-723-1066, 650-723-1067 (TTY)
info@drc.stanford.edu
http://www.stanford.edu/group/DRC
Disability Served: various
Available Accommodations/Facilities/Services: note takers; typists; scribes; readers; interpreters; captioning; alternative format production (including Braille, enlarged hardcopy, and electronic text); an assistive learning technology center (offering speech recognition software, specialized tape recorders, FM listening devices, portable word processors, text-to-speech screen

reading software, and alternative keyboards and mice); advocacy; academic and testing accommodations; a disability golf cart service for students with physical disabilities; and accessible classrooms and facilities. The university also has an assistive technology equipment and software loan library.

Staten Island, College of

Office of Disability Services
2800 Victory Boulevard, 1P-101
Staten Island, NY 10314
718-982-2510, 718-982-2515 (TTY)
Nielson@mail.csi.cuny.edu
http://www.csi.cuny.edu/disabilityservices/index2.html
Disability Served: various
Available Accommodations/Facilities/Services: priority registration, alternative testing, note takers, tutors, assistive technology, accessible facilities, advocacy and counseling, and more.

State University of New York-Binghamton

Services for Students with Disabilities
Box 6000
Binghamton, NY 13902-6000
607-777-2686 (Voice/TT)
bjfairba@ binghamton.edu
http://ssd.binghamton.edu
Disability Served: various
Available Accommodations/Facilities/Services: internship placements; advocacy and counseling; testing accommodations (e.g., extended time, accessible testing sites/seating, reading services, scribe services, adaptive technology, and alternative text formats); sign language interpreters; wheelchair-accessible transportation; disabled parking; and accessible facilities. The university's Bartle Library also offers an adaptive technology room that has assistive technology for loan and use on site.

State University of New York-Fredonia

Disability Support Services for Students
4th Floor, Reed Library
Fredonia, NY 14063
716-673-3270
disability.services@fredonia.edu
http://www.fredonia.edu/tlc/DSS/dss.htm
Disability Served: various
Available Accommodations/Facilities/Services: text on tape, expanded exam time, note takers, readers, scribes, tutoring services, accessible facilities, counseling and advocacy, and more.

St. John's University
Services for Students with Disabilities
Department of Student Life
8000 Utopia Parkway, University Center
Queens, NY 11439
718-990-6568
lochriej@stjohns.edu
http://www.stjohns.edu/campus/handbook/chapter6/
     disabilities.sju
Disability Served: various
Available Accommodations/Facilities/Services:
     counseling, accessible classrooms and facilities,
     extended test time, notetaking assistance, readers,
     scribes, sign language interpretation, tutoring, disabled
     parking, and more.

St. Mary's University
Atlantic Centre of Research, Access, and Support for
     Students with Disabilities
923 Robie Street, 3rd Floor
Halifax, NS B3H 3C3
Canada
902-420-5452, 902-425-1257 (TTY)
david.leitch@smu.ca
http://www.smu.ca/administration/studentservices/
     atlcentr/welcome.html
Disability Served: various
Available Accommodations/Facilities/Services: academic
     counseling, exam accommodations, American Sign
     Language/English interpreting, accessible computer
     workstations and facilities, assistive technology,
     and learning disability assessments. The university's
     Ferguson Library for Print-Handicapped Students has a
     collection of approximately 900 books on tape and 300
     e-text titles.

Syracuse University
Office of Disability Services
804 University Avenue, Suite 309
Syracuse, NY 13244-1120
315-443-4498, 315-443-1372 (TDD/TTY)
odssched@syr.edu
http://disabilityservices.syr.edu
Disability Served: various
Available Accommodations/Facilities/Services: note
     takers, tutors, books on tape, exam assistance,
     counseling and advocacy, accessible facilities, and
     adaptive technology (e.g., Braille printers, scanners,
     screen magnifiers, and voice-controlled computers).

Tarrant County College
Disability Support Services Office
1500 Houston Street
Fort Worth, TX 76102
817-515-4895
http://www.tccd.edu/neutral/DivisionDepartmentPage.
     asp?pagekey=53
Disability Served: various
Available Accommodations/Facilities/Services:
     counseling and advocacy, mobility assistants, note-
     takers, tutors, sign language interpreters, readers,
     media aids, wheelchairs, computer adaptations,
     alternative testing, accessible facilities, and disabled
     parking.

Temple University
Disability Resources and Services
1301 Cecil Moore Avenue, 100 Ritter Annex (003-00)
Philadelphia, PA 19122
215-204-1280
drs@temple.edu
http://www.temple.edu/disability
Disability Served: various
Available Accommodations/Facilities/Services:
     counseling and advocacy; accessible facilities;
     interpreting and captioning services; specialized
     software programs (e.g., screen-reading, screen
     enlargement, voice recognition, etc.); and adaptive
     computer equipment (e.g., raised workstations,
     desktop CCTVs, large monitors, optical scanners,
     Braille printers, alternate keystroke systems, portable
     electronic keyboards, and specialized, programmable
     CD players).

Tennessee-Knoxville, University of
Office of Disability Services
191 Hoskins Library
Knoxville, TN 37996
865-974-6087 (Voice/TTY)
ods@tennessee.edu
http://ods.utk.edu
Disability Served: various
Available Accommodations/Facilities/Services:
     alternative testing arrangements, books on tape,
     tape recorders, note takers, sign language and oral
     interpreters, transcribers, tutors, scribes, laboratory
     assistants, assistive listening equipment, assistive
     technology, counseling and advocacy, accessible
     facilities, and more.

Texas A&M University

Disability Services
Cain Hall, Room B118, 1224 TAMU
College Station, TX 77843-1224
979-845-1637
disability@tamu.edu
http://disability.tamu.edu
Disability Served: various
Available Accommodations/Facilities/Services: sign
  language interpreters, advocacy and counseling, an
  adaptive technology services computer laboratory,
  academic and testing accommodations, accessible
  facilities, paratransit services, and more.

Texas-Austin, University of

Services for Students with Disabilities
Office of the Dean of Students
Student Services Building, 4th Floor
Austin, TX 78713
512-471-6259, 512-471-4641 (TTY)
ssd@uts.cc.utexas.edu
http://deanofstudents.utexas.edu/ssd
Disability Served: various
Available Accommodations/Facilities/Services:
  alternative text formats; testing accommodations; an
  assistive technology laboratory that offers adaptive
  equipment and software; assistive technology rooms
  in the university's libraries; sign language interpreters;
  communication access real-time translation services;
  wheelchair mobility support; wheelchair maintenance
  and repair services; counseling and advocacy; and
  accessible facilities.

Texas Woman's University

Disability Support Services
PO Box 425966
Denton, TX 76204-5966
940-898-3835, 940-898-3830 (TTY)
dss@twu.edu
http://www.twu.edu/dss
Disability Served: various
Available Accommodations/Facilities/Services:
  alternative testing accommodations, sign language
  interpreters, readers, note takers, taped and large-
  print books, carbonless note taking paper, accessible
  facilities, and counseling and advocacy.

Toledo, University of

Office of Accessibility
1400 Snyder Memorial, Mail Stop # 110
Toledo, OH 43606
419-530-4981, 419-530-2612 (TTY)
kjohnso3@utnet.utoledo.edu
http://www.student-services.utoledo.edu/accessibility
Disability Served: various
Available Accommodations/Facilities/Services: an
  adaptive technology computer laboratory, note taking
  assistance, interpreters, and learning disability and
  attention deficit disability testing and referrals.

Tulane University

Office of Disability Services
Center for Educational Resources and Counseling
New Orleans, LA 70118-5698
504-862-8433
erc@tulane.edu
http://erc.tulane.edu/disability
Disability Served: various
Available Accommodations/Facilities/Services: note
  takers, interpreters, readers, priority seating, recorded
  lectures, testing accommodations, assistive technology,
  counseling, and accessible facilities.

Utah, University of

Center for Disability Services
162 Union Building, 200 South Central Campus Drive,
  Room 162
Salt Lake City, UT 84112-9107
801-581-5020 (Voice/TDD)
onadeau@sa.utah.edu
http://disability.utah.edu
Disability Served: various
Available Accommodations/Facilities/Services:
  campus orientation; sign language interpreters;
  real-time caption stenographers; readers; scribes;
  note takers; counseling and advocacy services; testing
  accommodations; accessible facilities; adaptive
  computer technology training; an alternative format
  textbook archive; adaptive equipment loans; assistance
  with admissions, registration, and graduation.

Utah Valley State College

Accessibility Services Department
Business Building (BU 146), 800 West University Parkway
Orem, UT 84058
801-863-8747, 801-221-0908 (TTY)
asd@uvsc.edu
http://www.uvsc.edu/asd
Disability Served: various

Available Accommodations/Facilities/Services: testing
accommodations (e.g., isolated test environments,
extended time, computer- or technology-aided
assistance, orthopedic accommodations, scribes, and
proctors); alternate formats for educational materials
(e.g., Braille, audio cassette tapes, and enlarged
text); academic accommodations (cued speech
transliterators, note takers, sign language interpreters,
stenographers, and transcribers); text on tape, auxiliary
aids and assistive devices (e.g., adaptive computer
software and hardware, auditory amplifiers, calculators,
computer screen enlarging programs, computer text
scanning equipment, computer voice synthesizers,
electronic spellers, speech recognition software, tape
recorders, and text enlarging devices); an accessible
computer laboratory; accessible facilities; and advocacy
and counseling.

Vermont, University of
Accommodation, Consultation, Collaboration and
Educational Support Services
Living Learning Center, A-170
Burlington, VT 05405
802-656-7753
access@uvm.edu
http://www.uvm.edu/~access
Disability Served: various
Available Accommodations/Facilities/Services: advocacy
and counseling, referral to diagnostic services, exam
accommodations, sign language interpreting, real-
time captioning services, accessible facilities, and an
adaptive technology laboratory.

Virginia, University of
Learning Needs and Evaluation Center
400 Brandon Avenue, PO Box 800760
Charlottesville, VA 22908-0760
434-243-5180, 434-243-5189 (TTY)
LNEC@virginia.edu
http://www.virginia.edu/studenthealth/lnec.html
Disability Served: various
Available Accommodations/Facilities/Services: priority
scheduling; note-takers; sign language interpreters;
scribes; taped readings of course textbooks (for students
with reading disabilities); academic and testing
accommodations; special computer equipment; access
to TTY phone service; computer-assisted real-time
transliteration; assistive amplification devices; and
accessible facilities.

Virginia State University
Students with Disabilities Program
Memorial Hall, Room 412, PO Box 9030
Blacksburg, VA 23806
804-524-5061, 804-524-5838 (TDD)
http://www.vsu.edu/pages/264.asp
Disability Served: various
Available Accommodations/Facilities/Services: priority
registration and scheduling; accessible facilities;
counseling and advocacy; note takers; readers; tutors;
alternative formats for printed materials; cassette-taped
lectures; cassette taping of texts and materials; auxiliary
aids; assistive technology; and extended time for exams,
papers, and projects.

Washington, University of
Disability Services Office
4045 Brooklyn Avenue, NE, Room 230
Seattle, WA 98195
206-543-6450, 206-543-6452 (TTY)
dso@u.washington.edu
http://www.washington.edu/admin/dso
Disability Served: various
Available Accommodations/Facilities/Services: accessible
facilities; assistive equipment; interpreters (e.g., sign
language, oral and tactile); academic and testing
accommodations; counseling and advocacy; and
disabled parking.

Waubonsee Community College
Access Center for Students with Disabilities
Collins Hall, Room 118
Sugar Grove, IL 60554-9799
630-466-7900, ext. 2564, 630-466-4649 (TTY)
ihansen@waubonsee.edu
http://www.waubonsee.edu/current_students/access_
center
Disability Served: various
Available Accommodations/Facilities/Services: accessible
facilities, academic and testing accommodations,
counseling and advocacy, and more.

Wayne State University
Educational Accessibility Services
583 Student Center Building, 5221 Gullen Mall
Detroit, MI 48202
313-577-1851, 313-577-3365 (TTY)
eas@teadmin.sa.wayne.edu
http://www.eas.wayne.edu

Disability Served: various

Available Accommodations/Facilities/Services: pre-enrollment consultation, alternative testing, advocacy, counseling, sign language interpreters, real-time reporters, disabled parking, and study rooms with adaptive equipment. The university also hosts the Developmental Disabilities Institute.

Western Connecticut State University

Office of Disability Services
Old Main 101
Danbury, CT 06810
203-837-8278, 203-837-8284 (TTY)
Disability Served: various
Available Accommodations/Facilities/Services: counseling and advocacy, accessible facilities, academic and testing accommodations, disabled parking, and more.

Western Michigan University

Disabled Students Resources and Services
1903 West Michigan Avenue, Mail Stop 5277
Kalamazoo, MI 49008-5277
269-387-2120, 269-387-2120 (TDD)
jennifer.lawson@wmich.edu
http://www.dsrs.wmich.edu
Disability Served: various
Available Accommodations/Facilities/Services: assistance with class scheduling, priority registration, academic and testing accommodations, a reader service, advocacy and counseling, adaptive computer equipment, accessible facilities, handi-van transportation, and adaptive computer equipment.

Western New Mexico University

Special Needs Services
Juan Chacon Building, #212
Silver City, NM 88062
505-538-6498, 505-538-6498 (TTY)
http://www.wnmu.edu/Special%20Needs%202/
specialneeds.htm
Disability Served: various
Available Accommodations/Facilities/Services: tutoring, typing of class notes in large print, reading services, interpreting, note taking, recording, transcribing, escort services for blind students, counseling and advocacy, accessible facilities, and academic and testing accommodations.

West Kentucky Community and Technical College

Disability Resource Office
Anderson Building, Room 114A
Paducah, KY 42002
270-534-3406
http://www.westkentucky.kctcs.edu/geninfo/special_
needs.shtml
Disability Served: various
Available Accommodations/Facilities/Services: wheelchair loans; tape recorder loans; note takers; interpreters; tutors; readers; writers; testing accommodations; large-print material; assistive technology (e.g., visual-text amplifiers, right-handed keyboards, left-handed keyboards, and lap desks for computer keyboards); large-print dictionaries and thesauri; counseling and advocacy; accessible facilities; and disabled parking.

West Texas A&M University

Student Disability Services
WTAMU Box 60923
Canyon, TX 79016-0001
806-651-2335
elathrop@mail.wtamu.edu
http://www.wtamu.edu/administrative/ss/ls/ds
Disability Served: various
Available Accommodations/Facilities/Services: limited diagnostic testing and/or referral, note takers, extended time on tests, alternate testing sites, scribe services, tutoring, textbooks on tape, enhanced computer software programs, advocacy and counseling, and accessible facilities.

West Virginia State College

Disability Services Office
123 Sullivan Hall East
Morgantown, WV 26506-6004
304-766-3083
blankenc@wvstateu.edu
http://www.wvstateu.edu/studentaffairs/saoffices/csc/
disabilityservices
Disability Served: various
Available Accommodations/Facilities/Services: accessible facilities, active listening devices, advocacy and counseling, cassette recorders, extended time for tests, note takers, oral/large-print exams, sign language interpreters, taped textbooks, text enlargers, TDDs, and tutoring services.

West Virginia University
Office of Disability Services
G-30 Mountainlair, PO Box 6423
Morgantown, WV 26506-6423
304-293-7740 (Voice/TDD)
access2@mail.wvu.edu
http://www.wvu.edu/~socjust/disability
Disability Served: various
Available Accommodations/Facilities/Services: advocacy;
    counseling; interpreters; closed captioning services;
    alternative formats for educational materials; and
    disabled parking, transportation, and facilities.

Wisconsin-Madison, University of
McBurney Disability Resource Center
1305 Linden Drive
Madison, WI 53706
608-263-2741, 608-263-6393 (TTY)
mcburney@uwmadmail.services.wisc.edu
http://www.mcburney.wisc.edu
Disability Served: various
Available Accommodations/Facilities/Services:
    priority registration, alternative testing, assistive
    listening devices, Braille services, computer-assisted
    transcription, note taking assistance, document
    conversion, interpreting services, laboratory assistance,
    library assistance, paratransit, class relocation
    recommendation, counseling and advocacy, and
    commencement accommodations.

Wright State University
Office of Disability Services
3640 Colonel Glenn Highway, E186 Student Union
Dayton, OH 45435-0001
937-775-5680, 937-775-5844 (TTY)
disability_services@wright.edu
http://www.wright.edu/students/dis_services
Disability Served: various
Available Accommodations/Facilities/Services: physical
    support services (such as personal assistance with daily
    hygiene requirements, disabled parking areas, acces-
    sible facilities, and the coordination of campus mobil-
    ity orientation); classroom accommodations (such as
    sign language interpreters, a reader/writer service, and
    laboratory assistance); a technology center (that offers
    classroom materials in alternative formats such as Braille,
    audio cassette tapes, computer disks, and image enhance-
    ment); and career and vocational support services.

Wyoming, University of
University Disability Support Services
1000 East University Avenue, Department 3808
Laramie, WY 82071
307-766-6189, 307-766-3073 (TTY)
udssc@uwyo.edu
http://www.uwyo.edu/udss
Disability Served: various
Available Accommodations/Facilities/Services: priority
    registration; campus orientation; an adaptive
    computer laboratory; assistive technology orientation
    and training; assistive listening systems; test-taking
    accommodations; note-taking services; taped texts or
    other alternative formats; interpreter services; tutoring
    services; advocacy and counseling; disabled parking;
    paratransit services; adaptive physical education; and
    accessible facilities.

York Technical College
Disability Services
452 South Anderson Road
Rock Hill, SC 29730
803-327-8000
http://www.yorktech.com
Disability Served: various
Available Accommodations/Facilities/Services: counsel-
    ing and advocacy, accessible facilities, academic and
    testing accommodations, disabled parking, and more.

EDUCATIONAL FUNDING RESOURCES

Following is a list of funding resources for persons with disabilities who wish to pursue postsecondary education. Included are grants, scholarships, and loans.

Alabama, University of
Office of Student Financial Aid
Box 870162, 106 Student Services Center
Tuscaloosa, AL 35487
205-348-6756
financialaid@ua.edu
http://financialaid.ua.edu
Disability Served: various
The university offers financial aid to help students (including those with disabilities) attend college. *Eligibility: Students who need financial assistance are eligible to apply. *Financial Details: Amounts vary according to need. *Number Awarded: Varies. *Deadline: Write or call for details.

Alabama Commission on Higher Education
PO Box 302000
Montgomery, AL 36130-2000
334-242-1998
http://www.ache.state.al.us
Disability Served: various
The commission provides financial aid to help students (including those with disabilities) attend college. *Eligibility: Alabama students who need financial assistance are eligible to apply. *Financial Details: Amounts vary according to need. *Number Awarded: Varies. *Deadline: Write or call for details.

Alabama Department of Veterans Affairs
PO Box 1509
Montgomery, AL 36102-1509
334-242-5077
willie.moore@va.alabama.gov
http://www.va.state.al.us
Disability Served: various
The department provides scholarships for the purpose of college study. *Eligibility: Children or spouses of Alabama military veterans who are disabled are eligible to apply. Recipients must attend a college or university in the state. *Financial Details: Amounts vary, but benefits are limited to cost of tuition and fees. Awards are renewable for up to four years. *Number Awarded: Varies each year. *Deadline: Write or call for details.

Alabama State University
Office of Financial Aid
PO Box 271
Montgomery, AL 36101
334-229-4323
http://www.alasu.edu
Disability Served: various
The university provides financial aid to help students (including those with disabilities) attend college. *Eligibility: Students who need financial assistance are eligible to apply. *Financial Details: Amounts vary according to need. *Number Awarded: Varies. *Deadline: Write or call for details.

Alaska Department of Education and Early Development
801 West 10th Street, Suite 200
Juneau, AK 99801-1894
907-465-8713
patricia_wherry@eed.state.ak.us
http://www.educ.state.ak.us
Disability Served: various
The department provides financial aid to help students (including those with disabilities) attend college. *Eligibility: Alaska students who need financial assistance are eligible to apply. *Financial Details: Amounts vary according to need. *Number Awarded: Varies. *Deadline: Write or call for details.

Alaska-Fairbanks, University of
Office of Financial Aid
101 Eielson Building
Fairbanks, AK 99775
888-474-7256
financialaid@uaf.edu
http://www.uaf.edu/finaid
Disability Served: physically disabled
The university offers a variety of financial aid programs to help students attend college, including the Eugene and Loretta Rafson Scholarship for Students with Disabilities. *Eligibility: Physically disabled students who need financial assistance are eligible to apply. *Financial Details: $750. *Number Awarded: Varies. *Deadline: Write or call for details.

Alaska Office of Veterans Affairs
Camp Denali, PO Box 5800
Fort Richardson, AK 99505-5800
907-428-6016
http://www.ak-prepared.com/vetaffairs
Disability Served: various
The office provides tuition waivers for the purpose of
college study. *Eligibility: Children of Alaska military
veterans who died as a result of military service,
or who have been declared missing in action, are
eligible to apply. Applicants must be residents
of Alaska and attend selected public colleges or
universities in the state. *Financial Details: Amounts
vary. *Number Awarded: Varies each year. *Deadline:
Write or call for details.

**Alexander Graham Bell Association for the Deaf
and Hard of Hearing**
Manager of Financial Aid and Scholarship Programs
3417 Volta Place, NW
Washington, DC 20007
202-337-5220
publications@agbell.org
http://www.agbell.org
Disability Served: hearing
The association provides a variety of scholarships
for the purpose of college study. *Eligibility:
Applicants must have a hearing loss and be able to
communicate orally. Other specifications may apply.
Contact the association to learn more. *Financial
Details: Scholarships range from $250 to $2,000.
*Number Awarded: Approximately 55 scholarships
each year. *Deadline: Deadline for applications is
February 15.

**American Academy of Allergy, Asthma
and Immunology**
555 East Wells Street, Suite 1100
Milwaukee, WI 53202-3823
414-272-6071
info@aaaai.org
http://www.aaaai.org
Disability Served: asthma
This organization offers Excellence Asthma Scholarships.
*Eligibility: High school seniors with asthma who
need financial assistance are eligible to apply.
*Financial Details: Awards range from $100 to $2,000.
*Number Awarded: At least 23. *Deadline: Contact
the academy for additional details.

American Cancer Society-Florida Division
1001 South McDill Avenue
Tampa, FL 33629
800-444-1410, ext. 405
mwestley@cancer.org
http://www.cancer.org
Disability Served: cancer patients and survivors
This organization provides R.O.C.K. College Scholarships
to help finance college training at an accredited
Florida university, community college, or vocational
technical school. *Eligibility: Florida residents who
have had cancer before age 21 are eligible to apply.
*Financial Details: Grants are for up to $2,000 plus
$300 for textbooks. *Number Awarded: Varies each
year. *Deadline: April 11.

American Council of the Blind
Scholarship Committee
1155 15th Street, NW, Suite 1004
Washington, DC 20005
800-424-8666
http://www.acb.org
Disability Served: vision
The council offers scholarships to help finance college
study via its state affiliates. *Eligibility: Students
who are blind or visually impaired and admitted to
an academic, vocational, technical, or professional
training program are eligible to apply. *Financial
Details: Awards vary. *Number Awarded: Varies.
*Deadline: Contact the Council for more information.

American Council of the Blind of Minnesota
PO Box 7341
Minneapolis, MN 55407
mmalver@visi.com
http://www.acb.org/minnesota/Scholarship.html
Disability Served: vision
The council offers educational scholarships to blind
students. *Eligibility: Legally blind students who
are residents of Minnesota are eligible to apply.
*Financial Details: $750. *Number Awarded: Two.
*Deadline: May 31.

American Council of the Blind of Ohio
ACBO Scholarship Committee
3114 Manning Avenue
Cincinnati, OH 45211
800-835-2226
kmorlock@gcfn.org

http://www.acbohio.org
Disability Served: vision
The council offers a variety of educational scholarships to blind students. *Eligibility: Blind students who are residents of Ohio (or who attend a school in Ohio) and have a GPA of at least 3.0 are eligible to apply. *Financial Details: Varies. *Number Awarded: Five. *Deadline: August 1.

American Council of the Blind of South Carolina
PO Box 481
Columbia, SC 29202
803-735-1052
http://www.acb.org/southcarolina
Disability Served: vision
The council offers an educational scholarship to blind students. *Eligibility: Blind full-time students who reside in South Carolina are eligible to apply. Scholarships are awarded based on academic achievement, community service, and financial need. *Financial Details: $1,000. *Number Awarded: Varies. *Deadline: Typically in September.

American Council of the Blind of Texas
Scholarship Committee Chairperson
374 County Road 2206
Texarkana, TX 75501
903-832-5038
http://www.acbtexas.org/scholarshipinfo.html
Disability Served: vision
The council offers educational scholarships to blind students. *Eligibility: Blind students who are residents of Texas and have a GPA of at least 2.75 are eligible to apply. *Financial Details: Varies. *Number Awarded: Varies. *Deadline: April 25.

American Foundation for the Blind
Scholarship Committee
11 Penn Plaza, Suite 300
New York, NY 10001
212-502-7600
afbinfo@afb.net
http://www.afb.org
Disability Served: vision
The foundation offers many scholarships for students who are legally blind and studying at the college level. *Eligibility: The Rudolph Dillman Memorial Scholarship is open to undergraduate and graduate students preparing for the rehabilitation field. The

Gladys C. Anderson Memorial Scholarship is open to undergraduate or graduate women studying classical or religious music. The Paul and Ellen Ruckes Scholarship is open to undergraduate or graduate students studying engineering or computer, physical, or life sciences. Additional scholarships are available. *Financial Details: The Dillman Scholarship is for $2,500. The Anderson Scholarship is worth $1,000. The Ruckes Scholarship awards up to $1,000. *Number Awarded: One for the Anderson and Ruckes Scholarships; four for the Dillman Scholarship. *Deadline: April 30.

American Legion Auxiliary
777 North Meridian Street, Third Floor
Indianapolis, IN 46204
317-955-3845
mpotts@legion-aux.org
http://www.legion-aux.org
Disability Served: various
The following national scholarships are available to help students finance college study: National President's Scholarship, Spirit of Youth Scholarship for Junior Members, and Non-Traditional Student Scholarship. *Eligibility: Children of veterans who served in the Armed Forces during eligibility dates specified by the Legion and who complete 50 hours of community service during high school may apply for the National President's Scholarship. Students who have been members of the American Legion Auxiliary for the immediate past three years may apply for the Spirit of Youth Scholarship for Junior Members. Students who plan to return to the classroom after an extended period of time or students who have completed at least one year of college, but are in need of financial aid to continue their education, may apply for the Non-Traditional Student Scholarship. Applicants must also be members of The American Legion, the American Legion Auxiliary, or Sons of The American Legion and be enrolled in at least six hours per semester or four hours per quarter. *Financial Details: National President's Scholarship: $2,500 and $2,000. Spirit of Youth Scholarship for Junior Members: $1,000. Non-Traditional Student Scholarship: $1,000. *Number Awarded: National President's Scholarship: 10. Spirit of Youth Scholarship for Junior Members: one. Non-Traditional Student Scholarship: three. *Deadline: Varies. Contact the auxiliary for details.

American Legion-Iowa Auxiliary

720 Lyon Street

Des Moines, IA 50309

515-282-7987

http://www.ialegion.org/ala

Disability Served: various

The Hoffman Memorial Scholarship is designed to help finance college training. *Eligibility: Dependents of a disabled veteran who are Iowa residents and who wish to pursue teaching careers are eligible. *Financial Details: The scholarship is for $400. *Number Awarded: Varies. *Deadline: Contact the auxiliary for additional details.

American Legion-Oregon Auxiliary

PO Box 1730

Wilsonville, OR 97070-1730

503-682-3162

Disability Served: various

The auxiliary provides a scholarship to help finance college study. *Eligibility: Oregon residents who are children of a disabled veteran and who plan to pursue post-secondary education at a school within the state are eligible. *Financial Details: Scholarships are for up to $1,000. *Number Awarded: Varies. *Deadline: Applications are due in March.

American Legion-Pennsylvania Auxiliary

PO Box 2643

Harrisburg, PA 17105

717-763-7545

paalad@hotmail.com

Disability Served: various

The auxiliary provides grants to help finance college study at a state college or university. *Eligibility: Pennsylvania high school seniors who are sons or daughters of disabled veterans are eligible to apply. Candidates must demonstrate financial need. *Financial Details: Grants are for $600 a year for four years. *Number Awarded: Two per year. *Deadline: Applications are due March 15.

American University

Financial Aid Building

4400 Massachusetts Avenue, NW

Washington, DC 20016-8001

202-885-6100

financialaid@american.edu

http://admissions.american.edu

Disability Served: various

The university provides financial aid to help students (including those with disabilities) attend college. *Eligibility: Students who need financial assistance are eligible to apply. *Financial Details: Amounts vary according to need. *Number Awarded: Varies. *Deadline: Write or call for details.

Aquinas College

Office of Financial Aid

1607 Robinson Road, SE

Grand Rapids, MI 49506

616-632-2893

financialaid@aquinas.edu

http://www.aquinas.edu/financialaid

Disability Served: various

This liberal arts college provides financial aid to help finance college study. *Eligibility: Students with disabilities are eligible to apply. *Financial Details: Amounts vary and depend on financial need. *Number Awarded: Varies. *Deadline: Write or call for details.

Arizona, University of

Disability Resource Center

1224 East Lowell Street

Tucson, AZ 85721

520-621-3268 (Voice/TTY)

uadrc@email.arizona.edu

http://drc.arizona.edu/drc/scholarship.shtml

Disability Served: various

The university's Disability Resource Center offers a variety of financial aid to disabled students. *Eligibility: Students who demonstrate financial need and have a minimum 2.5 cumulative GPA are eligible to apply. *Financial Details: Awards range from approximately $1,500 to $2,000. *Number Awarded: 10 to 12 annually. *Deadline: Mid-April.

Arizona Department of Education

1535 West Jefferson Street

Phoenix, AZ 85007

602-542-5393, 800-352-4558

http://www.ade.state.az.us

Disability Served: various

The department provides financial aid to help students (including those with disabilities) attend college. *Eligibility: Arizona students who need financial assistance are eligible to apply. *Financial Details: Amounts vary according to need. *Number Awarded: Varies. *Deadline: Contact the department for additional details.

Arizona Kidney Foundation
Scholarship Fund
4203 East Indian School Road, Suite 140
Phoenix, AZ 85018
602-840-1644
http://www.azkidney.org
Disability Served: kidney disease
The foundation offers the Bidstrug Scholarship.
 *Eligibility: Arizona residents who are undergoing
 dialysis treatment or who have had a kidney
 transplant are eligible to apply. *Financial Details:
 Amount varies. Write for further information.
 *Number Awarded: Varies. *Deadline: Contact the
 foundation for additional details.

Arizona State University
Disability Resource Center
PO Box 873202
Tempe, AZ 85287-3202
480-965-1234, 480-965-9000 (TDD)
Disability-Q@asu.edu
http://www.asu.edu/drc/scholarships.html
Disability Served: various
The university's Disability Resource Center offers a
 variety of scholarships for disabled students at the
 undergraduate level. *Eligibility: Students must have
 a GPA of at least 2.5, demonstrate financial need,
 and be pursuing full-time study. *Financial Details:
 Awards range from $200 to $1,987 per semester.
 *Number Awarded: Varies. *Deadline: June 1.

Arizona State University
Office of Financial Aid
PO Box 870412
Tempe, AZ 85287
480-965-3355
http://www.asu.edu
Disability Served: communication
The Sertoma Communicative Disorders Scholarship
 Program is available. *Eligibility: Full-time, graduate-
 level students at the University studying speech
 language pathology or audiology are eligible to
 apply. *Financial Details: The award ranges from
 $2,500 to 5,000. *Number Awarded: Varies. *Deadline:
 Applications are available from December through
 April 1.

Arkansas Department of Education
114 East Capitol
Little Rock, AR 72201

800-54-STUDY
finaid@adhe.arknet.edu
http://www.arkansashighered.com/aidprograms.html
Disability Served: various
The department provides financial aid to help students
 (including those with disabilities) attend college.
 *Eligibility: Arkansas students who need financial
 assistance are eligible to apply. *Financial Details:
 Amounts vary according to need. *Number Awarded:
 Varies. *Deadline: Contact the Department for
 additional details.

Arkansas Department of Veterans Affairs
Building 65, 2200 Fort Roots Drive, Room 119
North Little Rock, AR 72114
501-370-3820
http://www.nasdva.com/arkansas.html
Disability Served: various
The department provides tuition waivers for the purpose
 of college study. *Eligibility: Children of Arkansas
 military veterans who died as a result of military
 service, or who have been declared missing in action,
 are eligible to apply. Applicants must be residents of
 Arkansas and attend a public college or university in
 the state. *Financial Details: Amounts vary. *Number
 Awarded: Varies each year. *Deadline: Write or call for
 details.

Arkansas-Fayetteville, University of
Office of Financial Aid
518 Old Main
Fayetteville, AR 72701
479-575-4464
scholars@uark.edu
http://www.uark.edu/admin/fininfo
Disability Served: various
The university offers financial aid to help students
 (including those with disabilities) attend college.
 *Eligibility: Students who need financial assistance
 are eligible to apply. *Financial Details: Amounts
 vary according to need. *Number Awarded: Varies.
 *Deadline: Write or call for details.

**Arkansas Governor's Commission on People
 with Disabilities**
1616 Brookwood Drive
Little Rock, AR 72202-1704
501-296-1637
ibesh@ars.state.ar.us
Disability Served: various

The commission offers scholarships to students with disabilities. *Eligibility: Disabled students who live in Arkansas may apply. Scholarships are awarded based on severity of disability and resulting functional limitations, academic achievement, financial need, and applicants' contributions to the community. *Financial Details: Varies. *Number Awarded: Varies. *Deadline: Contact the Commission for details.

Arkansas State University
Office of Financial Aid
PO Box 1620
State University, AR 72467
870-972-2310
http://www.astate.edu
Disability Served: various
The university provides financial aid to help students (including those with disabilities) attend college. *Eligibility: Students who need financial assistance are eligible to apply. *Financial Details: Amounts vary according to need. *Number Awarded: Varies. *Deadline: Write or call for details.

Association for Education and Rehabilitation of the Blind and Visually Impaired
1703 North Beauregard Street, Suite 440
Alexandria, VA 22311
703-671-4500, ext. 201
bsherr@aerbvi.org
http://www.aerbvi.org
Disability Served: vision
The association awards the William and Dorothy Ferrell Scholarship to help finance college study. *Eligibility: Visually impaired individuals studying for a career in the field of services to persons who are blind or visually impaired are eligible. *Financial Details: Varies. *Number Awarded: Two. *Deadline: Applications are due March 15.

Association for Glycogen Storage Disease
PO Box 896
Durant, IA 52747
563-785-6038
maryc@agsdus.org
http://www.agsdus.org
Disability Served: Glycogen Storage Disease
The association offers scholarships to students with glycogen storage disease. *Eligibility: Students who have a confirmed diagnosis of glycogen storage disease and who are paid members of the Association (or whose parents are members) may apply *Financial Details: Varies. *Number Awarded: Varies. *Deadline: Contact the association for details.

Association for the Education and Rehabilitation of the Blind And Visually Impaired of Ohio
7012 Beresford Avenue
Parma Heights, OH 44130-5050
http://www.aerohio.org
Disability Served: vision
The association offers the David H. Newmeyer Post-Secondary Scholarship For Visually Impaired Students. *Eligibility: Blind students who are Ohio residents are eligible to apply. *Financial Details: Approximately $500. *Number Awarded: Varies. *Deadline: June 1.

Association of Blind Citizens
PO Box 246
Holbrook, MA 02343
781-961-1023
scholarship@assocofblindcitizens.org
http://www.assocofblindcitizens.org
Disability Served: vision
This organization offers the Reggie Johnson Memorial Scholarship. *Eligibility: Legally blind students who are U.S. legal residents are eligible to apply. *Financial Details: One $3,000 scholarship, three $2,000 scholarships, and 11 $1,000 scholarships. *Number Awarded: Fifteen. *Deadline: April 15.

Association of Universities and Colleges of Canada
350 Albert Street, Suite 600
Ottawa, ON K1R 1B1
Canada
613-563-1236
awards@aucc.ca
http://www.aucc.ca
Disability Served: various
The Mattinson Endowment Fund Scholarship for Disabled Students is designed to help finance college training. *Eligibility: Canadian college students with disabilities are eligible to apply. There is no restriction on the field of study, and the scholarship may be used at any undergraduate Canadian college or university. *Financial Details: $2,500. *Number Awarded: Varies based on funding. *Deadline: Varies. Contact the association for details.

Autism Society of America
7910 Woodmont Avenue, Suite 300
Bethesda, MD 20814-3067
301-657-0881, 800-328-8476
http://www.autism-society.org
Disability Served: autism
The society offers the Eden Services Charles H. Hoens, Jr.,
   Scholars Program. *Eligibility: Students with autism
   may apply. *Financial Details: $1,000. *Number
   Awarded: Varies. *Deadline: February 28.

Bank of America ADA Abilities Scholarship
PO Box 1465
Taylors, SC 29687
864-268-3363
allisonlee@bellsouth.net
http://www.scholarshipprograms.org
Disability Served: various
This organization offers the ADA Abilities Scholarship
   Program. *Eligibility: Applicant must have a minimum
   cumulative GPA of 2.5; plan to pursue a degree in
   finance, business, or computer systems, plan on
   a career with a banking institution, and be a U.S.
   citizen. *Financial Details: $5,000. *Number Awarded:
   Varies. *Deadline: April 1.

Bechtel Foundation
PO Box 193965
San Francisco, CA 94119-3965
http://www.bechtel.com/foundation.htm
Disability Served: hearing, physically disabled
The foundation provides funds to support educational
   programs for the hearing impaired and the physically
   disabled for grades K through 12. *Eligibility:
   Nonprofit organizations and educational institutions
   are eligible to apply. The Foundation is interested in
   supporting math, sciences, and technical educational
   programs. Preference is given to applicants from
   communities where Bechtel offices are located.
   *Financial Details: Amounts vary. *Number Awarded:
   Varies each year. *Deadline: Proposals are accepted
   throughout the year.

Blanche Fischer Foundation
1511 Southwest Sunset Boulevard, Suite 1-B
Portland, OR 97239
503-819-8205
bff@bff.org
http://www.bff.org

Disability Served: physically disabled
The foundation offers grants to physically disabled
   students. *Eligibility: Applicants who are physically
   disabled, reside in Oregon, and show financial need
   may apply. *Financial Details: Award varies. *Number
   Awarded: Varies. *Deadline: Contact the foundation
   for details.

Blinded Veterans Association
477 H Street, NW
Washington, DC 20001-2694
202-371-8880
bva@bva.org
http://www.bva.org
Disability Served: various
The Kathern F. Gruber Scholarship helps finance
   undergraduate or graduate study. *Eligibility:
   Children or spouses of blind veterans are eligible.
   *Financial Details: Eight scholarships of $2,000 and
   eight scholarships of $1,000. *Number Awarded: 16
   per year. *Deadline: Applications are due in April.

Blind Information Technology Specialists
c/o American Council of the Blind
1155 15th Street, NW, Suite 1004
Washington, DC 20005
800-424-8666
rrrogers@nuvox.net
http://www.acb.org/bits
Disability Served: vision
The Kellie Cannon Scholarship is offered by this
   organization. *Eligibility: Students with a visual
   impairment who wish to prepare for a career in
   the computer field are eligible. *Financial Details:
   Amount varies. *Number Awarded: One per year.
   *Deadline: Contact Blind Information Technology
   Specialists for details.

Boomer Esiason Foundation
c/o Jerry Cahill
417 Fifth Avenue, Second Floor
New York, NY 10016
646-344-3765
jcahill@esiason.org
http://www.cfambassador.com
Disability Served: cystic fibrosis
The foundation awards scholarships to students with
   cystic fibrosis. *Eligibility: Undergraduate and
   graduate students with cystic fibrosis may apply.

Scholarships are awarded based on academic achievement, community service, and financial need. *Financial Details: $500 to $2,000. *Number Awarded: 10 to 15 annually. *Deadline: Quarterly deadlines; contact the foundation for details.

Boston University
Office of Admissions
121 Bay State Road
Boston, MA 02215
617-353-2320
finaid@bu.edu
http://www.bu.edu/admissions/apply/finaid.html
Disability Served: various
The university offers financial aid to help students (including those with disabilities) attend college. *Eligibility: Students who need financial assistance are eligible to apply. *Financial Details: Amounts vary according to need. *Number Awarded: Varies. *Deadline: Write or call for details.

Brigham Young University
University Accessibility Center
1520 WSC
Provo, UT 84602
801-422-2767, 801-422-0436 (TTY)
scholarships@byu.edu
http://saas.byu.edu/depts/finaid
Disability Served: various
This university offers a few private scholarships to assist students with disabilities. *Eligibility: Disabled students who need financial assistance are eligible to apply. Applicants must provide documentation of their disability from a licensed professional. *Financial Details: Awards vary. *Number Awarded: Varies. *Deadline: Write or call for details.

Calhoun Community College
Office of Student Financial Services
PO Box 2216
Decatur, AL 35609-2216
205-306-2500
http://www.calhoun.edu/FinancialAid
Disability Served: various
This two-year college provides financial aid to help students (including those with disabilities) attend college. *Eligibility: Students who need financial assistance are eligible to apply. *Financial Details: Amounts vary according to need. *Number Awarded: Varies. *Deadline: Write or call for details.

California Association for Postsecondary Education and Disability
c/o Janet Shapiro, Disabled Students Programs and Services
721 Cliff Drive
Santa Barbara, CA 93109
805-965-0581, ext. 2365
shapiro@sbcc.net
http://www.caped.net/scholarship.html
Disability Served: various
The association offers many scholarships to disabled students. *Eligibility: Disabled students planning to enroll or currently enrolled at a California postsecondary institution may apply. Undergraduate applicants must have a minimum GPA of 2.5; graduate-level applicants must have a GPA of at least 3.0. *Financial Details: $1,000 or $1,500. *Number Awarded: Varies. *Deadline: September 1.

California Council of the Blind
578 B Street
Hayward, CA 94541
510-537-7877
ccotb@earthlink.net
http://www.ccbnet.org
Disability Served: vision
The council offers scholarships to help finance undergraduate or graduate training. *Eligibility: Residents of California who are legally blind may qualify for scholarships. Applicants must demonstrate financial need. *Financial Details: Scholarships of $300 to $3,000 are available. *Number Awarded: Varies. *Deadline: Contact the council for details.

California Department of Veterans Affairs
Division of Veterans Services
1227 O Street,
Sacramento, CA 95814
800-952-5626, 800-324-5966 (TDD)
http://www.cdva.ca.gov
Disability Served: various
The department offers scholarships to help finance college training. *Eligibility: California children of veterans with a service-related disability are eligible for financial aid to attend a California state college, university, or community college. Applicants must demonstrate financial need. *Financial Details: Full scholarships for tuition and fees plus a stipend of $100 a month are awarded. *Number Awarded: Varies. *Deadline: Contact the department for information.

California Governor's Committee on Employment of People with Disabilities

800 Capitol Mall, MIC 41
Sacramento, CA 95814
800-695-0350, 916-654-9820 (TTY)
http://www.disabilityemployment.org/youth.htm
Disability Served: various
The committee's Hal Connolly Scholarships are designed to help finance college study. *Eligibility: High school seniors who participated in varsity sports despite a disability are eligible. Recipients need not plan to take part in sports while in college. Applicants must be disabled, have a GPA of at least 2.8, and be age 19 or under on January 1 of the same calendar year in which they apply. *Financial Details: Awards of $1,000 are available. *Number Awarded: Six (three male, three female). *Deadline: Write or call for more information.

California Hawaii Elks Major Project Inc.

5450 East Lamona Avenue
Fresno, CA 93727-2224
599-255-4531
http://www.chea-elks.org/uspsd.html
Disability Served: various
This program awards stipends to disabled residents of California and Hawaii to help them finance college training. *Eligibility: California and Hawaii residents with physical impairments, neurological impairments, visual impairments, hearing impairments, and/or speech-language disorders are eligible. Applicants must be sponsored by an Elks member from California or Hawaii. *Financial Details: Stipends are for $1,000 or $2,000 and are renewable for up to four years. *Number Awarded: 20 to 30 per year. *Deadline: April 15.

California-Los Angeles, University of

Financial Aid Office
A129J Murphy Hall, PO Box 951435
Los Angeles, CA 90095-1435
310-206-0400
finaid@saonet.ucla.edu
http://www.fao.ucla.edu
Disability Served: various
The university offers financial aid to help students (including those with disabilities) attend college. *Eligibility: Students who need financial assistance are eligible to apply. *Financial Details: Amounts vary according to need. *Number Awarded: Varies. *Deadline: Write or call for details.

California-Santa Cruz, University of

Financial Aid Office
201 Hahn Student Services Building
Santa Cruz, CA 95064
831-459-4008
fin_aid@cats.ucsc.edu
http://www2.ucsc.edu/fin-aid
Disability Served: various
The university offers financial aid to help students (including those with disabilities) attend college. *Eligibility: Students who need financial assistance are eligible to apply. *Financial Details: Amounts vary according to need. *Number Awarded: Varies. *Deadline: Write or call for details.

California State Polytechnic University-San Luis Obispo

Financial Aid Office
Administration Building, Room 212
San Luis Obispo, CA 93407
805-756-2927
financialaid@calpoly.edu
http://www.ess.calpoly.edu/_finaid/home.html
Disability Served: various
The university provides financial aid to help students (including those with disabilities) attend college. *Eligibility: Students who need financial assistance are eligible to apply. *Financial Details: Amounts vary according to need. *Number Awarded: Varies. *Deadline: Write or call for details.

California State University

Office of the Chancellor
401 Golden Shore, Fourth Floor
Long Beach, CA 90802-4210
562-985-2692
http://www.calstate.edu/hr/flp
Disability Served: various
The Forgivable Loan/Doctoral Incentive Program is the largest program of its type in the nation. It is designed to increase the pool of qualified faculty candidates with the qualifications, motivation, and skill to teach the diverse student body in the California State University system. *Eligibility: Women and persons with disabilities preparing for academic teaching careers are eligible to apply. *Financial Details: Loans of $10,000 per year to a total of $30,000 are available. Twenty percent of the amount borrowed is forgiven for each year of college teaching. *Number Awarded: Varies. *Deadline:

Contact the program administrator for additional information.

California State University-Bakersfield

Office of Financial Aid and Scholarships
9001 Stockdale Highway
Bakersfield, CA 93311-1099
661-654-3016
financialaid@csub.edu
http://www.csub.edu/FinAid
Disability Served: various
This university offers a scholarship program for students with disabilities. *Eligibility: Disabled students who need financial assistance are eligible to apply. *Financial Details: Awards vary according to need. *Number Awarded: Varies. *Deadline: Write or call for details.

California State University-Fresno

Financial Aid Office
Joyal Building, 5150 North Maple Avenue, Room 296
Fresno, CA 93740
559-278-2182
http://studentaffairs.csufresno.edu/financial_aid
Disability Served: various
Among the financial aid awards is the Becky Honda Memorial Scholarship for students with disabilities. *Eligibility: Students with disabilities who demonstrate financial need are eligible. Other restrictions may apply. *Financial Details: Awards vary. *Number Awarded: Varies. *Deadline: Write or call for details.

California State University-Fullerton

Office of Financial Aid
PO Box 6804, UH 146
Fullerton, CA 92834-6804
714-278-3125
fa@fullerton.edu
http://www.fullerton.edu/financialaid
Disability Served: various
The university offers a variety of financial aid for students (including those with disabilities). *Eligibility: Students who need financial assistance are eligible to apply. *Financial Details: Awards vary according to need. *Number Awarded: Varies. *Deadline: Write or call for details.

California Student Aid Commission

PO Box 419027
Rancho Cordova, CA 95741-9027
888-224-7268
http://www.csac.ca.gov
Disability Served: various
The commission provides financial aid to help students (including those with disabilities) attend college. *Eligibility: California students who need financial assistance are eligible to apply. *Financial Details: Amounts vary according to need. *Number Awarded: Varies. *Deadline: Contact the commission for additional details.

Cancer Survivor's Fund

PO Box 792
Missouri City, TX 77459
281-437-7142
info@cancersurvivorsfund.org
http://www.cancersurvivorsfund.org
Disability Served: cancer
The fund awards scholarships to cancer survivors and those currently with cancer. *Eligibility: Applicants must reside in Texas, be enrolled in or accepted for enrollment in an undergraduate or graduate school, and write an essay. *Financial Details: Varies. *Number Awarded: Varies. *Deadline: June 30.

Canyons, College of the

Office of Admissions
26455 Rockwell Canyon Road
Santa Clarita, CA 91355
661-259-7800
http://www.canyons.edu
Disability Served: various
This two-year community college offers a financial aid program for students with disabilities. *Eligibility: Disabled students who need financial assistance are eligible to apply. *Financial Details: Awards vary according to need. *Number Awarded: Varies. *Deadline: Write or call for details.

Central Arkansas, University of

Office of Financial Aid
201 Donaghey Avenue, McCastlain 001
Conway, AR 72035
501-450-3140
finaid@uca.edu
http://www.uca.edu/divisions/admin/finaid
Disability Served: various
The university offers financial aid to help students (including those with disabilities) attend college. *Eligibility: Students who need financial assistance

are eligible to apply. *Financial Details: Amounts vary according to need. *Number Awarded: Varies. *Deadline: Write or call for details.

Central Intelligence Agency
PO Box 12727
Arlington, VA 22209-8727
800-368-3886
http://www.cia.gov/employment/student.html#usp
Disability Served: various
The agency offers the Undergraduate Scholarship Program. *Eligibility: High school seniors and college sophomores with disabilities are eligible to apply. Applicants must be at least 18 years of age by April 1 of their senior year; score 1000 or higher on the SAT, or 21 or higher on the ACT ; and demonstrate financial need. *Financial Details: Scholars are awarded a salary (students are required to work in Washington, D.C., for the CIA during their summer vacation) and up to $18,000 per school year for tuition, fees, books, and supplies. *Number Awarded: Varies each year. *Deadline: November 1.

Central Michigan University
Office of Scholarships and Financial Aid
Student Service Court
Mt Pleasant, MI 48859
888-392-0007
cmuosfa@cmich.edu
http://financialaid.cmich.edu
Disability Served: various
The university offers a variety of financial aid for students (including those with disabilities). *Eligibility: Students who need financial assistance are eligible to apply. *Financial Details: Awards vary according to need. *Number Awarded: Varies. *Deadline: Write or call for details.

Central Piedmont Community College (CPCC)
Office of Financial Aid and Veterans' Affairs
1201 Elizabeth Avenue
Charlotte, NC 28204-2240
704-330-6240
debbie.brooks@cpcc.edu
http://www.cpcc.edu/financial_aid
Disability Served: various
This college offers financial aid to its students (including those with disabilities). *Eligibility: Disabled students who need financial assistance are eligible to apply. *Financial Details: Awards vary according to need.

*Number Awarded: Varies. *Deadline: Write or call for details.

Central Texas College Foundation
Office of Financial Aid
PO Box 1800
Killeen, TX 76540-1800
800-792-3348
financial.aid@ctcd.edu
http://www.ctcd.edu/f_aid/index.htm
Disability Served: various
The foundation provides financial aid to help students (including those with disabilities) attend college. *Eligibility: Students who need financial assistance are eligible to apply. *Financial Details: Amounts vary according to need. *Number Awarded: Varies. *Deadline: Write or call for details.

Central Washington University
Office of Financial Aid
Barge Hall, 400 East University Way, Room 115
Ellensburg, WA 98926-7495
509-963-1611
finaid@cwu.edu
http://www.cwu.edu/~finaid
Disability Served: various
The university provides financial aid to help students (including those with disabilities) attend college. *Eligibility: Students who need financial assistance are eligible to apply. *Financial Details: Amounts vary according to need. *Number Awarded: Varies. *Deadline: Write or call for details.

Cerritos College
Financial Aid Office
11110 Alondra Boulevard
Norwalk, CA 90650
562-860-2451
http://www.cerritos.edu/finaid
Disability Served: various
This two-year college offers the Ron Fornier Scholarship to students who are enrolled in its Disabled Students Program. *Eligibility: Disabled students who need financial assistance are eligible to apply. *Financial Details: Awards vary according to need. *Number Awarded: Varies. *Deadline: Write or call for details.

Chairscholars Foundation Inc.
16101 Carancia Lane
Odessa, FL 33556

813-920-2737
info@chairscholars.org
http://www.chairscholars.org
Disability Served: physically disabled
This organization offers awards for students who are
severely physically challenged. *Eligibility: High
school seniors or college freshmen who are physically
challenged (although they do not have to be in a
wheelchair) who demonstrate strong financial need
are eligible to apply. Applicants must also have a
minimum B+ average, be under 21, and demonstrate
some form of major community service or social
contribution in the past. *Financial Details: $3,000
to $5,000 (with a maximum of $20,000 awarded
over four years of study). *Number Awarded: Varies.
*Deadline: March 1.

Charlotte W. Newcombe Foundation
35 Park Place
Princeton, NJ 08542
609-924-7022
Disability Served: various
The foundation provides grants to colleges and
universities for scholarship support. *Eligibility:
The foundation does not aid individual students,
but awards grants to colleges and universities in
Pennsylvania, New York, New Jersey, Delaware,
Maryland, and Washington, D.C., which, in turn, offer
scholarships of up to $600 a year to students with
disabilities. *Financial Details: A total of $276,000
was awarded to nine colleges and universities for the
2004-05 academic year. *Number Awarded: Varies
each year. *Deadline: Contact the financial aid offices
of participating colleges for additional information.

Cheff Therapeutic Riding Center
8450 North 43rd Street
Augusta, MI 49012
269-731-4471
sandi@cheffcenter.org
http://www.cheffcenter.com
Disability Served: various
The center teaches therapeutic horseback riding to
handicapped children and adults. Graduates of
the four-week program can become instructors of
horseback riding for individuals with disabilities.
*Eligibility: Disabled children and adults who have
an interest in horseback riding are eligible to apply
for scholarships. *Financial Details: Half-tuition
scholarships are available. *Number Awarded:

Varies. *Deadline: Contact the center for additional
information.

Christian Record Services Inc.
4444 South 52nd Street
Lincoln, NE 68516
402-488-0981
info@christianrecord.org
http://www.christianrecord.org
Disability Served: vision
This organization provides financial aid to help students
toward a bachelor's degree. *Eligibility: Candidates
who are legally blind are eligible to apply. Candidates
must show financial need and describe how college
will help them develop independence. *Financial
Details: Amount of grant varies from year to year.
*Number Awarded: Varies. *Deadline: Applications
are accepted between November 1 and April 1.

Cincinnati, University of
Office of Financial Aid
PO Box 210125
Cincinnati, OH 45221-0125
513-556-6816
http://www.financialaid.uc.edu
Disability Served: various
This university offers a financial aid program for students
with disabilities. *Eligibility: Disabled students who
need financial assistance are eligible to apply. *Finan-
cial Details: Awards vary according to need. *Number
Awarded: Varies. *Deadline: Write or call for details.

Colorado-Boulder, University of
Office of Financial Aid
556 UCB
Boulder, CO 80309-0556
303-492-5091
finaid@colorado.edu
http://www.colorado.edu/finaid
Disability Served: various
This university provides financial aid to help students
(including those with disabilities) attend college.
*Eligibility: Students who need financial assistance
are eligible to apply. *Financial Details: Amounts
vary according to need. *Number Awarded: Varies.
*Deadline: Write or call for details.

Colorado Department of Education
Competitive Grants and Awards Unit, Room 501
201 East Colfax Avenue

Denver, CO 80203-1799
303-866-6974
kalber_t@cde.state.co.us
http://www.cde.state.co.us
Disability Served: various
The department provides financial aid to help students
(including those with disabilities) attend college.
*Eligibility: Colorado students who need financial
assistance are eligible to apply. *Financial Details:
Amounts vary according to need. *Number Awarded:
Varies. *Deadline: Contact the department for
additional details.

Columbia State Community College
Office of Financial Aid
PO Box 1315
Columbia, TN 38402-1315
931-540-2722
http://www.columbiastate.edu/financialaid
Disability Served: various
This two-year college offers a scholarship program
to help students with disabilities. *Eligibility:
First-year students with disabilities are eligible.
*Financial Details: Amounts vary. *Number
Awarded: Varies. *Deadline: Write or call for
details.

Concordia University
Office of Financial Aid
1530 Concordia West
Irvine, CA 92612
949-854-8002
finaid@cui.edu
http://www.cui.edu
Disability Served: various
This private four-year college offers financial aid to
help students with disabilities. *Eligibility: Disabled
students who need financial assistance are eligible to
apply. *Financial Details: Amounts vary according to
need. *Number Awarded: Varies. *Deadline: Contact
the University for additional details.

Conference of Educational Administrators of Schools and Programs for the Deaf
PO Box 1778
St. Augustine, FL 32085-1778
904-810-5200
nationaloffice@ceasd.org
http://ceasd.org
Disability Served: hearing

This organization offers graduate scholarships to help
underrepresented ethnic and cultural groups who
are interested in careers in the education of deaf
students. *Eligibility: Minority students enrolled in an
approved graduate program in the area of deafness
are eligible. *Financial Details: $2,000. *Number
Awarded: Two per year. *Deadline: Contact the
organization for further information.

Connecticut Department of Higher Education
Office of Student Financial Aid
61 Woodland Street
Hartford, CT 06105
800-842-0229
http://www.ctdhe.org/SFA
Disability Served: various
The department awards financial aid for undergraduate college study. *Eligibility: Connecticut residents
(including those who are disabled) are eligible; other
requirements vary by program. *Financial Details: Varies by program. *Number Awarded: Varies. *Deadline:
Varies. Call or write for information. The Department
also offers grants to Connecticut residents who are
dependents of disabled Connecticut war veterans.

Connecticut Department of Veterans Affairs
287 West Street
Rocky Hill, CT 06067
860-529-2571, 800-447-0961
http://www.state.ct.us/ctva
Disability Served: various
The department provides tuition wavers for the purpose
of college study. *Eligibility: Connecticut military
veterans are eligible to apply. Applicants must be
residents of Connecticut and attend a public college
or university in the state. *Financial Details: Amounts
vary, but benefits are limited to cost of tuition.
*Number Awarded: Varies each year. *Deadline:
Contact the department for details.

Connecticut-Storrs, University of
Office of Student Financial Aid Services
233 Glenbrook Road, Unit 4116
Storrs, CT 06269-4116
860-486-2819
financialaid@uconn.edu
http://www.financialaid.uconn.edu/cnt-main/home.php
Disability Served: various
The university offers financial aid for students (including those with disabilities). *Eligibility: Students who

need financial assistance are eligible to apply. *Financial Details: Awards vary according to need. *Number Awarded: Varies. *Deadline: Write or call for details.

Council of Citizens with Low Vision International

1155 15 Street, NW, Suite 1004
Washington, DC 20005
800-733-2258
http://www.cclvi.org/scholarship.html
Disability Served: vision
The council offers the Fred Scheigert Scholarship to help finance college study. *Eligibility: High school seniors who have been accepted into college and current undergraduates with low vision are eligible to apply. Recipients must maintain a GPA of at least 3.0 and attend school full time. *Financial Details: Varies. *Number Awarded: Varies. *Deadline: April 15.

Crohn's and Colitis Foundation of America

386 Park Avenue South, 17th Floor
New York, NY 10016
800-932-2423
http://www.ccfa.org
Disability Served: physically disabled
The Foundation awards the Brudnick Scholarship to help finance college study. *Eligibility: Undergraduate college students with Crohn's disease, colitis, or an ostomy are eligible. Applicants must be under 24 years of age, and priority is given to an individual who can demonstrate how he or she has overcome major obstacles in life. *Financial Details: The Scholarship is for $2,500. *Number Awarded: One per year. *Deadline: Applications are due in January.

Curry College

Student Financial Services
1071 Blue Hill Avenue
Milton, MA 02186
800-669-0686
Fin-aid@curry.edu
http://www.curry.edu/Admissions/Financial+Aid
Disability Served: learning disabled
The college offers the Jennifer Ann Phillips Scholarship. *Eligibility: Sophomores, juniors, or seniors who are learning disabled or students who are interested in teaching the learning disabled may apply. Preference will be given to applicants with both qualifications. Recipients are under moral obligation to repay the grant (interest free) as soon as possible. *Financial Details: Up to $3,500. *Number Awarded:

Varies. *Deadline: Contact the student financial services for details.

Cuyamaca College

Student Services One-Stop Center
Building Z300
900 Rancho San Diego Parkway
El Cajon, CA 92019
619-660-4201
http://www.cuyamaca.edu/finaid
Disability Served: various
This two-year community college provides financial aid to help students (including those with disabilities) attend college. *Eligibility: Students who need financial assistance are eligible to apply. *Financial Details: Amounts vary according to need. *Number Awarded: Varies. *Deadline: Write or call for details.

Cystic Fibrosis Scholarship Foundation

2814 Grant Street
Evanston, IL 60201
847-328-0127
mkbcfsf@aol.com
http://www.cfscholarship.org
Disability Served: cystic fibrosis
The foundation provides financial aid to help students (including those with disabilities) attend college. *Eligibility: High school seniors and college students with cystic fibrosis who need financial assistance are eligible to apply. *Financial Details: $1,000 to $2,000. *Number Awarded: Varies. *Deadline: March 15.

Daughters of the American Revolution (DAR)

Committee Services Office, Attn: Scholarships
1776 D Street, NW
Washington, DC 20006-5303
202-879-3293
http://www.dar.org
Disability Served: learning disabled
The organization offers Margaret Howard Hamilton Scholarships to help finance college study. *Eligibility: High school students who plan to enroll in the Harvey and Bernice Jones Learning Center, at the University of the Ozarks-Clarksville, Arkansas, are eligible. Candidates must be sponsored by a local DAR chapter. *Financial Details: Scholarships are for $1,000 a year. *Number Awarded: Varies. *Deadline: April 15. The DAR offers a variety of additional scholarships.

David Lipscomb University
Office of Financial Aid
3901 Granny White Pike
Nashville, TN 37204
615-269-1791
http://www.lipscomb.edu
Disability Served: various
Among its other financial aid awards, the university
offers a scholarship for students who have a parent
with a disability. *Eligibility: Children of disabled
parents are eligible to apply. *Financial Details:
Amounts vary. *Number Awarded: One per year.
*Deadline: Call or write for additional details.

Davis and Elkins College
Office of Admissions
100 Campus Drive
Elkins, WV 26241
304-636-1900
admiss@davisandelkins.edu
http://www.davisandelkins.edu
Disability Served: various
This private four-year institution offers a financial aid
program for students with disabilities. *Eligibility:
Disabled students who need financial assistance
are eligible to apply. *Financial Details: Awards
vary according to need. *Number Awarded: Varies.
*Deadline: Write or call for details.

Daytona Beach Community College
Office of Financial Aid
1200 West International Speedway Boulevard
Daytona Beach, FL 32114
386-255-8131
http://www.dbcc.cc.fl.us/html/departments/finaid
Disability Served: various
This two-year community college provides financial aid
to help students (including those with disabilities)
attend college. *Eligibility: Students who need
financial assistance are eligible to apply. *Financial
Details: Amounts vary according to need. *Number
Awarded: Varies. *Deadline: Write or call for details.

De Anza College
Office of Financial Aid
21250 Stevens Creek Boulevard
Cupertino, CA 95014
408-864-8718
FinancialAid@deanza.edu
http://www.deanza.fhda.edu/financialaid
Disability Served: various
This two-year college offers a financial aid to students
(including those with disabilities). *Eligibility:
Students who need financial assistance are eligible
to apply. *Financial Details: Awards vary. *Number
Awarded: Varies. *Deadline: Write or call for details.

Defiance College
Office of Financial Aid
701 North Clinton Street
Defiance, OH 43512
419-784-4010
http://www.defiance.edu/pages/FA_home.html
Disability Served: various
This four-year institution offers financial aid to help
students (including those with disabilities) attend
college. *Eligibility: Students who need financial
assistance are eligible to apply. *Financial Details:
Amounts vary according to need. *Number Awarded:
Varies. *Deadline: Write or call for details.

Delaware Commission of Veterans Affairs
Robbins Building, 802 Silver Lake Boulevard, Suite 100
Dover, DE 19904
302-739-2792, 800-344-9900
http://www.state.de.us/veteran
Disability Served: various
The commission provides tuition wavers for the purpose
of college study. *Eligibility: Children of Delaware
military veterans who died as a result of military
service, or who have been declared missing in action,
are eligible to apply. Applicants must be residents of
Delaware and attend a public college or university
in the state. *Financial Details: $525 or the amount
of tuition per academic year, whichever is greater.
*Number Awarded: Varies each year. *Deadline:
Contact the commission for details. The commission
also offers scholarships for active members of the
Delaware National Guard.

Delaware Higher Education Commission
820 North French Street
Wilmington, DE 19801
302-577-3240, 800-292-7935
dhec@doe.k12.de.us
http://www.doe.state.de.us/high-ed
Disability Served: various
The commission provides financial aid to help students
(including those with disabilities) attend college.
*Eligibility: Delaware students who need financial

assistance are eligible to apply. *Financial Details: Amounts vary according to need. *Number Awarded: Varies. *Deadline: Contact the commission for additional details.

Delaware-Newark, University of
Scholarships & Financial Aid
Student Services Building
Newark, DE 19716
302-831-8761
finaid@udel.edu
http://www.udel.edu/admissions/viewbook/finance
Disability Served: various
The university provides financial aid to help students (including those with disabilities) attend college. *Eligibility: Students who need financial assistance are eligible to apply. *Financial Details: Amounts vary according to need. *Number Awarded: Varies. *Deadline: Write or call for details.

Delta Gamma Foundation
3250 Riverside Drive, PO Box 21397
Columbus, OH 43221
http://www.deltagamma.org/scholarships_fellowships_and_loans_2.shtml
Disability Served: vision
Delta Gamma offers the Wilma H. Wright Memorial Scholarship to help finance postsecondary training. *Eligibility: Members of Delta Gamma who are visually impaired or who wish to prepare to work with the visually impaired are eligible to apply. *Financial Details: Varies. *Number Awarded: One per year. *Deadline: Contact the sorority for more information.

Disabled American Veterans
PO Box 14301
Cincinnati, OH 45250
859-441-7300
http://www.dav.org
Disability Served: various
This organization offers scholarships to help finance college study. *Eligibility: Children of veterans with a service-related disability are eligible. Interested students may apply when finishing high school or during any of the first three years of college. Scholarships are awarded based on financial need and strong academic record. *Financial Details: Scholarships range from $200 to $3,000. *Number Awarded: Varies. *Deadline: Contact for more information.

Disabled American Veterans Auxiliary
3725 Alexandria Pike
Cold Springs, KY 41076
859-441-7300
http://www.dav.org/dava
Disability Served: various
The auxiliary provides loans to help finance college study. *Eligibility: Children whose mothers were or are members of the auxiliary are eligible. *Financial Details: Loans of up to $1,000 are renewable for up to four years and must be repaid within seven years after graduation. *Number Awarded: Varies. *Deadline: Write or call for details.

DuPage, College of
Student Financial Aid Office
Student Resource Center, Room 2050
Glen Ellyn, IL 60137
630-942-2251
financialaid@cdnet.cod.edu
http://www.cod.edu/dept/fin_aid
Disability Served: various
This two-year college offers financial aid for students with disabilities. *Eligibility: Disabled students who demonstrate financial need are eligible. *Financial Details: Awards vary according to need. *Number Awarded: Varies. *Deadline: Write or call for details.

The Ear Foundation
1817 Patterson Street
Nashville, TN 37203
800-545-HEAR (Voice/TDD)
info@earfoundation.org
http://www.earfoundation.org
Disability Served: hearing
The Minnie Pearl Scholarship helps students pay for college tuition. *Eligibility: Applicants must have a significant bilateral hearing loss, a minimum 3.0 GPA, and have attended regular schools. *Financial Details: Scholarships are for $2,500; a $500 bonus award is available to students who maintain a 3.5 cumulative GPA or higher during the school year. *Number Awarded: Varies. *Deadline: February 16.

East Central College
1964 Prairie Dell Road
Union, MO 63084
636-583-5193, 636-583-4581 (TDD)
http://www.eastcentral.edu/stuserv/finaid
Disability Served: various

This two-year public institution offers financial aid to help students (including those with disabilities) attend college. *Eligibility: Students who need financial assistance are eligible to apply. *Financial Details: Amounts vary according to need. *Number Awarded: Varies. *Deadline: Contact the college for additional details.

Eastern Amputee Golf Association
2015 Amherst Drive
Bethlehem, PA 18015-5606
888-868-0992
info@eaga.org
http://www.eaga.org
Disability Served: amputees
This organization offers scholarships for college study. *Eligibility: Amputee members and/or a member of his or her family who need financial assistance are eligible to apply. Award recipients must maintain a 2.0 GPA to continue receiving the scholarship over its four-year duration. *Financial Details: $1,000. *Number Awarded: Five. *Deadline: Contact for additional details.

Eastern Kentucky University
Office of Financial Aid
521 Lancaster Avenue
Richmond, KY 40475
859-622-2361
http://www.eku.edu
Disability Served: various
The university offers financial aid and scholarships for students with disabilities. *Eligibility: Disabled students who demonstrate financial need are eligible. *Financial Details: Awards vary according to need. *Number Awarded: Varies. *Deadline: Write or call for details.

East Los Angeles College
Financial Aid Office
1301 Avenida Cesar Chavez, C2-3
Monterey Park, CA 91754
323-265-8738
http://www.elac.edu/departments/financialaid
Disability Served: various
This two-year college offers financial aid for students, including those with disabilities. *Eligibility: Students who demonstrate financial need are eligible. *Financial Details: Awards vary according to need. *Number Awarded: Varies. *Deadline: Write or call for details.

Edinboro University of Pennsylvania
Financial Aid Office
Hamilton Hall
Edinboro, PA 16444
888-611-2680
finaid@edinboro.edu
http://piper.edinboro.edu/cwis/studaff/emr/finaid
Disability Served: various
The university provides the following financial aid options for disabled students: the Mabel Hamlett Scholarship, the Charlotte W. Newcombe Foundation Grants, the Charlotte W. Newcombe Scholarship, and the SGA Scholarship for Students with Disabilities. *Eligibility: Disabled students with a minimum 2.0 GPA who demonstrate financial need are eligible. *Financial Details: Awards vary according to need. *Number Awarded: Varies. *Deadline: Write or call for details.

Edmonds Community College
Edmonds Community College Foundation
20000 68th Avenue West
Lynnwood, WA 98036
425-640-1274
foundation@edcc.edu
http://foundation.edcc.edu
Disability Served: various
This two-year college offers a variety of financial aid, including the Crane Fund for Widows and Children Scholarship for needy and deserving widows and children who, at the death of their spouses, were left without adequate means of support. *Eligibility: Applicants who demonstrate financial need are eligible. *Financial Details: Awards vary. *Number Awarded: Varies. *Deadline: Applications are typically due in late March.

El Camino College
Office of Financial Aid
16007 Crenshaw Boulevard
Torrance, CA 90506
310-660-3493
eccfaid@elcamino.edu
http://www.elcamino.edu/student_services/FAO
Disability Served: various
This two-year college provides financial aid to help students, including those with disabilities, attend college. *Eligibility: Students who need financial assistance are eligible to apply. *Financial Details: Amounts vary according to need. *Number Awarded: Varies. *Deadline: Contact the college for additional details.

Eli Lilly and Company
c/o Lilly Secretariat
PMB 327, 310 Busse Highway
Park Ridge, IL 60068-3251
800-809-8202
lillyscholarships@reintegration.com
http://www.reintegration.com/resources/scholarships
Disability Served: mental health
This organization offers Lilly Reintegration Scholarships.
*Eligibility: Applicants must be diagnosed with
schizophrenia, schizophreniform, schizoaffective
disorder, or bipolar disorder and be currently
receiving medical treatment for the disease.
*Financial Details: Varies. *Number Awarded: Varies.
*Deadline: Contact Eli Lilly and Company for details.

Elizabeth City State University
Office of Financial Aid
1704 Weeksville Road
Elizabeth City, NC 27909
252-335-3283
http://www.ecsu.edu/prospective/financialaid.cfm
Disability Served: various
This university offers financial aid and vocational
rehabilitation scholarships for students with
disabilities. *Eligibility: Disabled students who
demonstrate financial need are eligible. *Financial
Details: Awards vary according to need. *Number
Awarded: Varies. *Deadline: Write or call for details.

Elks National Foundation
Scholarship Department
2750 North Lakeview Avenue
Chicago, IL 60614-1889
773-755-4732
scholarship@elks.org
http://www.elks.org/enf/scholars/ourscholarships.cfm
Disability Served: various
This fraternal organization offers the Emergency
Educational Grant program to help students finance
college study. *Eligibility: Children of deceased or
totally disabled Elks members may apply. *Financial
Details: Up to $4,000. *Number Awarded: Varies.
*Deadline: Applications should be filed between
July 1 and December 31. Additional scholarships are
available.

Erskine College
Office of Financial Aid
PO Box 337
Due West, SC 29639
864-379-8832
http://www.erskine.edu/admissions/financialaid
Disability Served: various
Among its other financial aid awards, the college
offers the William H. Dunlap Scholarship Program, a
scholarship for students whose parents are deceased
or who have a parent with a disability. *Eligibility:
Students who have a parent with a disability are
eligible. *Financial Details: Up to $4,000. *Number
Awarded: Varies. *Deadline: Contact the college for
details.

Ethel Louise Armstrong Foundation
2460 North Lake Avenue, PMB #128
Altadena, CA 91001
626-398-8840
executivedirector@ela.org
http://www.ela.org/scholarships/scholarships.html
Disability Served: physically disabled
This organization offers scholarships for college study.
*Eligibility: Women graduate students with physical
disabilities who are enrolled in a college or university
in the United States are eligible to apply. Students
must be active in a local, state, or national disability
organization. *Financial Details: Scholarships range
between $500 and $2,000. *Number Awarded: Varies.
*Deadline: June 1.

Faulkner State Community College
Office of Student Financial Assistance
1900 Highway 31 South
Bay Minette, AL 36507
251-580-2151
Financial_Aid@FaulknerState.edu
http://www.faulkner.cc.al.us
Disability Served: various
This two-year community college offers financial aid for
students, including those with disabilities. *Eligibility:
Students who demonstrate financial need are
eligible. *Financial Details: Awards vary according to
need. *Number Awarded: Varies. *Deadline: Write or
call for details.

Florida, University of
Student Financial Affairs
P-113 Peabody Hall, PO Box 114025
Gainesville, FL 32611-4025
352-392-1272 (Voice/TDD)
http://www.ufsa.ufl.edu/sfa

Disability Served: various

This state university provides financial aid to help students (including those with disabilities) attend college. *Eligibility: Students who need financial assistance are eligible to apply. *Financial Details: Amounts vary according to need. *Number Awarded: Varies. *Deadline: Write or call for details.

Florida Council of the Blind

2915 Circle Ridge Drive
Orange Park, FL 32065
800-262-4448
http://www.fcb.org
Disability Served: vision
The council offers scholarships for academic achievement and upward mobility, and a scholarship for a part-time student. *Eligibility: Florida residents who are legally blind are eligible (although they do not need to attend college in Florida to be eligible). Candidates must have a good prior academic record. *Financial Details: Awards range from $500 to $1,500. *Number Awarded: Three. *Deadline: Contact the council for dates.

Florida Department of Education

Office of Student Financial Assistance
1940 North Monroe Street, Suite 70
Tallahassee, FL 32303-4759
888-827-2004
http://www.floridastudentfinancialaid.org/osfahomepg.htm
Disability Served: various
The department provides scholarships covering tuition and fees at Florida's public colleges or universities. *Eligibility: Children of deceased or 100 percent disabled veterans pursuing or planning to pursue postsecondary education at a Florida's public college or university are eligible to apply. *Financial Details: Tuition and fees are covered. *Number Awarded: Approximately 90 scholarships are awarded per year. *Deadline: Apply by April 1. The department also offers the Florida Student Assistance Grant and Access to Better Learning and Education Grant Programs.

Florida Department of Veterans' Service

Mary Grizzle Building, 11351 Ulmerton Road, Room 311-K
Largo, FL 33778-1630
727-518-3202

http://www.floridavets.org
Disability Served: various
The department offers tuition waivers to help finance college. *Eligibility: Florida residents who are children of disabled veterans, or those who died in combat or as a result of combat-related injuries, are eligible. Participants must maintain a GPA of at least 2.0. *Financial Details: Full tuition. *Number Awarded: Varies. *Deadline: Varies. These awards are administered by the Florida Office of Student Financial Assistance (http://www.firn.edu/doe/osfa/cddvfactsheet.htm).

Florida International University

Financial Aid Office
University Park, PC 125
Miami, FL 33199
305-348-7272
finaid@fiu.edu
http://www.fiu.edu/orgs/finaid
Disability Served: various
The university offers financial aid to help students (including those with disabilities) defer the costs of college. *Eligibility: Students who need financial assistance are eligible to apply. *Financial Details: Amounts vary and depend on need. *Number Awarded: Varies. *Deadline: Write or call for details.

Florida State University

Office of Financial Aid
University Center, Suite 4400A
Tallahassee, FL 32306-2430
850-644-0539
ofacs@admin.fsu.edu
http://www.fsu.edu/prospective/undergraduate/finances.shtml
Disability Served: various
The university offers financial aid to help students (including those with disabilities) attend college. *Eligibility: Students who need financial assistance are eligible to apply. *Financial Details: Amounts vary according to need. *Number Awarded: Varies. *Deadline: Contact the university for additional details.

Fordham University School of Law

33 West 60th Street, 2nd Floor
New York, NY 10023
212-636-6815
financialaid@law.fordham.edu

http://law.fordham.edu/financialaid.htm
Disability Served: hearing, physically disabled, vision
The Amy Reiss Blind Student Scholarship is awarded to help finance law school. *Eligibility: Disabled (vision, hearing, mobility impaired, etc.) students who demonstrate financial need are eligible. Preference is given to blind or partially blind students. *Financial Details: The scholarship covers partial tuition for three years. *Number Awarded: One per year. *Deadline: Contact the university for dates. Additional scholarships may be available.

Forward Face
Scholarship Committee
317 East 34th Street, Suite 901A
New York, NY 10016
212-684-5860
info@forwardface.org
http://www.forwardface.org
Disability Served: physically disabled
Forward Face offers educational scholarships. *Eligibility: Students with craniofacial conditions who are at least 13 years old are eligible to apply. *Financial Details: $500 and $1,000 scholarships are available. *Number Awarded: Up to three. *Deadline: February 1.

Foundation for Physical Therapy
1111 North Fairfax Street
Alexandria, VA 22314-1488
800-999-2782, 703-683-6748 (TDD)
http://www.apta.org/Foundation
Disability Served: various
The Mary McMillan Scholarship helps students (including those with disabilities) who are entering a doctoral program. *Eligibility: Students who wish to prepare for careers in physical therapy are eligible. Applicants must be preparing to work in a clinical setting. *Financial Details: Varies. *Number Awarded: Varies. *Deadline: Write or call for application materials and additional information.

Foundation for Science and Disability
503 Northwest 89th Street
Gainesville, FL 32607-1400
352-374-5774
http://www.as.wvu.edu/~scidis/organizations/fsd_main. html
Disability Served: various
The foundation provides grants for the purpose of financing education. *Eligibility: Students with disabilities working toward graduate degrees in the sciences or related fields are eligible to apply. *Financial Details: Grants are for the amount of $1,000. *Number Awarded: One to two per year. *Deadline: December 15.

Foundation Northwest
Old City Hall, Suite 624
North 221 Wall Street
Spokane, WA 99201-0826
888-267-5606
admin@foundationnw.org
http://foundationnw.org
Disability Served: physically disabled
The foundation offers the Ren H. Rice Scholarship to help finance college study. *Eligibility: Spokane-area residents with physical disabilities are eligible. *Financial Details: The scholarship covers tuition, fees, and books at a Washington state college or university. Scholarships are renewable. *Number Awarded: Varies. *Deadline: Contact the foundation for more information.

Friends University
Office of Financial Aid
2100 West University Avenue
Wichita, KS 67213
316-295-5200, 800-794-6945
apply4$@friends.edu
http://www.friends.edu/FinancialAssistance
Disability Served: various
This liberal arts college provides financial aid to help students (including those with disabilities) attend college. *Eligibility: Students who need financial assistance are eligible to apply. *Financial Details: Amounts vary according to need. *Number Awarded: Varies. *Deadline: Write or call for details.

Frostburg State University
Disability Support Services
150 Pullen Hall
Frostburg, MD 21532
301-687-4483 (Voice/TTY)
lpullen@frostburg.edu
http://www.frostburg.edu/clife/dss/frontpage.htm
Disability Served: various
The university offers the Delta Chi Fraternity Scholarship to students with disabilities. *Eligibility: Students who are enrolled as full-time students, demonstrate academic ability, and have documented disabilities

are eligible to apply. *Financial Details: Amounts vary. *Number Awarded: Varies. *Deadline: March 1.

Gallaudet University
Financial Aid Office
800 Florida Avenue, NE
Washington, DC 20002
202-651-5290 (Voice/TTY), 800-995-0990 (Voice/TTY)
Financial.Aid@gallaudet.edu
http://financialaid.gallaudet.edu
Disability Served: hearing
This is the only general college established exclusively to serve the deaf. It offers a full liberal arts program and financial aid to needy students. *Eligibility: Deaf students in need of financial assistance are eligible to apply. *Financial Details: Awards vary and depend on need. *Number Awarded: Varies. *Deadline: Contact the university for details.

Gallaudet University Alumni Association
800 Florida Avenue, NE
Washington, DC 20002
202-651-5060
alumni.relations@gallaudet.edu
http://alumni.gallaudet.edu
Disability Served: hearing
The alumni association offers scholarships to help deaf and hard of hearing people finance graduate training. *Eligibility: Graduates of Gallaudet and others who are deaf and are pursuing doctoral studies are eligible. *Financial Details: Amounts vary. *Number Awarded: Varies. *Deadline: Applications are due April 20.

Galveston College
4015 Avenue Q
Galveston, TX 77550
409-944-4242
http://www.gc.edu/FinancialAid/index.html
Disability Served: various
This two-year community college offers a scholarship (sponsored by the Houston Metropolitan Area Diagnosticians) for students with disabilities. *Eligibility: Disabled students who need financial assistance are eligible to apply. *Financial Details: The scholarship is in the amount of $750. *Number Awarded: Two annually. *Deadline: Write or call for details.

Gardner-Webb University
Financial Planning Office
Boiling Springs, NC 28017

704-406-4243
http://wwwebb.gardner-webb.edu/fy/fa.html
Disability Served: various
This private university offers financial aid for students with disabilities. *Eligibility: Disabled students who need financial assistance are eligible to apply. *Financial Details: Awards vary according to need. *Number Awarded: Varies. *Deadline: Write or call for details.

GateWay Community College
Office of Student Financial Assistance
108 North 40th Street
Phoenix, AZ 85034
602-286-8300
finaid@gwmail.maricopa.edu
http://enroll.gatewaycc.edu
Disability Served: various
This two-year community college provides financial aid to help students (including those with disabilities) attend college. *Eligibility: Students who need financial assistance are eligible to apply. *Financial Details: Amounts vary according to need. *Number Awarded: Varies. *Deadline: Contact the college for additional details.

Gateway Community-Technical College
60 Sargent Drive
New Haven, CT 06511
203-285-2234, 203-285-2231
tpage@gwcc.commnet.edu
http://www.gwctc.commnet.edu
Disability Served: various
Disabled students planning to or currently attending this two-year community college are eligible for financial aid. *Eligibility: Disabled students who need financial assistance are eligible to apply. *Financial Details: Awards vary according to need. *Number Awarded: Varies. *Deadline: Write or call for details.

Geoffrey Foundation
PO Box 1112
Ocean Avenue
Kennebunkport, ME 04046
Disability Served: hearing
The foundation offers financial aid to help with the expenses of an auditory-verbal program. *Eligibility: Persons with a severe hearing loss who intend to enroll in an auditory-verbal program are eligible. *Financial Details: Amounts vary. *Number Awarded: Varies. *Deadline: End of March.

Geological Society of America

PO Box 9140
Boulder, CO 80301-9140
303-357-1028
awards@geosociety.org
http://www.geosociety.org
Disability Served: various
The society awards research grants to students
(including those with disabilities)*Eligibility: Geology
students who are studying at a university in the
southeastern, south central, or northeastern states
are eligible. *Financial Details: Research grants of
$400 to $2,500 are awarded. *Number Awarded:
Varies. *Deadline: Contact the society for details.

George Washington University

Office of Financial Assistance
2121 I Street, NW, #310
Washington, DC 20052
202-994-6620, 800-222-6242
finaid@gwu.edu
http://gwired.gwu.edu/finaid
Disability Served: various
The university provides financial aid to help students
(including those with disabilities) attend college.
*Eligibility: Students who need financial assistance
are eligible to apply. *Financial Details: Amounts
vary according to need. *Number Awarded: Varies.
*Deadline: Contact the university for additional
details.

Georgia, University of

Disability Resource Center
114 Clark Howell Hall
Athens, GA 30602-3338
706-542-8719, 706-542-8778 (TTY)
http://www.drc.uga.edu
Disability Served: various
The university's Disability Resource Center offers a
variety of scholarships for students with disabilities.
*Eligibility: Disabled students who need financial
assistance are eligible to apply; additional
requirements vary by scholarship. *Financial Details:
$500 to full tuition. *Number Awarded: Varies.
*Deadline: Contact the Disability Resource Center for
details.

Georgia Council of the Blind

Scholarship Committee Chair
1477 Nebo Road
Dallas, GA 30157
williamsdebk@wmconnect.com
http://www.georgiacounciloftheblind.com
Disability Served: vision
The council awards a scholarship to help vision-impaired
students pay for college. *Eligibility: Georgia students
with a visual impairment are eligible. High school
seniors or first year college students may apply.
Selection is based on academic record, with financial
need as a secondary factor. *Financial Details: Up to
$1,000. *Number Awarded: Varies. *Deadline: Contact
the council for information.

Georgia Institute of Technology

Office of Student Financial Planning and Services
225 North Avenue
Atlanta, GA 30332-0460
404-894-4160
finaid@gatech.edu
http://www.finaid.gatech.edu
Disability Served: various
The university offers the Roy and Zou Feagin Scholarship
for students with mobility impairments, hearing
impairments, visual impairments, learning disabilities,
psychological disabilities, and other disabilities.
*Eligibility: Disabled undergraduate students who
have a GPA of at least 2.0, show leadership qualities,
and demonstrate financial need may apply. *Financial
Details: Awards vary. *Number Awarded: Varies.
*Deadline: Write or call for details.

Georgia Southwestern University

Office of Financial Aid
Sanford Hall, 800 Wheatley Street, Room 207
Americus, GA 31709
229-928-1378
http://www.gsw.edu/~finaid
Disability Served: various
The university provides financial aid to help students
(including those with disabilities) attend college.
*Eligibility: Students who need financial assistance
are eligible to apply. *Financial Details: Amounts
vary according to need. *Number Awarded: Varies.
*Deadline: Write or call for details.

Georgia Student Finance Commission

2082 East Exchange Place, Suite 200
Tucker, GA 30084
770-724-9000, 800-505-GSFC
http://www.gsfc.org/Main/dsp_main.cfm

Disability Served: various

The Georgia Law Enforcement Personnel Dependents Grant and the Georgia Public Safety Memorial Grant help students meet college expenses. *Eligibility: Children of disabled police, fire, and prison guards in Georgia are eligible. Applicants must have resided in Georgia for at least one year and be attending college in Georgia. *Financial Details: Amount varies and is renewable. *Number Awarded: Varies. *Deadline: Contact the commission for more information.

Disability Served: various

Glendale Community College

Financial Aid Office
6000 West Olive Avenue
Glendale, AZ 85302
623-845-3366
http://www.gc.maricopa.edu/finaid
Disability Served: various

This two-year community college provides financial aid to help students (including those with disabilities) attend college. *Eligibility: Students who need financial assistance are eligible to apply. *Financial Details: Amounts vary according to need. *Number Awarded: Varies. *Deadline: Write or call for details.

Gordon College

Student Financial Services
255 Grapevine Road
Wenham, MA 01984
978-927-2300
http://www.gordon.edu/finance
Disability Served: various

This private four-year college provides financial aid to help students (including those with disabilities) attend college. *Eligibility: Students who need financial assistance are eligible to apply. *Financial Details: Amounts vary according to need. *Number Awarded: Varies. *Deadline: Contact the college for additional details.

Gore Family Memorial Foundation

4747 Ocean Drive, #204
Ft Lauderdale, FL 33308
Disability Served: various

The foundation provides grants to help with college costs. *Eligibility: Persons with severe disabilities are eligible to apply. Financial need is taken into consideration. *Financial Details: Most grants average $1,000 to $2,000. *Number Awarded: Varies. *Deadline: Write for additional information.

Grand Valley State University

Disability Support Services
1 Campus Drive, 200 STU
Allendale, MI 49401-9403
616-331-2490
http://www.gvsu.edu/dss
Disability Served: various

The university offers the Berkowitz Scholarship for Handicapped Students. *Eligibility: Full-time students with disabilities attending the university are eligible. *Financial Details: $500 or greater, depending on need and available funding. *Number Awarded: Varies. *Deadline: March 15.

Grays Harbor College

Financial Aid Office
1620 Edward Smith Drive
Aberdeen, WA 98520
800-562-4830, 360-538-4223 (TDD/TTY)
http://ghc.ctc.edu/finaid
Disability Served: various

This two-year college provides financial aid to help students (including those with disabilities) attend college. *Eligibility: Students who need financial assistance are eligible to apply. *Financial Details: Amounts vary according to need. *Number Awarded: Varies. *Deadline: Write or call for details.

Hannibal-La Grange College

Office of Financial Aid
2800 Palmyra Road
Hannibal, MO 63401
800-HLG-1119
http://www.hlg.edu/Admiss/financialaid.html
Disability Served: various

This four-year liberal arts college provides financial aid to help students (including those with disabilities) attend college. *Eligibility: Students who need financial assistance are eligible to apply. *Financial Details: Amounts vary according to need. *Number Awarded: Varies. *Deadline: Contact the college for additional details.

Harding University

Student Financial Services
PO Box 12282
Searcy, AR 72149-0001
800-477-3243
finaid@harding.edu
http://www.harding.edu/finaid

Disability Served: various

This university offers financial aid to help students (including those with disabilities) with college expenses. *Eligibility: Students who demonstrate financial need are eligible. *Financial Details: Awards vary. *Number Awarded: Varies. *Deadline: Write or call for details.

Harper College

Scholarships and Financial Assistance
Building C, 1200 West Algonquin Road, Room C102
Palatine, IL 60067-7398
847-925-6248
finaid@harpercollege.edu
http://www.harper.cc.il.us

Disability Served: various

The college offers several scholarships for students with disabilities. *Eligibility: Students with disabilities at Harper College are eligible to apply. *Financial Details: Awards vary. *Number Awarded: Varies. *Deadline: Contact the college for deadline information.

Hartford, University of

Office of Admission and Student Financial Assistance
200 Bloomfield Avenue
West Hartford, CT 06117-1599
800-947-4303
admission@mail.hartford.edu
http://admission.hartford.edu/overview.php

Disability Served: various

The university provides financial aid to help students (including those with disabilities) attend college. *Eligibility: Students who need financial assistance are eligible to apply. *Financial Details: Amounts vary according to need. *Number Awarded: Varies. *Deadline: Write or call for details.

Hawaii Community Foundation

1164 Bishop Street, Suite 800
Honolulu, HI 96813
888-731-3863
scholarships@hcf-hawaii.org
http://www.hawaiicommunityfoundation.org/scholar/
    scholar.php

Disability Served: various

The foundation offers several awards to help students (including those with disabilities). *Eligibility: Students who reside in Hawaii, demonstrate financial need, and have a GPA of at least 2.7 may

apply. *Financial Details: Amounts vary and depend on need. *Number Awarded: Varies. *Deadline: March 1.

Hawaii Department of Education

PO Box 2360
Honolulu, HI 96804
808-586-3230
doe_info@notes.k12.hi.us
http://doe.k12.hi.us/college_financialaid.htm

Disability Served: various

The department provides financial aid to help students (including those with disabilities) attend college. *Eligibility: Hawaiian students who need financial assistance are eligible to apply. *Financial Details: Amounts vary according to need. *Number Awarded: Varies. *Deadline: Contact the Department for additional details.

Hawaii-Hilo, University of

Office of Admissions
200 West Kawali Street
Hilo, HI 96720-4091
800-897-4456
uhhadm@hawaii.edu
http://www.uhh.hawaii.edu/studentaffairs/admissions

Disability Served: various

The university offers financial aid to help students (including those with disabilities) attend college. *Eligibility: Students who need financial assistance are eligible to apply. *Financial Details: Amounts vary according to need. *Number Awarded: Varies. *Deadline: Write or call for details.

Hawkeye Community College

Financial Aid Office-Hawkeye Center-Main Campus
1501 East Orange Road
Waterloo, IA 50704
800-670-4769, ext. 4020
finaid@hawkeyecollege.edu
http://www.hawkeyecollege.edu/currentstudents/
    financialaid.asp

Disability Served: various

This two-year college offers the following scholarships for students with disabilities: Civitan Club Scholarship (any disability) and Jimmie Robinson Scholarships (physical disabilities). *Eligibility: Disabled students who demonstrate financial need are eligible. *Financial Details: Civitan Club Scholarship: $250, Jimmie Robinson Scholarships: $350. *Number

Awarded: Four annually. *Deadline: Contact the college for details.

Hemophilia Federation of America

1405 West Pinhook Road, Suite 101
Lafayette, LA 70503
800-230-9797
info@hemophiliafed.org
http://www.hemophiliafed.org/scholarships.php
Disability Served: inherited bleeding disorders
The organization offers educational scholarships.
*Eligibility: Students with blood clotting disorders who plan to pursue postsecondary education either from a college, university, or trade school are eligible to apply. *Financial Details: $1,500. *Number Awarded: Four. *Deadline: Contact the federation for details. In addition to educational scholarships, the federation offers artistic encouragement grants for people with blood clotting disorders who are pursuing an artistic endeavor, parent continuing education scholarships for parents of children with blood clotting disorders, and sibling continuing education scholarships for siblings of a person with a blood clotting disorder who intend to pursue postsecondary education.

Hemophilia Foundation of Southern California

33 South Catalina Avenue, Suite 102
Pasadena, CA 91106
800-371-4123
hfsc@hemosocal.org
http://www.hemosocal.org
Disability Served: inherited bleeding disorders
The organization offers the Christopher Pitkin Memorial Scholarship. *Eligibility: Students with blood clotting disorders (as well as members of their family) who plan to pursue postsecondary education are eligible to apply. *Financial Details: $500 to $1,000. *Number Awarded: Varies. *Deadline: Contact the foundation for details.

Hemophilia Health Services

Financial Aid Services
PO Box 23737
Nashville, TN 37202-3737
615-850-5175
scholarship@hemophiliahealth.com
http://www.hemophiliahealth.com/consumers/
products_services/scholarship.htm
Disability Served: inherited bleeding disorders

This organization offers two scholarships via its HHS Memorial Scholarship Program. *Eligibility: Students with hemophilia and related bleeding disorders are eligible to apply; requirements vary by scholarship. *Financial Details: Awards start at $1,500. *Number Awarded: Varies. *Deadline: May 1.

Hofstra University

Office of Financial Aid
202 Memorial Hall
Hempstead, NY 11549
516-463-6680, option 2
http://www.hofstra.edu/StudentServ/Enroll/Financial_
Aid/index_Financial_Aid.cfm
Disability Served: various
The university provides financial aid to help students (including those with disabilities) attend college. *Eligibility: Students who need financial assistance are eligible to apply. *Financial Details: Amounts vary according to need. *Number Awarded: Varies. *Deadline: Write or call for details.

Holy Cross, College of the

Office of Financial Aid
1 College Street, Hogan Campus Center, Room 314
Worcester, MA 01610-2395
508-793-2265/2266
financialaid@holycross.edu
http://www.holycross.edu/departments/adm-fa-bur/
financial
Disability Served: various
The college provides financial aid to help students (including those with disabilities) attend college. *Eligibility: Students who need financial assistance are eligible to apply. *Financial Details: Amounts vary according to need. *Number Awarded: Varies. *Deadline: Contact the college for additional details.

Houston, University of

Office of Scholarships and Financial Aid
4800 Calhoun Road
Houston, TX 77204-2010
713-743-1010, Option 3
http://www.uh.edu/enroll/sfa
Disability Served: various
The university provides financial aid to help students (including those with disabilities) attend college. *Eligibility: Students who need financial assistance are eligible to apply. *Financial Details: Amounts

vary according to need. *Number Awarded: Varies. *Deadline: Contact the university for additional details.

Houston Community College (HCC) Foundation
PO Box 667517 (MC 1148)
Houston, TX 77266-7517
713-718-8494
http://www.hccs.edu/students/financialaid
Disability Served: various
The Houston Community College (HCC) Foundation offers financial aid for students attending schools in the HCC System. *Eligibility: Students who demonstrate financial need are eligible. *Financial Details: Awards vary according to need. *Number Awarded: Varies. *Deadline: Contact the foundation for details.

Humboldt State University
Financial Aid Office
1 Harpst Street
Arcata, CA 95521-8299
866-255-1390
finaid@humboldt.edu
http://www.humboldt.edu/%7Efinaid
Disability Served: various
This public university provides financial aid to help students (including those with disabilities) attend college. *Eligibility: Students who need financial assistance are eligible to apply. *Financial Details: Amounts vary according to need. *Number Awarded: Varies. *Deadline: Write or call for details.

Idaho, University of
Student Financial Aid Services
PO Box 444291
Moscow, ID 83844-4291
888-884-3246
finaid@uidaho.edu
http://www.students.uidaho.edu/finaid
Disability Served: various
This public university offers financial aid to help students (including those with disabilities) attend college. *Eligibility: Students who need financial assistance are eligible to apply. *Financial Details: Amounts vary according to need. *Number Awarded: Varies. *Deadline: Write or call for details.

Idaho State Board of Education
PO Box 83720
Boise, ID 83720-0037

http://www.idahoboardofed.org/scholarships.asp
Disability Served: various
The board provides financial aid to help students (including those with disabilities) attend college. *Eligibility: Idaho students who need financial assistance are eligible to apply. *Financial Details: Amounts vary according to need. *Number Awarded: Varies. *Deadline: Contact the Board for additional details.

Idaho State University
Office of Financial Aid and Scholarships
Campus Box 8077
Pocatello, ID 83209-8077
208-282-2981
finaidem@isu.edu
http://www.isu.edu/finaid
Disability Served: various
The university provides scholarships and other financial aid to help finance college study. *Eligibility: Students with disabilities may apply for this financial aid. *Financial Details: Amounts vary. *Number Awarded: Varies. *Deadline: Call or write for details.

Illinois Department of Veterans Affairs
PO Box 19432
Springfield, IL 62794-9432
217-782-6641
http://www.state.il.us/agency/dva
Disability Served: various
The department offers grants to help finance college training. *Eligibility: Children (ages 10-18) of disabled veterans whose disability occurred as the result of active service are eligible. *Financial Details: Varies. *Number Awarded: Grant numbers vary. *Deadline: Contact the department for details.

Illinois State University
Office of Financial Aid
231 Fell Hall, Campus Box 2320
Normal, IL 61790-2320
309-438-2231
askfao@ilstu.edu
http://www.fao.ilstu.edu
Disability Served: various
The university provides financial aid to help students (including those with disabilities) attend college. *Eligibility: Students who need financial assistance are eligible to apply. *Financial Details: Amounts vary according to need. *Number Awarded: Varies. *Deadline: Contact the university for additional details.

Illinois Student Assistance Commission
1755 Lake Cook Road
Deerfield, IL 60015-5209
800-899-4722, 800-526-0844 (TDD)
collegezone@isac.org
http://www.collegezone.com/studentzone/416_855.htm
Disability Served: various
The commission offers financial aid to help Illinois
   students (including those with disabilities) attend
   college. *Eligibility: Students who need financial
   assistance are eligible to apply. *Financial Details:
   Amounts vary. *Number Awarded: Varies. *Deadline:
   Contact the commission for additional details.

Illinois-Urbana-Champaign, University of
Division Of Rehabilitation-Education Services
1207 South Oak Street
Champaign, IL 61820
217-333-4603 (Voice/TTY)
disability@uiuc.edu
http://www.disability.uiuc.edu/services/scholarship
Disability Served: various
The university's Division Of Rehabilitation-Education
   Services provides scholarships to disabled students
   to help finance college study. *Eligibility: Students
   with disabilities who are attending the university are
   eligible to apply. *Financial Details: Amounts vary.
   *Number Awarded: Varies. *Deadline: May 1.

Illinois-Urbana-Champaign, University of
Office of Student Financial Aid
620 East John Street, MC-303
Champaign, IL 61820-5712
217-333-0100
http://www.osfa.uiuc.edu
Disability Served: physically disabled
The university offers the Joseph and Elizabeth Davey
   Scholarship. *Eligibility: Physically disabled students
   who demonstrate financial need are eligible. *Finan-
   cial Details: Awards vary according to need. *Number
   Awarded: Varies. *Deadline: Write or call for details.

Immune Deficiency Foundation
Attn: Scholarship/Medical Programs
40 West Chesapeake Avenue, Suite 308
Towson, MD 21204
800-296-4433
idf@primaryimmune.org
http://www.primaryimmune.org/services/scholarship.
   htm
Disability Served: immune deficiency disorders
The Foundation offers scholarships to help finance
   college study. *Eligibility: Undergraduate students
   attending or entering college or a technical
   training school with a diagnosed primary immune
   deficiency disease are eligible to apply. Selection is
   based on financial need. *Financial Details: $750 to
   $2,000. *Number Awarded: Forty-three. *Deadline:
   Applications are typically due at the end of March.

Indiana Department of Veterans' Affairs
302 West Washington Street, Room E120
Indianapolis, IN 46204-2738
317-232-3910, 800-400-4520
http://www.in.gov/veteran
Disability Served: various
The department provides tuition wavers for the
   purpose of college study. *Eligibility: Children of
   Indiana veterans who died or who are permanently
   disabled as a result of military service are eligible to
   apply. Applicants must be residents of Indiana and
   attend a college or university in the state. *Financial
   Details: Amounts vary, but benefits are limited to
   cost of tuition and fees. *Number Awarded: Varies
   each year. *Deadline: Contact the department for
   details.

Indiana State University
Office of Student Financial Aid
Tirey Hall, 200 North 17th Street., Room 150
Terre Haute, IN 47809
800-841-4744
finaid@indstate.edu
http://www.indstate.edu/join_us/money.htm
Disability Served: various
The university provides financial aid to help students
   (including those with disabilities) attend college.
   *Eligibility: Students who need financial assistance
   are eligible to apply. *Financial Details: Amounts
   vary according to need. *Number Awarded: Varies.
   *Deadline: Write or call for details.

Indiana University-Bloomington
Student Financial Assistance
Franklin Hall, 601 East Kirkwood Avenue, Room 208
Bloomington, IN 47405
812-855-0321
rsvposfa@indiana.edu
http://www.indiana.edu/~sfa
Disability Served: various

This university offers a wide range of financial assistance to its students (including those with disabilities). *Eligibility: Students who demonstrate financial need. *Financial Details: Amounts vary according to need. *Number Awarded: Varies. *Deadline: Contact the university for details.

Indiana University-Purdue University Fort Wayne
Office of Financial Aid
32010 East Coliseum Boulevard
Ft Wayne, IN 46805
260-481-6820
dahlv@ipfw.edu
http://www.ipfw.edu/financial/finaid/process
Disability Served: various
The Sidney and Viola Hutner Scholarships are available to help finance college study. *Eligibility: High school students with disabilities are eligible. *Financial Details: Amounts vary. *Number Awarded: Varies. *Deadline: Nominations from high school guidance counselors are required. The nomination deadline is in late March.

Indiana University-Purdue University Indianapolis
Office of Student Financial Aid Services
Cavanaugh Hall, 425 University Boulevard, Room 147
Indianapolis, IN 46202-5145
317-274-4162
finaid@iupui.edu
http://www.iupui.edu/finaid
Disability Served: various
This joint university venture offers degrees in a variety of fields through the doctorate. It offers financial aid to help students with disabilities. *Eligibility: Students with disabilities who need financial assistance are eligible. *Financial Details: Amounts depend on need. *Number Awarded: Varies. *Deadline: Contact the universities for more information.

International Alumnae of Delta Epsilon
Fellowship Award Committee
9406 Steeple Court
Laurel, MD 20723
fellowship@iades.org
http://www.iades.org/faf.html
Disability Served: hearing
The International Alumnae of Delta Epsilon offers a fellowship to help finance doctoral studies. *Eligibility: Deaf women enrolled in doctoral programs are eligible to apply. Candidates must have a GPA of at least 3.0. *Financial Details: The fellowship is for $1,200. *Number Awarded: One per year. *Deadline: Applications are due August 26.

International Christian Youth Exchange
Große Hamburger Str. 30
Berlin, D-10115
Germany
icye@icye.org
http://www.icye.org
Disability Served: various
This organization offers scholarships to help its members (including those with disabilities) finance study abroad. *Eligibility: Students with disabilities, in high school or college, who have been selected to take part in the program, are eligible. *Financial Details: Amounts vary. *Number Awarded: Varies. *Deadline: Contact the organization for more information.

Iowa, University of
Student Disability Services
3100 Burge Hall
Iowa City, IA 52242-1214
319-353-1462, 319-353-1498 (TTY)
http://www.uiowa.edu/~sds
Disability Served: various
The David Braverman Scholarship helps finance graduate or professional studies. *Eligibility: Students with disabilities may apply. Selection is based on need, prior academic record, and intention to serve the community. *Financial Details: An award of $1,500 is offered. *Number Awarded: Varies. *Deadline: Contact the university for deadlines.

Iowa College Student Aid Commission
200 - 10th Street, 4th Floor
Des Moines, IA 50309-2036
800-383-4222
info@iowacollegeaid.org
http://www.iowacollegeaid.org
Disability Served: various
The commission provides financial aid to help students (including those with disabilities) attend college. *Eligibility: Iowa students who need financial assistance are eligible to apply. *Financial Details: Amounts vary according to need. *Number Awarded: Varies. *Deadline: Contact the commission for additional details.

Iowa Commission of Veterans Affairs
7700 Northwest Beaver Drive
Johnston, IA 50131-1902
515-242-5331, 800-838-4092
info@icva.state.ia.us
http://www2.state.ia.us/icva
Disability Served: various
The commission provides tuition wavers for the purpose
of college study. *Eligibility: Children of Iowa veterans
who died as a result of military service are eligible
to apply. Applicants must be residents of Iowa and
attend selected public colleges or universities in
the state. *Financial Details: $600 per calendar year,
with a lifetime maximum benefit of $3,000. *Number
Awarded: Varies each year. *Deadline: Contact the
commission for details.

Iowa State University
Office of Student Financial Aid
0210 Beardshear Hall
Ames, IA 50011-2028
800-478-2998
financialaid@iastate.edu
http://www.financialaid.iastate.edu
Disability Served: various
The university provides financial aid to help students
(including those with disabilities) attend college.
*Eligibility: Students who need financial assistance
are eligible to apply. *Financial Details: Amounts
vary according to need. *Number Awarded: Varies.
*Deadline: Write or call for details.

Iowa Western Community College
Office of Financial Aid
2700 College Road
Council Bluffs, IA 51502
712-325-3200
http://iwcc.cc.ia.us/Enrollment_Services/financial_aid.
html
Disability Served: various
This public two-year college provides financial aid to
help students (including those with disabilities)
attend college. *Eligibility: Students who need
financial assistance are eligible to apply. *Financial
Details: Amounts vary according to need. *Number
Awarded: Varies. *Deadline: Contact the college for
additional details.

Irvine Valley College
Financial Aid Office
5500 Irvine Center Drive, Student Center, Room 120
Irvine, CA 92720
949-451-5287
financialaid@ivc.edu
http://www.ivc.edu/finaid
Disability Served: various
This public two-year college offers financial aid to help
students (including those with disabilities) attend
college. *Eligibility: Students attending the college
who have disabilities may apply. *Financial Details:
Amounts vary. *Number Awarded: Varies. *Deadline:
Write or call for details.

Italian Catholic Federation
675 Hegenberger Road, Suite 230
Oakland, CA 94621
888-ICF-1924
info@icf.org
http://www.icf.org/applications.html
Disability Served: developmentally disabled
This organization offers the Gifts of Love Scholarship.
*Eligibility: Students who are developmentally
disabled or those who work with the
developmentally disabled are eligible to apply.
Applicants must be of the Catholic faith and of Italian
heritage. *Financial Details: Scholarships start at
$400. *Number Awarded: Varies. *Deadline: Contact
the federation for details.

Kansas, University of
Office of Admissions and Scholarships
KU Visitor Center, 1502 Iowa
Lawrence, KS 66045-7576
785-864-3911
adm@ku.edu
http://www.admissions.ku.edu/scholarships
Disability Served: various
The university offers financial aid to help students
(including those with disabilities) attend college.
*Eligibility: Students who need financial assistance
are eligible to apply. *Financial Details: Amounts
vary according to need. *Number Awarded: Varies.
*Deadline: Write or call for details.

Kansas Board of Regents
1000 Southwest Jackson Street, Suite 520
Topeka, KS 66612-1368

785-296-3421
http://www.kansasregents.org/financial_aid
Disability Served: various
The board provides financial aid to help students (including those with disabilities) attend college. *Eligibility: Kansas students who need financial assistance are eligible to apply. *Financial Details: Amounts vary according to need. *Number Awarded: Varies. *Deadline: Contact the board for additional details.

Kansas Commission on Veterans' Affairs

Jayhawk Towers, 700 Southwest Jackson Street, Suite 701
Topeka, KS 66603-3714
785-296-3976
http://www.nasdva.com/kansas.html
Disability Served: various
The commission provides tuition waivers for the purpose of college study. *Eligibility: Children of Kansas veterans who are deceased as a result of military service, or missing in action, are eligible to apply. Applicants must be residents of Kansas and attend a public college or university in the state. *Financial Details: Full tuition. *Number Awarded: Varies each year. *Deadline: Contact the commission for details.

Kappa Kappa Gamma Foundation

530 East Town Street, PO Box 38
Columbus, OH 43216
866-KKG-1870
http://www.kappa.org
Disability Served: various
The foundation offers the Rose McGill Fund, which provides financial assistance to members faced with sudden illness or misfortune. *Eligibility: Members of the sorority in financial need are eligible to apply. *Financial Details: Varies. *Number Awarded: Varies. *Deadline: Call or write for information. The foundation also offers undergraduate and graduate scholarships.

Kendall College of Art and Design

Office of Scholarships and Financial Aid
17 Fountain Street, Student Services-Office 114E
Grand Rapids, MI 49503
800-676-2787
lori_deforest@ferris.edu
http://www.kcad.edu
Disability Served: physically disabled
The college provides financial aid to help students (including those with disabilities) attend college.

*Eligibility: Students who need financial assistance are eligible to apply. *Financial Details: Amounts vary according to need. *Number Awarded: Varies. *Deadline: Contact the college for additional details.

Kent State University

Student Disability Services
Michael Schwartz Center, Room 181
Kent, OH 44242-0001
330-672-3391 (Voice/TTY)
finaid@kent.edu
http://www.registrars.kent.edu/disability
Disability Served: spinal-cord injury
The college provides a variety of financial aid to students, including the Cunningham Award. *Eligibility: Students with a spinal cord injury who need financial assistance are eligible to apply. *Financial Details: $500. *Number Awarded: One. *Deadline: February 15.

Kentucky, University of

Disability Resource Center
2 Alumni Gym
Lexington, KY 40506-0029
859-257-2754
msfogg0@uky.edu
http://www.uky.edu/TLC/grants/uk_ed/services/drc.html
Disability Served: various
The university offers the following scholarships for students with disabilities: the Varney Scholarship and the Carol Adelstein Award. *Eligibility: Students with cystic fibrosis may apply for the Varney Scholarship. Faculty and staff nominate outstanding students with disabilities for the Carol Adelstein Award. *Financial Details: Varney Scholarship: Approximately $700. Carol Adelstein Award: Up to $2,000. *Number Awarded: Varies. *Deadline: Contact the university for additional details.

Kentucky Department of Veteran Affairs

1111 Louisville Road
Frankfort, KY 40601
800-572-6245
http://www.kdva.net
Disability Served: various
The department offers tuition waivers at public colleges and universities in the state of Kentucky. *Eligibility: Kentucky residents who are children of disabled veterans are eligible. *Financial Details: Full tuition.

*Number Awarded: Varies. *Deadline: Contact the department for details.

Kentucky Higher Education Assistance Authority

PO Box 798
Frankfort, KY 40602-0798
800-928-8926
http://www.kheaa.com
Disability Served: various
The authority provides financial aid to help students (including those with disabilities) attend college. *Eligibility: Kentucky students who need financial assistance are eligible to apply. *Financial Details: Amounts vary according to need. *Number Awarded: Varies. *Deadline: Contact the authority for additional details.

Kentucky State University

Office of Financial Aid
400 East Main Street
Frankfort, KY 40601
502-597-6000
http://www.kysu.edu/academics/enrollment_services/financial_aid
Disability Served: various
This public university provides financial aid to help students (including those with disabilities) attend college. *Eligibility: Students who need financial assistance are eligible to apply. *Financial Details: Amounts vary according to need. *Number Awarded: Varies. *Deadline: Write or call for details.

Lake-Sumter Community College

9501 US Highway 441
Leesburg, FL 34788
352-365-3512
FinAid@lscc.edu
http://www.lscc.edu/financialaid
Disability Served: various
This two-year community college provides financial aid to help students (including those with disabilities) attend college. *Eligibility: Students who need financial assistance are eligible to apply. *Financial Details: Amounts vary according to need. *Number Awarded: Varies. *Deadline: Write or call for details.

Lamar University

Office of Financial Aid
PO Box 10042
Beaumont, TX 77710
409-880-7011
finaid@hal.lamar.edu
http://dept.lamar.edu/financialaid
Disability Served: various
The university offers scholarships to students (including those with disabilities) to help finance college study. *Eligibility: Students who need financial assistance are eligible to apply. *Financial Details: Amounts vary according to need. *Number Awarded: Varies. *Deadline: Write or call for details.

Landmark College

River Road South
Putney, VT 05346
802-387-6736
cmullins@landmark.edu
http://www.landmarkcollege.org/
Disability Served: learning disabled
This is the nation's only college designed exclusively for dyslexic students and students with learning disabilities. It has approximately 200 students enrolled and offers several scholarships to help those with financial need. *Eligibility: Students attending the college who demonstrate financial need are eligible. *Financial Details: Amounts vary according to need. *Number Awarded: Varies. *Deadline: Contact the college for information.

Landscape Architecture Foundation

818 18th Street, NW, Suite 810
Washington, DC 20006
rfigura@lafoundation.org
http://www.laprofession.org
Disability Served: various
The foundation offers a variety of financial aid to students (including those with disabilities) studying landscape architecture. *Eligibility: Students who are studying landscape architecture may apply. Applicants must submit samples of work as a part of the application process. *Financial Details: Awards vary. *Number Awarded: Varies. *Deadline: Contact the foundation for details.

Las Positas College

Office of Financial Aid
3033 Collier Canyon Road
Livermore, CA 94550
510-373-4908
lpcfinaid@laspositascollege.edu
http://lpc1.clpccd.cc.ca.us/lpc/finaid

Disability Served: various
This two-year college offers financial aid to its students with disabilities. *Eligibility: Financially needy students with disabilities are eligible to apply. *Financial Details: Awards vary according to need. *Number Awarded: Varies. *Deadline: Write or call for details.

Lewis-Clark State College
Office of Financial Aid
500 Eighth Street
Lewiston, ID 83501
800-933-5272
http://www.lcsc.edu/financialaid
Disability Served: various
This public four-year institution offers financial aid to help students (including those with disabilities) attend college. *Eligibility: Financially needy students are eligible to apply. *Financial Details: Awards vary according to need. *Number Awarded: Varies. *Deadline: Contact the college for details.

Lighthouse International
Scholarship Awards Program
111 East 59th Street
New York, NY 10022-1202
212-821-9200, 800-829-0500
http://www.lighthouse.org/scholarship_awards.htm
Disability Served: vision
Lighthouse International provides scholarships to students who are legally blind. *Eligibility: Legally blind high school and college students who reside and attend school in the Greater New York area and New England states are eligible to apply. *Financial Details: Each scholarship is worth $5,000. *Number Awarded: Four per year. *Deadline: The deadline is typically at the end of March.

Lions Club International
300 West 22nd Street
Oak Brook, IL 60523-8842
630-571-5466
lcif@lionsclub.org
http://www.lionsclubs.org
Disability Served: vision
Local Lions Clubs often sponsor scholarships or other forms of assistance to aid blind persons in their area of academic interest. *Eligibility: Requirements vary from chapter to chapter; call or write for details.

*Financial Details: Amounts vary. *Number Awarded: Varies. *Deadline: For details on programs in your area, contact your local Lions Club.

Loma Linda University
Office of Financial Aid
11139 Anderson Street
Loma Linda, CA 92350
909-558-4509
finaid@univ.llu.edu
http://www.llu.edu/ssweb/finaid
Disability Served: various
This four-year university provides financial aid to help students (including those with disabilities) attend college. *Eligibility: Students who need financial assistance are eligible to apply. *Financial Details: Amounts vary according to need. *Number Awarded: Varies. *Deadline: Contact the university for additional details.

Los Medanos College
Financial Aid Office
2700 East Leland Road
Pittsburg, CA 94565
925-439-2181
http://www.losmedanos.net/studentservices/finaid
Disability Served: various
This public two-year institution offers financial aid to help students (including those with disabilities) attend college. *Eligibility: Financially needy students are eligible to apply. *Financial Details: Awards vary according to need. *Number Awarded: Varies. *Deadline: Contact the college for details.

Louisiana Department of Veterans Affairs
Capitol Station, PO Box 94095
Baton Rouge, LA 70804-9095
225-922-0500
http://www.vetaffairs.com
Disability Served: various
The department helps students (including those with disabilities) pay for college. *Eligibility: Children of Louisiana veterans who are 100 percent disabled as a result of wartime active duty service are eligible to apply. *Financial Details: Free tuition and fees at one of the state's public colleges and universities are awarded. *Number Awarded: Varies. *Deadline: Contact the department for information.

Louisiana-Lafayette, University of

Services for Students With Disabilities
PO Drawer 41650
Lafayette, LA 70504-1650
337-482-5252
http://disability.louisiana.edu
Disability Served: various
The university offers financial aid to help students
(including those with disabilities) attend college.
*Eligibility: Students who need financial assistance
are eligible to apply. *Financial Details: Amounts
vary according to need. *Number Awarded: Varies.
*Deadline: Contact the university for additional
details.

Louisiana Office of Student Financial Assistance

PO Box 91202
Baton Rouge, LA 70821-9202
800-259-5626
custserv@osfa.state.la.us
http://www.osfa.state.la.us
Disability Served: various
The office provides financial aid to help students
(including those with disabilities) attend college.
*Eligibility: Louisiana students who need financial
assistance are eligible to apply. *Financial Details:
Amounts vary according to need. *Number Awarded:
Varies. *Deadline: Contact the office for additional
details.

Louisiana State University

Office of Student Aid and Scholarships
202 Himes Hall
Baton Rouge, LA 70803
225-578-3103
financialaid@lsu.edu
http://appl003.lsu.edu/slas/studentaid.nsf/index
Disability Served: various
The university offers financial aid to students. *Eligibility:
Students whose parents have a disability are eligible
for financial aid. *Financial Details: Amounts vary
and depend on need. *Number Awarded: Varies.
*Deadline: Varies. Write or call for details.

Madonna University

Office of Financial Aid
36660 Schoolcraft Road
Livonia, MI 48150
734-432-5663
http://www.madonna.edu/pages/financialaid.cfm
Disability Served: various
This private four-year university offers financial aid to
its students with disabilities. *Eligibility: Financially
needy students with disabilities are eligible to apply.
*Financial Details: Awards vary according to need.
*Number Awarded: Varies. *Deadline: Write or call for
details.

Maharishi University of Management

1000 North Fourth Street
Fairfield, IA 52557
641-472-1156
finaid@mum.edu
http://www.mum.edu/financial_aid/welcome.html
Disability Served: cerebral palsy
The university offers the Shelley Hoffman Scholarship
to help finance college training. *Eligibility: Students
with cerebral palsy and/or creative writing skills may
apply. Recipients must maintain a 2.0 GPA to retain
the award. *Financial Details: Awards vary from $200
to $1,500 per year. *Number Awarded: One to four
per year. *Deadline: Applications are due May 15.

Maine-Augusta, University of

46 University Drive
Augusta, ME 04330
207-621-3066
http://www.uma.edu/financialaid1.html
Disability Served: various
The university provides financial aid to help students
(including those with disabilities) attend college.
*Eligibility: Students who need financial assistance
are eligible to apply. *Financial Details: Amounts
vary according to need. *Number Awarded: Varies.
*Deadline: Write or call for details.

Maine Bureau of Veterans' Services

117 State House Station
Augusta, ME 04333-0117
207-626-4464
http://www.mainebvs.org
Disability Served: physically disabled
This agency offers grants and tuition waivers to help
with the costs of college training. *Eligibility: Maine
residents who are children of severely disabled
veterans are eligible. *Financial Details: Varies.
*Number Awarded: Varies. *Deadline: Call or write for
information.

Maine Education Services (MES)
One City Center, 11th Floor
Portland, ME 04101
207-791-3600, 800-922-6352
info@mesfoundation.com
http://www.mesfoundation.com
Disability Served: various
MES is a private organization that provides financial aid
    to help students (including those with disabilities)
    attend college. *Eligibility: Maine students who need
    financial assistance are eligible to apply. *Financial
    Details: Amounts vary according to need. *Number
    Awarded: Varies. *Deadline: Contact MES for
    additional details.

Marin, College of
College of Marin Foundation
PO Box 446
Kentfield, CA 94914
415-485-9382
comf@marin.cc.ca.us
http://www.comf.org/scholarships.html
Disability Served: various
The college offers the Burke Sister Memorial Scholarship
    and the San Rafael Indoor Sports Club Scholarship.
    *Eligibility: Students with disabilities may apply.
    *Financial Details: Varies. *Number Awarded: Varies.
    *Deadline: Contact the college for details.

Marine Corps Scholarship Foundation
PO Box 3008
Princeton, NJ 08543-3008
800-292-7777
mcsfnj@mcsf.org
http://www.marine-scholars.org
Disability Served: various
The foundation offers scholarships to help defray the
    costs of college. *Eligibility: Children of a Marine,
    either on active duty or discharged, are eligible.
    Candidates must come from a family with a total
    annual income below $61,000. *Financial Details:
    Scholarships range from $500 to $2,500. *Number
    Awarded: Varies. *Deadline: April 15. Contact the
    foundation for information.

Marquette University
Office of Disability Services
PO Box 1881
Milwaukee, WI 53201-1881
414-288-1645

http://www.marquette.edu/oses/disabilityservices
Disability Served: various
This private four-year university offers financial aid
    and scholarships to its students with disabilities.
    *Eligibility: Financially needy students with
    disabilities are eligible to apply. *Financial Details:
    Awards vary according to need. *Number Awarded:
    Varies. *Deadline: Contact the university for details.

Marshalltown Community College
Financial Aid Office
3700 South Center Street
Marshalltown, IA 50158
641-752-7106, ext. 210
Nancy.Ellis@iavalley.edu
http://www.iavalley.cc.ia.us/mcc/FinancialAid
Disability Served: various
This two-year community college offers a variety of
    financial aid to its students, including the following
    scholarships for students with disabilities: Patti Bacino
    Memorial Scholarship and Legion of Guardsmen
    Auxiliary Scholarship. *Eligibility: Disabled students at
    the sophomore level who demonstrate financial need
    may apply for the Patti Bacino Memorial Scholarship.
    Female disabled students who are residents of
    Marshall County and who demonstrate financial need
    may apply for the Legion of Guardsmen Auxiliary
    Scholarship. *Financial Details: Awards vary. *Number
    Awarded: Varies. *Deadline: Contact the college for
    details.

Maryland-College Park, University of
Student Financial Services Center
1135 Lee Building
College Park, MD 20742
301-314-9000, 301-314-7017 (TTY)
http://www.financialaid.umd.edu
Disability Served: various
The university provides financial aid to help students
    (including those with disabilities) attend college.
    *Eligibility: Students who need financial assistance
    are eligible to apply. *Financial Details: Amounts
    vary according to need. *Number Awarded: Varies.
    *Deadline: Write or call for details.

Maryland-Eastern Shore, University of
Office of Financial Aid
Student Services Center Lane
Princess Anne, MD 21853
410-651-6172

http://www.umes.edu/financialaid
Disability Served: various
The university provides financial aid to help students (including those with disabilities) attend college. *Eligibility: Students who need financial assistance are eligible to apply. *Financial Details: Amounts vary according to need. *Number Awarded: Varies. *Deadline: Write or call for details.

Maryland Higher Education Commission
Office of Student Financial Assistance
839 Bestgate Road, Suite 400
Annapolis, MD 21401-3013
800-974-1024, 800-735-2258 (TTY)
osfamail@mhec.state.md.us
http://www.mhec.state.md.us/financialAid
Disability Served: various
The Edward Conroy Memorial Award helps finance college study at a state college in Maryland. *Eligibility: Children of a permanently disabled Maryland veteran, a disabled state or local public safety employee, or a deceased victim of the September 11 terrorist attacks may apply. *Financial Details: Up to full tuition and fees at a state college are awarded. *Number Awarded: Varies. *Deadline: Contact the commission for more information. The commission also offers a variety of other awards, grants, loans, and scholarships.

Massachusetts-Dartmouth, University of
Financial Aid Services Office
285 Old Westport Road
North Dartmouth, MA 02747
508-999-8857
FinancialAid@umassd.edu
http://www.umassd.edu/financialaid
Disability Served: various
This university offers a variety of financial aid for students (including those with disabilities). *Eligibility: Students who need financial assistance are eligible to apply. *Financial Details: Awards vary according to need. *Number Awarded: Varies. *Deadline: Contact the university for details.

Massachusetts Department of Veterans' Services
600 Washington Street, Suite 1100
Boston, MA 02111
617-210-5480
MDVS@vet.state.ma.us
http://www.state.ma.us/veterans

Disability Served: various
The department provides a wide variety of grants, loans, scholarships, and other financial aid to veterans and children of veterans. *Eligibility: Requirements vary by type of financial aid. Applicants must plan to attend a public institution in the state of Massachusetts. *Financial Details: Varies depending on type of aid. *Number Awarded: Varies each year. *Deadline: Contact the department for details.

Massachusetts Office of Student Financial Assistance
454 Broadway, Suite 200
Revere, MA 02151
617-727-9420
osfa@osfa.mass.edu
http://www.osfa.mass.edu
Disability Served: various
The Christian Herter Scholarship is designed to help fund college training for students who have faced mental, physical, geographic, or societal challenges. *Eligibility: Massachusetts residents who are in their second or third year of high school are eligible. Applicants must also demonstrate financial need and have a GPA of at least 2.5. *Financial Details: Up to $15,000. *Number Awarded: Varies. *Deadline: Applications are typically due in March. In addition to this opportunity, the Office of Student Financial Assistance offers a variety of grants, scholarships, and loans.

Mays Mission for the Handicapped
604 Colonial Drive
Heber Springs, AR 72545
501-362-7526
info@maysmission.org
http://www.maysmission.org/schol.html
Disability Served: various
Mays Mission for the Handicapped offers scholarships to students. *Eligibility: Applicants must be able to document a significant disability, have a score of 18 or better on the ACT or 870 on the SAT, and be enrolled in a four-year undergraduate program. Recipients must maintain a GPA of at least 2.7. *Financial Details: Awards vary. *Number Awarded: Seven. *Deadline: June 30.

McLennan Community College
Office of Financial Aid
1400 College Drive
Waco, TX 76708

254-299-8698
http://www.mclennan.edu/students/finasst
Disability Served: physically disabled
This two-year community college offers a variety of
financial aid for students, including the Herb Barsh
Hot Lions Scholarship for physically challenged stu-
dents. *Eligibility: Physically challenged students who
demonstrate financial need may apply. Applicants
must have a minimum high school "B" average, a GED
Score of 50, or a college GPA of 2.5. *Financial Details:
A $500 award. *Number Awarded: One annually.
*Deadline: Applications are due February 10.

Metropolitan Community Colleges

3200 Broadway
Kansas City, MO 64111
816-759-1000
http://www.kcmetro.cc.mo.us
Disability Served: various
This two-year community college system (with four
campuses) offers financial aid to its students with
disabilities. *Eligibility: Financially needy students
with disabilities are eligible to apply. *Financial
Details: Awards vary according to need. *Number
Awarded: Varies. *Deadline: The application deadline
for all scholarships is April 1.

Michigan, University of

Office of Financial Aid
2011 Student Activities Building
515 East Jefferson Street
Ann Arbor, MI 48109-1316
734-763-6600
financial.aid@umich.edu
http://www.finaid.umich.edu
Disability Served: various
The university provides financial aid to students, including the Thomas Komar Scholarship. *Eligibility:
Disabled students who need financial assistance are
eligible to apply. *Financial Details: Awards range
from $1,000 to $6,000. *Number Awarded: Six. *Deadline: Contact the university for additional details. The
university also offers several small disability-related
scholarships that are offered intermittently. Contact
the Financial Aid Office to be notified by email of
further information on these scholarships.

Michigan Association for Deaf, Hearing, and Speech Services

2929 Covington Court, Suite 200
Lansing, MI 48912-4939

800-YOUR-EAR
http://www.madhs.org
Disability Served: communication, hearing
The association awards Brian McCartney Memorial
Scholarships to help students finance college
training. *Eligibility: Michigan high school seniors
with hearing or speech impairments may apply.
Applicants must also have a minimum GPA of 2.5 and
be U.S. citizens. *Financial Details: Varies. *Number
Awarded: Varies. *Deadline: Applications are typically
due at the end of March.

Michigan Bureau of Student Financial Assistance

PO Box 30047
Lansing, MI 48909-7547
800-642-5626, ext. 39598
sfs@michigan.gov
http://www.michigan.gov/mistudentaid
Disability Served: various
The bureau provides financial aid to help students
(including those with disabilities) attend college.
*Eligibility: Michigan students who need financial
assistance are eligible to apply. *Financial Details:
Amounts vary according to need. *Number Awarded:
Varies. *Deadline: Contact the bureau for additional
details.

Michigan Commission for the Blind

Victor Building, 201 North Washington, 2nd Floor
PO Box 30652
Lansing, MI 48909
517-373-2062, 800-292-4200
Disability Served: vision
The fund offers the Roy Johnson Scholarship to help
finance graduate study at a college or university in
Michigan. *Eligibility: Blind students who hold a bachelor's degree from any college in the country who
plan to pursue graduate study at a college or university in Michigan may apply. *Financial Details: Awards
range from $250 to $1,000. *Number Awarded: Varies.
*Deadline: Applications are due in May.

Michigan Department of Military and Veterans Affairs

3411 Martin Luther King Boulevard
Lansing, MI 48906
517-335-6523
http://www.michigan.gov/dmva
Disability Served: various
The department provides tuition wavers for the purpose
of college study. *Eligibility: Children or spouses of

Michigan veterans who died or who are permanently disabled as a result of military service are eligible to apply. Applicants must be residents of Michigan, have a GPA of at least 2.25, and attend a college or university in the state full time. *Financial Details: Up to $2,800 annually. *Number Awarded: Varies each year. *Deadline: Contact the department for details.

Midlands Technical College
Student Financial Services
PO Box 2408
Columbia, SC 29202
803-922-8038, 803-822-3401(TDD)
AskSFS@midlandstech.com
http://www.mid.tec.sc.us/sfs
Disability Served: spinal-cord injury, traumatic brain injury
The college provides financial aid to students, including the Steven L. Ball Memorial Scholarship. *Eligibility: Full- or part-time students who have sustained a traumatic brain injury or a spinal injury are eligible to apply. *Financial Details: $300. *Number Awarded: One. *Deadline: Write or call for details.

Minnesota Department of Veterans Affairs
State Veterans Service Building
20 West 12th Street, Room 206C
St. Paul, MN 55155-2006
651-296-2562
http://www.mdva.state.mn.us
Disability Served: various
The department offers grants to help finance college training. *Eligibility: Disabled Minnesota veterans are eligible. *Financial Details: Varies. *Number Awarded: Varies. *Deadline: Contact the department for details. Additionally, grants of $750 are available to dependents of veterans who have died on active duty or as a result of a service-connected condition.

Minnesota Higher Education Services Office
1450 Energy Park Drive, Suite 350
St. Paul, MN 55108-5227
651-642-0567
http://www.mheso.state.mn.us
Disability Served: various
The office provides financial aid to help students (including those with disabilities) attend college. *Eligibility: Minnesota students who need financial assistance are eligible to apply. *Financial Details: Amounts vary according to need. *Number Awarded: Varies. *Deadline: Contact the office for additional details.

Minnesota-Twin Cities, University of
Office of Financial Aid
106 Pleasant Street, SE
Minneapolis, MN 55455
612-624-4037
http://www1.umn.edu/twincities
Disability Served: various
The university provides financial aid to help students (including those with disabilities) attend college. *Eligibility: Students who need financial assistance are eligible to apply. *Financial Details: Amounts vary according to need. *Number Awarded: Varies. *Deadline: Contact the university for additional details.

Miss Deaf America Pageant
c/o National Association of the Deaf
814 Thayer Avenue
Silver Spring, MD 20910-4500
mda@nad.org
http://www.nad.org/site/pp.asp?c=foINKQMBF&b=103756
Disability Served: hearing
This competition selects Miss Deaf America. *Eligibility: Deaf women between the ages of 18 and 28 are eligible to compete for the title of Miss Deaf America. Women compete first at the state level and later at the national competition. *Financial Details: Winners receive transportation to the national competition and small cash grants. *Number Awarded: Varies. *Deadline: Contact the organization for information. The competition is held every two years.

Mississippi, University of
Office of Financial Aid
257 Martindale, Student Services Center, PO Box 1848
University, MS 38677
800-891-4596
finaid@olemiss.edu
http://www.olemiss.edu/depts/financial_aid
Disability Served: various
The university provides financial aid to help students (including those with disabilities) attend college. *Eligibility: Students who need financial assistance are eligible to apply. *Financial Details: Amounts vary according to need. *Number Awarded: Varies. *Deadline: Contact the university for additional details.

Mississippi Office of Student Financial Aid
3825 Ridgewood Road
Jackson, MS 39211-6453
800-327-2980

sfa@ihl.state.ms.us
https://www.state.ms.us/sfa/Main.do
Disability Served: various
The office provides financial aid to help students
(including those with disabilities) attend college.
*Eligibility: Mississippi students who need financial
assistance are eligible to apply. *Financial Details:
Amounts vary according to need. *Number Awarded:
Varies. *Deadline: Contact the office for additional
details.

Mississippi State University
Department of Student Financial Aid
Garner Hall, PO Box 6035
Mississippi State, MS 39762
662-325-2450
financialaid@saffairs.msstate.edu
http://www.sfa.msstate.edu
Disability Served: various
The University offers financial aid to help students
(including those with disabilities) attend college.
*Eligibility: Students who need financial assistance
are eligible to apply. *Financial Details: Amounts
vary according to need. *Number Awarded: Varies.
*Deadline: Write or call for details.

Mississippi State Veterans Affairs Board
PO Box 5947
Pearl, MS 39288-5947
601-576-4850
grice@vab.state.ms.us
http://www.vab.state.ms.us
Disability Served: various
The department provides tuition wavers for the purpose
of college study. *Eligibility: Children of Mississippi
veterans who are officially classified as being either a
prisoner of a foreign government or missing in action
can receive an eight-semester scholarship. Applicants
must be residents of Mississippi and attend a college
or university in the state. *Financial Details: Amounts
vary. *Number Awarded: Varies each year. *Deadline:
Contact the board for details.

Missouri-Columbia, University of
Office of Disability Services
A038 Brady Commons
Columbia, MO 65211
573-882-4696, 573-882-8054 (TTY)
disabilityservices@missouri.edu
http://web.missouri.edu/~accesscm

Disability Served: physically disabled
The University offers a variety of financial aid to help
students attend college, including the Frank Hodges
Jr. Physical Disability Scholarship Fund. *Eligibility:
Students with documented physical disabilities who
have a minimum GPA of 2.0 are eligible to apply.
*Financial Details: Amount varies. *Number Awarded:
Varies. *Deadline: April 22.

Missouri Department of Higher Education
3515 Amazonas Drive
Jefferson City, MO 65109
573-751-2361
info@dhe.mo.gov
http://www.dhe.mo.gov
Disability Served: various
The department provides financial aid to help students
(including those with disabilities) attend college.
*Eligibility: Missouri students who need financial
assistance are eligible to apply. *Financial Details:
Amounts vary according to need. *Number Awarded:
Varies. *Deadline: Contact the department for
additional details.

Molloy College
Kellenberg Hall, 100 Hempstead Avenue
Rockville Centre, NY 11570
516-678-5000, ext. 6249
http://www.molloy.edu/fin_aid
Disability Served: various
This private four-year college provides financial aid
to help students (including those with disabilities)
attend college. *Eligibility: Students who
need financial assistance are eligible to apply.
*Financial Details: Amounts vary according to
need. *Number Awarded: Varies. *Deadline: Write
or call for details.

Montana, University of
Enrollment Services
Missoula, MT 59812
http://admissions.umt.edu/hottopics/money/
financialaid.htm
Disability Served: various
The university provides financial aid to help students
(including those with disabilities) attend college.
*Eligibility: Students who need financial assistance
are eligible to apply. *Financial Details: Amounts
vary according to need. *Number Awarded: Varies.
*Deadline: Write or call for details.

Montana Office of Public Instruction
PO Box 202501
Helena, MT 59620-2501
888-231-9393
http://www.opi.state.mt.us
Disability Served: various
The office provides financial aid to help students
    (including those with disabilities) attend college.
    *Eligibility: Montana students who need financial
    assistance are eligible to apply. *Financial Details:
    Amounts vary according to need. *Number Awarded:
    Varies. *Deadline: Contact the office for additional
    details.

Ms. Wheelchair America Program Inc.
8610 Glenfield Way
Louisville, KY 40241
http://www.mswheelchairamerica.org
Disability Served: physically disabled
This is a state and national competition for outstanding
    women who use wheelchairs on a regular basis.
    *Eligibility: Women who use wheelchairs may
    compete. *Financial Details: Winners at the state level
    receive approximately $100 and the national winner,
    $250. *Number Awarded: Varies. *Deadline: Contact
    the organization for additional details.

**National Aeronautics and Space Administration
    (NASA)**
NASA Langley Research Center
100 NASA Road
Hampton, VA 23681-2199
757-864-5209, 757-864-9701
http://edu.larc.nasa.gov
Disability Served: various
NASA awards grants to students pursuing advanced
    degrees in science and engineering while making
    significant contributions to aerospace efforts. *Eligi-
    bility: Disabled graduate students attending accred-
    ited U.S. universities on a full-time basis may apply.
    *Financial Details: The maximum yearly award is for
    $24,000. Awards are renewable for up to three years.
    *Number Awarded: Varies. *Deadline: February 1.

National Amputee Golf Association
Scholarship Grant Program
11 Walnut Hill Road
Amherst, NH 03031
info@nagagolf.org
http://www.nagagolf.org

Disability Served: amputees
The association offers a scholarship to help finance
    college study. *Eligibility: Members who have lost
    a limb, or their dependents, are eligible to apply.
    Applicants need not be serious golfers. A minimum
    GPA of 2.0 is required. *Financial Details: The award is
    for $1,000 a year, which may be renewed. *Number
    Awarded: One per year. *Deadline: Applications are
    due in August.

National Center for Learning Disabilities
381 Park Avenue South, Suite 1401
New York, NY 10016-8806
212-545-7510, ext.233
AFScholarship@ncld.org
http://www.ncld.org/awards/afscholarinfo.cfm
Disability Served: learning disabled
The Center offers the Anne Ford Scholarship. *Eligibility:
    High school seniors with an identified learning
    disability may apply. Applicants must have a GPA of
    at least 3.0, be U.S. citizens, and demonstrate financial
    need. *Financial Details: $10,000. *Number One.
    Varies. *Deadline: Typically in late December.

National Federation of Music Clubs
c/o Norma Alexander
1219 Forsyth Street
Winston-Salem, NC 27101-2403
http://www.nfmc-music.org
Disability Served: vision
The Linda Honigman Award for the Blind is intended to
    help finance musical studies. *Eligibility: Blind vocal
    or instrumental musicians who are between the ages
    of 16 and 25 are eligible to audition for the award.
    *Financial Details: $650 for the winner; $350 for the
    runner up. *Number Awarded: Varies. *Deadline:
    February 1.

National Federation of Music Clubs
c/o Sharon Booker, Chair
325 North Via Del Ceruelo
Green Valley, AZ 85614
http://www.nfmc-music.org
Disability Served: vision
The Music for the Blind Award is available to help finance
    postsecondary training. *Eligibility: Blind composers
    who are between the ages of 19 and 30 are eligible
    to apply. A fee of $3 per manuscript submission
    is required. *Financial Details: Award is for $200.
    *Number Awarded: Varies. *Deadline: March 1.

National Federation of Music Clubs

c/o Sharon Booker, Chair
325 North Via Del Ceruelo
Green Valley, AZ 85614
http://www.nfmc-music.org
Disability Served: vision
Regional scholarships are offered to blind musicians
in each area in which the National Federation
has affiliates. *Eligibility: Applicants must submit
a recommendation from a teacher as well as an
audiotape presenting at least three different
selections performed by the musician. *Financial
Details: Awards are for $200. *Number Awarded:
Varies. *Deadline: Contact the federation for
details.

National Federation of the Blind

1800 Johnson Street
Baltimore, MD 21230-4914
410-659-9314
http://www.nfb.org
Disability Served: vision
This organization offers scholarships for full-time,
postsecondary education. *Eligibility: Legally blind
students pursuing or planning to pursue full-time,
postsecondary education are eligible to apply. Other
restrictions may apply; contact the Federation for
further information. *Financial Details: Scholarships
ranging from $3,000 to $12,000 are available.
*Number Awarded: One for $10,000, three for $4,000
each, and 22 for $3,000 each are awarded annually.
*Deadline: March 30.

National Federation of the Blind of Alabama

Scholarship Committee
340 Shelton Mill Road
Auburn, AL 36830
334-501-2001
http://www.nfbofalabama.org
Disability Served: vision
This state affiliate of the National Federation of
the Blind offers a scholarship for college study.
*Eligibility: Graduating high school seniors and
college students who are blind or visually impaired
and residents of Alabama are eligible to apply.
Scholarships are awarded based on academic
excellence, community service, and financial need.
*Financial Details: $500. *Number Awarded: Varies.
*Deadline: April 1.

National Federation of the Blind of Arizona

4630 East Thomas Road, E-11
Phoenix, AZ 85018
602-956-0230
hodgdoe@extremezone.com
http://www.nfbarizona.com
Disability Served: vision
The Federation offers the James R. Carlock Scholarship
to blind students. *Eligibility: Blind students who are
Arizona residents or attending school in Arizona are
eligible to apply. *Financial Details: $1,000. *Number
Awarded: Varies. *Deadline: Typically in March.

National Federation of the Blind of California

175 East Olive Avenue, Suite 308
Burbank, CA 91502
818-558-6524
nfbcal@sbcglobal.net
http://www.nfbcal.org
Disability Served: vision
The federation awards national and state scholarships to
legally blind high school seniors and current college
students. *Eligibility: Visually impaired students
who are California residents are eligible to apply.
*Financial Details: Scholarships ranging from $3,000
to $12,000 are awarded each year. *Number Awarded:
The number of scholarships awarded varies annually.
*Deadline: March 31.

National Federation of the Blind of Colorado

2233 West Shepperd Avenue
Littleton, CO 80120
800-401-4NFB
http://www.nfbco.org
Disability Served: vision
The federation provides grants to help finance college
training. *Eligibility: Visually impaired students from
Colorado are eligible to apply. Selection is based on
academic record, need, and community involvement.
*Financial Details: Grants are for up to $1,500.
*Number Awarded: Varies each year. *Deadline:
Applications are due in May.

National Federation of the Blind of Connecticut

580 Burnside Avenue, Suite 1
East Hartford, CT 06108
860-289-1971
info@nfbct.org
http://www.nfbct.org/html/schinfo.htm

Disability Served: vision

This state affiliate of the National Federation of the Blind offers scholarships for college study. *Eligibility: Graduating high school seniors and college students who are blind or visually impaired and residents of Connecticut (or attending school in Connecticut) are eligible to apply. Scholarships are awarded based on academic excellence, community service, and financial need. *Financial Details: Awards range from $1,000 to $5,000. *Number Awarded: Varies. *Deadline: September 15.

National Federation of the Blind of Florida

121 Deer Lake Circle
Ormond Beach, FL 32174
888-282-5972
http://www.nfbflorida.org
Disability Served: vision
The federation offers an educational scholarship to blind students. *Eligibility: Blind students who reside in Florida and have a GPA of at least 2.70 are eligible to apply. *Financial Details: $1,000. *Number Awarded: Varies. *Deadline: Contact the federation for further details.

National Federation of the Blind of Idaho

1301 South Capitol Boulevard, Suite C
Boise, ID 83706-2926
208-343-1377
http://www.nfbidaho.org
Disability Served: vision
The federation offers an educational scholarship to blind students. *Eligibility: Blind students are eligible to apply. Scholarships are awarded based on academic excellence, community service, and financial need. *Financial Details: Varies. *Number Awarded: Varies. *Deadline: Contact the federation for the deadline.

National Federation of the Blind of Illinois

Chairman, NFBI Scholarship Committee
5817 North Nina
Chicago, IL 60631
http://www.nfbillinois.org
Disability Served: vision
The federation offers the Peter Grunwald Scholarship and the Kenneth Jernigan Scholarships to blind students. *Eligibility: Blind full-time students who are Illinois residents or attending school in the state are eligible to apply. Scholarships are awarded

based on academic excellence, community service, and financial need. *Financial Details: Gunwale Scholarship: $1,500. Jernigan Scholarships: $1,250. *Number Awarded: Gunwale Scholarship: One. Jernigan Scholarships: Two. *Deadline: Typically at the end of March.

National Federation of the Blind of Kansas

11905 Mohawk Lane
Leawood, KS 66209-1038
913-339-9341
circa1944@aol.com
http://www.nfbks.org/nfb-sklr.shtml
Disability Served: vision
This state affiliate of the National Federation of the Blind offers a scholarship for college study. *Eligibility: Graduating high school seniors and college students who are blind or visually impaired and residents of Kansas are eligible to apply. *Financial Details: Awards vary. *Number Awarded: Varies. *Deadline: Contact the federation for details.

National Federation of the Blind of Massachusetts

Scholarship Program
140 Wood Street
Somerset, MA 02726-5225
508-679-8543
nfbmass@earthlink.net
http://www.nfbmass.org
Disability Served: vision
This state affiliate of the National Federation of the Blind offers a scholarship for college study. *Eligibility: Graduating high school seniors and college students who are blind or visually impaired and residents of Massachusetts (or attending school in the state) are eligible to apply. Scholarships are awarded based on academic excellence, community service, and financial need. *Financial Details: Awards vary. *Number Awarded: Varies. *Deadline: February 6.

National Federation of the Blind of Missouri

3910 Tropical Lane
Columbia, MO 65202
http://www.nfbmo.org
Disability Served: vision
The federation offers educational scholarships to blind students. *Eligibility: Blind students who are residents of Missouri are eligible to apply. *Financial

Details: Varies. *Number Awarded: Varies. *Deadline: February 1.

National Federation of the Blind of New York State
PO Box 09-0363
Brooklyn, NY 11209
718-567-7821, 800-356-7713
nfbnys@aol.com
http://www.nfbny.org
Disability Served: vision
The federation provides a small number of scholarships to help defer postsecondary education expenses. *Eligibility: Blind students from New York are eligible to apply. *Financial Details: Awards vary. *Number Awarded: Three. *Deadline: Contact the federation for details.

National Federation of the Blind of Ohio
Blind of Ohio Scholarship Committee
2 Canterbury Street
Athens, OH 45701
740-593-4838
jsmith1@ohiou.edu
http://www.nfbohio.org
Disability Served: vision
The federation offers educational scholarships to blind students. *Eligibility: Blind full-time students are eligible to apply. Scholarships are awarded based on academic excellence, community service, and financial need. *Financial Details: One $1,500 and one $1,000 scholarship *Number Awarded: Two. *Deadline: June 1.

National Federation of the Blind of Oregon
NFBO Scholarship Committee
2005 Main Street
Springfield, OR 97478
541-726-6924
nfb_or@msn.com
http://www.nfb-or.org/scholarships.htm
Disability Served: vision
The federation offers educational scholarships to blind students. *Eligibility: Blind students who reside in Oregon are eligible to apply. Scholarships are awarded based on academic excellence, professional promise, and leadership potential. *Financial Details: One for $1,500, two for $1,000. *Number Awarded: Three. *Deadline: June 1.

National Federation of the Blind of South Dakota
901 South Chicago Street
Hot Springs, SD 57747

605-745-5599
Disability Served: vision
The Federation provides the Anna Marklund Scholarship to help defer postsecondary education expenses. *Eligibility: Blind students from South Dakota are eligible to apply. *Financial Details: $1,000. *Number Awarded: Varies. *Deadline: Varies each year; contact the federation for details.

National Federation of the Blind of Texas
Attn: Scholarship Committee
3805 Harley Avenue
Fort Worth, TX 76107
scholarship@nfb-texas.org
http://www.nfb-texas.org
Disability Served: vision
The federation offers several educational scholarships to blind students. *Eligibility: Blind full-time students who reside in Texas are eligible to apply. Scholarships are awarded based on academic excellence, community service, and financial need. *Financial Details: $1,000 to $2,000. *Number Awarded: Varies. *Deadline: June 15.

National Federation of the Blind of Utah
132 Penman Lane
Bountiful, UT 84010-7634
Disability Served: vision
The federation provides a small number of scholarships to help defer postsecondary education expenses. *Eligibility: Blind students from Utah are eligible to apply. *Financial Details: Awards vary. *Number Awarded: Varies. *Deadline: Contact the federation for details.

National Federation of the Blind of Vermont
PO Box 1354
Montpelier, VT 05601
802-279-5136
http://www.nfbvt.org
Disability Served: vision
The federation provides scholarships to help defer postsecondary education expenses. *Eligibility: Blind students from Vermont are eligible to apply. *Financial Details: The awards range from $300 to $600. *Number Awarded: Varies. *Deadline: Applications are typically due in the summer.

National Federation of the Blind of Washington
Scholarship Committee
1420 Fifth Avenue, Suite 2200

Seattle, WA 98101
206-224-7242
http://www.nfbw.org
Disability Served: vision
The federation offers educational scholarships to blind
students. *Eligibility: Blind students who are residents
of Washington are eligible to apply. *Financial Details:
Awards of $2,000 or $3,000 are available. *Number
Awarded: Varies. *Deadline: Typically in late August.

National FFA

6060 FFA Drive, PO Box 68960
Indianapolis, IN 46268-0960
317-802-6060
scholarships@ffa.org
http://www.ffa.org/programs/scholarships
Disability Served: physically disabled
The National FFA provides scholarships to help finance
college study, including the B.R.I.D.G.E Endowment
for physically disabled students. *Eligibility: Physically
disabled students who are members of the FFA and
pursuing a two- or four-year degree in any area of
agriculture may apply. *Financial Details: $5,000.
*Number Awarded: Approximately one. *Deadline:
Applications are typically due at the end of April.

National Foundation for Ectodermal Dysplasias

410 East Main Street, PO Box 114
Mascoutah, IL 62258-0114
618-566-2020
info@nfed.org
http://www.nfed.org/College.htm
Disability Served: ectodermal dysplasias
The council offers the Ectodermal Dysplasias Memorial
College Scholarship. *Eligibility: Students with
ectodermal dysplasias may apply. Scholarships
are awarded based on academic achievement,
community service, and financial need. *Financial
Details: Awards vary. *Number Awarded: Varies.
*Deadline: Applications are typically due in March.

National Fraternal Society of the Deaf

1118 South Sixth Street
Springfield, IL 62703
217-789-7429, 217-789-7438 (TTY)
thefrat@nfsd.com
http://www.nfsd.com
Disability Served: hearing
Scholarships to help finance college training are
offered by the society. *Eligibility: Persons who have

been a member of the Society for at least one year
are eligible to apply. Applicants must be hearing
impaired. *Financial Details: Scholarships are for
$1,000. *Number Awarded: Varies. *Deadline: Contact
the society for details.

National Institutes of Health (NIH)

Office of Loan Repayment and Scholarship
2 Center Drive, Room 2E24, MSC 0230
Bethesda, MD 20892-0230
888-352-3001
ugsp@nih.gov
http://ugsp.info.nih.gov
Disability Served: various
The NIH offers the Undergraduate Scholarship Program
to students (including those who are disabled) who
are committed to careers in biomedical, behavioral,
and social science health-related research. *Eligibility:
Disadvantaged students (defined as those having
"exceptional financial need") with disabilities are
eligible. For each paid scholarship year, students
are required to train for 10 weeks as a paid summer
research employee in an NIH research laboratory.
After graduation, they are expected to work one
year at a NIH facility for every year they received
a scholarship. *Financial Details: Up to $20,000
annually. *Number Awarded: Fifteen. *Deadline:
Typically in late March.

Nazareth College of Rochester

Financial Aid Office
4245 East Avenue
Rochester, NY 14618-3790
585-389-2310
finaid@naz.edu
http://www.naz.edu/dept/finaid
Disability Served: various
This private four-year college provides financial aid
to help students (including those with disabilities)
attend college. *Eligibility: Students who need
financial assistance are eligible to apply. *Financial
Details: Amounts vary according to need. *Number
Awarded: Varies. *Deadline: Write or call for details.

Nebraska Department of Education

PO Box 94987
Lincoln, NE 68509
402-471-2295
http://www.nde.state.ne.us
Disability Served: various

The department provides financial aid to help students (including those with disabilities) attend college. *Eligibility: Nebraska students who need financial assistance are eligible to apply. *Financial Details: Amounts vary according to need. *Number Awarded: Varies. *Deadline: Contact the department for additional details.

Nebraska Department of Veterans Affairs
PO Box 95083
Lincoln, NE 68509-5083
402-471-2458
http://www.nebraskaveteran.com
Disability Served: various
The department provides tuition wavers for the purpose of college study. *Eligibility: Children or spouses of Nebraska veterans who died or who are permanently disabled as a result of military service are eligible to apply. Applicants must be residents of Nebraska and attend a college or university in the state. *Financial Details: Full tuition. *Number Awarded: Varies each year. *Deadline: Contact the department for details.

Nebraska-Lincoln, University of
Office of Scholarships and Financial Aid
17 Canfield Administration Building, PO Box 880411
Lincoln, NE 68588-0411
800-742-8800, ext.2030
finaid2@unl.edu
http://www.unl.edu/scholfa
Disability Served: various
The university offers financial aid to help students (including those with disabilities) attend college. *Eligibility: Students who need financial assistance are eligible to apply. *Financial Details: Amounts vary according to need. *Number Awarded: Varies. *Deadline: Write or call for details.

Nevada-Las Vegas, University of
Student Financial Services
4505 Maryland Parkway, 232 Reynolds Student Services Center
Las Vegas, NV 89154-2016
702-895-3424
sfsssc@ccmail.nevada.edu
http://financialaid.unlv.edu
Disability Served: various
The university provides financial aid to help students (including those with disabilities) attend college. *Eligibility: Students who need financial assistance

are eligible to apply. *Financial Details: Amounts vary according to need. *Number Awarded: Varies. *Deadline: Contact the university for additional details.

Nevada Office of the State Treasurer
101 North Carson, #4
Carson City, NV 89701
775-684-5600
http://nevadatreasurer.gov
Disability Served: various
The office provides financial aid to help students (including those with disabilities) attend college. *Eligibility: Nevada students who need financial assistance are eligible to apply. *Financial Details: Amounts vary according to need. *Number Awarded: Varies. *Deadline: Contact the office for additional details.

New England Hemophilia Association
Scholarship Committee Chairperson
347 Washington Street, Suite 402
Dedham, MA 02026
800-800-6606, ext. 5175
scholarship@hemophiliaheatlh.com
http://www.newenglandhemophilia.org
Disability Served: inherited bleeding disorders
The association provides a variety of scholarships and grants to students. *Eligibility: Students with hemophilia who need financial assistance are eligible to apply. *Financial Details: Amounts vary according to need. *Number Awarded: Varies. *Deadline: Contact the association for additional details.

New Hampshire, University of
Financial Aid Office
Stoke Hall, 11 Garrison Avenue
Durham, NH 03824
603-862-3600
http://www.unh.edu/financial-aid
Disability Served: various
The university offers financial aid to help students (including those with disabilities) attend college. *Eligibility: Students who need financial assistance are eligible to apply. *Financial Details: Amounts vary according to need. *Number Awarded: Varies. *Deadline: Write or call for details.

New Hampshire Charitable Fund
37 Pleasant Street
Concord, NH 03301

Educational Funding Resources 253

603-225-6641
http://www.nhcf.org
Disability Served: various
The fund offers a wide range of financial aid to
New Hampshire students (including those with
disabilities). *Eligibility: New Hampshire residents
may apply; application requirements vary by award.
*Financial Details: Awards vary. *Number Awarded:
Varies. *Deadline: Contact the foundation for details.

**New Hampshire Postsecondary Education
Commission**
3 Barrell Court, Suite 300
Concord, NH 03301-8543
603-271-2555, 800-735-2964 (TDD)
http://www.state.nh.us/postsecondary/fin.html
Disability Served: various
The commission provides financial aid to help students
(including those with disabilities) attend college.
*Eligibility: New Hampshire students who need
financial assistance are eligible to apply. *Financial
Details: Amounts vary according to need. *Number
Awarded: Varies. *Deadline: Contact the commission
for additional details.

New Hampshire State Veterans Council
275 Chestnut Street, Room 321
Manchester, NH 03101-2411
603-624-9230, 800-622-9230
nhviold@vba.va.gov
http://www.state.nh.us/nhveterans
Disability Served: various
The council provides tuition wavers for the purpose of
college study. *Eligibility: Children of New Hampshire
veterans who are deceased as a result of a service-
connected disability or declared missing in action are
eligible to apply. Applicants must be residents of New
Hampshire and attend a public college or university
in the state. *Financial Details: Full tuition. *Number
Awarded: Varies each year. *Deadline: Contact the
council for details. Additional educational financial
aid programs are available to veterans.

New Jersey, College of
Office of Student Financial Assistance
Green Hall, Room 101, PO Box 7718
Ewing, NJ 08628
609-771-2211
osfa@tcnj.edu
http://www.tcnj.edu/%7Eosfa

Disability Served: various
The college offers financial aid to help students
(including those with disabilities) to attend college.
*Eligibility: Students who need financial assistance
are eligible to apply. *Financial Details: Amounts
vary according to need. *Number Awarded: Varies.
*Deadline: Write or call for details.

**New Jersey Commission for the Blind and Visually
Impaired**
153 Halsey Street, 6th Floor, PO Box 47017
Newark, NJ 07101
973-648-3333
http://www.state.nj.us/humanservices/cbvi
Disability Served: vision
The commission provides scholarships for the purpose
of financing schooling. *Eligibility: Visually impaired
residents of New Jersey are eligible for financial aid
to help them attend a public college in the state.
*Financial Details: Awards vary according to need.
*Number Awarded: Varies. *Deadline: Contact the
commission for details.

**New Jersey Higher Education Student Assistance
Authority**
PO Box 540
Trenton, NJ 08625
800-792-8670
http://www.nj.gov/highereducation/njhesaa.htm
Disability Served: various
The authority provides financial aid to help students
(including those with disabilities) attend college.
*Eligibility: New Jersey students who need financial
assistance are eligible to apply. *Financial Details:
Amounts vary according to need. *Number Awarded:
Varies. *Deadline: Contact the authority for additional
details.

New Mexico, University of
Student Financial Aid Office
Mesa Vista Hall North, 1 University of New Mexico,
MSC06 3610
Albuquerque, NM 87131
505-277-2041
finaid@unm.edu
http://www.unm.edu/%7efinaid
Disability Served: various
The university offers financial aid to help students
(including those with disabilities) attend college.
*Eligibility: Students who need financial assistance

are eligible to apply. *Financial Details: Amounts vary according to need. *Number Awarded: Varies. *Deadline: Contact the university for additional details.

New Mexico Department of Veterans' Services
PO Box 2324
Santa Fe, NM 87504
505-827-6300, 866-433-8387
http://www.state.nm.us/veterans/vschome.html
Disability Served: various
The department provides tuition wavers for the purpose of college study. *Eligibility: Children of New Mexico veterans who died as a result of military service are eligible to apply. Applicants must be residents of New Mexico and attend a public college or university in the state. *Financial Details: Financial aid includes tuition, required fees, and books not to exceed an amount equal to the highest resident tuition charged by a state institution. *Number Awarded: Varies each year. *Deadline: Contact the department for details. The department also offers Vietnam Veterans Scholarship for veterans who have resided in New Mexico for a minimum of 10 years and are in receipt of the Vietnam Service Medal.

New Mexico Higher Education Department
1068 Cerrillos Road
Santa Fe, NM 87501
800-279-9777
http://hed.state.nm.us/collegefinance/index.asp
Disability Served: various
The department provides financial aid to help students (including those with disabilities) attend college. *Eligibility: New Mexico students who need financial assistance are eligible to apply. *Financial Details: Amounts vary according to need. *Number Awarded: Varies. *Deadline: Contact the department for additional details.

New York State Division of Veterans Affairs
116 West 32nd Street, 5th Floor
New York, NY 10001
888-838-7697
http://www.veterans.state.ny.us/benefits.htm
Disability Served: various
The division offers tuition awards to help finance college training. *Eligibility: New York residents who are children of disabled veterans, or those who died in combat or as a result of combat-related injuries,

are eligible. *Financial Details: $500/semester for part-time study; $1,000/semester for full-time study. *Number Awarded: Varies. *Deadline: Contact the division for details. These awards are administered by the New York State Higher Education Services Corporation (http://www.hesc.com).

New York State Higher Education Services Corporation
99 Washington Avenue
Albany, NY 12255
888-697-4372
http://www.hesc.state.ny.us
Disability Served: various
The corporation provides financial aid to help students (including those with disabilities) attend college. *Eligibility: New York students who need financial assistance are eligible to apply. *Financial Details: Amounts vary according to need. *Number Awarded: Varies. *Deadline: Contact the corporation for additional details.

New York University
Office of Financial Aid
25 West 4th Street
New York, NY 10012-1119
212-998-4444
financial.aid@nyu.edu
http://www.nyu.edu/financial.aid
Disability Served: various
The university offers financial aid to help students (including those with disabilities) attend college. *Eligibility: Students who need financial assistance are eligible to apply. *Financial Details: Amounts vary according to need. *Number Awarded: Varies. *Deadline: Contact the university for additional details.

Nicholls State University
Office of Financial Aid
PO Box 20005
Thibodeaux, LA 70310
985-448-4048
finaid@nicholls.edu
http://www.nicholls.edu/finaid
Disability Served: various
The university provides financial aid to help students (including those with disabilities) attend college. *Eligibility: Students who need financial assistance are eligible to apply. *Financial Details: Amounts

vary according to need. *Number Awarded: Varies.
*Deadline: Write or call for details.

Northampton Community College
Office of Admissions
3835 Green Pond Road
Bethlehem, PA 18017
610-861-5342
adminfo@northampton.edu
http://www.northampton.edu
Disability Served: various
This two-year community college has student support
services and a financial aid program open to students
with disabilities. *Eligibility: Disabled students who
need financial assistance are eligible. *Financial
Details: Amounts vary according to need. *Number
Awarded: Varies. *Deadline: Write or call for details.

North Carolina-Chapel Hill, University of
Office of Scholarships and Student Aid
300 Pettigrew Hall, CB #2300, PO Box 1080
Chapel Hill, NC 27514-1080
919-962-8396
aidinfo@unc.edu
http://studentaid.unc.edu/studentaid
Disability Served: various
The university provides financial aid to help students
(including those with disabilities) attend college.
*Eligibility: Students who need financial assistance
are eligible to apply. *Financial Details: Amounts
vary according to need. *Number Awarded: Varies.
*Deadline: Write or call for details.

North Carolina Division of Services for the Blind
309 Ashe Avenue, 2601 Mail Service Center
Raleigh, NC 27699-2601
http://www.dhhs.state.nc.us/dsb
Disability Served: vision
The division provides financial aid to help cover college
tuition and fees. *Eligibility: Legally blind residents of
the state who demonstrate financial need are eligible.
*Financial Details: Amounts vary and depend on
need. *Number Awarded: Varies. *Deadline: Contact
the division for information.

North Carolina Division of Veterans Affairs
325 North Salisbury Street
Raleigh, NC 27699-1315
919-733-3851
http://www.nasdva.com/northcarolina.html

Disability Served: various
The division offers tuition waivers to help finance college
training. *Eligibility: North Carolina residents who are
children of disabled veterans, or those who died in
combat, or as a result of combat-related injuries are
eligible. *Financial Details: Varies. *Number Awarded:
Varies. *Deadline: Contact the division for details.

North Carolina Division of Vocational Rehabilitation Services
2801 Mail Service Center
Raleigh, NC 27699-2801
919-855-3500
dvr.info@ncmail.net
http://dvr.dhhs.state.nc.us
Disability Served: various
The Division of Vocational Rehabilitation Services
provides assistance with tuition and fees for
postsecondary training. *Eligibility: Residents
of North Carolina with disabilities may apply.
Interested parties may apply at any of the local
vocational rehabilitation unit offices or they can
contact the state office. *Financial Details: Amounts
vary according to need. *Number Awarded: Varies.
*Deadline: Contact the division for information.

North Carolina State Education Assistance Authority
PO Box 14103
Research Triangle Park, NC 27709
919-549-8614
information@ncseaa.edu
http://www.ncseaa.edu
Disability Served: various
The authority provides financial aid to help students
(including those with disabilities) attend college.
*Eligibility: North Carolina students who need
financial assistance are eligible to apply. *Financial
Details: Amounts vary according to need. *Number
Awarded: Varies. *Deadline: Contact the authority for
additional details.

North Dakota, University of
Student Financial Aid Office
216 Twamley Hall, PO Box 8371
Grand Forks, ND 58202-8371
800-CALL-UND, ext. 73121
sfa@mail.und.nodak.edu
http://www.und.edu/dept/finaid
Disability Served: various
The university offers financial aid to help students

(including those with disabilities) attend college. *Eligibility: Students who need financial assistance are eligible to apply. *Financial Details: Amounts vary according to need. *Number Awarded: Varies. *Deadline: Contact the university for additional details.

North Dakota Association of the Blind (NDAB)

NDAB Scholarship Committee
1412 5th Street, SW
Minot, ND 58701
http://www.ndab.org/Scholarship.html
Disability Served: vision
The council offers the College Scholarship and the Emma Skogen Scholarship to blind students. *Eligibility: Legally blind, second-year-through-post-graduate students who are residents of North Dakota are eligible to apply for College Scholarships. Scholarships are awarded based on financial need and academic achievements. Blind or visually impaired students who are planning to attend a vocational or trade school are eligible to apply for the Emma Skogen Scholarship. Students must demonstrate financial need. *Financial Details: College Scholarship: One $1,000 and two $500 scholarships. Emma Skogen Scholarship: One $400 scholarship. *Number Awarded: Four. *Deadline: March 15.

North Dakota Department of Public Instruction

600 East Boulevard Avenue, Department 201
Bismarck, ND 58505-0440
701-328-2260
http://www.dpi.state.nd.us
Disability Served: various
The department provides financial aid to help students (including those with disabilities) attend college. *Eligibility: North Dakota students who need financial assistance are eligible to apply. *Financial Details: Amounts vary according to need. *Number Awarded: Varies. *Deadline: Contact the department for additional details.

North Dakota Department of Veterans Affairs

1411 32nd Street South, PO Box 9003
Fargo, ND 58106-9003
701-239-7165, 866-634-8387
http://www.state.nd.us/veterans
Disability Served: various
The department offers tuition/fee waivers to help

finance college. *Eligibility: North Dakota residents who are children of disabled veterans, those who died in combat, those who died as a result of combat-related injuries, or those who are have been declared missing in action are eligible. *Financial Details: Full tuition. *Number Awarded: Varies. *Deadline: Contact the department for details.

North Dakota State College of Science

Haverty Hall, Room 115
Wahpeton, ND 58076
800-342-4325
ndscs.fin.aid@ndscs.nodak.edu
http://www.ndscs.nodak.edu/student/finaid
Disability Served: various
This public two-year community college provides financial aid to help students (including those with disabilities) attend college. *Eligibility: Students who need financial assistance are eligible to apply. *Financial Details: Amounts vary according to need. *Number Awarded: Varies. *Deadline: Contact the college for additional details.

Northern Arizona State University

Office of Financial Aid
PO Box 4108
Flagstaff, AZ 86001-4108
928-523-4951
Financial.Aid@nau.edu
http://www4.nau.edu/finaid
Disability Served: various
The university provides financial aid to help students (including those with disabilities) attend college. *Eligibility: Students who need financial assistance are eligible to apply. *Financial Details: Amounts vary according to need. *Number Awarded: Varies. *Deadline: Write or call for details.

North Harris College

2700 W.W. Thorne Drive
Houston, TX 77073-3499
281-618-5400
nhc.startcollege@nhmccd.edu
http://wwwnhc.nhmccd.cc.tx.us
Disability Served: various
This two-year community college provides financial aid to students (including those with disabilities). *Eligibility: Financially needy students who are attending the College are eligible to apply. *Financial Details: Amounts vary and depend on need. *Number

Awarded: Varies. *Deadline: Contact the college for details.

North Lake College

Office of Financial Aid and Veterans Affairs
5001 North MacArthur Boulevard
Irving, TX 75038
972-273-3320
http://www.northlakecollege.edu/adreg/FinAid_
    VetAffairs.htm
Disability Served: various
This public two-year college provides financial aid to
    help students (including those with disabilities)
    attend college. *Eligibility: Students who need
    financial assistance are eligible to apply. *Financial
    Details: Amounts vary according to need. *Number
    Awarded: Varies. *Deadline: Contact the college for
    additional details.

Northwestern University

Office of Undergraduate Financial Aid
1801 Hinman Avenue
Evanston, IL 60208-1270
847-491-7400
ug-finaid@northwestern.edu
http://ug-finaid.northwestern.edu
Disability Served: various
This private four-year university provides financial
    aid to students (including those with disabilities).
    *Eligibility: Financially needy students are eligible to
    apply. *Financial Details: Amounts vary and depend
    on need. *Number Awarded: Varies. *Deadline:
    Contact the university for details.

Northwest Nazarene College

623 Holly Street
Nampa, ID 83686
208-467-8644
FinancialAid@NNU.edu
http://www.nnu.eduDisability Served: various
This private four-year college offers financial aid to help
    students (including those with disabilities) attend
    college. *Eligibility: Students who need financial assis-
    tance are eligible to apply. *Financial Details: Amounts
    vary according to need. *Number Awarded: Varies.
    *Deadline: Contact the college for additional details.

Norwalk Community-Technical College

188 Richards Avenue
Norwalk, CT 06854

203-857-7023
NK-FinAid@ncc.commnet.edu
http://www.ncc.commnet.edu/finaid.asp
Disability Served: various
This public, two-year college provides financial aid to
    help students (including those with disabilities)
    attend college. *Eligibility: Students who need
    financial assistance are eligible to apply. *Financial
    Details: Amounts vary according to need. *Number
    Awarded: Varies. *Deadline: Contact the college for
    additional details.

NuFACTOR

41093 County Center Drive
Temecula, CA 92591
800-323-6832
http://www.nufactor.com/web_pages/edostie_
    scholarship.html
Disability Served: inherited bleeding disorders
This company offers the Eric Dostie Memorial College
    Scholarship. *Eligibility: Students with hemophilia
    who demonstrate scholastic achievement,
    community service, and financial need may apply.
    *Financial Details: $1,000. *Number Awarded: Ten.
    *Deadline: Contact NuFACTOR for details.

Oakland City University

138 North Lucretia Street
Oakland City, IN 47660
800-737-5125
http://www.oak.edu
Disability Served: various
This private four-year college provides financial aid
    to students (including those with disabilities).
    *Eligibility: Financially needy students are eligible to
    apply. *Financial Details: Amounts vary and depend
    on need. *Number Awarded: Varies. *Deadline: Write
    or call for details.

Oakland Community College

2480 Opdyke Road
Bloomfield Hills, MI 48304
248-341-2000
http://www.oaklandcc.edu/FutureStudents/Cost.htm
Disability Served: various
This two-year college provides financial aid to students
    (including those with disabilities). *Eligibility: Finan-
    cially needy students are eligible to apply. *Financial
    Details: Amounts vary and depend on need. *Number
    Awarded: Varies. *Deadline: Write or call for details.

Odessa College
Financial Aid Office
Student Union Building, 201 West University Odessa,
  Room 203
Odessa, TX 79764
915-335-6433
http://www.odessa.edu/dept/financial
Disability Served: various
This two-year college provides financial aid to students
  (including those with disabilities). *Eligibility:
  Financially needy students are eligible to apply.
  *Financial Details: Amounts vary and depend on
  need. *Number Awarded: Varies. *Deadline: Contact
  the college for details.

Ohio Board of Regents
State Grants and Scholarships Department
PO Box 182452
Columbus, OH 43218-2452
888-833-1133
http://www.regents.state.oh.us/sgs
Disability Served: various
The board provides financial aid to help students
  (including those with disabilities) attend college.
  *Eligibility: Ohio students who need financial
  assistance are eligible to apply. *Financial Details:
  Amounts vary according to need. *Number Awarded:
  Varies. *Deadline: Contact the board for additional
  details.

Ohio State University
Office of Student Financial Aid
PO Box 183029
Columbus, OH 43218-3029
614-292-0300
sfa-finaid@osu.edu
http://sfa.osu.edu
Disability Served: various
This public four-year university provides financial
  aid to students (including those with disabilities).
  *Eligibility: Financially needy students are eligible to
  apply. *Financial Details: Amounts vary and depend
  on need. *Number Awarded: Varies. *Deadline:
  Contact the university for details.

Ohio University
Office of Student Financial Aid and Scholarships
020 Chubb Hall
Athens, OH 45701
740-593-4141

financial.aid@ohio.edu
http://www-sfa.chubb.ohiou.edu
Disability Served: various
The university offers financial aid to help students
  (including those with disabilities) attend college.
  *Eligibility: Students who need financial assistance
  are eligible to apply. *Financial Details: Amounts
  vary according to need. *Number Awarded: Varies.
  *Deadline: Contact the university for additional
  details.

Oklahoma, University of
Buchanan Hall, 1000 Asp Avenue, Room 216
Norman, OK 73019-4078
405-325-4521
http://www.financialaid.ou.edu
Disability Served: various
The university offers several scholarships to disabled
  students. *Eligibility: Students who demonstrate
  strong academic performance and financial need
  may apply. *Financial Details: $1,000 or $1,200.
  *Number Awarded: Varies. *Deadline: Contact the
  university for additional details.

Oklahoma Department of Veterans Affairs
2311 North Central Avenue
Oklahoma City, OK 73105
405-521-3684
sclymer@odva.state.ok.us
http://www.odva.state.ok.us
Disability Served: various
The department provides tuition waivers for those with
  disabilities. *Eligibility: Oklahoma veterans who
  have a service-related disability and are planning to
  attend an Oklahoma vocational or technical school
  are eligible. *Financial Details: Free tuition for up to
  36 months is awarded. *Number Awarded: Varies.
  *Deadline: Contact the department for information.

**Oklahoma State Regents for Higher Education
  (OSRHE)**
655 Research Parkway, Suite 200
Oklahoma City, OK 73104
405-225-9100
rstokes@osrhe.edu
http://www.okhighered.org/student%2Dcenter/
  financial%2Daid
Disability Served: various
This agency provides financial aid to help students
  (including those with disabilities) attend college.

*Eligibility: Oklahoma students who need financial assistance are eligible to apply. *Financial Details: Amounts vary according to need. *Number Awarded: Varies. *Deadline: Contact the agency for additional details.

Oklahoma State University

Office of Disability Services
315 Student Union
Stillwater, OK 74078
405-744-7116
http://www.okstate.edu/ucs/stdis/scholarship.html
Disability Served: various
This four-year university provides more than 15 scholarships to disabled students. *Eligibility: Financially needy students with disabilities attending the University are eligible to apply. *Financial Details: Amounts vary and depend on need. *Number Awarded: Varies. *Deadline: Write or call for details.

Old Dominion University

Disability Services
1525 Webb Center
Norfolk, VA 23529
757-683-4655
http://www.odu.edu/disabilityservices
Disability Served: various
This four-year university provides scholarships to students with disabilities. *Eligibility: Students with disabilities attending the university are eligible to apply. *Financial Details: Amount varies. *Number Awarded: Varies. *Deadline: Write or call for details.

Olivet Nazarene University

Office of Financial Aid
One University Avenue
Bourbonnais, IL 60914-2345
800-648-1463
http://www.olivet.edu/services/financialaid
Disability Served: various
The university offers awards to help students with disabilities. *Eligibility: Students with disabilities in a vocational rehabilitation program may apply. *Financial Details: Amounts vary. *Number Awarded: Varies. *Deadline: Write or call for details.

Oregon, University of

Office of Student Financial Aid and Scholarships
1278 University of Oregon
Eugene, OR 97403-1278

800-760-6953
fawww@uoregon.edu
http://financialaid.uoregon.edu
Disability Served: various
The university offers financial aid to help students (including those with disabilities) attend college. *Eligibility: Students who need financial assistance are eligible to apply. *Financial Details: Amounts vary according to need. *Number Awarded: Varies. *Deadline: Write or call for details.

Oregon Council of the Blind

4730 Auburn Road, NE, Suite 52
Salem, OR 97301
503-362-4151
http://www.acboforegon.org
Disability Served: vision
The council awards scholarships to help finance college study. *Eligibility: High school seniors who are blind are eligible to apply. *Financial Details: Scholarships of $2,500 are given. *Number Awarded: Two. *Deadline: Varies. Write or call for information.

Oregon Student Assistance Commission

1500 Valley River Drive, Suite 100
Eugene, OR 97401
541-687-7400, 800-452-8807
awardinfo@mercury.osac.state.or.us
http://www.osac.state.or.us or http://www.getcollegefunds.org
Disability Served: vision
The commission offers the Harry Ludwig Memorial Scholarship to blind students, as well as general financial aid that disabled students may apply for. *Eligibility: Blind students who are Oregon residents planning to enroll in full-time undergraduate or graduate studies are eligible to apply. *Financial Details: Varies. *Number Awarded: Varies. *Deadline: Contact the commission for details.

Paralyzed Veterans of America (PVA)

801 18th Street, NW
Washington, DC 20006-3517
800-424-8200, ext. 619
TrishH@pva.org
http://www.pva.org/member/scholar.htm
Disability Served: physically disabled
This organization provides scholarships to finance education. *Eligibility: Organization members and their dependents under 24 years of age pursuing

college degrees are eligible to apply. *Financial Details: Awards vary. *Number Awarded: Varies each year. *Deadline: Applications are due by June 1.

Patient Advocate Foundation

Attn: Vice President of Special Programs
700 Thimble Shoals Boulevard, Suite 200
Newport News, VA 23606
800-532-5274
help@patientadvocate.org
http://www.patientadvocate.org
Disability Served: various
The foundation offers the following scholarships: the Cheryl Grimmel Award, the Monica Bailes Award, and Scholarships for Survivors. *Eligibility: Students whose education has been interrupted or delayed by a diagnosis of cancer or another critical or life-threatening disease may apply. Recipients must enroll full time, maintain a GPA of at least 3.0, and complete 20 hours of community service for each year covered by a scholarship. *Financial Details: $2,000. *Number Awarded: 10. *Deadline: May 1.

P. Buckley Moss Society

20 Stoneridge Drive
Waynesboro, VA 22980
540-943-5678
society@mosssociety.org
http://www.mosssociety.org
Disability Served: learning disabled
The society offers the Anne and Matt Harbison Scholarship. *Eligibility: Graduating high school seniors with certified language-related learning disabilities who are pursuing postsecondary education may apply. *Financial Details: $1,000. *Number Awarded: One. *Deadline: March 31.

Pennsylvania, University of

Student Financial Services
3451 Walnut Street
Philadelphia, PA 19104-6270
215-898-1988
sfsmail@sfs.upenn.edu
http://www.sfs.upenn.edu
Disability Served: various
This private four-year university provides financial aid to help students (including those with disabilities) attend college. *Eligibility: Students who need financial assistance are eligible to apply. *Financial Details: Amounts vary according to need. *Number

Awarded: Varies. *Deadline: Contact the university for additional details.

Pennsylvania Department of Military and Veterans' Affairs

Fort Indiantown Gap, Building P-O-47
Annville, PA 17003-5002
717-861-8901
http://www.dmva.state.pa.us/dmvanew
Disability Served: various
The department offers tuition waivers to help finance college training. *Eligibility: Pennsylvania residents who are children of disabled veterans or those who died in combat or as a result of combat-related industries are eligible. *Financial Details: Tuition waivers are awarded. *Number Awarded: Varies. *Deadline: Contact the department for details.

Pennsylvania Higher Education Assistance Agency

1200 North 7th Street
Harrisburg, PA 17102-1444
800-692-7392
http://www.pheaa.org
Disability Served: various
The agency provides financial aid to help students (including those with disabilities) attend college. *Eligibility: Pennsylvania students who need financial assistance are eligible to apply. *Financial Details: Amounts vary according to need. *Number Awarded: Varies. *Deadline: Contact the agency for additional details.

Pennsylvania State University

Office of Student Aid
105 Booker Building
University Park, PA 16802
814-863-1807
http://www.psu.edu/dept/studentaid
Disability Served: cancer patients and survivors
This four-year university provides a variety of financial aid to students, including the American Cancer Society's Sy Barash Coaches vs. Cancer Scholarship. *Eligibility: Student whose studies have been interrupted by cancer, whether their own or that of an immediate family member, are eligible. Students must also demonstrate academic achievement, be a full-time undergraduate student, and be enrolled or plan to enroll at Penn State-University Park. Contact the Office of Student Aid for further info. *Financial Details: Amounts vary. *Number Awarded: One to

three annually. *Deadline: Submit an application by May 15.

Pennsylvania State University-Harrisburg
Office of Financial Aid
777 West Harrisburg Pike
Middletown, PA 17057
717-948-6307
hbgfinaid@psu.edu
http://www.hbg.psu.edu/hbg/hbgfinaid.html
Disability Served: various
This four-year university offers financial aid to help students (including those with disabilities) attend college. *Eligibility: Students who need financial assistance are eligible to apply. *Financial Details: Amounts vary according to need. *Number Awarded: Varies. *Deadline: Contact the university for additional details.

Pfizer Epilepsy Scholarship Award Center
c/o The Eden Communications Group
515 Valley Street, Suite 200
Maplewood, NJ 07040
800-292-7373
czoppi@edencomgroup.com
http://www.epilepsy-scholarship.com
Disability Served: epilepsy
This pharmaceutical company offers the Pfizer Epilepsy Scholarship Award. *Eligibility: High school seniors and college students who have overcome the challenges of epilepsy and who have been successful in school and in the community are eligible to apply. *Financial Details: $3,000. *Number Awarded: Sixteen. *Deadline: March 1.

Pilot International Foundation
PO Box 4844
Macon, GA 31208-4844
478-743-7403
pifinfo@pilothq.org
http://www.pilotinternational.org
Disability Served: various
The foundation sponsors three scholarship programs, The PIF/Lifeline Scholarship, The Marie Newton Sepia Memorial Scholarship, and The Pilot International Foundation Scholarship. *Eligibility: Students preparing to work with individuals with disabilities/brain related disorders are eligible to apply. Applicants must also have a GPA of 3.25 on a 4.0 scale and be sponsored by a local Pilot Club. *Financial

Details: Grants of up to $1,500 a year are available. Grants may be renewed. *Number Awarded: Varies each year. *Deadline: Applications are due in April.

Portland State University
Office of Graduate Studies
117 Cramer Hall
Portland, OR 97207-0751
503-725-8410
grad@pdx.edu
http://www.pdx.edu/finaid
Disability Served: physically disabled
The Robert and Rosemary Law Memorial Scholarship is reserved for full-time graduate students. *Eligibility: Full-time graduate students with physical disabilities and good academic records are eligible to apply. *Financial Details: Amounts vary. *Number Awarded: One per year. Scholarships may not be awarded every year. *Deadline: Applications are due by April 15.

Potomac State College of West Virginia University
Office of Enrollment Services
One Grand Central Business Center, Suite 2090
Keyser, WV 26726
800-262-7332
go2psc@mail.wvu.edu
http://www.potomacstatecollege.edu/admissions/financing.html
Disability Served: various
This two-year community college offers financial aid to help students (including those with disabilities) attend college. *Eligibility: Students who need financial assistance are eligible to apply. *Financial Details: Amounts vary according to need. *Number Awarded: Varies. *Deadline: Write or call for details.

Purdue University
Division of Financial Aid Services and Information
Schleman Hall of Student Services, 475 Stadium Mall Drive, Room 305
West Lafayette, IN 47907-2050
765-494-3886
facontact@purdue.edu
http://www.purdue.edu/DFA
Disability Served: various
The university provides financial aid to help students (including those with disabilities) attend college. *Eligibility: Students who need financial assistance are eligible to apply. *Financial Details: Amounts

vary according to need. *Number Awarded: Varies. *Deadline: Contact the university for additional details.

Quota Club of Candlewood Valley

PO Box 565
Danbury, CT 06813
quota@quotacv.org
http://www.quotacv.org/community.htm
Disability Served: hearing
This chapter of Quota offers a scholarship for college study. *Eligibility: Graduating high school seniors, college students, and graduate students who are either deaf or hard of hearing or who are hearing students preparing to work in the field of deafness are eligible to apply. Applicants must be residents of the Danbury, Connecticut-area. *Financial Details: $1,000 and $2,000. *Number Awarded: Two. *Deadline: Contact the club for details.

Quota Club of the Mississippi Gulf Coast

Scholarship Chairperson
PO Box 8001
Gulfport, MS 39501
228-594-3738
http://www.orgsites.com/ms/quotamsgc
Disability Served: hearing
This chapter of Quota offers a scholarship for college study. *Eligibility: Graduating high school seniors, college students, and graduate students who are either deaf or hard of hearing or who are hearing students preparing to work in the field of deafness are eligible to apply. Applicants must be residents of the Mississippi Gulf Coast. *Financial Details: $750. *Number Awarded: Two. *Deadline: April 1.

Quota International of Plantation, Florida

Scholarship Committee
1600 Northeast 49 Street
Oakland Park, FL 33334
QuotaPlantation@aol.com
http://members.aol.com/QuotaPlantation/Scholars.html
Disability Served: hearing
This chapter of Quota offers a scholarship for college study. *Eligibility: Deaf high school seniors or deaf graduates from South Florida high schools are eligible to apply. Applicants must have a GPA of at least 2.7 and plan to attend college full time. *Financial Details: Amount varies. *Number Awarded: Varies. *Deadline: April 17.

Randolph Community College

Office of Financial Aid
PO Box 1009
Asheboro, NC 27203
336-633-0205
jacruthis@randolph.edu
http://www.randolph.cc.nc.us/edprog/fin_aid.html
Disability Served: various
This two-year community college offers financial aid to help students (including those with disabilities) attend college. *Eligibility: Students who need financial assistance are eligible to apply. *Financial Details: Amounts vary according to need. *Number Awarded: Varies. *Deadline: Write or call for details.

Rhode Island, University of

Office of Financial Aid
Green Hall, 35 Campus Avenue
Kingston, RI 02881
401-874-9500
esmail@etal.uri.edu
http://www.uri.edu/es/students/finance/info.html
Disability Served: various
The university offers the Paul DePace Scholarship. *Eligibility: Students who have a permanent disability may apply. *Financial Details: Varies. *Number Awarded: Varies. *Deadline: Contact the Office of Financial Aid for details.

Rhode Island Higher Education Assistance Authority

560 Jefferson Boulevard
Warwick, RI 02886
800-922-9855, 401-734-9481 (TDD)
info@riheaa.org
http://www.riheaa.org
Disability Served: various
The authority provides financial aid to help students (including those with disabilities) attend college. *Eligibility: Rhode Island students who need financial assistance are eligible to apply. *Financial Details: Amounts vary according to need. *Number Awarded: Varies. *Deadline: Contact the authority for additional details.

Roane State Community College

Office of Financial Aid
276 Patton Lane
Harriman, TN 37748
866-GO2-RSCC, ext. 4545

FinancialAid_orbc@roanestate.edu

http://www.roanestate.edu/keyword.asp?keyword=financial%20Aid

Disability Served: various

This two-year college offers financial aid to help students (including those with disabilities) attend college. *Eligibility: Students who need financial assistance are eligible to apply. *Financial Details: Amounts vary according to need. *Number Awarded: Varies. *Deadline: Write or call for details.

Roosevelt University

430 South Michigan Avenue

Chicago, IL 60605

312-341-3566

http://www.roosevelt.edu/financialaid

Disability Served: various

This private four-year university provides financial aid to students (including those with disabilities). *Eligibility: Financially needy students are eligible to apply. *Financial Details: Amounts vary and depend on need. *Number Awarded: Varies. *Deadline: Contact the university for details.

Rutgers, The State University of New Jersey

Office of Financial Aid

620 George Street

New Brunswick, NJ 08901-1175

732-932-7057

http://studentaid.rutgers.edu

Disability Served: various

The university offers financial aid to help students (including those with disabilities) attend college.*Eligibility: Students who need financial assistance are eligible to apply.*Financial Details: Amounts vary according to need.*Number Awarded: Varies.*Deadline: Contact the university for additional details.

Saint Anselm College

Office of Financial Aid

100 Saint Anselm Drive

Manchester, NH 03102

603-641-7110

financial_aid@anselm.edu

http://www.anselm.edu/admission/Financial+Aid

Disability Served: various

This private four-year college offers financial aid to help students (including those with disabilities) attend college. *Eligibility: Students who need financial

assistance are eligible to apply.*Financial Details: Amounts vary according to need.*Number Awarded: Varies.*Deadline: Write or call for details.

Saint Cloud State University

106 Administrative Services, 720 Fourth Avenue South

St Cloud, MN 56301-4498

320-308-2047

financialaid@stcloudstate.edu

http://www.stcloudstate.edu/financialaid

Disability Served: various

This public four-year university provides financial aid to students (including those with disabilities). *Eligibility: Financially needy students are eligible to apply.*Financial Details: Amounts vary and depend on need.*Number Awarded: Varies.*Deadline: Contact the university for details.

Saint Elizabeth, College of

Office of Financial Aid

2 Convent Road

Convent Station, NJ 07960-6989

973-290-4445

http://www.cse.edu/financialaid.htm

Disability Served: various

This women's college provides financial aid to help students (including those with disabilities) attend college. *Eligibility: Students who need financial assistance are eligible to apply.*Financial Details: Amounts vary according to need.*Number Awarded: Varies.*Deadline: Write or call for details.

Salisbury State University

Financial Aid Office

1101 Camden Avenue

Salisbury, MD 21801

410-543-6165

finaid@salisbury.edu

http://www.salisbury.edu/admissions/finaid

Disability Served: various

The university offers the Rick Dudley Scholarship Fund for Graduate Students with Disabilities. *Eligibility: Applicants must be accepted into a graduate program at the university and must meet one or more of the following disability-required criteria: inability to ambulate without assistive devices, cerebral palsy, legally blind, profoundly deaf, inability of speech to be understood by the average person, or require personal assistance with the daily activities of living. *Financial Details: Scholarships of $1,500,

$3,000, and $5,000 are awarded.*Number Awarded: Varies.*Deadline: Contact the university for details.

San Diego Christian College
Financial Aid Office
2100 Greenfield Drive
El Cajon, CA 92019
619-590-1786
http://www.christianheritage.edu/fao
Disability Served: various
The college provides financial aid to help students (including those with disabilities) attend college. *Eligibility: Students who need financial assistance are eligible to apply.*Financial Details: Amounts vary according to need.*Number Awarded: Varies.*Deadline: Write or call for details.

San Diego City College
Financial Aid Office
1313 Park Boulevard, Room A-113
San Diego, CA 92101
619-388-3501
cityaid@sdccd.net
http://www.sdcity.edu/studentresources/financialaid
Disability Served: various
This public two-year college offers financial aid to help students (including those with disabilities) attend college. *Eligibility: Students who need financial assistance are eligible to apply.*Financial Details: Amounts vary according to need.*Number Awarded: Varies.*Deadline: Contact the college for additional details.

San Francisco, University of
Office of Financial Aid
2130 Fulton Street
San Francisco, CA 94117
415-422-6303
http://www.usfca.edu/acadserv/academic/finaid
Disability Served: various
The university provides financial aid to help students (including those with disabilities) attend college. *Eligibility: Students who need financial assistance are eligible to apply. *Financial Details: Amounts vary according to need. *Number Awarded: Varies. *Deadline: Write or call for details.

San Jose State University
Financial Aid and Scholarships Office, Student Services Center
One Washington Square

San Jose, CA 95192-0036
408-283-7500
scholarships@sjsu.edu
http://www2.sjsu.edu/depts/finaid
Disability Served: various
This four-year university offers the Donna Ellis Honorary Award to disabled students who are in their junior or senior years. *Eligibility: Financially needy students with disabilities who are attending the university and have at least one semester of education remaining are eligible to apply. Must have minimum GPA of 2.0. *Financial Details: Amounts vary and depend on need. *Number Awarded: Varies. *Deadline: Write or call for details.

Schenectady County Community College
Office of Financial Aid
78 Washington Avenue
Schenectady, NY 12305
518-381-1352
http://www.sunysccc.edu/adm-fin/financial.htm
Disability Served: various
This public two-year college has a financial aid program to help students (including those with disabilities) finance college training. *Eligibility: Students who need financial assistance are eligible. *Financial Details: Amounts vary and depend on need. *Number Awarded: Varies. *Deadline: Contact the college for details.

Scripps College
Office of Financial Aid
1030 Columbia Avenue
Claremont, CA 91711
909-621-8275
finaid@scrippscollege.edu
http://www.scrippscol.edu/dept/admission/financing.html
Disability Served: vision
This private liberal-arts women's college offers the Juliet King Esterly '34 Scholarship Fund. *Eligibility: The scholarship is awarded to students with financial need, with strong preference given to those who are visually impaired or blind. The recipient must demonstrate scholastic achievement and possess character and personal qualities that indicate future success in his/her chosen field. Applicants who are not blind or visually handicapped may be considered if they have chosen a field of interest related to the service of those with physical challenges. *Financial Details: Amount varies. *Number Awarded: Varies. *Deadline: Contact the college for details.

Sertoma International
1912 East Meyer Boulevard
Kansas City, MO 64132
816-333-8300
infosertoma@sertoma.org
http://www.sertoma.org/%5EScholarships/Scholarships.htm
Disability Served: hearing
Sertoma offers the Hearing Impaired Scholarship. *Eligibility: Applicants must have documented hearing loss, be U.S. residents, have a GPA of at least 3.2, and plan to or be currently pursuing a bachelor's degree. *Financial Details: $1,000. *Number Awarded: Varies. *Deadline: May 1.

Shawnee State University
940 Second Street
Portsmouth, OH 45662
740-354-3205
http://www.shawnee.edu
Disability Served: various
This public university has a financial aid program to help students (including those with disabilities) pay for their college education. *Eligibility: Students who need financial assistance are eligible. *Financial Details: Amounts vary and depend on need. *Number Awarded: Varies. *Deadline: Contact the university for details.

Shenandoah University
Office of Financial Aid
1460 University Drive
Winchester, VA 22601
540-665-4538, 800-432-2266
finaid@su.edu
http://www.su.edu/financialaid
Disability Served: various
The university offers financial aid to help students (including those with disabilities) attend college. *Eligibility: Students who need financial assistance are eligible to apply. *Financial Details: Amounts vary according to need. *Number Awarded: Varies. *Deadline: Write or call for details.

Sickle Cell Disease Association of America
Kermit B. Nash Academic Scholarship Selection Committee
16 South Calvert Street, Suite 600
Baltimore, MD 21202
410-528-1555
scdaa@sicklecelldisease.org
http://www.sicklecelldisease.org/programs/nash_scholarship.phtml
Disability Served: sickle cell anemia
The organization offers the Kermit B. Nash, Jr. Academic Scholarship. *Eligibility: Graduating high school seniors who have sickle cell disease and plan to attend a four-year accredited college may apply. *Financial Details: $5,000 a year for up to four years. *Number Awarded: Varies. *Deadline: Contact the Selection Committee for details.

Sickle Cell Disease Foundation of California
Attn: Program Administrator
6133 Bristol Parkway, Suite 240
Culver City, CA 90230
310-693-0247
deborahg@scdfc.org
http://www.scdfc.org/program_services/LifeSteps/Scott_Zuniga_Scholarship.htm
Disability Served: sickle cell anemia
The foundation offers the Scott Zuniga Memorial Scholarship to help finance college training. *Eligibility: Applicants must be residents of Los Angeles, Orange, Riverside, San Bernardino or Ventura counties in California and have sickle cell disease. Awardees must maintain a GPA of at least 2.0 and complete at least 2.5 to 15 hours of community service at the foundation. *Financial Details: Ranges from $250 to $1,500. *Number Awarded: Varies. *Deadline: Contact the foundation for details.

Sierra College
Financial Services Office
5000 Rocklin Road
Rocklin, CA 95677
916-781-0568, 800-242-4004
http://www.sierra.cc.ca.us/ed_programs/student_support_services/financial_services/financial_aid
Disability Served: various
This public two-year college offers a variety of financial aid to students, including the Ken Holt Memorial Scholarship, the Billy Hanley Memorial Scholarship, and the Success For The Physically Challenged Scholarship. *Eligibility: Students with disabilities who are involved in athletics may apply for the Ken Holt Memorial Scholarship. Applicants must have a minimum GPA of 2.0, meet enrollment requirements, and be a member of Students Overcoming Challenges. Incoming freshmen with disabilities who have a minimum GPA of 2.0 and meet enrollment requirements may apply for the Billy Hanley

Memorial Scholarship. Incoming freshmen with learning or physical disabilities who have a minimum GPA of 2.75 and meet enrollment requirements may apply for the Success For The Physically Challenged Scholarship. *Financial Details: Ken Holt Memorial Scholarship: $200. Billy Hanley Memorial Scholarship: $1,000. Success For The Physically Challenged Scholarship: $200. *Number Awarded: Varies. *Deadline: February 7.

Sigma Alpha Iota Philanthropies Inc.

Attn: Director, Visually Impaired Scholarship
One Tunnel Road
Asheville, NC 28805
hadley@exis.net
http://www.sai-national.org/phil/philschs.html
Disability Served: vision
This music fraternity offers the Visually Impaired Scholarship. *Eligibility: Legally blind members of Sigma Alpha Iota enrolled in an undergraduate or graduate degree program in music are eligible to apply. A non-refundable application fee of $25 is required. *Financial Details: $1,000. *Number Awarded: Varies. *Deadline: March 15.

Solvay Pharmaceuticals Inc.

CREON Family Scholarship Program Coordinator
901 Sawyer Road
Marietta, GA 30062
http://www.solvaypharmaceuticals-us.com/products/
    cfscholarships/0,,14635-2-0,00.htm
Disability Served: cystic fibrosis
This pharmaceutical company offers the CREON Family Scholarship. *Eligibility: Students with cystic fibrosis may apply. Scholarships are awarded based on academic achievement, financial need, and students' ability to serve as a role model for others with cystic fibrosis. *Financial Details: $2,000 for two years. *Number Awarded: Thirty. *Deadline: June 24.

Soroptomist International of the Americas

1709 Spruce Street
Philadelphia, PA 19103-6103
215-893-9000
http://www.soroptimist.org
Disability Served: physically disabled
The Venture Clubs Scholarships help finance college study. *Eligibility: Physically disabled students between 15 and 40 years old are eligible to apply. Applicants must demonstrate financial need and the capacity to profit from further education. *Financial Details: The award is given at the local-level where award amounts vary. *Number Awarded: Varies. *Deadline: Write or call for information. This award is administered by local, participating Venture clubs and is not available in all communities. Soroptimist national headquarters does not distribute or accept applications. Look for the Venture Student Aid Award advertised in your area.

South Carolina, University of

Office of Student Aid and Scholarships
1714 College Street
Columbia, SC 29208
803-777-8134
USCFAID@sc.edu
http://www.sc.edu/financialaid
Disability Served: various
The university offers financial aid to help students (including those with disabilities) attend college. *Eligibility: Students who need financial assistance are eligible to apply. *Financial Details: Amounts vary according to need. *Number Awarded: Varies. *Deadline: Write or call for details.

South Carolina Commission on Higher Education

1133 Main Street, Suite 200
Columbia, SC 29201
803-737-2260
http://www.che.sc.gov/StudentServices/FinAHome.htm
Disability Served: various
The commission provides financial aid to help students (including those with disabilities) attend college. *Eligibility: South Carolina students who need financial assistance are eligible to apply. *Financial Details: Amounts vary according to need. *Number Awarded: Varies. *Deadline: Contact the commission for additional details.

South Carolina Department of Veterans Affairs

1205 Pendleton Street, Suite 477
Columbia, SC 29201
803-255-4255
va@oepp.sc.gov
http://www.govoepp.state.sc.us/vetaff.htm
Disability Served: various
The department offers scholarships to help finance college. *Eligibility: Children of South Carolina veterans who died in combat, those who died as a result of combat-related injuries, those who are

disabled as a result of service, or those who are have been declared missing in action are eligible to apply. Applicants must be residents of South Carolina and attend a public college or university in the state. *Financial Details: Free tuition. *Number Awarded: Varies. *Deadline: Contact the department for details.

South Dakota, University of

Financial Aid Office
414 East Clark Street
Vermillion, SD 57069
877-269-6837
http://www.usd.edu/finaid
Disability Served: various
The university offers financial aid to help students (including those with disabilities) attend college. *Eligibility: Students who need financial assistance are eligible to apply. *Financial Details: Amounts vary according to need. *Number Awarded: Varies. *Deadline: Write or call for details.

South Dakota Board of Regents

306 East Capitol Avenue, Suite 200
Pierre, SD 57501-2545
605-773-3455
info@ris.sdbor.edu
http://www.ris.sdbor.edu
Disability Served: various
The board offers the South Dakota Opportunity Scholarships for students (including those with disabilities) who plan to pursue postsecondary education. *Eligibility: Residents of South Dakota attending any public college or university in the state may apply. Applicants must have an ACT score of 24 or higher or an SAT score of 1110 or higher. *Financial Details: $5,000 over four years. *Number Awarded: Varies. *Deadline: Varies. Contact the board for more information.

South Dakota Division of Veterans Affairs

425 East Capitol Avenue
Pierre, SD 57501
605-773-4981
http://www.state.sd.us/military/VetAFfairs/sdmva.htm
Disability Served: various
The division offers tuition waivers to help finance college training. *Eligibility: South Dakota residents who are children of disabled veterans, those who died in combat, those who died as a result of combat-related injuries, or those who are have been declared missing

in action are eligible. *Financial Details: Full tuition. *Number Awarded: Varies. *Deadline: Contact the division for details.

South Dakota School of Mines and Technology

Financial Aid Office
501 East Saint Joseph Street
Rapid City, SD 57701-3995
605-394-2274, 800-544-8162, ext. 224
financialaid@sdsmt.edu
http://www.hpcnet.org/sdsmt/ProspectiveStudents
Disability Served: various
This technical school provides financial aid to students (including those with disabilities). *Eligibility: Financially needy students are eligible to apply. *Financial Details: Amounts vary and depend on need. *Number Awarded: Varies. *Deadline: Contact the school for additional details.

South Dakota State University

Office of Financial Aid
PO Box 2201
Brookings, SD 57000-0001
605-688-4496
sdsu_financialaid@sdstate.edu
http://www.sdstate.edu
Disability Served: various
This four-year university provides financial aid to students (including those with disabilities). *Eligibility: Financially needy students are eligible to apply. *Financial Details: Amounts vary and depend on need. *Number Awarded: Varies. *Deadline: Write or call for details.

Southern Idaho, College of

Student Financial Aid Office
PO Box 1238
Twin Falls, ID 83303-1238
208-732-6273
mdoolittle@csi.edu
http://www.csi.edu/prospectiveStudents_/moneyMatters/financialAid
Disability Served: various
This two-year college provides financial aid to help students (including those with disabilities) attend college. *Eligibility: Students who need financial assistance are eligible to apply. *Financial Details: Amounts vary according to need. *Number Awarded: Varies. *Deadline: Contact the college for additional details.

Southern Illinois University-Carbondale

Financial Aid Office
Woody Hall, 900 South Normal Avenue, B Wing,
    Third Floor
Carbondale, IL 62901-4702
618-453-8738
fao@siu.edu
http://www.siu.edu/~fao
Disability Served: vision
This four-year university provides financial aid to
    students, including a scholarship in cooperation
    with The Chicago Lighthouse For People Who Are
    Blind Or Visually Impaired. *Eligibility: Financially
    needy students who are blind or visually impaired
    are eligible to apply. *Financial Details: Amounts vary
    and depend on need. *Number Awarded: Varies.
    *Deadline: Write or call for details.

Southern Indiana, University of

Office of Admission
8600 University Boulevard
Evansville, IN 47712
812-464-8600
http://www.usi.edu/admissn
Disability Served: various
The university provides the Roy W. & Adelaide D.
    Daudistal Sanders Scholarship to help students
    with disabilities finance college study. *Eligibility:
    Applicants must have a minimum high school GPA
    of 3.5, minimum test scores of 1800 on the SAT and
    28 on the ACT, and enroll for at least three-quarter
    time (nine semester hours). *Financial Details: $2,000.
    Since it is renewable, the scholarship is awarded only
    once every four years. *Number Awarded: One every
    four years. *Deadline: Write or call for details.

Southern Vermont College

Financial Aid Office
982 Mansion Drive
Bennington, VT 05201-6002
877-563-6076
svc@vsac.org
http://www.svc.edu/financialaid
Disability Served: various
This private four-year college provides financial aid
    to students (including those with disabilities).
    *Eligibility: Financially needy students are eligible to
    apply. *Financial Details: Amounts vary and depend
    on need. *Number Awarded: Varies. *Deadline: Write
    or call for details.

South Mountain Community College

7050 South 24th Street
Phoenix, AZ 85042
602-243-8000, 602-245-5727 (TDD)
http://www.southmountaincc.edu/Registration/
    FinancialAid
Disability Served: various
This two-year community college provides financial
    aid to students (including those with disabilities).
    *Eligibility: Financially needy students are eligible to
    apply. *Financial Details: Amounts vary and depend
    on need. *Number Awarded: Varies. *Deadline: Write
    or call for details.

Southwest Missouri State University

Office of Financial Aid
901 South National
Springfield, MO 65804
417-836-5262, 800-283-4243
financialaid@smsu.edu
http://www.smsu.edu/financialaid
Disability Served: various
This university provides financial aid to students
    (including those with disabilities). *Eligibility:
    Financially needy students are eligible to apply.
    *Financial Details: Amounts vary and depend on
    need. *Number Awarded: Varies. *Deadline: Contact
    the university for details.

Spina Bifida Association of America (SBAA)

4590 MacArthur Boulevard, NW, Suite 250
Washington, DC 20007
202-944-3285, 800-621-3141
http://www.sbaa.org
Disability Served: spina bifida
The association provides the following educational
    scholarships: the Lazof Family Foundation
    Scholarship, the SBAA Four-Year Scholarship, and the
    SBAA One-Year Scholarship. *Eligibility: High school
    juniors and seniors with spina bifida are eligible to
    apply for the Lazof Family Foundation Scholarship
    and the SBAA Four-Year Scholarship. High school
    graduates or those who possess a GED and who have
    been diagnosed with spina bifida may apply for the
    SBAA One-Year Scholarship. *Financial Details: Lazof
    Family Foundation Scholarship: $2,500 every year for
    four years. SBAA Four-Year Scholarship: up to $5,000
    every year for four years. SBAA One-Year Scholarship:
    $2,000 for one year. *Number Awarded: Varies each
    year. *Deadline: March 1.

Spina Bifida Association of Connecticut

Attn: Allocations Committee
PO Box 2545
Hartford, CT 06146-2545
800-574-6274
sbac@sbac.org
http://www.sbac.org
Disability Served: spina bifida
The association offers an educational scholarship.
  *Eligibility: Applicants who have spina bifida and
  plan to or are currently enrolled in a postsecondary
  institution may apply. Scholarships are awarded
  based on academic achievement, community
  service, and financial need. *Financial Details: $1,000.
  *Number Awarded: Varies. *Deadline: April 15.

Spoon River College

23235 North County Road 22
Canton, OH 61520
800-334-7337
info@spoonrivercollege.edu
http://www.spoonrivercollege.net/admis/assistance.
  html
Disability Served: various
This two-year institution provides financial aid to
  students (including those with disabilities).
  *Eligibility: Financially needy students are eligible to
  apply. *Financial Details: Amounts vary and depend
  on need. *Number Awarded: Varies. *Deadline: Write
  or call for details.

State Council Higher Education for Virginia

101 North 14th Street
Richmond, VA 23219
804-225-2600
http://www.schev.edu
Disability Served: various
The council provides financial aid to help students
  (including those with disabilities) attend college.
  *Eligibility: Virginia students who need financial
  assistance are eligible to apply. *Financial Details:
  Amounts vary according to need. *Number Awarded:
  Varies. *Deadline: Contact the council for additional
  details.

Staten Island, College of

Student Financial Aid Office
2800 Victory Boulevard, 2A-401
Staten Island, NY 10314
718-982-2030
finaid@postbox.csi.cuny.edu
http://www.csi.cuny.edu/finaid
Disability Served: various
The college provides financial aid to help students
  (including those with disabilities) attend college.
  *Eligibility: Students who need financial assistance
  are eligible to apply. *Financial Details: Amounts
  vary according to need. *Number Awarded: Varies.
  *Deadline: Write or call for details.

State Student Assistance Commission of Indiana

150 West Market Street, Suite 500
Indianapolis, IN 46204
317-232-2350
grants@ssaci.in.gov
http://www.in.gov/ssaci
Disability Served: various
The commission provides financial aid to help students
  (including those with disabilities) attend college.
  *Eligibility: Indiana students who need financial
  assistance are eligible to apply. *Financial Details:
  Amounts vary according to need. *Number Awarded:
  Varies. *Deadline: Contact the Commission for
  additional details.

State University of New York-Binghamton

Office of Student Financial Aid and Employment
PO Box 6000
Binghamton, NY 13902-6000
607-777-2428
finaid@binghamton.edu
http://bingfa.binghamton.edu
Disability Served: various
The university provides financial aid to help students
  (including those with disabilities) attend college.
  *Eligibility: Students who need financial assistance
  are eligible to apply. *Financial Details: Amounts
  vary according to need. *Number Awarded: Varies.
  *Deadline: Write or call for details.

State University of New York-Fredonia

Financial Aid Office
215 Maytum Hall
Fredonia, NY 14063
716-673-3253
Financial.Aid@fredonia.edu
http://www.fredonia.edu/finaid
Disability Served: various
The university provides financial aid to help students
  (including those with disabilities) attend college.

*Eligibility: Students who need financial assistance are eligible to apply. *Financial Details: Amounts vary according to need. *Number Awarded: Varies. *Deadline: Write or call for details.

Sterling College

Office of Financial Aid
PO Box 98
Sterling, KS 67579
800-346-1017
http://sterling.edu
Disability Served: various
This private four-year college provides scholarships to students. *Eligibility: Students with disabilities who are attending the college are eligible to apply. *Financial Details: Amounts vary. *Number Awarded: Varies. *Deadline: Contact the college for details.

Stony Wold-Herbert Fund

136 East 57th Street, Room 1705
New York, NY 10022
212-753-6565
http://www.stonywoldherbertfund.com
Disability Served: physically disabled
This organization offers financial aid to help students pay for college costs. *Eligibility: Students with respiratory diseases from the Greater New York area are eligible to apply. *Financial Details: Awards are approximately $10,000 over four years. *Number Awarded: Varies. *Deadline: Call or write for information.

Sussex County Community College

Office of Admissions
One College Hill Road
Newton, NJ 07860
973-300-2225
http://sussex.edu/studentlife/financialaid
Disability Served: various
This public two-year community college provides financial aid to students (including those with disabilities). *Eligibility: Financially needy students are eligible to apply. *Financial Details: Amounts vary and depend on need. *Number Awarded: Varies. *Deadline: Contact the college for details.

Syracuse University

Office of Disability Services
804 University Avenue, Suite 309
Syracuse, NY 13244-1120

315-443-4498, 315-443-1372 (TDD/TTY)
odssched@syr.edu
http://www.syr.edu
Disability Served: various
This four-year university has a scholarship program for students with disabilities. *Eligibility: Students with disabilities who are attending the university are eligible to apply. *Financial Details: Amounts vary. *Number Awarded: Varies. *Deadline: Write or call for details.

Tarrant County College

Office of Financial Aid
828 Harwood Road
Hurst, TX 76054
817-788-6333
fahelp@tccd.edu
http://www.tccd.edu
Disability Served: various
This two-year institution provides financial aid to students (including those with disabilities). *Eligibility: Financially needy students are eligible to apply. *Financial Details: Amounts vary and depend on need. *Number Awarded: Varies. *Deadline: Write or call for details.

Temple University

Disability Resources and Services
1300 Cecile Moore Avenue, 100 Ritter Annex (003-00)
Philadelphia, PA 19122
215-204-1280
drs@temple.edu
http://www.temple.edu/disability
Disability Served: various
This four-year university provides scholarships to students with disabilities, including the Charlotte W. Newcombe Scholarship. *Eligibility: Enrolled students with a permanent disability are eligible to apply. Applicants must have a minimum GPA of 2.0 and demonstrate financial need. *Financial Details: Amounts vary. *Number Awarded: Varies. *Deadline: Applications are due the first Friday of each semester.

Tennessee Department of Veterans Affairs

215 Eighth Avenue North
Nashville, TN 37243
615-741-6663
Donald.Samuels@state.tn.us
http://www.state.tn.us/veteran

Disability Served: various

The department offers scholarships to help finance college. *Eligibility: Children of disabled military service veterans whose disability occurred as the result of active service are eligible. Applicants must reside in Tennessee. *Financial Details: Varies. *Number Awarded: Varies. *Deadline: Contact the department for details.

Tennessee Hemophilia and Bleeding Disorders Foundation

203 Jefferson Street
Smyrna, TN 37167
615-220-4868
mail@tennesseehemophilia.org
http://www.thbdf.org
Disability Served: inherited bleeding disorders

The foundation offers the Dudgale/Van Eys Scholarship. *Eligibility: Students with hemophilia who reside in Tennessee are eligible to apply. *Financial Details: Approximately $2,000. *Number Awarded: Varies. *Deadline: Typically in May.

Tennessee-Knoxville, University of

Office of Disability Services
191 Hoskins Library
Knoxville, TN 37996-4007
865-974-6087 (Voice/TTY)
ods@tennessee.edu
http://ods.utk.edu
Disability Served: various

The university's Office of Disability Services offers the following scholarships for disabled students: the Scholarship for Students With Visual Impairments, the Charles Jackson Scholarship, and the Robert L. and Helen Johnson Scholarship. *Eligibility: Students with documented visual impairments who maintain a minimum GPA of 2.0 and are enrolled as full-time undergraduate students are eligible to apply for the Scholarship for Students With Visual Impairments. Students with documented disabilities who maintain a minimum GPA of 2.5 and are classified as juniors or seniors are eligible to apply for the Charles Jackson Scholarship. Students with documented disabilities who maintain a minimum GPA of 2.0 and are Knox County residents are eligible to apply for the Robert L. and Helen Johnson Scholarship. *Financial Details: Varies. *Number Awarded: Varies. *Deadline: May 1.

Tennessee Student Assistance Corporation

Parkway Towers, 404 James Robertson Parkway, Suite 1950
Nashville, TN 37243-0820
615-741-1346
Disability Served: various

The nonprofit organization offers financial aid to help Tennessee students (including those with disabilities) attend college. *Eligibility: Students who need financial assistance are eligible to apply. *Financial Details: Amounts vary. *Number Awarded: Varies. *Deadline: Contact the corporation for additional details.

Texas A&M University

Department of Student Financial Aid
PO Box 30016
College Station, TX 77842-3016
979-845-3982
http://financialaid.tamu.edu
Disability Served: various

This four-year university offers financial aid to help disabled students through its Opportunity Award program. *Eligibility: Students who have overcome significant traumatic life experiences, including, but not limited to, cancer, traumatic brain injury, leukemia, learning disabilities, orthopedic disabilities, and HIV/AIDS are eligible to apply. *Financial Details: Amounts vary according to need. *Number Awarded: Varies. *Deadline: Write or call for details.

Texas-Austin, University of

Office of Student Financial Services
PO Box 7758, UT Station
Austin, TX 78713-7758
512-475-6282
http://bealonghorn.utexas.edu/bal/financial_aid. WBX
Disability Served: various

This four-year university provides a variety of financial aid to students, including the Will Rogers Scholarship and the Carole Patterson Endowed Scholarship. *Eligibility: Disabled students and those preparing to work with handicapped children are eligible to apply for the Will Rogers Scholarship. Scholarships are awarded based on financial need. Physically disabled students taking at least six hours of credit at the University are eligible to apply for the Carole Patterson Endowed Scholarship. Preference will be given to mobility-impaired students. *Financial

Details: Will Rogers Scholarship: $400 to $1,000. Carole Patterson Endowed Scholarship: $500 to $2,000. *Number Awarded: Varies. *Deadline: Contact the university for details.

Texas Higher Education Coordinating Board
PO Box 12788
Austin, TX 78711
512-427-6101
http://www.collegefortexans.com
Disability Served: hearing, vision
The board offers the Blind/Deaf Student Exemption Program. *Eligibility: Blind or deaf students attending public colleges and universities in Texas are eligible. Applicants must otherwise qualify for admission. *Financial Details: Tuition and fees are waived. *Number Awarded: 2,929 awards were made in 2002-2003. *Deadline: Write or call for details.

Texas Veterans Commission
PO Box 12277
Austin, TX 78711-2277
800-252-8387
info@tvc.state.tx.us
http://www.tvc.state.tx.us
Disability Served: various
The commission provides tuition wavers for the purpose of college study. *Eligibility: Veterans (including those who are disabled) of the Spanish-American War through the Persian Gulf War who were legal residents of Texas at the time they entered military service are eligible to apply. Applicants must have exhausted all federal educational benefits, be current residents of Texas, and plan to attend a public college or university in the state. *Financial Details: Amounts vary. *Number Awarded: Varies each year. *Deadline: Contact the commission for details.

Texas Woman's University
Financial Aid Office
PO Box 425408
Denton, TX 76204-5408
940-898-3064
FINAID@twu.edu
http://www.twu.edu/finaid
Disability Served: various
This four-year university provides financial aid to students (including those with disabilities). *Eligibility: Financially needy students who are attending the university are eligible to apply.

*Financial Details: Amounts vary and depend on need. *Number Awarded: Varies. *Deadline: Write or call for details.

Toledo, University of
Office of Student Financial Aid
2801 West Bancroft Street, Mail Stop 314
Toledo, OH 43606-3390
419-530-8700
utfinaid@utnet.utoledo.edu
http://www.financialaid.utoledo.edu
Disability Served: hearing, physically disabled, vision
This public four-year university offers a variety of financial aid to students, including the following scholarships for students with disabilities: Paula Marie Kuehn Endowed Scholarship for blind, hearing impaired, or wheelchair-bound students and the Toledo Host Lions Club Welfare Inc. Endowed Scholarship for students who are legally disabled due to sight impairment or blindness. *Eligibility: Kuehn Scholarship: Applicants must have a GPA of 2.5 or higher and must demonstrate financial need. Toledo Host Scholarship: applicants must be full-time students and U.S citizens who reside in Northwest Ohio or Southeast Michigan. Entering freshmen must have a high school GPA of 3.0 or higher. *Financial Details: Amounts vary and depend on need. *Number Awarded: Varies. *Deadline: April 1.

Travelers Protective Association (TPA) of America
c/o Scholarship Trust for the Deaf and Near Deaf
3755 Lindell Boulevard
St. Louis, MO 63108-3476
314-371-0533
support@tpahq.org
http://www.tpahq.org
Disability Served: hearing
The organization offers the Scholarship Trust for the Deaf and Near Deaf. *Eligibility: Deaf or hearing-impaired children and adults who need assistance in obtaining mechanical devices, medical or specialized treatment, or specialized education are eligible to apply. *Financial Details: Varies. *Number Awarded: Varies. *Deadline: March 1.

Twitty, Milsap, Sterban Foundation
600 Renaissance Center, Suite 1300, PO Box 43517
Detroit, MI 48243
Disability Served: vision
The foundation offers scholarships to help finance

undergraduate or graduate training. *Eligibility: Blind or visually impaired students with strong academic records and achievements are eligible. *Financial Details: $500 or more is awarded. *Number Awarded: Varies. *Deadline: Applications are due September 1.

Ulman Cancer Fund for Young Adults
PMB #505, 4725 Dorsey Hall Drive, Suite A
Ellicott City, MD 21042
410-964-0202
scholarship@ulmanfund.org
http://www.ulmanfund.org/Services/Scholarship/
    scholarship_main.htm
Disability Served: cancer patients and survivors
This organization offers the Matt Stauffer Memorial Scholarship. *Eligibility: College students who are currently battling or who have overcome cancer and who demonstrate financial need are eligible to apply. *Financial Details: $1,000. *Number Awarded: Varies. *Deadline: April 1. The fund also offers the Marilyn Yetso Memorial Scholarship for college students who have a parent who has cancer or is a survivor of cancer, or who have lost a parent to cancer and the Cancer Teach Us Scholarship for Chicago, Illinois-residents who are currently battling or who have overcome cancer.

United Cerebral Palsy Research and Educational Foundation
1660 L Street, NW, Suite 700
Washington, DC 20036
800-872-5827, 202-973-7197 (TTY)
http://www.ucp.org
Disability Served: cerebral palsy
This organization provides grants for the research of cerebral palsy, its treatment, diagnosis, and prevention. *Eligibility: Eligibility requirements vary. Contact the foundation for application materials. *Financial Details: Awards vary. *Number Awarded: Varies. *Deadline: Contact the foundation for additional details.

Utah, University of
Center for Disability Services
162 Union Building, 200 South Central Campus Drive, Room #162
Salt Lake City, UT 84112-9107
801-581-5020 (Voice/TDD)
onadeau@sa.utah.edu
http://disability.utah.edu/scholarship.htm

Disability Served: various
The University of Utah offers several scholarships for students with disabilities through its Center for Disability Services. These include the Louise J. Snow Scholarship, the Keaton Walker Scholarship, and the Drake Briggs Scholarship. *Eligibility: Louise J. Snow Scholarship: any disabled student with a GPA of at least 2.5. Keaton Walker Scholarship: students with visual (preference) and physical disabilities who have a GPA of at least 2.5. Drake Briggs Scholarship: legally deaf high school seniors and college students, must be a resident of Utah, and have a GPA of at least 2.5. *Financial Details: Amounts vary. *Number Awarded: Varies each year. *Deadline: February 1.

Utah Higher Education Assistance Authority
60 South 400 West
Salt Lake City, UT 84101-1284
877-336-7378
uheaa@utahsbr.edu
http://www.uheaa.org
Disability Served: various
The authority provides financial aid to help students (including those with disabilities) attend college. *Eligibility: Utah students who need financial assistance are eligible to apply. *Financial Details: Amounts vary according to need. *Number Awarded: Varies. *Deadline: Contact the authority for additional details.

Utah Valley State College
Office of Financial Aid
800 West University Parkway
Orem, UT 84058
801-863-8442
http://www.uvsc.edu/finaid
Disability Served: various
This public four-year college provides financial aid to help students (including those with disabilities) attend college. *Eligibility: Students who need financial assistance are eligible to apply. *Financial Details: Amounts vary according to need. *Number Awarded: Varies. *Deadline: Write or call for details.

Vermont, University of
Financial Aid Office
330 Waterman Building, 85 South Prospect Street
Burlington, VT 05405
802-656-5700
FinancialAid@uvm.edu

http://www.uvm.edu/financialaid
Disability Served: various
The university provides financial aid to help students (including those with disabilities) attend college. *Eligibility: Students who need financial assistance are eligible to apply. *Financial Details: Amounts vary according to need. *Number Awarded: Varies. *Deadline: Write or call for details.

Vermont Association for the Blind and Visually Impaired (VABVI)

VABVI Scholarship
PO Box 2000, Champlain Mill
Winooski, VT 05404
http://www.vabvi.org/scholar.htm
Disability Served: vision
The federation offers the Charles E. Leonard Memorial Scholarship to blind students. *Eligibility: Blind students who are Vermont residents are eligible to apply. Scholarships are awarded based on academic achievement and financial need. *Financial Details: Approximately $2,000. *Number Awarded: Varies. *Deadline: May 1.

Vermont Student Assistance Corporation

PO Box 999
Winooski, VT 05404
800-798-8722
info@vsac.org
http://services.vsac.org/ilwwcm/connect/VSAC
Disability Served: various
The nonprofit organization offers financial aid to help students (including those with disabilities) attend college. *Eligibility: Students who need financial assistance are eligible to apply. *Financial Details: Amounts vary. *Number Awarded: Varies. *Deadline: Contact the corporation for additional details.

Very Special Arts

818 Connecticut Avenue, NW
Washington, DC 20006
202-628-2800, 800-933-8721, 202-737-0645 (TDD)
info@vsarts.org
http://www.vsarts.org
Disability Served: various
The arts-focused organization for people with disabilities provides scholarships to finance the study of music and playwriting. *Eligibility: Students of music and playwriting who are disabled are eligible to apply.

*Financial Details: Award amounts vary. *Number Awarded: Four scholarships are given in music (two in the United States and two internationally), and two scholarships are given in playwriting. *Deadline: Contact Very Special Arts for details.

Virginia, University of

Office of Student Financial Services
PO Box 400204
Charlottesville, VA 22904-4204
434-982-6000
faid@virginia.edu
http://www.virginia.edu/financialaid
Disability Served: various
The university offers financial aid to help students (including those with disabilities) attend college. *Eligibility: Students who need financial assistance are eligible to apply. *Financial Details: Amounts vary according to need. *Number Awarded: Varies. *Deadline: Write or call for details.

Virginia Department of Veterans Affairs

270 Franklin Road, SW, Room 503
Roanoke, VA 24011
540-857-7104
pmignard131@worldnet.att.net
http://www.vdva.vipnet.org/education_benefits.htm
Disability Served: various
The department provides tuition wavers for the purpose of college study. *Eligibility: Children of Virginia veterans who are deceased, disabled, or declared missing in action as a result of military service are eligible to apply. Applicants must be residents of Virginia and attend a public college or university in the state. *Financial Details: Full tuition. *Number Awarded: Varies each year. *Deadline: Contact the department for details. Additional educational financial aid programs are available to veterans.

Virginia State University

Office of Student Financial Aid
102 Gandy Hall
Blacksburg, VA 23806
800-823-7214
http://www.vsu.edu/pages/203.asp
Disability Served: various
The university provides financial aid to help students (including those with disabilities) attend college. *Eligibility: Students who need financial assistance

are eligible to apply. *Financial Details: Amounts vary according to need. *Number Awarded: Varies. *Deadline: Write or call for details.

Virgin Islands Board of Education
No. 44-46 Kongens Gade
Charlotte Amalie, VI 00802
340-774-0100
http://www.usvi.org/education
Disability Served: various
The board offers financial aid to help students (including those with disabilities) attend college. *Eligibility: Students who need financial assistance are eligible to apply. *Financial Details: Amounts vary according to need. *Number Awarded: Varies. *Deadline: Contact the board for additional details.

Wal-Mart Foundation
702 Southwest 8th Street
Bentonville, AR 72716-0150
http://www.walmartfoundation.org
Disability Served: various
The foundation provides scholarships to help high school seniors and college students (including those who are disabled) fund college education. *Eligibility: Applicants must have a GPA of at least 2.5 and demonstrate financial need. *Financial Details: Scholarships range from $1,000 to $10,000. *Number Awarded: Varies each year. *Deadline: February 1.

Washington, University of
Office of Student Financial Aid
Box 355880
Seattle, WA 98195-5880
206-543-6101
osfa@u.washington.edu
http://www.washington.edu/students/osfa
Disability Served: various
The university provides financial aid to help students (including those with disabilities) attend college. *Eligibility: Students who need financial assistance are eligible to apply. *Financial Details: Amounts vary according to need. *Number Awarded: Varies. *Deadline: Contact the university for additional details. Additionally, the university offers a very small number of disability-specific scholarships based on funding availability. Contact the Office of Student Financial Aid for details.

Washington Council of the Blind
Attn: Scholarship Committee Chair
7356 34th Avenue, NE
Seattle, WA 98115
206-527-4527
http://www.wcbinfo.org
Disability Served: vision
The council offers educational scholarships to blind students. *Eligibility: Blind students who reside and pursue an education in Washington are eligible to apply. *Financial Details: Awards of at least $2,000 are available. *Number Awarded: Varies. *Deadline: June 1.

Washington Department of Veterans Affairs
Republic Building, 505 East Union, 1st Floor,
     PO Box 41155
Olympia, WA 98504-1155
360-586-1070, 800-562-2308
http://www.dva.wa.gov
Disability Served: various
The department provides tuition wavers for the purpose of college study. *Eligibility: Children of Washington veterans who are disabled as a result of military service are eligible to apply. Applicants must be residents of Washington and attend public colleges or universities in the state. *Financial Details: Varies based on degree of disability and length of service. *Number Awarded: Varies each year. *Deadline: Contact the department for details.

Washington Higher Education Coordinating Board
917 Lakeridge Way, PO Box 43430
Olympia, WA 98504-3430
360-753-7800
info@hecb.wa.gov
http://www.hecb.wa.gov/paying
Disability Served: various
The board provides financial aid to help students (including those with disabilities) attend college. *Eligibility: Washington students who need financial assistance are eligible to apply. *Financial Details: Amounts vary according to need. *Number Awarded: Varies. *Deadline: Contact the board for additional details.

Waubonsee Community College
Route 47 at Waubonsee Drive
Sugar Grove, IL 60554-9799

630-466-7900
financialaid@waubonsee.edu
http://www.waubonsee.edu/prostudents/financial_aid
Disability Served: various
This large public community college offers a financial
    aid program to help students (including those with
    disabilities) finance college. *Eligibility: Students
    who need financial assistance are eligible to apply.
    *Financial Details: Awards vary according to need.
    *Number Awarded: Varies. *Deadline: Write or call for
    details.

Wayne State University
Office of Student Financial Aid
42 West Warren Avenue, PO Box 2340
Detroit, MI 48202-0340
313-577-3378
financialaid@wayne.edu
http://www.financialaid.wayne.edu
Disability Served: various
The university provides financial aid to help students
    (including those with disabilities) attend college.
    *Eligibility: Students who need financial assistance
    are eligible to apply. *Financial Details: Amounts
    vary according to need. *Number Awarded: Varies.
    *Deadline: Contact the university for additional
    details.

Western Connecticut State University
Office of Financial Aid
181 White Street
Danbury, CT 06810
203-837-8580
wcsufinancialaid@wcsu.edu
http://www.wcsu.ctstateu.edu/finaid
Disability Served: various
The university provides financial aid to help students
    (including those with disabilities) attend college.
    *Eligibility: Students who need financial assistance
    are eligible to apply. *Financial Details: Amounts
    vary according to need. *Number Awarded: Varies.
    *Deadline: Write or call for details.

Western Michigan University
Student Financial Aid Office
1903 West Michigan Avenue
Kalamazoo, MI 49008-5337
269-387-6000
finaid-info@wmich.edu
http://www.wmich.edu/finaid

Disability Served: various
This public four-year university provides financial aid
    to help students (including those with disabilities)
    attend college. *Eligibility: Students who need
    financial assistance are eligible to apply. *Financial
    Details: Amounts vary according to need. *Number
    Awarded: Varies. *Deadline: Write or call for details.

Western New Mexico University
Office of Financial Aid
PO Box 680
Silver City, NM 88062
505-538-6173
finaid@wnmu.edu
http://www.wnmu.edu/financialAid
Disability Served: various
This four-year university provides financial aid to
    students (including those with disabilities).
    *Eligibility: Financially needy students are eligible to
    apply. *Financial Details: Amounts vary and depend
    on need. *Number Awarded: Varies. *Deadline:
    Contact the university for additional details.

West Kentucky Community and Technical College
4810 Alben Barkley Drive
Paducah, KY 42002-7380
270-534-3248
WKAdmissions@westkentucky.kctcs.edu
http://www.westkentucky.kctcs.edu/financial/finaid.
    shtml
Disability Served: various
This two-year college provides financial aid to help
    students (including those with disabilities) attend
    college. *Eligibility: Students who need financial
    assistance are eligible to apply. *Financial Details:
    Amounts vary according to need. *Number Awarded:
    Varies. *Deadline: Write or call for details.

West Texas A&M University
Office of Financial Aid
WTAMU Box 60939
Canyon, TX 79016-0001
806-651-2055
financial@mail.wtamu.edu
http://www.wtamu.edu/administrative/vpa/sfs
Disability Served: various
This public university provides financial aid to help
    students (including those with disabilities) attend
    college. *Eligibility: Students who need financial
    assistance are eligible to apply. *Financial Details:

Amounts vary according to need. *Number Awarded: Varies. *Deadline: Write or call for details.

West Virginia State College
Financial Aid Office
PO Box 6004
Morgantown, WV 26506-6004
304-293-5242
finaid@mail.wvu.edu
http://www.finaid.wvu.edu
Disability Served: various
This four-year college provides financial aid to help students (including those with disabilities) attend college. *Eligibility: Students who need financial assistance are eligible to apply. *Financial Details: Amounts vary according to need. *Number Awarded: Varies. *Deadline: Write or call for details.

West Virginia University
PO Box 6004
Morgantown, WV 26506-6004
304-293-5242
finaid@mail.wvu.edu
http://www.finaid.wvu.edu
Disability Served: various
The university offers financial aid to help students (including those with disabilities) attend college. *Eligibility: Students who need financial assistance are eligible to apply. *Financial Details: Amounts vary according to need. *Number Awarded: Varies. *Deadline: Contact the university for additional details.

Winston-Salem Foundation
Student Aid Committee
860 West Fifth Street
Winston-Salem, NC 27101-2506
336-725-2382
info@wsfoundation.org
http://www.wsfoundation.org
Disability Served: various
The Foundation offers the Marcus Raper Zimmerman Scholarship. *Eligibility: Students with disabilities from select counties in North Carolina are eligible. Applicants must have a minimum GPA of 2.5. Nondisabled persons who wish to prepare for careers serving persons with disabilities are also eligible. *Financial Details: Awards of up to $1,000 are available. *Number Awarded: Varies. *Deadline: August 31.

Wisconsin Council of the Blind
754 Williamson Street
Madison, WI 53703
800-783-5213
sue@wcblind.org
http://www.wcblind.org/Scholarships.htm
Disability Served: vision
The council offers the Lloyd P. Foote Scholarship to blind students. *Eligibility: Applicants who are blind, reside in Wisconsin, have completed at least one year carrying a full academic load, and maintain a GPA of at least 2.5 may apply. *Financial Details: $1,000. *Number Awarded: Seven. *Deadline: Contact the council for details.

Wisconsin Department of Veterans Affairs
30 West Mifflin Street, PO Box 7843
Madison, WI 53707-7843
608-266-1311, 800-947-8387
wdvaweb@dva.state.wi.us
http://dva.state.wi.us
Disability Served: various
The department provides a wide variety of grants, loans, scholarships, and other financial aid to veterans and children of veterans (including those with disabilities). *Eligibility: Requirements vary by type of financial aid. Applicants must plan to attend a public institution in the state of Wisconsin. *Financial Details: Varies depending on type of aid. *Number Awarded: Varies each year. *Deadline: Contact the department for details.

Wisconsin Higher Educational Aids Board
PO Box 7885
Madison, WI 53707-7885
608-267-2206
HEABmail@heab.state.wi.us
http://www.heab.state.wi.us
Disability Served: hearing, vision
The Hearing & Visually Handicapped Student Grant Program awards grants to help defer college expenses. *Eligibility: Wisconsin residents with hearing- and/or vision-related disabilities may apply. *Financial Details: Awards range from $250 to $1,800. *Number Awarded: Varies. *Deadline: Write or call for details. A loan program is also available for students who plan to teach the visually or hearing impaired.

Wisconsin-Madison, University of
McBurney Disability Resource Center
1305 Linden Drive

Madison, WI 53706
608-263-2741, 608-263-6393 (TTY)
mcburney@uwmadmail.services.wisc.edu
http://www.mcburney.wisc.edu
Disability Served: various
This state university offers the McBurney Disability
Scholarship for students with disabilities. *Eligibility:
Students with a documented disability (physical,
psychological, sensory, or learning, as verified by the
McBurney Disability Resource Center) are eligible to
apply. *Financial Details: $500 to $2,500. *Number
Awarded: Up to 20 annually. *Deadline: April 15.

Wisconsin-Madison, University of
Office of Student Financial Services
432 North Murray Street
Madison, WI 53706-1496
608-262-3060
finaid@finaid.wisc.edu
http://www.finaid.wisc.edu
Disability Served: various
The university offers a variety of financial aid for students
(including those with disabilities). *Eligibility:
Students who need financial assistance are eligible
to apply. *Financial Details: Awards vary according to
need. *Number Awarded: Varies. *Deadline: Write or
call for details.

Woodrow Wilson National Fellowship Foundation
5 Vaughn Drive, Suite 300, CN5281
Princeton, NJ 08543-5281
609-452-7007
http://www.woodrow.org
Disability Served: various
The Charlotte Newcome Doctoral Dissertation
Fellowships help finance doctoral studies. *Eligibility:
Disabled students pursuing doctoral degrees in the
humanities and social sciences may apply. *Financial
Details: The fellowship is worth approximately
$18,500. *Number Awarded: Varies. *Deadline:
Request an application by December 6.

World TeamTennis
1776 Broadway, Suite 600
New York, NY 10019
212-586-3444
http://www.wtt.com/charities/donnelly.asp
Disability Served: diabetes
Novo Nordisk, a pharmaceutical company, offers the
Novo Nordisk Donnelly Awards in cooperation with

World TeamTennis. The scholarship was established
by tennis great Billie Jean King to encourage
diabetic children to lead an active life and compete
in tennis. *Eligibility: Students ages 14-21 who
have diabetes and play tennis competitively
in tournaments or on their school team may
apply. Applicants must show strong personal
character, values, sportsmanship, and community
involvement, as well as demonstrate financial need.
*Financial Details: $5,000. *Number Awarded: Two.
*Deadline: June 1.

Wright State University
Office of Financial Aid
3640 Colonel Gleen Highway, E136 Student Union
Dayton, OH 45435-0001
877-978-3243
financialaid@wright.edu
http://www.wright.edu/admissions/finaid
Disability Served: various
The university offers financial aid to help students
(including those with disabilities) attend college.
*Eligibility: Students who need financial assistance
are eligible to apply. *Financial Details: Amounts
vary according to need. *Number Awarded: Varies.
*Deadline: Write or call for details.

Wyoming, University of
Office of Student Financial Aid
Department 3335, 1000 East University Avenue
Laramie, WY 82071
307-766-2118
http://uwadmnweb.uwyo.edu/SFA
Disability Served: various
Among the other financial aid programs administered
by the University is the Wyoming War Orphans
Scholarship. *Eligibility: Children of disabled veterans
are eligible to apply. *Financial Details: Amounts
vary. *Number Awarded: One scholarship is awarded
each year. *Deadline: Contact the Office of Student
Financial Aid for details.

Wyoming, University of
University Disability Support Services
Department 3808, 1000 East University Avenue
Laramie, WY 82071
307-766-6189, 307-766-3073 (TTY)
udssc@uwyo.edu
http://www.uwyo.edu/udss
Disability Served: various

The institution's University Disability Support Services offers scholarships, such as the Bernadette Smith Memorial Scholarship, to assist students with disabilities. *Eligibility: Students with disabilities attending the university may apply. *Financial Details: Amounts vary. *Number Awarded: Varies. *Deadline: Contact University Disability Support Services for more information.

Wyoming Commission of Veterans Affairs

5905 Cy Avenue, Room 101
Casper, WY 82604
307-265-7372
wvac@bresnan.net
http://www.nasdva.com/wyoming.html
Disability Served: various

The commission provides tuition wavers for the purpose of college study. *Eligibility: Residents of Wyoming who served in the U.S. military during the Vietnam War are eligible to apply. Applicants must be residents of Wyoming and attend a public college or university in the state either full or part time. *Financial Details: Full tuition for not more than 10 semesters of credit classes. *Number Awarded: Varies each year. *Deadline: Contact the commission for details.

Wyoming Department of Education

Hathaway Building, 2300 Capitol Avenue, 2nd Floor
Cheyenne, WY 82002-0050
307-777-6265
lpicke@educ.state.wy.us
http://www.k12.wy.us
Disability Served: various

The department provides financial aid to help students (including those with disabilities) attend college. *Eligibility: Wyoming students who need financial assistance are eligible to apply. *Financial Details: Amounts vary according to need. *Number Awarded: Varies. *Deadline: Contact the department for additional details.

Yes I Can! Foundation for Exceptional Children

1110 North Glebe Road, Suite 300
Arlington, VA 22201-5704
800-224-6830, ext. 450
http://yesican.cec.sped.org
Disability Served: various

The foundation offers the Stanley E. Jackson Scholarship Awards and the Sara Conlon Memorial Scholarship Award to students with disabilities. *Eligibility: The applicant must be disabled, enrolling in full-time, postsecondary education or training for the first time, and provide evidence of financial need. There are five categories for these awards: scholarship for students with disabilities, scholarship for ethnic minority students with disabilities, scholarship for talented and gifted students with disabilities, scholarship for ethnic minority talented and gifted students with disabilities, and scholarship for disabled students who are committed to pursuing a major in Education. *Financial Details: $500. *Number Awarded: Varies each year. *Deadline: February 1.

York Technical College

Financial Aid Office
452 South Anderson Road
Rock Hill, SC 29730
803-327-8005
http://www.yorktech.com/financial.asp
Disability Served: various

This two-year institution provides financial aid to help students (including those with disabilities) attend college. *Eligibility: Students who need financial assistance are eligible to apply. *Financial Details: Amounts vary according to need. *Number Awarded: Varies. *Deadline: Write or call for details.

EDUCATION ORGANIZATIONS

The following organizations provide educational assistance, information, programs, and materials for persons with disabilities.

ACT Inc.
500 ACT Drive, PO Box 168
Iowa City, IA 52243-0168
319-337-1332
http://www.act.org
Disability Served: *various*
This organization develops educational programs, exams, and services for students and educational institutions. The most frequently used program is the ACT Assessment. Students with documented disabilities may be eligible for testing accommodations.

American School Health Association
PO Box 708
Kent, OH 44240-0708
330-678-1601
asha@ashaweb.org
http://www.ashaweb.org
Disability Served: *various*
This organization disseminates information on school health to parents and professionals.

Association on Higher Education and Disability
PO Box 540666
Waltham, MA 02454
781-788-0003 (Voice/TTY)
ahead@ahead.org
http://www.ahead.org
Disability Served: *various*
This organization works toward the full participation of the disabled in postsecondary education.

Banyan Tree Learning Center
9636 Tierra Grande, Suite 200-201
San Diego, CA 92126
858-578-6616
http://www.banyantlc.com
Disability Served: *learning disabled*
This school offers instruction in the basics of reading, written language, mathematics, and study/organizational skills to students with learning disabilities.

Canadian Association of Disability Service Providers in Post-Secondary Education
4 Cataraqui Street, Suite 310
Kingston, ON K7K 1Z7

Canada
613-531-9210
http://www.cacuss.ca/en/cadsppe.html
Disability Served: *various*
This association seeks to improve accessibility and enhance the postsecondary education of students with disabilities in Canada.

Child Development Institute
3528 East Ridgeway Road
Orange, CA 92867
714-998-8617
sales@childdevelopmentinfo.com
http://www.cdipage.com
Disability Served: *learning disabled*
The Institute offers free resources at its Web site, as well as books, tapes, games, and computer software for children with learning and other related disabilities.

College Board
45 Columbus Avenue
New York, NY 10023
212-713-8000
sat@info.collegeboard.org
http://www.collegeboard.com
Disability Served: *various*
The College Board offers test-taking accommodations for persons with disabilities.

Distance Education and Training Council
1601 18th Street, NW
Washington, DC 20009-2529
202-234-5100
http://www.detc.org
Disability Served: *various*
The council provides information on correspondence and distance education.

Educational Resources Information Center (ERIC)
c/o Computer Sciences Corporation
4483-A Forbes Boulevard
Lanham, MD 20706
800-538-3742
http://www.eric.ed.gov
Disability Served: *various*

The ERIC database contains more than 1.1 million education-related documents, including those that cover disability issues.

Equal Access to Software and Information
PO Box 818
Lake Forest, CA 92609
949-916-2837
info@easi.cc
http://www.rit.edu/~easi
Disability Served: various
This organization offers online courses for people with disabilities who are interested in learning about information technology.

Federal Resource Center for Special Education
Academy for Educational Development
1825 Connecticut Avenue, NW
Washington, DC 20009
202-884-8215, 202-884-8200 (TTY)
thampton@aed.org
http://www.dssc.org/frc
Disability Served: various
The center provides information and technical assistance to students with disabilities.

FREE Application for Federal Student Aid Web Site
U.S. Department of Education
400 Maryland Avenue, SW
Washington, DC 20202
800-433-3243, 800-730-8913 (TTY)
http://www.fafsa.ed.gov
Disability Served: various
The center provides information on financial aid to fund a college education.

Gallaudet University
800 Florida Avenue, NE
Washington, DC 20002
202-651-5000 (Voice/TTY)
admissions.office@gallaudet.edu
http://www.gallaudet.edu
Disability Served: hearing
This is the only general college established exclusively to serve the deaf. It offers a full liberal arts program and financial aid to students.

Gifted Child Society
190 Rock Road
Glen Rock, NJ 07452-1736

201-444-6530
admin@gifted.org
http://www.gifted.org
Disability Served: various
The society offers training programs for gifted children, as well as educators of special needs children.

HEATH Resource Center
2121 K Street, NW, Suite 220
Washington, DC 20037
202-973-0904 (Voice/TTY)
askheath@gwu.edu
http://www.heath.gwu.edu
Disability Served: various
The center serves as a national clearinghouse on post-secondary education for individuals with disabilities.

Institute on Disability
University of New Hampshire
10 West Edge Drive
Durham, NH 03824
603-862-4320
http://iod.unh.edu
Disability Served: various
The Institute advocates for improved services and programs for the disabled.

Learning Disabilities Association
4156 Library Road
Pittsburgh, PA 15234-1349
412-341-1515
http://www.ldanatl.org
Disability Served: attention deficit disorder, dyslexia, learning disabled
This nonprofit organization assists individuals with learning disabilities. It has more than 200 state and local affiliates in 42 states and Puerto Rico.

Multisensory Learning Associates
One Katherine Road
Rehoboth, MA 02769
508-252-6482
multilearn@hotmail.com
http://mlaog.homestead.com
Disability Served: developmentally disabled, physically disabled
This organization provides services and training programs to parents and teachers in reading, writing, spelling, and phonological awareness. It also gives consultations, presentations, and workshops

anywhere in the world. An extensive catalog of teaching materials is available.

National Association of Private Special Education Centers

1522 K Street, NW, Suite 1032
Washington, DC 20005
202-408-3338
napsec@aol.com
http://www.napsec.org
Disability Served: various
This organization represents private providers of special education services for preschool, elementary, and secondary aged children and adult learners.

National Center for Learning Disabilities

381 Park Avenue South, Suite 1401
New York, NY 10016
212-545-7510, 888-575-7373
http://www.ld.org
Disability Served: learning disabled
This organization provides a wealth of information to people with learning disabilities.

National Center on Secondary Education and Transition

Institute on Community Integration
University of Minnesota
150 Pillsbury Drive, SE, 6 Pattee Hall
Minneapolis, MN 55455
612-624-2097
ncset@umn.edu
http://www.ncset.org
Disability Served: various
The center helps disabled students achieve academic success at the secondary level. It also helps students to transition to postsecondary education, employment, or other settings.

National Council on Rehabilitation Education

5005 North Maple Avenue, ED 3
Fresno, CA 93740-8026
http://www.rehabeducators.org
Disability Served: various
The council represents educators, researchers, and others, and promotes the education of persons with disabilities. The council also provides vocational rehabilitation services and develops standards for rehabilitation personnel.

National Disabled Student Union

430 North East 16th Avenue
Portland, OR 97343
803-524-6029
http://www.disabledstudents.org
Disability Served: various
This organization for students who are disabled works toward achieving social justice for all.

National Dissemination Center for Children with Disabilities

PO Box 1492
Washington, DC 20013
800-695-0285 (Voice/TTY)
nichcy@aed.org
http://nichcy.org
Disability Served: various
The center provides a variety of information on special education, The No Child Left Behind Act (as it relates to children with disabilities), and research on effective educational practices.

National Educational Association of Disabled Students

Carleton University
1125 Colonel By Drive, Unicentre, Room 426
Ottawa, ON K1S 5B6
Canada
613-526-8008 (Voice/TTY)
info@neads.ca
http://www.neads.ca
Disability Served: various
This organization advocates for the rights of postsecondary students with disabilities in Canada.

National Rehabilitation Information Center

4200 Forbes Boulevard, Suite 202
Lanham, MD 20706
800-346-2742, 301-459-5984 (TTY)
naricinfo@heitechservices.com
http://www.naric.com
Disability Served: various
This organization provides a variety of resources for the disabled, including information on education.

National Technical Institute for the Deaf (NTID)

52 Lomb Memorial Drive
Rochester, NY 14623-5604
585-475-6400

http://www.rit.edu/ntid
Disability Served: hearing
The NTID provides postsecondary education to students who are deaf or hard of hearing.

Parent Advocacy Coalition for Educational Rights Center

8161 Normandale Boulevard
Minneapolis, MN 55437
952-838-9000, 952-838-0190 (TTY)
pacer@pacer.org
http://www.pacer.org
Disability Served: various
This nonprofit advocacy organization of parents of children with disabilities seeks to improve educational opportunities for the disabled.

Special Education Technology-British Columbia

105-1750 West 75th Avenue
Vancouver, BC V6P 6G2
Canada
604-261-9450
http://www.setbc.org
Disability Served: various
This program provides assistive technology services to school districts, including consultation, evaluation of student needs, and program planning.

TASH: The Association for Persons with Severe Handicaps

29 West Susquehanna Avenue, Suite 210
Baltimore, MD 21204
410-828-8274
http://www.tash.org
Disability Served: various
TASH is a membership organization of educators, parents, administrators, and other educational professionals. TASH provides numerous publications, materials, and resources.

United States Department of Education

Office of Special Education Programs
400 Maryland Avenue, SW
Washington, DC 20202-7100
202-245-7459
http://www.ed.gov/about/offices/list/osers/osep/index.
html?src=mr
Disability Served: various
This government organization works to improve the educational success of disabled children and youth from birth through age 21.

United States Department of Education

TRIO Programs
400 Maryland Avenue, SW
Washington, DC 20202
800-872-5327, 800-437-0833 (TTY)
http://www.ed.gov/about/offices/list/ope/trio/index.
html
Disability Served: various
TRIO Programs (Upward Bound, Talent Search, Educational Opportunity Centers, and Student Support Services) operate to aid students with disabilities. Contact local schools for details on programs in your area.

TEACHING RESOURCES

This section lists publications of interest to teachers of students wth disabilities.

Accommodating Students with Dyslexia in All Classroom Settings
International Dyslexia Association
Chester Building, 8600 LaSalle Road, Suite 382
Baltimore, MD 21286-2044
410-296-0232
http://www.interdys.org
Disability Served: *dyslexic*
This online brochure features advice for teachers about working with students with dyslexia in the classroom.

ADD/ADHD Behavior-Change Resource Kit: Ready-to-Use Strategies & Activities for Helping Children with Attention Deficit Disorder
Jossey-Bass
Customer Care Center-Consumer Accounts
10475 Crosspoint Boulevard
Indianapolis, IN 46256
877-762-2974
http://www.josseybass.com
Disability Served: *attention deficit disorder*
This kit offers strategies to help students with attention deficit disorder learn academic, social, and personal skills.

The ADD/ADHD Checklist
Jossey-Bass
Customer Care Center-Consumer Accounts
10475 Crosspoint Boulevard
Indianapolis, IN 46256
877-762-2974
http://www.josseybass.com
Disability Served: *attention deficit disorder*
This is a useful statistical-based reference for parents and educators.

Addressing the Challenging Behavior of Children with High-Functioning Autism/Asperger Syndrome in The Classroom: A Guide for Teachers and Parents
Taylor & Francis Group
270 Madison Avenue
New York, NY 10016
212-216-7800
http://www.taylorandfrancisgroup.com
Disability Served: *Asperger Syndrome, autism*

This guide offers suggestions on how to create optimal learning environments for students with autism or Asperger Syndrome.

Advanced Language Tool Kit
Educators Publishing Service
PO Box 9031
Cambridge, MA 02139-9031
800-225-5750
http://www.epsbooks.com
Disability Served: *communication*
This set of cards and teacher's manual is designed to teach reading and spelling to students with language disabilities and with skills that are beyond the elementary level.

Answers to Questions Teachers Ask about Sensory Integration
Future Horizons Inc.
721 West Abram Street
Arlington, TX 76013
800-489-0727
info@futurehorizons-autism.com
http://www.futurehorizons-autism.com
Disability Served: *autism*
This publication provides answers to frequently asked questions about working with children who have sensory integration challenges.

Asperger Syndrome: A Practical Guide for Teachers
Future Horizons,Inc.
721 West Abram Street
Arlington, TX 76013
800-489-0727
info@futurehorizons-autism.com
http://www.futurehorizons-autism.com
Disability Served: *Asperger Syndrome, autism*
This is a useful text for teachers working with students with Asperger Syndrome in the classroom.

Basic Course in American Sign Language
TJ Publishers Inc.
817 Silver Spring Avenue, Suite 206
Silver Spring, MD 20910
301-585-4440, 800-999-1168
tjpubinc@aol.com
Disability Served: *hearing*

This book and videotape package provides teaching tools for American Sign Language.

Breakthroughs: How to Reach Students with Autism
Research Press
Department 25W, PO Box 9177
Champaign, IL 61826
217-352-3273, 800-519-2707
rp@researchpress.com
http://www.researchpress.com
Disability Served: autism
This how-to guide covers math, reading, fine motor, self-help, vocational, and social skills.

Children and Youth Assisted by Medical Technology in Educational Settings
Paul H. Brookes Publishing Company
PO Box 10624
Baltimore, MD 21285-0624
410-337-9580, 800-638-3775
custserv@brookespublishing.com
http://www.pbrookes.com
Disability Served: various
This book is designed to inform school nurses, educators, parents, health aides, and others who work with disabled students about medical procedures that may need to be performed in educational settings.

Choice Magazine Listening
85 Channel Drive, Department 16
Port Washington, NY 11050
516-883-8280, 888-724-6423
choicemag@aol.com
http://www.choicemagazinelistening.org
Disability Served: dyslexic, physically disabled, vision
This free, bimonthly audio magazine provides articles, short stories, and nationwide news from a variety of sources for the blind, physically disabled, and dyslexic. Available on special-speed cassette tape.

Choosing Options and Accommodations for Children: A Guide to Educational Planning for Students with Disabilities
Paul H. Brookes Publishing Company
PO Box 10624
Baltimore, MD 21285-0624
410-337-9580, 800-638-3775
custserv@brookespublishing.com
http://www.pbrookes.com
Disability Served: various

This reference manual assists the teacher in implementing inclusive education.

Classroom Listening and Speaking: Preschool
Pro-Ed Inc.
8700 Shoal Creek Boulevard
Austin, TX 78757-6897
800-897-3202
http://www.proedinc.com
Disability Served: communication, learning disabled
This book helps teachers target reinforced learning for preschool students via 11 themes, including Self and Senses; Family, Home, and Friend; School and Community; Colors and Other Concepts; and Animals; Clothes; and Holidays.

Classroom Success for the LD and ADHD Child
John F. Blair, Publisher
1406 Plaza Drive
Winston-Salem, NC 27103
800-222-9796
http://www.blairpub.com
Disability Served: attention deficit disorder, learning disabled
Provides information to teachers who work with LD/ADHD children. Includes diagnostic tools, suggestions on adjusting teaching techniques, and advice on testing and grading.

Classroom Success or the Learning Disabled
John F. Blair, Publisher
1406 Plaza Drive
Winston-Salem, NC 27103-1470
336-768-1374
http://www.blairpub.com
Disability Served: learning disabled
This book provides teaching methods, strategies, and other helpful information for teachers of learning disabled students.

Cognitive Strategy Instruction for Middle and High Schools
Brookline Books
34 University Road
Brookline, MA 02445
617-734-6772
http://www.brooklinebooks.com
Disability Served: learning disabled
This text provides teaching strategies and procedures.

Come Sign with Us: Sign Language Activities for Children
Gallaudet University Press
800 Florida Avenue, NE
Washington, DC 20002
202-651-5488 (Voice/TTY)
valencia.simmons@gallaudet.edu
http://gupress.gallaudet.edu
Disability Served: hearing
This publication provides a variety of activities that
educators can use to teach children sign language.

**Commonsense Methods for Children with Special
Needs: Strategies for the Regular Classroom**
Falmer Press
270 Madison Avenue
New York, NY 10016
http://www.routledgefalmer.com
Disability Served: various
This text offers ideas for teachers of special needs
children in regular classrooms.

Communication Intervention: Birth to Three
Alexander Graham Bell Association of the Deaf
3417 Volta Place, NW
Washington, DC 20007
202-337-5220, 202-337-5221 (TTY)
publications@agbell.org
http://www.agbell.org
Disability Served: hearing
This publication addresses communication-based
intervention for children under the age of three.

**Communication Skills for Visually Impaired Learners:
Braille, Print, and Listening Skills for Students Who
Are Visually Impaired**
Charles C. Thomas, Publisher
2600 South First Street
Springfield, IL 62704
800-258-8980
books@ccthomas.com
http://www.ccthomas.com
Disability Served: vision
This text seeks to provide a strong foundation for
educators teaching reading, writing, and listening
skills to students with visual impairments.

**Complete Learning Disabilities Handbook: Ready-to-
Use Strategies & Activities for Teaching Students
with Learning Disabilities**
Jossey-Bass
Customer Care Center-Consumer Accounts

10475 Crosspoint Boulevard
Indianapolis, IN 46256
877-762-2974
http://www.josseybass.com
Disability Served: learning disabled
This resource for educators provides diagnostic tools,
remedial techniques, sample lessons, and worksheets
to help identify and work with students who have
learning deficits.

Comprehensive Test of Nonverbal Intelligence
Pro-Ed Inc.
8700 Shoal Creek Boulevard
Austin, TX 78757-6897
800-897-3202
http://www.proedinc.com
Disability Served: learning disabled
This test is designed to assess intelligence, aptitude, and
reasoning skills through problem-solving tasks. It
contains the following subtests: Pictorial Analogies,
Geometric Analogies, Pictorial Categories, Geometric
Categories, Pictorial Sequences, and Geometric
Sequences.

**Cooperative Learning and Strategies for Inclusion:
Celebrating Diversity in the Classroom**
Paul H. Brookes Publishing Company
PO Box 10624
Baltimore, MD 21285-0624
410-337-9580, 800-638-3775
custserv@brookespublishing.com
http://www.pbrookes.com
Disability Served: various
This book offers strategies for teaching and tailoring
curricula to accommodate students from various
backgrounds.

**Curricular and Instructional Approaches for Persons
with Severe Disabilities**
Allyn & Bacon
75 Arlington Street, Suite 300
Boston, MA 02116
800-852-8024
http://www.ablongman.com
Disability Served: various
This text offers information for teachers working with
students who have severe disabilities.

Curriculum Based Assessment: A Primer
Charles C. Thomas, Publisher
2600 South First Street

Springfield, IL 62704
800-258-8980
books@ccthomas.com
http://www.ccthomas.com
Disability Served: *learning disabled*
This is an overview of curriculum-based assessment for educators.

A Curriculum for Profoundly Handicapped Students
Pro-Ed Inc.
8700 Shoal Creek Boulevard
Austin, TX 78757-6897
800-897-3202
http://www.proedinc.com
Disability Served: *various*
This curriculum provides advice to teachers on how to successfully work with students with profound disabilities.

Decreasing Behaviors of Persons with Severe Retardation and Autism
Research Press
Department 25W, PO Box 9177
Champaign, IL 61826
217-352-3273, 800-519-2707
rp@researchpress.com
http://www.researchpress.com
Disability Served: *autism, developmentally disabled*
This book, geared toward educators of students with mental disabilities, provides strategies and guidelines for decreasing undesirable behaviors. Techniques include satiation, extinction, physical restraint, punishment, time-out, and overcorrection.

Developmental Variation and Learning Disorders
Educators Publishing Service Inc.
PO Box 9031
Cambridge, MA 02139-9031
800-225-5750
customer_service@epsbooks.com
http://www.epsbooks.com
Disability Served: *developmentally disabled, learning disabled*
This book provides information on the stages of development and academic proficiency and how this relates to the development of disabilities in children.

Dyslexia over the Lifespan
Educators Publishing Service Inc.
PO Box 9031
Cambridge, MA 02139-9031

800-225-5750
customer_service@epsbooks.com
http://www.epsbooks.com
Disability Served: *dyslexic*
This book provides profiles of more than 50 male students with dyslexia who attended a school that had one of the pioneering programs for treating dyslexia.

Educating Children with Autism
National Academies Press
500 Fifth Street, NW, Lockbox 285
Washington, DC 20055
888-624-8373
zjones@nas.edu
http://books.nap.edu
Disability Served: *autism*
This publication offers advice and information for educators who teach children with autism.

Educating Deaf Students: From Research to Practice
Oxford University Press
198 Madison Avenue
New York, NY 10016
212-726-6000
http://www.oup.com/us/?view=usa
Disability Served: *hearing*
This accessible text provides advice to educators about working with deaf students.

Educational Care: A System for Understanding and Helping Children with Learning Differences at Home and in School
Educators Publishing Service Inc.
PO Box 9031
Cambridge, MA 02139-9031
800-225-5750
customer_service@epsbooks.com
http://www.epsbooks.com
Disability Served: *learning disabled*
This book is designed to provide educators and parents with information regarding learning disabilities and how the educational system can work for students with these disorders.

Educational Games for Visually Impaired and Sighted Children
Love Publishing Company
9101 East Kenyon Avenue, Suite 2200
Denver, CO 80237
303-221-7333

lpc@lovepublishing.com
http://www.lovepublishing.com
Disability Served: vision
This publication details more than 100 games and
  activities for sighted and visually impaired children in
  grades one through eight.

Effective Curriculum for Students with Emotional and Behavioral Disorders
Love Publishing Company
9101 East Kenyon Avenue, Suite 2200
Denver, CO 80237
303-221-7333
lpc@lovepublishing.com
http://www.lovepublishing.com
Disability Served: behavioral disorders, developmentally
  disabled, emotionally disabled adolescents
This curriculum provides advice for educators on how
  to create specialized instruction based on the
  individualized needs of students with emotional and
  behavioral disorders.

Explode the Code Books: A Supplementary Program for Beginning Readers
Educators Publishing Service Inc.
PO Box 9031
Cambridge, MA 02139-9031
800-225-5750
customer_service@epsbooks.com
http://www.epsbooks.com
Disability Served: communication
This series of workbooks is designed to help educators
  teach reading to students in grades K through four.
  The books help children learn the sounds of letters
  and how to recognize and distinguish them.

Fun to Grow On: Engaging Play Activities for Kids with Teachers, Parents and Grandparents
Alexander Graham Bell Association of the Deaf
3417 Volta Place, NW
Washington, DC 20007
202-337-5220, 202-337-5221 (TTY)
publications@agbell.org
http://www.agbell.org
Disability Served: various
This set features 167 classroom and at-home interactive
  activities that will stimulate sensory and body
  awareness, enhance spatial/perceptual skills, and
  build large and small motor skills.

Helping Adolescents with ADHD & Learning Disabilities: Ready-to-Use Tips, Techniques, and Checklists for School Success
Jossey-Bass
Customer Care Center-Consumer Accounts
10475 Crosspoint Boulevard
Indianapolis, IN 46256
877-762-2974
http://www.josseybass.com
Disability Served: attention deficit disorder, learning
  disabled
This is a useful guide for teachers who are looking for
  ways to improve ADD/LD teens' academic and social
  skills.

How to Find and Select an Academic Therapist
International Dyslexia Association
Chester Building, 8600 LaSalle Road, Suite 382
Baltimore, MD 21286-2044
410-296-0232
http://www.interdys.org
Disability Served: dyslexic
This online brochure provides advice to parents on
  finding an academic therapist. A Spanish-language
  version is also available.

How to Reach and Teach ADD/ADHD Children: Practical Techniques, Strategies and Interventions for Helping Children with Attention Problems and Hyperactivity
Council for Exceptional Children
1110 North Glebe Road, Suite 300
Arlington, VA 22201-5704
service@cec.sped.org
http://www.cec.sped.org
Disability Served: attention deficit disorder, behavioral
  disorders
This text offers tips on educating ADD/ADHD children,
  including teaching reading, writing, and math.

How to Reach and Teach All Students in the Inclusive Classroom: Ready-to-Use Strategies Lessons and Activities Teaching Students with Diverse Learning Needs
Jossey-Bass
Customer Care Center-Consumer Accounts
10475 Crosspoint Boulevard
Indianapolis, IN 46256
877-762-2974
http://www.josseybass.com

Disability Served: various

This publication offers suggestions and tips to teachers working with disabled students in inclusive educational settings.

How to Reach and Teach Children and Teens with Dyslexia: A Parent and Teacher Guide to Helping Students of All Ages Academically, Socially, and Emotionally

Jossey-Bass
Customer Care Center-Consumer Accounts
10475 Crosspoint Boulevard
Indianapolis, IN 46256
877-762-2974
http://www.josseybass.com
Disability Served: dyslexic, learning disabled

This is a useful resource that helps teachers and parents working with young people who are dyslexic. Includes 50 full-page activity sheets.

How to Reach and Teach Children with ADD/ADHD: Practical Techniques, Strategies, and Interventions

Jossey-Bass
Customer Care Center-Consumer Accounts
10475 Crosspoint Boulevard
Indianapolis, IN 46256
877-762-2974
http://www.josseybass.com
Disability Served: attention deficit disorder

This publication features interviews, real-life case studies, and student intervention plans for children with ADD/ADHD.

How to Teach Spelling

Educators Publishing Service
PO Box 9031
Cambridge, MA 02139-9031
800-225-5750
http://www.epsbooks.com
Disability Served: learning disabled

This product consists of a comprehensive resource manual and four grade-level workbooks for students in grades one through 12.

Human Exceptionality: School, Community, and Family

Allyn & Bacon
75 Arlington Street, Suite 300
Boston, MA 02116
800-852-8024
http://www.ablongman.com

Disability Served: various

This textbook discusses all aspects of the field of special education. Includes stories about the disabled and those who work with them.

I Can't Hear You in the Dark: How to Learn and Teach Lipreading

Alexander Graham Bell Association of the Deaf
3417 Volta Place, NW
Washington, DC 20007
202-337-5220, 202-337-5221 (TTY)
publications@agbell.org
http://www.agbell.org
Disability Served: hearing

This text provides an overview of lipreading for teachers and potential learners of this communication method.

Implementing Cognitive Strategy Instruction across the School: The Benchmark Manual for Teachers

Brookline Books
34 University Road
Brookline, MA 02445
617-734-6772
http://www.brooklinebooks.com
Disability Served: learning disabled

This book is designed to help teachers who have students with reading problems.

Including Students with Severe and Multiple Disabilities in Typical Classrooms: Practical Strategies for Teachers

Paul H. Brookes Publishing Company
PO Box 10624
Baltimore, MD 21285-0624
800-638-3775
http://www.brookespublishing.com
Disability Served: various

This text for educators provides strategies for successful inclusion.

Including Students with Severe Disabilities

Allyn & Bacon
75 Arlington Street, Suite 300
Boston, MA 02116
800-852-8024
http://www.ablongman.com
Disability Served: various

This book offers advice on integrating students with severe disabilities into general education classrooms.

Inclusion and School Reform: Transforming America's Classrooms
Paul H. Brookes Publishing Company
PO Box 10624
Baltimore, MD 21285-0624
800-638-3775
http://www.brookespublishing.com
Disability Served: various
This book provides a history of inclusive education.

Inclusive Materials Mini-Kit
The Educational Equity Center at The Academy for
   Educational Development
100 Fifth Avenue, 8th Floor
New York, NY 10011
212-243-1110 (Voice/TTY)
information@edequity.org
http://www.edequity.org/inclusive.php
Disability Served: various
This packet is designed to help the teacher who will
   implement mainstreaming.

Inclusive Programming for Elementary Students with Autism
Future Horizons Inc.
721 West Abram Street
Arlington, TX 76013
800-489-0727
info@futurehorizons-autism.com
http://www.futurehorizons-autism.com
Disability Served: autism
This text offers useful suggestions for teachers who work
   with autistic students at the elementary level.

Inclusive Programming for Middle School Students with Autism
Future Horizons Inc.
721 West Abram Street
Arlington, TX 76013
800-489-0727
info@futurehorizons-autism.com
http://www.futurehorizons-autism.com
Disability Served: autism
This publication offers useful suggestions for teachers
   who work with autistic students at the middle-school
   level.

Increasing Behaviors of Persons with Severe Retardation and Autism
Research Press
Department 25W, PO Box 9177
Champaign, IL 61826
217-352-3273, 800-519-2707
rp@researchpress.com
http://www.researchpress.com
*Disability Served: autism, developmentally disabled,
   mental retardation*
This book, geared toward educators of students with
   mental disabilities, provides strategies and guidelines
   for increasing desirable behaviors. Techniques
   include shaping, prompting, fading, modeling,
   backward chaining, and graduated guidance.

Individualizing Instruction for the Educationally Handicapped
Charles C. Thomas, Publisher
2600 South First Street
Springfield, IL 62704
800-258-8980
books@ccthomas.com
http://www.ccthomas.com
Disability Served: learning disabled
This text offers advice for setting up individualized
   educational instruction for educationally
   handicapped children.

I Need Help with School!
Future Horizons Inc.
721 West Abram Street
Arlington, TX 76013
800-489-0727
info@futurehorizons-autism.com
http://www.futurehorizons-autism.com
Disability Served: Asperger Syndrome, autism
This book offers advice and information for parents on
   designing an appropriate educational program for
   children with autism or Asperger Syndrome.

Information from HEATH
George Washington University, HEATH Resource Center
2121 K Street, NW, Suite 220
Washington, DC 20037
202-973-0904 (Voice/TTY), 800-544-3284
askheath@gwu.edu
http://www.heath.gwu.edu
Disability Served: various
This quarterly newsletter offers information regarding postsecondary education for individuals with disabilities.

Keeping A Head in School
Educators Publishing Service Inc.
PO Box 9031

Cambridge, MA 02139-9031
800-225-5750
customer_service@epsbooks.com
http://www.epsbooks.com
Disability Served: *learning disabled*
This book helps students with learning disabilities gain
self-confidence and overcome obstacles.

Keys to Success for Teaching Students with Autism
Future Horizons
721 West Abram Street
Arlington, TX 76013
800-489-0727
info@futurehorizons-autism.com
http://www.futurehorizons-autism.com
Disability Served: *autism*
This publication details six keys to success in teaching
students with autism.

Language Learning Practices with Deaf Children
Pro-Ed Inc.
8700 Shoal Creek Boulevard
Austin, TX 78757-6897
800-897-3202
http://www.proedinc.com
Disability Served: *hearing*
This book provides teaching methods and language development theories that can be used with deaf children.

Language Tool Kit
Educators Publishing Service Inc.
PO Box 9031
Cambridge, MA 02139-9031
800-225-5750
customer_service@epsbooks.com
http://www.epsbooks.com
Disability Served: *learning disabled*
This set of cards and teacher's manual is designed to
teach reading and spelling to first through third
grade students with language disabilities.

LCCE: Life Centered Career Education and All Related Products
Council for Exceptional Children
1110 North Glebe Road, Suite 300
Arlington, VA 22201-5704
conteduc@cec.sped.org
http://www.cec.sped.org
Disability Served: *learning disabled, mentally disabled*
This publication provides a functional curriculum for
general education students, students with learning

disabilities, students with mild mental disabilities,
and at-risk students.

The LD and the ADHD Child: Ways Parents and Professionals Can Help
John F. Blair, Publisher
1406 Plaza Drive
Winston-Salem, NC 27103
800-222-9796
http://www.blairpub.com
Disability Served: *attention deficit disorder, learning
disabled*
This publication provides a useful overview of LD/ADHD
for teachers and parents.

Learning a Living: A Guide to Planning Your Career and Finding a Job for People with Learning Disabilities, Attention Deficit Disorder, and Dyslexia
Council for Exceptional Children
1110 North Glebe Road, Suite 300
Arlington, VA 22201-5704
service@cec.sped.org
http://www.cec.sped.org
Disability Served: *attention deficit disorder, dyslexic,
learning disabled*
This guide helps educators learn more about special
work accommodations and planning necessary
for those with learning disabilities, dyslexia, and
attention deficit disorder.

Learning Disabilities and Challenging Behaviors: A Guide to Intervention and Classroom Management
Paul H. Brookes Publishing Co. Inc.
PO Box 10624
Baltimore, MD 21285-0624
800-638-3775
custserv@brookespublishing.com
http://www.pbrookes.com
Disability Served: *behavioral disorders, learning disabled*
This book provides an overview of the Building Blocks
model in classrooms to effectively educate those with
learning disabilities and challenging behaviors.

Let's Read: A Linguistic Reading Program
Educators Publishing Service Inc.
PO Box 9031
Cambridge, MA 02139-9031
800-225-5750
customer_service@epsbooks.com
http://www.epsbooks.com
Disability Served: *learning disabled*

This manual teaches reading skills using the linguistic reading approach.

Literacy Learning for Children Who Are Deaf or Hard of Hearing
Alexander Graham Bell Association of the Deaf
3417 Volta Place, NW
Washington, DC 20007
202-337-5220, 202-337-5221 (TTY)
publications@agbell.org
http://www.agbell.org
Disability Served: hearing
This guide is for educators who teach reading to hearing-impaired students.

Literacy Program
Educators Publishing Service Inc.
PO Box 9031
Cambridge, MA 02139-9031
800-225-5750
customer_service@epsbooks.com
http://www.epsbooks.com
Disability Served: learning disabled
This series is designed to teach reading skills to older students and adults whose reading skills are below a sixth grade level.

Meeting the ADD Challenge a Practical Guide for Teachers
Research Press
Department 25W, PO Box 9177
Champaign, IL 61826
217-352-3273, 800-519-2707
rp@researchpress.com
http://www.researchpress.com
Disability Served: attention deficit disorder
This guide covers the needs and treatment of children and adolescents with ADD.

Multisensory Teaching Approach
Educators Publishing Service Inc.
PO Box 9031
Cambridge, MA 02139-9031
800-225-5750
customer_service@epsbooks.com
http://www.epsbooks.com
Disability Served: learning disabled
This kit contains tools to teach reading, writing, spelling, and alphabet skills.

The New Language of Toys: Teaching Communication Skills to Children with Special Needs: A Guide for Parents and Teachers
Alexander Graham Bell Association of the Deaf
3417 Volta Place, Northwest
Washington, DC 20007
202-337-5220, 202-337-5221 (TTY)
publications@agbell.org
http://www.agbell.org
Disability Served: communication
This guide gives advice to teachers and parents on using toys and play to teach communication skills to children with special needs.

1001 Great Ideas for Teaching and Raising Children with Autism Spectrum
Future Horizons Inc.
721 West Abram Street
Arlington, TX 76013
800-489-0727
info@futurehorizons-autism.com
http://www.futurehorizons-autism.com
Disability Served: autism
This publication provides useful suggestions for teachers of students with autism and related syndromes.

Our Forgotten Children: Hard of Hearing Pupils in the Schools
Alexander Graham Bell Association of the Deaf
3417 Volta Place, NW
Washington, DC 20007
202-337-5220, 202-337-5221 (TTY)
publications@agbell.org
http://www.agbell.org
Disability Served: hearing
This publication covers educational issues for parents and teachers. Includes a discussion of early intervention, the medical aspects of hearing loss, classroom acoustics, cutting-edge hearing assistance technology, cochlear implants, and federal regulations, including the Individuals with Disabilities Education Act.

Pediatric Examination of Educational Readiness
Educators Publishing Service Inc.
PO Box 9031
Cambridge, MA 02139-9031
800-225-5750
customer_service@epsbooks.com

http://www.epsbooks.com
Disability Served: various
This test is designed to assess the developmental levels of students not yet in the first grade.

Pediatric Exam of Educational Readiness at Middle Childhood
Educators Publishing Service Inc.
PO Box 9031
Cambridge, MA 02139-9031
800-225-5750
customer_service@epsbooks.com
http://www.epsbooks.com
Disability Served: various
This test is designed to assess neurological and motor skills of students in grades four through 10.

Pediatric Extended Examination at Three
Educators Publishing Service Inc.
PO Box 9031
Cambridge, MA 02139-9031
800-225-5750
customer_service@epsbooks.com
http://www.epsbooks.com
Disability Served: various
This test assesses general developmental levels of preschoolers.

PEEX II-Pediatric Early Elementary Examination
Educators Publishing Service Inc.
PO Box 9031
Cambridge, MA 02139-9031
800-225-5750
customer_service@epsbooks.com
http://www.epsbooks.com
Disability Served: various
This test assesses general developmental levels of students in grades two through four.

Practical Strategies for Including High School Students with Behavioral Disabilities
Research Press
Department 25W, PO Box 9177
Champaign, IL 61826
217-352-3273, 800-519-2707
rp@researchpress.com
http://www.researchpress.com
Disability Served: behavioral disorders, emotionally disabled adolescents

This publication provides advice to educators on working with high school students with emotional and behavioral disabilities.

Preschool Language Disorders: Resource Guide
Alexander Graham Bell Association of the Deaf
3417 Volta Place, NW
Washington, DC 20007
202-337-5220, 202-337-5221 (TTY)
publications@agbell.org
http://www.agbell.org
Disability Served: communication
This guide provides an overview of preschool language disorders for educators.

Preventing Academic Failure
Educators Publishing Service Inc.
PO Box 9031
Cambridge, MA 02139-9031
800-225-5750
customer_service@epsbooks.com
http://www.epsbooks.com
Disability Served: communication
This book is designed to aid the teacher of students with language disabilities. It offers curriculum guidelines, reading techniques, phonics, and more.

Questions Teachers Ask: A Guide for The Mainstream Classroom Teacher with a Hearing-Impaired Student
Alexander Graham Bell Association of the Deaf
3417 Volta Place, NW
Washington, DC 20007
202-337-5220, 202-337-5221 (TTY)
publications@agbell.org
http://www.agbell.org
Disability Served: hearing
This guide offers useful information and advice for mainstream teachers who work with hearing-impaired students.

Reaching the Child with Autism through Art
Future Horizons Inc.
721 West Abram Street
Arlington, TX 76013
800-489-0727
info@futurehorizons-autism.com
http://www.futurehorizons-autism.com
Disability Served: autism

This publication provides useful suggestions to teachers and parents on using art to improve autistic children's self-esteem, spatial relationships, form discrimination, fine motor skills, eye contact, directionality, and other abilities.

Reading Practices With Deaf Learners
Pro-Ed Inc.
8700 Shoal Creek Boulevard
Austin, TX 78757-6897
800-897-3202
http://www.proedinc.com
Disability Served: hearing
This guide helps educators teach reading to deaf and hard-of-hearing students.

Reasoning And Reading
Educators Publishing Service Inc.
PO Box 9031
Cambridge, MA 02139-9031
800-225-5750
customer_service@epsbooks.com
http://www.epsbooks.com
Disability Served: learning disabled
This workbook series is designed to help students in grades three through eight build reading comprehension skills.

Recommended Reading for Professionals
International Dyslexia Association
Chester Building, 8600 LaSalle Road, Suite 382
Baltimore, MD 21286-2044
410-296-0232
http://www.interdys.org
Disability Served: dyslexic
This online brochure suggests dyslexic-related publications for educators.

Self-Esteem and Adjusting with Blindness: The Process of Responding to Life's Demands
Charles C. Thomas, Publisher
2600 South First Street
Springfield, IL 62704
800-258-8980
books@ccthomas.com
http://www.ccthomas.com
Disability Served: vision
This is a useful text for professionals in education, social work, vocational counseling, rehabilitation, recreation therapy, ophthalmology, and optometry.

A Self-Regulated Learning Approach for Children with Learning/Behavior Disorders
Charles C. Thomas, Publisher
2600 South First Street
Springfield, IL 62704
800-258-8980
books@ccthomas.com
http://www.ccthomas.com
Disability Served: behavioral disorders, learning disabled
This text uses Piaget's study of constructivism to help educators assist children with learning/behavioral disorders.

Slingerland Screening Tests for Identifying Children with Specific Language Disability
Educators Publishing Service Inc.
PO Box 9031
Cambridge, MA 02139-9031
800-225-5750
customer_service@epsbooks.com
http://www.epsbooks.com
Disability Served: communication
These tests are designed to identify students in grades one through six who have language disabilities.

Social and Cultural Perspectives on Blindness: Barriers to Community Integration
Charles C. Thomas, Publisher
2600 South First Street
Springfield, IL 62704
800-258-8980
books@ccthomas.com
http://www.ccthomas.com
Disability Served: vision
This book examines different attitudes that people throughout the world have about blindness.

Solving Language Difficulties
Educators Publishing Service Inc.
PO Box 9031
Cambridge, MA 02139-9031
800-225-5750
customer_service@epsbooks.com
http://www.epsbooks.com
Disability Served: communication
This workbook is designed to teach reading to students with language disabilities who are in grades five and up.

The Special Educator's Book of Lists
Jossey-Bass
Customer Care Center-Consumer Accounts
10475 Crosspoint Boulevard
Indianapolis, IN 46256
877-762-2974
http://www.josseybass.com
Disability Served: various
This text provides 192 reproducible lists that cover
assessment, diagnosis, remediation, and legal and
procedural information.

Speech and the Hearing-Impaired Child
Alexander Graham Bell Association of the Deaf
3417 Volta Place, NW
Washington, DC 20007
202-337-5220, 202-337-5221 (TTY)
publications@agbell.org
http://www.agbell.org
Disability Served: hearing
This text provides methods and strategies for teaching
language and speech skills to hearing-impaired
students.

Strategies for Teaching Learners with Special Needs
Prentice Hall
375 Hudson Street
New York, NY 10014
Disability Served: various
This guide is designed to assist special education
teachers.

**Successfully Educating Preschoolers with Special
Needs: Ages 2-1/2 To 5: A Guide for Parents,
A Tool for Teachers**
Paul H. Brookes Publishing Co. Inc.
PO Box 10624
Baltimore, MD 21285-0624
800-638-3775
custserv@brookespublishing.com
http://www.pbrookes.com
Disability Served: various
This video for educators and parents offers practical
information about preschool education and special
education services for children ages 2-1/2 to five.

**Survival Guide for the First-Year Special Education
Teacher**
Council for Exceptional Children
1110 North Glebe Road, Suite 300

Arlington, VA 22201-5704
888-CEC-SPED, 866-915-5000 (TTY)
service@cec.sped.org
http://www.cec.sped.org
Disability Served: various
This guide is designed to prepare and help new special
education teachers.

**A Teacher's Guide to Including Students with
Disabilities in Regular Physical Education**
Paul H. Brookes Publishing Company
PO Box 10624
Baltimore, MD 21285-0624
410-337-9580, 800-638-3775
custserv@brookespublishing.com
http://www.pbrookes.com
Disability Served: various
This book provides strategies for including students with
disabilities in physical education programs.

Teaching Adolescents with Learning Disabilities
Love Publishing Company
9101 East Kenyon Avenue, Suite 2200
Denver, CO 80237
303-221-7333
lpc@lovepublishing.com
http://www.lovepublishing.com
Disability Served: learning disabled
This book provides teachers with strategies and methods
for successfully instructing learning disabled
adolescents.

Teaching and Mainstreaming Autistic Children
Love Publishing Company
9101 East Kenyon Avenue, Suite 2200
Denver, CO 80237
303-221-7333
lpc@lovepublishing.com
http://www.lovepublishing.com
Disability Served: autism
This text offers the author's views on successfully
teaching autistic children, which includes
maintaining a highly structured environment and
placing emphasis on parents and teachers working
cooperatively.

Teaching Exceptional Children
Council for Exceptional Children
1110 North Glebe Road, Suite 300
Arlington, VA 22201-5704

888-CEC-SPED, 866-915-5000 (TTY)
service@cec.sped.org
http://www.cec.sped.org
Disability Served: various
This quarterly journal focuses on the teaching of students with disabilities.

Teaching Individuals with Physical or Multiple Disabilities

Prentice Hall
375 Hudson Street
New York, NY 10014
http://vig.prenhall.com
Disability Served: physically disabled
This teacher's guide provides background information on the needs of the disabled and offers teaching strategies.

Teaching Language-Disabled Children: A Communication/Games Intervention

Brookline Books
34 University Road
Cambridge, MA 02445
617-734-6772
http://www.brooklinebooks.com
Disability Served: behavioral disorders, learning disabled
This text provides communication games designed to teach language skills to students with language disabilities.

Teaching Learners with Mild Disabilities: Integrating Research and Practice

Thomson Learning
PO Box 6904
Florence, KY 41022-6904
800-354-9706
http://www.thomson.com
Disability Served: various
This book presents hypothetical case studies of the interaction between teachers and students with mild disabilities.

Teaching Self-Determination to Students with Disabilities: Basic Skills for Successful Transition

Paul H. Brookes Publishing Company
PO Box 10624
Baltimore, MD 21285-0624
410-337-9580, 800-638-3775
custserv@brookespublishing.com
http://www.pbrookes.com

Disability Served: various
This book provides tips and strategies to help educators prepare high school students with disabilities for adult life.

Teaching Students with Learning and Behavior Problems

Pro-Ed Inc.
8700 Shoal Creek Boulevard
Austin, TX 78757-6897
800-897-3202
http://www.proedinc.com
Disability Served: various
This text provides an overview of common methods for instructing students with learning and behavior problems.

Teaching Students with Learning Problems

Prentice Hall
375 Hudson Street
New York, NY 10014
http://vig.prenhall.com
Disability Served: learning disabled
This book provides methods and strategies to help teachers of learning disabled students.

Teaching Students with Mental Retardation: Providing Access to the General Curriculum

Paul H. Brookes Publishing Co. Inc.
PO Box 10624
Baltimore, MD 21285-0624
800-638-3775
custserv@brookespublishing.com
http://www.pbrookes.com
Disability Served: developmentally disabled
This publication offers advice on developing a person-centered approach; a review of four instruction types (teacher-mediated, peer-mediated, technology-mediated, and activity-anchored); and other information that will help educators provide the mentally retarded with access to the general curriculum.

Teaching Teens with ADD and ADHD

Council for Exceptional Children
1110 North Glebe Road, Suite 300
Arlington, VA 22201-5704
service@cec.sped.org
http://www.cec.sped.org
Disability Served: attention deficit disorder

This publication offers advice on teaching teenagers who have ADD/ADHD.

Teaching the Kids with High-Tech Ears
Alexander Graham Bell Association of the Deaf
3417 Volta Place, NW
Washington, DC 20007
202-337-5220, 202-337-5221 (TTY)
publications@agbell.org
http://www.agbell.org
Disability Served: hearing
This video for teachers illustrates a school district's three-year study of the implementation of general and special education collaboration practices for educating students who have cochlear implants.

Teaching Visually Impaired Children
Charles C. Thomas, Publisher
2600 South First Street
Springfield, IL 62704
800-258-8980
books@ccthomas.com
http://www.ccthomas.com
Disability Served: vision
This text combines practical instruction for educators with discussions of learning theory and the educational process.

Teach Your Tot to Sign: The Parents' Guide to American Sign Language
Gallaudet University Press
800 Florida Avenue, NE
Washington, DC 20002
202-651-5488 (Voice/TTY)
valencia.simmons@gallaudet.edu
http://gupress.gallaudet.edu
Disability Served: communication, hearing
This is a pocket-size guide of more than 500 basic American Sign Language signs.

Test of Mathematical Abilities for Gifted Students
Pro-Ed Inc.
8700 Shoal Creek Boulevard
Austin, TX 78757-6897
800-897-3202
http://www.proedinc.com
Disability Served: learning disabled
This test is designed to assess the math skills of gifted students in grades K through 6.

Textbooks and the Student Who Can't Read Them: A Guide for Teaching Content
Brookline Books
34 University Road
Brookline, MA 02445
617-734-6772
http://www.brooklinebooks.com
Disability Served: learning disabled
This teacher's guide provides strategies for using regular reading textbooks for students with low-level reading skills.

Thirteen Keys To a Successful High School Experience: Guidelines for Students with Hearing Impairments or Auditory Processing Problems in Mainstream Education
Alexander Graham Bell Association of the Deaf
3417 Volta Place, NW
Washington, DC 20007
202-337-5220, 202-337-5221 (TTY)
publications@agbell.org
http://www.agbell.org
Disability Served: hearing
This publication offers useful guidelines for hearing-impaired students who are involved in mainstream education.

Transition from School to Post-School Life for Individuals with Disabilities
Charles C. Thomas, Publisher
2600 South First Street
Springfield, IL 62704
800-258-8980
books@ccthomas.com
http://www.ccthomas.com
Disability Served: various
This text covers the transition of people with disabilities from school to work using an educational and school psychological perspective.

The Transition Handbook: Strategies High School Teachers Use That Work!
Paul H. Brookes Publishing Co. Inc.
PO Box 10624
Baltimore, MD 21285-0624
800-638-3775
custserv@brookespublishing.com
http://www.pbrookes.com
Disability Served: various

This handbook provides more than 500 research-based, teacher-tested, transition support strategies for high school teachers faced with transitioning disabled students to adulthood.

Understanding and Teaching Emotionally Disturbed Children and Adolescents

Pro-Ed Inc.
8700 Shoal Creek Boulevard
Austin, TX 78757-6897
800-897-3202
http://www.proedinc.com
Disability Served: emotionally disabled adolescents
This book discusses how various theoretical treatment approaches—such as cognitive, behavioral, ecological, and humanistic psychology—can be applied to the education of emotionally disturbed children and adolescents.

Understanding Asperger's Syndrome: Fast Facts

Future Horizons Inc.
721 West Abram Street
Arlington, TX 76013
800-489-0727
info@futurehorizons-autism.com
http://www.futurehorizons-autism.com
Disability Served: Asperger Syndrome, autism
This is a fact-filled overview of Asperger Syndrome for teachers and other educators.

Understanding College Students with Autism

HEATH Resource Center, George Washington University
2121 K Street, NW, Suite 220
Washington, DC 20037
202-973-0904 (Voice/TTY), 800-544-3284
askheath@gwu.edu
http://www.heath.gwu.edu/FactSheets.htm
Disability Served: autism
This free online resource, written by an individual with autism, details what education professionals should expect from students with autism in terms of learning styles, behavior, testing, and housing.

Understanding Dyslexia and the Reading Process: A Guide for Educators and Parents

Allyn & Bacon
75 Arlington Street, Suite 300
Boston, MA 02116
800-852-8024
http://www.ablongman.com

Disability Served: dyslexic
This guide provides an overview of the history, nature, and improvement of reading instruction as it relates to dyslexia.

Visual Impairment in the Schools

Charles C. Thomas, Publisher
2600 South First Street
Springfield, IL 62704
800-258-8980
books@ccthomas.com
http://www.ccthomas.com
Disability Served: vision
This text is designed for those planning to teach the visually impaired, as well as educators who are seeking to update their knowledge regarding visual disabilities.

The Volta Review

Alexander Graham Bell Association of the Deaf
3417 Volta Place, NW
Washington, DC 20007
202-337-5220
publications@agbell.org
http://www.agbell.org
Disability Served: hearing
This professional journal for those who teach students with hearing impairments includes articles on speech reading, using residual hearing, and more.

What Every Teacher Should Know about ADD

Research Press
Department 25W, PO Box 9177
Champaign, IL 61826
217-352-3273, 800-519-2707
rp@researchpress.com
http://www.researchpress.com
Disability Served: attention deficit disorder, behavioral disorders
This video provides management strategies for disruptive, inattentive, or hyperactive pre-school and elementary students.

What Every Teacher Should Know about Students with Special Needs

Research Press
Department 25W, PO Box 9177
Champaign, IL 61826
217-352-3273, 800-519-2707
rp@researchpress.com

http://www.researchpress.com
Disability Served: various
This publication provides more than 500 classroom-tested, teacher-friendly tips for helping special education students find success in school.

Why Home School a Dyslexia Child?
International Dyslexia Association
Chester Building, 8600 LaSalle Road, Suite 382
Baltimore, MD 21286-2044
410-296-0232
http://www.interdys.org
Disability Served: dyslexic
This online brochure outlines the benefits of home schooling a dyslexic child. It also provides instructions on how to set up a home-based educational program.

The Words They Need: Welcoming Children Who Are Deaf and Hard of Hearing to Literacy
Pro-Ed Inc.
8700 Shoal Creek Boulevard
Austin, TX 78757-6897
800-897-3202
http://www.proedinc.com
Disability Served: hearing
This book discusses the development of reading skills in deaf and hearing-impaired students.

Working with Challenging Parents of Students with Special Needs
Research Press
Department 25W, PO Box 9177
Champaign, IL 61826
217-352-3273, 800-519-2707
rp@researchpress.com
http://www.researchpress.com
Disability Served: various
This book provides advice for educators facing stressful or demanding interactions with parents of children with special needs.

Working with Visually Impaired Young Students: A Curriculum Guide for Birth to 3 Year Olds
Charles C. Thomas, Publisher
2600 South First Street
Springfield, IL 62704
800-258-8980
books@ccthomas.com
http://www.ccthomas.com

Disability Served: vision
This guide provides methods for educating students up to the age of three who have visual impairments.

Working with Visually Impaired Young Students: A Curriculum Guide for 3 to 5 Year Olds
Charles C. Thomas, Publisher
2600 South First Street
Springfield, IL 62704
800-258-8980
books@ccthomas.com
http://www.ccthomas.com
Disability Served: vision
This guide provides methods for educating students from three to five who have visual impairments.

Writing Better: Effective Strategies for Teaching Students with Learning Difficulties
Paul H. Brookes Publishing Co. Inc.
PO Box 10624
Baltimore, MD 21285-0624
800-638-3775
custserv@brookespublishing.com
http://www.pbrookes.com
Disability Served: learning disabled
This publication offers advice for teachers on how to improve the writing skills of learning disabled students.

You're Going to Love This Kid: Teaching Students with Autism in the Inclusive Classroom
Paul H. Brookes Publishing Co. Inc.
PO Box 10624
Baltimore, MD 21285-0624
800-638-3775
custserv@brookespublishing.com
http://www.pbrookes.com
Disability Served: autism
This handbook offers strategies for educators who work with students with autism in both primary and secondary school classrooms.

VOCATIONAL ASSISTANCE AND EMPLOYMENT ORGANIZATIONS

These organizations and agencies provide job training, vocational rehabilitation, job placement programs, supported employment, job skills assessment, and educational services to persons with disabilities and other barriers to employment.

ALABAMA

Alabama Department of Labor
RSA Union, 6th Floor, PO Box 303500
Montgomery, AL 36130-3500
334-242-3460
http://www.alalabor.state.al.us
Disability Served: various

Alabama Department of Rehabilitation Services
2129 East South Boulevard
Montgomery, AL 36116-2455
334-281-8780, 800-543-3098
http://www.rehab.state.al.us
Disability Served: various

Alabama Division of Employment Service
1060 East South Boulevard
Montgomery, AL 36116
334-286-1746
Disability Served: various

Alabama Governor's Committee on Employment of People with Disabilities
PO Box 11586
Montgomery, AL 36111-0586
334-281-8780 (Voice/TTY)
Disability Served: various

Easter Seals Alabama Achievement Center
510 West Thomason Circle
Opelika, AL 36801
205-745-3501
info@achievement-center.org
http://www.achievement-center.org
Disability Served: various

Easter Seals Alabama Opportunity Center
217 West 13th Street
Anniston, AL 36202
256-820-9960
http://www.alabama.easter-seals.org
Disability Served: various

Fort Payne-Dekalb Rehab Center
311 North Gault Avenue
Fort Payne, AL 35967
256-845-9367
Disability Served: various

Janice Capilouto Center for the Deaf
5950 Monticello Drive
Montgomery, AL 36117
334-244-8090, 334-272-6754 (TTY)
http://www.jccd.org
Disability Served: hearing

Mobile Association for the Blind
2440 Gordon Smith Drive
Mobile, AL 36617
251-473-3585, 877-292-5463
Sales@Mobile Blind.com
http://www.mobileblind.com
Disability Served: vision

United States Equal Employment Opportunity Commission (Birmingham District Office)
1130 22nd Street South, Suite 2000
Birmingham, AL 35205
205-212-2100, 205-212-2112 (TTY)
Disability Served: various

Wiregrass Rehabilitation Center Inc.
795 Ross Clark Circle, NE, PO Box 338
Dothan, AL 36302-0338
334-792-0022
wrcadmin@ala.net
Disability Served: various

Workshops Inc.
240 Commerce Parkway
Pelham, AL 35124
205-987-2133
http://www.workshopsinc.com
Disability Served: various

Workshops Inc.
4244 Third Avenue South
Birmingham, AL 35222
205-592-9683, 888-805-9683, 205-592-8006 (TTY)
http://www.workshopsinc.com
Disability Served: various

ALASKA

Alaska Department of Labor and Workforce Development
PO Box 21149
Juneau, AK 99802-1149
907-465-2700
http://www.labor.state.ak.us
Disability Served: various

Alaska Division of Vocational Rehabilitation
801 West 10th Street, Suite A
Juneau, AK 99801-1894
907-465-2814, 800-478-2815
anne_knight@labor.state.ak.us
http://www.labor.state.ak.us/dvr/home.htm
Disability Served: various

Alaska Governor's Committee on Employment and Rehabilitation of People with Disabilities
801 West 10th Street, Suite A
Juneau, AK 99801-1894
800-478-2815
http://www.labor.state.ak.us/govscomm/home.htm
Disability Served: various

ARIZONA

Arizona Department of Economic Security
1789 West Jefferson, 4th Floor SC
Phoenix, AZ 85007
602-542-5678
http://www.de.state.az.us
Disability Served: various

Arizona Fair Employment Practices Agency
Attorney General Civil Rights Division
South Building, 402 West Congress, #215
Tucson, AZ 85701
520-628-6500
http://www.attorney-general.state.az.us/civil_rights
Disability Served: various

Arizona Governor's Committee on Employment of People with Disabilities
PO Box 16404
Phoenix, AZ 85011
602-266-6752
Disability Served: various

Arizona Rehabilitation Services Administration
1789 West Jefferson
Phoenix, AZ 85007
602-542-3332, 602-542-6049 (TTY)
http://www.azdes.gov/rsa
Disability Served: various

Beacon Group
308 West Glenn
Tucson, AZ 85703
520-622-4874
shilkemeyer@tetracorp.com
http://www.tetracorp.com
Disability Served: various

Industrial Commission of Arizona
800 West Washington Street
Phoenix, AZ 85007
602-542-4515
LaborAdmin@ica.state.az.us
http://www.ica.state.az.us/Labor/labortop.htm
Disability Served: various

United States Equal Employment Opportunity Commission (Phoenix District Office)
3300 North Central Avenue, Suite 690
Phoenix, AZ 85012-2504
602-640-5000, 602-640-5072 (TTY)
Disability Served: various

Yavapai Rehabilitation Center
436 North Washington Avenue
Prescott, AZ 86301
520-445-0991
Disability Served: various

ARKANSAS

Arkansas Department of Labor
10421 West Markham
Little Rock, AR 72205
501-682-4500
asklabor@arkansas.gov

http://www.arkansas.gov/labor
Disability Served: various

Arkansas Division of Services for the Blind
700 Main Street, PO Box 3237
Little Rock, AR 72203
800-960-9270, 501-682-0093 (TDD)
http://www.arkansas.gov/dhs/dsb/NEWDSB
Disability Served: vision

Arkansas Employment Security Department
#1 Pershing Circle
North Little Rock, AR 72114
501-682-2121
artee.williams.aesd@mail.state.ar.us
http://www.state.ar.us/esd
Disability Served: various

Arkansas Governor's Commission on Employment of People with Disabilities
1616 Brookwood Drive
Little Rock, AR 72202
501-296-1626 (Voice/TTY)
Disability Served: various

Easter Seals Arkansas Adult Services Center
11801 Fairview Road
Little Rock, AR 72212
501-221-8400
http://ar.easterseals.com
Disability Served: various

Hot Springs Rehabilitation Center
PO Box 1358
Hot Springs, AR 71902
501-624-4411
ktaylor@ars.state.ar.us
http://www.arsinfo.org/hsrehab.html
Disability Served: various

United States Equal Employment Opportunity Commission (Little Rock Area Office)
820 Louisiana Street, Suite 200
Little Rock, AR 72201
501-324-5060, 501-324-5481 (TTY)
Disability Served: various

CALIFORNIA

Ability First
1300 Green Street
Pasadena, CA 91106

626-396-1010
http://abilityfirst.com
Disability Served: physically disabled

California Department of Employment Development
800 Capitol Mall, MIC 83
Sacramento, CA 95814
http://www.edd.ca.gov/eddpwd.htm
Disability Served: various

California Department of Industrial Relations
455 Golden Gate Avenue
San Francisco, CA 94102
415-703-5070
http://www.dir.ca.gov
Disability Served: various

California Department of Rehabilitation
2000 Evergreen Street, PO Box 944222
Sacramento, CA 95815
916-263-8981, 916-263-7477 (TTY)
http://www.rehab.cahwnet.gov
Disability Served: various

California's Governor's Committee on Employment of People with Disabilities
800 Capitol Mall, MIC 83
Sacramento, CA 95814
http://www.edd.ca.gov/gcedpind.htm
Disability Served: various

Career Assessment and Placement Center
9401 South Painter Avenue
Whittier, CA 90605
310-698-8121
Disability Served: various

CHARO Industries
4301 East Valley Boulevard
Los Angeles, CA 90032
213-343-9520, 323-343-9520
Disability Served: developmentally disabled

Desert Haven Enterprises
43437 Copeland Circle
Lancaster, CA 93535
805-948-8402
http://www.deserthaven.org
Disability Served: developmentally disabled

Do-It-Leisure-Work Training Center
621 1/2 Mangrove Avenue
Chico, CA 95926
530-343-6055
http://www.wtcinc.org/doit.htm
Disability Served: developmentally disabled, mental health

Imperial County Work Training Center
210 Wake Avenue
El Centro, CA 92243
619-352-6181
Disability Served: various

Jeff Malmuth and Company
870 Market Street, Suite 588
San Francisco, CA 94102
415-362-7005
http://www.jmalmuth.com
Disability Served: various

Konocti Industries
4195 Lakeshore Boulevard
Lakeport, CA 95453
707-263-3811
peopleservices@mindspring.com
Disability Served: various

Motherlode Rehabilitation Enterprises
399 Placerville Drive
Placerville, CA 95667
916-622-4848
Disability Served: various

Mt. Diablo Vocational Services
490 Golf Club Road
Pleasant Hill, CA 94523
925-687-9675
Disability Served: various

Napa Valley PSI
651 Trabajo Lane
Napa, CA 94559
707-255-0177
Disability Served: developmentally disabled

NCI Affiliates Inc.
1434 Chestnut Street
Paso Robles, CA 93446
805-238-6630
info@nciaffiliates.org

http://www.nciaffiliates.org
Disability Served: various

Porterville Sheltered Workshop
187 West Olive Avenue
Porterville, CA 93257
559-784-1399
marketing@pswrehab.com
http://www.pswrehab.com
Disability Served: various

Sacramento Vocational Services
6950 21st Avenue
Sacramento, CA 95820
916-381-1300
Disability Served: various

Saddleback Community Enterprises
26041 Pala
Mission Viejo, CA 92691
714-837-7280
Disability Served: various

San Francisco Arc
1500 Howard Street
San Francisco, CA 94103
415-255-7200
http://www.thearcsanfrancisco.org
Disability Served: various

Sensory Access Foundation
1142 West Evelyn Avenue
Sunnyvale, CA 94086
408-245-7330
http://www.sensoryaccess.com
Disability Served: vision

Shasta County Opportunity Center
1265 Redwood Boulevard
Redding, CA 96003
530-225-5781
info@oppcenter.org
http://www.oppcenter.org
Disability Served: various

Tulare County Training Center Able Industries
8127 Avenue 304
Visalia, CA 93291
559-651-8150
info@ableindustries.org
http://www.ableindustries.org
Disability Served: various

United States Equal Employment Opportunity Commission (Fresno Local Office)
1265 West Shaw Avenue, Suite 103
Fresno, CA 93711
559-487-5793, 559-487-5837 (TTY)
Disability Served: various

United States Equal Employment Opportunity Commission (Los Angeles District Office)
255 East Temple Street, 4th Floor
Los Angeles, CA 90012
213-894-1000, 213-894-1121 (TTY)
Disability Served: various

United States Equal Employment Opportunity Commission (Oakland Local Office)
1301 Clay Street, Suite 1170-N
Oakland, CA 94612-5217
510-637-3230, 510-637-3234 (TTY)
Disability Served: various

United States Equal Employment Opportunity Commission (San Diego Area Office)
401 B Street, Suite 510
San Diego, CA 92101
619-557-7235, 619-557-5748 (TTY)
Disability Served: various

United States Equal Employment Opportunity Commission (San Francisco District Office)
350 The Embarcadero, Suite 500
San Francisco, CA 94105-1260
415-625-5600, 415-625-5610 (TTY)
Disability Served: various

United States Equal Employment Opportunity Commission (San Jose Local Office)
96 North Third Street, Suite 200
San Jose, CA 95112
408-291-7352, 408-291-7374 (TTY)
Disability Served: various

Unyeway Inc.
2330 Main Street, Suite E
Ramona, CA 92065-2595
760-789-5960
Disability Served: developmentally disabled

Valley Light Industries Inc.
5358 North Irwindale, Suite 4B
Irwindale, CA 91706

626-337-6200
Disability Served: various

Vocational Improvement Inc.
8675 Boston Place
Rancho Cucamonga, CA 91730
909-483-5924
http://www.vipsolutions.com
Disability Served: various

Work Training Center for the Handicapped
2255 Fair Street
Chico, CA 95928
530-343-7994
http://www.wtcinc.org
Disability Served: various

Work Training Programs Inc.
9430 Topanga Canyon Boulevard, Suite 103
Chatsworth, CA 91311
818-773-9570
Disability Served: various

COLORADO

Bayaud Industries Inc.
1600 Downing Street, Suite 300
Denver, CO 80218
303-830-6885
mary.page@bayaudindustries.org
http://www.bayaudindustries.org
Disability Served: various

Colorado Commission for the Deaf and Hard of Hearing
1575 Sherman Street, 2nd Floor
Denver, CO 80203
303-866-4824, 303-866-4734 (TTY)
Deaf.Commission@state.co.us
http://www.cdhs.state.co.us/DeafCommission
Disability Served: hearing

Colorado Department of Labor and Employment
1515 Arapahoe, Tower 2, Suite 400
Denver, CO 80202
303-318-8000
http://www.coworkforce.com
Disability Served: various

Colorado Division of Vocational Rehabilitation
1575 Sherman Street, 4th Floor
Denver, CO 80023

303-866-4150 (Voice/TDD)
http://www.cdhs.state.co.us/ods/dvr/ods_dvr1.html
Disability Served: various

Colorado Fair Employment Practice Agency
1560 Broadway, Suite 1050
Denver, CO 80202
303-894-2997
http://www.dora.state.co.us/civil-rights
Disability Served: various

**Colorado Governor's Advisory Council for Persons
    with Disabilities**
PO Box 172
Denver, CO 80201-0172
Disability Served: various

Developmental Disabilities Resource Center
11177 West 8th Avenue, Suite 300
Lakewood, CO 80215
303-233-3363
ahogling@ddrcco.com
http://www.ddrcco.com
Disability Served: developmentally disabled

Easter Seals Colorado
5755 West Alameda Avenue
Lakewood, CO 80226-3500
303-233-1666
info@eastersealscolorado.org
http://co.easterseals.com
Disability Served: various

Goodwill Industries of Colorado Springs
2320 West Colorado Avenue
Colorado Springs, CO 80934
719-635-4483
jhansen@goodwill-colosprings.org
http://www.goodwill-colosprings.org
Disability Served: various

Hope Center Inc.
3475 Holly Street
Denver, CO 80207
303-321-0997
gghope@qwest.net
http://www.hopecenterinc.org
Disability Served: developmentally disabled

JFK Partners
University of Colorado Health Sciences Center
4200 East 9th Avenue, C221

Denver, CO 80262
http://www.jfkpartners.org
Disability Served: developmentally disabled

Las Animas County Rehabilitation Center
1205 Congress Drive
Trinidad, CO 81082
719-846-3388
Disability Served: various

**United States Equal Employment Opportunity
    Commission (Denver District Office)**
303 East 17th Avenue, Suite 510
Denver, CO 80203
303-866-1300, 303-866-1950 (TTY)
Disability Served: various

CONNECTICUT

Allied Community Services Inc.
Three Pearson Way
Enfield, CT 06082
860-741-3701 (Voice/TTY)
info@alliedgroup.org
Disability Served: developmentally disabled

Area Cooperative Educational Services
205 Skiff Street
Hamden, CT 06517
203-407-4448
mcaruso@aces.k12.ct.us
Disability Served: various

Central Connecticut Arc Inc.
950 Slater Road
New Britain, CT 06053
860-229-6665 (Voice/TDD)
http://ccarc.com
Disability Served: mental retardation

Cheshire Occupational and Career Center
615 West Johnson Avenue, Building #3
Cheshire, CT 06410
203-272-5607
Disability Served: various

**Connecticut Board of Education and Services
    for the Blind**
184 Windsor Avenue
Windsor, CT 06095
860-602-4000, 860-602-4221 (TDD)

besb@po.state.ct.us
http://www.besb.state.ct.us
Disability Served: vision

Connecticut Department of Labor
200 Folly Brook Boulevard
Wethersfield, CT 06109
860-263-6000, 860-263-6074 (TTY/TDD)
http://www.ctdol.state.ct.us
Disability Served: various

Connecticut Division of Vocational Rehabilitation
25 Sigourney Street
Hartford, CT 06106
800-842-1508, 800-842-4524 (TDD/TTY)
judith.moeckel@po.state.ct.us
http://www.dss.state.ct.us
Disability Served: various

Connecticut Governor's Committee on Employment of Disabled Persons
200 Folly Brook Boulevard
Wethersfield, CT 06109
860-263-6593, 860-263-6074 (TTY)
Disability Served: various

Connecticut Institute for the Blind
120 Holcomb Street
Hartford, CT 06112
860-242-2274
http://www.ciboakhill.org
Disability Served: vision

Connecticut Vocational Rehabilitation for Persons Who Are Visually Impaired
184 Windsor Avenue
Windsor, CT 06095
860-602-4000, 800-842-4510
http://www.dss.state.ct.us/regions.htm
Disability Served: vision

Easter Seals Goodwill Industries Recreation Center
95 Hamilton Street
New Haven, CT 06511
203-777-2000
Disability Served: various

Goodwill Industries of Western Connecticut
165 Ocean Terrace
Bridgeport, CT 06605

203-581-5335
Disability Served: various

Healthways Inc.
435 East Main Street
Ansonia, CT 06401
203-736-2601
Disability Served: various

Kennedy Center Inc.
2440 Reservoir Avenue
Trumbull, CT 06611
203-365-8522, 203-339-3034 (TDD)
hr@kennedyctr.org
http://www.thekennedycenterinc.org
Disability Served: various

Meriden-Wallingford Society for the Handicapped
224-226 Cook Avenue
Meriden, CT 06451
203-237-9975
info@mwsinc.org
http://www.mwsinc.org
Disability Served: various

Varca Inc.
5 Coon Hollow Road
Derby, CT 06418
203-735-8727
http://www.varcainc.com
Disability Served: developmentally disabled

West Haven Community House
227 Elm Street
West Haven, CT 06516
203-934-5221
http://www.whcommunityhouse.org
Disability Served: developmentally disabled

DELAWARE

Delaware Department of Labor
4425 North Market Street, 4th Floor
Wilmington, DE 19802
http://www.delawareworks.com
Disability Served: various

Delaware Division for the Visually Impaired
1901 North duPont Highway, Biggs Building
New Castle, DE 19720

302-255-9800
dhssinfo@state.de.us
http://www.dhss.delaware.gov/dhss/dvi
Disability Served: vision

Delaware Division of Vocational Rehabilitation
4425 North Market Street
Wilmington, DE 19802
302-761-8300
http://www.delawareworks.com/dvr
Disability Served: various

Delaware Governor's Committee on Employment of People with Disabilities
PO Box 9969
Wilmington, DE 19809-0969
302-761-8275
Disability Served: various

Easter Seals Delaware Dover Enterprise
61 Corporate Circle
New Castle, DE 19720
800-677-3800
http://de.easterseals.com
Disability Served: various

Opportunity Center Inc.
3030 Bowers Street
Wilmington, DE 19802
302-762-0300
http://www.oppctr.com
Disability Served: various

DISTRICT OF COLUMBIA
District of Columbia Employment Service
609 H Street, NE
Washington, DC 20001
202-724-7000, 202-698-4817 (TDD)
http://www.does.dc.gov
Disability Served: various

District of Columbia Fair Employment Practice Agencies
1350 Pennsylvania Avenue, NW
Washington, DC 20004
202-727-1000
http://ohr.dc.gov/ohr
Disability Served: various

District of Columbia Rehabilitation Services Administration
1350 Pennsylvania Avenue, NW
Washington, DC 20004
202-442-8400, 202-442-8600 (TTY/TDD)
http://dhs.dc.gov/dhs/cwp/view,a,3,q,492432.asp
Disability Served: various

Goodwill of Greater Washington
2200 South Dakota Avenue, NE
Washington, DC 20018
202-636-4225
http://www.dcgoodwill.org
Disability Served: various

Operation Job Match
2021 K Street, NW, Suite 715
Washington, DC 20006
202-296-5363
information@msandyou.org
http://www.msandyou.org
Disability Served: multiple sclerosis

FLORIDA
Abilities Inc. of Florida
2735 Whitney Road
Clearwater, FL 33760
727-538-7370
http://servicesrcsub3.timberlakepublishing.com
Disability Served: various

ARC Broward Achievement and Rehabilitation Centers
10250 Northwest 53rd Street
Sunrise, FL 33351
954-746-9400, 954-577-4101 (TTY/TDD)
http://www.arcbroward.com
Disability Served: developmentally disabled

Easter Seals Miami-Dade
1475 Northwest 14th Avenue
Miami, FL 33125-1692
305-325-0470
http://www.miami.easter-seals.org
Disability Served: various

Florida Agency for Workforce Innovation
107 East Madison Street, Caldwell Building
Tallahassee, FL 32399

850-245-7105
http://www.floridajobs.org
Disability Served: various

Florida Division of Vocational Rehabilitation
2002 Old Saint Augustine Road, Building A
Tallahassee, FL 32301
850-245-3399 (Voice/TDD)
http://www.rehabworks.org
Disability Served: various

Florida Fair Employment Practice Agency
2009 Apalachee Parkway, Suite 100
Tallahassee, FL 32301
800-955-8770, 800-955-1339 (TDD)
fchrinfo@dms.state.fl.us
http://fchr.state.fl.us
Disability Served: various

**Florida Governor's Alliance for the Employment
of Citizens with Disabilities**
106 East College Avenue, Suite 820
Tallahassee, FL 32301
850-224-4493
Disability Served: various

Jewish Vocational Service Inc.
735 Northeast 125th Street
North Miami, FL 33161
305-899-1587
Disability Served: various

Lighthouse Central Florida
215 East New Hampshire
Orlando, FL 32804
407-898-2483
http://www.cite-fl.com
Disability Served: vision

Primrose Center Inc.
2733 South Fern Creek Avenue
Orlando, FL 32806
407-898-7201
Disability Served: various

**United States Equal Employment Opportunity
Commission (Miami District Office)**
2 South Biscayne Boulevard, Suite 2700
Miami, FL 33131

305-536-4491, 305-536-5721 (TTY)
Disability Served: various

**United States Equal Employment Opportunity
Commission (Tampa Area Office)**
501 East Polk Street, Suite 1000
Tampa, FL 33602
813-228-2310, 813-228-2003 (TTY)
Disability Served: various

GEORGIA

Easter Seals North Georgia
5600 Roswell Road, Prado North, Suite 100
Atlanta, GA 30342
http://www.northgeorgia.easterseals.com
Disability Served: various

**Georgia Committee on Employment of People
with Disabilities Inc.**
PO Box 1090
Fortson, GA 31808
706-324-2150
Disability Served: various

Georgia Department of Labor
404-232-7300
http://www.dol.state.ga.us/find_voc_rehab_offices.htm
Disability Served: various

Georgia Industries for the Blind
700 Faceville Highway
Bainbridge, GA 39818-0218
229-248-2666
rehab@dol.state.ga.us
http://www.vocrehabga.org/indus.html
Disability Served: vision

Georgia Rehabilitation Services
148 Andrew Young International Boulevard, NE
Atlanta, GA 30303
404-232-3910, 877-709-8185
http://www.vocrehabga.org
Disability Served: various

**Goodwill Industries of North Georgia Inc./Vocational
Transitions**
PO Box 447
Ellijay, GA 30540

706-276-4722
http://www.ging.org
Disability Served: various

Griffin Area Resource Center
931 Hamilton Boulevard
Griffin, GA 30223
404-228-3766
Disability Served: various

Kelley Diversified Inc.
265 Newton Bridge Road
Athens, GA 30607
706-549-4398
http://www.kelleydiversified.org
Disability Served: various

New Ventures Inc.
306 Fort Drive
LaGrange, GA 30240
770-882-7723
Disability Served: various

**United States Equal Employment Opportunity
    Commission (Atlanta District Office)**
100 Alabama Street, SW, Suite 4R30
Atlanta, GA 30303
404-562-6800, 404-562-6801 (TTY)
Disability Served: various

**United States Equal Employment Opportunity
    Commission (Savannah Local Office)**
410 Mall Boulevard, Suite G
Savannah, GA 31406-4821
912-652-4234, 912-652-4439 (TTY)
Disability Served: various

HAWAII

ASSETS School
One Ohana Nui Way
Honolulu, HI 96818
808-423-1356
info@assets-school.net
http://www.assets-school.net
Disability Served: dyslexia

Easter Seals Hawaii
710 Green Street
Honolulu, HI 96813

808-536-3765
http://www.EasterSealsHawaii.org
Disability Served: various

Hawaii Department of Labor and Industrial Relations
830 Punchbowl Street, Room 320
Honolulu, HI 96813
808 586-8842
dlir-info@dlir.state.hi.us
http://hawaii.gov/labor
Disability Served: various

**Hawaii Vocational Rehabilitation and Services
    for the Blind Division**
PO Box 339
Honolulu, HI 96809
808-586-5355
http://www.state.hi.us/dhs/vr.pdf
Disability Served: vision

Ho'opono Workshop for the Blind
1901 Bachelot Street
Honolulu, HI 96817
808-586-5286
Disability Served: vision

Lanakila Rehabilitation Center
1809 Bachelot Street
Honolulu, HI 96817
808-531-0555
communityrelations@lanakilahawaii.org
http://www.lanakilahawaii.org
Disability Served: various

**United States Equal Employment Opportunity
    Commission (Honolulu Local Office)**
300 Ala Moana Boulevard, Room 7-127, PO Box 50082
Honolulu, HI 96850-0051
808-541-3120, 808-541-3131 (TTY)
Disability Served: various

IDAHO

Easter Seals Idaho-Goodwill Staffing Services
1465 South Vinnell Way
Boise, ID 83709
208-373-1299
http://www.esgw-nrm.easterseals.com
Disability Served: various

Idaho Commission for the Blind and Visually Impaired
PO Box 83720
Boise, ID 83720-0012
800-542-8688
http://www.icbvi.state.id.us
Disability Served: vision

Idaho Department of Commerce and Labor
317 West Main Street
Boise, ID 83735
208-332-3570
http://cl.idaho.gov/portal
Disability Served: various

Idaho Division of Vocational Rehabilitation
PO Box 83720
Boise, ID 83720
208-287-6443
rthomas@idvr.state.id.us
http://www.state.id.us/idvr/ldvrhome.htm
Disability Served: various

Idaho Governor's Committee on Employment of People with Disabilities
PO Box 21
Boise, ID 83703
208-332-3570
Disability Served: various

ILLINOIS

Ada S. McKinley Vocational Services
1863 South Wabash Avenue
Chicago, IL 60621
312-326-1229
http://www.adasmckinley.org
Disability Served: developmentally disabled

Anixter Center
6610 North Clark Street
Chicago, IL 60626-4062
773-973-7900, ext. 226
AskAnixter@anixter.org
http://www.anixter.org
Disability Served: various

Carle Community Re-Entry Program
611 West Park Street
Urbana, IL 61801

217-383-3360
Disability Served: various

Chicago Light House Industries
1850 West Roosevelt Road
Chicago, IL 60608-1298
800-842-8624
http://www.chicagolighthouse.org
Disability Served: vision

Donka Inc.
400 North County Farm Road
Wheaton, IL 60187
630-665-8169
info@donkainc.org
http://www.donkainc.org
Disability Served: various

Easter Seals Missouri/Southwestern Illinois
602 East 3rd Street
Alton, IL 62002
618-462-7325
http://mo.easterseals.com
Disability Served: various

Edgewater Uptown Work Center
4425 North Clark Street
Chicago, IL 60640
773-334-2211
Disability Served: various

Fulton County Rehab Center
500 North Main Street
Canton, IL 61520
309-647-6510
Disability Served: various

Illinois Department of Labor
160 North LaSalle, Suite C-1300
Chicago, IL 60601
312-793-2800
http://www.state.il.us/agency/idol
Disability Served: various

Illinois Division of Rehabilitation Services
100 South Grand Avenue East
Springfield, IL 62794
800 843-6154
http://www.dhs.state.il.us/ors
Disability Served: various

Illinois Fair Employment Practice Agency
100 West Randolph, Suite 10-100
Chicago, IL 60601
312-814-6245, 800-662-3942
http://www.state.il.us/dhr
Disability Served: various

Jewish Vocational Services
216 West Jackson Boulevard, Suite 700
Chicago, IL 60606
312-673-3400
jvshr@jvschicago.org
http://www.jvschicago.org
Disability Served: various

Jo Daviess Workshop Inc.
706 West Street
Galena, IL 61036
815-777-2211
jdwi@jdwi.org
http://www.jdwi.org
Disability Served: various

Kankakee County Training Center
333 South Schuyler Avenue
Bradley, IL 60915
815-932-4022
Disability Served: various

Lambs Farm
14245 West Rockland Road
Libertyville, IL 60048
847-362-4636
http://www.lambsfarm.org
Disability Served: developmentally disabled

Occupational Development Center
1201 East Bell Street
Bloomington, IL 61701
309-820-0891 (Voice/TDD)
http://www.ODCworks.com
Disability Served: various

Pioneer Center of McHenry County
4001 Dayton Street
McHenry, IL 60050
815-344-1230
http://www.pioneercenter.org
Disability Served: various

Sertoma Centre
4343 West 123rd Street
Alsip, IL 60803
708-371-9700
info@sertomacentre.org
http://www.sertomacentre.org
Disability Served: various

Shore Training Center
8035 North Austin Avenue
Morton Grove, IL 60053
847-581-0200
shoretrctr@fsi.net
Disability Served: various

Skills Inc.
1122 Fifth Avenue
Moline, IL 61265
309-797-3586
Disability Served: various

St. Coletta's of Illinois Foundation
18350 Crossing Drive, Suite 103
Tinley Park, IL 60477
708-342-5246
info@stcolettail.org
http://www.stcolettail.org
Disability Served: developmentally disabled

**United States Equal Employment Opportunity
    Commission (Chicago District Office)**
500 West Madison Street, Suite 2800
Chicago, IL 60661
312-353-2713, 312-353-2421 (TTY)
Disability Served: various

Washington County Vocational Workshop
781 East Holzhauer Drive, PO Box 273
Nashville, IL 62263
618-327-4461
Disability Served: developmentally disabled, mental
    health

INDIANA
**Easter Seals Indiana Crossroads Rehabilitation
    Center**
4740 Kingsway Drive
Indianapolis, IN 46205-1521
Disability Served: various

Indiana Civil Rights Commission
100 North Senate Avenue, Room N103
Indianapolis, IN 46204
317-232-2600, 800-628-2909
http://www.state.in.us/icrc
Disability Served: various

Indiana Department of Labor
402 West Washington Street, Room W195
Indianapolis, IN 46204
800-743-3333 (Voice/TTY)
http://www.in.gov/labor
Disability Served: various

Indiana Department of Workforce Development
10 North Senate Avenue
Indianapolis, IN 46214
888-WORK-ONE
http://www.in.gov/dwd/workforce_serv/workone
Disability Served: various

**Indiana Governor's Council for People with
   Disabilities**
150 West Market Street, Suite 628
Indianapolis, IN 46204
317-232-7770
GPCPD@gpcpd.org
http://www.in.gov/gpcpd
Disability Served: various

Indiana Vocational Rehabilitation Agency
402 West Washington Street, Room W-451, PO Box 7083
Indianapolis, IN 46207
317-232-1147
scook3@fssa.state.in.us
http://www.in.gov/fssa/servicedisabl/ddars
Disability Served: various

Michiana Resources Inc.
4315 East Michigan Boulevard
Michigan City, IN 46360
219-874-4288
michiana@michianaresources.com
http://www.michianaresources.org
Disability Served: various

**United States Equal Employment Opportunity
   Commission (Indianapolis District Office)**
101 West Ohio Street, Suite 1900
Indianapolis, IN 46204

317-226-7212, 317-226-5162 (TTY)
Disability Served: various

IOWA

Easter Seals Iowa Center
2920 30th Street
Des Moines, IA 50310
515-274-1529, 515-274-8348 (TTY)
info@eastersealsia.org
http://www.ia.easterseals.com
Disability Served: various

Iowa Civil Rights Commission
400 East 14th Street
Des Moines, IA 50319
515-281-4121
http://www.state.ia.us/government/crc
Disability Served: various

Iowa Division of Persons with Disabilities
321 East 12th Street
Des Moines, IA 50319
888-219-0471 (Voice/TTY)
dhr.disabilities@iowa.gov
http://www.state.ia.us/government/dhr/pd
Disability Served: various

Iowa Vocational Rehabilitation Services
510 East 12th Street
Des Moines, IA 50319
515-281-4211 (Voice/TTY)
http://www.dvrs.state.ia.us
Disability Served: various

Iowa Workforce Development
1000 East Grand Avenue
Des Moines, IA 50319-0209
800-JOB-IOWA, 800-831-1399 (TTY)
http://www.iowaworkforce.org
Disability Served: various

Options of Linn County
1019 7th Street, SE
Cedar Rapids, IA 52401
319-892-5800
options@linncounty.org
http://www.co.linn.ia.us/dhrm/options
Disability Served: various

KANSAS

Big Lakes Developmental Center Inc.
1416 Hayes Drive
Manhattan, KS 66502
785-776-9201
http://www.biglakes.org
Disability Served: developmentally disabled

Easter Seals Kansas
3636 North Oliver
Wichita, KS 67220
888-337-6287, 316-744-0158 (TTY)
http://www.easterseals.com/site/PageServer?JServSess
  ionIdr005=o1kwp7gsc1.app26b&pagename=KSDR_
  homepage
Disability Served: various

Kansas Commission on Disability Concerns
1430 Southwest Topeka Boulevard
Topeka, KS 66612-1877
785-296-1722
http://www.hr.state.ks.us/dc
Disability Served: various

**Kansas Department of Social and Rehabilitation
  Services**
915 Harrison Street
Topeka, KS 66612
785-296-3777, 785-296-1491 (TTY)
http://www.srskansas.org/rehab
Disability Served: various

**Rehabilitation Engineering Research Center
  on Modifications to Worksites**
Cerebral Palsy Research Foundation of Kansas Inc.
5111 East 21st Street N
Wichita, KS 67208
316-688-1888
info@cprf.org
http://www.cprf.org
Disability Served: various

**United States Equal Employment Opportunity
  Commission (Kansas City Area Office)**
4th & State Avenue, 9th Floor
Kansas City, KS 66101
913-551-5655, 913-551-5657 (TTY)
Disability Served: various

KENTUCKY

Easter Seals Employment Connections-Pennyrile
755 Industrial Road
Madisonville, KY 42431
270-625-4840
Disability Served: various

**Kentucky Committee on Employment of People
  with Disabilities**
275 East Main Street, 2nd Floor West
Frankfort, KY 40621
502-564-5331 (Voice/TTY)
Disability Served: various

**Kentucky Department for Employment Service
  and Job Training Program Liaison**
275 East Main Street, 2-West
Frankfort, KY 40621
502-564-5331
Disability Served: various

Kentucky Department of Labor
1047 US Highway 127 South, Suite 4
Frankfort, KY 40601
502-564-3070
http://www.kylabor.net
Disability Served: various

Kentucky Office for the Blind
209 St. Clair Street, PO Box 757
Frankfort, KY 40602-0757
800-321-6668, 502-564-2929 (TDD)
http://blind.ky.gov
Disability Served: vision

Kentucky Office of Vocational Rehabilitation
209 St. Clare Street
Frankfort, KY 40601
502-564-4440 (Voice/TTY)
wfd.vocrehab@mail.state.ky.us
http://ovr.ky.gov
Disability Served: various

Pioneer Vocational/Industrial Services
590 Stanford Road
Danville, KY 40422
859-236-8413, 859-236-1251 (TTY)
pioneer@pioneerservices.org
http://www.pioneerservices.org
Disability Served: various

United States Equal Employment Opportunity Commission (Louisville Area Office)
600 Dr. Martin Luther King, Jr. Place, Suite 268
Louisville, KY 40202
502-582-6082, 502-582-6285 (TTY)
Disability Served: various

LOUSIANA

Jefferson Parish Workforce Connection
1900 Lafayette Street
Gretna, LA 70053
504-227-1283
http://www.jeffparish.net/index.cfm?DocID=1164
Disability Served: various

Louisiana Department of Labor
1001 North 23rd Street
Baton Rouge, LA 70804-9094
225-342-3111, 800-259-5154 (TDD)
http://www.ldol.state.la.us
Disability Served: various

Louisiana Governor's Office of Disability Affairs
PO Box 94004
Baton Rouge, LA 70804
225-219-7547, 225-219-7550 (TTY)
disabilityaffairs@gov.state.la.us
http://www.gov.state.la.us/disabilityaffairs/default.asp
Disability Served: various

Louisiana Rehabilitation Services
3651 Cedarcrest Avenue
Baton Rouge, LA 70816-4010
800-737-2959
http://www.dss.state.la.us/departments/lrs/Vocational_
    Rehabilitation.html
Disability Served: various

Port City Enterprises
836 North 7th Street
Port Allen, LA 70767
504-344-1142
Disability Served: various

United States Equal Employment Opportunity Commission (New Orleans District Office)
701 Loyola Avenue, Suite 600
New Orleans, LA 70113-9936

504-589-2329, 504-589-2958 (TTY)
Disability Served: various

MAINE

Creative Work Systems
443 Congress Street
Portland, ME 04101
207-879-1140
cws@gwi.net
http://www.creativeworksystems.com
Disability Served: various

Maine Bureau of Rehabilitation Services
150 State House Station
Augusta, ME 04333-0150
207-624-5950, 888 755-0023 (TTY)
http://www.state.me.us/rehab
Disability Served: various

Maine Department of Labor
PO Box 259
Augusta, ME 04332-0259
207-624-6400, 800-794-1110 (TTY)
mdol@maine.gov
http://www.state.me.us/labor
Disability Served: various

Maine Human Rights Commission
51 State House Station
Augusta, ME 04333-0051
207-624-6050, 207-624-6064 (TTY/TTD)
http://www.state.me.us/mhrc
Disability Served: various

Northeast Occupational Exchange Inc.
29 Franklin Street
Bangor, ME 04401
207-942-3816, 800-857-0500, 207-992-2248 (TTY)
http://www.noemaine.org
Disability Served: chemical dependency, mental health

MARYLAND

Ardmore Enterprises Inc.
3010 Lottsford Vista Road
Mitchellsville, MD 20721
301-577-2575
Disability Served: various

Blind Industries and Services of Maryland

3345 Washington Boulevard
Baltimore, MD 21227
410-737-2600, 888-322-4567
http://bism.org
Disability Served: vision

Goodwill Industries International Inc.

15810 Indianola Drive
Rockville, MD 20855
301-530-6500
ContactUs@goodwill.org
http://www.goodwill.org
Disability Served: various

Maryland Department of Disabilities

217 East Redwood Street, Suite 1300
Baltimore, MD 21202
410-767-3660 (Voice/TTY), 800-637-4113 (Voice/TTY)
mdod@mdod.state.md.us
http://www.mdtap.org/oid.html
Disability Served: various

Maryland Department of Labor, Licensing, and Regulation

500 North Calvert Street, #401
Baltimore, MD 21202
410-230-6001
http://www.dllr.state.md.us
Disability Served: various

Maryland Division of Rehabilitation Services

2301 Argonne Drive
Baltimore, MD 21218-1696
888-554-0334, 410-554-9411 (TTY)
dors@dors.state.md.us
http://www.dors.state.md.us/dors
Disability Served: various

National Federation of the Blind

1800 Johnson Street
Baltimore, MD 21230
410-659-9314
nfb@nfb.org
http://www.nfb.org/default.htm
Disability Served: vision

TransCen Inc.

451 Hungerford Drive, Suite 700
Rockville, MD 20850
301-424-2002, 301-309-2435 (TDD)
inquiries@transcen.org
http://www.transcen.org
Disability Served: various

United States Equal Employment Opportunity Commission (Baltimore District Office)

10 South Howard Street, Third Floor
Baltimore, MD 21201
410-962-3932, 410-962-6065 (TTY)
Disability Served: various

MASSACHUSETTS

Easter Seals Massachusetts

89 South Street
Boston, MA 02111
800-244-2756, 800-564-9700 (TTY)
http://ma.easterseals.com
Disability Served: various

Gateway Arts

Vinfen Corporation
60-62 Harvard Street
Brookline, MA 02445
617-734-1577
gatewayarts@vinfen.org
http://www.gatewayarts.org
Disability Served: various

Just-A-Start Summer Program

432 Columbia Street
Cambridge, MA 02141
617-494-0444
info@justastart.org
http://www.justastart.org
Disability Served: various

Massachusetts Commission for the Blind

48 Boylston Street
Boston, MA 02116-4718
800-392-6450, 800-392-6556 (TTY)
http://www.mass.gov/mcb
Disability Served: vision

Massachusetts Departments of Labor and Workforce Development

One Ashburton Place, Room 2112
Boston, MA 02108

617-727-6573, 617-727-4404 (TTY)
dlwd@state.ma.us
http://www.mass.gov/dlwd
Disability Served: various

**Massachusetts Governor's Commission on
     Employment of People with Disabilities**
19 Stanford Street, 3rd Floor
Boston, MA 02114
617-626-5190
Disability Served: various

Massachusetts Rehabilitation Commission
27 Wormwood Street
Boston, MA 02210-1616
800-245-6543 (Voice/TDD)
http://www.mass.gov/portal/index.jsp?pageID=eohhs2
     agencylanding&L=4&L0=Home&L1=Government&
     L2=Departments+and+Divisions&L3=Massachuset
     ts+Rehabilitation+Commission&sid=Eeohhs2
Disability Served: various

**United States Equal Employment Opportunity
     Commission (Boston Area Office)**
475 Government Center
Boston, MA 02203
617-565-3200, 617-565-3204 (TTY)
Disability Served: various

Work Inc.
3 Arlington Street
North Quincy, MA 02171
617-691-1500
workinc@workinc.org
http://www.workinc.org
Disability Served: various

MICHIGAN

Christian Horizons Inc.
PO Box 3381
Grand Rapids, MI 49501-3381
616-956-7063
info@christianhorizonsinc.org
http://www.christianhorizonsinc.org
Disability Served: developmentally disabled

Michigan Commission for the Blind Training Center
1541 Oakland Drive
Kalamazoo, MI 49008

269-337-3848
http://www.michigan.gov/cis/0,1607,7-154-28077_
     28313_33124-110979--,00.html
Disability Served: vision

Michigan Commission on Disability Concerns
320 North Washington Square
Lansing, MI 48913
517-334-8000, 877-499-6232
mcdc@michigan.gov
http://www.michigan.gov/cis/0,1607,7-154-28077_
     28545---,00.html
Disability Served: various

Michigan Department of Labor and Economic Growth
611 West Ottawa, PO Box 30004
Lansing, MI 48909
517-373-1820
http://www.michigan.gov/cis
Disability Served: various

Michigan Rehabilitation Services
201 North Washington Square, 4th Floor, PO Box 30010
Lansing, MI 48909
800-605-6722, 888-605-6722 (TTY)
http://www.michigan.gov/mdcd/0,1607,7-122-25392---
     ,00.html
Disability Served: various

Mid-Michigan Industries Inc.
2426 Parkway Drive
Mt Pleasant, MI 48858
517-773-6918
clerical@mmionline
http://www.mmionline.com
Disability Served: various

**United States Equal Employment Opportunity
     Commission (Detroit District Office)**
477 Michigan Avenue, Room 865
Detroit, MI 48226
313-226-4600, 313-226-7599 (TTY)
Disability Served: various

MINNESOTA

AccessAbility Inc.
360 Hoover Street, NE
Minneapolis, MN 55413
612-331-5958

http://www.accessability.org
Disability Served: various

Choice Inc.
470 Water Street
Excelsior, MN 55331
952-474-9510
http://www.choicejobs.org
Disability Served: developmentally disabled

Courage Center Courageworks
3915 Golden Valley Road
Golden Valley, MN 55422-4249
888-846-8253
courageinfo@courage.org
http://www.courage.org
Disability Served: physically disabled

Goodwill/Easter Seals Minnesota
553 Fairview Avenue
St. Paul, MN 55104
651-379-5800, 800-669-6719
http://mnges.easterseals.com
Disability Served: various

Goodwill Industries Vocational Enterprises
700 Garfield Avenue
Duluth, MN 55802
218-722-6351
Disability Served: various

Jewish Family and Children's Service of Minneapolis
13100 Wayzata Boulevard, Suite 400
Minnetonka, MN 55305
952-591-0300
http://www.iajvs.org
Disability Served: various

Lambert Vocational Services
375 East Kellogg Boulevard
Saint Paul, MN 55101-1411
651-225-9425, 651-290-4615 (TTY)
info@lambertvocational.com
http://www.lambertvocational.com
Disability Served: various

Minnesota Department of Labor and Industry
443 Lafayette Road North
St. Paul, MN 55155-4307
800-342-5354, 651-297-4198 (TTY)

http://www.doli.state.mn.us
Disability Served: various

Minnesota Rehabilitation Services Branch
332 Minnesota Street, Suite E200
St Paul, MN 55101
800-328-9095, 800-657-3973 (TTY)
http://www.deed.state.mn.us/rehab/vr/main_vr.htm
Disability Served: various

Minnesota State Council on Disability
121 East 7th Place, Suite 107
St. Paul, MN 55101
651-296-6785 (Voice/TTY), 800-945-8913 (Voice/TTY)
http://www.disability.state.mn.us
Disability Served: various

Minnesota State Services for the Blind
2200 University Avenue, Suite 240
Saint Paul, MN 55114
800-652-9000 (Voice/TTY)
http://www.mnssb.org
Disability Served: vision

United States Equal Employment Opportunity Commission (Minneapolis Area Office)
330 South Second Avenue, Suite 430
Minneapolis, MN 55401-2224
612-335-4040, 612-335-4045 (TTY)
Disability Served: various

MISSISSIPPI

Mississippi Department of Rehabilitation Services
PO Box 1698
Jackson, MS 39215-1698
http://www.mdrs.state.ms.us/about
Disability Served: various

Mississippi Office of Special Disability Programs
1281 Highway 51 North
Madison, MS 39110
http://www.mdrs.state.ms.us/client/ind_general.html
Disability Served: various

United States Equal Employment Opportunity Commission (Jackson Area Office)
100 West Capitol Street, Suite 207
Jackson, MS 39269
601-965-4537, 601-965-4915 (TTY)
Disability Served: various

MISSOURI

Adaptive Computer and Communication Technology Program
The Rehabilitation Institute
3011 Baltimore
Kansas City, MO 64108
816-751-7950
dana.chatlin@rehabkc.org
http://www.rehabkc.org
Disability Served: various

Missouri Assistive Technology
4731 South Cochise, Suite 114
Independence, MO 64055-6975
816-373-5193, 816-373-9315 (TTY)
matpmo@swbell.net
http://www.at.mo.gov
Disability Served: various

Missouri Department of Labor and Industrial Relations
3315 West Truman Boulevard, Room 213,
   PO Box 504
Jefferson City, MO 65102-0504
573-751-4091
publicaffairs@dolir.mo.gov
http://www.dolir.state.mo.us
Disability Served: various

Missouri Division of Vocational Rehabilitation
3024 Dupont Circle
Jefferson City, MO 65109-0525
877-222-8963, 573-751-0881 (TDD)
http://www.vr.dese.state.mo.us
Disability Served: various

Missouri Governor's Council on Disability
301 West High Street, Room 250-A, PO Box 1668
Jefferson City, MO 65102
573-751-2600, 800-877-8249 (Voice/TTY)
beth.whaley@oa.mo.gov
http://www.gcd.oa.mo.gov
Disability Served: various

Missouri Rehabilitation Services for the Blind
615 Howerton Court, PO Box 2320
Jefferson City, MO 65102
573-751-4249, 800-735-2966 (TTD)
http://dss.missouri.gov/fsd/rsb
Disability Served: vision

United States Equal Employment Opportunity Commission (St. Louis District Office)
1222 Spruce Street, Room 8.100
St. Louis, MO 63103
314-539-7800, 314-539-7803 (TTY)
Disability Served: various

MONTANA

Displaced Homemaker Program
Walt Sullivan Building, 1327 Lockey, PO Box 1728
Helena, MT 59624
406-444-4100
Disability Served: various

Easter Seals-Goodwill
4400 Central Avenue
Great Falls, MT 59405
406-761-3680
gwbillings@mcn.net
http://esgw-nrm.easterseals.com
Disability Served: various

Montana Department of Labor and Industry
PO Box 1728
Helena, MT 59624-1728
406-444-2840
dliquestions@mt.gov
http://dli.state.mt.us
Disability Served: various

Montana Disability Services Division
111 Sanders, Suite 307, PO Box 4210
Helena, MT 59604-4210
406-444-2590 (Voice/TTY), 877-296-1197
http://www.dphhs.mt.gov/dsd
Disability Served: various

Montana Governor's Advisory Council on Disability
PO Box 200127
Helena, MT 59620-0127
406-444-3794
Disability Served: various

NEBRASKA

Easter Seals Nebraska
2727 West 2nd, Suite 471
Hastings, NE 68901
800-650-9880, 402-462-4721 (TTY)

http://ne.easterseals.com
Disability Served: various

Nebraska Department of Labor
550 South 16th Street, PO Box 94600
Lincoln, NE 68509-4600
402-471-2600
http://www.dol.state.ne.us
Disability Served: various

Nebraska Governor's Committee on Employment of People with Disabilities
PO Box 94600
Lincoln, NE 68509
402-471-3405
Disability Served: various

Nebraska Vocational Rehabilitation
PO Box 94987
Lincoln, NE 68509
402-471-3644, 877-637-3422
s_chapin@vocrehab.state.ne.us
http://www.vocrehab.state.ne.us
Disability Served: various

NEVADA
Easter Seals Southern Nevada
6200 West Oakey Boulevard
Las Vegas, NV 89146
702-870-7050, 702-870-7050 (TTY)
info@eastersealssn.org
http://sn.easterseals.com
Disability Served: various

Nevada Bureau of Services to the Blind and Visually Impaired
1933 North Carson Street
Carson City, NV 89701
775-684-0432
http://detr.state.nv.us/rehab/bvi_offl.htm
Disability Served: vision

Nevada Department of Employment, Training, and Rehabilitation
500 East 3rd Street
Carson City, NV 89713
775-684-3911, 775-687-5353 (TTY)
http://detr.state.nv.us
Disability Served: various

Nevada Division of Rehabilitation
505 East King Street, Room 502
Carson City, NV 89701-3705
775-684-4040, 775-684-8400 (TTY)
detrvr@nvdetr.org
http://www.detr.state.nv.us/rehab/reh_index.htm
Disability Served: various

Nevada Fair Employment Practice Agency
1515 East Tropicana, Suite 590
Las Vegas, NV 89158
702-486-7161
http://detr.state.nv.us/nerc/NERC_index.htm
Disability Served: various

Nevada Governor's Committee on the Employment of People with Disabilities
4001 Kietzke Lane, Suite F-154
Reno, NV 89502
775-688-1111
http://www.state.nv.us/b&i/gb
Disability Served: various

NEW HAMPSHIRE
Easter Seals New Hampshire
555 Auburn Street
Manchester, NH 03103
603-623-8863
http://nh.easterseals.com
Disability Served: various

New Hampshire Bureau of Vocational Rehabilitation
21 South Fruit Street
Concord, NH 03301
603-271-3471 (Voice/TTY), 800-339-9900
http://www.ed.state.nh.us/VR
Disability Served: various

New Hampshire Department of Labor
95 Pleasant Street
Concord, NH 03301
603-271-3176
http://www.labor.state.nh.us
Disability Served: various

New Hampshire Employment Security
32 South Main Street
Concord, NH 03301
603-228-4191, 800-852-3400

http://www.nhes.state.nh.us
Disability Served: various

**New Hampshire Governor's Commission
  on Disability**
57 Regional Drive
Concord, NH 03301
603-271-2773 (Voice/TTY), 800-852-3405
http://www.state.nh.us/disability
Disability Served: various

New Hampshire Human Rights Commission
2 Chenell Drive
Concord, NH 03301
603-271-2767
http://www.state.nh.us/hrc
Disability Served: various

NEW JERSEY
Easter Seals New Jersey
1 Kimberley Road
East Brunswick, NJ 08816
732-257-66626
http://nj.easterseals.com
Disability Served: various

First Occupational Center of New Jersey
391 Lakeside Avenue
Orange, NJ 07050
973-672-5800
info@ocnj.org
http://www.ocnj.org
Disability Served: various

LIFT Inc.
PO Box 4264
Warren, NJ 07059
908-707-9840
liftinc@aol.com
http://www.lift-inc.org
Disability Served: physically disabled

**New Jersey Commission for the Blind and Visually
  Impaired**
153 Halsey Street, 6th Floor, PO Box 47017
Newark, NJ 07101
973-648-2324, 973-648-3333
 http://www.state.nj.us/humanservices/cbvi
Disability Served: vision

**New Jersey Department of Labor and Workforce
  Development**
PO Box 110
Trenton, NJ 08625-0110
http://www.state.nj.us/labor
Disability Served: various

**New Jersey Division of Vocational Rehabilitation
  Services**
135 East State Street, PO Box 398
Trenton, NJ 08625-0398
609-292-5987, 609-292-2919 (TTY)
http://www.wnjpin.state.nj.us
Disability Served: various

**United States Equal Employment Opportunity
  Commission (Newark Area Office)**
One Newark Center, 21st Floor
Newark, NJ 07102-5233
973-645-6383, 973-645-3004 (TTY)
Disability Served: various

NEW MEXICO
**New Mexico Department of Labor, Job Training
  Division**
1596 Pacheco Street, PO Box 4218
Santa Fe, NM 87502
505-827-6827
http://www.dol.state.nm.us
Disability Served: various

New Mexico Division of Vocational Rehabilitation
435 St Michael's Drive, Building D
Santa Fe, NM 87505
505-827-3500, 800-224-7005
http://www.state.nm.us/dvr
Disability Served: various

**New Mexico Governor's Committee on Concerns
  of the Handicapped**
491 Old Santa Fe Trail, Suite 117
Santa Fe, NM 87501
505-827-6465, 505-827-6329 (TDD)
http://www.state.nm.us/gcch/gcch.htm
Disability Served: various

**United States Equal Employment Opportunity
  Commission (Albuquerque Area Office)**
505 Marquette, NW, Suite 900, 9th Floor
Albuquerque, NM 87102

505-248-5201, 505-248-5240 (TTY)
Disability Served: various

NEW YORK

Easter Seals New York
11 West 42nd Street
New York, NY 10036
800-727-8785
info@ny.easter-seals.org
http://ny.easterseals.com
Disability Served: various

Fedcap Rehabilitation Services Inc.
211 West 14th Street
New York, NY 10011
212-727-4200, 212-727-4384 (TTY)
info@fedcap.org
http://www.fedcap.org
Disability Served: various

Industries for the Blind of New York State
518-456-8671, 800-421-9010
info@ibnys.org
http://www.ibnys.org
Disability Served: vision

Just One Break Inc.
120 Wall Street, 20th Floor
New York, NY 10005
212-785-7300, 212-785-4515 (TTY)
http://www.justonebreak.com
Disability Served: various

National Business and Disability Council
201 I.U. Willets Road
Albertson, NY 11507
516-465-1515
http://www.business-disability.com
Disability Served: various

National Technical Institute for the Deaf Center on Employment
52 Lomb Memorial Drive
Rochester, NY 14623-5604
585-475-6219 (Voice/TTY)
ntidcoe@rit.edu
http://www.ntid.rit.edu/nce
Disability Served: hearing

New York Commission for the Blind and Visually Handicapped
40 North Pearl Street
Albany, NY 11243
518-474-7079, 518-474-7501 (TTY)
http://www.ocfs.state.ny.us/main/cbvh
Disability Served: vision

New York Employment Services and Job Training Program Liaison
State Office Building Campus, Room 288
Albany, NY 12240
518-457-2741
Disability Served: various

New York State Department of Labor
State Office Building Campus, Room 500
Albany, NY 12240-0003
518-457-9000
http://www.labor.state.ny.us
Disability Served: various

New York State Vocational and Educational Services for Individuals with Disabilities
One Commerce Plaza
Albany, NY 12234
518-474-2714, 800-222-5627
http://www.vesid.nysed.gov
Disability Served: various

United States Equal Employment Opportunity Commission (Buffalo Local Office)
6 Fountain Plaza, Suite 350
Buffalo, NY 14202
716-551-4441, 716-551-5923 (TTY)
Disability Served: various

United States Equal Employment Opportunity Commission (New York District Office)
33 Whitehall Street
New York, NY 10004
212-336-3620, 212-336-3622 (TTY)
Disability Served: various

NORTH CAROLINA

Easter Seals UCP North Carolina
2315 Myron Drive
Raleigh, NC 27607-3399
800-662-7119

info@nc.eastersealsucp.com
http://nc.easterseals.com
Disability Served: various

North Carolina Department of Labor
1101 Mail Service Center
Raleigh, NC 27699-1101
800-NCLABOR
http://www.dol.state.nc.us
Disability Served: various

North Carolina Division of Services for the Blind
2601 Mail Service Center, 309 Ashe Avenue
Raleigh, NC 27699
919-733-9822
Disability Served: vision

North Carolina Division of Vocational Rehabilitation
803 Mail Service Center 27699
Raleigh, NC 27611
919-733-7807, 800-215-7227
http://dvr.dhhs.state.nc.us
Disability Served: various

North Carolina Employment Network
2801 Mail Service Center
Raleigh, NC 27699
919-855-3500
Disability Served: various

North Carolina Governor's Advocacy Council for Persons with Disabilities
1314 Mail Service Center
Raleigh, NC 27699-1314
919-733-9250
http://www.gacpd.com
Disability Served: various

Rowan County Vocational Workshop Inc.
642 South Shaver Street, PO Box 137
Salisbury, NC 28145
704-633-6223
Disability Served: various

Rutherford Life Service
230 Fairground Road
Spindale, NC 28160
828-286-4352
elbrown@rutherfordlifeservices.com
http://www.rutherfordlifeservices.com
Disability Served: developmentally disabled, mental health

Transylvania Vocational Services Inc.
11 Mountain Industrial Drive, PO Box 1115
Brevard, NC 28712
828-884-3195
http://www.tvsinc.org
Disability Served: various

United States Equal Employment Opportunity Commission (Charlotte District Office)
129 West Trade Street, Suite 400
Charlotte, NC 28202
704-344-6682, 704-344-6684 (TTY)
Disability Served: various

United States Equal Employment Opportunity Commission (Greensboro Local Office)
2303 West Meadowview Road, Suite 201
Greensboro, NC 27407
336-547-4188, 336-547-4035 (TTY)
Disability Served: various

United States Equal Employment Opportunity Commission (Raleigh Area Office)
1309 Annapolis Drive
Raleigh, NC 27608-2129
919-856-4064, 919-856-4296 (TTY)
Disability Served: various

Webster Enterprises Inc.
PO Box 220
Webster, NC 28788
828-586-8981
Disability Served: various

NORTH DAKOTA

North Dakota Department of Labor
600 East Boulevard Avenue, Department 406
Bismarck, ND 58505-0340
800-582-8032, 800-366-6888 (TTY)
labor@state.nd.us
http://www.state.nd.us/labor
Disability Served: various

North Dakota Employment Service and Job Training Program Liaison
Job Service North Dakota
1000 East Divide Avenue, PO Box 5507
Bismarck, ND 58506
701-328-2836
Disability Served: various

North Dakota Governor's Committee on Employment of Disabled Persons
600 South 2nd Street, Suite 1B
Bismarck, ND 58504
701-328-8952
Disability Served: various

North Dakota Vocational Rehabilitation Agency
600 East Boulevard Avenue, Department 325
Bismarck, ND 58505
701-328-2310
http://discovernd.com
Disability Served: various

OHIO

Cornucopia Inc.
18120 Sloane Avenue
Lakewood, OH 44107
216-521-4600
chris.yurick@cornucopia-inc.org
http://www.cornucopia-inc.org
Disability Served: various

Cuyahoga East Vocational Education Consortium
211 Alpha Park Drive
Highland Heights, OH 44143
440-995-7450
http://www.mayfield.k12.oh.us/schools/cevec
Disability Served: various

Easter Seals West Central Ohio
1511 Kuntz Road
Dayton, OH 45404
937-461-4800, 937-461-4447 (TTY)
communications@goodwilldayton.org
http://www.eastersealswestcentralohio.org
Disability Served: various

Ohio Governor's Council on People with Disabilities
400 East Campus View Boulevard
Columbus, OH 43235
800-282-4536, ext. 1391, 614-438-1391 (Voice/TTD)
http://gcpd.ohio.gov
Disability Served: various

Ohio Rehabilitation Services Commission
400 East Campus View Boulevard
Columbus, OH 43235
614-438-1200 (Voice/ TTY)
http://www.state.oh.us/rsc
Disability Served: various

United States Equal Employment Opportunity Commission (Cincinnati Area Office)
550 Main Street, 10th Floor
Cincinnati, OH 45202
513-684-2851, 513-684-2074 (TTY)
Disability Served: various

United States Equal Employment Opportunity Commission (Cleveland District Office)
1660 West Second Street, Suite 850
Cleveland, OH 44113-1412
216-522-2003, 216-522-8441 (TTY)
Disability Served: various

OKLAHOMA

National Clearinghouse of Rehabilitation Training Materials
206 West Sixth Street
Stillwater, OK 74078-4080
405-744-2000, 800-223-5219, 405-744-2002 (TDD)
http://www.nchrtm.okstate.edu
Disability Served: various

Oklahoma Department of Labor
4001 North Lincoln Boulevard
Oklahoma City, OK 73105
405-528-1500, 888-269-5353
http://www.state.ok.us/~okdol
Disability Served: various

Oklahoma Department of Rehabilitation Services
3535 Northwest 58th Street, Suite 500
Oklahoma City, OK 73112
405-951-3400, 800-845-8476
http://www.okrehab.org
Disability Served: various

Oklahoma Governor's Committee on Employment of People with Disabilities
2401 Northwest 23rd Street, Suite 90
Oklahoma City, OK 73107
405-521-3756 (Voice/TTY)
http://www.state.ok.us/~ohc
Disability Served: various

United States Equal Employment Opportunity Commission (Oklahoma Area Office)
210 Park Avenue, Suite 1350
Oklahoma City, OK 73102
405-231-4911, 405-231-5745 (TTY)
Disability Served: various

OREGON

Easter Seals CARES
5757 Southwest Macadam Avenue
Portland, OR 97239
503-228-5108
CARES@or.easterseals.com
http://or.easterseals.com
Disability Served: various

Hiring Individuals Ready for Employment
155 Cottage Street, NE U-30
Salem, OR 97301
503-378-8344, 503-378-4672 (TTY)
hrsd.information@state.or.us
http://www.oregon.gov/DAS/HR/hire.shtml
Disability Served: various

Oregon Bureau of Labor and Industries
800 Northeast Oregon Street, Suite 1045
Portland, OR 97232
503-731-4200
BOLI.MAIL@state.or.us
http://www.boli.state.or.us
Disability Served: various

Oregon Disabilities Commission
1257 Ferry Street, SE
Salem, OR 97301
503-378-3142 (Voice/TTY)
http://www.odc.state.or.us
Disability Served: various

Oregon Fair Employment Practice Agency
800 Northeast Oregon, Suite 1045
Portland, OR 97232
503-731-4200
http://egov.oregon.gov/BOLI/CRD/about_us.shtml
Disability Served: various

Oregon Industries for the Blind
905 Southeast Ankeny Street
Portland, OR 97214
503-236-2147
http://home.teleport.com/~oib
Disability Served: vision

Oregon Office of Vocational Rehabilitation Services
500 Summer Street, NE, E-87
Salem, OR 97310-1018
877-277-0513, 503-945-5894 (TTY)
vrinfo@state.or.us
http://www.oregon.gov/DHS/vr
Disability Served: various

PENNSYLVANIA

Devereux National Vocational Rehabilitation Center
444 Devereux Drive, PO Box 638
Villanova, PA 19085
800-345-1292
http://www.devereux.org
Disability Served: various

Easter Seals of Southeastern Pennsylvania
3975 Conshohocken Avenue
Philadelphia, PA 19131
215-879-1000
http://sepa.easterseals.com
Disability Served: various

Pennsylvania Department of Labor and Industry
7th and Forster Streets, Room 1700
Harrisburg, PA 17120
717-787-5279
http://www.dli.state.pa.us
Disability Served: various

Pennsylvania Governor's Committee on Employment of People with Disabilities
1521 North Sixth Street
Harrisburg, PA 17102
717-772-1658, 717-787-4885 (TTY)
Disability Served: various

Pennsylvania Human Relations Commission
301 Chestnut Street, Suite 300
Harrisburg, PA 17101
717-787-4412, 717-783-9308
http://www.phrc.state.pa.us
Disability Served: various

Pennsylvania Office of Vocational Rehabilitation
Labor and Industry Building, Seventh and Forster Streets
Harrisburg, PA 17120
800-442-6351, 800-233-3008 (TTY)
ovr@dli.state.pa.us
http://www.dli.state.pa.us/ovr
Disability Served: various

United States Equal Employment Opportunity Commission (Philadelphia District Office)
21 South Fifth Street, Suite 400
Philadelphia, PA 19106

215-440-2600, 215-440-2610 (TTY)
Disability Served: various

**United States Equal Employment Opportunity
    Commission (Pittsburgh Area Office)**
1001 Liberty Avenue, Suite 300
Pittsburgh, PA 15222-4187
412-644-3444, 412-644-2720 (TTY)
Disability Served: various

RHODE ISLAND
**Rhode Island Commission on the Deaf and Hard
    of Hearing**
One Capitol Hill, Ground Level
Providence, RI 02908-5850
401-222-1204, 401-222-1205 (TTY)
cdhh@cdhh.ri.gov
http://www.cdhh.ri.gov
Disability Served: hearing

Rhode Island Department of Labor and Training
1511 Pontiac Avenue
Cranston, RI 02920
401-462-8000, 401-462-8006 (TDD)
mmadonna@dlt.state.ri.us
http://www.dlt.state.ri.us
Disability Served: various

**Rhode Island Governor's Commission on
    Disabilities**
41 Cherry Dale Court
Cranston, RI 02920
401-462-0100
http://www.gcd.state.ri.us
Disability Served: various

Rhode Island Office of Rehabilitation Services
40 Fountain Street
Providence, RI 02903
401-421-7005, 401-421-4016 (TTY)
http://www.ors.state.ri.us
Disability Served: various

SOUTH CAROLINA
**South Carolina Department of Labor, Licensing,
    and Regulation**
PO Box 11329
Columbia, SC 29211
803-896-4300

http://www.llr.state.sc.us
Disability Served: various

**South Carolina Governor's Committee on
    Employment of People with Disabilities**
1410 Boston Avenue, PO Box 15
West Columbia, SC 29171
803-896-6500
Disability Served: various

South Carolina Vocational Rehabilitation Department
1410 Boston Avenue, PO Box 15
West Columbia, SC 29171
803-896-6500
info@scvrd.state.sc.us
http://www.scvrd.net
Disability Served: various

**United States Equal Employment Opportunity
    Commission (Greenville Local Office)**
301 North Main Street, Suite 1402
Greenville, SC 29601-9916
864-241-4400, 864-241-4403 (TTY)
Disability Served: various

SOUTH DAKOTA
Black Hills Workshop and Training Center
3650 Range Road
Rapid City, SD 57702
605-343-4550
http://www.bhws.com
Disability Served: various

Easter Seals South Dakota
1351 North Harrison Avenue
Pierre, SD 57501-2373
605-224-5879
http://sd.easterseals.com
Disability Served: various

Service to the Blind and Visually Impaired
3800 East Highway 34
Pierre, SD 57501
605-773-4644 (Voice/TTY)
http://www.state.sd.us/dhs/sbvi
Disability Served: vision

South Dakota Department of Labor
700 Governors Drive
Pierre, SD 57501

605-773-3094
http://www.state.sd.us/dol
Disability Served: various

South Dakota Division of Rehabilitation Services
500 East Capitol
Pierre, SD 57501-5070
605-773-3195
eric.weiss@state.sd.us
http://www.state.sd.us/dhs/drs
Disability Served: various

South Dakota Industries for the Blind
801 North Lake Avenue
Sioux Falls, SD 57104
800-223-5145
info@sdib.org
http://www.sdib.org
Disability Served: vision

South Dakota Rehabilitation Center for the Blind
800 West Avenue North
Sioux Falls, SD 57104
605-367-5260
http://www.state.sd.us/dhs/sbvi/SDRC.htm
Disability Served: vision

TENNESSEE
Easter Seals Tennessee Adult Services
99 Monroe Street
Lexington, TN 38351
731-968-6037
eseal@netease.net
http://tn.easterseals.com
Disability Served: various

Easter Seals Tennessee AgrAbility Project (Spring City)
463 Porter Lake Road
Spring City, TN 37381
423-452-0130
http://tn.easterseals.com
Disability Served: various

Easter Seals Tennessee AgrAbility Project (Trenton)
1252 Manufacturers Row
Trenton, TN 38382
731-855-7637
http://tn.easterseals.com
Disability Served: various

Tennessee Committee for Employment of Persons with Disabilities
400 Deaderick Street
Nashville, TN 37248
615-313-4891, 615-313-5695
http://www.state.tn.us/humanserv/TCEPD.html
Disability Served: various

Tennessee Council for the Deaf and Hard of Hearing
400 Deaderick Street, 11th Floor
Nashville, TN 37248-6000
615-313-4918, 800-270-1349 (TTY)
http://www.state.tn.us/humanserv/TCDHH.htm
Disability Served: hearing

Tennessee Department of Labor and Workforce Development
Andrew Johnson Tower, 8th Floor
Nashville, TN 37243
615-741-6642
http://www.state.tn.us/labor-wfd
Disability Served: various

Tennessee Services for the Blind and Visually Impaired
400 Deaderick Street, 11th Floor
Nashville, TN 37248-6000
615-313-4914
http://www.state.tn.us/humanserv/vis-home.html
Disability Served: vision

Tennessee Vocational Rehabilitation Services
400 Deaderick Street, Citizens Plaza Building, Room 1100
Nashville, TN 37248-0001
615-313-4714
Disability Served: various

United States Equal Employment Opportunity Commission (Memphis District Office)
1407 Union Avenue, Suite 621
Memphis, TN 38104
901-544-0115, 901-544-0112 (TTY)
Disability Served: various

United States Equal Employment Opportunity Commission (Nashville Area Office)
50 Vantage Way, Suite 202
Nashville, TN 37228-9940
615-736-5820, 615-736-5870 (TTY)
Disability Served: various

TEXAS

Easter Seals Central Texas Workforce Development
315 West St. Elmo Road
Austin, TX 78745
512-440-7819
http://www.centraltx.easterseals.com
Disability Served: various

Texas Department of Assistive and Rehabilitative Services
4800 North Lamar Boulevard, 3rd Floor
Austin, TX 78756
800-252-5204
DARS.Inquiries@dars.state.tx.us
http://www.dars.state.tx.us
Disability Served: various

Texas Division for Blind Services
4800 North Lamar Boulevard
Austin, TX 78756
800-628-5115
http://www.dars.state.tx.us/dbs
Disability Served: vision

Texas Governor's Committee on People with Disabilities
PO Box 12428
Austin, TX 78711
512-463-5739, 512-463-5746 (TTY)
http://www.governor.state.tx.us/disabilities
Disability Served: various

United States Equal Employment Opportunity Commission (Dallas District Office)
207 South Houston Street, 3rd Floor
Dallas, TX 75202
214-253-2700, 214-253-2710 (TTY)
Disability Served: various

United States Equal Employment Opportunity Commission (El Paso Area Office)
300 East Main Drive, Suite 500
El Paso, TX 79901
915-534-6700, 915-534-6710 (TTY)
Disability Served: various

United States Equal Employment Opportunity Commission (Houston District Office)
1919 Smith Street, Suite 600
Houston, TX 77002-8049
713-209-3320, 713-209-3439 (TTY)
Disability Served: various

United States Equal Employment Opportunity Commission (San Antonio District Office)
5410 Fredericksburg Road, Suite 200
San Antonio, TX 78229
210-281-7600, 210-281-7610 (TTY)
Disability Served: various

UTAH

Easter Seals Utah
638 East Wilmington Avenue
Salt Lake City, UT 84106-1491
800-388-1991, 801-486-3778 (TTY)
http://ut.easterseals.com
Disability Served: various

Utah Department of Workforce Services
PO Box 45249
Salt Lake City, UT 84145
801-526-9675
dwscontactus@utah.gov
http://jobs.utah.gov/edo/dwsdefault.asp
Disability Served: various

Utah Division of Services for the Blind and Visually Impaired
PO Box 144200
Salt Lake City, UT 84114-4200
800-473-7530, 801-538-7530 (Voice/TTY)
http://www.usor.utah.gov/dsbvi.htm
Disability Served: vision

Utah Governor's Council for People with Disabilities
155 South 300 West, Suite 100
Salt Lake City, UT 84101
801-533-3965
http://www.gcpd.org
Disability Served: various

Utah State Office of Rehabilitation
250 East 500 South
Salt Lake City, UT 84111
801-538-7530
http://www.usor.state.ut.us
Disability Served: various

VERMONT

Vermont Department of Labor and Industry
National Life Building, Drawer 20
Montpelier, VT 05620-3401
802-828-2288
http://www.state.vt.us/labind
Disability Served: various

Vermont Division for the Blind and Visually Impaired
Osgood Building, 103 South Main Street
Waterbury, VT 05671
802-241-2210
http://www.dad.state.vt.us/dbvi
Disability Served: vision

Vermont Division of Vocational Rehabilitation
Osgood II Building, 103 South Main Street
Waterbury, VT 05671-2303
866-879-6757 (Voice/TTY)
janetr@dad.state.vt.us
http://www.vocrehabvermont.org
Disability Served: various

Vermont Governor's Committee on Employment of People with Disabilities
1187 Maple Street
Waterbury Center, VT 05677
802-241-2612
http://www.hireus.org
Disability Served: various

VIRGINIA

APSE: The Network on Employment
1627 Monument Avenue, Room 301
Richmond, VA 23220
804-278-9187
apse@apse.org
http://www.apse.org
Disability Served: various

Campagna Center
418 South Washington Street
Alexandria, VA 22314
703-549 0111
http://www.campagnacenter.org
Disability Served: various

Didlake Inc.
8641 Breeden Avenue
Manassas, VA 22110

703-361-4195
http://www.didlake.com
Disability Served: various

Easter Seals Virginia
201 East Main Street
Salem, VA 24153
800-365-1656
info@va.easter-seals.org
http://va.easterseals.com
Disability Served: various

National Rehabilitation Association of Job Placement and Development
633 South Washington Street
Alexandria, VA 22314
703-836-0850, 703-836-0849, 703-836-0849 (TDD)
info@nationalrehab.org
http://www.nationalrehab.org
Disability Served: various

NISH National
8401 Old Courthouse Road
Vienna, VA 22182-5200
571-226-4660
http://www.nish.org
Disability Served: various

Rehabilitation Research and Training Center on Supported Employment
Virginia Commonwealth University
1314 West Main Street, PO Box 2011
Richmond, VA 23284-2011
804-828-1851
http://www.worksupport.com
Disability Served: various

United States Equal Employment Opportunity Commission (Norfolk Area Office)
200 Granby Street, Suite 739
Norfolk, VA 23510
757-441-3470, 757-441-3578 (TTY)
Disability Served: various

United States Equal Employment Opportunity Commission (Richmond Area Office)
830 East Main Street, 6th Floor
Richmond, VA 23219
804-771-2200, 804-771-2227 (TTY)
Disability Served: various

Virginia Board for People with Disabilities
202 North 9th Street, 9th Floor
Richmond, VA 23219
800-846-4464 (Voice/TTY)
http://www.vaboard.org
Disability Served: various

Virginia Department for the Blind and Vision Impaired
397 Azalea Avenue
Richmond, VA 23227-3623
800-622-2155 (Voice/TTY)
http://www.vdbvi.org
Disability Served: vision

Virginia Department for the Deaf and Hard of Hearing
1602 Rolling Hills Drive
Richmond, VA 23229-5012
800-552-7917 (Voice/TTY)
frontdsk@vddhh.virginia.gov
http://www.vddhh.org
Disability Served: hearing

Virginia Department of Labor and Industry
13 South Thirteenth Street
Richmond, VA 23219-4101
804-371-2327, 804-786-2376 (TDD)
http://www.dli.state.va.us
Disability Served: various

Virginia Department of Rehabilitative Services
8004 Franklin Farms Drive
Richmond, VA 23288
800-552-5019
800-464-9950(TTY)
drs@drs.virginia.gov
http://vadrs.org
Disability Served: various

WASHINGTON
Easter Seals Washington
1740 Northeast Riddell Road, Suite 315
Bremerton, WA 98310-3870
360-373-2502, 360-373-2502 (TTY)
http://wa.easterseals.com
Disability Served: various

School of Piano Technology for the Blind
Building 17, Airdustrial Park, PO Box 43105
Olympia, WA 98504-3105
360-753-5673

http://www.pianotuningschool.org
Disability Served: vision

United States Equal Employment Opportunity Commission (Seattle District Office)
909 First Avenue, Suite 400
Seattle, WA 98104-1061
206-220-6883, 206-220-6882 (TTY)
Disability Served: various

Washington Department of Labor and Industries
PO Box 44000
Olympia, WA 98504-4000
800-547-8367, 360-902-5797 (TDD)
http://www.lni.wa.gov
Disability Served: various

Washington Department of Services for the Blind
402 Legion Way, Suite 100, PO Box 40933
Olympia, WA 98504-0933
800-552-7103
http://www.dsb.wa.gov
Disability Served: vision

Washington Division of Vocational Rehabilitation
PO Box 45340
Olympia, WA 98504-5340
800-637-5627, 360-438-8000
http://www1.dshs.wa.gov/dvr/aboutdvr/dvr-right-you.htm
Disability Served: various

Washington Governor's Committee on Disability Issues and Employment
PO Box 9046
Olympia, WA 98507
360-438-3168, 360-438-3167 (TTY)
http://www.wa.gov/esd/gcde
Disability Served: various

Washington Office of the Deaf and Hard of Hearing
PO Box 45301
Olympia, WA 98504-5301
800-422-7930 (Voice/TTY)
http://www1.dshs.wa.gov/hrsa/odhh
Disability Served: hearing

WEST VIRGINIA
International Center for Disability Information
PO Box 6122
Morgantown, WV 26506-6122

304-293-7186
jan@jan.wvu.edu
http://www.jan.wvu.edu
Disability Served: various

West Virginia Division of Labor
Building 6, State Capitol Complex, Room B749
Charleston, WV 25305
304-558-7890
http://www.wv.gov/offsite.aspx?u=http://www.labor.
  state.wv.us
Disability Served: various

West Virginia Division of Rehabilitation Services
State Capitol, PO Box 50890
Charleston, WV 25305-0890
304-766-4601, 800-642-8207
http://www.wvdrs.org
Disability Served: various

WISCONSIN

Easter Seals Wisconsin FARM Program
101 Nob Hill Road, Suite 301
Madison, WI 53713
800-422-2324, 608-277-8031 (TTY)
http://wi.easterseals.com
Disability Served: various

**United States Equal Employment Opportunity
  Commission (Milwaukee District Office)**
310 West Wisconsin Avenue, Suite 800
Milwaukee, WI 53203-2292
414-297-1111, 414-297-1115 (TTY)
Disability Served: various

Wisconsin Department of Workforce Development
PO Box 7946
Madison, WI 53707-7946
608-266-3131
http://www.dwd.state.wi.us
Disability Served: various

Wisconsin Division of Vocational Rehabilitation
201 East Washinton Avenue, PO Box 7852
Madison, WI 53707
608-261-0050, 800-877-5939 (TTY)
http://www.dwd.state.wi.us/dvr
Disability Served: various

**Wisconsin Governor's Committee for People
  with Disabilities**
PO Box 7851
Madison, WI 53707
608-266-7974, 608-267-9880 (TTY)
http://dhfs.wisconsin.gov/Disabilities/Physical/gcpd.htm
Disability Served: various

WYOMING

Easter Seals Wyoming-Sheridan Center
991 Joe Street
Sheridan, WY 82801
307-672-2816
http://esgw-nrm.easterseals.com
Disability Served: various

Wyoming Department of Employment
1510 East Pershing Boulevard
Cheyenne, WY 82002
http://wydoe.state.wy.us
Disability Served: various

**Wyoming Governor's Committee on Employment
  of People with Disabilities**
Herschler Building, Room 1126
Cheyenne, WY 82002
307-777-7191 (Voice/TTY)
GCHILD@missc.state.wy.us
Disability Served: various

Wyoming Vocational Rehabilitation Division
1100 Herschler Building
Cheyenne, WY 82002
307-777-7389
http://wyomingworkforce.org/who/disabled.aspx
Disability Served: various

PUERTO RICO

Puerto Rico Department of Labor
Prudencio Rivera Martínez Building
505 Muñoz Rivera Avenue, 21st Floor
Hato Rey, PR 00918
Disability Served: various

Puerto Rico Division of Vocational Rehabilitation
PO Box 191118
Hato Rey, PR 00919

787-728-6550
Disability Served: various

Puerto Rico Governor's Committee on Employment of People with Disabilities
PO Box 41309
San Juan, PR 00940
787-725-2333, ext. 2070, 787-725-4014 (TTY)
http://www.oppi.gobierno.pr
Disability Served: various

United States Equal Employment Opportunity Commission (San Juan Area Office)
525 F.D. Roosevelt Avenue, Plaza Las Americas, Suite 1202
San Juan, PR 00918-8001
787-771-1464, 787-771-1484 (TTY)
Disability Served: various

VIRGIN ISLANDS

Virgin Islands Division of Disabilities and Vocational Rehabilitation Services
1303 Hospital Ground, Knud Hansen Complex, Building A
St. Thomas, VI 00802
Disability Served: various

CANADA

Vocational and Rehabilitation Research Institute
3304 - 33 Street, NW
Calgary, AB T2L 2A6
Canada
http://www.vrri.org
Disability Served: various

WORKink
c/o Canadian Council on Rehabilitation and Work
111 Richmond Street West, Suite 401
Toronto, ON M5H 2G4
Canada
416-260-3060, 800-664-0925
http://www.workink.com
Disability Served: various

INTERNATIONAL

Global Applied Disability Research Network for Employment and Training
info@gladnet.org
http://www.gladnet.org
Disability Served: various

FUNDING RESOURCES

FUNDING FOR NONPROFITS

The following organizations and foundations provide funding to nonprofit organizations to support charitable projects and programs. Eligibility requirements vary widely.

Abbott Laboratories Fund
100 Abbott Park Road
Abbott Park, IL 60064-3500
847-937-7075
http://www.abbott.com/citizenship/fund/fund.cfm
Disability Served: various
Purpose: The fund provides grants in the areas of education, health and welfare, and culture. *Eligibility: Nonprofit organizations are eligible to apply. *Financial Details: Awards vary. *Number Awarded: Varies. *Deadline: Visit the fund's Web site to complete a grant application.

Abell-Hanger Foundation
PO Box 430
Midland, TX 79702-0430
432-684-6655
ahf@abell-hanger.org
http://www.abell-hanger.org
Disability Served: various
Purpose: The foundation provides grants in the areas of health, education, human services, arts, culture, and humanities. *Eligibility: Nonprofit organizations in Texas are eligible to apply. *Financial Details: Awards vary. *Number Awarded: Varies. *Deadlines: February, May, August, and November. Visit the foundation's Web site for more information.

Adolph Coors Foundation
4100 East Mississippi Avenue, Suite 1850
Denver, CO 80246
303-388-1636
generalinfo@acoorsfdn.org
http://www.adolphcoors.org
Disability Served: various
Purpose: The foundation provides grants in the areas of health, education, culture, youth, community, and human services. *Eligibility: Charitable organizations that have not applied for a grant from the foundation in the last year are eligible to apply. *Financial Details: Awards vary. *Number Awarded: Varies. *Deadline: Contact the foundation for additional details.

Agnes M. Lindsay Trust
660 Chestnut Street
Manchester, NH 03104

603-669-1366, 866-669-1366
admin@lindsaytrust.org
http://www.lindsaytrust.org
Disability Served: various
Purpose: The trust offers grants to fund programs in health, recreation, and education. *Eligibility: Charitable organizations in Maine, Massachusetts, New Hampshire, and Vermont that have not applied for a grant from the trust in the past 12 months are eligible to apply. *Financial Details: Amounts vary. *Number Awarded: Varies. *Deadline: Grant applications are reviewed monthly. Contact the trust for details.

Ahmanson Foundation
9215 Wilshire Boulevard
Beverly Hills, CA 90210
310-278-0770
Disability Served: various
Purpose: The foundation provides grants for the improvement of the quality of life of Los Angeles County and southern California. *Eligibility: Charitable organizations in southern California working in arts and humanities, education, medicine and health, and human services are eligible to apply. *Financial Details: Awards vary. z*Number Awarded: Varies. *Deadline: Contact the foundation for details.

The Alaska Community Foundation
701 West Eighth Avenue, Suite 230
Anchorage, AK 99501
907-265-6044
mhastings@ak.org
http://www.alaskacf.org
Disability Served: various
Purpose: The foundation provides grants to improve the quality of life in Alaska. Areas of interest include the elderly, youth, education, and the arts. *Eligibility: Nonprofits in Alaska are eligible to apply. *Financial Details: Grants rarely exceed $10,000. *Number Awarded: Varies. *Deadlines: Letters of inquiry are due April 15 and October 15. Visit the foundation's Web site for more information.

Albuquerque Community Foundation
PO Box 36960
Albuquerque, NM 87176-6960

505-883-6240
acf@albuquerquefoundation.org
http://www.albuquerquefoundation.org
Disability Served: various
Purpose: The foundation provides grants to improve the quality of life in the greater Albuquerque, New Mexico, area. Areas of interest include education, health and human services, arts and culture, and environmental and historic preservation. *Eligibility: Nonprofits that serve the greater Albuquerque area are eligible to apply. *Financial Details: Grants range from $2,000 to $20,000. *Number Awarded: Varies. *Deadline: May 2. Visit the foundation's Web site for more information.

Alexander and Margaret Stewart Trust
888 Seventeenth Street, NW, Suite 210
Washington, DC 20006-3313
Disability Served: various
Purpose: The trust provides funds for cancer treatment and the treatment of children who are physically or mentally ill, or otherwise disabled. *Eligibility: Nonprofit organizations in the Washington, D.C., area may apply. *Financial Details: Amounts vary. *Number Awarded: Varies. *Deadline: Varies. Contact the trust for details.

Alice Tweed Tuohy Foundation
PO Box 1328
Santa Barbara, CA 93102-1328
atuohyfdn@aol.com
Disability Served: various
Purpose: The foundation provides grants for the purpose of rehabilitation, recreation, or constructing new buildings in Santa Barbara County. *Eligibility: Charitable organizations in the Santa Barbara area are eligible to apply. *Financial Details: Amounts vary. *Number Awarded: Varies. *Deadline: Varies. Contact the foundation for additional details.

American Express Philanthropic Program
http://home3.americanexpress.com/corp/giving_back.asp
Disability Served: various
Purpose: The foundation supports programs in a variety of fields, including community service, cultural heritage, and economic independence. *Eligibility: Charitable organizations in the following six service areas are eligible to apply: Ft. Lauderdale or Miami, Florida; Greensboro, North Carolina; Minneapolis, Minnesota; New York, New York; Phoenix, Arizona; and Salt Lake City, Utah. (See the foundation's Web site for contact information for each service area.) Organizations that are outside of these areas, and that have a project that is national in scope, are eligible to apply for grants through an internal process by which applicants receive an endorsement from an American Express employee in their area. *Financial Details: Amounts vary widely. *Number Awarded: Varies. *Deadline: Contact the foundation for more information.

Anheuser-Busch Foundation
One Busch Place
St. Louis, MO 63118
314-577-7368
Disability Served: various
Purpose: The foundation provides grants in the areas of community affairs, environment, conservation, and more. *Eligibility: Nonprofit organizations are eligible to apply. *Financial Details: Amounts vary depending on project need. *Number Awarded: Varies. *Deadline: Varies. Contact the foundation for more information.

Ann Arbor Area Community Foundation
201 South Main, Suite 501
Ann Arbor, MI 48104
734-663-0401
info@aaacf.org
http://www.aaacf.org
Disability Served: various
Purpose: The foundation provides financial support for projects designed to improve the quality of life for residents of Washtenaw County, Michigan. Grant areas include education, health care, basic human services, transportation, the arts, and youth and senior programs. *Eligibility: Charitable organizations serving the Washtenaw County area may apply. *Financial Details: Amounts vary and depend on project need. *Number Awarded: Varies. *Deadline: Contact the foundation for details.

Anschutz Family Foundation
555 17th Street, Suite 2400
Denver, CO 80202
303-293-2338
info@anschutzfamilyfoundation.org
http://www.anschutzfamilyfoundation.org
Disability Served: various
Purpose: The foundation provides grants for the purpose of improving conditions for the elderly, the young, and the economically disadvantaged. *Eligibility: Charitable organizations in Colorado that are dedicated to helping the elderly, young, and economically disadvantaged and that have not applied for a grant from the

foundation in the past 12 months are eligible to apply. *Financial Details: Grants range from $2,500 to $10,000. *Number Awarded: Varies. *Deadlines: January 15 and August 1. Contact the foundation for details.

Archstone Foundation
401 East Ocean Boulevard, Suite 1000
Long Beach, CA 90802
562-590-8655
archstone@archstone.org
http://www.archstone.org
Disability Served: elderly
*Purpose: The foundation offers grants for projects dealing with the health and welfare of the elderly. *Eligibility: Nonprofit organizations dedicated to helping the elderly are eligible. *Financial Details: Amounts vary according to project need. *Number Awarded: Varies each year. *Deadline: Applications are accepted throughout the year. Funding decisions are made in March, June, September, and December .*

Argyros Foundation
949 South Coast Drive, #600
Costa Mesa, CA 92626
714-481-5000
Disability Served: communication, hearing, physically disabled
*Purpose: The foundation provides grants to support a number of projects in southern California. *Eligibility: Charitable organizations dedicated to helping the physically disabled, speech impaired, and hearing impaired are eligible to apply. *Financial Details: Amounts vary. *Number Awarded: Varies each year. *Deadline: Contact the foundation for more information.*

Arizona Community Foundation
2201 East Camelback Road, Suite 202
Phoenix, AZ 85016
602-381-1400, 800-222-8221
grants@azfoundation.org
http://www.azfoundation.org
Disability Served: various
*Purpose: The foundation provides grants to improve the quality of life in Arizona. Areas of interest include health and mental health, children and youth, family and elders, human services, and social welfare. *Eligibility: Nonprofits in Arizona are eligible to apply. *Financial Details: Awards vary by type of project. *Number Awarded: Varies. *Deadline: Varies. Visit the foundation's Web site to download a grant application.*

Arkansas Community Foundation Inc.
700 South Rock Street
Little Rock, AR 72202
501-372-1116
arcf@arcf.org
http://www.arcf.org
Disability Served: various
*Purpose: The foundation provides grants to improve the quality of life in Arkansas. Areas of interest include education, health, human services, community development, arts and humanities, the environment, and religion. *Eligibility: Nonprofits in Arkansas are eligible to apply. *Financial Details: Awards vary by type of project. *Number Awarded: Varies. *Deadline: Varies. Visit the foundation's Web site for more information.*

AT&T Foundation
32 Avenue of the Americas, 6th Floor
New York, NY 10013
http://www.att.com/foundation
Disability Served: various
*Purpose: The foundation supports projects in the areas of education, arts and culture, and civic and community service. *Eligibility: Nonprofit organizations involved in the above areas are eligible. *Financial Details: Amounts vary according to project need. *Number Awarded: Varies each year. *Deadline: Applications and proposals are accepted throughout the year.*

Atherton Family Foundation
1164 Bishop Street, Suite 800
Honolulu, HI 96813
888-731-3863
foundations@hcf-hawaii.org
http://hawaiicommunityfoundation.org/atherton
Disability Served: various
*Purpose: This private foundation provides funds for charitable purposes. Areas of interest include education, health and welfare, social services, and religious concerns. *Eligibility: Nonprofit organizations in Hawaii are eligible to apply. *Financial Details: Amounts vary and depend on the project. *Number Awarded: Varies. *Deadlines: February 1, April 1, August 1, October 1, and December 1. Contact the foundation for more information.*

Atkinson Foundation
1720 South Amphlett Boulevard, Suite 100
San Mateo, CA 94402-2710
650-357-1101

atkinfdn@aol.com
Disability Served: *various*
Purpose: *The foundation provides grants for community service, education, and civic organizations in San Mateo County, California. *Eligibility: Charitable organizations in San Mateo County dedicated to helping the elderly, youth, the disadvantaged, and persons needing rehabilitation are eligible to apply. *Financial Details: Amounts vary, but average $5,000 each. *Number Awarded: Varies. *Deadline: Varies. Contact the foundation for more information.*

Autry Foundation
4383 Colfax Avenue
Studio City, CA 91604
818-752-7770
Disability Served: *various*
Purpose: *The foundation supports charitable projects in Los Angeles, Riverside, and Orange Counties in southern California. *Eligibility: Nonprofit organizations serving the counties listed above may apply. *Financial Details: Amounts vary and depend on financial need. *Number Awarded: Varies. *Deadline: Varies. Contact the foundation for more information.*

Ball Brothers Foundation
222 South Mulberry Street, PO Box 1408
Muncie, IN 47308-1408
765-741-5500
http://www.ballfdn.org
Disability Served: *various*
Purpose: *The foundation provides grants for charitable, religious, or educational purposes. *Eligibility: Organizations in the state of Indiana are eligible to apply. Grants are not given to individuals. *Financial Details: A total amount of $5,100,000 was awarded in a recent year. *Number Awarded: Varies. Thirty-nine grants were awarded in a recent year. *Deadline: Contact the foundation for deadline information.*

Baltimore Community Foundation
2 East Read Street, 9th Floor
Baltimore, MD 21202
410-332-4171
grants@bcf.org
http://www.bcf.org
Disability Served: *various*
Purpose: *The foundation has a goal of improving the quality of life in the Baltimore, Maryland region by awarding of grants in the following areas: children and families, community development, and arts and culture. *Eligibility: Nonprofit organizations serving the Baltimore region are eligible to apply. *Financial Details: Varies. *Number Awarded: Varies. *Deadlines: March 1, June 1, and December 1. Contact the foundation for more information.*

Bank of America Foundation
888-488-9802
http://www.bankofamerica.com/foundation
Disability Served: *various*
Purpose: *The foundation offers grants in the areas of arts and culture, health and human services, community investment, education, and conservation and the environment. *Eligibility: Charitable organizations in 28 states and the District of Columbia that are involved in the areas listed above are eligible to apply. *Financial Details: Amounts vary and depend on project need. *Number Awarded: Varies. *Deadline: Contact the foundation for details.*

Bill and Melinda Gates Foundation
PO Box 23350
Seattle, WA 98102
206-709-3140
info@gatesfoundation.org
http://www.gatesfoundation.org
Disability Served: *various*
Purpose: *The foundation provides grants in the areas of global health, education, library programs, and special projects. *Eligibility: Charitable organizations are eligible to apply. *Financial Details: Amounts vary. *Number Awarded: Varies each year. *Deadline: Varies. Contact the foundation for details.*

Blowitz-Ridgeway Foundation
1701 East Woodfield Road, Suite 201
Schaumburg, IL 60173
847-330-1020
laura@blowitzridgeway.org
http://www.blowitzridgeway.org
Disability Served: *mental health, physically disabled*
Purpose: *The foundation provides grants designed to support projects for the physically or mentally disabled. *Eligibility: Organizations serving the disabled (including children) that have not applied for a grant from the foundation in the past 12 months are eligible to apply. Preference is given to applicants from Illinois. *Financial Details: Amounts vary. *Number Awarded: Varies. *Deadline: Applications are accepted throughout the year. Contact the foundation for more information.*

Bothin Foundation
Presidio Building 1016, Suite 300, PO Box 29906
San Francisco, CA 94129-0906
415-561-6540
mcallender@pfs-llc.net
http://www.pfs-llc.net/bothin
Disability Served: various
Purpose: The foundation provides grants to charitable
organizations in the California counties of San
Francisco, Marin, Sonoma, and San Mateo. Areas of
interest include health services, community concerns,
and education. *Eligibility: Charitable organizations
serving the counties listed above are eligible. Priority
is given to organizations concerned with the elderly,
youth, and the disabled. *Financial Details: Amounts
vary. *Number Awarded: Varies. *Deadline: Visit the
foundation's Web site for more information.

The Brown Foundation Inc.
PO Box 130646
Houston, TX 77219-0646
713-523-6867
bfi@brownfoundation.org
http://www.brownfoundation.org
Disability Served: various
Purpose: The foundation offers grants in the areas of
arts and humanities, civic and public affairs, human
services, and medicine/science. *Eligibility: Nonprofit
organizations and schools in Texas (especially Houston)
that have not applied for a grant from the foundation
in the past 12 months are eligible; a small number or
grants are awarded to organizations from outside of
Texas. *Financial Details: Varies. *Number Awarded:
Varies. *Deadline: Contact the foundation for details.

Burlington Resources Foundation
717 Texas Avenue, Suite 2100
Houston, TX 77002
Disability Served: various
Purpose: The foundation provides funding in the areas of
community affairs, education, youth organizations,
medical facilities, arts and culture, and human services.
*Eligibility: Nonprofit organizations are eligible to
apply. *Financial Details: Amounts vary. *Number
Awarded: Varies. *Deadline: Contact the foundation for
application forms and deadlines.

Bushrod H. Campbell and Adah F. Hall Charity Fund
111 Huntington Avenue at Prudential Center
Boston, MA 02199-7613
617-239-0556

Disability Served: various
Purpose: The fund provides grants in the areas of health
care, population control, and the aged. *Eligibility:
Nonprofit organizations in the Greater Boston area
are eligible to apply. *Financial Details: Amounts vary.
*Number Awarded: Varies. *Deadline: Varies. Contact
the fund for more information.

California Community Foundation
445 South Figueroa, Suite 3400
Los Angeles, CA 90071-1638
213-413-4130
http://www.calfund.org
Disability Served: various
Purpose: The foundation provides grants to support
programs dedicated to improving the lives of the
residents of Los Angeles County, California. *Eligibility:
Nonprofit organizations serving Los Angeles County are
eligible. *Financial Details: Amounts vary depending on
program need. *Number Awarded: Varies. *Deadline:
Deadlines vary. Contact the foundation for application
materials.

The California Wellness Foundation
6320 Canoga Avenue, Suite 1700
Woodland Hills, CA 91367-7111
818-593-6600
http://www.tcwf.org
Disability Served: various
Purpose: This private foundation awards grants in
the areas of diversity in the health professions,
environmental health, healthy aging, mental health,
teenage pregnancy prevention, violence prevention,
women's health, and work and health. *Eligibility:
Nonprofit organizations in California with a focus on
the areas listed above are eligible to apply. *Financial
Details: Grants range from $20,000 to approximately
$300,000 for a one-to-three-year period; a three-year
grant does not usually exceed $150,000. *Number
Awarded: Varies. *Deadline: Proposals are accepted
throughout the year. Contact the foundation for more
information.

Campbell Soup Foundation
Attn: Grant Administrator
One Campbell Place, Box 60-D
Camden, NJ 08103
800-257-8443
http://www.campbellsoupcompany.com/community_
center.asp?cpovisq=
Disability Served: various

Purpose: The foundation supports projects in the areas of education, health and nutrition, arts and culture, and youth. *Eligibility: Nonprofit organizations devoted to community service in the areas listed above are eligible to apply. Priority is given to organizations in the New Jersey area. *Financial Details: Amounts vary. *Number Awarded: Varies. *Deadline: Varies. Contact the foundation for further details.

Cannon Foundation Inc.
PO Box 548
Concord, NC 28026-0548
704-786-8216
http://www.thecannonfoundationinc.org
Disability Served: various
Purpose: The foundation supports projects in healthcare, higher education, and community service that serve the residents of North Carolina. *Eligibility: Charitable organizations in North Carolina are eligible. *Financial Details: Amounts vary. *Number Awarded: Varies each year. *Deadlines: January 5, April 5, July 5, and October 5. Contact the foundation for more information.

The Champlin Foundations
300 Centerville Road, Suite 300S
Warwick, RI 02886-0226
401-736-0370
http://fdncenter.org/grantmaker/champlin
Disability Served: various
Purpose: This organization provides grants for charitable purposes in many areas, including youth/fitness, hospitals/healthcare, education, libraries, and social services. *Eligibility: Nonprofit organizations serving Rhode Island are eligible. *Financial Details: Amounts vary according to need. *Number Awarded: Varies each year. *Deadline: Applications are accepted between March 1 and June 30.

Charles Bloom Foundation Inc.
240 Eucalyptus Hill Drive
Santa Barbara, CA 93108-1851
Disability Served: various
Purpose: The foundation offers grants in the areas of health, education, and community services. *Eligibility: Charitable organizations may apply. *Financial Details: Amounts vary according to project needs. *Number Awarded: Varies. *Deadline: Varies. Contact the foundation for more information.

Chatlos Foundation Inc.
PO Box 915048
Longwood, FL 32791-5048

407-862-5077
cj@chatlos.org
http://www.chatlos.org
Disability Served: various
Purpose: The foundation provides grants in the areas of higher education, social causes, and medical issues. *Eligibility: Nonprofit organizations and universities that have not received a grant from the foundation in the past 12 months are eligible to apply. Emphasis is placed on overall mission statements rather than individual projects. *Financial Details: Awards range from $2,500 to $50,000. *Number Awarded: Varies. *Deadline: Varies. Contact the foundation for more information.

Chicago Community Trust
111 East Wacker Drive, Suite 1400
Chicago, IL 60601
312-616-8000, 312-856-1703 (TDD)
info@cct.org
http://www.cct.org
Disability Served: various
Purpose: The trust disseminates grants on behalf of organizations or individuals wishing to provide funds for charitable purposes in the following areas: basic human needs, health, education, community development, and arts and culture. *Eligibility: Nonprofit organizations serving Cook County, Illinois, are eligible to apply. Other requirements may apply; contact the trust for information. *Financial Details: Grants can range from several hundred dollars to more than $1 million. *Number Awarded: Varies. *Deadline: Contact the trust for details.

Chichester DuPont Foundation
3120 Kennett Pike
Wilmington, DE 19807-3052
302-658-5244
Disability Served: various
Purpose: The foundation provides grants in the areas of education, health, and culture. *Eligibility: Nonprofit organizations may apply. *Financial Details: Amounts vary. *Number Awarded: Varies. *Deadline: Varies. Contact the foundation for more information.

Clark-Winchcole Foundation
3 Bethesda Metro Center, Suite 550
Bethesda, MD 20814-5358
301-654-3607
Disability Served: hearing, physically disabled
Purpose: The foundation provides grants to programs for the deaf and physically disabled. *Eligibility: Charitable

organizations in the Washington, D.C., area may apply. *Financial Details: Amounts vary. *Number Awarded: Varies. *Deadline: Varies. Contact the foundation for more information.

Clipper Ship Foundation Inc.
77 Summer Street, Eighth Floor
Boston, MA 02110
617-426-7080
tteich@grantsmanagement.com
http://www.agmconnect.org/clipper1.html
Disability Served: various
Purpose: The foundation provides financial assistance to organizations dedicated to helping the homeless, the poor, the sick, the disabled, children, the elderly, or those with special needs. *Eligibility: Charitable organizations serving the people of the Boston area are eligible. *Financial Details: Awards range from $5,000 to $25,000. *Number Awarded: Varies each year. *Deadlines: March 1, May 10, August 10, and November 15. Contact the foundation for more information.

Clorox Company Foundation
c/o East Bay Community Foundation
200 Frank Ogawa Plaza
Oakland, CA 94612
510-836-3223
cloroxfndt@eastbaycf.org
http://www.thecloroxcompany.com/community
Disability Served: various
Purpose: The foundation provides grants for the purpose of improving the quality of life in communities where Clorox employees live and work. *Eligibility: Charitable organizations serving a community where Clorox has an operating facility or where its employees reside are eligible to apply. *Financial Details: Varies. *Number Awarded: Varies. *Deadlines: January 1, April 1, July 1, and October 1. Visit the foundation's Web site to apply online.

The Cockrell Foundation
Attn: Executive Vice President
1000 Main Street, Suite 3250
Houston, TX 77002
foundation@cockrell.com
http://www.cockrell.com/foundation
Disability Served: various
Purpose: The foundation provides grants in the areas of health, higher education, cultural programs, social services, and youth services. *Eligibility: Nonprofit organizations serving the Houston area may apply.

*Financial Details: Grants range from $1,000 to more than $2 million—the average grant in 2004 was approximately $125,000. *Number Awarded: Approximately 50 annually. *Deadline: Applications are accepted throughout the year. Visit the foundation's Web site for more information.

The Commonwealth Fund
Attn: Director of Grants Management
One East 75th Street
New York, NY 10021
212-606-3800
cmwf@cmwf.org
http://www.cmwf.org
Disability Served: various
Purpose: The fund provides grants in the areas of health care, elderly issues, children and youth, and minority concerns. *Eligibility: Nonprofit organizations involved in the areas listed above are eligible to apply. *Financial Details: Amounts vary. *Number Awarded: Varies. *Deadline: Letters of inquiry are accepted throughout the year. Contact the fund for more information.

Communities Foundation of Texas
5500 Caruth Haven Lane
Dallas, TX 75225-8146
214-750-4222
Reckhoff@cftexas.org
http://www.cftexas.org
Disability Served: various
Purpose: This foundation provides grants for charitable purposes in the areas of health care, elder care, and care of the homeless. *Eligibility: Nonprofit organizations serving residents in the Greater Dallas metropolitan area of North Texas are eligible. *Financial Details: Amounts vary. *Number Awarded: Varies. *Deadlines: January 15 and September 15. Contact the foundation for additional details.

Community Foundation of Broward
1401 East Broward Boulevard
Ft Lauderdale, FL 33301
954-761-9503, ext. 103
http://www.cfbroward.org
Disability Served: various
Purpose: The foundation provides grants in order to improve the quality of life for citizens of Broward County, Florida. Areas of interest include AIDS/HIV prevention, cancer and arthritis research, youth and families, independent living, and animal welfare.

*Eligibility: Charitable organizations serving Broward County may apply. *Financial Details: Grants range from $4,000 to $50,000. *Number Awarded: Varies. *Deadline: Varies. Visit the foundation's Web site to download a grant application.

Community Foundation of Greater Jackson
525 East Capitol Street, Suite 5B
Jackson, MS 39201
601-974-6044
info@cfgreaterjackson.org
http://www.cfgreaterjackson.org
Disability Served: various
Purpose: The foundation provides grants to improve the quality of life in the central Mississippi counties of Hinds, Madison, and Rankin. Areas of interests include health, education, families and children, arts and humanities, community building, and the environment. *Eligibility: Nonprofit organizations, schools, churches, and governmental entities in Hinds, Madison, or Rankin County, Mississippi, are eligible to apply. *Financial Details: Grants range from $100 to $20,000. *Number Awarded: Varies. *Deadline: Applications are accepted throughout the year. Visit the foundation's Web site to download a grant application.

Community Foundation of Greater Memphis
1900 Union Avenue
Memphis, TN 38104
901-722-0054
mwolowicz@cfgm.org
http://www.cfgm.org
Disability Served: various
Purpose: The foundation provides grants to improve the quality of life in eastern Arkansas, northern Mississippi, and western Tennessee. Areas of interest include children with disabilities and visually impaired individuals. *Eligibility: Nonprofits in eastern Arkansas, northern Mississippi, and western Tennessee are eligible to apply. *Financial Details: Grants range from $5,000 to $50,000 or more. *Number Awarded: Twenty-five to 40 annually. *Deadline: Varies. Contact the foundation for more information.

Community Foundation of New Jersey
Knox Hill Road, PO Box 338
Morristown, NJ 07963-0338
973-267-5533
http://www.cfnj.org
Disability Served: various

Purpose: The foundation provides funds in the areas of health care, education, youth programs, human services, community development, and public affairs. *Eligibility: Nonprofit organizations serving New Jersey are eligible. *Financial Details: Amounts vary. *Number Awarded: Varies. *Deadlines: Varies. Contact the foundation for more information.

Community Foundation of Shreveport-Bossier
Attn: Director of Programs
401 Edwards, Suite 105
Shreveport, LA 71101
318-221-0582
adams@comfoundsb.org
http://www.comfoundsb.org
Disability Served: various
Purpose: The foundation provides grants in the areas of education, the environment, arts, youth services, the elderly, and other social and cultural areas. It serves the parishes of Caddo and Bossier in Louisiana. *Eligibility: Nonprofit organizations in Louisiana are eligible to apply. *Financial Details: Varies. *Number Awarded: Varies. *Deadlines: Typically in late March and late July. Visit the foundation's Web site to download a grant application.

Community Foundation of the Virgin Islands
PO Box 11790
Charlotte Amalie, VI 00801
340-774-6031
http://www.cfvi.net
Disability Served: various
Purpose: The foundation provides grants to improve the quality of life in the Virgin Islands. Areas of interest include education, early childcare, the arts, and the environment. *Eligibility: Private groups and nonprofits in the Virgin Islands are eligible to apply. *Financial Details: Amounts vary. *Number Awarded: Varies. *Deadline: Typically in March. Visit the foundation's Web site to download a grant application.

Community Foundation Silicon Valley
60 South Market Street, Suite 1000
San Jose, CA 95113
408-278-2200
http://www.cfsv.org
Disability Served: various
Purpose: The foundation provides grants in the areas of education and lifelong learning, arts and cultural participation, neighborhoods and civic engagement,

and self-reliant individuals and families. *Eligibility: Nonprofit organizations serving Santa Clara County and southern San Mateo County may apply. *Financial Details: Amounts vary. *Number Awarded: Varies each year. *Deadline: Varies. Contact the foundation for more information.

Connecticut Community Foundation
81 West Main Street
Waterbury, CT 06702
203-753-1315
http://www.conncf.org
Disability Served: various
Purpose: The foundation provides grants to improve the quality of life in Connecticut. Areas of interest include education, health, human services, and community development. *Eligibility: Nonprofits in the following Connecticut towns are eligible to apply: Beacon Falls, Bethlehem, Bridgewater, Cheshire, Goshen, Litchfield, Middlebury, Morris, Naugatuck, New Milford, Oxford, Prospect, Roxbury, Southbury, Thomaston, Warren, Washington, Waterbury, Watertown, Wolcott, and Woodbury. *Financial Details: Awards range from $1,000 to $50,000. *Number Awarded: Varies. *Deadlines: January, April, and September. Visit the foundation's Web site for more information.

Crail-Johnson Foundation
222 West 6th Street, #1010
San Pedro, CA 90731
310-519-7413
carolyn-johnson@crail-johnson.org
http://www.crail-johnson.org
Disability Served: various
Purpose: The foundation funds projects that benefit children in the areas of education, health, and social services. *Eligibility: Charitable organizations dedicated to helping children in the Los Angeles area are eligible. *Financial Details: Awards vary. *Number Awarded: Varies. *Deadline: Varies.

Crescent Porter Hale Foundation
655 Redwood Highway, Suite 301
Mill Valley, CA 94941
415-388-2333
Disability Served: various
Purpose: The foundation supports projects that benefit the residents of the San Francisco Bay area, primarily in the areas of education, youth concerns, human services, and capital funding. *Eligibility: Nonprofit organizations

involved in projects that serve the San Francisco Bay area community are eligible. *Financial Details: Amounts vary. *Number Awarded: Varies. *Deadline: Contact the foundation for more information.

The Cullen Foundation
Attn: Executive Director
601 Jefferson Street, 40th Floor
Houston, TX 77002
713-651-8837
http://www.cullenfdn.org
Disability Served: various
Purpose: The foundation provides funds for charitable projects in Texas; grants are primarily given to Houston-based nonprofit organizations. *Eligibility: Nonprofit organizations in Texas are eligible. *Financial Details: Amounts vary and depend on program need. *Number Awarded: Varies. *Deadline: Applications are accepted throughout the year. Contact the foundation for details.

David and Lucile Packard Foundation
300 Second Street
Los Altos, CA 94022
650-948-7658
cfc@packard.org
http://www.packard.org
Disability Served: various
Purpose: This private foundation provides funding in the areas of science, children, families, communities, conservation, film and arts preservation, and education. *Eligibility: Charitable organizations are eligible. Other restrictions may apply; contact the foundation for details. *Financial Details: Amounts vary. *Number Awarded: Varies. *Deadline: Varies. Visit the foundation's Web site to complete an online letter of inquiry.

Delaware Community Foundation
100 West 10th Street, Suite 115, PO Box 1636
Wilmington, DE 19899
302-571-8004
info@delcf.org
http://www.delcf.org
Disability Served: various
Purpose: The foundation provides grants to improve the quality of life in metropolitan Washington, D.C. Areas of interest include healthcare, adolescent needs, affordable housing, homelessness, arts stabilization, and violence prevention. *Eligibility: Nonprofits in metropolitan Washington, D.C., are eligible to apply. *Financial Details: Awards vary by type of project.

*Number Awarded: Varies. *Deadline: Varies. Visit the foundation's Web site for more information.

The Deutsch Foundation
2444 Wilshire Boulevard, Suite 600
Santa Monica, CA 90403-5813
310-453-0055
Disability Served: various
Purpose: The foundation supports projects that improve the quality of life of California residents. *Eligibility: Nonprofit organizations in California are eligible. *Financial Details: Amounts vary according to project need. *Number Awarded: Varies each year. *Deadline: Varies. Contact the foundation for more information.

DeWitt Wallace-Reader's Digest Fund
5 Penn Plaza
New York, NY 10001
212-251-9700
http://www.wallacefunds.org
Disability Served: various
Purpose: This private foundation provides grants to improve the quality of educational opportunities for school-age youth, especially those in low-income communities. *Eligibility: Nonprofit organizations are eligible. *Financial Details: Awards vary, but in general, the fund does not make grants of less than $100,000. *Number Awarded: Varies. *Deadline: Letters of inquiry are accepted throughout the year, but the fund rarely, if ever, makes grants to unsolicited projects.

Douglas County Community Foundation
900 Massachusetts, Suite 406
Lawrence, KS 66047
785-843-8727
http://www.dccfoundation.org
Disability Served: various
Purpose: The foundation provides grants in the areas of health, youth, education, human services, and arts/culture to organizations serving the needs of the communities of Douglas County, Kansas, (which includes Lawrence, Baldwin City, Lecompton, and Eudora). *Eligibility: Nonprofit organizations in Kansas are eligible to apply. *Financial Details: Grants of up to $25,000 are awarded; the median award is $5,000. *Number Awarded: Varies. *Deadline: December 1. Visit the foundation's Web site to download a grant application.

Duke Endowment
100 North Tryon Street, Suite 3500
Charlotte, NC 28202-4012
704-376-0291
http://www.dukeendowment.org
Disability Served: various
Purpose: This charitable trust provides support in the areas of education, health care, childcare, and religion. *Eligibility: Nonprofit organizations serving North and South Carolina are eligible. Other restrictions may apply; contact the endowment for details. *Financial Details: Amounts vary. *Number Awarded: Varies. *Deadline: Letters of inquiry are accepted throughout the year.

East Bay Community Foundation
200 Frank Ogawa Plaza
Oakland, CA 94612
510-836-3223
communityinvestment@eastbaycf.org
http://www.eastbaycf.org
Disability Served: various
Purpose: The foundation provides grants to support programs designed to better the lives of the residents of the East Bay area of San Francisco. Grant areas include community health, education and youth development, strengthening families, arts and culture, neighborhood and community building, and the environment. *Eligibility: Nonprofit organizations in Alameda and Contra Costa counties are eligible. *Financial Details: Awards range from $500 to $12,000. *Number Awarded: Varies. *Deadline: Varies. Call or write for details.

Eckerd Corporation Foundation
6501 Legacy Drive, MS 1203
Plano, TX 75024-3698
972-431-2159
Disability Served: various
Purpose: The foundation offers funds to support projects in areas where Eckerd operates stores. *Eligibility: Nonprofit organizations, primarily health organizations, pharmaceutical colleges, and organizations benefiting women and children, are eligible. *Financial Details: Amounts vary. *Number Awarded: Varies. *Deadline: Varies. Contact the foundation for details.

Edna McConnell Clark Foundation
415 Madison Avenue, 10th Floor
New York, NY 10017
212-551-9100
info@emcf.org
http://www.emcf.org
Disability Served: various

Purpose: The foundation seeks to improve conditions and opportunities for people who live in poor and disadvantaged communities. *Eligibility: Nonprofit organizations are eligible to apply. *Financial Details: Grants range from $25,000 to $250,000. *Number Awarded: Varies. *Deadline: There is no deadline. Grant-seeking youth organizations can visit the foundation's Web site to complete a youth organizations survey, which will be reviewed by foundation officials for possible funding opportunities.

Edyth Bush Charitable Foundation
199 East Welbourne Avenue, PO Box 1967
Winter Park, FL 32790-1967
407-647-4322
http://www.edythbush.org
Disability Served: various
Purpose: The foundation provides grants to support projects that help underprivileged and needy people. *Eligibility: Nonprofit organizations operating in Orange, Seminole, and Osceola counties, Florida, are eligible. *Financial Details: Amounts vary, but grants average between $5,000 and $50,000. *Number Awarded: Varies. *Deadline: Applications are accepted throughout the year. Contact the foundation for details.

Elizabeth Firth Wade Endowment Fund
114 East De La Guerra Street, Suite 7
Santa Barbara, CA 93101
805-963-8822
Disability Served: various
Purpose: The foundation provides grants for charitable purposes in the areas of human services, arts and culture, youth projects, and education. *Eligibility: Nonprofit organizations may apply. *Financial Details: Amounts vary and depend on need. *Number Awarded: Varies. *Deadline: Varies. Contact the foundation for details.

E. L. Wiegand Foundation
165 West Liberty Street
Reno, NV 89501
775-333-0310
Disability Served: various
Purpose: The foundation provides grants for charitable purposes. *Eligibility: Educational institutions and health organizations are eligible to apply. *Financial Details: Amounts vary, depending on program need. *Number Awarded: Varies. *Deadline: Varies. Contact the foundation for more information.

Equifax Foundation
1550 Peachtree Street, NW
Atlanta, GA 30309
kirby.thompson@equifax.com
Disability Served: various
Purpose: The foundation provides grants in the areas of health and welfare, arts and culture, civic and community services, and education. *Eligibility: Charitable organizations in areas where Equifax operates are eligible. *Financial Details: Amounts vary. *Number Awarded: Varies each year. *Deadline: Contact the foundation for further information.

Ethel Louise Armstrong Foundation
Attn: Executive Director
2460 North Lake Avenue, PMB #128
Altadena, CA 91001
626-398-8840
info@ela.org
http://www.ela.org
Disability Served: various
Purpose: The foundation "promotes, through grants and scholarships, the inclusion of people with disabilities in the areas of arts, advocacy, and education." *Eligibility: Nonprofit organizations are eligible to apply. *Financial Details: Awards vary. *Number Awarded: Varies. *Deadlines: May 1 and November 1. Visit the foundation's Web site for more information.

ExxonMobil Foundation
5959 Las Colinas Boulevard
Irving, TX 75039-2298
972-444-1106
http://www.exxonmobil.com/corporate/Citizenship/
Corp_citizenship_Com_foundation.asp
Disability Served: various
Purpose: The foundation provides funds to help support programs dedicated to improving the quality of education, health, and arts and culture in the United States. *Eligibility: Charitable organizations and schools are eligible to apply. *Financial Details: Amounts vary and depend on project need. *Deadline: Varies. An online grant application is available at the foundation's Web site.

Field Foundation of Illinois
200 South Wacker Drive, Suite 3860
Chicago, IL 60606
312-831-0910
jross@fieldfoundation.org
http://www.fieldfoundation.org
Disability Served: various

Purpose: The foundation offers grants in the areas of health, education, urban and community affairs, culture, community welfare, and the environment. The grants are awarded primarily to organizations in the Chicago metropolitan area. *Eligibility: Nonprofit organizations involved in the areas mentioned above may apply. Organizations that have received a grant from the foundation in the past 12 months are not eligible to apply. *Financial Details: Amounts vary, but do not typically exceed $50,000. *Number Awarded: Varies. *Deadlines: January 15, May 15, and September 15. Contact the foundation for more information.

Florence V. Burden Foundation
10 East 3rd Street, 32nd Floor
New York, NY 10022
212-872-1150
Disability Served: various
Purpose: This private foundation provides grants in a variety of areas, including education, environment, family care giving, and employment and volunteer opportunities for the elderly. *Eligibility: Charitable organizations and schools are eligible to apply. *Financial Details: Amounts vary and depend on program need. *Number Awarded: Varies. *Deadline: Varies. Contact the foundation for details.

Foundation for Seacoast Health
100 Campus Drive, Suite 1
Portsmouth, NH 03801
603-422-8200
ffsh@communitycampus.org
http://www.ffsh.org
Disability Served: various
Purpose: The foundation provides grants to support programs in health and wellness in the Portsmouth, New Hampshire-area. *Eligibility: Charitable organizations serving the Portsmouth area are eligible. *Financial Details: Up to $5,000. *Number Awarded: Varies each year. *Deadlines: March 1 and June 1. Contact the foundation for more information.

Foundation for the Carolinas
217 South Tryon Street
Charlotte, NC 28202
704-973-4500, 800-973-7244
oscott@fftc.org
http://www.fftc.org
Disability Served: various

Purpose: The foundation provides grants to improve the quality of life in communities in North and South Carolina. It also provides specialized grant programs in children's medicine, medical research, and education. *Eligibility: Nonprofits in North Carolina (including the Lexington area and Cabarrus, Cleveland, Iredell, Lincoln, Mecklenburg, Richmond, Salisbury, Stanly and Union Counties) and South Carolina (including Cherokee, Lancaster, and York Counties) are eligible to apply. *Financial Details: Awards vary. *Number Awarded: Varies. *Deadline: Varies. Visit the foundation's Web site for more information.

Frank Adam Foundation
7733 Forsyth Boulevard, Suite 900
St. Louis, MO 63105-1898
Disability Served: various
Purpose: The foundation provides grants to help fund projects in the areas of medicine and health services, child welfare, and more. *Eligibility: Nonprofit organizations and medical facilities are eligible. Other restrictions may apply; contact the foundation for details. *Financial Details: Amounts vary according to project need. *Number Awarded: Varies each year. *Deadline: Contact the foundation for details.

Fred Gellert Family Foundation
361 Third Street, Suite A
San Rafael, CA 94901
415-256-5433
foundation@fredgellert.com
http://fdncenter.org/grantmaker/fredgellert
Disability Served: various
Purpose: The foundation provides funding in the areas of health, the environment, arts and humanities, and youth, seniors, and family services. The purpose is to advance positive forces for social change to ensure quality of life for future generations. *Eligibility: Funding is limited to San Francisco, San Mateo, and Marin counties in California. Grants are available to nonprofit organizations only (no funds are given to individuals). *Financial Details: Amounts vary. *Number Awarded: Varies. *Deadline: The foundation is currently reevaluating its grant process; visit its Web site for an update regarding grant applications.

Gebbie Foundation
111 West Second Street, Suite 1100
Jamestown, NY 14701
716-487-1062

info@gebbie.org
http://www.gebbie.org
Disability Served: various
Purpose: The foundation provides grants for charitable purposes in the areas of human services, community development, the arts, and children and education. *Eligibility: Nonprofit organizations in western New York are eligible to apply. *Financial Details: Amounts vary. *Number Awarded: Varies each year. *Deadlines: April 1, August 1, and December 1.

GE Foundation
3135 Easton Turnpike
Fairfield, CT 06431
203-373-3216
gefoundation@ge.com
http://www.ge.com/foundation
Disability Served: various
Purpose: The foundation provides grants to fund programs in higher education. *Eligibility: Charitable organizations are eligible to apply. *Financial Details: Grants range from $10,000 to $100,000. In 2003, more than $50 million in grants was awarded. *Number Awarded: Varies each year. *Deadline: Proposals are accepted throughout the year.

Giant Food Foundation Inc.
6300 Sheriff Road
Landover, MD 20785
301-341-4171
Disability Served: various
Purpose: The foundation provides grants in the areas of health, recreation, community programs, art, and education. *Eligibility: Charitable organizations in the greater Washington, D.C., area may apply. *Financial Details: Amounts vary depending on project need. *Number Awarded: Varies each year. *Deadline: Varies. Contact the foundation for more information.

Gladys Brooks Foundation
1055 Franklin Avenue
Garden City, NY 11530
http://www.gladysbrooksfoundation.org
Disability Served: various
Purpose: The foundation provides grants to hospitals, clinics, educational institutions, and nonprofit libraries. *Eligibility: Nonprofit organizations in the District of Columbia and the following states are eligible: Connecticut, Delaware, Indiana, Maine, Maryland,

Massachusetts, New Hampshire, New Jersey, New York, Ohio, Pennsylvania, Rhode Island, Tennessee, Vermont, Virginia, and West Virginia. *Financial Details: Grants range from $50,000 to $100,000. *Number Awarded: Varies. *Deadline: Varies. Visit the foundation's Web site to download an application.

Grover Hermann Foundation
1000 Hillgrove, Suite 200
Western Springs, IL 60558
708-246-8331
Disability Served: various
Purpose: The foundation's primary areas of interest are education, public policy, community affairs, health care, and religious groups. *Eligibility: Charitable organizations with a focus on the areas listed above may apply. *Financial Details: Amounts vary. *Number Awarded: Varies. *Deadline: Varies. Contact the foundation for more information.

Hall Family Foundation
2501 McGee, MD 323
Kansas City, MO 64108
816-274-5615
Disability Served: various
Purpose: The Foundation provides grants to help improve the quality of life for citizens of the Kansas City area. *Eligibility: Charitable organizations in the Kansas City area are eligible. *Financial Details: Amounts vary and depend on project need. *Number Awarded: Varies. *Deadline: Varies. Contact the Foundation for more information.

Harry and Grace Steele Foundation
441 Old Newport Boulevard, Suite 301
Newport Beach, CA 92663
949-631-0418
Disability Served: various
Purpose: The foundation provides grants for charitable purposes. *Eligibility: Nonprofit organizations serving southern California may apply. *Financial Details: Amounts vary. *Number Awarded: Varies. *Deadline: Varies. Contact the foundation for further details.

Hartford Foundation for Public Giving
85 Gillett Street
Hartford, CT 06105
860-548-1888
hfpg2@hfpg.org
http://www.hfpg.org

Disability Served: various
Purpose: *This community foundation provides grants in the areas of health, education, family and social services, the arts and culture, and other areas. *Eligibility: Nonprofit organizations serving the Hartford area are eligible to apply. *Financial Details: Amounts vary, but the foundation normally does not make grants in excess of $75,000 to a new organization or in excess of $400,000 to an established organization. *Number Awarded: Varies. *Deadline: Applications may be submitted throughout the year.*

Hawai'i Community Foundation
1164 Bishop Street, Suite 800
Honolulu, HI 96813
808-537-6333, 888-731-3863
http://www.hawaiicommunityfoundation.org
Disability Served: various
Purpose: *The foundation provides grants to improve the quality of life in Hawaii. Areas of interest include education, health and medical research, human services, disability, culture and art, and natural resources conservation. *Eligibility: Nonprofits in Hawaii are eligible to apply. *Financial Details: Awards vary by type of project. *Number Awarded: Varies. *Deadline: Varies. Visit the foundation's Web site to download a grant application.*

The Hawley Foundation
PO Box 1017
Saratoga Springs, NY 12866
518-584-3355
scottjohnson@tfgjlaw.com
http://www.hawleyfoundation.com
Disability Served: various
Purpose: *The foundation provides grants to organizations that serve the neediest children in Saratoga County, New York. *Eligibility: Nonprofit organizations in Saratoga County may apply. *Financial Details: Amounts vary. Number Awarded: Varies. *Deadline: May 1. Visit the foundation's Web site to download an application.*

Herbst Foundation
30 Van Ness Avenue, Suite 3600
San Francisco, CA 94102
415-252-1220
Disability Served: various
Purpose: *The foundation provides funds for building projects and facilities in San Francisco County. *Eligibility: Nonprofit organizations involved in education and children's projects serving San Francisco County may apply. *Financial Details: Amounts vary and depend on project need. *Number Awarded: Varies each year. *Deadline: Applications are accepted throughout the year. Contact the foundation for more information.*

Hill Foundation
1740 Broadway, MAC C7300-483
Denver, CO 80274
720-947-6820
Disability Served: various
Purpose: *The foundation provides grants to help finance projects in higher education, culture, and health and human services. *Eligibility: Charitable and university organizations are eligible to apply. *Financial Details: Amounts vary. *Number Awarded: Varies each year. *Deadline: Varies. Contact the foundation for more information.*

Houston Endowment
Attn: Grant Department
600 Travis Street, Suite 6400
Houston, TX 77002-3000
713-238-8100
info@houstonendowment.org
http://www.houstonendowment.org
Disability Served: various
Purpose: *The foundation makes grants to Houston-area nonprofit organizations in the areas of education, health, human services, neighborhood development, the arts, and the environment. *Eligibility: Organizations serving Harris County and contiguous counties may apply. *Financial Details: Amounts vary. *Number Awarded: Varies. *Deadline: Applications are accepted throughout the year.*

Howard Heinz Endowment
625 Liberty Avenue, 30 Dominion Tower
Pittsburgh, PA 15222
412-281-5777
info@heinz.org
http://www.heinz.org
Disability Served: various
Purpose: *The foundation provides grants in the areas of arts and culture, education, economic opportunity, health and human services, and the environment. *Eligibility: Nonprofit organizations serving southwestern Pennsylvania may apply. *Financial Details: Amounts vary and depend on need. *Number Awarded: Varies. *Deadline: The committee meets*

twice per year. Call or write for dates. Applicants may complete an online application or submit a traditional letter of inquiry.

Hugh J. Andersen Foundation

Attn: Program Director
342 Fifth Avenue North, White Pine Building
Bayport, MN 55003
651-439-1557, 888-439-9508
hjafdn@srinc.biz
http://www.srinc.biz/hja
Disability Served: various
Purpose: The foundation provides grants for the purpose of improving the community. Focus areas include programs for the developmentally or physically disabled, seniors, children and youth, and other groups. *Eligibility: Charitable organizations in the St. Croix Valley and Washington County in Minnesota and Pierce, Polk, and St. Croix Counties in Wisconsin are eligible to apply. *Financial Details: Recent grants ranged from $1,500 to $200,000. *Number Awarded: Varies. *Deadlines: March 15, June 15, September 15, and November 15. Visit the foundation's Web site to download an application.

Humboldt Area Foundation

373 Indianola Road
Bayside, CA 95524
707-442-2993
http://hafoundation.org
Disability Served: various
Purpose: This community foundation provides grants to improve the quality of life for residents of the counties of Humboldt, Del Norte, Siskiyou, and Trinity, California. *Eligibility: Charitable organizations serving the North Coast area may apply. *Financial Details: Amounts vary and depend on need. *Number Awarded: Varies. *Deadline: Varies. Visit the foundation's Web site for more information.

Idaho Community Foundation

PO Box 8143
Boise, ID 83707
208-342-3535, 800-657-5357
info@idcomfdn.org
http://www.idcomfdn.org
Disability Served: various
Purpose: The foundation provides grants in the areas of health, human services, arts and culture, education, public projects, and the environment. *Eligibility:

Nonprofit organizations in Idaho are eligible to apply. *Financial Details: Awards vary. *Number Awarded: Varies. *Deadlines: February, May, August, and November. Visit the foundation's Web site to download a grant application.

The Invacare Foundation

One Invacare Way
Elyria, OH 44036
440-329-6102
Disability Served: various
Purpose: The foundation provides grants intended to improve the lives of people with disabilities. *Eligibility: Charitable organizations are eligible to apply. Contact the foundation for additional eligibility requirements. *Financial Details: Amounts vary. *Number Awarded: Varies each year. *Deadline: The application review committee meets during the first week of January, March, May, July, September, and November. Applications must be received no later than three weeks prior to a scheduled meeting.

James S. Copley Foundation

PO Box 1530
La Jolla, CA 92038-1530
858-454-0411
Disability Served: various
Purpose: The foundation provides support for community and civic services in the immediate circulation areas of Copley newspapers. Areas of interest include education, the arts, health and human services, youth development, and urban affairs. *Eligibility: Nonprofit organizations serving the Copley newspapers' immediate circulation areas may apply. *Financial Details: Amounts vary and depend on need and available funds. *Number Awarded: Varies each year. *Deadline: Varies. Contact the foundation for more information.

J. B. and Emily Van Nuys Charities

PO Box 2946
Palos Verdes Peninsula, CA 90274
310-544-8045
Disability Served: physically disabled
Purpose: The charities provide grants to help finance programs for the physically disabled. *Eligibility: Charitable organizations and independent living programs are eligible. *Financial Details: Amounts vary. *Number Awarded: Varies. *Deadline: Varies. Contact the charities for details.

Jefferson Lee Ford III Memorial Foundation

c/o Suntrust Bank, Trust Department
9600 Collins Avenue
PO Box 546487
Bal Harbour, FL 33154
Disability Served: various
Purpose: The foundation provides grants for charitable
purposes. *Eligibility: Nonprofit organizations
concerned with the welfare of disabled children and
persons with hearing and communicative impairments
are eligible. *Financial Details: Amounts vary. *Number
Awarded: Varies. *Deadline: Varies. Contact the
foundation for more information.

Jessie Ball duPont Fund

One Independent Drive, Suite 1400
Jacksonville, FL 32202-0511
904-353-0890, 800-252-3452
contactus@dupontfund.org
http://www.dupontfund.org
Disability Served: various
Purpose: The foundation awards grants in many areas,
including health, education, religion, the arts, social
service, and the environment. *Eligibility: This grant
making foundation limits its grant making to 327
eligible organizations to which Mrs. duPont personally
contributed during 1960 through 1964; visit the
foundation's Web site for a complete list. *Financial
Details: $10,000 per award. *Number Awarded: Varies.
*Deadline: Varies. Visit the foundation's Web site for
more information.

Johnson Controls Foundation

5757 North Green Bay Avenue, PO Box 591
Milwaukee, WI 53201
414-524-2296
http://www.johnsoncontrols.com/corpvalues/
foundation.htm
Disability Served: various
Purpose: The foundation awards grants in many areas,
including health, education, the arts, and social service.
*Eligibility: Charitable organizations are eligible to
apply. *Financial Details: Amounts vary. *Number
Awarded: Varies each year. *Deadline: Applications are
accepted throughout the year. Contact the foundation
for details.

Joseph Drown Foundation

1999 Avenue of the Stars, Suite 2330
Los Angeles, CA 90067
310-277-4488

http://www.jdrown.org
Disability Served: various
Purpose: The foundation provides funds to help improve
the quality of life for residents of the Los Angeles
area. *Eligibility: Charitable organizations serving
the Los Angeles area may apply. *Financial Details:
Amounts range from $5,000 to $1 million. *Number
Awarded: Varies. *Deadlines: January 15, April 15, July
15, and October 15. Contact the foundation for more
information.

Kenneth T. and Eileen L. Norris Foundation

11 Golden Shore, Suite 450
Long Beach, CA 90802
562-435-8444
grants@ktn.org
http://www.norrisfoundation.org
Disability Served: various
Purpose: The foundation offers grants in the areas of
medicine, education, community, youth, and the
arts. *Eligibility: Nonprofit organizations serving the
southern California area are eligible. *Financial Details:
Amounts vary, but average $5,000. *Number Awarded:
Varies. *Deadline: Varies. An online application is
available at the foundation's Web site.

Kinney-Lindstrom Foundation Inc.

PO Box 520
Mason City, IA 50401
Disability Served: various
Purpose: The foundation provides grants for charitable
purposes, primarily in the areas of arts and culture,
programs for the physically disabled, and the Special
Olympics. *Eligibility: Nonprofit organizations in Iowa
may apply. *Financial Details: Amounts vary. *Number
Awarded: Varies. *Deadline: Varies. Contact the
foundation for more information.

Kiplinger Foundation Inc.

1729 H Street, NW
Washington, DC 20006
202-887-6559
foundation@kiplinger.com
Disability Served: various
Purpose: The foundation provides grants to fund programs
in education, cultural projects, social welfare, and community activities. *Eligibility: Nonprofit organizations in
the Greater Washington, D.C., area are eligible to apply.
*Financial Details: Amounts vary and depend on project
need. *Number Awarded: Varies. *Deadline: Varies.
Contact the foundation for more information.

Kresge Foundation
3215 West Big Beaver
Troy, MI 48084
248-643-9630
http://www.kresge.org
Disability Served: various
Purpose: *The foundation offers grants for capital projects, such as building renovation, construction, and the purchase of science equipment. *Eligibility: Nonprofit organizations are eligible. *Financial Details: Awards vary by project. *Number Awarded: Varies. *Deadline: Applications are accepted throughout the year. Contact the foundation for more information.*

Levi Strauss Foundation
1155 Battery Street, LS7N
San Francisco, CA 94111
415-501-6579
http://www.levistrauss.com/responsibility/
foundation
Disability Served: AIDS
Purpose: *The foundation provides funds in the areas of AIDS, economic empowerment, youth empowerment, and social justice. *Eligibility: Charitable organizations involved in projects that serve areas where Levi Strauss and Company has facilities are eligible to apply. *Financial Details: Awards vary and depend on project need. *Number Awarded: Varies. *Deadline: Visit the foundation's Web site for current priorities and application information.*

The Liz Claiborne Foundation
1441 Broadway
New York, NY 10018
http://www.lizclaiborneinc.com/foundation/default.asp
Disability Served: various
Purpose: *The foundation supports projects in the areas of social welfare, education, health (including women who are HIV-positive or have AIDS), culture, and the environment. *Eligibility: Charitable organizations involved in the areas listed above are eligible. *Financial Details: Award amounts vary. *Number Awarded: Varies. *Deadline: Varies. Contact the foundation for further details.*

Longwood Foundation Inc.
100 West 10th Street, Suite 1109
Wilmington, DE 19801
Disability Served: mental retardation, physically disabled
Purpose: *The foundation offers grants to support projects for the mentally and physically disabled in Delaware.*

*Eligibility: Nonprofit organizations dedicated to helping the mentally and physically disabled in Delaware are eligible. *Financial Details: Amounts vary. *Number Awarded: Varies. *Deadline: Varies. Contact the foundation for more information.*

Maine Community Foundation
245 Main Street
Ellsworth, ME 04605
207-667-9735, 877-700-6800
http://www.mainecf.org
Disability Served: various
Purpose: *The foundation provides grants to improve the quality of life in Maine. *Eligibility: Nonprofit organizations in Maine are eligible to apply. *Financial Details: Varies. *Number Awarded: Varies. *Deadline: Varies. Visit the foundation's Web site to download a grant application.*

Mary A. Crocker Trust
Attn: Program Officer
233 Post Street
San Francisco, CA 94108
415-982-0138
mact@best.com
http://www.mactrust.org
Disability Served: various
Purpose: *The trust provides funds in the areas of education and the environment. *Eligibility: Charitable organizations in the San Francisco Bay area may apply. The Bay area is defined as the following nine counties: Alameda, Contra Costa, Marin, Napa, San Francisco, San Mateo, Santa Clara, Solano, and Sonoma. *Financial Details: Amounts vary, but grants usually range from $10,000 to $25,000. Continuing support is not awarded. *Number Awarded: Varies. *Deadlines: Letters of intent are due at the end of January and the end of August. Contact the trust for details.*

Mary Reynolds Babcock Foundation Inc.
2920 Reynolda Road
Winston-Salem, NC 27106
336-748-9222
info@mrbf.org
http://www.mrbf.org
Disability Served: various
Purpose: *The foundation provides grants to support community projects. *Eligibility: Nonprofit organizations serving communities in the Southeast are eligible to apply. *Financial Details: Grassroots organizations: one-time, one-year grants that range*

from $20,000 to $50,000. Established organizations: $50,000 to $200,000 annually over two to 10 years. *Number Awarded: Varies each year. *Deadlines: February 1 and July 1. Interested parties should visit the foundation's Web site to complete an online summary in advance of submitting an application.

McKesson Foundation Inc.
One Post Street
San Francisco, CA 94104
415-983-8300
community.relations@mckesson.com
http://www.mckesson.com/foundation.html
Disability Served: various
Purpose: The foundation provides funds that help improve the quality of healthcare for low-income children and youth. *Eligibility: Nonprofit organizations involved in the area mentioned above may apply. *Financial Details: Varies depending on need, but grants range from $1,500 to $200,000. *Number Awarded: Varies. *Deadline: Applications are accepted throughout the year. Contact the foundation for additional information.

McKnight Foundation
710 South Second Street, Suite 400
Minneapolis, MN 55401
612-333-4220
http://www.mcknight.org
Disability Served: various
Purpose: The foundation provides grants in a number of areas, including social services, arts, housing, family services, the disadvantaged, rural development, child development, child welfare, women, youth, AIDS, community funds, environment, homeless, and international development. *Eligibility: Charitable organizations in Minnesota may apply. *Financial Details: Amounts vary. *Number Awarded: Varies. *Deadline: Varies. Visit the foundation's Web site for more information.

The Meadows Foundation
Attn: Vice President for Grants
3003 Swiss Avenue
Dallas, TX 75204
214-826-9431, 800-826-9431
http://www.mfi.org
Disability Served: various
Purpose: The foundation provides grants in the areas of education, health, human services, arts and

culture, and civic and public affairs. *Eligibility: Nonprofit organizations serving the people of Texas are eligible. *Financial Details: Grant amounts vary. Number Awarded: Varies. *Deadline: Grant proposals are accepted throughout the year. An online grant application is available at the foundation's Web site.

Metzger-Price Fund Inc.
230 Park Avenue, Suite 2300
New York, NY 10169
Disability Served: various
Purpose: This organization provides funds to help organizations in New York City care for the needy, elderly, and infirm. *Eligibility: Nonprofit organizations in the New York metropolitan area are eligible. *Financial Details: Amounts vary. *Number Awarded: Varies. *Deadline: Contact the fund for more information.

Meyer Foundation
1400 16th Street, NW, Suite 360
Washington, DC 20036
202-483-8294
meyer@meyerfdn.org
http://www.meyerfoundation.org
Disability Served: various
Purpose: The foundation provides grants to help finance projects having to do with health and mental health, education, community service, and other areas. *Eligibility: Nonprofit organizations in the metropolitan area of Washington, D.C., are eligible. *Financial Details: Grants range from $1,500 to $50,000 or more. *Number Awarded: Varies. *Deadline: Varies. Contact the foundation for more information.

Mildred Andrews Fund
925 Euclid Avenue, Suite 2000
Cleveland, OH 44115-1407
Disability Served: various
Purpose: The foundation provides grants to support charitable projects in the Cleveland area. *Eligibility: Nonprofit organizations serving the Cleveland area are eligible to apply. *Financial Details: Amounts vary. *Number Awarded: Varies each year. *Deadline: Varies. Contact the foundation for more information.

Mitsubishi Electric America Foundation
1560 Wilson Boulevard, Suite 1150
Arlington, VA 22209
703-276-8240
http://www.meaf.org

Disability Served: *learning disabled, mental retardation, and physically disabled*

Purpose: *The foundation provides grants to organizations that improve the lives of the learning disabled, the mentally disabled, and the physically disabled. *Eligibility: Nonprofit organizations are eligible to apply. *Financial Details: Awards vary. *Number Awarded: Varies. *Deadline: Concept papers may be submitted throughout the year. Visit the foundation's Web site for more information.*

Montana Community Foundation

101 North Last Chance Gulch, Suite 211
Helena, MT 59601
406-443-8313
http://www.mtcf.org
Disability Served: *various*
Purpose: *The foundation provides grants to improve the quality of life in Montana. Areas of interest include education, basic human needs, arts and culture, economic development, natural resources and conservation, leadership development, and tolerance. *Eligibility: Nonprofits in Montana are eligible to apply. *Financial Details: Varies. *Number Awarded: Approximately 150 annually. *Deadline: Varies. Contact the foundation for more information.*

Morris Stulsaft Foundation

100 Bush Street, Suite 825
San Francisco, CA 94104-3911
415-986-7117
stulsaft@aol.com
http://www.stulsaft.org
Disability Served: *various*
Purpose: *The foundation offers grants to support projects for children and youth, specifically in the areas of physical and mental health, education, arts, recreation, and social services. *Eligibility: Charitable organizations serving the youth of the San Francisco Bay area (which is defined as Alameda, Contra Costa, Marin, San Francisco, San Mateo, and Santa Clara Counties) are eligible. *Financial Details: Amounts vary, but grants generally range from $5,000 to $25,000. *Number Awarded: 150 to 200 annually. *Deadline: Applications are accepted throughout the year and are reviewed six times per year. Visit the foundation's Web site to download an application.*

Nebraska Community Foundation

317 South 12th Street, Suite 200, PO Box 83107
Lincoln, NE 68501

402-323-7330
http://www.nebcommfound.org
Disability Served: *various*
Purpose: *The foundation provides grants to improve the quality of life in Nebraska. Areas of interest include education, health, and community development. *Eligibility: Nonprofits in Nebraska are eligible to apply. *Financial Details: Varies. *Number Awarded: Varies. *Deadline: Contact the foundation for more information.*

NEC Foundation of America

2950 Express Drive South, Suite 102
Islandia, NY 11749-1412
631-232 2212
http://www.necfoundation.org
Disability Served: *various*
Purpose: *The foundation provides grants to organizations that provide assistive technology to people with disabilities. *Eligibility: Nonprofit organizations are eligible to apply. *Financial Details: Grants range from $1,500 to $75,000—the average grant is $30,000. *Number Awarded: Varies. *Deadlines: March 1 and September 1. Applicants may submit preliminary proposals online at the foundation's Web site.*

New Hampshire Charitable Foundation

37 Pleasant Street
Concord, NH 03301
603-225-6641, ext. 229
la@nhcf.org
http://www.nhcf.org
Disability Served: *various*
Purpose: *The Foundation provides grants to improve the quality of life in New Hampshire. Areas of interest include education, health, and human services. *Eligibility: Nonprofits in New Hampshire are eligible to apply. *Financial Details: Awards vary by type of project. *Number Awarded: Varies. *Deadline: Varies. Visit the Foundation's Web site for more information.*

North Carolina Community Foundation

200 South Salisbury Street
Raleigh, NC 27602-2828
919-828-4387, 800-201-9533
http://www.nccommf.org
Disability Served: *various*
Purpose: *The foundation provides grants to improve the quality of life in North Carolina. Areas of interest include human services, education, health, arts, religion,*

civic affairs, and the conservation and preservation of historical, cultural, and environmental resources. *Eligibility: Nonprofits in North Carolina are eligible to apply. *Financial Details: Awards vary by type of project. *Number Awarded: Varies. *Deadline: Varies. Visit the foundation's Web site for more information.

North Dakota Community Foundation
1025 North Third Street, PO Box 387
Bismarck, ND 58502-0387
701-222-8349
http://www.ndcf.net
Disability Served: various
Purpose: The foundation provides grants to improve the quality of life in North Dakota communities. Areas of interest include aging, education, health, human services, children and youth, arts and culture, conservation, and the environment. *Eligibility: Nonprofits that serve North Dakota communities are eligible to apply. *Financial Details: Varies. *Number Awarded: Varies. *Deadline: Applicants should submit proposals by August 15. Visit the foundation's Web site for more information.

Ordean Foundation
501 Ordean Building
Duluth, MN 55802
218-726-4785
Disability Served: various
Purpose: The foundation provides grants for projects in a number of areas, including health, youth programs, and aid for the economically disadvantaged. *Eligibility: Nonprofit organizations servicing the Duluth and St. Louis County areas are eligible. *Financial Details: Amounts vary. *Number Awarded: Varies. *Deadline: Varies. Contact the foundation for more information.

The Oregon Community Foundation
1221 Southwest Yamhill, Suite 100
Portland, OR 97205
503-227-6846, ext. 414
info@ocf1.org
http://www.ocf1.org
Disability Served: various
Purpose: The foundation provides grants to improve the quality of life in Oregon communities. Areas of interest include education, nursing home care, and early childhood. *Eligibility: Nonprofits that serve Oregon communities are eligible to apply. *Financial Details: Grants range from $5,000 to $50,000. *Number

Awarded: More than 200 annually. *Deadlines: February 1 and August 1. Visit the foundation's Web site for more information.

Parker Foundation
Attn: Assistant Secretary
4365 Executive Drive, Suite 1100
San Diego, CA 92121-2133
858-677-1431
http://www.theparkerfoundation.org
Disability Served: various
Purpose: The foundation provides grants for charitable purposes in San Diego County. *Eligibility: Nonprofit organizations serving San Diego County may apply. *Financial Details: Grants range from $5,000 to $100,000. *Number Awarded: Varies. *Deadline: Varies. Visit the foundation's Web site to download an application.

The Pasadena Community Foundation
260 South Robles Avenue, Suite 119
Pasadena, CA 91101
626-796-2097
pcfstaff@pasadenacf.org
http://www.pasadenacf.org
Disability Served: various
Purpose: The foundation provides funds to help improve the quality of life in the Pasadena, California area. *Eligibility: Nonprofit organizations serving the communities of Pasadena, Altadena, and Sierra Madre are eligible. *Financial Details: Grants range from $25 to $50,000. *Number Awarded: Varies. *Deadline: Varies. Visit the foundation's Web site to download a grant application.

The Philadelphia Foundation
1234 Market Street, Suite 1800
Philadelphia, PA 19107
215-563-6417
parkow@philafound.org
http://www.philafound.org
Disability Served: various
Purpose: This community foundation provides grants in the areas of education, culture, health, housing and economic development, children and families, community affairs, and social services. *Eligibility: Nonprofit organizations serving the Pennsylvania counties of Bucks, Chester, Delaware, Montgomery, and Philadelphia are eligible. *Financial Details: Amounts vary. *Number Awarded: Varies each year. *Deadlines: May 2 and November 1.

The Prudential Foundation
751 Broad Street, 15th Floor
Newark, NJ 07102-3777
973-802-4791
community.resources@prudential.com
http://www.prudential.com/community
Disability Served: various
*Purpose: The foundation provides grants for charitable projects in the areas of children's issues, community development, education, health and human services, business and civic affairs, and arts and culture. *Eligibility: Nonprofit organizations may apply. Priority is given to organizations in New Jersey and in cities where Prudential has a significant presence. *Financial Details: Grants range from $25,000 to $1 million. *Number Awarded: Varies. *Deadline: Varies. A grant application is available at the foundation's Web site.*

Public Welfare Foundation Inc.
1200 U Street, NW
Washington, DC 20037
202-965-1800
http://www.publicwelfare.org
Disability Served: various
*Purpose: The foundation supports grant programs in the following areas: health, youth, reproductive and sexual health, welfare reform, community development, civic participation, criminal justice, environment, and human rights/global security. *Eligibility: Nonprofit organizations that work in these areas may apply. *Financial Details: Grants range from $25,000 to $100,000 or more. *Number Awarded: Approximately 145 annually. *Deadline: Visit the foundation's Web site to complete an online letter of inquiry.*

Ralph M. Parsons Foundation
Attn: Executive Director
1055 Wilshire Boulevard, Suite 1701
Los Angeles, CA 90017
213-482-3185
http://www.rmpf.org
Disability Served: various
*Purpose: The foundation supports projects in the areas of education, social issues, health, and civic and cultural affairs. *Eligibility: Charitable organizations in Los Angeles County may apply. *Financial Details: Amount range from $25,000 to $50,000. *Number Awarded: Approximately 200 annually. *Deadline: Varies. Proposals are accepted throughout the year. Write or call for information.*

Rasmuson Foundation
301 West Northern Lights Boulevard, Suite 400
Anchorage, AK 99503
907-297-2700
rasmusonfdn@rasmuson.org
http://www.rasmuson.org
Disability Served: various
*Purpose: The foundation offers grants for recreation programs and projects designed to increase the quality of life of people in Alaska. *Eligibility: Charitable organizations in Alaska are eligible. *Financial Details: Grants range from $1,500 to $25,000 or more. *Number Awarded: Varies. *Deadline: Varies. Contact the foundation for details.*

R. C. Baker Foundation
PO Box 6150
Orange, CA 92863-6150
Disability Served: various
*Purpose: The foundation provides grants for charitable causes. Historically, aid has been given to educational institutions, scientific facilities, religious organizations, and youth programs. *Eligibility: Nonprofit organizations may apply. *Financial Details: Amounts vary and depend on need. *Number Awarded: Varies. *Deadline: Contact the foundation for more information.*

The Retirement Research Foundation
8765 West Higgins Road, Suite 430
Chicago, IL 60631-4170
773-714-8080
info@rrf.org
http://www.rrf.org
Disability Served: elderly
*Purpose: This private foundation provides grants to support projects for the elderly. *Eligibility: Charitable organizations dedicated to improving the lives of the aged are eligible. Nonprofit agencies in Illinois, Indiana, Iowa, Kentucky, Missouri, Wisconsin, and Florida are eligible to apply, with organizations located in the Chicago area receiving the highest priority. *Financial Details: In 2003, grants ranged from $1,000 to $213,000—the average grant was $53,000. *Number Awarded: Varies. *Deadlines: February 1, May 1, and August 1. Contact the foundation for more information.*

The Rhode Island Foundation
One Union Station
Providence, RI 02903

401-274-4564
http://www.rifoundation.org/matriarch
Disability Served: *various*
Purpose: *The foundation provides grants to improve the quality of life in Rhode Island. Areas of interest include children and families, economic/community development, and education. *Eligibility: Nonprofits in Rhode Island are eligible to apply. *Financial Details: Awards range from $500 to $50,000. *Number Awarded: Varies. *Deadline: Varies. Visit the foundation's Web site for more information.*

Robert Sterling Clark Foundation
135 East 64th Street
New York, NY 10021
212-288-8900
http://www.rsclark.org
Disability Served: *various*
Purpose: *Principal funding areas of this private foundation include reproductive health information and services, cultural institutions, and government accountability. *Eligibility: Nonprofit organizations involved in the areas listed above are eligible. *Financial Details: Amounts vary. *Number Awarded: Approximately 100 annually. *Deadline: Proposals are accepted throughout the year. Contact the foundation for more information.*

The San Diego Foundation
1420 Kettner Boulevard, Suite 500
San Diego, CA 92101
619-235-2300
info@sdfoundation.org
http://www.sdfoundation.org
Disability Served: *various*
Purpose: *The foundation funds projects designed to benefit the residents of the San Diego region. Areas of interest include health and human services, arts and culture, the environment, urban affairs, and education. *Eligibility: Nonprofit organizations involved in the areas described above may apply. *Financial Details: Amounts vary and depend on project need. *Number Awarded: Varies. *Deadline: Varies. Contact the foundation for dates.*

The San Francisco Foundation
225 Bush Street, Suite 500
San Francisco, CA 94104
415-733-8500
rec@sff.org
http://www.sff.org
Disability Served: *various*

Purpose: *The foundation provides grants to support projects that benefit the residents of the San Francisco Bay area (including Alameda, Contra Costa, Marin, San Francisco, and San Mateo Counties). Grant making areas include community health, education, neighborhood and community development, arts and culture, the environment, and social justice. *Eligibility: Nonprofit organizations serving the San Francisco Bay area are eligible to apply. *Financial Details: Amounts vary. *Number Awarded: Varies. *Deadline: Varies. Contact the foundation for details.*

Santa Fe Community Foundation
Attn: Program Director
PO Box 1827
Santa Fe, NM 87504-1827
505-988-9715
DRoybal@SantaFeCF.org
http://www.santafecf.org
Disability Served: *various*
Purpose: *The foundation provides grants to improve the quality of life in Santa Fe and northern New Mexico. Areas of interest include health and human services, education, the environment, arts, and civic affairs. *Eligibility: Nonprofits that serve Santa Fe, Los Alamos, Mora, Rio Arriba, San Miguel, and Taos Counties are eligible to apply. *Financial Details: Varies. *Number Awarded: Varies. *Deadline: July 1. Visit the foundation's Web site for more information.*

Sarkeys Foundation
530 East Main Street
Norman, OK 73071
405-364-3703
sarkeys@sarkeys.org
http://www.sarkeys.org
Disability Served: *various*
Purpose: *The foundation offers grants to help improve the quality of life in Oklahoma and the Southwest. Areas of interest include arts and culture, social service, health concerns, and education. *Eligibility: Nonprofit organizations in Oklahoma are eligible to apply. *Financial Details: Up to $50,000. *Number Awarded: Varies. *Deadline: Applications are accepted from December 15 through February 1. A grant application is available at the foundation's Web site.*

The Seattle Foundation
1200 Fifth Avenue, Suite 1300
Seattle, WA 98101-3151

206-622-2294
grantmaking@seattlefoundation.org
http://www.seattlefoundation.org
Disability Served: various
Purpose: The foundation provides grants to organizations
that focus on health, human services, education,
the environment, and community improvements.
Eligibility: Nonprofit organizations in the Seattle
metropolitan area are eligible to apply. *Financial
Details:* Amounts vary. *Number Awarded:* Varies each
year. *Deadlines:* January 1, April 1, July 1, and October
1. Visit the foundation's Web site for more information.

S. H. Cowell Foundation
120 Montgomery Street, Suite 2570
San Francisco, CA 94104
415-397-0285
http://www.shcowell.org
Disability Served: various
Purpose: The foundation supports projects that focus on
the underlying causes of poverty and social problems.
Areas of interest include education, health, youth
development, and affordable housing. *Eligibility:*
Nonprofit organizations in northern California that are
involved in the areas listed above may apply. *Financial
Details:* Grants range from $15,000 to $700,000.
Number Awarded: Varies. *Deadline:* There are no
deadlines; applications are accepted throughout the
year. Contact the foundation for more information.

Sidney Stern Memorial Trust
PO Box 893
Pacific Palisades, CA 90272
310-459-2117
Disability Served: various
Purpose: The trust provides grants in the areas of
community affairs, youth services, arts and culture,
health and science, education, and programs for
the mentally and physically disabled. *Eligibility:*
Nonprofit organizations serving California may apply.
Financial Details: Amounts vary. *Number Awarded:*
Varies. *Deadline:* Varies. Contact the trust for more
information.

South Dakota Community Foundation
207 East Capitol, Box 296
Pierre, SD 57501
605-224-1025, 800-888-1842
ginger@sdcommunityfoundation.org
http://www.sdcommunityfoundation.org/home.php

Disability Served: various
Purpose: The foundation provides grants to improve
the quality of life in South Dakota. Areas of interest
include human services, health, education, economic
development, and cultural programs. *Eligibility:*
Nonprofits in South Dakota are eligible to apply.
Financial Details: Grants range from $2,000 to $25,000.
Number Awarded: Varies. *Deadline:* Applications are
accepted throughout the year. Visit the foundation's
Web site to download a grant application.

Square D Foundation
1415 South Roselle Road
Palatine, IL 60067
847-397-2600
Disability Served: various
Purpose: The foundation provides funds in a number
of areas, including education, civic and community
affairs, health services, and arts and culture. *Eligibility:*
Nonprofit organizations may apply. *Financial Details:*
Amounts vary. Funds may be used for operating support
or capital development. *Number Awarded:* Varies.
Deadline: Varies. Contact the foundation for more
information.

SunTrust Bank Atlanta Foundation
Community and Government Affairs
PO Box 4418, Mail Code 041
Atlanta, GA 30302
404-588-8250
http://www.suntrustatlantafoundation.org/funds.html
Disability Served: various
Purpose: The foundation serves as the administrator for
four funds/trusts. Grants are awarded in the fields
of education, health, general welfare, and culture.
Eligibility: Charitable organizations in Atlanta are
eligible to apply. *Financial Details:* Amounts vary.
Number Awarded: Varies. *Deadline:* Contact the
foundation for details. An online application is available
at the foundation's Web site.

Toby Wells Foundation
17083 Old Coach Road
Poway, CA 92064
858-391-2973
adrienne@tobywells.org
http://www.tobywells.org
Disability Served: various
Purpose: The foundation provides grants to organizations
in San Diego County that serve persons with disabilities,

youth, and animals. *Eligibility: Nonprofit organizations in San Diego County are eligible to apply. *Financial Details: Varies. *Number Awarded: Varies. *Deadline: Grant proposals are accepted throughout the year. Contact the foundation for more information.

The Tull Charitable Foundation
50 Hurt Plaza, Suite 1245
Atlanta, GA 30303
404-659-7079
jan@tullfoundation.org
http://www.tullfoundation.org
Disability Served: various
Purpose: The foundation provides funds to support major projects in the following areas: health and human services, education and schools, youth development, civic improvement, and art and culture. *Eligibility: Nonprofit organizations in Georgia may apply. *Financial Details: Amounts vary. Funds may not be used for operating support. *Number Awarded: Approximately 60 annually. *Deadlines: January 1, April 1, July 1, and October 1. Contact the foundation for details.

Van Ameringen Foundation Inc.
509 Madison Avenue
New York, NY 10022-5501
212-758-6221
http://www.vanamfound.org
Disability Served: mental health
Purpose: The foundation provides grants in the areas of mental health and social welfare. *Eligibility: Nonprofit organizations serving the metropolitan New York and Philadelphia areas may apply. *Financial Details: Single-year grants in the range of $10,000 to $50,000 are awarded. *Number Awarded: Varies. *Deadlines: Six weeks prior to board meetings, which take place in March, June, and November. Visit the foundation's Web site for more information.

The Vermont Community Foundation
Three Court Street, PO Box 30
Middlebury, VT 05753
802-388-3355
info@vermontcf.org
http://www.vermontcf.org
Disability Served: various
Purpose: The foundation provides grants to improve the quality of life in Vermont. Areas of interest include health, education, social services, arts and humanities, the environment, public affairs and community

development, and historic resources. *Eligibility: Nonprofits in Vermont are eligible to apply. *Financial Details: Grants range from $100 to $25,000. *Number Awarded: Varies. *Deadline: Varies. Contact the foundation for more information.

West Virginia Community Foundations Consortium
c/o West Virginia Grantmakers Association
202 Main Avenue, Suite 213, PO Box 985
Weston, WV 26452
304-517-1450
info@GiveToWestVirginia.org
http://givetowestvirginia.org
Disability Served: various
Purpose: The consortium is a network of West Virginia's 26 community foundations and county funds. These organizations provide grants to improve the quality of life in West Virginia. Areas of interest include education, health, children, improving living and working conditions, scientific research, and public recreation. *Eligibility: Nonprofits in West Virginia are eligible to apply. *Financial Details: Awards vary depending on project. *Number Awarded: Varies. *Deadline: Varies. Contact the foundation for more information.

Weyerhaeuser Company Foundation
EC2-2A8, PO Box 9777
Federal Way, WA 98063-9777
253-924-3159
http://www.weyerhaeuser.com/citizenship/philanthropy
Disability Served: various
Purpose: The foundation provides grants that improve the quality of life in areas that have Weyerhaeuser facilities. *Eligibility: Nonprofit organizations are eligible to apply. *Financial Details: Amounts vary. *Number Awarded: Varies. *Deadline: Applications are accepted throughout the year. A grant application is available at the foundation's Web site.

William G. Selby and Marie Selby Foundation
1800 Second Street, Suite 750
Sarasota, FL 34236
941-957-0442
http://www.selbyfdn.org
Disability Served: various
Purpose: The foundation supports capital projects in education, health and human services, and arts and culture. *Eligibility: Nonprofit organizations in Sarasota, Manatee, DeSoto, and Charlotte counties in Florida are eligible. *Financial Details: Grants ranged

from $10,000 to $350,000 in 2004—the average grant was $90,555. *Number Awarded: Approximately 20 annually. *Deadlines: February 1 and August 1. Visit the foundation's Web site to download a grant application.

William Randolph Hearst Foundations

888 Seventh Avenue, 45th Floor
New York, NY 10106
212-586-5404
http://www.hearstfdn.org
Disability Served: *various*
Purpose: *The foundations provide grants in the areas of education, health, social service, and culture. *Eligibility: Nonprofit organizations are eligible to apply. *Financial Details: Awards vary. *Number Awarded: Varies. *Deadline: Letters of inquiry are accepted throughout the year. Visit the foundation's Web site for more information.*

William Stamps Farish Fund

1100 Louisiana, Suite 1200
Houston, TX 77002
Disability Served: *various*
Purpose: *The fund provides grants for charitable purposes. *Eligibility: Nonprofit organizations in Texas are eligible to apply. *Financial Details: Amounts vary. *Number Awarded: Varies. *Deadline: Varies. Contact the fund for details.*

Winthrop Rockefeller Foundation

308 East Eighth Street
Little Rock, AR 72202
501-376-6854
programstaff@wrfoundation.org
http://www.wrockefellerfoundation.org
Disability Served: *various*
Purpose: *The foundation provides grants for the improvement of the quality of life in Arkansas. *Eligibility: Nonprofit organizations dedicated to making changes and improvements in education, economic development, or civic affairs in Arkansas are eligible to apply. *Financial Details: Grant amounts vary. *Number Awarded: Varies from year to year. *Deadline: There are no application deadlines. Concept papers, budgets, request information forms, and evidence of eligibility may be submitted throughout the year. Contact the foundation for more information.*

W. P. and H. B. White Foundation

540 Frontage Road, Suite 3240
Northfield, IL 60093
847-446-1441
Disability Served: *mental health, vision*
Purpose: *The foundation gives to organizations in the Chicago metropolitan area. *Eligibility: Nonprofit groups in Chicago involved with the visually impaired, youth, and those with mental illnesses are eligible. *Financial Details: Amounts vary. *Number Awarded: Varies. *Deadline: Varies. Contact the foundation for more information.*

Wyoming Community Foundation

221 Ivinson Avenue, Suite 202
Laramie, WY 82070-3038
307-721-8300
wcf@wycf.org
http://www.wycf.org
Disability Served: *various*
Purpose: *The foundation provides grants to improve the quality of life in Wyoming. Areas of interest include health and human services, education, arts and culture, civic projects, and conservation and natural resources. *Eligibility: Nonprofits in Wyoming are eligible to apply. *Financial Details: Varies. *Number Awarded: Varies. *Deadlines: March 1, July 1, and November 1. Visit the foundation's Web site to download a grant application.*

PUBLICATIONS ON FUNDING

The following section lists publications of interest to people with disabilities and their caregivers, as well as resources for private and public organizations that serve the disabled.

Aging News Alert
CD Publications
8204 Fenton Street
Silver Spring, MD 20910
301-588-6380, 800-666-6380
info@cdpublications.com
http://www.cdpublications.com
Disability Served: elderly
This bimonthly publication provides information on federal legislation and actions that affect the elderly. It features articles on funding opportunities, long-term care, prescription drug coverage, and other topics.

America's Nonprofit Sector
The Foundation Center
79 Fifth Avenue
New York, NY 10003
212-620-4230
orders@fdncenter.org
http://fdncenter.org
Disability Served: various
This publication provides information on the nonprofit sector.

The Buck Starts Here: A Guide to Assistive Technology Funding in Kentucky
Kentucky Assistive Technology Service Network Coordinating Center
Charles McDowell Center
8412 Westport Road
Louisville, KY 40242
502-429-4484, 800-327-5287
http://www.katsnet.org/fundingbook.html
Disability Served: various
This publication discusses public and private funding sources for assistive technology in Kentucky and beyond. It is available for free download at the center's Web site.

California Foundations: A Profile of the State's Grantmaking Community
The Foundation Center
79 Fifth Avenue
New York, NY 10003
212-620-4230
orders@fdncenter.org
http://fdncenter.org
Disability Served: various
This publication profiles California foundations by type, size, and geographic focus.

Catalog of Federal Domestic Assistance
United States General Services Administration
1800 F Street, NW
Washington, DC 20405
800-827-1000
http://12.46.245.173/cfda/cfda.html
Disability Served: various
This online publication provides access to a database of all federal programs that are available to state and local governments (including the District of Columbia); federally recognized Indian tribal governments; territories (and possessions) of the United States; domestic public, quasi-public, and private profit and nonprofit organizations and institutions; specialized groups; and individuals.

Children & Youth Funding Report
CD Publications
8204 Fenton Street
Silver Spring, MD 20910
301-588-6380, 800-666-6380
info@cdpublications.com
http://www.cdpublications.com
Disability Served: various
This bimonthly publication details public and private grant opportunities in a wide range of areas, including health care, children with disabilities, education, mental health, and nutrition.

Chronicle Guide to Grants
The Chronicle of Philanthropy
1255 23rd Street, NW, Suite 700
Washington, DC 20037
202-466-1200
help@philanthropy.com
http://philanthropy.com/grants
Disability Served: various
This Guide provides a comprehensive listing of grants. It is a fee-based electronic database of all corporate and foundation grants listed in *The Chronicle of Philanthropy.*

Community Health Funding Week
CD Publications
8204 Fenton Street
Silver Spring, MD 20910
301-588-6380, 800-666-6380
info@cdpublications.com
http://www.cdpublications.com
Disability Served: various
This newsletter (formerly known as the *Community Health Funding Report*) for nonprofit executive directors, program coordinators, and development directors details legislative and federal policy developments and provides information on federal, regional and private funding sources.

Consumer Reports Complete Guide to Health Services for Seniors: What Your Family Needs to Know about Finding and Financing Medicare, Assisted Living, Nursing Homes, Home Care, and Adult Day Care
Three Rivers Press
280 Park Avenue
New York, NY 10017
800-733-3000
http://www.randomhouse.com/crown/trp.html
Disability Served: elderly
This book provides advice and resources on funding health care for seniors.

Directory of Funding Resources for Assistive Technology in Minnesota
Minnesota STAR Program
50 Sherburne Avenue, Room 309
St Paul, MN 55155
651-296-2771, 651-296-9478 (TTY)
http://www.admin.state.mn.us/assistivetechnology
Disability Served: various
This guide lists statewide resources that offer either funding or assistive technology loans in Minnesota. This publication is also available as a searchable, online database.

Directory of Missouri Grantmakers
The Foundation Center
79 Fifth Avenue
New York, NY 10003
212-620-4230
orders@fdncenter.org
http://fdncenter.org
Disability Served: various
This is a directory of 1,400 grantors in the state and 400 grantors across the United States that fund Missouri nonprofit agencies.

Disability Funding Week
CD Publications
8204 Fenton Street
Silver Spring, MD 20910
301-588-6380, 800-666-6380
info@cdpublications.com
http://www.cdpublications.com
Disability Served: various
This newsletter (formerly known as the *Disability Funding News),* provides information on public and private funding opportunities for a wide range of disability programs, including those serving people with emotional disabilities, physical handicaps, learning disabilities, visual impairment, autism, and speech impairment.

Family Foundations: A Profile of Funders and Trends
The Foundation Center
79 Fifth Avenue
New York, NY 10003
212-620-4230
orders@fdncenter.org
http://fdncenter.org
Disability Served: various
This book provides an overview of the United States family foundations.

Federal Grants & Contracts Weekly
LRP Publications
PO Box 24668, West
Palm Beach, FL 33416-4668
800-341-7874
custserve@lrp.com
http://www.shoplrp.com
Disability Served: various
This weekly publication provides information on new grant opportunities, profiles of foundations and programs, advice on writing grants, and more. The publication focuses on the fields of research, training, and services. It is available in both print and online versions.

Financial Aid for Individuals with Disabilities
HEATH Resource Center
2121 K Street, NW, Suite 220
Washington, DC 20037
202-973-0904 (Voice/TTY), 800-544-3284

askheath@gwu.edu
http://www.heath.gwu.edu/PDFs/FinancialAid05.pdf
Disability Served: various
This publication discusses funding sources, including
    funding for assistive technology for college students.
    It is available as a PDF document at HEATH's Web site.

Financial Aid for Individuals with Learning Disabilities
HEATH Resource Center
2121 K Street, NW, Suite 220
Washington, DC 20037
202-973-0904 (Voice/TTY), 800-544-3284
askheath@gwu.edu
http://www.heath.gwu.edu/PDFs/Financial%20Aid%20
    for%20Individuals%20with%20Learning%20Disabili
    ties.pdf
Disability Served: learning disabled
This fact sheet provides information on funding for
    students with learning disabilities. It is available as a
    PDF document at HEATH's Web site.

Financial Aid for the Disabled and Their Families
Reference Service Press
5000 Windplay Drive, Suite 4
El Dorado Hills, CA 95762-9600
916-939-9620
info@rspfunding.com
http://www.rspfunding.com
Disability Served: various
This book provides comprehensive information on
    financial aid sources for the disabled, including
    scholarships, grants, and loans.

Finding Funding: Grantwriting from Start to Finish, Including Project Management and Internet Use
Corwin Press
2455 Teller Road
Thousand Oaks, CA 91320
800-818-7243
http://www.corwinpress.com
Disability Served: various
This book provides an overview of grant writing.

The First-Time Grantwriter's Guide to Success
Corwin Press
2455 Teller Road
Thousand Oaks, CA 91320
800-818-7243
http://www.corwinpress.com
Disability Served: various

This publication provides an overview of grant writing
    for the first-time grant writer. It includes information
    on the application package, writing tips, and advice
    on developing a budget.

The Foundation Center's Guide to Grantseeking on the Web
The Foundation Center
79 Fifth Avenue
New York, NY 10003
212-620-4230
orders@fdncenter.org
http://fdncenter.org
Disability Served: various
This book provides 3,000 annotated listings of
    foundations, corporate grant makers, public charities,
    and other important philanthropic Internet links.

The Foundation Center's Guide to Proposal Writing
The Foundation Center
79 Fifth Avenue
New York, NY 10003
212-620-4230
orders@fdncenter.org
http://fdncenter.org
Disability Served: various
This publication provides information and advice on
    writing a grant proposal.

The Foundation Center's Guide to Winning Proposals
The Foundation Center
79 Fifth Avenue
New York, NY 10003
212-620-4230
orders@fdncenter.org
http://fdncenter.org
Disability Served: various
This book features 20 grant proposals that were funded
    by some of the most influential grant makers in the
    United States. A discussion of the strengths and
    weaknesses of each proposal is provided.

The Foundation Directory
The Foundation Center
79 Fifth Avenue
New York, NY 10003
212-620-4230
orders@fdncenter.org
http://fndcenter.org
Disability Served: various

This directory lists the top 10,000 corporate, independent, and community foundations that award grants.

Foundation Fundamentals
The Foundation Center
79 Fifth Avenue
New York, NY 10003
212-620-4230
orders@fdncenter.org
http://fndcenter.org
Disability Served: various
This guide provides general information about foundations and how to write grants.

Foundation Grants to Individuals
The Foundation Center
79 Fifth Avenue
New York, NY 10003
212-620-4230
orders@fdncenter.org
http://fdncenter.org
Disability Served: various
This publication provides information on more than 6,000 corporate and independent foundations that award grants to individuals. An online, subscription-based version is also available.

The Foundation 1000
The Foundation Center
79 Fifth Avenue
New York, NY 10003
212-620-4230
orders@fdncenter.org
http://fdncenter.org
Disability Served: various
This publication offers in-depth profiles of 1,000 foundations in the United States.

Funding for Persons with Visual Impairments
Reference Service Press
5000 Windplay Drive, Suite 4
El Dorado Hills, CA 95762-9600
916-939-9620
info@rspfunding.com
http://www.rspfunding.com
Disability Served: vision
This book provides comprehensive information on financial aid sources, including scholarships, fellowships, grants, and loans, for people with visual impairments. A large-print edition, as well as an electronic version, is available.

Funding Technology for People with Disabilities: A Manual
Illinois Assistive Technology Project
1 West Old State Capitol Plaza, Suite 100
Springfield, IL 62701
217-522-7985, 800-852-5110 (Voice/TTY)
http://www.iltech.org
Disability Served: various
This publication provides detailed information on more than 50 public and alternative funding sources in Illinois.

Grants for Children and Youth
The Foundation Center
79 Fifth Avenue
New York, NY 10003
212-620-4230
orders@fdncenter.org
http://fdncenter.org
Disability Served: various
This guide lists foundations and corporate giving programs that award funds to projects focused on children, youth, and families. The publication also lists sample grants.

Grants for Elementary and Secondary Education
The Foundation Center
79 Fifth Avenue
New York, NY 10003
212-620-4230
orders@fdncenter.org
http://fdncenter.org
Disability Served: various
This publication lists more than 870 foundations and corporate giving programs that award grants to projects supporting elementary and secondary education (including the education of special populations, such as disabled children).

Grants for Higher Education
The Foundation Center
79 Fifth Avenue
New York, NY 10003
212-620-4230
orders@fdncenter.org
http://fdncenter.org
Disability Served: various

This guide lists more than 3,000 foundations and corporate giving programs that award grants to universities, colleges, graduate programs, and research facilities.

Grants for Libraries and Information Services
The Foundation Center
79 Fifth Avenue
New York, NY 10003
212-620-4230
orders@fdncenter.org
http://fdncenter.org
Disability Served: various
This publication provides details on more than 610 foundations that provide grants to libraries and information services.

Grants for Mental Health, Addictions and Crisis Services
The Foundation Center
79 Fifth Avenue
New York, NY 10003
212-620-4230
orders@fdncenter.org
http://fdncenter.org
Disability Served: mental health, substance abuse
This publication provides information on funding sources for drug and alcohol abuse programs, as well as mental health services.

Grants for the Physically and Mentally Disabled
The Foundation Center
79 Fifth Avenue
New York, NY 10003
212-620-4230
orders@fdncenter.org
http://fdncenter.org
Disability Served: mental health, physically disabled
This publication provides an overview of more than 745 foundations that provide grants to organizations that work with the mentally and physically disabled.

Grants for Women and Girls
The Foundation Center
79 Fifth Avenue
New York, NY 10003
212-620-4230
orders@fdncenter.org
http://fdncenter.org
Disability Served: various
This publication lists foundations and corporate giving programs that provide grants to projects supporting women and girls.

The Grantwriter's Internet Companion: A Resource for Educators and Others Seeking Grants and Funding
Corwin Press
2455 Teller Road
Thousand Oaks, CA 91320
800-818-7243
http://www.corwinpress.com
Disability Served: various
This book provides an overview of grant writing resources on the Internet.

Grant Writing For Dummies
John Wiley & Sons
10475 Crosspoint Boulevard
Indianapolis, IN 46256
877-762-2974
http://www.dummies.com/WileyCDA
Disability Served: various
This book includes information on government and foundation grants, writing cover letters and abstracts, presenting a budget, and much more.

Guide to Alabama Grantmakers
Alabama Giving/Alabama Funders Forum
PO Box 530727
Birmingham, AL 35253-0727
205-313-4830
Disability Served: various
This publication features profiles of more than 765 funders in Alabama and 107 funders outside the state with a geographic focus that includes Alabama.

Guide to Funding for International and Foreign Programs
The Foundation Center
79 Fifth Avenue
New York, NY 10003
212-620-4230
orders@fdncenter.org
http://fdncenter.org
Disability Served: various
This is a directory of 1,500 grant makers that are focused on funding international and foreign programs.

Guide to Greater Washington D.C. Grantmakers on CD-ROM
The Foundation Center
79 Fifth Avenue
New York, NY 10003
212-620-4230
orders@fdncenter.org
http://fdncenter.org
Disability Served: various
This directory of grant making foundations profiles 1,900 grant makers located in the Washington, D.C., region and funders in 39 different states that have an interest in funding Washington, D.C., nonprofit organizations.

Guide to Ohio Grantmakers on CD-ROM
The Foundation Center
79 Fifth Avenue
New York, NY 10003
212-620-4230
orders@fdncenter.org
http://fdncenter.org
Disability Served: various
This publication profiles more than 3,500 foundations in Ohio, plus more than 300 funders outside the state that award grants in Ohio.

Guide to U.S. Foundations, Their Trustees, Officers, and Donors
The Foundation Center
79 Fifth Avenue
New York, NY 10003
212-620-4230
orders@fdncenter.org
http://fdncenter.org
Disability Served: various
The guide provides profiles of more than 68,000 foundations across the nation.

How to Write a Grant Proposal (Wiley Nonprofit Law, Finance and Management Series)
John Wiley & Sons
10475 Crosspoint Boulevard
Indianapolis, IN 46256
877-762-2974
http://www.wiley.com/WileyCDA
Disability Served: various
This publication offers tips on writing effective grants. It includes completed grant proposals and case studies.

International Encyclopedia of Foundations
Greenwood Press
88 Post Road West
Westport, CT 06881
800-225-5800
http://www.greenwood.com
Disability Served: various
This publication provides profiles of 145 foundations located outside the United States. Thirty-one countries are covered.

International Grantmaking III: An Update on U.S. Foundation Trends
The Foundation Center
79 Fifth Avenue
New York, NY 10003
212-620-4230
orders@fdncenter.org
http://fdncenter.org
Disability Served: various
This publication provides information on international grants.

The Michigan Foundation Directory
Council of Michigan Foundations
PO Box 599
Grand Haven, MI 49417
616-842-7080
cmf@cmif.org
http://www.cmif.org
Disability Served: various
This directory offers profiles of more than 2,200 foundations that fund in Michigan. It is also available on CD-ROM.

National Directory of Corporate Giving
The Foundation Center
79 Fifth Avenue
New York, NY 10003
212-620-4230
orders@fdncenter.org
http://fdncenter.org
Disability Served: various
The directory profiles of corporations that provide grant funding.

National Guide to Funding for Community Development
The Foundation Center
79 Fifth Avenue

New York, NY 10003
212-620-4230
orders@fdncenter.org
http://fdncenter.org
Disability Served: various
This is a directory of grants available for community
development.

**National Guide to Funding for Libraries and
    Information Services**
The Foundation Center
79 Fifth Avenue
New York, NY 10003
212-620-4230
orders@fdncenter.org
http://fdncenter.org
Disability Served: various
This guide provides a listing of more than 1,500
    foundations and corporate giving programs that
    award grants to libraries.

National Guide to Funding in Aging
The Foundation Center
79 Fifth Avenue
New York, NY 10003
212-620-4230
orders@fdncenter.org
http://fdncenter.org
Disability Served: elderly
This publication offers information on foundations,
    organizations, and federal and state programs that
    provide funding for projects for the elderly.

National Guide to Funding in AIDS
The Foundation Center
79 Fifth Avenue
New York, NY 10003
212-620-4230
orders@fdncenter.org
http://fdncenter.org
Disability Served: AIDS
This publication provides information on foundations,
    public charities, and corporate giving programs
    that provide funding for AIDS-related services and
    research.

National Guide to Funding in Arts and Culture
The Foundation Center
79 Fifth Avenue
New York, NY 10003

212-620-4230
orders@fdncenter.org
http://fdncenter.org
Disability Served: various
This guide provides a listing of more than 9,600
    foundations and corporate giving programs that
    award grants for programs in the arts.

National Guide to Funding in Health
The Foundation Center
79 Fifth Avenue
New York, NY 10003
212-620-4230
orders@fdncenter.org
http://fdncenter.org
Disability Served: various
This publication provides a listing of more than 11,500
    foundations and corporate giving programs
    that award funds to research centers, hospitals,
    universities, and other medical projects.

**New York Metropolitan Area Foundations:
    A Profile of the Grantmaking Community**
The Foundation Center
79 Fifth Avenue
New York, NY 10003
212-620-4230
orders@fdncenter.org
http://fdncenter.org
Disability Served: various
This is a directory of foundations based in the eight-
    county New York metropolitan area.

**The Only Grant Writing Book You'll Ever Need: Top
    Grant Writers and Grant Givers Share Their Secrets!**
Carroll & Graf Publishers
245 West 17th Street, 11th Floor
New York, NY 10011-5300
212-981-9919
http://www.carrollandgraf.com
Disability Served: various
This book provides tips on grant writing from experts
    in the field. It includes a grant checklist, a glossary,
    sample grant forms, and a list of community
    foundations.

**The PRI Directory: Charitable Loans and Other
    Program-Related Investments by Foundations**
The Foundation Center
79 Fifth Avenue

New York, NY 10003
212-620-4230
orders@fdncenter.org
http://fdncenter.org
Disability Served: various
This directory lists leading program-related investing
foundations.

Raise More Money for Your Nonprofit Organization
The Foundation Center
79 Fifth Avenue
New York, NY 10003
212-620-4230
http://fdncenter.org
Disability Served: various
This guide provides useful information regarding fund-
raising for nonprofit organizations.

Simplified Grantwriting
Corwin Press
2455 Teller Road
Thousand Oaks, CA 91320
800-818-7243
http://www.corwinpress.com
Disability Served: various
This is a step-by-step guide for schools and community
organizations that are interested in obtaining
program funding.

Southeastern Foundations II: A Profile of the Region's Grantmaking Community
The Foundation Center
79 Fifth Avenue
New York, NY 10003
212-620-4230
http://fdncenter.org
Disability Served: various
This book profiles foundations in the southeastern
United States by type, size, geographic focus, and
program focus.

The Student Guide
Federal Student Aid Information Center
400 Maryland Avenue, SW
Washington, DC 20202
800-433-3243
http://studentaid.ed.gov
Disability Served: various
The guide provides a listing of student aid programs
administered by the United States Department of

Education. It is available in both print and electronic
versions.

Substance Abuse Funding Week
CD Publications
8204 Fenton Street
Silver Spring, MD 20910
301-588-6380, 800-666-6380
http://www.cdpublications.com
Disability Served: substance abuse
This newsletter (formerly known as the *Substance Abuse
Funding News*) announces new funding sources for
chemical dependency programs.

Technology for Students with Disabilities: A School Leader's Resource Guide
National School Boards Association
1680 Duke Street
Alexandria, VA 22314
703-838-6722, 800-706-6722
http://www.nsba.org
Disability Served: various
This publication discusses strategies for teaching and
learning with assistive technology and obtaining
funding for educational technology.

Who Pays?: Taking the Maze out of Funding
Minnesota Children with Special Health Needs
PO Box 64975
St. Paul, MN 55164-0975
http://www.health.state.mn.us/divs/fh/mcshn/pdfdocs/
maze0105.pdf
Disability Served: various
This online publication provides information on funding
for families of children with special health needs.

Winning Grants: Step by Step
John Wiley & Sons
10475 Crosspoint Boulevard
Indianapolis, IN 46256
877-762-2974
http://www.josseybass.com/WileyCDA
Disability Served: various
This workbook offers a general, systematic approach to
writing grant proposals. Topics include developing
the proposal idea, writing the proposal summary,
developing relationships with funders, how to
evaluate a proposal through a funder's eyes, and
helpful Web sites for grant seekers.

RESEARCH FUNDING

The following organizations and foundations provide funds to research facilities and university organizations for research that is often scientific or medical in nature.

American Cancer Society
1599 Clifton Road
Atlanta, GA 30329
800-ACS-2345, 866-228-4327 (TTY)
http://www.cancer.org
Disability Served: cancer patients and survivors
The society provides research grants for research related to cancer.

American Hearing Research Foundation
8 South Michigan Avenue, Suite 814
Chicago, IL 60603-4539
312-726-9670
lkoch@american-hearing.org
http://www.american-hearing.org/index.jsp
Disability Served: hearing
This organization provides grants for the purpose of research to help hearing-impaired people.

The Arc
1010 Wayne Avenue, Suite 650
Silver Spring, MD 20910
301-565-3842
http://www.thearc.org
Disability Served: developmentally disabled, mental retardation
This organization provides research grants for the study of the prevention of mental retardation.

Bireley Foundation
130 North Brand Boulevard, Suite 405
Glendale, CA 91203-2617
Disability Served: various
This organization provides grants for the purpose of medical research on adolescent medicine.

Burroughs Wellcome Fund
PO Box 13901
Research Triangle Park, NC 27709-3901
919-991-5100
http://www.bwfund.org
Disability Served: various
The fund provides grants to research institutions or facilities to support biomedical research.

Christopher Reeve Paralysis Foundation
500 Morris Avenue
Springfield, NJ 07081
973-379-2690, 800-225-0292
info@paralysis.org
http://www.paralysis.org
Disability Served: spinal-cord injury
This nonprofit organization supports research to find a cure for paralysis caused by spinal cord injury and other central nervous system disorders.

Cystic Fibrosis Foundation
6931 Arlington Road
Bethesda, MD 20814
301-951-4422, 800-FIGHT-CF
info@cff.org
http://www.cff.org
Disability Served: cystic fibrosis
The foundation provides grants for research related to cystic fibrosis.

E. Matilda Ziegler Foundation for the Blind
20 Thorndal Circle, 1st Floor
Darien, CT 06820
203-656-8000
Disability Served: vision
This organization provides grants for research on blindness.

Foundation Fighting Blindness
11435 Cronhill Drive
Owings Mills, MD 21117-2220
888-394-3937, 800-683-5555 (TDD)
info@blindness.org
http://www.blindness.org
Disability Served: vision
The foundation offers funding for medical research dedicated to finding the causes, cures, and prevention of diseases that effect vision.

Jane Coffin Childs Memorial Fund for Medical Research
333 Cedar Street, LW300-SHM
New Haven, CT 06510

203-785-4612
info@jccfund.org
http://info.med.yale.edu/jccfund
Disability Served: cancer patients and survivors
The fund supports medical research projects that relate
to cancer treatment and prevention.

May Mitchell Royal Foundation
PO Box 75000, MC 3302
Detroit, MI 48275-3302
Disability Served: vision
This organization provides funds for the purpose of eye
research.

Multiple Sclerosis Foundation Inc.
6350 North Andrews Avenue
Ft. Lauderdale, FL 33309-2130
954-776-6805, 800-225-6495
admin@msfocus.org
http://www.msfacts.org
Disability Served: multiple sclerosis
The foundation provides grants to universities for
the research of the cause, cure, prevention, and
treatment of multiple sclerosis.

National Ataxia Foundation
2600 Fernbrook Lane, Suite 119
Minneapolis, MN 55447
763-553-0020
naf@ataxia.org
http://www.ataxia.org
Disability Served: physically disabled
The foundation provides grants for the research of ataxia.

National Hemophilia Foundation
116 West 32nd Street, 11th Floor
New York, NY 10001
800-42-HANDI
info@hemophilia.org
http://www.hemophilia.org
Disability Served: inherited bleeding disorders
The foundation provides scholarships and grants for the
purpose of researching hemophilia.

National Parkinson Foundation
1501 Northwest 9th Avenue, Bob Hope Road
Miami, FL 33136-1494
800-327-4545
contact@parkinson.org
http://www.parkinson.org
Disability Served: Parkinson's Disease
This organization provides grants for the research of
Parkinson's disease.

Phil N. Allen Charitable Trust
PO Box 63954, MAC 0103-179
San Francisco, CA 94163
Disability Served: multiple sclerosis
The trust offers grants for multiple sclerosis research.

Prevent Blindness America
211 West Wacker Drive, Suite 1700
Chicago, IL 60606
800-331-2020
info@preventblindness.org
http://www.preventblindness.org
Disability Served: vision
This organization provides grants to fund research
activities in the field of blindness prevention.

W. M. Keck Foundation
550 South Hope Street, Suite 2500
Los Angeles, CA 90071
213-680-3833
info@wmkeck.org
http://www.wmkeck.org
Disability Served: various
The foundation supports scientific, engineering, and
medical research programs at accredited universities
and colleges.

TECHNOLOGY FUNDING

These organizations provde funding to help persons with disabilities purchase assistive technology and necessary equipment.

Adaptive Equipment Loan Program and Finance Authority of Maine
Alpha One
127 Main Street
South Portland, ME 04106
207-767-2189
kadams@alphaonenow.org
http://www.alpha-one.org
Disability Served: various
This organization offers financial assistance to persons with disabilities in Maine for the purchase of assistive technology devices.

Alabama STAR System for Alabamians with Disabilities
Ability Loan Program
2129 East South Boulevard
Montgomery, AL 36116-2455
334-281-8780, 800-441-7607
http://www.rehab.state.al.us/star
Disability Served: various
This organization offers financial assistance to persons with disabilities in Alabama for the purchase of assistive technology devices.

Arizona Loan$ for Assistive Technology
Institute for Human Development
Northern Arizona University
2400 North Central Avenue, Suite 300
Phoenix, AZ 85004
800-477-9921, 602-728-9536 (TTY)
http://www.azlat.org
Disability Served: various
Arizona Loan$ for Assistive Technology offers financial assistance to persons with disabilities in Arizona for the purchase of assistive technology devices.

Arkansas Technology Alternative Financing Project
Arkansas Rehabilitation Services
4601 West Markham
Little Rock, AR 72205
501-683-3008
Disability Served: various
This organization offers financial assistance to persons with disabilities in Arkansas for the purchase of assistive technology devices.

Assistive Technology Loan Fund Authority
1602 Rolling Hills Drive, Suite 107
Richmond, VA 23229
804-662-9000, 866-835-5976
atlfa@atlfa.org
http://www.atlfa.org
Disability Served: various
The Assistive Technology Loan Fund Authority offers financial assistance to persons with disabilities in Virginia for the purchase of assistive technology devices.

Assistive Technology of Minnesota Micro-Loan Program
Assistive Technology of Minnesota
1800 Pioneer Creek Center, Box 310
Maple Plain, MN 55359-0310
763-479-8239
Disability Served: various
This organization offers financial assistance to persons with disabilities in Minnesota for the purchase of assistive technology devices.

Assistive Technology of Ohio
445 East Dublin-Granville Road, Building L
Worthington, OH 43085
800-784-3425
http://www.atohio.org
Disability Served: various
Assistive Technology of Ohio offers financial assistance to persons with disabilities in Ohio for the purchase of assistive technology devices.

Assistive Technology Resource Centers of Hawaii
414 Kuwili Street, Suite 104
Honolulu, HI 96817
808-532-7110 (Voice/TTY)
atrc-info@atrc.org
http://www.atrc.org
Disability Served: various
This organization offers financial assistance to persons with disabilities in Hawaii for the purchase of assistive technology devices.

Association of Blind Citizens
PO Box 246
Holbrook, MA 02343

781-961-1023

http://www.blindcitizens.org

Disability Served: vision

The association offers the assistive technology fund, which provide funds to pay for 50 percent of the retail cost of adaptive devices or software.

BPO Elks of the USA

2750 North Lakeview Avenue

Chicago, IL 60614-1889

773-755-4700

http://www.elks.org

Disability Served: physically disabled

This organization occasionally offers grants and loans to disabled people who do not have the financial means to purchase assistive technology. Contact your local club for more information.

Colorado Assistive Technology Project

1245 East Colfax Avenue, Suite 200

Denver, CO 80218

http://www.uchsc.edu/atp/projects/catp/catp.htm

Disability Served: various

This organization offers information on assistive technology funding resources available in Colorado.

Connecticut Tech Act Project

Department of Social Services, Bureau of Rehabilitation Services

25 Sigourney Street, 11th Floor

Hartford, CT 06106

Disability Served: various

This organization offers financial assistance to persons with disabilities in Connecticut for the purchase of assistive technology devices.

DakotaLink

1161 Deadwood Avenue, Suite 5

Rapid City, SD 57702

800-645-0673 (Voice/TDD)

http://dakotalink.tie.net/content/default.htm

Disability Served: various

DakotaLink offers financial assistance to persons with disabilities in South Dakota for the purchase of assistive technology devices.

Delaware Assistive Technology Initiative

University of Delaware/Alfred I. duPont Hospital for Children

Center for Applied Science and Engineering

1600 Rockland Road, PO Box 269

Wilmington, DE 19899-0269

800-870-DATI, 302-651-6794 (TDD)

http://www.dati.org

Disability Served: various

This organization offers financial assistance to persons with disabilities in Delaware for the purchase of assistive technology devices.

Disabled Children's Relief Fund

PO Box 89

Freeport, NY 11520

http://www.dcrf.com

Disability Served: physically disabled

This organization provides financial assistance to the disabled to fund assistive devices, rehabilitative services, and arts and humanities projects.

Entrepreneurs with Disabilities Program

4177 Alyssa Court, SW, #1

Iowa City, IA 52240

866-720-3863

http://www.abilitiesfund.org/iowa_ewd_program/about_ewd.php

Disability Served: various

The Entrepreneurs with Disabilities Program provides financial assistance to entrepreneurs with disabilities.

Florida Alternative Financing Program

Florida Alliance for Assistive Services and Technology

325 John Knox Road, Building 400, Suite 402

Tallahassee, FL 32303

850-487-3278, 888-788-9216

http://www.faast.org/AlternativeFinancing.cfm

Disability Served: various

This organization offers financial assistance to persons with disabilities in Florida for the purchase of assistive technology devices.

Georgia Credit-Able

Tech-Able, Inc.

1114 Brett Drive, Suite 100

Conyers, GA 30094

404-638-0385

gregsams@mindspring.com

Disability Served: various

Georgia Credit-Able offers financial assistance to persons with disabilities in Georgia for the purchase of assistive technology devices.

GiveTech.org
4630 Geary Boulevard, Suite 101
San Francisco, CA 94118
415-750-2576
http://givetech.org
Disability Served: physically disabled
This organization helps people with severe physical disabilities obtain assistive technology for computer access.

Idaho Assistive Technology Project
129 West Third Street
Moscow, ID 83843
208-885-3573
http://www.educ.uidaho.edu/idatech
Disability Served: various
This organization offers financial assistance to persons with disabilities in Idaho for the purchase of assistive technology devices.

Illinois Assistive Technology Project
TechConnect Low Interest Loan Program
1 West Old State Capitol Plaza, Suite 100
Springfield, IL 62701-1200
217-522-7985, 217-522-9966 (TTY)
https://techconnect.iltech.org/Home.aspx
Disability Served: various
The Illinois Assistive Technology Project offers financial assistance to persons with disabilities in Illinois for the purchase of assistive technology devices.

Jim Mullen Foundation
9450 Bryn Mawr Avenue, Suite 520
Rosemont, IL 60018
847-233-9880 (Voice/TTY)
http://www.jimmullen.com
Disability Served: physically disabled
The Jim Mullen Foundation works with a variety of technology companies to provide computers to the physically disabled.

Kansas Assistive Technology Cooperative
Alternative Financing Program
625 Merchant, Suite 205
Emporia, KS 66801
866-465-2826 (Voice/TTY)
http://www.katco.net
Disability Served: various
This organization offers financial assistance to persons with disabilities in Kansas for the purchase of assistive technology devices.

Kentucky Assistive Technology Loan Corporation
209 St. Clair Street
Frankfort, KY 40601
http://www.katlc.ky.gov
Disability Served: various
The Kentucky Assistive Technology Loan Corporation offers financial assistance to persons with disabilities in Kentucky for the purchase of assistive technology devices.

Lions Clubs International
300 West 22nd Street
Oak Brook, IL 60523-8842
http://www.lionsclubs.org
Disability Served: physically disabled
Lions Clubs International occasionally offers grants and loans to disabled people who do not have the financial means to purchase assistive technology. Contact your local club for more information.

Louisiana Assistive Technology Access Network
Assistive Technology Loan Program
3042 Old Forge Drive
Baton Rouge, LA 70808
800-270-6185
http://www.latan.org
Disability Served: various
This organization offers financial assistance to persons with disabilities in Louisiana for the purchase of assistive technology devices.

Maryland Technology Assistance Program
Assistive Technology Guaranteed Loan Program
2301 Argonne Drive, Room T-17
Baltimore, MD 21218
800-832-4827, 866-881-7488 (TTY)
mdtap@mdod.state.md.us
http://www.mdtap.org
Disability Served: various
The Maryland Technology Assistance Program offers financial assistance to persons with disabilities in Maryland for the purchase of assistive technology devices.

Massachusetts Assistive Technology Loan Program
Easter Seals Massachusetts
484 Main Street
Worcester, MA 01608
800-922-8290, 800-564-9700 (TTY)
http://www.smallworldgraphics.com/easterseals.htm

Disability Served: various

This organization offers financial assistance to persons with disabilities in Massachusetts for the purchase of assistive technology devices.

Medicare Program
Centers for Medicare & Medicaid Services
7500 Security Boulevard
Baltimore, MD 21244-1850
http://www.medicare.gov
Disability Served: various
The Medicare program provides payment/reimbursement for the purchase or rental of assistive technology.

Michigan Assistive Technology Loan Fund
United Cerebal Palsy of Michigan
3401 East Saginaw, Suite 216
Lansing, MI 48912
800-828-2714
http://www.mi-atlf.org/atlf/index.htm
Disability Served: various
This organization offers financial assistance to persons with disabilities in Michigan for the purchase of assistive technology devices.

Missouri Assistive Technology
$how Me Loans
4731 South Cochise, #114
Independence, MO 64055-6975
816-373-5193, 816-373-9315 (TTY)
matpmo@swbell.net
http://www.at.mo.gov
Disability Served: various
Missouri Assistive Technology offers financial assistance to persons with disabilities in Missouri for the purchase of assistive technology devices.

MonTECH
Rural Institute on Disabilities
University of Montana
634 Eddy Avenue, CHS 009
Missoula, MT 59812-6696
406-243-5467 (Voice/TTY)
http://montech.ruralinstitute.umt.edu
Disability Served: various
This organization offers financial assistance to persons with disabilities in Montana for the purchase of assistive technology devices.

Nebraska Loan Program
Nebraska Easter Seals
638 North 109th Plaza
Omaha, NE 68154
402-345-2200, ext. 6
Disability Served: various
This organization offers financial assistance to persons with disabilities in Nebraska for the purchase of assistive technology devices.

Nevada Assistive Technology Loan Fund
CareChest
7910 North Virginia Street
Reno, NV 89506
775-829-2273
loans@carechest.com
Disability Served: various
This organization offers financial assistance to persons with disabilities in Nevada for the purchase of assistive technology devices.

New Hampshire Assistive Technology Partnership Project
10 Ferry Street, #14
Concord, NH 03301
800-228-2048
http://www.iod.unh.edu/projects/nh_assistive_technology.html
Disability Served: various
The New Hampshire Assistive Technology Partnership Project offers financial assistance to persons with disabilities in New Hampshire for the purchase of assistive technology devices.

New Jersey Technology Assistance Resource Program
210 South Broad Street, 3rd Floor
Trenton, NJ 08608
856-777-0945
elence@njpanda.org
Disability Served: various
This organization offers financial assistance to persons with disabilities in New Jersey for the purchase of assistive technology devices.

New Mexico Loan Program
San Juan Center for Independence
3535 East 30th, Suite 101
Farmington, NM 87402
505-566-5831
Disability Served: various

This organization offers financial assistance to persons with disabilities in New Mexico for the purchase of assistive technology devices.

North Carolina Assistive Technology Project
Division of Vocational Rehabilitation Services
1110 Navaho Drive, Suite 101
Raleigh, NC 27609-7322
919-850-2787
jmedlicott@ncatp.org
http://www.ncatp.org
Disability Served: various
The North Carolina Assistive Technology Project provides information on assistive technology funding resources available in North Carolina.

North Dakota Assistive Technology Loan Program
North Dakota Association for the Disabled
2660 South Columbia Road
Grand Forks, ND 58201
800-532-6323
http://www.ndad.org
Disability Served: various
This organization offers financial assistance to persons with disabilities in North Dakota for the purchase of assistive technology devices.

Oklahoma Alternative Financing Program
Oklahoma ABLE Tech
1514 West Hall of Fame
Stillwater, OK 74078
800-257-1705 (Voice/TDD)
http://okabletech.okstate.edu
Disability Served: various
The Oklahoma Alternative Financing Program offers financial assistance to persons with disabilities in Oklahoma for the purchase of assistive technology devices.

Parents, Let's Unite for Kids Family Guide to Assistive Technology
516 North 32nd Street
Billings, MT 59101-6003
800-222-7585
plukinfo@pluk.org
http://www.pluk.org/AT1.html#6
Disability Served: various
This guide provides an overview of assistive technology and methods of obtaining funding.

Pennsylvania Assistive Technology Foundation
1004 West Ninth Avenue, 1st Floor
King of Prussia, PA 19406
888-744-1938, 877-693-7271 (TTY)
patf@amexcenters.com
http://www.patf.us
Disability Served: various
This organization offers financial assistance to persons with disabilities in Pennsylvania for the purchase of assistive technology devices.

South Carolina Assistive Technology Financial Loan Program
Vocational Rehabilitation Department
1410 Boston Avenue
West Columbia, SC 29171
803-896-5978
http://www.scvrd.net/atloans.htm
Disability Served: various
This organization offers financial assistance to persons with disabilities in South Carolina for the purchase of assistive technology devices.

Tennessee Technology Access Project
400 Deadrick Street, Citizens Plaza Office Building, 14th Floor
Nashville, TN 37248
615-313-5183, 615-741-4566
TN.TTAP@state.tn.us
http://www.state.tn.us/humanserv/ttap_index.htm
Disability Served: various
The Tennessee Technology Access Project offers financial assistance to persons with disabilities in Tennessee for the purchase of assistive technology devices.

Texas Technology Access Project
University of Texas-Austin
4030 West Braker Lane, Building 2, Suite 220, Mail Code L4000
Austin, TX 78759
512-232-0740, 800-828-7839
http://tatp.edb.utexas.edu/funding.html
Disability Served: various
This organization provides information on assistive technology funding resources available in Texas.

United Cerebral Palsy Foundation
1660 L Street, NW, Suite 700
Washington, DC 20036

800-872-5827, 202-776-0406 (TTY)
http://www.ucp.org
Disability Served: various
Visit the foundation's Web site for a variety of resources on obtaining funding for assistive technology for people with cerebral palsy and other disabilities. Its state chapters often work with government organizations to provide funding for assistive technology. Visit the foundation's Web site for a complete list of chapters.

United States Department of Veterans Affairs-Vocational Rehabilitation

125 South State Street, Federal Building, PO Box 11500
Salt Lake City, UT 84147
801-524-5450, ext. 1
http://www.va.gov
Disability Served: various
This government organization provides funds to veterans for the purchase of necessary equipment or supplies in relation to an occupational goal.

University Legal Services Assistive Technology Program for the District of Columbia

220 I Street, NE, Suite 130
Washington, DC 20002
202-547-0198, 202-547-2657 (TTY)
atpdc@uls-dc.com
Disability Served: various
This organization offers financial assistance to persons with disabilities in the District of Columbia for the purchase of assistive technology devices.

Utah Assistive Technology Foundation

6835 Old Main Hill
Logan, UT 84322-6835
800-524-5152
uatf@cpd2.usu.edu
http://www.uatf.org
Disability Served: various
This organization offers financial assistance to persons with disabilities in Utah for the purchase of assistive technology devices.

Vermont Assistive Technology Fund

103 South Main Street
Waterbury, VT 05671
800-750-6355
http://www.dad.state.vt.us/atp

Disability Served: various
The Vermont Assistive Technology Fund offers financial assistance to persons with disabilities in Vermont for the purchase of assistive technology devices.

Washington Assistive Technology Foundation

1823 East Madison, Suite 1000
Seattle, WA 98122
800-214-8731 (Voice/TTY)
info@watf.org
http://watf.org
Disability Served: various
This organization offers financial assistance to persons with disabilities in Washington for the purchase of assistive technology devices.

West Virginia Technology-Related Assistance Revolving Loan Fund

West Virginia Department of Rehabilitative Services
PO Box 1004
Institute, WV 25112-1004
304-766-4702
This organization offers financial assistance to persons with disabilities in West Virginia for the purchase of assistive technology devices.

WisLoan

Independence First
600 West Virginia Street, Suite 401
Milwaukee, WI 53204-1516
414-226-8306, 877-463-3778
http://www.dhfs.wisconsin.gov/disabilities/wistech/wisloan.htm
Disability Served: various
WisLoan offers financial assistance to persons with disabilities in Wisconsin for the purchase of assistive technology devices.

Wyoming Technology Access Program

Wyoming Independent Living Rehabilitation, Inc.
305 West First Street
Casper, WY 82601
800-735-8322
khof@trib.com
Disability Served: various
This organization offers financial assistance to persons with disabilities in Wyoming for the purchase of assistive technology devices.

GOVERNMENT BODIES

FEDERAL BODIES

These federal government agencies provide free programs to help people with disabilities find employment, pursue an education, receive legal representation and social services, and gain greater independence in their communities.

Division of Aging and Seniors
Address Locator 1908A1
Ottawa, ON KIA 1B4
Canada
613-952-7606
seniors@phac-aspc.gc.ca
http://www.phac-aspc.gc.ca/seniors-aines/index_pages/
   whatsnew_e.htm
Disability Served: elderly

National Council on Disability
1331 F Street, NW, Suite 850
Washington, DC 20004
202-272-2004, 202-272-2074 (TTY)
info@ncd.gov
http://www.ncd.gov
Disability Served: various

Public Health Agency of Canada
130 Colonnade Road, Address Locator 6501H
Ottawa, ON K1A 0K9
Canada
http://www.phac-aspc.gc.ca/about_apropos
Disability Served: various

Social Security Administration
6401 Security Boulevard
Baltimore, MD 21235
800-772-1213, 800-325-0778 (TTY)
http://www.ssa.gov
Disability Served: various

Social Security Administration Region I-Boston
JFK Federal Building, Room 1211B
Boston, MA 02203
617-565-2881, 800-772-1213, 800-325-0778 (TTY)
http://www.socialsecurity.gov/boston
Disability Served: various
This region includes the following states: Connecticut, Maine, Massachusetts, New Hampshire, Rhode Island, and Vermont.

Social Security Administration Region II-New York
26 Federal Plaza, Room 749
New York, NY 10278

212-264-2500, 800-772-1213, 800-325-0778 (TTY)
http://www.socialsecurity.gov/ny
Disability Served: various
This region includes New Jersey and New York, the Commonwealth of Puerto Rico, and the U.S. Virgin Islands.

Social Security Administration Region III-Philadelphia
Suite South Independence Mall West
Philadelphia, PA 19106
215-597-0596, 800-772-1213, 800-325-0778 (TTY)
http://www.socialsecurity.gov/phila
Disability Served: various
This region serves Delaware, Maryland, Pennsylvania, Virginia, and West Virginia and the District of Columbia.

Social Security Administration Region IV-Atlanta
101 Marietta Street
Atlanta, GA 30323
404-331-2998, 800-772-1213, 800-325-0778 (TTY)
http://www.socialsecurity.gov/atlanta/southeast
Disability Served: various
This region includes the following states: Alabama, Florida, Georgia, Kentucky, Mississippi, North Carolina, South Carolina, and Tennessee.

Social Security Administration Region V-Chicago
175 West Jackson Boulevard
Chicago, IL 60604
312-353-3230, 800-772-1213, 800-325-0778 (TTY)
http://www.socialsecurity.gov/chicago
Disability Served: various
This region includes the following states: Illinois, Indiana, Michigan, Minnesota, Ohio, and Wisconsin.

Social Security Administration Region VI-Dallas
1200 Main Tower Building
Dallas, TX 75202
214-767-4281, 800-772-1213, 800-325-0778 (TTY)
http://www.socialsecurity.gov/dallas
Disability Served: various
This region includes the following states: Arkansas, Louisiana, New Mexico, Oklahoma, and Texas.

Social Security Administration Region VII-Kansas City
601 East Twelfth Street, Room 436
Kansas City, MO 64106
816-426-6191, 800-772-1213, 800-325-0778 (TTY)
http://www.socialsecurity.gov/kc
Disability Served: various
This region includes the following states: Iowa, Nebraska,
Kansas, and Missouri.

Social Security Administration Region VIII-Denver
1961 Stout Street
Denver, CO 80294-3538
303-844-4441, 800-772-1213, 800-325-0778 (TTY)
http://www.socialsecurity.gov/denver
Disability Served: various
This region includes the following states: Colorado,
Montana, North Dakota, South Dakota, Utah, and
Wyoming.

**Social Security Administration Region IX-
San Francisco**
100 Van Ness Avenue
San Francisco, CA 94102
415-744-4896, 800-772-1213, 800-325-0778 (TTY)
SF.RPA@ssa.gov
http://www.socialsecurity.gov/sf
Disability Served: various
This region includes California, Arizona, Nevada, and
Hawaii; Guam; American Samoa; and the Northern
Mariana Islands.

Social Security Administration Region X-Seattle
1321 Second Avenue
Seattle, WA 98121
206-615-2105, 800-772-1213, 800-325-0778 (TTY)
http://www.socialsecurity.gov/seattle
Disability Served: various
This region includes the following states: Alaska, Idaho,
Oregon, and Washington.

Social Security Disability Determination Service
6401 Security Boulevard
Baltimore, MD 21235
800-772-1213, 800-325-0778 (TTY)
http://www.ssa.gov/disability
Disability Served: various

United States Administration on Aging
330 Independence Avenue, SW
Washington, DC 20201
202-619-0724
AoAInfo@aoa.hhs.gov
http://www.aoa.dhhs.gov
Disability Served: elderly

**United States Administration on Developmental
Disabilities**
370 L'Enfant Promenade, SW, Mail Stop: HHH 405-D
Washington, DC 20447
202-690-6590
http://www.acf.hhs.gov/programs/add
Disability Served: developmentally disabled

United States Center for Mental Health Services
PO Box 42557
Rockville, MD 20015
800-789-2647, 866-889-2647 (TDD)
http://www.mentalhealth.samhsa.gov
Disability Served: mental health

**United States Centers for Medicare and Medicaid
Services**
7500 Security Boulevard
Baltimore, MD 21244-1850
877-267-2323, 866-226-1819 (TTY)
http://www.cms.hhs.gov
Disability Served: various

United States Department of Education
400 Maryland Avenue, SW
Washington, DC 20202
800-872-5327, 800-437-0833 (TTY)
http://www.ed.gov
Disability Served: various

**United States Department of Health and Human
Services**
200 Independence Avenue, SW
Washington, DC 20201
202-619-0257, 877-696-6775
http://www.hhs.gov
Disability Served: various

United States Department of Veterans Affairs
810 Vermont Avenue, NW
Washington, DC 20420
800-827-1000, 800-829-4833 (TDD)
http://www.va.gov
Disability Served: various

United States Equal Employment Opportunity Commission
PO Box 7033
Lawrence, KS 66044
800-669-4000, 800-669-6820 (TTY)
info@ask.eeoc.gov
http://www.eeoc.gov
Disability Served: various

United States National Institutes of Health
9000 Rockville Pike
Bethesda, MD 20892
301-496-4000, 301-402-9612 (TTY)
NIHinfo@od.nih.gov
http://www.nih.gov
Disability Served: various

United States Office of Disability Employment Policy
200 Constitution Avenue, NW
Washington, DC 20210
866-633-7365, 877-889-5627 (TTY)
http://www.dol.gov/odep
Disability Served: various

United States Office of Special Education and Rehabilitative Services
400 Maryland Avenue, SW
Washington, DC 20202-7100
202-245-7468
http://www.ed.gov/about/offices/list/osers
Disability Served: various

United States Office of Workers' Compensation Programs
200 Constitution Avenue, NW
Washington, DC 20210
866-4-USA-DOL, 877-889-5627 (TTY)
http://www.dol.gov/esa/owcp_org.htm
Disability Served: various

STATE BODIES

These state government agencies provide free programs to help people with disabilities find employment, pursue an education, receive legal representation and social services, and gain greater independence in their communities.

ALABAMA

Alabama Council for Developmental Disabilities
100 North Union Street, PO Box 301410
Montgomery, AL 36130-1410
334-242-3973, 800-232-2158
addpc@mh.state.al.us
http://www.acdd.org
Disability Served: developmentally disabled

Alabama Department of Education
50 North Ripley Street, PO Box 302101
Montgomery, AL 36104
334-242-9700
http://www.alsde.edu/html/home.asp
Disability Served: various

Alabama Department of Mental Health and Mental Retardation
PO Box 301410
Montgomery, AL 36130-1410
800-367-0955
DMHMR@mh.state.al.us
http://www.mh.state.al.us
Disability Served: mental health, mental retardation

Alabama Department of Public Health
PO Box 303017
Montgomery, AL 36130-3017
334-613-5300
http://www.adph.org
Disability Served: various

Alabama Department of Rehabilitation Services
2129 East South Boulevard
Montgomery, AL 36116-2455
334-281-8780, 800-441-7607
http://www.rehab.state.al.us
Disability Served: various

Alabama Department of Senior Services
770 Washington Avenue, RSA Plaza, Suite 470
Montgomery, AL 36130-1851
334-242-5743, 877-425-2243
ageline@adss.state.al.us
http://www.adss.state.al.us
Disability Served: elderly

Alabama Institute for Deaf and Blind
205 East South Street
Talladega, AL 35160
205-761-3201
http://www.aidb.org
Disability Served: hearing, vision

Alabama Social Security Disability Determination Service (Birmingham)
PO Box 830300
Birmingham, AL 35283-0300
800-292-8106
http://www.ssa.gov/disability
Disability Served: various

Alabama Social Security Disability Determination Service (Mobile)
PO Box 2371
Mobile, AL 36615
800-292-6743
http://www.ssa.gov/disability
Disability Served: various

Alabama Workers' Compensation Division
649 Monroe Street
Montgomery, AL 36131
334-242-2868
http://dir.alabama.gov/wc
Disability Served: various

ALASKA

Alaska Commission on Aging
PO Box 110693
Juneau, AK 99811-0693
907-465-3250
http://www.alaskaaging.org
Disability Served: elderly

Alaska Department of Education and Early Development
801 West 10th Street, Suite 200
Juneau, AK 99801-1878
907-465-2800
http://www.educ.state.ak.us
Disability Served: various

Alaska Department of Health and Social Services
350 Main Street, Room 404, PO Box 110601
Juneau, AK 99811-0601
907-465-3030, 907-586-4265 (TDD/TTY)
http://www.hss.state.ak.us
Disability Served: various

Alaska Division of Behavioral Health
PO Box 110620
Juneau, AK 99811
907-465-3370
http://www.hss.state.ak.us/dbh
Disability Served: mental health

Alaska Division of Senior and Disability Services
240 Main Street, Suite 601
Juneau, AK 99801
907-465-3372, 866-465-3165
http://www.hss.state.ak.us/dsds
Disability Served: developmentally disabled, elderly, physically disabled

Alaska Division of Vocational Rehabilitation
801 West 10th Street, Suite A
Juneau, AK 99801-1894
907-465-2814, 800-478-2815
anne_knight@labor.state.ak.us
http://www.labor.state.ak.us/dvr
Disability Served: various

Alaska Governor's Council on Disabilities and Special Education
3601 C Street, Suite 740
Anchorage, AK 99524-0249
907-269-8990
http://www.hss.state.ak.us/gcdse
Disability Served: various

Alaska Social Security Disability Determination Service
619 East Ship Creek Avenue, Suite 305
Anchorage, AK 99501
907-777-8100, 800-577-3334
http://www.ssa.gov/disability
Disability Served: various

Alaska Workers' Compensation Division
PO Box 25512
Juneau, AK 99802
907-465-2790
http://www.labor.state.ak.us/wc
Disability Served: various

ARIZONA

Arizona Commission for the Deaf and the Hard of Hearing
1400 West Washington, Room 126
Phoenix, AZ 85007
602-542-3323, 602-364-0990 (TTY)
http://acdhh.org
Disability Served: hearing

Arizona Department of Education
1535 West Jefferson Street
Phoenix, AZ 85007
602-542-5393, 800-352-4558
http://www.ade.state.az.us
Disability Served: various

Arizona Department of Health Services
150 North 18th Avenue
Phoenix, AZ 85007
602-542-1001
http://www.azdhs.gov
Disability Served: various

Arizona Division of Aging and Community Services
1789 West Jefferson, Site Code 950A
Phoenix, AZ 85007
602-542-4446
askdesaaa@mail.de.state.az.us
http://www.de.state.az.us/aaa
Disability Served: elderly

Arizona Division of Behavioral Health Services
150 North 18th Avenue, 2nd Floor
Phoenix, AZ 85007
602-364-4558
http://www.azdhs.gov/bhs
Disability Served: mental health

Arizona Division of Developmental Disabilities
1789 West Jefferson Street
Phoenix, AZ 85005
866-229-5553
http://www.de.state.az.us/ddd
Disability Served: developmentally disabled

Arizona Governor's Council on Developmental Disabilities
3839 North Third Street, Suite 306 (SC074Z)
Phoenix, AZ 85012
866-771-9378, 602-277-4949 (TTY)
http://www.azgcdd.org
Disability Served: developmentally disabled

Arizona Rehabilitation Services Administration
1789 West Jefferson, 2NW
Phoenix, AZ 85007
602-542-3332, 602-542-6049 (TTY)
http://www.azdes.gov/rsa
Disability Served: various

Arizona Social Security Disability Determination Service (Phoenix)
3310 North 19th Avenue
Phoenix, AZ 85015-5701
602-264-2644
http://www.ssa.gov/disability
Disability Served: various

Arizona Social Security Disability Determination Service (Tucson)
5441 East 22nd Street, Suite 135
Tucson, AZ 85711
520-790-2580
http://www.ssa.gov/disability
Disability Served: various

ARKANSAS
Arkansas Department of Education
4 Capitol Mall
Little Rock, AR 72201
http://arkedu.state.ar.us
Disability Served: various

Arkansas Department of Health
4815 West Markham
Little Rock, AR 72205
501-661-2000
http://www.healthyarkansas.com
Disability Served: various

Arkansas Division of Aging and Adult Services
PO Box 1437, Slot S-530
Little Rock, AR 72203-1437

501-682-2441
ron.tatus@mail.state.ar.us
http://www.arkansas.gov/dhs/aging
Disability Served: elderly

Arkansas Division of Behavioral Health Services
4313 West Markham
Little Rock, AR 72205
877-227-0007
sheila.duncan@mail.state.ar.us
http://www.arkansas.gov/dhs/dmhs
Disability Served: mental health

Arkansas Division of Developmental Disabilities Services
PO Box 1437, Slot N503
Little Rock, AR 72203-1437
501-682-8665, 501-682-1332 (TDD)
http://www.arkansas.gov/dhs/ddds
Disability Served: developmentally disabled

Arkansas Division of Services for the Blind
700 Main Street, PO Box 3237
Little Rock, AR 72203
800-960-9270, 501-682-0093 (TDD)
http://www.arkansas.gov/dhs/dsb/NEWDSB
Disability Served: vision

Arkansas Governor's Developmental Disabilities
Planning Council
5800 West 10th Street, Suite 805
Little Rock, AR 72204
800-482-5400, ext. 2589 (Voice/TDD)
http://www.ddcouncil.org
Disability Served: developmentally disabled

Arkansas Rehabilitation Services
1616 Brookwood Drive, PO Box 3781
Little Rock, AR 72203
501-296-1600, 501-296-1669 (TDD)
http://www.arsinfo.org
Disability Served: various

Arkansas Social Security Disability Determination Service
701 Pulaski Street
Little Rock, AR 72201
501-682-3030
http://www.ssa.gov/disability
Disability Served: various

Arkansas Workers' Compensation Commission
324 Spring Street, PO Box 950
Little Rock, AR 72203-0950
501-682-3930, 800-622-4472, 800-285-1131 (TDD)
http://www.awcc.state.ar.us
Disability Served: various

CALIFORNIA

California Department of Aging
1300 National Drive
Sacramento, CA 95834
916-419-7500, 800-735-2929 (TTY)
http://www.aging.state.ca.us
Disability Served: elderly

California Department of Education
1430 N Street
Sacramento, CA 95814
916-319-0800
http://www.cde.ca.gov
Disability Served: various

California Department of Health Services
PO Box 997413
Sacramento, CA 95899-7413
916-445-4171
http://www.dhs.ca.gov
Disability Served: various

California Department of Mental Health
1600 Ninth Street, Room 151
Sacramento, CA 95814
800-896-4042, 800-896-2512 (TTY)
dmh@dmhhq.state.ca.us
http://www.dmh.cahwnet.gov
Disability Served: mental health

California Department of Rehabilitation
2000 Evergreen Street, PO Box 944222
Sacramento, CA 95815
916-263-8981, 916-263-7477 (TTY)
http://www.rehab.cahwnet.gov
Disability Served: various

California Division of Workers' Compensation
1515 Clay Street
Oakland, CA 94612
510-286-7143

http://www.dir.ca.gov/dwc/dwc_home_page.htm
Disability Served: various

California Social Security Disability Determination Service (Bay Area Branch)
PO Box 24539
Oakland, CA 94623-1539
510-622-3296
http://www.ssa.gov/disability
Disability Served: various

California Social Security Disability Determination Service (Central Valley)
PO Box 28937
Fresno, CA 93729-8937
559-440-5000
http://www.ssa.gov/disability
Disability Served: various

California Social Security Disability Determination Service (Golden Gate Branch)
PO Box 24225
Oakland, CA 94623-1225
510-622-3506
http://www.ssa.gov/disability
Disability Served: various

California Social Security Disability Determination Service (La Jolla)
PO Box 85501
San Diego, CA 92186-5501
619-278-4550
http://www.ssa.gov/disability
Disability Served: various

California Social Security Disability Determination Service (Los Angeles East)
PO Box 513819
Los Angeles, CA 90051-1819
213-736-7900
http://www.ssa.gov/disability
Disability Served: various

California Social Security Disability Determination Service (Los Angeles North)
PO Box 54800
Los Angeles, CA 90054-0800
213-736-7000
http://www.ssa.gov/disability
Disability Served: various

California Social Security Disability Determination Service (Los Angeles South)
PO Box 60396
Los Angeles, CA 90060-0396
213-736-4086
http://www.ssa.gov/disability
Disability Served: various

California Social Security Disability Determination Service (Los Angeles West)
PO Box 60999
Los Angeles, CA 90060-0999
213-736-7500
http://www.ssa.gov/disability
Disability Served: various

California Social Security Disability Determination Service (Roseville)
PO Box 619020
Roseville, CA 95678-9861
916-774-4100
http://www.ssa.gov/disability
Disability Served: various

California Social Security Disability Determination Service (Sacramento)
PO Box 997120
Sacramento, CA 95899-7120
916-263-5000
http://www.ssa.gov/disability
Disability Served: various

California Social Security Disability Determination Service (San Diego)
PO Box 85273
San Diego, CA 92186-5273
619-278-4300
http://www.ssa.gov/disability
Disability Served: various

California Social Security Disability Determination Service (Sierra)
PO Box 28937-8937
Fresno, CA 93720
559-440-5200
http://www.ssa.gov/disability
Disability Served: various

California State Council on Developmental Disabilities
1507 21st Street, Suite 210
Sacramento, CA 95814

866-802-0514, 916-324-8420 (TDD)
council@scdd.ca.gov
http://www.scdd.ca.gov
Disability Served: developmentally disabled

COLORADO

Colorado Department of Education
201 East Colfax Avenue
Denver, CO 80203-1799
303-866-6600
http://www.cde.state.co.us
Disability Served: various

Colorado Department of Public Health and Environment
4300 Cherry Creek Drive South
Denver, CO 80246-1530
303-692-2000
cdphe.information@state.co.us
http://www.cdphe.state.co.us/cdphehom.asp
Disability Served: various

Colorado Division for Developmental Disabilities
3824 West Princeton Circle
Denver, CO 80236
303-866-7450, 303-866-7471 (TDD)
http://www.cdhs.state.co.us/ohr/dds/DDS_center.html
Disability Served: developmentally disabled

Colorado Division of Aging and Adult Services
1575 Sherman Street, 10th Floor
Denver, CO 80203
303-866-2800
http://www.cdhs.state.co.us/ADRS/AAS/about1.html
Disability Served: elderly

Colorado Division of Mental Health
3824 West Princeton Circle
Denver, CO 80236
303-866-7400
http://www.cdhs.state.co.us/ohr/mhs
Disability Served: mental health

Colorado Division of Vocational Rehabilitation
1575 Sherman Street, 4th Floor
Denver, CO 80023
303-866-4150 (Voice/TDD)
keri.wells@state.co.us
http://www.cdhs.state.co.us/ODS/dvr
Disability Served: various

Colorado Division of Workers' Compensation
633 17th Street
Denver, CO 80202
303-318-8700, 888-390-7936
http://www.coworkforce.com/DWC
Disability Served: various

Colorado Social Security Disability Determination Service
2530 South Parker Road, Suite 500
Aurora, CO 80014-1641
303-368-4100, 800-332-8087
http://www.ssa.gov/disability
Disability Served: various

CONNECTICUT

Connecticut Board of Education and Services for the Blind
184 Windsor Avenue
Windsor, CT 06095
860-602-4000, 860-602-4221 (TDD)
besb@po.state.ct.us
http://www.besb.state.ct.us
Disability Served: vision

Connecticut Commission on the Deaf and Hearing Impaired
67 Prospect Avenue, 3rd Floor
Hartford, CT 06106-2980
800-708-6796 (Voice/TTY)
http://www.state.ct.us/cdhi
Disability Served: hearing

Connecticut Council on Developmental Disabilities
460 Capitol Avenue
Hartford, CT 06106-1308
860-418-6160, 860-418-6172 (TTY)
http://www.ct.gov/ctcdd
Disability Served: developmentally disabled

Connecticut Department of Education
165 Capitol Avenue
Hartford, CT 06145
860-713-6548
http://www.state.ct.us/sde
Disability Served: various

Connecticut Department of Mental Health a nd Addiction Services
410 Capitol Avenue, PO Box 341431
Hartford, CT 06134

800-446-7348, 860-418-6707 (TDD)
http://www.dmhas.state.ct.us
Disability Served: chemical dependency, mental health

Connecticut Department of Mental Retardation
460 Capitol Avenue
Hartford, CT 06106
860-418-6000, 860-418-6079 (TDD)
dmrct.co@po.state.ct.us
http://www.dmr.state.ct.us
Disability Served: developmentally disabled

Connecticut Department of Public Health
410 Capitol Avenue, PO Box 340308
Hartford, CT 06134-0308
860-509-8000, 860-509-7191 (TDD)
http://www.dph.state.ct.us
Disability Served: various

Connecticut Elderly Services Division
25 Sigourney Street, 10th Floor
Hartford, CT 06106
800-994-9422
ctelderlyserv.dss@po.state.ct.us
http://www.ctelderlyservices.state.ct.us
Disability Served: elderly

Connecticut Social Security Disability Determination Service
PO Box 2363
Hartford, CT 06146-2363
800-842-8320
http://www.ssa.gov/disability
Disability Served: various

Connecticut Workers' Compensation Commission
21 Oak Street
Hartford, CT 06106
860-493-1500
wcc.chairmansoffice@po.state.ct.us
http://wcc.state.ct.us
Disability Served: various

DELAWARE

Delaware Department of Education
401 Federal Street, Suite 2, Townsend Building
Dover, DE 19901
302-739-4601
http://www.doe.state.de.us
Disability Served: various

Delaware Developmental Disabilities Council
410 Federal Street, Suite 2
Dover, DE 19901
302-739-3333
http://www.state.de.us/ddc
Disability Served: developmentally disabled

Delaware Division for the Visually Impaired
1901 North DuPont Highway, Biggs Building
New Castle, DE 19720
302-255-9800
dhssinfo@state.de.us
http://www.dhss.delaware.gov/dhss/dvi
Disability Served: vision

Delaware Division of Developmental Disabilities Services
1056 South Governor's Avenue, Suite 101
Dover, DE 19904
302-744-9600
dhssinfo@state.de.us
http://www.dhss.delaware.gov/dhss/ddds
Disability Served: developmentally disabled

Delaware Division of Public Health
417 Federal Street
Dover, DE 19901
302-744-4700, 888-459-2943
dhssinfo@state.de.us
http://www.dhss.delaware.gov/dhss/dph
Disability Served: various

Delaware Division of Services for the Aging and Adults with Physical Disabilities
1901 North DuPont Highway
New Castle, DE 19720
800-223-9074, 302-453-3837 (TTY)
DSAAPDinfo@state.de.us
http://www.dhss.delaware.gov/dhss/dsaapd
Disability Served: elderly, physically disabled

Delaware Division of Substance Abuse and Mental Health
1901 North DuPont Highway, Main Building
New Castle, DE 19720
302-255-9399
dhssinfo@state.de.us
http://www.dhss.delaware.gov/dhss/dsamh
Disability Served: chemical dependency, mental health

Delaware Division of Vocational Rehabilitation
4425 North Market Street
Wilmington, DE 19802
302-761-8300 (Voice/TTY)
http://www.delawareworks.com/dvr
Disability Served: various

Delaware Office of Workers' Compensation
PO Box 9954
Wilmington, DE 19809-9954
302-761-8200
http://www.delawareworks.com/industrialaffairs/
services/workerscomp.shtml
Disability Served: various

Delaware Social Security Disability Determination Service
PO Box 8862
Wilmington, DE 19899
302-761-8325
http://www.ssa.gov/disability
Disability Served: various

DISTRICT OF COLUMBIA

District of Columbia Department of Health
825 North Capitol Street, NE
Washington, DC 20002
202-671-5000
http://dchealth.dc.gov
Disability Served: various

District of Columbia Department of Mental Health
64 New York Avenue, NE, 4th Floor
Washington, DC 20002
202-673-7440, 888-793-4357
http://dmh.dc.gov/dmh
Disability Served: mental health

District of Columbia Mental Retardation and Developmental Disabilities Administration
1350 Pennsylvania Avenue, NW
Washington, DC 20004
202-673-4500, 202-673-3580 (TTY/TDD)
http://dhs.dc.gov/dhs/cwp/view,a,3,q,492425.asp
Disability Served: developmentally disabled

District of Columbia Office of Workers' Compensation
64 New York Avenue, NE, 2nd Floor
Washington, DC 20002

202-671-1000
http://does.dc.gov/does/cwp/view,a,1232,q,537428.
asp
Disability Served: various

District of Columbia Office on Aging
441 4th Street, NW, Suite 900S
Washington, DC 20001
202-724-5622
http://dcoa.dc.gov/dcoa
Disability Served: elderly

District of Columbia Public Schools
825 North Capitol Street, NE
Washington, DC 20002
202-724-4222
http://www.k12.dc.us/dcps
Disability Served: various

District of Columbia Rehabilitation Services Administration
1350 Pennsylvania Avenue, NW
Washington, DC 20004
202-442-8400, 202-442-8600 (TTY/TDD)
http://dhs.dc.gov/dhs/cwp/view,a,3,q,492432.asp
Disability Served: various

District of Columbia Social Security Disability Determination Service
810 1st Street, NE, Room 8019
Washington, DC 20002
202-442-8500
http://www.ssa.gov/disability
Disability Served: various

FLORIDA
Florida Agency for Health Care Administration
2727 Mahan Drive
Tallahassee, FL 32308
888-419-3456
http://www.fdhc.state.fl.us
Disability Served: various

Florida Agency for Persons with Disabilities
4030 Esplanade Way, Suite 380
Tallahassee, FL 32399-0950
http://apd.myflorida.com
Disability Served: developmentally disabled

Florida Department of Education
Turlington Building, 325 West Gaines Street, Suite 1514
Tallahassee, FL 32399
850-245-0505
http://www.firn.edu/doe
Disability Served: various

Florida Department of Elder Affairs
4040 Esplanade Way
Tallahassee, FL 32399-7000
850-414-2000
information@elderaffairs.org
http://elderaffairs.state.fl.us
Disability Served: elderly

Florida Developmental Disabilities Council
124 Marriott Drive, Suite 203
Tallahassee, FL 32301-2981
800-580-7801, 888-488-8633 (TDD)
fddc@fddc.org
http://www.fddc.org
Disability Served: developmentally disabled

Florida Division of Workers' Compensation
200 East Gaines Street
Tallahassee, FL 32399-4228
800-413-1601
http://www.fldfs.com/wc
Disability Served: various

Florida Mental Health Program Office
2639 North Monroe Street, Suite 200-A
Tallahassee, FL 32303
http://www.dcf.state.fl.us/mentalhealth
Disability Served: mental health

Florida Social Security Disability Determination Service (Jacksonville)
PO Box 10375
Jacksonville, FL 32247-0375
800-821-8122
http://www.ssa.gov/disability
Disability Served: various

Florida Social Security Disability Determination Service (Miami)
PO Box 839001
Miami, FL 33283
800-223-6820

http://www.ssa.gov/disability
Disability Served: various

Florida Social Security Disability Determination Service (Orlando)
3438 Lawton Road, Chandler Building, Suite 100
Orlando, FL 32803
800-342-2065
http://www.ssa.gov/disability
Disability Served: various

Florida Social Security Disability Determination Service (Tallahassee)
2729 Fort Knox Boulevard, Building 2, Suite 205
Tallahassee, FL 32399-5340
800-342-1824
http://www.ssa.gov/disability
Disability Served: various

Florida Social Security Disability Determination Service (Tampa)
PO Box 292923
Tampa, FL 33687
800-223-1172
http://www.ssa.gov/disability
Disability Served: various

GEORGIA

Georgia Board of Workers' Compensation
270 Peachtree Street, NW
Atlanta, GA 30303-1299
404-656-2048
http://sbwc.georgia.gov
Disability Served: various

Georgia Department of Education
2066 Twin Towers East
Atlanta, GA 30334
404-656-2800, 800-311-3627
http://www.doe.k12.ga.us
Disability Served: various

Georgia Division of Aging Services
Two Peachtree Street, NW , Suite 9385
Atlanta, GA 30303-3142
404-657-5258
http://aging.dhr.georgia.gov
Disability Served: elderly

Georgia Division of Mental Health, Developmental Disabilities and Addictive Diseases
Two Peachtree Street, NW, 22nd Floor
Atlanta, GA 30303
404-657-5737
glwilson@dhr.state.ga.us
http://mhddad.dhr.georgia.gov
Disability Served: chemical dependency, developmentally disabled, mental health

Georgia Social Security Disability Determination Service (Athens)
394 South Milledge Avenue, Suite 205
Athens, GA 30605
706-227-5455
http://www.ssa.gov/disability
Disability Served: various

Georgia Social Security Disability Determination Service (Savannah)
450 Mall Boulevard, Suite C
Savannah, GA 31416
912-351-3511
http://www.ssa.gov/disability
Disability Served: various

Georgia Social Security Disability Determination Service (Stone Mountain)
PO Box 57
Stone Mountain, GA 30086
678-476-7000
http://www.ssa.gov/disability
Disability Served: various

Georgia Social Security Disability Determination Service (Thomasville)
1317 East Jackson Street
Thomasville, GA 31792
800-350-5279
http://www.ssa.gov/disability
Disability Served: various

HAWAII
Hawaii Council on Developmental Disabilities
919 Ala Moana Boulevard, Suite 113
Honolulu, HI 96814
808-586-8100
council@hiddc.org
http://www.hiddc.org
Disability Served: developmentally disabled

Hawaii Department of Education
PO Box 2360
Honolulu, HI 96804
808-586-3230
doe_info@notes.k12.hi.us
http://doe.k12.hi.us
Disability Served: various

Hawaii Department of Health
1250 Punchbowl Street
Honolulu, HI 96813
808-586-4400
http://www.state.hi.us/health
Disability Served: various

Hawaii Developmental Disabilities Division
1250 Punchbowl Street, Room 463
Honolulu, HI 96813
808-586-5840
http://www.hawaii.gov/health/disability-services/
developmental
Disability Served: developmentally disabled

Hawaii Disability Compensation Division
830 Punchbowl Street
Honolulu, HI 96813
808 586-8842
dlir-info@dlir.state.hi.us
http://hawaii.gov/labor
Disability Served: various

Hawaii Division of Adult Mental Health
1250 Punchbowl Street, #256
Honolulu, HI 96813
808-586-4686
admin@amhd.org
http://www.amhd.org
Disability Served: mental health

Hawaii Executive Office on Aging
250 South Hotel Street, Room 406
Honolulu, HI 96813-2831
808-586-0100
eoa@health.state.hi.us
http://www2.state.hi.us/eoa
Disability Served: elderly

Hawaii Social Security Disability Determination Service
PO Box 2458
Honolulu, HI 96804
808-973-2244
http://www.ssa.gov/disability
Disability Served: various

IDAHO
Idaho Bureau of Mental Health and Substance Abuse
450 West State Street
Boise, ID 83720-0036
208-334-5500
http://www.healthandwelfare.idaho.gov
Disability Served: chemical dependency, mental health

Idaho Commission for the Blind and Visually Impaired
341 West Washington
Boise, ID 83702
800-542-8688
http://www.icbvi.state.id.us
Disability Served: vision

Idaho Commission on Aging
PO Box 83720
Boise, ID 83720-0007
208-334-3833, 877-471-2777
senglesby@icoa.state.id.us
http://www.state.id.us/icoa
Disability Served: elderly

Idaho Council for the Deaf and Hard of Hearing
1720 Westgate Drive, Suite A
Boise, ID 83704
800-433-1323, 800-433-1361 (TDD/TTY)
http://www2.state.id.us/cdhh/cdhh1.htm
Disability Served: hearing

Idaho Council on Developmental Disabilities
802 West Bannock
Boise, ID 83702-5840
800-544-2433, 208-334-2179 (TTY)
http://www2.state.id.us/icdd
Disability Served: developmentally disabled

Idaho Department of Education
PO Box 83720
Boise, ID 83720-0027
208-332-6800
http://www.sde.state.id.us/Dept
Disability Served: various

Idaho Department of Health and Welfare
450 West State Street
Boise, ID 83720-0036
208-334-5500
contactus@idhw.state.id.us
http://www.healthandwelfare.idaho.gov
Disability Served: various

Idaho Department of Vocational Rehabilitation
PO Box 83720
Boise, ID 83720-0096
208-334-3390
rthomas@idvr.state.id.us
http://www.state.id.us/idvr
Disability Served: various

Idaho Industrial Commission
PO Box 83720
Boise, ID 83720-0041
208-334-6000
sraeder@iic.state.id.us
http://www2.state.id.us/iic/index.htm
Disability Served: various

Idaho Social Security Disability Determination Service
PO Box 21
Boise, ID 83707
208-327-7333, 800-626-2681
http://www.ssa.gov/disability
Disability Served: various

ILLINOIS
Illinois Board of Education
100 North First Street
Springfield, IL 62777
866-262-6663
http://www.isbe.state.il.us
Disability Served: various

Illinois Department of Public Health
535 West Jefferson Street
Springfield, IL 62761
217-782-4977, 800-547-0466 (TTY)
http://www.idph.state.il.us
Disability Served: various

Illinois Department on Aging
421 East Capitol Avenue, #100
Springfield, IL 62701-1789

217-785-3356
http://www.state.il.us/aging
Disability Served: elderly

Illinois Division of Developmental Disabilities Services
100 South Grand Avenue East
Springfield, IL 62762
217-524-0260, 800-447-6404 (TTY)
http://www.dhs.state.il.us/mhdd/dd
Disability Served: developmentally disabled

Illinois Division of Mental Health Services
100 South Grand Avenue East
Springfield, IL 62762
217-524-0260
http://www.dhs.state.il.us/mhdd/mh
Disability Served: mental health

Illinois Division of Rehabilitation Services
100 South Grand Avenue East
Springfield, IL 62762
800-843-6154, 800-447-6404 (TTY)
DRS@dhs.state.il.us
http://www.dhs.state.il.us/ors
Disability Served: various

Illinois Social Security Disability Determination Service
PO Box 19250
Springfield, IL 62794-9250
800-225-3607
http://www.ssa.gov/disability
Disability Served: various

Illinois Workers' Compensation Commission
100 West Randolph Street, #8-200
Chicago, IL 60601
866-352-3033, 312-814-2959 (TDD)
iwccinfo@mail.state.il.us
http://www.state.il.us/agency/iic
Disability Served: various

INDIANA
Indiana Department of Education
Room 229, State House
Indianapolis, IN 46204-2798
317-232-6610
http://www.doe.state.in.us
Disability Served: various

Indiana Department of Health
Two North Meridian Street
Indianapolis, IN 46204
317-233-1325
http://www.state.in.us/doh
Disability Served: various

Indiana Division of Disability, Aging, and Rehabilitative Services
PO Box 7083
Indianapolis, IN 46207-7083
800-545-7763
SBell@fssa.state.in.us
http://www.ai.org/fssa/servicedisabl/ddars
Disability Served: various

Indiana Division of Mental Health
PO Box 7083
Indianapolis, IN 46207-7083
317-233-4454
SBell@fssa.state.in.us
http://www.ai.org/fssa/servicemental
Disability Served: chemical dependency, mental health

Indiana Social Security Disability Determination Service
PO Box 7069
Indianapolis, IN 46207-7069
800-622-4968, ext. 2007
http://www.state.in.us/fssa/servicedisabl/ddars/ddb.html
Disability Served: various

Indiana Workers' Compensation Board
402 West Washington Street, Room W-196
Indianapolis, IN 46204
800-824-COMP
http://www.in.gov/workcomp
Disability Served: various

IOWA
Iowa Deaf Services Commission of Iowa
321 East 12th Street, Lucas State Office Building
Des Moines, IA 50319
888-221-3724 (voice/TTY)
dhr.dsci@iowa.gov
http://www.state.ia.us/government/dhr/ds
Disability Served: hearing

Iowa Department for the Blind
524 Fourth Street
Des Moines, IA 50309-2364
800-362-2587, 515-281-1355 (TTY)
http://www.blind.state.ia.us
Disability Served: vision

Iowa Department of Education
Grimes State Office Building
Des Moines, IA 50319-0146
515-281-5294
http://www.state.ia.us/educate
Disability Served: various

Iowa Department of Elder Affairs
Clemens Building, 200 Tenth Street, Third Floor
Des Moines, IA 50309-3609
515-242-3333, 515-242-3302 (TTY)
Sherry.James@iowa.gov
http://www.state.ia.us/elderaffairs
Disability Served: elderly

Iowa Department of Public Health
321 East Twelfth Street, Lucas State Office Building
Des Moines, IA 50319
515-281-7689
http://www.idph.state.ia.us
Disability Served: various

Iowa Division of Mental Health and Developmental Disabilities
Hoover State Office Building, 1305 East Walnut, Fifth Floor
Des Moines, IA 50319-0114
800-972-2017
http://www.dhs.state.ia.us/mhdd
Disability Served: developmentally disabled, mental health

Iowa Division of Persons with Disabilities
321 East 12th Street
Des Moines, IA 50319
888-219-0471 (Voice/TTY)
dhr.disabilities@iowa.gov
http://www.state.ia.us/government/dhr/pd
Disability Served: various

Iowa Division of Vocational Rehabilitation Services
510 East 12th Street
Des Moines, IA 50319-0240
515-281-4211 (Voice/TTY)

http://www.dvrs.state.ia.us
Disability Served: various

Iowa Division of Workers' Compensation
1000 East Grand Avenue
Des Moines, IA 50319
800-JOB-IOWA, 515-281-4748 (TDD)
iwd.dwc@iwd.state.ia.us
http://www.iowaworkforce.org/wc
Disability Served: various

Iowa Social Security Disability Determination Service
510 East 12th Street
Des Moines, IA 50319
515-281-4474, 800-532-1223
http://www.ssa.gov/disability
Disability Served: various

KANSAS

Kansas Commission for the Deaf and Hard of Hearing
3640 Southwest Topeka Boulevard, Suite 150
Topeka, KS 66611
800-432-0698 (Voice/TTY)
http://www.srskansas.org/kcdhh
Disability Served: hearing

Kansas Commission on Disability Concerns
1430 Southwest Topeka Avenue
Topeka, KS 66612-1877
800-295-5232, 877-340-5874 (TTY)
http://www.hr.state.ks.us/dc
Disability Served: various

Kansas Council on Developmental Disabilities
915 Southwest Harrison, Room 141
Topeka, KS 66612-1570
785-296-2608
http://www.nekesc.org/kcdd.html
Disability Served: developmentally disabled

Kansas Department of Education
120 Southeast 10th Avenue
Topeka, KS 66612-1182
785-296-3201
http://www.ksbe.state.ks.us
Disability Served: various

Kansas Department of Social and Rehabilitation Services
915 Southwest Harrison Street
Topeka, KS 66612
785-296-3959, 785-296-1491 (TTY)
http://www.srskansas.org
Disability Served: various

Kansas Department on Aging
503 South Kansas Avenue, New England Building
Topeka, KS 66603-3404
800-432-3535, 785-291-3167 (TTY)
wwwmail@aging.state.ks.us
http://www.agingkansas.org
Disability Served: elderly

Kansas Division of Health
1000 Southwest Jackson, Suite 300
Topeka, KS 66612-1365
785-296-1086
http://www.kdhe.state.ks.us/health
Disability Served: various

Kansas Division of Workers' Compensation
800 Southwest Jackson, Suite 600
Topeka, KS 66612-1227
785-296-2996
anita.ramirez@dol.ks.gov
http://www.dol.ks.gov/wc/html/wc_ALL.html
Disability Served: various

Kansas Social Security Disability Determination Service
3640 Southwest Topeka Boulevard, Suite 100
Topeka, KS 66611-2367
785-267-4440, 800-685-0122
http://www.ssa.gov/disability
Disability Served: various

KENTUCKY
Kentucky Cabinet for Family and Health Services
275 East Main Street
Frankfort, KY 40621
800-372-2973, 800-627-4702 (TTY)
http://chfs.ky.gov
Disability Served: various

Kentucky Commission on the Deaf and Hard of Hearing
632 Versailles Road
Frankfort, KY 40601
800-372-2907 (Voice/TTY)
http://www.kcdhh.org
Disability Served: hearing

Kentucky Council on Developmental Disabilities
100 Fair Oaks Lane, 4E-F
Frankfort, KY 40601
877-367-5332
http://chfs.ky.gov/kcdd
Disability Served: developmentally disabled

Kentucky Department of Education
500 Mero Street
Frankfort, KY 40601
800-533-5372, 502-564-4970 (TTY)
http://www.education.ky.gov/KDE
Disability Served: various

Kentucky Department of Workers' Claims
657 Chamberlin Avenue
Frankfort, KY 40601
502-564-5550
http://labor.ky.gov/dwc
Disability Served: various

Kentucky Division of Aging Services
275 East Main Street
Frankfort, KY 40621
800-372-2973, 800-627-4702 (TTY)
http://chfs.ky.gov/dhss/das
Disability Served: elderly

Kentucky Office for the Blind
209 St. Clair Street, PO Box 757
Frankfort, KY 40602-0757
800-321-6668, 502-564-2929 (TDD)
http://blind.ky.gov
Disability Served: vision

Kentucky Office of Vocational Rehabilitation
209 St. Clair Street
Frankfort, KY 40601
502-564-4440 (Voice/TTY)
http://ovr.ky.gov
Disability Served: various

Kentucky Social Security Disability Determination Service (Frankfort)
PO Box 1000
Frankfort, KY 40601
800-928-8050
http://www.ssa.gov/disability
Disability Served: various

Kentucky Social Security Disability Determination Service (Louisville)
PO Box 1061
Louisville, KY 40201
800-928-3202
http://www.ssa.gov/disability
Disability Served: various

LOUISIANA

Louisiana Commission for the Deaf
8225 Florida Boulevard
Baton Rouge, LA 70806
800-256-1523 (Voice/TDD)
froy1@dss.state.la.us
http://www.dss.state.la.us/departments/lrs/
    Commission_For_the_Deaf.html
Disability Served: hearing

Louisiana Department of Education
PO Box 94064
Baton Rouge, LA 70804-9064
877-453-2721
http://www.doe.state.la.us/lde
Disability Served: various

Louisiana Department of Health and Hospitals
1201 Capitol Access Road, PO Box 629
Baton Rouge, LA 70821-0629
225-342-9500
webadmin@dhh.la.gov
http://www.dhh.state.la.us
Disability Served: various

Louisiana Office for Citizens with Developmental Disabilities
1201 Capitol Access Road
Baton Rouge, LA 70821-0629
225-342-9500
webadmin@dhh.la.gov
http://www.dhh.louisiana.gov
Disability Served: developmentally disabled

Louisiana Office of Mental Health
PO Box 4049, Bin #12
Baton Rouge, LA 70821
225-342-2540
http://www.dhh.state.la.us/offices/?ID=62
Disability Served: mental health

Louisiana Rehabilitation Services
3651 Cedarcrest Avenue
Baton Rouge, LA 70816-4010
800-737-2959
http://www.dss.state.la.us/departments/lrs/Vocational_
    Rehabilitation.html
Disability Served: various

**Louisiana Social Security Disability Determination
    Service (Baton Rouge)**
755 3rd Street, A. Z. Young Building
Baton Rouge, LA 70802
225-925-3522
http://www.dss.state.la.us
Disability Served: various

**Louisiana Social Security Disability Determination
    Service (Metairie)**
PO Box 5916
Metairie, LA 70009
504-838-5000
http://www.ssa.gov/disability
Disability Served: various

**Louisiana Social Security Disability Determination
    Service (Shreveport)**
2920 Knight Street, Suite 232
Shreveport, LA 71105
318-869-6400
http://www.ssa.gov/disability
Disability Served: various

Louisiana Workers' Compensation Administration
PO Box 94040
Baton Rouge, LA 70804-9040
225-342-7555
owca@ldol.state.la.us
http://www.ldol.state.la.us/wrk_owca.asp
Disability Served: various

MAINE

Maine Bureau of Elder and Adult Services
442 Civic Center Drive, 11 State House Station
Augusta, ME 04333

800-262-2232, 888-720-1925 (TTY)
http://www.maine.gov/dhhs/beas/health.htm
Disability Served: various

Maine Bureau of Health
286 Water Street, Station 11
Augusta, ME 04333-0011
207-287-8016
http://www.maine.gov/dhhs/boh
Disability Served: various

**Maine Department of Behavioral and Developmental
    Services**
40 State House Station
Augusta, ME 04333-0040
207-287-4200, 207-287-2000 (TTY)
http://www.maine.gov/dhhs/bds
Disability Served: chemical dependency, developmentally
    disabled, mental health

Maine Department of Education
23 State House Station
Augusta, ME 04333-0023
207-624-6600, 207-624-6800 (TTY)
http://www.state.me.us/education
Disability Served: various

**Maine Social Security Disability Determination
    Service**
State House Station, #116
Augusta, ME 04333
207-377-9500
http://www.ssa.gov/disability
Disability Served: various

Maine Workers' Compensation Board
27 State House Station
Augusta, ME 04333-0027
207-287-3751
melinda.porter@maine.gov
http://www.state.me.us/wcb
Disability Served: various

MARYLAND

Maryland Blind Industries and Services
3345 Washington Boulevard
Baltimore, MD 21227
410-737-2600, 888-322-4567
http://bism.org
Disability Served: vision

Maryland Department of Disabilities
217 East Redwood Street, Suite 1300
Baltimore, MD 21202
800-637-4113 (Voice/TTY)
mdod@mdod.state.md.us
http://www.mdtap.org/oid.html
Disability Served: various

Maryland Department of Education
200 West Baltimore Street
Baltimore, MD 21201
410-767-0600
http://www.marylandpublicschools.org/msde
Disability Served: various

Maryland Department of Health and Mental Hygiene
201 West Preston Street
Baltimore, MD 21201
877-463-3464
http://www.dhmh.state.md.us
Disability Served: various

Maryland Developmental Disabilities Council
217 East Redwood Street, Suite 1300
Baltimore, MD 21202
800-305-6441
info@md-council.org
http://www.md-council.org
Disability Served: developmentally disabled

Maryland Division of Rehabilitation Services
2301 Argonne Drive
Baltimore, MD 21218-1696
888-554-0334, 410-554-9411 (TTY)
dors@dors.state.md.us
http://www.dors.state.md.us/dors
Disability Served: various

Maryland Office on Aging
301 West Preston Street, Suite 1007
Baltimore, MD 21201
410-767-1100, 800-243-3425
http://www.mdoa.state.md.us
Disability Served: elderly

Maryland Social Security Disability Determination Service
PO Box 6338
Timonium, MD 21094-6338
410-308-4350

http://www.ssa.gov/disability
Disability Served: various

Maryland Worker's Compensation Commission
10 East Baltimore Street
Baltimore, MD 21202-1641
410-864-5100
info@wcc.state.md.us
http://www.wcc.state.md.us
Disability Served: various

MASSACHUSETTS

Massachusetts Commission for the Blind
48 Boylston Street
Boston, MA 02116-4718
800-392-6450, 800-392-6556 (TTY)
http://www.mass.gov/mcb
Disability Served: vision

Massachusetts Commission for the Deaf and Hard of Hearing
210 South Street, Fifth Floor
Boston, MA 02111
617-695-7500
http://www.mass.gov
Disability Served: hearing

Massachusetts Department of Education
350 Main Street
Malden, MA 02148-5023
781-338-3000
http://www.doe.mass.edu
Disability Served: various

Massachusetts Department of Mental Health
500 Harrison Avenue
Boston, MA 02118
617-727-5608, 617-624-7783 (TTY)
Info@state.ma.us
http://mass.gov
Disability Served: mental health

Massachusetts Department of Mental Retardation
500 Harrison Avenue
Boston, MA 02118
617-727-5608, 617-624-7783 (TTY)
Info@state.ma.us
http://mass.gov
Disability Served: developmentally disabled

Massachusetts Department of Public Health
250 Washington Street
Boston, MA 02108-4619
617-624-6000, 617-624-6001 (TTY)
http://www.mass.gov/dph
Disability Served: various

Massachusetts Developmental Disabilities Council
1150 Hancock Street, Third Floor, Suite 300
Quincy, MA 02169-4340
617-770-7676, 617-770-9499 (TTY)
http://www.mass.gov/mddc
Disability Served: developmentally disabled

Massachusetts Disabled Person Protection Commission
50 Ross Way
Quincy, MA 02169
617-727-6465, 800-426-9009 (Voice/TTY)
http://www.mass.gov/dppc
Disability Served: various

Massachusetts Executive Office of Elder Affairs
One Ashburton Place, Fifth Floor
Boston, MA 02108
800-243-4636, 800-872-0166 (TDD/TTY)
elder.affairs@state.ma.us
http://mass.gov
Disability Served: elderly

Massachusetts Rehabilitation Commission
27 Wormwood Street
Boston, MA 02210-1616
617-204-3762 (Voice/TDD)
http://www.mass.gov
Disability Served: various

Massachusetts Social Security Disability Determination Service (Boston)
110 Chauncy Street
Boston, MA 02111
617-727-1600, 800-882-2040
http://www.ssa.gov/disability
Disability Served: various

Massachusetts Social Security Disability Determination Service (Worcester)
22 Front Street, PO Box 8009
Worcester, MA 01614-9981
508-752-5001, 800-551-5532

http://www.ssa.gov/disability
Disability Served: various

MICHIGAN

Michigan Department of Community Health
320 South Walnut Street
Lansing, MI 48913
517-373-3740, 517-373-3573 (TDD)
http://www.michigan.gov/mdch
Disability Served: various

Michigan Department of Education
608 West Allegan Street, PO Box 30008
Lansing, MI 48909
517-373-3324
MDEweb@michigan.gov
http://www.michigan.gov/mde
Disability Served: various

Michigan Developmental Disabilities Council
1033 South Washington Avenue
Lansing, MI 48910
517-334-6123, 517-334-7354 (TDD)
vanhornr@michigan.gov
http://www.michigan.gov/mdch/1%2C1607%2C7-132-2941_4868_4897-14614--%2C00.html
Disability Served: developmentally disabled

Michigan Office of Services to the Aging
PO Box 30676
Lansing, MI 48909-8176
517-373-8230, 517-373-4096 (TDD)
http://www.miseniors.net/MiSeniors+Home
Disability Served: elderly

Michigan Social Security Disability Determination Service (Detroit)
PO Box 345
Detroit, MI 48231
800-383-7155
http://www.ssa.gov/disability
Disability Served: various

Michigan Social Security Disability Determination Service (Kalamazoo)
PO Box 4020
Kalamazoo, MI 49003
800-829-7763
http://www.ssa.gov/disability
Disability Served: various

Michigan Social Security Disability Determination Service (Lansing)
PO Box 30011
Lansing, MI 48909
800-366-3404
http://www.ssa.gov/disability
Disability Served: various

Michigan Social Security Disability Determination Service (Traverse City)
PO Box 1200
Traverse City, MI 49685
800-632-1097
http://www.ssa.gov/disability
Disability Served: various

Michigan Workers' Compensation Agency
PO Box 30016
Lansing, MI 48909
888-396-5041
wcinfo@michigan.gov
http://www.michigan.gov/wca
Disability Served: various

MINNESOTA

Minnesota Board on Aging
444 Lafayette Road North
St. Paul, MN 55155-3843
651-296-2770, 800-627-3529 (TTY)
mba@state.mn.us
http://www.mnaging.org
Disability Served: elderly

Minnesota Deaf and Hard of Hearing Services Division
444 Lafayette Road North
St. Paul, MN 55155
651-296-3980, 651-297-1506 (TTY/TDD)
DHS.Info@state.mn.us
http://www.dhs.state.mn.us/main/groups/disabilities/
    documents/pub/DHS_id_000081.hcsp
Disability Served: hearing

Minnesota Department of Education
1500 Highway 36 West
Roseville, MN 55113-4266
651-582-8200
http://education.state.mn.us/html/mde_home.htm
Disability Served: various

Minnesota Department of Health
PO Box 64975
St. Paul, MN 55164-0975
651-215-5800, 651-215-8980 (TDD)
http://www.health.state.mn.us
Disability Served: various

Minnesota Department of Human Services
444 Lafayette Road North
Saint Paul, MN 55155
651-296-6117
DHS.Info@state.mn.us
http://www.dhs.state.mn.us/main/groups/disabilities/
    documents/pub/dhs_Disabilities.hcsp
Disability Served: various

Minnesota Governor's Council on Developmental Disabilities
658 Cedar Street, 370 Centennial Office Building
St. Paul, MN 55155
651-296-4018, 877-348-0505
admin.dd@state.mn.us
http://www.mnddc.org
Disability Served: developmentally disabled

Minnesota Mental Health Division
444 Lafayette Road
St. Paul, MN 55155
651-296-4497
http://www.dhs.state.mn.us/main/groups/disabilities/
    documents/pub/DHS_id_000085.hcsp
Disability Served: mental health

Minnesota Rehabilitation Services
332 Minnesota Street, Suite E200
St. Paul, MN 55101
800-328-9095, 800-657-3973 (TTY)
http://www.deed.state.mn.us/rehab
Disability Served: various

Minnesota Social Security Disability Determination Service
1st National Bank Building, Suite E200
St. Paul, MN 55101-1351
800-657-3858
http://www.ssa.gov/disability
Disability Served: various

Minnesota State Council on Disability
121 East 7th Place, Suite 107
St. Paul, MN 55101

800-945-8913 (Voice/TTY)
http://www.disability.state.mn.us
Disability Served: various

Minnesota State Services for the Blind
2200 University Avenue West, Suite 240
St. Paul, MN 55114-1840
651-642-0500, 651-642-0506 (TTY)
http://www.mnssb.org
Disability Served: vision

Minnesota Vocational Rehabilitation Unit
443 Lafayette Road
St. Paul, MN 55155
888-772-5500
DLI.Vocrehab@state.mn.us
Disability Served: various

Minnesota Workers' Compensation Division
443 Lafayette Road
St. Paul, MN 55155
651-284-5005, 800-342-5354
DLI.Workcomp@state.mn.us
http://www.doli.state.mn.us/workcomp.html
Disability Served: various

MISSISSIPPI
Mississippi Department of Education
PO Box 771
Jackson, MS 39205
601-359-3513
webhelp@mde.k12.ms.us
http://www.mde.k12.ms.us
Disability Served: various

Mississippi Department of Health
PO Box 1700
Jackson, MS 39215-1700
601-576-7400, 866-458-4948
http://www.msdh.state.ms.us
Disability Served: various

Mississippi Department of Mental Health
239 North Lamar Street
Jackson, MS 39201
601-359-1288, 601-359-6230 (TDD)
http://www.dmh.state.ms.us
Disability Served: mental health

Mississippi Department of Rehabilitation Services
PO Box 1698
Jackson, MS 39215-1698
601-853-5100
http://www.mdrs.state.ms.us
Disability Served: various

Mississippi Developmental Disabilities Council
239 North Lamar Street, 1101 Robert E. Lee Building
Jackson, MS 39201
601-359-1270, 601-359-6230 (TDD)
Disability Served: developmentally disabled

Mississippi Division of Aging and Adult Services
750 North State Street
Jackson, MS 39205
800-948-3090, 800-676-4154 (TDD)
http://www.mdhs.state.ms.us/aas.html
Disability Served: elderly

Mississippi Social Security Disability Determination Service
PO Box 1271
Jackson, MS 39215-1271
800-962-2230
http://www.ssa.gov/disability
Disability Served: various

Mississippi Workers' Compensation Commission
PO Box 5300
Jackson, MS 39296-5300
601-987-4200
http://www.mwcc.state.ms.us
Disability Served: various

MISSOURI
Missouri Commission for the Deaf and Hard of Hearing
1103 Rear Southwest Boulevard
Jefferson City, MO 65109
573-526-5205 (Voice/TTY)
MCDHH@mcdhh.mo.gov
http://www.mcdhh.state.mo.us
Disability Served: hearing

Missouri Department of Elementary and Secondary Education
PO Box 480
Jefferson City, MO 65102

573-751-4212
pubinfo@dese.mo.gov
http://www.dese.state.mo.us
Disability Served: various

Missouri Department of Health and Senior Services
PO Box 570
Jefferson City, MO 65102
573-751-6400
info@dhss.mo.gov
http://www.health.state.mo.us
Disability Served: various

Missouri Department of Mental Health
PO Box 687
Jefferson City, MO 65101
800-364-9687
dmhmail@dmh.mo.gov
http://www.dmh.missouri.gov
Disability Served: chemical dependency, developmentally disabled, mental health

Missouri Division of Mental Retardation and Developmental Disabilities
PO Box 687
Jefferson City, MO 65102
800-364-9687
dmhmail@dmh.mo.gov
http://www.dmh.mo.gov/mrdd/mrddindex.htm
Disability Served: developmentally disabled

Missouri Division of Vocational Rehabilitation
3024 DuPont Circle
Jefferson City, MO 65109-0525
877-222-8963, 573-751-0881 (TDD)
http://www.vr.dese.state.mo.us
Disability Served: various

Missouri Division of Workers' Compensation
PO Box 58
Jefferson City, MO 65102-0058
573-751-4231
workerscomp@dolir.mo.gov
http://www.dolir.state.mo.us/wc
Disability Served: various

Missouri Governor's Council on Disability
301 West High Street, Room 250-A, PO Box 1668
Jefferson City, MO 65102

800-877-8249 (Voice/TTY)
http://www.gcd.oa.mo.gov
Disability Served: various

Missouri Rehabilitation Services for the Blind
615 Howerton Court
PO Box 2320
Jefferson City, MO 65102
573-751-4249, 800-735-2966 (TTD)
http://dss.missouri.gov/fsd/rsb
Disability Served: vision

Missouri Social Security Disability Determination Service (Cape Girardeau)
3014 Blattner
Cape Girardeau, MO 63701
573-290-5710
http://www.ssa.gov/disability
Disability Served: various

Missouri Social Security Disability Determination Service (Jefferson City)
1500-B Southridge Drive
Jefferson City, MO 65109
573-751-2929
http://www.ssa.gov/disability
Disability Served: various

Missouri Social Security Disability Determination Service (Kansas City)
8500 East Bannister Road
Kansas City, MO 64134
816-325-1200
http://www.ssa.gov/disability
Disability Served: various

Missouri Social Security Disability Determination Service (Springfield)
2530-I South Campbell Avenue
Springfield, MO 65807
417-888-4070
http://www.ssa.gov/disability
Disability Served: various

Missouri Social Security Disability Determination Service (St. Louis North)
4040 Seven Hills Drive, Suite 237
Florissant, MO 63033
314-877-3100

http://www.ssa.gov/disability
Disability Served: various

Missouri Social Security Disability Determination Service (St. Louis South)
7545 South Lindbergh, Suite 220
St. Louis, MO 63125
314-416-2803
http://www.ssa.gov/disability
Disability Served: various

MONTANA

Montana Council on Developmental Disabilities
PO Box 526
Helena, MT 59624
406-443-4332
http://www.mtcdd.org
Disability Served: developmentally disabled

Montana Department of Public Health and Human Services
PO Box 4210
Helena, MT 59604
406-444-2590, 877-296-1197
http://www.dphhs.state.mt.us
Disability Served: various

Montana Disability Services Division
111 Sanders, Suite 307, PO Box 4210
Helena, MT 59604-4210
406-444-2590 (Voice/TTY), 877-296-1197
http://www.dphhs.mt.gov/dsd
Disability Served: various

Montana Office of Addictive and Mental Disorders
PO Box 202905
Helena, MT 59620-2905
406-444-3964
http://www.dphhs.state.mt.us/aboutus/divisions/
addictivementaldisorders
Disability Served: chemical dependency, mental health

Montana Office of Public Instruction
PO Box 202501
Helena, MT 59620-2501
888-231-9393
http://www.opi.state.mt.us
Disability Served: various

Montana Senior and Long Term Care Division
111 North Sanders, Room 210
Helena, MT 59604
406-444-4077, 800-332-2272
http://www.dphhs.state.mt.us/sltc
Disability Served: elderly

Montana Social Security Disability Determination Service
PO Box 4189
Helena, MT 59604-4189
406-444-3054, 800-545-3054
http://www.ssa.gov/disability
Disability Served: various

Montana Workers' Compensation Court
PO Box 537
Helena, MT 59624-0537
406-444-7794
http://wcc.dli.state.mt.us
Disability Served: various

NEBRASKA

Nebraska Department of Education
PO Box 94987
Lincoln, NE 68509
402-471-2295
http://www.nde.state.ne.us
Disability Served: various

Nebraska Department of Health and Human Services
PO Box 95044
Lincoln, NE 68509-5044
402-471-2306
http://www.hhs.state.ne.us/svc/svcindex.htm
Disability Served: various

Nebraska Developmental Disability System
PO Box 98925
Lincoln, NE 68509-8925
402-479-5247
http://www.hhs.state.ne.us/dip/ded/dedindex.htm
Disability Served: developmentally disabled

Nebraska Division of Aging and Disability Services
PO Box 95044
Lincoln, NE 68509-5044
402-471-4623, 800-942-7830 (Nebraska only)

http://www.hhs.state.ne.us/ags/agsindex.htm
Disability Served: elderly

Nebraska Office of Mental Health, Substance Abuse, and Addiction Services
PO Box 98925
Lincoln, NE 68509-8925
402-479-5583
http://www.hhs.state.ne.us/beh/mhsa.htm
Disability Served: chemical dependency, mental health

Nebraska Social Security Disability Determination Service
PO Box 82530
Lincoln, NE 68501-2530
800-331-5616
http://www.ssa.gov/disability
Disability Served: various

Nebraska Vocational Rehabilitation
PO Box 94987
Lincoln, NE 68509
402-471-3644, 877-637-3422 (Nebraska only)
s_chapin@vocrehab.state.ne.us
http://www.vocrehab.state.ne.us
Disability Served: various

Nebraska Workers' Compensation Court
PO Box 98908
Lincoln, NE 68509-8908
800-599-5155
http://www.wcc.ne.gov
Disability Served: various

NEVADA

Nevada Department of Education
700 East Fifth Street
Carson City, NV 89701-5096
775-687-9200
http://www.doe.nv.gov
Disability Served: various

Nevada Division for Aging Services
505 East King Street
Carson City, NV 89701
775-486-3545
http://www.aging.state.nv.us
Disability Served: elderly

Nevada Division of Industrial Relations Workers' Compensation Section
1301 North Green Valley Parkway, Suite 200
Henderson, NV 89074
702-486-9080
http://dirweb.state.nv.us/WCS/wcs.htm
Disability Served: various

Nevada Division of Mental Health and Development Services
505 East King Street, Room 602
Carson City, NV 89701-3790
775-684-5943
http://mhds.state.nv.us
Disability Served: developmentally disabled, mental health

Nevada Division of Rehabilitation
505 East King Street, Room 502
Carson City, NV 89701-3705
775-684-4040, 775-684-8400 (TTY)
detrvr@nvdetr.org
http://www.detr.state.nv.us/rehab/reh_index.htm
Disability Served: various

Nevada Governor's Committee on the Employment of People with Disabilities
4001 Kietzke Lane, Suite F-154
Reno, NV 89502
775-688-1111
http://www.state.nv.us/b&i/gb
Disability Served: various

Nevada Governor's Council on Developmental Disabilities
3656 Research Way
Carson City, NV 89701
775-687-4452, 775-687-3388 (TDD)
Disability Served: developmentally disabled

Nevada Social Security Disability Determination Service
1050 East William Street, Suite 300
Carson City, NV 89701-3102
800-882-4430
http://www.ssa.gov/disability
Disability Served: various

Nevada State Health Division
505 East King Street, Room 201
Carson City, NV 89701

775-684-4200
jflamm@nvhd.state.nv.us
http://health2k.state.nv.us
Disability Served: various

NEW HAMPSHIRE

New Hampshire Bureau of Behavioral Health
105 Pleasant Street
Concord, NH 03301-3857
603-271-5007, 800-735-2964 (TDD)
http://www.dhhs.state.nh.us/DHHS/BBH
Disability Served: mental health

New Hampshire Bureau of Elderly and Adult Services
129 Pleasant Street
Concord, NH 03301-3857
603-271-4680
http://www.dhhs.state.nh.us/DHHS/BEAS
Disability Served: elderly

New Hampshire Bureau of Vocational Rehabilitation Services
21 South Fruit Street, Suite 20
Concord, NH 03301
603-271-3471(Voice/TTY), 800-299-1647
http://www.ed.state.nh.us/VR
Disability Served: various

New Hampshire Department of Education
101 Pleasant Street
Concord, NH 03301-3860
603-271-6646
http://www.ed.state.nh.us/education/disabilities
Disability Served: various

New Hampshire Department of Health and Human Services
129 Pleasant Street
Concord, NH 03301-3857
603-271-4331
llovering@ed.state.nh.us
http://www.dhhs.state.nh.us/DHHS/DHHS_SITE
Disability Served: various

New Hampshire Developmental Disabilities Council
21 South Fruit Street, Room 290
Concord, NH 03301-2451
603-271-3236
http://www.dhhs.state.nh.us/DHHS/DDCOUNCIL
Disability Served: developmentally disabled

New Hampshire Governor's Commission on Disability
57 Regional Drive
Concord, NH 03301
800-852-3405, 603-271-2774 (TTY)
http://www.nh.gov/disability
Disability Served: various

New Hampshire Services for Blind and Visually Impaired
21 South Fruit Street, Suite 20
Concord, NH 03301
603-271-3471 (Voice/TTY), 800-581-6881
http://www.ed.state.nh.us/education/doe/organization/adultlearning/VR/BlindandVisuallyImpaired.htm
Disability Served: vision

New Hampshire Services for Chronically Ill Children and Adolescents
105 Pleasant Street
Concord, NH 03301-3857
603-271-5034
http://www.dhhs.state.nh.us/DHHS/DDCHRONICILLCHD
Disability Served: various

New Hampshire Social Security Disability Determination Service
PO Box 452
Concord, NH 03302-0452
603-271-3341
http://www.ssa.gov/disability
Disability Served: various

New Hampshire Workers' Compensation Division
95 Pleasant Street
Concord, NH 03301
603-271-3176, 800-272-4353
Disability Served: various

NEW JERSEY

New Jersey Commission for the Blind and Visually Impaired
153 Halsey Street, PO Box 47017
Newark, NJ 07102
973-648-2324
http://www.state.nj.us/humanservices/cbvi
Disability Served: vision

New Jersey Department of Education
PO Box 500
Trenton, NJ 08625-0500
609-292-4469
http://www.state.nj.us/education
Disability Served: various

New Jersey Department of Health and Senior Services
PO Box 360
Trenton, NJ 08625-0360
609-292-7837
http://www.state.nj.us/health
Disability Served: various

New Jersey Division of Developmental Disabilities
PO Box 700
Trenton, NJ 08625
609-987-0800, 800-832-9173
http://www.state.nj.us/humanservices/ddd
Disability Served: developmentally disabled

New Jersey Division of Disability Services
PO Box 700
Trenton, NJ 08625-0700
888-285-3036, 609-292-1210 (TTY)
http://www.state.nj.us/humanservices/dds
Disability Served: various

New Jersey Division of Mental Health Services
PO Box 727
Trenton, NJ 08625-0727
800-382-6717
http://www.state.nj.us/humanservices/dmhs/index.html
Disability Served: mental health

New Jersey Division of the Deaf and Hard of Hearing
PO Box 700
Trenton, NJ 08625
609-984-7281 (Voice/TTY)
http://www.state.nj.us/humanservices/ddhh
Disability Served: hearing

New Jersey Division of Workers' Compensation
PO Box 381
Trenton, NJ 08625-0381
609-292-2515
http://www.nj.gov/labor/wc/wcindex.html
Disability Served: various

New Jersey Social Security Disability Determination Service (Newark)
PO Box 649
Newark, NJ 07101
973-648-2889
http://www.ssa.gov/disability
Disability Served: various

New Jersey Social Security Disability Determination Service (New Brunswick)
506 Jersey Avenue
New Brunswick, NJ 08901
732-246-5866
http://www.ssa.gov/disability
Disability Served: various

New Jersey Social Security Disability Determination Service (Trenton)
PO Box 378
Trenton, NJ 08625
609-943-4423
http://www.ssa.gov/disability
Disability Served: various

NEW MEXICO

New Mexico Aging and Long-Term Services Department
2550 Cerrillos Road
Santa Fe, NM 87505
505-476-4799, 866-451-2901
nmaoa@state.nm.us
http://www.nmaging.state.nm.us
Disability Served: elderly

New Mexico Commission for Deaf and Hard of Hearing Persons
2055 South Pacheco Street, Suite 450
Santa Fe, NM 87505
505-827-7270
http://www.nmcdhh.org
Disability Served: hearing

New Mexico Commission for the Blind
2905 Rodeo Park Drive, East Building 4, Suite 100
Santa Fe, NM 87505
888-513-7968
http://www.state.nm.us/cftb
Disability Served: vision

New Mexico Department of Education
300 Don Gaspar
Santa Fe, NM 87501-2786
505-827-5800
http://sde.state.nm.us
Disability Served: various

New Mexico Department of Health
1190 St. Francis Drive
Santa Fe, NM 87502-6110
505-827-2613
http://www.health.state.nm.us
Disability Served: various

New Mexico Division of Vocational Rehabilitation
435 St. Michaels Drive, Building D
Santa Fe, NM 87505
505-954-8500, 800-224-7005
http://www.dvrgetsjobs.com
Disability Served: various

New Mexico Office of Disability and Health
New Mexico Department of Health
1190 St. Francis Drive
Santa FE, NM 87502-6110
susan.gray@state.nm.us
http://www.health.state.nm.us/dhp/odhhome.htm
Disability Served: various

New Mexico Social Security Disability Determination Service
PO Box 4588
Albuquerque, NM 87196
505-841-5600
http://www.ssa.gov/disability
Disability Served: various

New Mexico Workers' Compensation Administration
2410 Centre Avenue, SE, PO Box 27198
Albuquerque, NM 87125-7198
505-841-6000
http://www.state.nm.us/wca
Disability Served: various

NEW YORK
New York Social Security Disability Determination Service (Albany)
PO Box 165
Albany, NY 12260-0165

518-473-9320, 866-586-5750
http://www.ssa.gov/disability
Disability Served: various

New York Social Security Disability Determination Service (Buffalo)
PO Box 5030
Buffalo, NY 14205-5030
716-847-5007, 866-586-5750
http://www.ssa.gov/disability
Disability Served: various

New York Social Security Disability Determination Service (Endicott)
PO Box 9009
Endicott, NY 13761-9009
607-741-4195, 866-586-5750
http://www.ssa.gov/disability
Disability Served: various

New York Social Security Disability Determination Service (Jamaica)
92-31 Union Hall Street
Jamaica, NY 11433
718-262-4323, 866-586-5750
http://www.ssa.gov/disability
Disability Served: various

New York Social Security Disability Determination Service (New York)
22 Cortlandt Street
New York, NY 10007
212-240-3456, 866-586-5750
http://www.ssa.gov/disability
Disability Served: various

New York State Commission for the Blind and Visually Handicapped
52 Washington Street
Rensselaer, NY 12144-279
866-871-3000, 866-871-6000 (TDD)
http://www.ocfs.state.ny.us/main/cbvh
Disability Served: vision

New York State Commission on Quality of Care and Advocacy for Persons with Disabilities
401 State Street
Schenectady, NY 12305-2397
800-624-4143
http://www.cqc.state.ny.us
Disability Served: various

New York State Department of Education
89 Washington Avenue
Albany, NY 12234
518-474-3852
http://www.nysed.gov
Disability Served: various

New York State Department of Health
Corning Tower, Empire State Plaza
Albany, NY 12237
518-474-2011
http://www.health.state.ny.us
Disability Served: various

New York State Office of Aging
Building Two, Empire State Plaza
Albany, NY 12223-1251
518-474-4425
http://aging.state.ny.us
Disability Served: elderly

New York State Office of Mental Health
44 Holland Avenue
Albany, NY 12229
800-597-8481
http://www.omh.state.ny.us
Disability Served: mental health

**New York State Office of Mental Retardation
   and Developmental Disabilities**
44 Holland Avenue
Albany, NY 12229
518-473-9689
http://www.omr.state.ny.us
Disability Served: developmentally disabled

**New York State Vocational and Educational Services
   for Individuals with Disabilities**
One Commerce Plaza
Albany, NY 12234
518-474-2714
http://www.vesid.nysed.gov
Disability Served: various

New York State Workers' Compensation Board
180 Livingston Street
Brooklyn, NY 11248
518-474-6670
http://www.wcb.state.ny.us
Disability Served: various

NORTH CAROLINA
North Carolina Council on Developmental Disability
3801 Lake Boone Trail, Suite 250
Raleigh, NC 27607
919-420-7901
http://www.nc-ddc.org
Disability Served: developmentally disabled

**North Carolina Department of Health and Human
   Services**
2001 Mail Service Center
Raleigh, NC 27699-2001
919-733-4534
http://www.dhhs.state.nc.us
Disability Served: various

North Carolina Department of Public Instruction
301 North Wilmington Street
Raleigh, NC 27601-2825
919-807-3300
http://www.dpi.state.nc.us
Disability Served: various

North Carolina Division of Aging and Adult Services
2101 Mail Service Center
Raleigh, NC 27699-2101
919-733-3983
http://www.dhhs.state.nc.us/aging
Disability Served: elderly

**North Carolina Division of Mental Health,
   Developmental Disabilities, and Substance
   Abuse Services**
3001 Mail Service Center
Raleigh, NC 27699-3001
919-733-7011
http://www.dhhs.state.nc.us/mhddsas
*Disability Served: chemical dependency, developmentally
   disabled, mental health*

North Carolina Division of Services for the Blind
309 Ashe Avenue
Raleigh, NC 27699-2601
919-733-9822
http://www.dhhs.state.nc.us/dsb
Disability Served: vision

**North Carolina Division of Services for the Deaf
   and Hard of Hearing**
2301 Mail Service Center
Raleigh, NC 27699-2301

919-773-2963 (Voice/TTY)
http://dsdhh.dhhs.state.nc.us
Disability Served: hearing

North Carolina Division of Vocational Rehabilitation Services
2801 Mail Service Center
Raleigh, NC 27699-2801
919-855-3500
http://www.dhhs.state.nc.us/docs/divinfo/dvr.htm
Disability Served: various

North Carolina Industrial Commission
4340 Mail Service Center
Raleigh, NC 27699-4340
919-807-2500
http://www.comp.state.nc.us
Disability Served: various

North Carolina Social Security Disability Determination Service
PO Box 243
Raleigh, NC 27602-0243
919-212-3222, 800-443-9360
http://www.ssa.gov/disability
Disability Served: various

NORTH DAKOTA
North Dakota Department of Health
600 East Boulevard Avenue
Bismarck, ND 58505-0200
701-328-2372
http://www.health.state.nd.us
Disability Served: various

North Dakota Department of Public Instruction
600 East Boulevard Avenue, Department 201
Bismarck, ND 58505-0440
701-328-2260
http://www.dpi.state.nd.us
Disability Served: various

North Dakota Disability Services Division
1237 West Divide Avenue
Bismarck, ND 58501-1208
800-755-8529, 701-328-8968 (TTY)
http://www.state.nd.us/humanservices/services/
    disabilities
Disability Served: various

North Dakota Division of Aging Services
600 East Boulevard Avenue, Department 325
Bismarck, ND 58505-0250
701-328-4601, 701-328-3480 (TTY)
dhsaging@state.nd.us
http://www.state.nd.us/humanservices/services/
    adultsaging
Disability Served: elderly

North Dakota Division of Mental Health and Substance Abuse Services
1237 West Divide Avenue, Suite 1C
Bismarck, ND 58501-1208
701-328-8920, 800-755-2719
dhsmhsas@state.nd.us
http://www.state.nd.us/humanservices/services/
    mentalhealth
Disability Served: chemical dependency, mental health

North Dakota Social Security Disability Determination Service
600 South Second Street
Bismarck, ND 58504-5729
7701-328-8700, 800-543-204
http://www.ssa.gov/disability
Disability Served: various

North Dakota Workforce Safety and Insurance
1600 East Century Avenue, Suite 1
Bismarck, ND 58503-0644
800-777-5033
http://www.workforcesafety.com
Disability Served: various

OHIO
Ohio Bureau of Workers' Compensation
30 West Spring Street
Columbus, OH 43215-2256
800-644-6292, 800-292-4833 (TTY)
http://www.bwc.state.oh.us
Disability Served: various

Ohio Department of Aging
50 West Broad Street, Ninth Floor
Columbus, OH 43215-3363
614-466-5500, 614-466-6190 (TTY)
http://www.goldenbuckeye.com
Disability Served: elderly

Ohio Department of Education
25 South Front Street
Columbus, OH 43215-4183
877-644-6338
http://www.ode.state.oh.us
Disability Served: various

Ohio Department of Health
246 North High Street
Columbus, OH 43216-0118
614-466-3543
http://www.odh.ohio.gov
Disability Served: various

Ohio Department of Mental Health
30 East Broad Street, Eighth Floor
Columbus, OH 43215-3430
614-466-2596
http://www.mh.state.oh.us
Disability Served: mental health

Ohio Department of Mental Retardation and Developmental Disabilities
1810 Sullivant Avenue
Columbus, OH 43223-1239
877-464-6733
http://odmrdd.state.oh.us
Disability Served: developmentally disabled

Ohio Developmental Disabilities Council
8 East Long Street, 12th Floor
Columbus, OH 43215
800-766-7426, 614-644-5530 (TTY)
http://www.ddc.ohio.gov
Disability Served: developmentally disabled

Ohio Rehabilitation Services Commission
400 East Campus View Boulevard
Columbus, OH 43235-4604
614-438-1200 (Voice/TTY)
http://www.rsc.ohio.gov
Disability Served: various

Ohio Social Security Disability Determination Service
PO Box 359001
Columbus, OH 43235-9001
614-438-1200 (Voice/TTY), 800-282-4536 (Voice/TTY)
http://www.rsc.ohio.gov/VR_Services/BDD/bdd.asp
Disability Served: various

OKLAHOMA

Oklahoma Aging Services Division
2401 Northwest 23rd, Suite 40
Oklahoma City, OK 73107-2422
405-521-2327
http://www.okdhs.org/aging
Disability Served: elderly

Oklahoma Department of Education
2500 North Lincoln Boulevard
Oklahoma City, OK 73105-4599
405-521-3301
http://www.sde.state.ok.us
Disability Served: various

Oklahoma Department of Health
1000 Northeast 10th Street
Oklahoma City, OK 73117-1299
405-271-4200
http://www.health.state.ok.us
Disability Served: various

Oklahoma Department of Mental Health and Substance Abuse Services
1200 Northeast 13th Street, PO Box 53277
Oklahoma City, OK 73152
405-522-3908
http://www.odmhsas.org
Disability Served: chemical dependency, mental health

Oklahoma Department of Rehabilitation Services
3535 Northwest 58th Street, Suite 500
Oklahoma City, OK 73112-4815
405-951-3400, 800-845-8476
http://www.okrehab.org
Disability Served: various

Oklahoma Developmental Disabilities Services Division
4545 North Lincoln Boulevard, #102
Oklahoma City, OK 73105
405-521-6267, 800-522-1064
http://www.okdhs.org/ddsd
Disability Served: developmentally disabled

Oklahoma Office of Handicapped Concerns
2401 Northwest 23rd, Suite 90
Oklahoma City, OK 73107-2423
800-522-8224, 405-522-6706 (TDD)
http://www.state.ok.us/~ohc
Disability Served: various

Oklahoma Social Security Disability Determination Service
9801 North Kelley Avenue
Oklahoma City, OK 73131
405-419-2200, 800-877-9977
http://www.ssa.gov/disability
Disability Served: various

Oklahoma Workers' Compensation Court
1915 North Stiles Avenue
Oklahoma City, OK 73105-4918
405-522-8600
http://www.owcc.state.ok.us
Disability Served: various

OREGON
Oregon Commission for the Blind
535 Southeast 12th Avenue
Portland, OR 97214
888-202-5463, 503-731-3224 (TDD)
ocbmail@state.or.us
http://www.cfb.state.or.us
Disability Served: vision

Oregon Council on Developmental Disabilities
540 24th Place, NE
Salem, OR 97301-4517
503-945-9941, 800-292-4154
ocdd@ocdd.org
http://www.ocdd.org
Disability Served: developmentally disabled

Oregon Department of Education
255 Capitol Street, NE
Salem, OR 97310-0203
503-378-3569, 503-378-2892 (TDD)
ode.frontdesk@ode.state.or.us
http://www.ode.state.or.us
Disability Served: various

Oregon Disabilities Commission
1257 Ferry Street, SE
Salem, OR 97301-4278
800-358-3117 (Voice/TTY)
odc@state.or.us
http://www.odc.state.or.us
Disability Served: various

Oregon Division of Seniors and People with Disabilities
500 Summer Street, NE, E15
Salem, OR 97301-1097
503-945-5811, 800-282-8096 (TTY)
dhs.info@state.or.us
http://egov.oregon.gov/DHS/spwpd
Disability Served: elderly, physically disabled

Oregon Health Services
500 Summer Street, NE, E15
Salem, OR 97301-1097
503-945-5944, 503-947-5330 (TTY)
dhs.info@state.or.us
http://www.oregon.gov/DHS/aboutdhs/structure/
   hs.shtml
Disability Served: various

Oregon Office of Mental Health and Addiction Services
500 Summer Street, NE, E15
Salem, OR 97301-1097
503-945-5944, 503-947-5330 (TTY)
http://www.oregon.gov/DHS/mentalhealth
Disability Served: chemical dependency, mental health

Oregon Social Security Disability Determination Service
3150 Lancaster Drive, NE
Salem, OR 97305-1350
503-945-5878, 800-452-2147
http://www.ssa.gov/disability
Disability Served: various

Oregon Workers' Compensation Division
350 Winter Street, NE, PO Box 14480
Salem, OR 97309-0405
503-947-7810, 503-947-7993 (TTY)
workcomp.questions@state.or.us
http://www.cbs.state.or.us/external/wcd
Disability Served: various

PENNSYLVANIA
Pennsylvania Bureau of Workers' Compensation
1171 South Cameron Street, Room 324
Harrisburg, PA 17104-2501
717-783-5421, 800-362-4228 (TTY)
http://www.dli.state.pa.us
Disability Served: various

Pennsylvania Department of Aging
555 Walnut Street, 5th Floor
Harrisburg, PA 17101-1919
717-783-1550
aging@state.pa.us
http://www.aging.state.pa.us
Disability Served: elderly

Pennsylvania Department of Education
333 Market Street
Harrisburg, PA 17126
717-783-6788
http://www.pde.state.pa.us
Disability Served: various

Pennsylvania Department of Health
PO Box 90
Harrisburg, PA 17108
877-PA-HEALTH
http://www.dsf.health.state.pa.us/health
Disability Served: various

Pennsylvania Developmental Disabilities Council
8500 Brooktree Road, Suite 100
Wexford, PA 15090
724-933-1655
http://www.paddc.org
Disability Served: developmentally disabled

Pennsylvania Social Security Disability Determination Service (Greensburg)
351 Harvey Avenue
Greensburg, PA 15605
724-836-5100
http://www.ssa.gov/disability
Disability Served: various

Pennsylvania Social Security Disability Determination Service (Harrisburg)
1171 South Cameron Street, Room 104
Harrisburg, PA 17104
717-783-3620
http://www.ssa.gov/disability
Disability Served: various

Pennsylvania Social Security Disability Determination Service (Wilkes-Barre)
PO Box R
Wilkes-Barre, PA 18702

570-824-8971
http://www.ssa.gov/disability
Disability Served: various

RHODE ISLAND
Rhode Island Commission on the Deaf and Hard of Hearing
One Capitol Hill, Ground Level
Providence, RI 02908-5850
401-222-1204, 401-222-1205 (TTY)
cdhh@cdhh.ri.gov
http://www.cdhh.ri.gov
Disability Served: hearing

Rhode Island Department of Elderly Affairs
35 Howard Avenue
Cranston, RI 02920
http://www.dea.state.ri.us
Disability Served: elderly

Rhode Island Department of Elementary and Secondary Education
255 Westminster Street
Providence, RI 02903
401-222-4600
http://www.ridoe.net
Disability Served: various

Rhode Island Department of Health
Three Capitol Hill
Providence, RI 02908
401-222-2231
library@doh.state.ri.us
http://www.health.state.ri.us
Disability Served: various

Rhode Island Department of Mental Health, Retardation, and Hospitals
14 Harrington Road
Cranston, RI 02920-3080
401-462-3201, 401-462-6087 (TDD)
http://www.mhrh.state.ri.us
Disability Served: developmentally disabled, mental health

Rhode Island Developmental Disabilities Council
400 Bald Hill Road, Suite 515
Warwick, RI 02886
401-737-1238 (Voice/TDD)

riddc@riddc.org
http://www.riddc.org
Disability Served: developmentally disabled

Rhode Island Division of Workers' Compensation
1511 Pontiac Avenue, Building 69, Second Floor,
   PO Box 20190
Cranston, RI 02920-0942
401-462-8100
WCEdcUnit@DLT.state.ri.us
http://www.dlt.ri.gov/wc
Disability Served: various

Rhode Island Governor's Advisory Council for the Blind
40 Fountain Street
Providence, RI 02903
401-421-7005, 401-421-7016 (TDD)
http://www.ors.ri.gov/Governors_Advisory_Council_for_
   the_Blind.htm
Disability Served: vision

Rhode Island Governor's Commission on Disabilities
41 Cherry Dale Court
Cranston, RI 02920-3049
401-462-0100, 401-462-0101 (TTY)
disabilities@gcd.ri.gov
http://www.gcd.ri.gov
Disability Served: various

Rhode Island Office of Rehabilitation Services
40 Fountain Street
Providence, RI 02903
401-421-7005, 401-421-7016 (TDD)
http://www.ors.ri.gov
Disability Served: various

Rhode Island Social Security Disability Determination Service
40 Fountain Street
Providence, RI 02903
401-222-3182
http://www.ssa.gov/disability
Disability Served: various

SOUTH CAROLINA
South Carolina Department of Disabilities and Special Needs
PO Box 4706
Columbia, SC 29240

803-898-9600 (Voice/TTY)
http://www.state.sc.us/ddsn
Disability Served: various

South Carolina Department of Education
1429 Senate Street
Columbia, SC 29201
803-734-8500
info@sde.state.sc.us
http://www.myscschools.com
Disability Served: various

South Carolina Department of Health and Human Services
PO Box 8206
Columbia, SC 29202-8206
803-898-2500
info@dhhs.state.sc.us
http://www.dhhs.state.sc.us
Disability Served: various

South Carolina Department of Mental Health
2414 Bull Street
Columbia, SC 29202
803-898-8581
http://www.state.sc.us/dmh
Disability Served: mental health

South Carolina Developmental Disabilities Council
1205 Pendleton Street, Suite 372
Columbia, SC 29201
803-734-0465, 803-734-1147 (TTY)
http://www.scddc.state.sc.us
Disability Served: developmentally disabled

South Carolina Mental Retardation Division
3440 Harden Street Extension, PO Box 4706
Columbia, SC 29240
888-376-4636, 803-898-9600 (Voice/TTY)
http://www.state.sc.us/ddsn/mr/mrdd.htm
Disability Served: developmentally disabled

South Carolina Office on Aging
1301 Gervais Street
Columbia, SC 29201
803-734-9900
   http://www.state.sc.us/ltgov/aging/OfficeOnAging/
      OfficeOnAging.htm
Disability Served: elderly

South Carolina Social Security Disability Determination Service (Charleston)
2070 North Rivers Business Center
Charleston, SC 29406
843-953-0300
http://www.ssa.gov/disability
Disability Served: various

South Carolina Social Security Disability Determination Service (Columbia)
1410 Boston Avenue, PO Box 15
West Columbia, SC 29171
803-896-6500
info@scvrd.state.sc.us
http://www.scvrd.net/dds03.htm
Disability Served: various

South Carolina Social Security Disability Determination Service (Greenville)
PO Box 3090
Greenville, SC 29602
864-242-1950
http://www.ssa.gov/disability
Disability Served: various

South Carolina Vocational Rehabilitation Department
1410 Boston Avenue, PO Box 15
West Columbia, SC 29171
803-896-6500
info@scvrd.state.sc.us
http://www.scvrd.net
Disability Served: various

South Carolina Workers' Compensation Commission
1612 Marion Street, PO Box 1715
Columbia, SC 29202-1715
803-737-5700
http://www.wcc.state.sc.us
Disability Served: various

SOUTH DAKOTA

South Dakota Adult Services and Aging
700 Governors Drive
Pierre, SD 57501
605-773-3656, 866-854-5465
ASA@STATE.SD.US
http://www.state.sd.us/social/ASA
Disability Served: elderly

South Dakota Council on Developmental Disabilities
500 East Capitol
Pierre, SD 57501-5070
605-773-6369
Info@DDC
http://www.state.sd.us/dhs/ddc
Disability Served: developmentally disabled

South Dakota Department of Education
700 Governors Drive
Pierre, SD 57501-2291
605-773-3134
http://www.state.sd.us/deca
Disability Served: various

South Dakota Department of Health
600 East Capitol Avenue
Pierre, SD 57501-2536
605-773-3361, 800-738-2301
http://www.state.sd.us/doh
Disability Served: various

South Dakota Division of Labor and Management
700 Governors Drive, Kneip Building
Pierre, SD 57501-2291
605-773-3681
james.marsh@state.sd.us
http://www.state.sd.us/dol/dlm/dlm-home.htm
Disability Served: various

South Dakota Division of Mental Health
500 East Capitol
Pierre, SD 57501-5070
800-265-9684
infoMH@state.sd.us
http://www.state.sd.us/dhs/dmh
Disability Served: mental health

South Dakota Division of Rehabilitation Services
500 East Capitol
Pierre, SD 57501-5070
605-773-3195
eric.weiss@state.sd.us
http://www.state.sd.us/dhs/drs
Disability Served: various

South Dakota Service to the Blind and Visually Impaired
500 East Capitol
Pierre, SD 57501
605-773-5990, 605-773-6412 (TTY)

http://www.state.sd.us/dhs/sbvi
Disability Served: vision

South Dakota Social Security Disability Determination Service
811 East 10th Street, Department 24
Sioux Falls, SD 57103-1650
605-367-5499, 800-658-2272
http://www.ssa.gov/disability
Disability Served: various

TENNESSEE

Tennessee Commission on Aging and Disability
500 Deaderick Street, Eighth Floor
Nashville, TN 37243-0860
615-741-2056
tnaging.tnaging@state.tn.us
http://www.state.tn.us/comaging
Disability Served: elderly

Tennessee Council for the Deaf and Hard of Hearing
400 Deaderick Street, 15th Floor
Nashville, TN 37248-6000
615-313-4700918, 800-270-1349 (TTY)
http://www.state.tn.us/humanserv/TCDHH.htm
Disability Served: hearing

Tennessee Department of Education
Andrew Johnson Tower, Sixth Floor
Nashville, TN 37243-0375
615-741-2731
Education.Comments@state.tn.us
http://www.state.tn.us/education
Disability Served: various

Tennessee Department of Health
425 Fifth Avenue, North, Cordell Hull Building, 3rd Floor
Nashville, TN 37247
615-741-3111
TN.health@state.tn.us
http://www.state.tn.us/health
Disability Served: various

Tennessee Department of Mental Health and Developmental Disabilities
425 Fifth Avenue North, Cordell Hull Building, 5th Floor
Nashville, TN 37243-0675
615-532-6610
opie.tdmhdd@state.tn.us

http://www.tennessee.gov/mental
Disability Served: developmentally disabled, mental health

Tennessee Division of Mental Retardation Services
500 Deaderick Street, Andrew Jackson Building, 15th Floor
Nashville, TN 37243
800-535-9725
http://www.state.tn.us/dmrs
Disability Served: developmentally disabled

Tennessee Services for the Blind and Visually Impaired
400 Deaderick Street, 11th Floor
Nashville, TN 37248-6200
615-313-4914
Disability Served: vision

Tennessee Social Security Disability Determination Service
400 Deaderick Street, 15th Floor
Nashville, TN 37248-0001
615-743-7300, 800-342-1117
http://www.state.tn.us/humanserv/DDS-HOME.html
Disability Served: various

Tennessee Vocational Rehabilitation Services
400 Deaderick Street
Nashville, TN 37248-0001
615-313-4714
Disability Served: various

Tennessee Workers' Compensation Division
Andrew Johnson Tower, 8th Floor
Nashville, TN 37243-0655
615-741-2395
wc.info@state.tn.us
http://www.state.tn.us/labor-wfd/wcomp.html
Disability Served: various

TEXAS

Texas Department of Aging and Disability Services
PO Box 149030
Austin, TX 78714-9030
512-438-3011
mail@dads.state.tx.us
http://www.dads.state.tx.us
Disability Served: various

Texas Department of Assistive and Rehabilitative Services
4800 North Lamar Boulevard, 3rd Floor
Austin, TX 78756
800-628-5115
DARS.Inquiries@dars.state.tx.us
http://www.dars.state.tx.us
Disability Served: various

Texas Department of State Health Services
1100 West 49th Street
Austin, TX 78756-3199
800-735-2989
http://www.dshs.state.tx.us
Disability Served: various

Texas Division for Blind Services
4800 North Lamar Boulevard, 3rd Floor
Austin, TX 78756
800-628-5115
http://www.dars.state.tx.us/dbs
Disability Served: vision

Texas Education Agency
1701 North Congress Avenue
Austin, TX 78701
512-463-9734
http://www.tea.state.tx.us
Disability Served: various

Texas Social Security Disability Determination Service
PO Box 149198
Austin, TX 78714-9198
512-437-8000
http://www.ssa.gov/disability
Disability Served: various

Texas Workers' Compensation Commission
7551 Metro Center Drive
Austin, TX 78744-1609
512-804-4000
http://www.twcc.state.tx.us
Disability Served: various

UTAH

Utah Department of Health
PO Box 141010
Salt Lake City, UT 84114-1010

801-538-6101, 801-538-9936 (TTY)
http://health.utah.gov
Disability Served: various

Utah Division of Aging and Adult Services
120 North 200 West, Room 325
Salt Lake City, UT 84103
877-424-4640
DAAS@utah.gov
http://www.hsdaas.state.ut.us
Disability Served: elderly

Utah Division of Services for People with Disabilities
120 North 200 West, Room 411
Salt Lake City, UT 84103
801-538-4200, 801-538-4192 (TTY)
dspd@utah.gov
http://www.hsdspd.state.ut.us
Disability Served: various

Utah Division of Services for the Blind and Visually Impaired
PO Box 144200
Salt Lake City, UT 84114-4200
800-473-7530, 801-538-7530 (Voice/TTY)
http://www.usor.utah.gov/dsbvi.htm
Disability Served: vision

Utah Division of Substance Abuse and Mental Health
120 North 200 West, Room 209
Salt Lake City, UT 84103
801-538-3939
http://www.hsmh.state.ut.us
Disability Served: chemical dependency, mental health

Utah Governor's Council for People with Disabilities
155 South 300 West, Suite 100
Salt Lake City, UT 84101
801-533-3965
http://www.gcpd.org
Disability Served: various

Utah Services to the Deaf and Hard of Hearing
5709 South 1500 West
Taylorsville, UT 84123
801-263-4860 (Voice/TTY)
http://www.deafservices.utah.gov
Disability Served: hearing

Utah Social Security Disability Determination Service
PO Box 144032
Salt Lake City, UT 84111-4032
801-321-6500, 800-221-3493
http://www.ssa.gov/disability
Disability Served: various

Utah State Office of Education
250 East 500 South, PO Box 144200
Salt Lake City, UT 84114-4200
801-538-7500
http://www.usoe.k12.ut.us
Disability Served: various

Utah State Office of Rehabilitation
PO Box 144200
Salt Lake City, UT 84114-4200
800-473-7530, 801-538-7530 (Voice/TTY)
http://www.usor.utah.gov
Disability Served: various

VERMONT

Vermont Department of Disabilities, Aging and Independent Living
103 South Main Street
Waterbury, VT 05671
802-241-2400
http://www.dad.state.vt.us
Disability Served: various

Vermont Department of Education
120 State Street
Montpelier, VT 05620-2501
802-828-3154
edinfo@education.state.vt.us
http://www.state.vt.us/educ
Disability Served: various

Vermont Department of Health
108 Cherry Street, PO Box 70
Burlington, VT 05402-0070
802-863-7200, 800-464-4343
http://www.healthyvermonters.info
Disability Served: various

Vermont Developmental Disabilities Council
103 South Main Street
Waterbury, VT 05671-0206

802-241-2613, 888-317-2006 (Voice/TDD)
vtddc@ahs.state.vt.us
http://www.ahs.state.vt.us/vtddc
Disability Served: developmentally disabled

Vermont Division for the Blind and Visually Impaired
103 South Main Street, Osgood Building
Waterbury, VT 05671-2304
802-241-2210
http://www.dad.state.vt.us/dbvi
Disability Served: vision

Vermont Division of Children With Special Health Needs
108 Cherry Street, PO Box 70
Burlington, VT 05402-0070
802-863-7200, 800-464-4343
http://www.healthyvermonters.info/hi/cshn/cshn.shtml
Disability Served: various

Vermont Division of Mental Health
108 Cherry Street, PO Box 70
Burlington, VT 05402-0070
802-863-7200, 800-464-4343
http://www.healthyvermonters.info
Disability Served: mental health

Vermont Division of Vocational Rehabilitation
103 South Main Street, Osgood II Building
Waterbury, VT 05671-2303
866-879-6757 (Voice/TTY)
janetr@dad.state.vt.us
http://www.vocrehabvermont.org
Disability Served: various

Vermont Social Security Disability Determination Service
2 Pilgrim Park Road, 2nd Floor
Waterbury, VT 05676
802-241-2463
http://www.ssa.gov/disability
Disability Served: various

Vermont Workers' Compensation Division
National Life Building, Drawer 20
Montpelier, VT 05620-3401
802-828-2286
wcomp@labind.state.vt.us
http://www.state.vt.us/labind/wcindex.htm
Disability Served: various

VIRGINIA

Virginia Board for People with Disabilities
202 North 9th Street, 9th Floor
Richmond, VA 23219
800-846-4464 (Voice/TTY)
http://www.vaboard.org
Disability Served: developmentally disabled

Virginia Department for the Aging
1610 Forest Avenue, Suite 100
Richmond, VA 23229
800-552-3402 (Voice/TTY)
aging@vda.virginia.gov
http://www.aging.state.va.us
Disability Served: elderly

Virginia Department for the Blind and Vision Impaired
397 Azalea Avenue
Richmond, VA 23227-3623
800-622-2155 (Voice/TTY)
http://www.vdbvi.org
Disability Served: vision

Virginia Department for the Deaf and Hard of Hearing
1602 Rolling Hills Drive
Richmond, VA 23229-5012
800-552-7917 (Voice/TTY)
frontdsk@vddhh.virginia.gov
http://www.vddhh.org
Disability Served: hearing

Virginia Department of Education
PO Box 2120
Richmond, VA 23216-2120
804-371-0576
http://www.pen.k12.va.us
Disability Served: various

Virginia Department of Health
PO Box 2448
Richmond, VA 23218-2448
866-531-3065
http://www.vdh.state.va.us
Disability Served: various

Virginia Department of Mental Health, Mental Retardation, and Substance Abuse Services
PO Box 1797
Richmond, VA 23218-1797
804-786-3921, 804-371-8977 (TDD)

http://www.dmhmrsas.virginia.gov
Disability Served: chemical dependency, developmentally disabled, xmental health

Virginia Department of Rehabilitative Services
8004 Franklin Farms Drive
Richmond, VA 23229
800-552-5019 (Voice/TTY)
drs@drs.virginia.gov
http://vadrs.org
Disability Served: various

Virginia Social Security Disability Determination Service (Central Region)
5211 West Broad Street, Suite 200
Richmond, VA 23230
800-523-5007
http://www.ssa.gov/disability
Disability Served: various

Virginia Social Security Disability Determination Service (Northern Region)
11150 Main Street, Suite 200
Fairfax, VA 22030
800-379-9548
http://www.ssa.gov/disability
Disability Served: various

Virginia Social Security Disability Determination Service (Southwest Region)
111 Franklin Road, SE, Suite 250
Roanoke, VA 24011
800-627-1288
http://www.ssa.gov/disability
Disability Served: various

Virginia Social Security Disability Determination Service (Tidewater Region)
5700 Thurston Avenue, Suite 107
Virginia Beach, VA 23455
800-379-4403
http://www.ssa.gov/disability
Disability Served: various

Virginia Workers' Compensation Commission
1000 DMV Drive
Richmond, VA 23220
877-664-2566
http://www.vwc.state.va.us
Disability Served: various

WASHINGTON
Washington Department of Public Instruction
Old Capitol Building, PO Box 47200
Olympia, WA 98504-7200
360-725-6000, 360-664-3631 (TTY)
http://www.k12.wa.us
Disability Served: various

Washington Division of Developmental Disabilities
PO Box 45310
Olympia, WA 98504-5310
360-725-3413
dddcoreception@dshs.wa.gov
http://www1.dshs.wa.gov/ddd
Disability Served: developmentally disabled

Washington Division of Vocational Rehabilitation
PO Box 45340
Olympia, WA 98504
800-637-5627, 888-788-9802 (TTY)
http://www1.dshs.wa.gov/dvr
Disability Served: various

Washington Industrial Insurance Division
PO Box 44850
Olympia, WA 98504-4850
800-547-8367
http://www.lni.wa.gov/ClaimsIns
Disability Served: various

Washington Office of the Deaf and Hard of Hearing
PO Box 45301
Olympia, WA 98504-5301
800-422-7930 (Voice/TTY)
http://www1.dshs.wa.gov/hrsa/odhh
Disability Served: hearing

Washington Social Security Disability Determination Service
PO Box 9303-MS-45550
Olympia, WA 98507-9303
360-664-7500, 800-562-6074
http://www.ssa.gov/disability
Disability Served: various

Washington State Aging and Disability Services Administration
PO Box 45130
Olympia, WA 98504-5130
800-422-3263, 800-737-7931 (TDD)
http://www.aasa.dshs.wa.gov
Disability Served: elderly

Washington State Department of Health
PO Box 47890
Olympia, WA 98504-7890
800-525-0127
http://www.doh.wa.gov
Disability Served: various

WEST VIRGINIA
West Virginia Bureau of Public Health
350 Capitol Street, Room 702
Charleston, WV 25301-3712
304-558-2971
http://www.wvdhhr.org/bph
Disability Served: various

West Virginia Bureau of Senior Services
1900 Kanawha Boulevard East
Charleston, WV 25305
304-558-3317
http://www.state.wv.us/seniorservices
Disability Served: elderly

West Virginia Department of Education
1900 Kanawha Boulevard East
Charleston, WV 25305
304-558-2681
http://wvde.state.wv.us
Disability Served: various

West Virginia Developmental Disabilities Council
110 Stockton Street
Charleston, WV 25312
304-558-0416, 304-558-2376 (TDD)
http://www.wvddc.org
Disability Served: developmentally disabled

West Virginia Division of Rehabilitation Services
State Capitol Complex, PO Box 50890
Charleston, WV 25305-0890
304-766-4601
http://www.wvdrs.org
Disability Served: various

West Virginia Social Security Disability Determination Service (Charleston)
500 Quarrier Street, Suite 500
Charleston, WV 25301

304-558-5340
janiej@mail.drs.state.wv.us
http://www.wvdrs.org
Disability Served: various

West Virginia Social Security Disability Determination Service (Clarksburg)
320 West Pike Street, Suite 120
Clarksburg, WV 26301
304-624-0200
janiej@mail.drs.state.wv.us
http://www.wvdrs.org
Disability Served: various

West Virginia Workers' Compensation Division
4700 MacCorkle Avenue, SE
Charleston, WV 25304
888-498-2667
http://www.wvwcc.org
Disability Served: various

WISCONSIN
Wisconsin Bureau of Aging and Long Term Care Resources
1 West Wilson Street, Room 450, PO Box 7851
Madison, WI 53707-7851
608-267-9880
http://www.dhfs.state.wi.us/aging/baltcr_aging.htm
Disability Served: elderly, physically disabled

Wisconsin Bureau of Developmental Disabilities Services
1 West Wilson Street, Room 418, PO Box 7851
Madison, WI 53707-7851
608-266-0805
http://www.dhfs.state.wi.us/bdds
Disability Served: developmentally disabled

Wisconsin Bureau of Mental Health and Substance Abuse Services
PO Box 7851
Madison, WI 53707-7851
608-267-7792
http://www.dhfs.state.wi.us/MH_BCMH
Disability Served: chemical dependency, mental health

Wisconsin Department of Health and Family Services
1 West Wilson Street
Madison, WI 53702

608-266-1865, 608-267-7371 (TTY)
http://www.dhfs.state.wi.us
Disability Served: various

Wisconsin Department of Public Instruction
125 South Webster Street, PO Box 7841
Madison, WI 53707-7841
800-441-4563
http://www.dpi.state.wi.us
Disability Served: various

Wisconsin Division of Vocational Rehabilitation
201 East Washington Avenue, PO Box 7852
Madison, WI 53707-7852
800-442-3477, 888-877-5939 (TTY)
dwddvr@dwd.state.wi.us
http://www.dwd.state.wi.us/dvr
Disability Served: various

Wisconsin Social Security Disability Determination Service
PO Box 7886
Madison, WI 53707-7886
800-423-1938, 800-462-8817 (TTY)
WI.DD.MADISON@ssa.gov
http://www.ssa.gov/disability
Disability Served: various

Wisconsin Workers' Compensation Division
PO Box 7901
Madison, WI 53707-7901
608-266-1340
http://www.dwd.state.wi.us/wc
Disability Served: various

WYOMING
Wyoming Department of Education
Hathaway Building, Second Floor, 2300 Capitol Avenue
Cheyenne, WY 82002-0050
307-777-7675
http://www.k12.wy.us
Disability Served: various

Wyoming Department of Workforce Services
122 West 25th Street, Herschler Building, 2E
Cheyenne, WY 82002
307-777-8650
http://www.wyomingworkforce.org/
Disability Served: various

Wyoming Division of Aging
6101 Yellowstone Road, Room 259B
Cheyenne, WY 82002
307-777-7986, 800-442-2766
cnoon@state.wy.us
http://wdhfs.state.wy.us/aging
Disability Served: elderly

**Wyoming Division of Developmental Disabilities
Division**
186E Qwest Building, 6101 Yellowstone Road
Cheyenne, WY 82002
307-777-7115
http://wdh.state.wy.us/DDD
Disability Served: developmentally disabled

Wyoming Mental Health Division
6101 Yellowstone Road, Room 259B
Cheyenne, WY 82002
307-777-7094
msmith@state.wy.us
http://mhd.state.wy.us
Disability Served: mental health

Wyoming Relay/Deaf Services Program
122 West 25th Street, Herschler Building, 2E
Cheyenne, WY 82002
307-777-8650
http://www.wyomingworkforce.org/
Disability Served: hearing

**Wyoming Social Security Disability Determination
Service**
821 West Pershing Boulevard
Cheyenne, WY 82002
307-777-7341, 800-438-5788
 http://www.wyomingworkforce.org/how/vr_ssdds.aspx
Disability Served: various

**Wyoming Workers' Safety and Compensation
Division**
1510 East Pershing Boulevard
Cheyenne, WY 82002
307-777-7441
http://wydoe.state.wy.us/doe.asp?ID=9
Disability Served: various

PUERTO RICO

**Puerto Rico Social Security Disability Determination
Service**
PO Box 71301
San Juan, PR 00936-8401
787-754-8989, ext. 2275
http://www.ssa.gov/disability
Disability Served: various

VIRGIN ISLANDS

**Virgin Islands Social Security Disability
Determination Service**
Nisky Center, 1st Floor, Suite 2
St. Thomas, VI 00802
340-774-7375
http://www.ssa.gov/disability
Disability Served: various

WESTERN PACIFIC ISLANDS

**Western Pacific Islands (includes American Samoa,
Guam, & Northern Mariana Islands) Social
Security Disability Determination Service**
655 Harmon Loop Road, Suite 300
Dededo, Guam 96929
671-635-4779
http://www.ssa.gov/disability
Disability Served: various

ORGANIZATION NAME INDEX